GAMES
NATIONS
PLAY

GAMES
NATIONS
PLAY

FOURTH EDITION

ANALYZING INTERNATIONAL POLITICS

John Spanier

HOLT, RINEHART AND WINSTON
New York   Chicago   San Francisco   Philadelphia
Montreal   Toronto   London   Sydney   Tokyo   Mexico City
Rio de Janeiro   Madrid

Library of Congress Cataloging in Publication Data

Spanier, John W
  Games nations play.

  Bibliography: p. 578
  Includes index.
  1. International relations.   I.   Title.
JX1391.S7   1981   327   81-996
ISBN 0-03-058172-9   AACR2

Address correspondence to:
383 Madison Avenue, New York, N.Y. 10017

1 2 3 4 5   144   9 8 7 6 5 4 3 2

CBS COLLEGE PUBLISHING
Holt, Rinehart and Winston
The Dryden Press
Saunders College Publishing

PREFACE

As its title suggests, the purpose of this book is to teach the reader—primarily the college student—*how to think about international politics*. The average undergraduate takes a course in international politics primarily to gain some understanding of the contemporary world and, in particular, of the role played by his or her own country. Many, of course, are interested in finding out more about particular events and issues, such as the Cold War, détente, Afghanistan, Iran, OPEC, the Middle East, or SALT. The one thing that many students do not expect when they enroll in a course of international politics is abstract analyses of the nature of such politics in order to learn how to *analyze* events for themselves. It is precisely because current events so soon become "ancient history" that my aim has been to provide readers with those tools of analysis that will enable them to analyze tomorrow's events for themselves. I hope that, in the end, they will have gained a deeper comprehension of some of the external and internal problems that states confront and why frequently they act as they do, whether they are capitalist or communist, highly industrialized or economically underdeveloped.

This book is thus about the "games nations play." Its objective, furthermore, is to convey to the student that there are many different ways to think about the subject, not simply one "right" way. To this end, I employ three levels of analysis; one focused on the state system, with its emphasis on balance of power; one focused on the national system, with its domestic priorities; and one focused on the decision-making system, with its dependence both on policy makers' perceptions of reality and on the institutions that formulate and execute policy. This three-dimensional approach, which involves a modification of Kenneth N. Waltz's "three images" and J. David Singer's "levels of analysis," enables the student to view a single policy or set of policies from three different—and often conflicting—perspectives. It is hoped that this approach will afford him or her a greater understanding of the complexities of the international system, as well as a more sophisticated basis for prediction, criticism, and interpretation of nations' behavior and the interactions among nation-states.

This threefold scheme also reflects my own view that international events must be analyzed not only in the context of the environment, or state system, in which they occur but also in terms of the purposes of nations and their general behavior as it is shaped by their societies and the specific policy makers who conduct foreign policy at particular times. The environment has a powerful impact upon states—for example, upon their objectives and their degrees of choice among alternative policies—but their internal character and politics also exert a major influence. Although Clausewitz somewhat exaggerated, we can paraphrase him and say that foreign policy is the conduct of domestic politics by other means.

This emphasis on the state system does not mean a neglect of nonstate actors, transnational forces, or analysis of "world order" politics. Since the disillusionment of Vietnam and the OPEC shock of 1973, emphasis on interdependence and "new forces" in world politics has become quite fashionable. Yet the focus of our analysis remains on interstate politics. For the scholar familiar with the "new forces" this book may therefore appear dated and old-fashioned. But for the readers for whom it was written, who are unfamiliar with the state system and the behavior of the states that have been the primary international actors for more than 300 years, knowledge of the "older forces" is a prerequisite for understanding. Such knowledge is also indispensable for any comprehension and evaluation of the "new international politics." How can such comprehension be achieved when the student is unaware of why some scholars are so critical of the traditional state system and at times become fervent advocates of the "new forces"? Third, and closely related to such evaluation, the student has to make up his or her own mind on a fundamental issue posed by critics of the state-centered analysis:

> . . . it is an open question which is the most striking feature of the international order—the extent and rapidity of change or the astonishing persistence of tradition. As a matter of fact, if one can criticize some recent studies it is not because they fail to take account of change but because they exaggerate its impact to the point of losing sight of the aspects of continuity and of successful resistance to change that are equally conspicuous in our day.[1]

My views on this matter will be found in a detailed analysis of interdependence in Chapter 20.

It should be clear, then, that this book is not a book on American foreign policy or a contemporary diplomatic history. Nevertheless, a sufficient amount of historical material is interwoven for two purposes. One is to give the student a broad picture of the modern era, for, although the world is truly one that the present generation did not make, it is nonetheless one with which it must cope. An understanding of the forces and events that have shaped the modern world should help to make this generation more successful in coping with it than past generations have been. Second, and perhaps even more important, analytical frameworks and concepts are useless unless they have some bearing on the "real" world. Some years ago William Newman wrote that "history is useless, or even in a very real sense nonexistent, without some degree of conceptualization of what is to be looked for; at the same time the true meaning and understanding of a concept can only come from a detailed knowledge of those events that are relevant to that concept.[2]

In writing a book, the author is always indebted to many people. The undergraduates at the University of Florida who over the years have taken my introductory international-politics course and have been exposed to a number of different ways of organizing the material—and who have often been kind and gentle in suggesting helpful improvements and criticisms—are certainly entitled to a word of thanks. This book has also been immeasurably improved by my editor, whose suggestions on substance, organization, and style have been invaluable.

J.S.

Gainesville, Florida
January 1981

---

[1]Arnold Wolfers, *Discord and Collaboration* (Baltimore: John Hopkins Press, 1962), p. xvii.
[2]William J. Newman, *The Balance of Power in the Inter-War Years, 1919–1939* (New York: Random House, 1968), p. ix.

CONTENTS

I

ANALYTIC APPROACHES TO THE STUDY OF INTERNATIONAL POLITICS 1

ix

III

THE NATURE OF POWER: NEW ROLES AND LIMITATIONS   129

V

FROM STATE SYSTEM TO INTERDEPENDENCE AND THE "NEW INTERNATIONAL POLITICS" 467

GAMES NATIONS PLAY

I

ANALYTIC APPROACHES TO THE STUDY OF INTERNATIONAL POLITICS

Making Sense of International Politics 1

FOR DOVES AND HAWKS—AS WELL AS PARROTS, CUCKOOS, AND VULTURES

I nternational politics makes no sense to many people, even though it affects their daily lives more and more. It is the purpose of this book to help change that.

In this century, international politics has increasingly refused to leave the United States alone. Events in far-away places, places most Americans have never heard of and could not place on a map, have repeatedly pulled the country out of its isolationist posture. The assassination of an Austrian archduke in Serbia (now part of Yugoslavia) precipitated World War I. The German invasion of Poland started World War II. The Soviet consolidation of power in Poland and other eastern European countries and attempts to convert Iran and Turkey into satellite states as well initiated the Cold War between Russia and the United States after World War II. Events in eastern Europe—in far-away places and among peoples of whom we know nothing, to paraphrase a former British prime minister—have had a magnetic effect on the United States.

Yet during the Cold War most international events did not "touch" the majority of Americans. The Korean and Vietnamese wars did; although "limited wars," they aroused increasing opposition as they dragged on, seemingly with no victory in sight, and as loss of life, inflation, and tax increases mounted. The frequent crises between the United States and the Soviet Union also drew American attention as tensions rose sharply and the possibility of nuclear war became a

4   genuine reality: The superpowers confronted each other over the Western presence in Berlin or Soviet missiles in Cuba. But these instances of the use or the threat of force were exceptions. Most events during the Cold War—and since—received little, if any, mass attention. Many citizens were hardly aware of or, if aware, did not understand the significance of the Marshall Plan or could not name the principal members of the North Atlantic Treaty Organization (NATO), despite the publicity both received. More recently, how many people, busy with their own lives, know where Angola, Somalia, and Ethiopia are and what is happening in these countries? How many understand the strategic-arms limitation talks (SALT), if they have heard of them at all? For many, foreign affairs remain precisely that—"foreign." Polls from time to time show the sizable percentages of people who do not even know that mainland China is communist or think that Israel is an Arab nation! They also show that about half the American population thinks that the United States' population is larger than those of Russia or China.

    Since 1973 the impact of foreign policy on our individual lives has become more painfully obvious. The Arab oil producers' embargo against the United States and fourfold increase in oil prices imposed by the Organization of Petroleum Exporting Countries (OPEC) in that year have left no one untouched: the United States' economic growth, unemployment levels, and inflation rates are now basically determined overseas. Everyone's style of life has been deeply affected: Lower speed limits, less travel, home heating set lower and air conditioning set higher, and a generally declining standard of living are among the chief consequences.

    Furthermore, this change was only the beginning. Almost any event anywhere in the world suddenly appeared to affect and involve the United States. Since December 1978, for example, the overthrow of the Shah of Iran resulted in a 100 percent increase in oil prices in one year, a tremendous outpouring of dollars to pay for oil for the West, a sharp drop in the dollar's value, and a corresponding additional rise in inflation—all traceable to the fall of one man. And, as if this change were not enough, when the deposed Shah, for a time a man without a country as one nation after another refused to offer him shelter, came to New York for medical treatment of cancer, a mob of Iranian students in Teheran stormed the American embassy and held its personnel hostage for over one year to humiliate the United States and demonstrate its impotence. Nothing any more seems to pass the United States by, from a racial situation in South Africa and Zimbabwe (formerly Rhodesia), which the United States neither created nor approved, to a border war between Somalia and Ethiopia; domestic politics in Israel; a Soviet invasion of Afghanistan; or the attempts of a fanatical Islamic religious leader seeking to govern Iran. One shudders to think what would happen if the sheiks in Saudi Arabia or neighboring oil states were overthrown.

    It is one thing, however, to recognize that foreign events increasingly affect our daily lives; it is another to understand them. How can the average person understand the many events and masses of data that daily bombard him or her in the newspapers and on television? Workers, farmers, businessmen, retired people, and parents can all understand the "reality" they experience every day and can hold informed, even structured, opinions about political and social policies that directly affect them: busing of school children, parity prices for farm products, social-security payments, the increasing impact of big corporations that manufacture their products overseas on the job situation in this country. But few people have personal experience with foreign affairs. They often react emotionally: "They can't do that to us!" "Let's show them," "Send the marines," or—the modern version—"Nuke 'em." Attacks on the nation stir strong feelings. Frequently, the reaction is frustration and anger. As individuals we cannot do much; we seem powerless. But collectively, as a nation, we feel that we can do—or at least ought to be able to do—anything we set out to do. Together, are we not very powerful, even invincible, if only we have the will to exercise our power?

Understanding, however, is an intellectual process, and the beginning of understanding international politics comes with the recognition that, as in more familiar areas, we must organize the bits and pieces of information we hear and see every day. Making sense of international politics, therefore, starts with learning how to cope with large amounts of fragmented information. Each one of us perceives "reality" by means of abstracting from the totality of experience those parts that he or she considers relevant. Our perceptions are selective. They are bound to be, for obviously no one sees every aspect of reality; the world is too complex and perplexing, so that we are forced to simplify it if we are even to begin to understand it. We all have "pictures in our heads" by means of which we see the world and attempt to explain it.(Our perceptions of reality may be called *models* of the real world. They help us to organize information; select the relevant facts; arrange these facts in some order; and, in the process, interpret them.)

(We commonly use such models, sometimes called "analytical frameworks," to provide us with insight into events.)A model airplane is a representation of a real airplane. Its smaller size allows us to examine the attributes of an airplane in greater detail. Because of the difference in size, however, a model airplane is hardly a *true* representation of a real airplane (for one thing, it uses considerably less gas!). But, in its basic features, the model is indeed an airplane and thus can help us to gain a clearer picture of, for example, how the various parts of the aircraft are related to one another. Indeed, when an American toy manufacturer first started selling a model of the navy's nuclear submarine, one of its biggest initial purchasers was reportedly the Russian embassy. Because this particular plastic model, with its cutaway sections, revealed in detail the locations of the missile tubes, torpedoes, power plant, and other quarters of the submarine at a time when the Soviet Union did not yet have such a vessel, the model may have been of some interest to Soviet naval designers and engineers.

(In political analysis, in any event, a model fulfills three functions. The first is *classification* of political events and actors into categories.) We describe certain political systems, for example, as "democracies," "totalitarian states," "nation-states," and "empires." Or we describe international systems as "bipolar" or "multipolar" state systems and states as "superpowers," "secondary powers," and "small powers."(In assigning states or state systems to certain categories we must, of course, first describe the characteristics that each possesses, a task not always as simple as it sounds.)If we wanted to describe democracy, we might list such standard

6   characteristics as competitive parties, regular free elections, majority rule, and minority protection. But, as the performance of American democracy has come to be measured against continued racial discrimination, poverty, urban blight, and environmental pollution, these rather formal features—as well as such informal features as social pluralism—have been questioned. In its actual operations, the American political system is now frequently described as élitist, controlled by vested interests, and committed to the social and economic status quo ("to those who have shall be given").[1]

So how, then, do we describe democracy? What is the line of demarcation between democratic and nondemocratic states? By "democracy," do we mean free elections, majority rule, minority rights, or equality of resources? Suppose that two of these criteria come into conflict—as, for example, when a majority votes to deprive a minority group of certain rights (as American blacks were long prevented from voting in many parts of the South). And what about such supposedly totalitarian states as the German Democratic Republic (East Germany) and the Democratic Republic of Vietnam? Are these countries democracies? Because people have conflicting ideas of what "democracy" is, these questions may appear futile. If we develop a model of democracy, however, we are basically talking about how we use the term "democracy." What does the concept *communicate* to us about the characteristics of a political system? If we find that the concept is too vague to let us differentiate democratic from nondemocratic systems, then we must either choose another concept or try to refine our notion of what a democracy is.

A second function of a model is *explanation* of political happenings and behavior. We organize what would otherwise seem isolated occurrences into meaningful and understandable patterns. It has been argued, for instance, that a democracy acts peacefully unless it is provoked by aggression, but, once that happens, its foreign policy tends to become a crusade to punish the aggressor so completely that it will never dare attack again.[2] By taking a number of "facts" and relating them—a democracy with peace and a democracy with war—we offer two explanations of the behavior of a democracy under two quite different conditions. In fact, we generalize and say that a certain set of conditions will tend to produce a certain type of behavior.

Because this generalization may not hold true 100 percent of the time, we do not call it a "law" of behavior. We call it a "hypothesis," and we then test its accuracy by means of observation and, if possible, experimentation. These procedures may support the hypothesis, refute it, or require it to be more refined or qualified, so that it explains more accurately what kind of behavior is likely to occur in what kinds of conditions. The hypothesis can then be stated as an *"if, then"* proposition (*if* conditions A and B exist, *then* X type of behavior or action will most probably follow). A model in this sense is a creative tool, for its purpose

---

[1] See, for example, Theodore J. Lowi, *The End of Liberalism* (New York: Norton, 1969); Thomas R. Dye and L. Harmon Ziegler, *The Irony of Democracy* (Belmont, Calif.: Wadsworth, 1970); and Duane Lockard, *The Perverted Priorities of American Politics* (New York: Macmillan, 1970).

[2] George F. Kennan, *American Diplomacy 1900–1950* (Chicago: University of Chicago Press, 1951), pp. 65–66.

is to permit us to construct a framework that the mind can handle in such a manner as to be able to perceive relationships in the form of hypotheses, which can then be tested for their validity. *If* certain conditions exist, *then* certain types of behavior are likely to occur. Similarly, one could plan and construct different types of model airplane and obtain some idea of what happens when certain fuselage shapes are combined with various types of wings and other design features. An airplane manufacturer in fact builds such prototype models, which are then tested and changed in various ways until they become the prototypes of the real planes that will be built.

(Finally, a model offers the capacity for qualified *prediction* of future behavior, which is not as difficult as it may seem. Much depends on the ability to state accurately the conditions under which certain events will occur.) We can predict with considerable certainty that, if people suddenly notice the building they are in is on fire, they will scramble for the exits; that, if a state is attacked, it will fight back—and, if it is a democratic state and if our previous hypothesis is correct, it is likely to fight a total war for the enemy's unconditional surrender. These examples are not intended to suggest that predictions are easy. Indeed, policy makers who try to predict how other states will react to certain acts of their own may at times have good reason to doubt the predictive utility of any model. Had President Lyndon B. Johnson, for example, been able to predict accurately the costs of the Vietnam war, it is doubtful that he would have escalated American intervention so drastically in 1965. Nevertheless, prediction is one of the possible functions of a model, although the model builder should always be mindful, first, that the possibility of successful prediction depends on the quality of the model (and the information fed into it) and, second, that prediction is based not on certainties but on probabilities.

This explanation may sound rather formal and perhaps forbidding. The fact is that most of us do from time to time express our feelings and opinions about one or another international event. Although such views may not reveal a structured or organized way of thinking about the event, they do reflect some pattern of thought. Most of us do not really perceive the international political world as a mere set of random "happenings" that bear no relation to one another. We "theorize" even while we are unaware of doing so. For example, at the end of a war we may say that the victor should offer the vanquished nation a generous peace treaty. In saying so, we may be expressing implicitly the theory that a hostile state may change its behavior if the winner holds out a hand of reconciliation. Or we may say that a punitive peace treaty ought to be imposed. This statement suggests a belief that the hostile state will repeat its aggressive behavior unless it is severely punished.

We may approve or disapprove of a whole range of past, present, and future actions—strategic arms limitation; an expression in favor of human rights in Russia or Chile; a presidential order of economic or military sanctions against a country that has insulted and humiliated the Unites States, as Iran has done; the establishment of a Palestinian state on Israel's borders; or more foreign aid to less developed countries. If we were required to explain why we favor a particular course

8

of action or not, our explanation would probably begin, "Well, we think that . . . ," and then we would elaborate an opinion that would betray the "picture in our head" of how nations in general do or should behave or, more specifically, how Americans, Russians, or Arabs act or are said to act. Such an analytical framework is implicit, and it may be reliable or flimsy. What this textbook offers is a number of *explicit* conceptualizations; it is hoped that they are, on the whole, useful and offer insights that will help the reader to analyze international politics for himself or herself. The political scientist, however, is not interested only in specific issues as they occur. Unlike many historians who engage in detailed examination of the interstate politics of a particular period and tend to regard the occurrences of that period as unique—the reflections of specific men, social and economic forces, opinions of the time, and other factors—the political scientist tends to look for *recurrent* patterns of behavior. Despite the unique sets of happenings of different historical periods, including the contemporary one, he or she looks for similarities in conditions and behavior.)

For instance, we have referred to different ways in which a victor ought to treat a vanquished nation if a rematch is to be avoided. The fact remains that peace settlements often leave one or more states dissatisfied. If the defeated state has grievances, it may seek to remedy them militarily and also to gain revenge for its humiliation. But the state that renews aggression may also be one of the former victors, if what it perceives as its interests are not met when peace is made; dissatisfaction is likely to be enhanced if fellow victors seem to make greater gains. Such reasons contributed greatly to the outbreak of World War II. Germany, defeated in 1918, and Italy, one of the victors in 1918, joined forces in the late 1930s against the major victors of World War I, Britain and France. On the other hand, after World War II the Cold War erupted before peace conferences with Germany and Japan could even be arranged. Nor was this eruption accidental: American–Soviet differences over peace terms helped to precipitate intense conflict, which was perhaps kept cold only by the desire of both superpowers to avoid a suicidal nuclear conflagration.

From these two illustrations, we can suggest two generalizations about state behavior and the possible occurrence of wars (hot or cold): First, wars tend to result when defeated major powers are discontented with peace terms imposed upon them after previous wars, and, second, wars may be spawned when victorious nations quarrel over the terms for ending a war. We thus move from the examination of a specific war and the specific reasons why it broke out to generalizing about certain conditions that, *if* they materialize, are *then* likely to produce war. With such hypotheses in mind, we can examine a whole series of wars and sort them out according to these and other conditions that tend to lead to war; in our examinations, we may be able to refine our hypotheses further and to suggest more specifically for each condition why sometimes the sequel is war and why on other occasions it is not.

(How, then, can we organize and interpret the "reality" that we call international politics? First, we simplify this reality because we cannot possibly describe all aspects of international politics; we must be selective. We isolate and emphasize certain aspects of this reality and throw them into bold relief, thus enabling ourselves to make a "conceptual blueprint" of the political life among states.) In a sense, we act as does a painter viewing a panorama. He cannot draw every detail; rather, he will select and highlight certain parts of the view he sees, relegate others to the background, and omit yet others. The finished picture will be the landscape as seen by the painter's eyes, from his particular physical position and mental perspective. The painting is, in this respect, like the model airplane, a partial representation of actuality. If many intricate details are lost in the smaller canvas or model, that is the price we must pay for using a model to help us explain and understand something. (A model is always—if we may be excused for mixing metaphors—an "incomplete picture" that emphasizes those features we most want to communicate, the factors we believe critical in comparing events and objects.)

(Second, we view the picture from different perspectives, or "levels of analysis." The problem is one of scope and emphasis. Our view is three-dimensional, involving the state system, the nation-state, and decision making.[3] At the first level we consider the behavior of states, as determined by the system in which they exist and rules of which they must respect if they are to survive and be secure. At the second level we explain state behavior not as the outcome of the external environment but as a reflection of the state's own nature (whether capitalist or socialist, democratic or totalitarian, developed or underdeveloped). At the third level foreign policy is also explained as a product of the domestic system, but the focus is not on social, economic, political, and cultural characteristics; rather, it is on the men involved in the making and execution of foreign-policy decisions.)

(More specifically, on each of these three levels information is *organized* by means of boundaries between subjects (as between different types of international systems) and by selection of key variables (power, national style, social class) that allow us to focus on relevant data (and put the rest aside), in order to permit some meaningful synthesis that will aid us in our understanding and explanation of international politics *at that level of analysis*. Together, the three levels give us a comprehensive picture of the "games nations play"—particularly, why they play the game, how they play it, and some of the efforts they make to regulate and moderate the game, to play it differently, or to abolish it altogether.) ·

Rather than continue in this abstract fashion, let us take a preliminary look with examples at each level of analysis before we turn to study of each one in greater detail. It is to be hoped that, by the end of this book, the reader will no longer have to rely upon the teacher or news commentator to analyze world events for him or her.

[3.] The basic organization of this book was suggested by Kenneth N. Waltz's notion of "three images," introduced in *Man, the State and War* (New York: Columbia University Press, 1959). Also see J. David Singer, "The Level-of-Analysis Problem in International Relations," *World Politics*, October 1961, pp. 78–80. Only two changes have been introduced here: the order of the three images or levels of analysis has been reversed, and Waltz's first image (our third level), based on the traditional and behavioral analysis of man, has been replaced by emphasis on official policy makers and decision making.

2

The Three Levels of Analysis: A Framework for the Study of International Politics

THE SYSTEMIC LEVEL

The term "systemic level" refers to the international or state system comprising all existing political units that interact with one another according to some regular and observable pattern of relations. Some analysts add such phrases as "[and] all capable of being implicated in a generalized war"[1] and "[so that] system-centered behavior becomes to a large extent predictable."[2] The term "system" is used for two reasons. First, it encompasses all the sovereign states and therefore possesses the virtue of being comprehensive. The other two levels of analysis are more limited in scope. Second, it helps us to focus on the relations or interactions among the component units. The behavior of each state depends upon the behavior of other states. In gamesmanship, every player's move or "strategy"—the set of moves he or she must make to win—depends on the moves of every other player. A system, then, is simply an abstract but convenient way of representing some part of reality for purposes of analysis. We speak, for example, of a human being's "circulatory system," the parts of which—the veins, arteries, organs, and cells—must all work properly if the larger system is to give peak performance or to run at all. Similarly, we speak of the cooling system, ignition system, electrical system, and exhaust system of a car.

---

[1] Raymond Aron, *Peace and War* (New York: Holt, Rinehart and Winston, 1967), p. 94.

[2] Charles O. Lerche, Jr., and Abdul A. Said, *Concepts of International Politics* (Englewood Cliffs, N.J.: Prentice-Hall, 1963), p. 95.

Each system, in turn, has subsystems. The electrical system includes a battery, alternator, and spark plugs. Each system may, however, also be considered a subsystem, or smaller part, of the larger system, or car. All the parts must work together if the car is to run properly; the failure of one part affects all other parts.

(In the game of international politics, the key point is that each state in the system is the guardian of its own security and independence.[3] Each regards other states as potential enemies that may threaten fundamental interests. Consequently, states generally feel insecure and regard one another with a good deal of apprehension and distrust. All become very concerned about their strengths, or power. In order to prevent an attack, a state must be as powerful as potential aggressors, for disproportion of power may tempt another state to attack. A "balance of power," or equilibrium, however, makes victory in war unlikely. Therefore equilibrium will in all probability deter attack. "Equilibrium is balanced power, and balanced power is neutralized power."[4] A balance of power is thus the prerequisite for each nation's security, if not for its survival, as well as for the preservation of the system itself. Any attempt by any nation to expand its power and attain dominance or hegemony, which would allow it to impose its will upon the other states, will be resisted. When the balance is disturbed, the tendency will be to take responsive action in order to return to a position of equilibrium. States are actors whose purpose is to play the roles the system has "assigned" them in maintaining this equilibrium. If they fail in their assignment, if they disregard the operational rule that power must be counterbalanced, they place their own security in jeopardy. *The balance of power is therefore an empirical description of how states do act (or, more cautiously, how most of them, especially the great powers, act most of the time) and also a prescription for how states should act.*)

The impact of a shift in the distribution of power is clearly apparent in the United States' involvement in the two world wars of this century and in the Cold War. Our historical isolation from European "power politics" during most of the nineteenth century and the early twentieth century was the product of a balance of power on the European continent. A threat to this isolationism arose from the possibility that one state or a coalition of states might conquer most of Europe, organize its vast resources of manpower and industrial strength, and use those resources to menace the United States. England, to protect its own security, had long opposed any state's hegemony and had thus made it possible for the United States to remain what today is called "nonaligned." But when, in 1870, Germany was unified and launched a massive program of industrialization, British power declined relative to that of Germany. Indeed, World War I showed clearly that British and French power could not contain Germany. As czarist Russia collapsed, the transfer of as many as 2 million German soldiers from the eastern

---

[3] A fuller presentation of the state system will be found in Chapter 4.

[4] Nicholas J. Spykman, *America's Strategy in World Politics: The United States and the Balance of Power* (New York, Harcourt, 1942), p. 21. For a more extensive discussion of the various ways in which the term "balance of power" is used by analysts, see Ernst B. Haas, "The Balance of Power: Prescription, Concept, or Propaganda," *World Politics*, July 1953, pp. 442–477; and Inis L. Claude, Jr., *Power and International Relations* (New York: Random House, 1962), pp. 11–39.

12   to the western front raised the distinct possibility of a German victory. It was at that point that Germany's unrestricted submarine warfare, which included attacks on American shipping, precipitated American intervention, and it was this intervention that made it possible to contain the German spring offensive of 1918 and led to Germany's defeat.[5]

Just over two decades later, the United States—which after its earlier victory had retreated into isolationism again—was once more compelled to concern itself with the European balance. The unexpected German defeat of France in 1940 confronted the United States once again with the specter of an invasion and defeat of England, despite the latter's large navy. President Franklin D. Roosevelt therefore undertook a number of measures to strengthen Britain to withstand any Nazi assault.[6] He sent fifty old destroyers to help defend the English Channel, and he set up the Lend-Lease program, which made the United States "the arsenal of democracy." But there was no point in "leasing" Britain the war materials it needed unless they could reach their destination. By the time of Pearl Harbor, therefore, the United States was already engaged in an undeclared naval war with Germany in the Atlantic. American warships, convoying American supply ships for American troops in Iceland, allowed British merchantmen filled with war supplies to join convoys as far as that island; there the British navy took over escort duty. American merchant ships were later permitted to sail to English harbors; the American navy even reported the positions of German submarines to British warships and shot at the submarines when they allegedly shot first. The balance of power had made this increasing commitment to Britain necessary, even though such actions increased the risk of American war with Germany. In fact, war with Germany was merely a matter of time: German submarines would sooner or later start sinking American ships in order to compel Britain's surrender. The German invasion of Russia in 1941 briefly postponed the Battle of the Atlantic, and when the battle did take place, the United States was already at war. But had Hitler, in 1940–1941, given the order to sink all ships bound for England, President Roosevelt, like President Woodrow Wilson before him, would have had to ask Congress for a declaration of war.

(Nowhere, however, do the *continuity* of a policy and the degree to which the distribution of power *narrow a nation's range of choice* in its foreign policy show more clearly than in the eruption of the Cold War.) During World War II the United States, allied to Russia, believed it had established the basis for a postwar era of harmony and peace.[7] American policy makers recognized that the Soviet

---

[5] Edward H. Buehrig, *Woodrow Wilson and the Balance of Power* (Bloomington, Ind.: Indiana University Press, 1955); and Arthur S. Link, *Wilson the Diplomatist* (Baltimore.: Johns Hopkins Press, 1957), *passim*, esp. pp. 61–90.

[6] For the period from 1937 to 1941, the most detailed analysis will be found in William L. Langer and S. Everett Gleason, *The Challenge to Isolation* (New York: Harper & Row, 1952); and *The Undeclared War* (New York: Harper & Row, 1953). A briefer study is Robert A. Divine, *The Reluctant Belligerent* (New York: Wiley, 1965).

[7] William H. McNeill, *America, Britain and Russia—Their Cooperation and Conflict, 1941–1946* (London: Oxford University Press, 1953), written for the Royal Institute of International Affairs; Herbert Feis, *Churchill-Roosevelt-Stalin: The War They Waged and the Peace They Sought* (Princeton: Princeton University Press, 1957). A shorter study is Gaddis Smith, *American Diplomacy During the Second World War, 1941–1945* (New York: Wiley, 1965).

rulers had reasons to be suspicious of the West: Western intervention in the civil war that broke out upon the communists' seizure of power; the *cordon sanitaire* established by the French in the 1920s in alliance with a number of east European states and aimed at keeping the Russians out of Europe; Western appeasement of Hitler, especially the Munich agreement, which gave the Nazi dictator the Sudetenland in Czechoslovakia—and eventually the rest of the country—and which the Kremlin might well have viewed as a Western attempt to "open the gates to the East." But President Roosevelt believed that four years of wartime cooperation with the United States and England had dissolved Soviet suspicion of Western intentions and had replaced it with sufficient mutual respect and confidence to ensure that possible conflicts between Russia and the Western nations could be resolved amicably.

Before one of the wartime conferences between Prime Minister Churchill and President Roosevelt, American intelligence forecasters had concluded that the Soviet Union would be the dominant power in postwar Europe:

> With Germany crushed, there is no power in Europe to oppose her tremendous military forces. . . . The conclusions from the foregoing are obvious. Since Russia is the decisive factor in the war, she must be given every assistance, and every effort must be made to obtain her friendship. Likewise, since without question she will dominate Europe on the defeat of the Axis, it is even more essential to develop and maintain the most friendly relations with Russia.[8]

The significance of this forecast is clear: American policy makers were apparently unable to conceive that the Soviet Union, the acknowledged new dominant power in Europe, would replace Germany as the gravest threat to the European and global balance of power. During the war the American government had therefore not aimed at reestablishing a European balance of power in order to safeguard the United States. It had expected such security to result from a new era of Russo-American good feeling.

At a conference with Stalin held at the Black Sea port of Yalta in February 1945, amicable relations with Soviet Russia were established. "Uncle Joe" made several concessions on vital postwar issues—the United Nations Organization, German occupation policy, and self-government and free elections for the countries of eastern Europe, as set forth in the Declaration on Liberated Europe. He also promised good will for the future. No wonder that, at the end of the conference, the American delegation felt "supreme exaltation." President Roosevelt's closest adviser, Harry Hopkins, later recounted:

> We really believed in our hearts that this was the dawn of the new day we had all been praying for and talking about for so many years. We were absolutely certain that we had won the first great victory of the peace—and, by "we," I mean *all* of us, the whole civilized human race. The Russians has proved that they

---

[8] Robert E. Sherwood, *Roosevelt and Hopkins: An Intimate History* (New York: Harper & Row, 1948), p. 748.

14

could be reasonable and far-seeing, and there wasn't any doubt in the minds of the President or any of us that we could live with them peacefully for as far into the future as any of us could imagine.[9]

The American Secretary of State at that time, Cordell Hull, was even more optimistic: "There will no longer," he said, "be need for spheres of influence, for alliances, balance of power, or any other of the special arrangements through which, in the unhappy past, the nations strove to safeguard their security or promote their interests."[10]

Unlike the United States, with its long isolationist tradition, Russia had been a long-time player of "power politics." The Soviet Union was therefore bound to feel fearful. If conflict was inherent in the system, Russia had to ensure itself of a strong position in the struggle that it could expect after Germany's collapse. Russia had, after all, capitulated to Germany during World War I and had come close to defeat during World War II; more than a century earlier, Napoleon had invaded and almost defeated it. In fact, Russia's experience and fear of invasion and defeat were quite old and left the country, which had never possessed a natural frontier to protect it (like England's channel or the Atlantic ocean), with a double legacy: internally, the establishment of an authoritarian government that sought to centralize power in order to provide the country with a better defense and a greater degree of security and, externally, a "defensive expansionism" to obtain "security belts" beyond its frontiers.[11]

Stalin was well aware both of the state system's rules of behavior and of Russia's historical experience. In 1931, even before the German threat had reappeared, he had urged full speed ahead on Soviet industrialization because

> . . . to slacken the pace would mean to lag behind; and those who lag behind are beaten. We do not want to be beaten. No, we don't want to. The history of old . . . Russia [was that] she was ceaselessly beaten for her backwardness. She was beaten by the Mongol Khans, she was beaten by Turkish Beys, she was beaten by Swedish feudal lords, she was beaten by Polish-Lithuanian Pans, she was beaten by Anglo-French capitalists, she was beaten by Japanese barons, she was beaten by all—for her backwardness. For military backwardness, for industrial backwardness, for agricultural backwardness. She was beaten because to beat her was profitable and went unpunished. You remember the words of the prerevolutionary poet: "Thou art poor and thou art plentiful, thou art mighty, and thou art helpless, Mother Russia." . . . We are fifty or a hundred years behind the advanced countries. We must make good this lag in ten years. Either we do it or they crush us.[12]

Stalin was right. Hitler almost crushed Soviet Russia, just as World War I had, in fact, helped bring down the czarist system. And, as World War II was ending,

---

[9] *Ibid.*, p. 70.

[10] Cordell Hull, *The Memoirs of Cordell Hull* (New York: Macmillan, 1948), 2: 1314–1315.

[11] Louis J. Halle, *The Cold War as History* (New York: Harper & Row, 1967), pp. 10–19.

[12] Quoted by Isaac Deutscher, *Stalin: A Political Biography* (New York: Oxford University Press, 1949), p. 328.

Russia confronted yet another Western power, whose population was almost as big as its own, whose industrial strength was far greater, and whose enormous military power had, in the closing days of the war, been augmented by the discovery of how to split the atom.

As World War II came to a close and in the months immediately afterward, Russia's actions were typical of a great power, regardless of its ideology: imposition of Russian control over Poland, Hungary, Bulgaria, and Rumania, which turned them into satellites (Yugoslavia was already under Tito's control, and Czechoslovakia was living under the Red Army's shadow); attempts to dominate Iran; and attempts to effect a breakthrough to the Mediterranean by pressuring Turkey and supporting a guerrilla war in Greece; demands for administration of the Italian colony of Libya in North Africa and a share in the control of the Ruhr industry in West Germany along with insistence on unilateral control of East Germany. Above all, Soviet power advanced behind the retreating German armies and ended up in the center of Europe.

These actions led to the American policy of containment. As weary and devastated as Russia was by the war, it emerged as the major power in the Eurasian land mass. Its armed forces were reduced—according to Khrushchev's report in 1960—from 12 million to 3 million men; Western estimates in the late 1940s were 1 million to 2 million men higher, exclusive of approximately half a million security troops.[13] Still, all the other former major powers in Europe had collapsed. Germany was in ruins, France had never recovered from its defeat and occupation, and Britain foundered soon after victory. Nowhere in Europe was there any countervailing power. The only such power lay outside Europe. The United States may have wanted to turn its back on the international scene and to concentrate once more on domestic affairs. It had demobilized psychologically and militarily (American armed forces had been reduced from 11.5 million to just short of 1.5 million men, and the military budget had been cut from the 1945 high of $81 billion to a low of $11 billion in 1948—a full year after the announcement of the containment policy).[14] But this preference was not decisive. The distribution of power in the state system left the United States no choice. It was not what the government wished to do that was to matter; it was what it *had* to do. A new balance had to be established.

The postwar falling out among the Allies and their ensuing rivalry amounted almost to a replay of the conflict that had occurred after disintegration of the coalition that had defeated Napoleon. At the end of that lengthy war, czarist Russia, after an exhausting struggle, had soldiers in Paris and a close ally in Prussia. The czar was particularly adamant about retaining control of Poland (with boundaries quite different from those of contemporary Poland). All entreaties that he withdraw his troops behind his own frontiers were in vain. (Stalin himself later controlled East Germany, of which Prussia had been a large part before World War II. When an American said to Stalin that it must be gratifying to be in Berlin

---

    [13]. Thomas W. Wolfe, *Soviet Power and Europe, 1945–1970* (Baltimore: Johns Hopkins Press, 1970), p. 10.

    [14]. *Ibid.*, p. 11; and Samuel P. Huntington, *The Common Defense* (New York: Columbia University Press, 1961), pp. 33–39.

after such a bloody war, Stalin curtly replied, "Czar Alexander got to Paris."[15]) It was only after Britain, Austria, and a defeated France had signed a triple alliance and were reputedly ready to go to war if the czar remained stubborn, that a new balance satisfactory to all the great powers had been worked out (including a part of Poland for the czar) and ratified at the Congress of Vienna in 1815.

(In simple terms, the post-1945 conflict substituted Soviet Russia for czarist Russia and the United States for Britain.[16] The differences in ideology between the two Russias or the differences in political complexion and economic systems between the two English-speaking nations, were, in the context of balance-of-power analysis, *not* the key factors in breaking up the respective wartime alliances against Napoleon and Hitler and aligning the principal powers on opposite sides. The key issue in each instance was the postwar distribution of power. In the logic of the state system, even had Russia in 1945 been a capitalist state like the United States (or the latter country a communist state like Russia), the bipolar division of power after Germany's defeat would have brought on the Cold War. The two nations became enemies because, as the only two powerful states left, each had the ability to inflict enormous damage on the other. As Paul Seabury has noted, bipolarity was "a contradiction in which two powers—America and Russia—were by historical circumstances thrown into a posture of confrontation which neither had actually 'willed,' yet one from which extrication was difficult."[17] Or, as Louis Halle has pointed out, the historical circumstances of 1945 "had an ineluctable quality that left the Russians little choice but to move as they did. Moving as they did, they compelled the United States and its allies to move in response. And so the Cold War was joined." As Halle has suggested, "This is not fundamentally a case of the wicked against the virtuous. Fundamentally . . . we [the observers] may properly feel sorry for both parties, caught, as they are, in a situation of irreducible dilemma."[18]

One point still has to be illustrated in connection with this level of analysis: The price of failure to heed the operational rule of balancing the power of a potential opponent is a loss of security and probably war. Churchill once called World War II "the unnecessary war," by which he meant that it could have been prevented if Britain and France had remobilized sufficient forces and acted against Germany's various moves to upset the European balance: the reintroduction of conscription (the German forces had been limited to 100,000 men under the Treaty of Versailles); the occupation of the Rhineland—an area neutralized at Versailles because Germany had twice launched its attacks on France from there; demands for the return of the Sudetenland—a mountainous area that, despite its sizable German population, was at Versailles given to the new state of Czechoslovakia,

---

[15] W. Averell Harriman, *America and Russia in a Changing World: A Half Century of Personal Observation* (Garden City, N.Y.: Doubleday, 1971), p. 44.

[16] See, for example, Harold Nicolson, *The Congress of Vienna* (New York: Harcourt, 1946); and Edward V. Gulick, *Europe's Classical Balance of Power* (New York: Norton, 1967).

[17] Paul E. Seabury, *The Rise and Decline of the Cold War* (New York: Basic Books, 1967), p. 59.

[18] Halle, *op. cit.*, p. xiii.

so that it could better defend itself against its large German neighbor; and, finally, the demand for the return of land given to Poland in 1918. Each of these moves was designed to change the distribution of power in Europe in Germany's favor. Conscription would rebuild Germany's military strength. The militarization of the Rhineland would permit Germany to build the Siegfried line; hold the Western Front against France with minimal strength; and concentrate German power against the countries of eastern Europe in order to blackmail them into submission once they could no longer count on their French ally. And the first prize of this policy— the acquisition of the Sudetenland in 1938—dismembered Czechoslovakia, left the rest of that unhappy country prostrate for Germany to swallow a few months later, and strengthened the vise around Poland that was to pressure it into submission.[19]

Not until after Hitler had taken over the whole of Czechoslovakia did England's leaders decide that he could not be allowed to go any farther. Hitler, however, believing that England's announced support of Poland was meaningless and that his latest challenge would go unmet as before, attacked Poland. England then declared war on Germany, as did France. World War II thus began under the worst of all possible circumstances for the Western powers: After Germany's rearmament, the building of the Siegfried line, the loss of Czechoslovakia, and the demoralization of France's other allies in eastern Europe, when Germany was no longer the weak power it had been at the time of Hitler's first expansionist moves in the mid-1930s.

The outbreak of World War II, therefore, stands as a monument to a single lesson: Decent personal motives, like those of Prime Minister Neville Chamberlain, who wanted nothing more than to spare his countrymen the horror of another war, do not necessarily produce successful policies. At the very least, they require an understanding of the nature of the state system, its demands upon national leaders, and the rules of its operation. The American conduct of World War II was to underline the importance of such understanding. American leaders did not expect the Western coalition with Russia to collapse after Germany's defeat. They did not understand that, once the common purpose had been achieved, the partners would have to concern themselves with securing their own protection in a new balance of power; they did not recognize that even during the war, each alliance member had to take precautionary steps, in anticipation of possible future conflict and perhaps even war, to ensure itself of a strong postwar position.

(In summing up, three points about the state-system level of analysis should be noted briefly. First, to a very significant extent, state behavior can be explained by the ever-changing distribution of power in the system. As that distribution between any two powers changes, the behavior and alignment of third powers also change. According to this analysis, states have relatively limited ranges of choice about the kinds of foreign policy they adopt. Second, emphasis on the balance of power as the principal variable explaining a state's conduct suggests that domestic

[19] William J. Newman, *The Balance of Power in the Interwar Years, 1919–1939* (New York: Random House, 1968); Arnold Wolfers, *Britain and France between Two Wars* (New York: Norton, 1966); and Winston S. Churchill, *The Second World War, I. The Gathering Storm* (Boston: Houghton Mifflin, 1948), p. 90.

18   factors, like a state's political complexion, economic organization, social structure, and public opinion, have no noticeable impact on policy. All states are viewed as monolithic units, identical to all other states in interest, motivation, and behavior. Third, perhaps the most appropriate way of characterizing analysis of the state system is to repeat that, in many instances, the model clearly does seem to explain why states act as they do. But equally clearly it does not explain other significant instances. By itself, the model can explain neither British policy in the late 1930s nor American policy during World War II. These examples demonstrate that the systemic model is not so much "scientific" (in the sense that it can account for the behavior of the participating states) as it is *prescriptive*. It can at times tell us that states did behave as they behaved; but at other times the best it can tell us is that states did not behave as they *should have done*.[20] In Inis Claude's words, "From all this there emerges a general principle of action: When any state or bloc becomes powerful, or threatens to become inordinately powerful, other states *should* recognize this as a threat to their security and respond by taking equivalent measures, individually or jointly, to enhance their power."[21] Because states frequently do not do what they should do, we must look to other levels of analysis for alternative or supplementary explanations.)

THE NATION-STATE LEVEL

(As distinct from the state-system level of analysis, with its emphasis on the *external* determinants of state behavior, the nation-state level attributes such behavior to *internal* characteristics: the political system, the nature of the economy, or the social structure. The emphasis is not on the likeness of states, the similarity of their motives, the insignificant impact of domestic attributes but on differences in motivation, attitudes, and internal composition or domestic structure among nations. We therefore categorize states, for example, as capitalist, democratic, revolutionary, new, and so forth. Political scientists and diplomatic historians have frequently attributed certain characteristic patterns of behavior to such categories.)

Let us go back to our example of British policy during the 1930s and the principal point of our earlier analysis: that Britain did not pursue the policy it *should* have. Why? Our second-level analysis suggests one possible answer: England was a democracy in which mass preferences were expressed regularly through general elections. Successive British governments were therefore sensitive to public opinion and a mood that was throughout the entire period between the two world wars overwhelmingly influenced by memories of World War I; there was a widespread popular demand that another such bloodletting be avoided if at all possible.

It would be difficult to exaggerate the impact of the cataclysmic experience of the Great War. World War I had been the first total war—with the possible

---

[20] Charles A. McClelland, *Theory and the International System* (New York: Macmillan, 1966), p. 67.

[21] Claude, *op. cit.*, p. 43; italics added.

exception of the French Revolution and the Napoleonic wars—that Europe had experienced since the Treaty of Westphalia in 1648 had ended the slaughter of the Thirty Years' War. Although Europe had, to be sure, witnessed a number of wars during the nineteenth century, they had been minor and of brief duration. Then, after almost 100 years of relative peace since 1815, Europe had suffered the shock of another major war and a terrible bloodletting. Once the initial German offensive into France had been halted, the war on the Western Front bogged down in the trenches. First one side, then the other tried to break through the opponent's lines; neither was successful. Successive lines of barbed wire protected enemy trenches, and murderous machine-gun and rapid-rifle fire mowed down row after row of advancing infantry. Breakthroughs became impossible.

World War I was not a war of mobility and maneuver; it was a war of attrition—an organized, four-year attempt by both sides to gain victory simply by bleeding each other to death. It was an unsophisticated strategy and the losses were catastrophic. An English attempt to pierce German lines in 1916 resulted in the five-month Battle of the Somme. Although they pounded the German lines for eight days with artillery before the troops were even sent into battle, the British gained only 120 square miles—at the cost of 420,000 men, that is, 3,500 men per square mile. German losses were even greater: 445,000 men. Some estimates place the total Somme casualties at 1.2 million men, the highest for any battle in history. At Ypres in 1917 the British bombardment lasted nineteen days; 321 trainloads of shells were fired, the equivalent of a year's production by 55,000 war workers. That time the English forces captured forty-five square miles—at the cost of 370,000 men, or 8,222 men per square mile. By comparison, total British Empire casualties during the six years of World War II were almost 1.25 million, including 350,000 dead and 91,000 missing. Approximately 9 million men in uniform were killed during the four years of the Great War, and the number of dead civilians totaled several million more.[22]

But the impact of war cannot be measured by citing statistics of the dead. The real impact can be understood only psychologically. Losses are not just quantitative; they are qualitative as well. A nation can ill afford to lose millions of its men. It can even less afford to lose almost its entire youth. Is it any wonder that the nations of Europe, having lost so many of their men—and especially their young men and the children they would have fathered—also lost their *élan*, their self-confidence, their hope for the future? For the men who would have supplied this vigor and optimism—had they grown up and become the leaders of government, business, labor, and science—lay dead in Flanders fields. And those who returned from the battlefields, where they had left the corpses of their comrades in arms, were haunted by the war. In the interwar period they remained politically passive, withdrawing into their private worlds, avoiding public involvement. Erich Maria Remarque dedicated his famous novel *All Quiet on the Western Front* to this

---

[22] On the slaughter of World War I, see Theodore Ropp, *War in the Modern World* (rev. ed.; New York: Collier, 1962); Hanson W. Baldwin, *World War I: An Outline History* (New York: Harper & Row, 1962); Leon Wolff, *In Flanders Field* (New York: Viking, 1958); and particularly Alistair Horne, *The Price of Glory: Verdun 1916* (New York: St. Martin's, 1962).

20   "generation of men who, even though they may have escaped its shells, were destroyed by the war."[23]

As a result of this slaughter, England, its people, and almost all its political leaders were concerned above all with avoiding another war. "No more war, no more war" become their cry. And who could blame them? Prime Ministers Baldwin and Chamberlain were not concerned about their own personal survival. They were men of honorable intentions and decent motives, greatly concerned about the welfare of their fellow men and repelled by the senselessness of modern war. It is easy today to sneer at the appeasement of Hitler, but to the survivors of World War I another war could have meant only more slaughter and more useless sacrifices, more Verduns and Sommes. They still heard the "soldiers marching, all to die." And they remembered that the strain of the war had brought collapse to four of Europe's great empires: Austria-Hungary, Ottoman Turkey, imperial Russia, and imperial Germany. They also recalled that, despite Germany's grievous losses, its opponents had suffered twice as many—and their populations were smaller than that of Germany. If fighting another war would involve another such blood bath, surely they would be signing their nations' death warrants. Their social structures and morale could not absorb such losses for the second time in two generations.

To most men who had lived through the tragic war years, peace thus became a supreme value. The appeasement of Hitler during the 1930s was to them not just the best policy—it was an absolute necessity. Surely it was "saner" to resolve differences with reason than with guns. Would it not be better to understand one another's legitimate grievances and to settle differences in a spirit of good will, rather than by war? Was it not preferable to make mutual concessions, thus diminishing distrust and fear and building the mutual confidence that could be the only basis for a firm peace? For most of the men who had survived 1914–1918, to ask these questions was to answer them. Between the alternatives of appeasement and war, no man of good will and humanity had a choice.

British leaders thought they had no choice anyway. The antiwar mood was far too pervasive. In 1933 the students of the Oxford Union passed their resolution refusing "to fight for King and country"; in 1935 there were the Peace Ballot and a general election in which the Prime Minister, knowing that Britain should rearm, pledged not to do so because he felt certain that favoring rearmament would lose the election for the Conservatives; in 1938 cheering English crowds welcomed Prime Minister Chamberlain, who, they were assured, had brought them "peace in our time"; and in 1939, a few months before the outbreak of war and several months after Munich and Hitler's violation of it, the Labour Party—which had been pacifist throughout the 1930s—was still opposing military conscription.[24]

This scrutiny of a single democratic nation's foreign policy remains, nevertheless, a single instance and therefore does not provide a sufficient basis for gen-

---

[23] Erich Maria Remarque, *All Quiet on the Western Front*, trans. by A. W. Wheen (Boston: Little, Brown, 1929), pp. 289–290.

[24] Among other sources on this period, see Churchill, *op. cit.*; Charles L. Mowat, *Britain between the Wars 1918–1940* (Chicago: University of Chicago Press, 1955); and A. J. P. Taylor, *English History, 1914–1945* (New York: Oxford University Press, 1965).

erating broader generalizations about democracies' foreign-policy behavior. Klaus Knorr, a political scientist, has, however, gone beyond one example and has hypothesized that modern industrial societies like Britain—regardless of their earlier war experiences—tend on the whole to be peaceful societies.[25] (Before the scientific and industrial revolutions, he argues, a state could add to its power and wealth by adding territory and population. But such conquest has become unattractive because the "political and economic leaders of industrial and wealthy countries are now aware that domestic savings and investment and the advancement of education, science, and technology are the most profitable means and the most secure avenues to the attainment of wealth and welfare."[26]) Indeed, in modern societies, in which leaders are generally responsive to mass preferences, the policy emphasis shifts from "high" policy concerns with security and prestige to "low" policy concentration on wealth and welfare. Economic development, in short, turns the nation's attention and energy primarily toward the further domestic production of "butter" under conditions of peace. Modern societies have evolved into welfare states in which extensive domestic demands on government lower the priority of external aims. These social-service countries are, as a result, primarily inwardly oriented; in the absence of readily visible threats to their security, they view the spending of large sums on arms as a waste.[27] Popular interest in foreign affairs is at best sporadic, responding to specific crises; only then will money for defensive purposes be allocated. But the aggressive and acquisitive use of force by an affluent state that is geared to public and private expenditures for personal and family comfort will be rare and, if it occurs, disapproved. In addition, such modern societies tend to emphasize values, like health, education, and welfare, that are in conflict with the conduct of foreign policies that emphasize force, killing, or exploitation. Man is not to be treated as an object of aggression or oppression.

If this hypothesis about modernization and foreign-policy behavior is correct—and, given the industrial nature of Nazi Germany, Knorr's hypothesis would probably be more accurate if the term "modern industrialized societies" were preceded by the adjective "democratic"—Britain's policies during the 1930s then become even more understandable. For Britain would, by its very nature, be an essentially inward-looking nation, and this propensity would have been intensified by the Great Depression. The need to concentrate on domestic problems and to do something about the economy—an economy that even before the Depression

---

[25] Klaus Knorr, *On the Uses of Military Power in the Nuclear Age* (Princton: Princeton University Press, 1966), pp. 21–23, 29–30, 46–50; and Edward L. Morse, "The Transformation of Foreign Policies: Modernization, Interdependence, and Externalization," *World Politics* (April 1970), pp. 377–385.

[26] Knorr, *Uses of Military Power*, p. 22.

[27] Walter Lippmann has defined the role of democratic public opinion more negatively than Knorr. Precisely because of their emphasis on wealth and welfare, Lippman argues, democracies make it difficult to take the necessary preparations to avoid war: "The rule to which there are few exceptions . . . is that at the critical junctures, when the stakes are high, the prevailing mass opinion [in a democracy] will impose what amounts to a veto upon changing the course on which the government is at the time proceeding. Prepare for war in time of peace? No. It is bad to raise taxes, to unbalance the budget, to take men away from their schools or their jobs, to provoke the enemy." Lippmann, *The Public Philosophy* (Boston: Little, Brown, 1955), pp. 19–20.

22 was suffering large-scale unemployment—was bound to make foreign policy a secondary matter. Memories of 1914–1918 only augmented this existing scale of priorities, so that not until Hitler made the immense threat to Britain's security clear to both the public and its leaders was the priority of domestic over foreign policy reversed.

The war that broke out in September 1939 was the second in twenty years to have been precipitated by Germany. It was also the twentieth century's second total war, a war fought for the total destruction and unconditional surrender of the enemy. Again, our democratic typology may be used to analyze what happened. George Kennan, a famous American diplomat and scholar, has noted that, when democracies turn from their inward, peaceful preoccupations toward the external arena and are compelled to fight, they become ferocious.

> A democracy is peace-loving. It does not like to go to war. It is slow to rise to provocation. When it has once been provoked to the point where it must grasp the sword, it does not easily forgive its adversary for having produced this situation. The fact of the provocation then becomes itself the issue. Democracy fights in anger—it fights for the very reason that it was forced to go to war. It fights to punish the power that was rash enough and hostile enough to provoke it—to teach that power a lesson it will not forget, to prevent the thing from happening again. Such a war must be carried to the bitter end.[28]

Various reasons have been adduced to support this hypothesis about the warlike nature of democracy once it is engaged in military conflict. If war and violence are considered evil—the very denial of democracy's humanitarian ideals—their use demands a moral stance; when it becomes necessary to resort to force, it must be for defensive and noble reasons. The complete destruction of the aggressor regime, particularly if its way of life is authoritarian (as was that of Germany) and therefore by democratic standards inferior, immoral, and warlike, becomes a spiritually uplifting cause. Once destroyed, the vanquished nation can be sent to democratic reform school and transformed into a peaceful state. But beyond this general need for moral justification lies the reality of war. War disturbs the scale of social priorities in an individualistic and materialistic culture. It separates families, it kills and wounds, it demands economic sacrifice, and it imposes regimentation and discipline. If a society that emphasizes individual dignity and the pursuit of individual, family, and social welfare and affluence must go to war, the sacrifices demanded must be commensurate with some wholesome, ennobling, and morally transcending goal. Total victory, in this context, becomes the minimum aim.

Whatever the reasons for democracies to fight total wars, the consequences of such wars in this century have been dramatic. Kennan has even attributed the Communist seizure of power in Russia to the drive for total victory by the Allies in World War I.[29] After the collapse of the czarist state during that war, the February

---

[28] George F. Kennan, *American Diplomacy 1900–1950* (Chicago: University of Chicago Press, 1951), pp. 65–66.

[29] Kennan, *Russia and the West under Lenin and Stalin* (Boston: Little, Brown, 1961), pp. 33–36.

Revolution of 1917 established a provisional government composed of liberals and moderate conservatives and led by Alexander Kerensky. According to Kennan, if the war had been concluded immediately, the new government might have been able to consolidate its position and Russia would then have been able to evolve in a democratic direction. But Kerensky's government felt honor-bound not to break the czar's pledge to the Western powers that Russia would not sign a separate peace treaty with Germany—which would have left the Allies to confront Germany's overwhelming power alone. And the Western Allies would not release Russia from that pledge. They needed Russia's help to achieve total victory. Yet a conclusion of the war was a prerequisite for any possible stabilization of the domestic turmoil. The Russian people were weary of fighting. Above all else, they wanted peace. The army had already declared its desire for an end to the massacre by "voting with its feet": Large numbers of soldiers had simply left the front lines and returned home. Even more important, the provisional government could not implement a land-reform program while simultaneously trying to conduct a war. Yet this program was the key to long-term success. Nine tenths of all Russians lived on the land, and peasant land hunger had long agitated the czarist regime and eroded peasant loyalty to the autocracy. In the absence of a serious start on land redistribution, the new government was unable to rally popular support. Lenin exploited these circumstances, promising that, when the Communists assumed power they would end hostilities and grant every peasant his own piece of land. In November 1917 the Communist Party seized power in a second revolution. Russia's continued participation in the war had been fatal for Kerensky's provisional government. The incompatibility between Allied war aims and Russia's own domestic needs was thus resolved in the Communists' favor.

If the Western powers' addiction to total war after World War I had resulted in the collapse of Russia, leaving it in the hands of a regime that was to become openly hostile to the West, it also made World War II all but inevitable.[30] For, as we now know, a second result of the exhausting experience of World War I was the grave weakening of Britain and France. A third consequence was the collapse of Austria-Hungary and the birth of a small number of unstable Eastern and European states that would not contribute to the continent's equilibrium. Their independence was only temporary, lasting until Russia and Germany recovered their strength; these two great powers then shared a common interest in destroying the states between them, after which they could engage in a contest for supremacy over the entire area. A final consequence of the complete defeat of Germany was the fall of the monarchy. Although the kaiser had led his country into war, the new regime created at Weimar led it out, accepting the punitive terms imposed by the Treaty of Versailles. As a result, the German people identified the new democratic Weimar Republic with humiliation and defeat. Amid the great social unrest that followed the runaway inflation of the early 1920s and the Great Depression of a few years later, Germany had no traditional institutions to which to cling as it sought to weather the crisis. These conditions offered fertile ground for Hitler,

---

[30] Kennan, *American Diplomacy*, pp. 55–57, 68–69.

24   who gained power by exploiting nationalist frustration, impoverishment, and uncertainty.

Although democratic behavior, according to Kennan's interpretation,
helped to give birth to Soviet Russia, Soviet Russia represented—in a classification
coined by Henry Kissinger—a revolutionary state.[31] Whether democratic France
in the late eighteenth and early nineteenth centuries or communist Russia in our
century, the revolutionary state presents a total challenge to the international order.
It repudiates the existing order because it rejects the domestic structures of the
major powers in the system. The revolutionary state's leaders pose two questions:
Why do the masses live in poverty, ill health, and ignorance? Why is mankind
constantly cursed by war? Their leaders point to the *ancien régime*. The majority
of men are destitute because they are exploited by a privileged minority. Wars are
fought because they pay dividends in the form of enhanced prestige, territorial
acquisition, and economic gains. Although the few profit, it is the masses who are
compelled to do most of the fighting and dying. Man can thus be freed from
economic exploitation, political subjugation, and international violence only by
the destruction of the existing system. Only after the overthrow of the ruling classes
in all states can man achieve freedom from want, despotism, and war. The revolutionary state assumes responsibility for the liberation of mankind from bondage.

(By the very nature of its belief, the revolutionary state is presumably
committed to "permanent revolution"—that is, to the total defeat of the prevailing
political, economic, and cultural system that has condemned man to eternal slavery.
Only a worldwide victory of the "new order" can lead to the establishment of a
universal society in which man will, for the first time in history, be truly free from
oppression and need. Characteristic of the revolutionary state as a messianic power
engaged in a "just war" to establish eternal domestic social justice and international
peace is the proclamation issued by the National Convention of the Republic after
the French Revolution:

> The French Nation declares that it will treat as enemies every people who, refusing
> liberty and equality or renouncing them, may wish to maintain, recall, or treat
> with the prince and the privileged classes; on the other hand, it engages not to
> subscribe to any treaty and not to lay down its arms until the sovereignty and
> independence of the people whose territory the troops of the Republic shall have
> entered shall be established, and until the people shall have adopted the principles
> of equality and founded a free and democratic government.[32])

If this typology of the revolutionary state is valid, Stalinist Russia would
in the years immediately after World War II have viewed the United States not as
just another state trapped by the same security problem but as a capitalist state that
had to be eliminated. And, in fact, Moscow rejected the notion that national

---

[31.] Henry A. Kissinger, *Nuclear Weapons and Foreign Policy* (New York: Harper & Row,
1957), p. 316; and Kissinger, *A World Restored* (New York: Grosset & Dunlap, 1964).

[32.] Quoted from Carlton J. H. Hayes, *The Historical Evolution of Modern Nationalism* (New
York: Macmillan, 1950), p. 40.

insecurity and international conflict were the result *only*—or even primarily—of the state system. Its spokesmen believed that international antagonism and hostility, as well as domestic poverty, unemployment, ill health, and ignorance, are *also* due—indeed, primarily due—to the internal nature of the leading states in the system. Capitalism is viewed as the cause of all social evil. Only in a political system in which the Communist party, representing the exploited majority, the proletariat, has control and in which all the forces of production are removed from private ownership so that they may be used for the benefit of all men, instead of for the profit of the privileged few, can mankind finally live free from social injustice, deprivation, and war. As a total critique of capitalist society and a promise to deliver men from evil and bring them domestic justice and external peace, communism in fact constitutes a secular religion of damnation and salvation. It has conferred upon the Soviet Union the messianic duty of converting all men to the "true faith."

Consequently, according to this interpretation of the foreign-policy behavior of a revolutionary state, Soviet Russia was engaged in a constant and irreconcilable "holy war" with all noncommunist states, seeking hegemony in the state system. Soviet hostility toward the West, it must be emphasized, predated 1945 because it was to a large degree ideological and preconceived.[33] It was a hostility Lenin and Stalin had felt even before they seized power in Russia and before Western governments had adopted anti-Soviet policies. It was an enmity deduced from first principles and based not on what Western governments did but on what they were alleged to be. Western actions were almost irrelevant. Once noncommunist states were declared hostile and official declarations and policies formulated upon that assumption, it was hardly astounding that Western reactions were less than friendly and that the Soviet leaders reaped the fruits of the policies that they had sown. Communist ideology thus raised the level of mutual fear and suspicion resulting from the state system and caused Stalinist Russia to undertake both "defensive expansionism" (owing to its enhanced apprehension of foreign attack) and "offensive expansionism" (owing to its determination to shrink the capitalist world). Any *modus vivendi* like the one finally worked out between czarist Russia and the monarchies of Britain, France, and Austria-Hungary in 1815 was, in the circumstances of 1945, therefore excluded. The war was hardly over when the President of the Soviet Union, Mikhail Kalinin, was saying:

> But even now, after the greatest victory known to history, we cannot for one minute forget the basic fact that our country remains the one socialist state in the world. . . . The victory achieved does not mean that all dangers to our state structure and social order have disappeared. Only the most concrete, most immediate danger, which threatened us from Hitlerite Germany, has disappeared. In order that the danger of war may really disappear for a long time, it is necessary to consolidate our victory.[34]

---

[33] Kennan, *Russia and the West*, p. 181.

[34] Quoted by Paul E. Zinner, "The Ideological Bases of Soviet Foreign Policy," *World Politics*, July 1952, p. 497.

26 And in February 1946, a year before the promulgation of the Truman Doctrine, in what liberal Supreme Court Justice William O. Douglas called "the declaration of World War III," Stalin warned the Soviet people that further sacrifices were necessary to increase Russia's industrial strength, for

> it would be a mistake to believe that the second world war broke out accidentally or as a result of mistakes. . . . Actually the war came about as an inevitable result of the development of international economic and political forces on the basis of modern monopoly capitalism. Marxists have repeatedly explained that the capitalist system of world economy contains the elements of a general crisis and armed conflicts, that consequently the development of international capitalism in our time takes place not peacefully and evenly but through crises and war catastrophes.[35]

According to the second level of analysis, then, the Cold War would have erupted regardless of the emergence of bipolarity, because Russia had become *Soviet* Russia and its aims and objectives extended far beyond those historically entertained by the czars.

(As with the model of the state system, the typologies depicted in this section are helpful in explaining and predicting the behavior of particular classifications of states. The hypothesis about the peaceful behavior of a democracy helps in part to explain the reasons for Britain's appeasement of Hitler before World War II— that is, why it did not behave as it would have done had it heeded the systemic norms related to the distribution of power. Presumably, industrialized democracies look outward only when they perceive themselves as gravely provoked by external challenges that leave them little choice but to respond in their own defense against challengers clearly labeled as aggressors. Once the challenge has been met, they will demobilize and look inward again.)

(Similarly, if it is true that total wars are the kinds of wars that democracies fight with a fair degree of domestic unity and moral certitude, as only a high moral purpose can justify a democracy's waging of war,[36] it may have been predictable that the United States would experience internal dissension and moral anguish fighting "limited wars," especially wars that had not begun with clearly visible and overt aggression and in which the main ally was hardly a paragon of democratic rectitude. If a democracy prefers either to abstain from the use of power and to concentrate on its business at home or to use its power fully in a righteous cause so that the war will end as quickly as possible and permit return to domestic affairs, then one might have foreseen, in the event of a lengthy limited war, an extreme bifurcation in public opinion. On the one hand would be those who would say the country should never have become involved in the first place and should immediately withdraw; on the other, those who would advocate escalation of the

---

[35] *Ibid.*

[36] This penchant has led Paul Seabury to remark on the ultimate irony: "The pity of this is that in consequence, only huge wars, raising huge ethical issues, are worthy of moral approbation," *Rise and Decline of the Cold War,* p. 88.

conflict, a quick military victory, then withdrawal. Under these conditions, a president's early popular support for such a war is destined to erode.*)*

THE DECISION-MAKING LEVEL

*(*Up to now we have analyzed international politics in terms of such largely abstract units as the state system, in which roles are delegated to member units, especially principal actors, in order to preserve the balance of power among different classes of states. We have personified states, but common sense tells us that "the United States" does not make decisions; certain men who occupy the official political positions responsible for making foreign-policy decisions do.*)*

*(*It is this level of analysis that is probably most familiar to many people. At election time we debate the virtues of the leading candidates, their expressed and implied views, their alleged values, and groups to which they may be beholden. We watch how they handle themselves on television—whether or not they have "substance," are sincere, remain "cool" under pressure. Apparently, who is president matters. It affects the priorities between domestic and foreign policies, the kinds of foreign policies that will be adopted, the extensiveness of foreign commitments, and the weapons to be produced.*)*

*(*We shall emphasize three aspects of decision making: the policy maker's perceptions of the world,[37] the different kinds of decisions made, and the various types of decision-making systems. The first of these three is very important for the obvious reason that it is the link between the external environment and policy decisions; the real world is the world perceived, whether that perception is correct or not. This distinction between things as they *appear* and things as they *are* raises a key question: Is the objective environment as such more important—as we suggested in our analysis of the state system—or are the policy makers' subjective perceptions and definitions of that environment more important? In the terminology of Harold and Margaret Sprout, should we focus analysis on the "psycho milieu," the perceived world, or on the "operational milieu," the world that exists outside decision makers' values and beliefs?[38] Clearly, the gap between the two can range from very large to nonexistent. In the operational milieu presumably the number of feasible policies that can be implemented is limited; nevertheless, alternative policies are likely to exist, and the policy makers' perceptions will be crucial in selecting particular courses of action.*)*

---

[37] See, for example, Ross Stagner, *Psychological Aspects of International Conflict* (Belmont, Calif.: Brooks–Cole, 1967); and Joseph H. de Rivera, *The Psychological Dimension of Foreign Policy* (Columbus: Merrill, 1968). The effects of personality on foreign-policy makers' perceptions may be pursued in Alexander L. and Juliette L. George, *Woodrow Wilson and Colonel House: A Personality Study* (New York: Dover, 1964); and the study of Secretary of State John Foster Dulles in Ole R. Holsti *et al.*, eds., *Enemies in Politics* (Chicago: Rand-McNally, 1967), pp. 25–96.

[38] Harold and Margaret Sprout, *The Ecological Perspective on Human Affairs* (Princeton: Princeton University Press, 1965), pp. 28–30.

28

Prime Minister Chamberlain thus not only shared the general British desire in the 1930s to avoid another total war but thought that his policy of appeasing Hitler's demands would achieve that end. The reason: He saw Hitler as one of his own kind, a statesman who, like himself, had been born and bred in a system founded upon nationalism. He could even cite a supporting precedent, for Otto von Bismarck, after Germany's unification in 1870, had declared that Germany was satisfied and would thereafter support the new European status quo. Hitler talked in terms of national self-determination, and why should Chamberlain not believe that the new German leader was merely a cruder version of the Prussian aristocrat; that he, too, would be sated once he had achieved his apparently nationalistic aims? If Nazi Germany had, in fact, been merely a nationalist state, the differences between it and France and England could probably have been resolved without precipitating a war. But Hitler harbored aims beyond restoring Germany's 1914 frontiers.

Churchill, on the other hand, was steeped in British history, and he knew that Britain's foreign policy had long been one of opposition to any power seeking to dominate Europe, whether Philip II of Spain, Louis XIV or Napoleon of France, or the German kaiser. He perceived each of Hitler's limited demands and moves as part of a larger pattern, which would lead to Germany's destruction of the European equilibrium. For this reason, he counseled opposition, condemned the Munich agreement, and ridiculed Chamberlain's claim that he had brought back "peace in our time." "We have sustained a total and unmitigated defeat," he said bluntly.[39] As Churchill himself intimated, had he been Prime Minister in the late 1930s, World War II might have been avoided. Churchill's perception of Hitler and Nazi objectives was correct, Chamberlain's perception mistaken. Possibly Churchill could have explained to the British public the true nature of the Nazi regime, placed the German dictator's repeated demands in their proper perspective, and led Britain to oppose his moves and speed up rearmament.

The more recent American war in Vietnam illustrates the issue of perception even more poignantly. American intervention in the Vietnam war, which ranks with the Korean war as one of the most unpopular wars in American history, has often been cited as an instance of misperception by the administrations of Presidents Kennedy and Johnson. President Kennedy's inaugural address, it is said, was permeated with a sense of the bipolar conflict and confrontation of the 1940s and 1950s.[40] He pledged that the United States was "unwilling to witness or permit the slow undoing of those human rights to which this nation has always been committed, and to which we are committed today at home and around the world. . . . We shall pay any price, bear any burden, meet any hardship, support any friend, oppose any foe, in order to assure the survival and success of liberty." His conviction that the nation confronted a united and aggressive Communist bloc

---

[39] The drama of Munich is captured by John Wheeler-Bennett, *Munich: Prologue to Tragedy* (London: Macmillan, 1948).

[40] Townsend Hoopes, *The Limits of Intervention* (New York: McKay, 1969), pp. 7–13. A critique in depth of Washington's alleged misconceptions will be found in Ralph K. White, *Nobody Wanted War* (Garden City, N.Y.: Doubleday, 1968).

was reinforced by analysis of Khrushchev's famous speech of January 1961, in which the Soviet leader distinguished among three kinds of warfare: nuclear war, which would end in catastrophe for both superpowers; limited conventional wars, which were dangerous because they could escalate into American-Soviet nuclear confrontation; and wars of "national liberation," which, he declared, were "'just wars" and would have Russia's full support. Not surprisingly, therefore, when such a war was discovered in South Vietnam, the administration thought that the Russians or Chinese had instigated it and from 1961 on, sent in more than 16,000 military "advisers."[41] A few weeks before his death, President Kennedy declared that, if South Vietnam fell, it would "give the impression that the wave of the future in Southeast Asia was China and the Communists."[42] President Johnson, who relied for his policy advice principally upon his predecessor's counselors, certainly saw the issue that way and, in 1965, began massive American intervention.

Critics of the war claim that the commitment of half a million troops by Johnson and of military advisers by Kennedy was based upon the "old myths" of the Cold War instead of the "new realities" that had begun to emerge in the middle 1960s.[43] One of the new realities was that the communist bloc was badly fragmented along nationalistic lines. An extension of Hanoi's control to South Vietnam did not therefore mean parallel extension of Soviet or Chinese power; indeed, it was argued, a nationalistic communist Vietnam would be a barrier to extension of Chinese power. Nor would the loss of Saigon mean the collapse of neighboring nations; whether or not successful guerrilla wars occurred in those countries would depend on their indigenous conditions. Even a successful counterguerrilla war in South Vietnam would therefore not necessarily "teach the communists a lesson" and rule out other such conflicts, if internal factors in some of those states were conducive to wars of national liberation. In short, had the perceptions of the policy makers during the Kennedy–Johnson period more accurately reflected the changing nature of the international system, the United States could have avoided becoming involved in South Vietnam.

Different policy makers are, of course, involved in different types of decisions. We shall distinguish two kinds of decisions and policies: crisis and security policies (this distinction, though discussed here specifically in the context of American foreign policy, is broadly applicable to other democracies).[44] Crisis policy is related primarily to great-power confrontations, especially direct American-Russian confrontations; security policy refers to annually debated and funded policies such as foreign aid and defense spending. In the American governmental system, crisis policy is usually handled by the executive branch and security policy by both the

---

[41.] Hoopes, *Limits of Intervention.*, pp. 13–16.

[42.] Tom Wicker, *JFK and LBJ: The Influence of Personality upon Politics* (Baltimore: Penguin, 1969), p. 192.

[43.] Among many others, see J. William Fulbright, *The Arrogance of Power* (New York: Vintage, 1967), Part II; Arthur M. Schlesinger, Jr., *The Bitter Heritage* (New York: Fawcett, 1967); and Theodore Draper, *Abuse of Power* (New York: Viking, 1966).

[44.] Roger Hilsman, "The Foreign-Policy Consensus: An Interim Research Report," *Journal of Conflict Resolution*, December 1959, pp. 376–377.

30 executive and legislative branches. In the nuclear age crisis decisions are the most crucial, because their mismanagement may well precipitate nuclear conflict. A crisis is by definition some action of another state that the policy makers of the target nation view as threatening to their vital security interests; the threat is unexpected, and rapid counteraction is seen to be required.

Crisis decision making, whether in the Cold War period or before World War I, has received a fair amount of attention and study, and many hypotheses have been offered—some rather obvious, others more suggestive and stimulating. Although it is clear that crisis decisions require considerably more study, some hypotheses[45] are that, in moments of crises, decisions are made by a few men (the President, selected official advisers, and trusted friends and counselors from outside the government); that, as decision making "goes to the top," the foreign policy bureaucracies are "short-circuited"; that the decision makers feel under enormous pressure because crises tend to be short-lasting phenomena, which further raises the already high level of tension; that inaction permits the situation to worsen, so that the disposition is to act; that consequences of nonviolent responses are depreciated and the effects of violent action overestimated; that policy makers tend to have relatively little information at their disposal and, the less information they have, the greater their reliance on broad stereotypes or emotional images of the enemy; that they see themselves as having few alternative courses of action and the opponent as holding a number of options; and finally, that executive policy makers, feeling the need to act quickly, tend not to seek legislative approval, which may entail lengthy debate that would rule out speedy action and therefore lower domestic and allied morale.

Clearly, if American and Soviet policy makers in a confrontation do not, for example, have sufficient time to obtain information and evaluate the meanings of their opponents' intentions, as well as to plan tactics to meet threats to their security while simultaneously avoiding the ultimate catastrophe of nuclear war, a dangerous miscalculation becomes a definite possibility. During the 1962 Cuban missile crisis, President Kennedy's administration had one week for deliberation.[46] Had it not received intelligence photos of the Soviet missile construction before the installation was completed, had it instead been confronted by a Moscow announcement of Soviet missile strength in Cuba accompanied by a renewed demand for the West to leave West Berlin, nuclear war might have erupted. Washington might perhaps have decided to bomb the missile sites, as some of Kennedy's advisers counseled in the early stages of the deliberations, but that would have killed Soviet personnel, and the Kremlin might have felt compelled to retaliate to avenge the Soviet dead.

By contrast, security decisions on basic courses of policy involve far larger numbers of participants and take longer. In the United States, again, the various foreign-policy bureaucracies have grown to two-score agencies, each with personnel

---

[45] Holsti, "The 1914 Case," *American Political Science Review*, June 1965, pp. 365–378; and Glen D. Paige, *The Korean Decision* (New York: Free Press, 1968), pp. 273 ff.

[46] For further analysis of the Cuban missile crisis, see Chapter 7.

abroad, each reporting to different departments, and all competing for money and influence—especially for influence in the White House. This situation is noticeably changed since 1781, when the Continental Congress established a Department of Foreign Affairs to carry out "all correspondence and business" with other states and authorized it to hire "one or more clerks." Second, and of growing importance as presidents have increasingly wanted to direct American foreign policy, are those members of the White House staff concerned with national security affairs and led by the President's personally chosen assistant. A third set of decision makers includes Congress, especially the Senate. Power, however, is highly dispersed among committees in both chambers, committees that are, in addition, frequently jealous of one another. To mobilize the various factions in Congress in support of his policies is therefore a time-consuming and often frustrating affair for the President, tempting him to make his own policies and to sweep Congress along in the name of national unity. Fourth are the many interest groups—economic, veteran, religious, and others—that may be interested in influencing policies of concern to them. Finally, on the outer fringes, is the "public," whose opinions or moods the different policy makers take into account in varying degrees, depending on the particular issue and the scope of public interest. When there is little interest, the decision makers are relatively free to pursue the courses they believe best; when there is a great deal of interest, when mass opinion is aroused and does not fully support government policy, the freedom of the responsible officials is more restricted.

There is one final distinction among different kinds of governmental structures that should be stressed: Governmental organization for decision making leaves its imprint upon policy "output" in a number of different ways. Henry Kissinger has, for example, argued that the personal experience of the Soviet leaders in a totalitarian system affect their attitudes toward foreign policy. The absence of a constitutionally defined procedure for political succession (to positions of real, as opposed to formal, power) means continuous conflict over policy and power at the apex of the Soviet political structure. The rules of the game are usually quite nasty, for climbing upward usually means elimination of one's opponents. Stalin murdered most of his former rivals and associates. Khrushchev purged many of those who had helped him to power bureaucratically, and Brezhnev and Kosygin deposed and then denounced their former mentor, Khrushchev. The requisites for upward mobility in the Soviet system of government are therefore an enormous appetite for power, a single-minded dedication to attaining it, and a willingness to denounce colleagues and confront the unpleasant, even dangerous, consequences of losing. "Nothing in the personal experience of Soviet leaders would lead them to accept protestations of goodwill at face value. Suspicion is inherent in their domestic position. It is unlikely that their attitude toward the outside world is more benign than toward their own colleagues or that they would expect more consideration from it."[47]

This nonideological analysis, based upon interactions among the Soviet political élite, suggests, for instance, that long, tough, and patient bargaining is

---

[47.] Kissinger, *American Foreign Policy*, pp. 36–37.

necessary in negotiating with the Soviet leadership. Making concessions in order to earn good will and elicit later reciprocal concessions is a poor bargaining strategy, for the Soviets are unlikely to respond.(Only a strategy of *quid pro quo* on each item will have a chance of success and that only after the Soviet rulers are convinced, on the one hand, of the opponent's firmness and that no more concessions can be extracted and, on the other, that their self-interest is incorporated in any resulting agreement. Material interests are not sacrificed on the altar of good will and fellowship.)

Yet it was precisely upon avowals of good will that President Roosevelt relied to dissipate Soviet suspicions of the West. Roosevelt, a man of great personal charm and persuasiveness, was addicted to personal diplomacy. He could say "my friend" in eleven languages, and soon after meeting Stalin he was calling him Uncle Joe.[48] The President never doubted his ability to win Stalin's cooperation in the postwar world. He was too shrewd a politician and too good at manipulating men to fail; mutual good feeling and some hard bargaining had won over many an obstreperous congressman. The difficulty was that Roosevelt's technique, so well suited for success domestically, could not be equally successful in the quite different international arena.

> Disagreements in domestic affairs were over means, not basic objectives. All Americans desired a healthy economy, an end to unemployment, and a broadening of security among the whole population. There were no disagreements that could not be faced and thrashed out by reasonable men of good will. But how different the conduct of international affairs, especially in the emergency conditions of a world war. The nations in uneasy coalition against the Axis disagreed not only on the means of winning the war, but also on fundamental objectives for the future. Differences were too profound to be dissolved by geniality, and disgruntled allies, unlike subordinates, could not be ignored. Roosevelt either forgot these truths, or else believed that his power to make friends was so irresistible that all opposition could be charmed out of existence. He was wrong.[49]

More commonly, governmental organization affects policies in such broad categories as totalitarian (or dictatorial) governments and democratic governments. The former, it is sometimes claimed, have certain advantages over the latter because power and decision making are highly centralized and they can therefore act quickly and flexibly, adjusting policies as circumstances arise or changing and harnessing the resources necessary to support foreign-policy objectives. Democratic governments, on the other hand, are said to be deliberate, slow to change their minds once decisions have been made and sometimes unable to muster the necessary resources because of the electorate's demands for prior satisfaction of domestic needs. One of the earliest and most astute observers of the United States, Alexis de Tocqueville, suggested that a democratic government would be incapable of persevering on a fixed course in foreign policy; such policy would be constantly at

---

[48.] Richard Hofstadter, *American Political Tradition* (New York: Vintage, 1954), p. 316.

[49.] Smith, *op. cit.*, p. 9.

the mercy of domestic politics and the momentary whims of public opinion.
Whether or not democratic governments are thus handicapped in their competition
with dictatorial regimes is, of course, a matter of judgment and of continuing
debate among scholars and laymen alike.

COMBINING THE THREE LEVELS

The question that remains is Which level of analysis should be used in understanding international politics? In this book, we shall be using all three. Although
the state-system level is fundamental, it cannot by itself explain the world politics
of the postwar era. To understand why, let us look one final time at three different
and previously mentioned historical experiences that have molded our present-day
world.

First, as we stressed earlier in discussion of British policy toward Germany
in the late 1930s, first-level analysis will tell us that Britain did not adopt the
policies it ought to have adopted, largely because of the pacifist mood of the British
public and Prime Minister Chamberlain's misperception of Hitler's intentions.
Second- and third-level analyses explain why Chamberlain pursued the policies he
did. And we have also suggested that, if Churchill had been leader of His Majesty's
government, war might have been avoided, for Churchill perceived Hitler's aims
correctly. Had the British leader been able to explain to the British public the dire
threat to the island nation's security with his customary eloquence and persuasiveness, Britain might have stood up to Hitler.

But is this analysis of what would have happened likely? It is doubtful.
Memories of World War I were too vivid, the desire to avoid its repetition too
strong. Chamberlain's policy of appeasement was quite representative of British
opinion. How horrible, he had said in a radio address when war loomed with
Germany over Czechoslovakia, that the British should be digging trenches and
trying on gas masks because of a quarrel in a faraway country between people of
whom they knew nothing.[50] When Hitler's message that he would see Chamberlain
at Munich arrived, the Prime Minister was addressing the House of Commons;
interrupting his speech with the news, he was cheered by the Commons. "At once
pandemonium broke forth. Everyone was on his feet, cheering, tossing his order
papers in the air, some members in tears. It was an unprecedented and most
unparliamentary outburst of mass hysteria and relief, in which only a few did not
join."[51] Upon his return from Germany, he was met by a jubilant crowd. Roosevelt
sent a message: "Good man."

Perhaps the most significant and symbolic aspect of Churchill's career
during the late 1930s was precisely that he was not a member of the government.
Like Cassandra, he stood with a small group warning of "the gathering storm" over

---

[50] *The Times* (London), September 28, 1938; and Wheeler-Bennett, *op. cit.*, pp. 157–158.

[51] Mowat, *op. cit.*, p. 617.

34   Europe. But Britain did not want to hear him. Churchill was widely condemned as a warmonger in the 1930s. Even when war erupted, Churchill did not take over the prime ministry from the man whose policies had failed so dismally. Chamberlain did not fall until after Germany's unexpected takeover of Denmark and the defeat of British forces in Norway in the spring of 1940. It took both the outbreak of war and a disaster to make Churchill prime minister. Although the state-system level of analysis can suggest what Britain should have done, the nation-state and decision-making levels can best explain and could have predicted what did happen. (The state-system level correctly predicted that failure to play by the rules of the game would mean loss of security and the necessity to fight a war to recover it) But the climate of British democracy ruled out doing what should have been done. As this example shows, we must be careful not to exaggerate the importance of a nation's leader.(Foreign policy is not simply a reflection of his or her preferences and perceptions. He or she makes policy within the confines of a state system, a national political system, and a specific policy process.)

Second, immediate postwar American policy provides a striking example of the mutually reinforcing nature of all three levels of analysis. "Rarely has freedom been more clearly the recognition of necessity," Stanley Hoffmann has said, "and statesmanship the imaginative exploitation of necessity. America rushed to those gates at which Soviet power was knocking."[52] At the nation-state and decision-making levels policy makers ended up doing what they had to do, but that was by no means a certainty at the end of World War II. A period of eighteen months passed after the surrender of Japan before the official declaration of the containment policy, though throughout 1946 American policy had been changing slowly toward an anti-Soviet stance. Perhaps the time lag in the reversal of American policy from its wartime emphasis on alliance with the Soviet Union is not surprising. Democratic opinion does not normally shift overnight. The American desire for peace, symbolized by massive postwar demobilization, was too intense. Hostile Soviet acts were necessary before American admiration for the Soviet Union, the result of the latter's heroic wartime resistance, could be transformed. Not until Britain's support for Greece and Turkey was withdrawn in early 1947 did President Harry S. Truman confront the fact that only the United States possessed the power to establish a new balance that would secure both Europe and the United States while preserving the peace. Whenever in this century British power had weakened and Germany had stood on the verge of attaining European hegemony, the United States had become involved in order to reestablish equilibrium; with Britain's complete collapse after two world wars, the United States had no choice but to take over Britain's former responsibility.[53]

President Truman also showed that he had a keen awareness of the strategic significance of the eastern Mediterranean. When General Dwight Eisenhower, at

---

[52.] Stanley Hoffmann, *The State of War* (New York: Holt, Rinehart and Winston, 1965), p. 163.

[53.] For a detailed account of America's assumption of its new role, see Joseph M. Jones, *The Fifteen Weeks* (New York: Viking, 1955).

a meeting with the President, showed his concern that Truman might not fully understand the gravity of the course he was embarking on in an area so far removed from the United States, the President responded by pulling an obviously well-worn map of the Middle East out of a desk drawer and proceeding to give a group of top government officials, including Eisenhower, a "masterful" lecture on the historical and strategic importance of the area. Finishing, he turned to Eisenhower and good-humoredly asked whether or not the General was satisfied; Eisenhower joined in the laughter and said that he was.[54] By later going before a joint session of Congress and explaining to the whole country the new situation facing the United States, President Truman was able to mobilize both congressional and popular support. (In this example, therefore, the state-system level is of primary importance in explaining American policy. The nation-state and decision-making levels tell us how accurately the policy makers perceived "reality" and how they were able in a democratic society to mobilize popular support for the new containment policy)

In the remainder of this book, the three levels of analysis are discussed in three sections. In Parts II and III we focus on the state system; in Part IV we concentrate on the second and third levels (Part V then deals with the possible transformation of the state system). In fact, the division is not quite that neat. While analyzing the state system, we cannot separate it, for example, from the policy makers' perceptions of the system or from crisis decision making. And, in analyzing the second and third levels, it is not always possible to keep the specific political system separate from decision-making institutions and processes. Nevertheless, our broad distinction between the external environment in which states exist and the internal characteristics of the specific actors remains paramount.

HUMAN NATURE AND WAR

It is necessary to deal briefly with one final point in this chapter: human nature. As an explanation of the international system, it has been deliberately omitted, yet, because of its recent prominence in popular interpretations of the "ultimate" reason for the almost incessant international conflicts and wars of the twentieth century, it deserves a few words. (Periodically human nature—or rather, the aggressive instinct—is resurrected as the explanation for wars and violence.) Many years ago, Sigmund Freud declared

> that men are not gentle, friendly creatures wishing for love, who simply defend themselves if they are attacked, but that a powerful measure of desire for aggression has to be reckoned as a part of their instinctual endowment. . . . *Homo homini lupus*; who has the courage to dispute it in the face of all the evidence in his own life and in history? This aggressive cruelty usually lies in wait for some provocation. . . . In circumstances that favour it [it] manifests itself spontaneously and reveals men as savage beasts to whom the thought of sparing their own kind is alien.

[54] *Ibid.*, pp. 63–64.

36   Who can doubt Freud's claim, given human history from Genghis Khan to Hitler and the use of such horrible modern weapons as atomic bombs and napalm by humans against other humans? Life, Freud continued, is a struggle between Eros, which seeks to unite humankind, and Death, whose principal derivative is the instinct for aggression. "And it is this battle of the Titans that our nurses and governesses try to compose with their lullaby-song of Heaven!"[55]

(Freud's attribution of conflict and war to inherent human aggressiveness has in recent times received support from studies of animal life. The instinct for aggression, viewed not merely in Freud's way, as a means of destruction, but also as a means of preserving the various species, is claimed to be universal. It characterizes humanity, as well as the animals, and it is said that we must recognize that our behavior too obeys the laws of nature, that humans are not unique and are neither born in innocence nor possessed of noble souls. A human being is, in the final analysis, a naked ape. As Robert Ardrey has suggested, our ancestry is rooted in the animal world, and our legacy was bequeathed to us by the killer apes. "Man is a predator whose natural instinct is to kill with a weapon, [an animal with] an overpowering enthusiasm for things that go boom."[56])

(Others have attributed human strife to a human nature based on a desire for power.) The late Hans Morgenthau, the foremost proponent of "realism" among post-war American political scientists interested in the study of international politics, declares that this ("lust for power" is as basic a human drive as the drive to live and propagate.) The "struggle for power," he has written, "is universal in time and space"[57] But all societies establish rules of conduct and institutional means (like competitive examinations and elections) for controlling these power drives, either to divert them into channels where they will not endanger society or to weaken and possibly suppress them. The result, Morgenthau has argued, is that most people cannot satisfy their desires for power within the nation; they therefore project their unsatisfied aspirations onto the international arena and identify themselves with their country's power drives. Feeling impotent and insignificant domestically, the citizen gains a sense of pride and satisfaction from his or her nation's power and the successful use of that power. "My country, right or wrong" becomes the normal response to foreign policy, and the citizen calls those who disagree disloyal, if not traitors.[58] "International politics, like all politics, is [therefore] a struggle for power," though the political actor seeks to conceal the true nature of his or her actions by justifying himself or herself ideologically in terms of moral and legal principles.[59]

Morgenthau's view was similar to that of J. William Fulbright, former senator and chairman of the Senate Foreign Relations Committee. The causes of

---

[55] Sigmund Freud, *Civilization and Its Discontents*, trans. by Joan Riviere (Garden City, N.Y.: Doubleday, 1951), pp. 60–61, 75.

[56] Robert Ardey, *African Genesis* (New York: Dell, 1967), pp. 1, 325.

[57] Hans J. Morgenthau, *Politics among Nations: The Struggle for Power and Peace* (4th ed.; New York: Knopf, 1967), pp. 25–33, 97–105.

[58] *Ibid.*, pp. 97–105.

[59] *Ibid.*, pp. 83–86.

war, the senator suggested, may have more to do with pathology than with politics, with irrational pride rather than with rational calculations of advantage. It is not so much the defense of great principles, territories, or markets that has precipitated conflicts and hostilities among states as "certain unfathomable drives of human nature," which (Fulbright called the "arrogance of power." Powerful nations, confusing their power with their virtue, tend to believe that they have been selected by God or history to make other states equally wise, happy, and rich. They seem to have a psychological need to prove that they are bigger, better, and stronger than other nations. All nations, capitalist or communist, democratic or totalitarian, presumably suffer from this arrogance.[60])

The key question, however, is whether or not international politics can be ascribed so simply and directly to "human nature." A number of points may be made. First, the whole concept of instinctual behavior is questionable. In 1971 a tribe of twenty-seven people, the Tasaday, was discovered in the Philippines after its members had lived for at least six centuries in isolation. They had knives but no spears or bows and arrows, which they found inefficient for collecting food. Their diet of fruit and fish was shared equally among them. Their vocabulary included no words for war, weapons, or even anger.[61] Aggressive behavior was not part of their pattern of life. Not that biological factors cannot be important in explaining human behavior, but psychologists and others generally see this behavior as intimately related to social or environmental factors. Second, even when aggressive behavior—whatever its cause—manifests itself, it can take various forms. Konrad Lorenz, for example, suggests that human fighting behavior may be redirected through such other channels as sports; at the level of nations, such instincts may be rechanneled into the competitive peaceful development of space or underdeveloped countries.[62] Third, it is questionable whether or not one can argue from animal to human behavior and, even more, from individual to collective behavior. If human beings, individually or collectively, were really motivated by an aggressive instinct or power drive, how can we explain Sweden's policy of neutrality, India's nonalignment, the United States' historical isolationism, and Britain's appeasement of Hitler? Why do states that usually go to war only after careful consideration have to draft their citizens and resort to propaganda in order to arouse their supposedly aggressive populations and even give dishonorable discharges or courts-martial to soldiers who do not care to fight and may even desert? More fundamentally, however, why do events on some occasions result in war but on others do not?

Perhaps if humanity were constantly at war, this state of affairs might well be attributable to " human nature." But human beings are not always fighting; they also enjoy peace, though perhaps less so in this century than in some previous centuries. If human nature causes war, then it must surely also be the cause of the intervening periods of peace. To attribute both war and peace to human nature, however, is hardly helpful in analyzing why nations are sometimes at peace and

---

[60] Fulbright, *op. cit.*, pp. 4–9.

[61] L. S. Stavrianos, "Myths of our Time, *The New York Times*, May 8, 1976.

[62] Konrad Lorenz, *On Aggression* (New York: Bantam, 1967), pp. 269–273.

38 at other times engaged in conflict. Human nature is, in fact, too broad an explanation.[63] Explaining everything, it explains nothing. The factors that produce conflict and warfare among states must therefore be found in human social and political behavior, and we can explain this behavior in international politics better by means of our three levels of analysis.

[63] Kenneth N. Waltz, *Man, State, and War* (New York: Columbia University Press, 1959), pp. 27–28.

II

THE STATE SYSTEM

Of States and Other Actors

3

THE CHARACTERISTICS OF STATES

Since the Peace of Westphalia in 1648 the primary political actor in the state system has been the sovereign *state.* More recently, the number of states has more than doubled since 1945, when there were fifty-one members in the United Nations—nineteen from Europe and related areas, twenty from Latin America, only twelve from Asia and Africa. Twenty-five years later, the less developed countries (LDCs) of Asia and Africa alone constituted more than half of the total United Nations membership. If the Latin American states are included, the economically underdeveloped countries constitute a sizable majority. Altogether there are about 155 states today, including a few that are not members of the United Nations. Some forecasters predict a possible 200 states by the turn of the twenty-first century.

What distinguishes a state from any other actor on the international scene? This question has become important because of the increasing numbers of international actors since World War II. The first characteristic of a state is its territorial base. Frontiers separate one state from another. When crossing a border or flying from one country to another, one normally has to show immigration officials some sort of identification and proof of citizenship (of another country) and have one's luggage searched for items that cannot be imported, at least without some sort of duty that has to be paid to customs officials. Sometimes crossing a border can be grim business, as when going through the Berlin Wall: The frontier dividing East and West Germany is marked by barbed wire, watchtowers, and armed guards.

42   One may, of course, be forbidden entry into some countries, and sometimes citizens may be prevented from leaving unless they risk escape. Most frontiers, admittedly, are not like that. Nor does the existence of frontiers mean that they are not disputed or, on occasion, contested.

(Second, each state is considered sovereign. Its own government—not that of some other state—decides how it will manage domestic and foreign problems. Presumably, a government seeks to provide peace within its jurisdiction, promote the welfare of its citizens, and provide security from external danger as well.) In the American Constitution, the government is defined as seeking to "insure domestic tranquility, provide for the common defence, promote the general welfare. . . ." (John Herz has likened national frontiers to a "hard shell" the purpose of which has been to protect the citizens living within it from foreign invasion and penetration.[1]) All governments reject foreign interference in their domestic affairs, as the Soviets have rejected President Carter's human-rights campaign on behalf of Soviet dissidents. Nevertheless, governments interfere in one another's affairs frequently, whether by condemning the treatment of a nation's people—for example, the blacks in South Africa—or by supporting a political leader or faction seeking control of a government. In addition, sovereignty, especially in smaller states, is severely constrained by dependence upon neighboring great powers for security or markets in which to sell goods. (Sovereignty thus hardly confers upon states the power to do as they please when they please. Nevertheless, within existing limits, governments preserve the right to determine their own futures, including the right to use force should that be necessary to achieve their foreign-policy objectives. Only a defeat in war, the breakdown of the protective shell, may permit a foreign state to take over sovereign control, to make and enforce rules for the vanquished state's people (as the United States, for example, did in Japan for a number of years after World War II).)

(Third, a state is usually officially recognized by other states when it is perceived as having established control over the people within its boundaries; at that time ambassadors are exchanged and agreements undertaken. Actually, matters are not always so straightforward.) The state of Israel has existed since 1948, but of the Arab states, only Egypt finally recognized it and its government, in 1978. The other Arab states still refuse to recognize Israel's existence, even though they have fought four wars with it. (Recognition means acceptance of a state as a legitimate political entity.) The United States did not recognize mainland China until 1979. Just as the Arabs have negotiated cease-fires and prisoner exchanges with Israel, so the United States negotiated the end of the Korean war with Peking, attended the great-power conference ending the first Indochina war in 1954, and met with Chinese officials to explore certain issues from time to time before recognition was a possibility. (Diplomatic relations with governments that have not yet been recognized as legitimate are thus possible, but such relations are intermittent and do not easily permit accurate assessment of one another's intentions and capabilities.)

[1.] John Herz, *International Politics in the Atomic Age* (New York: Columbia University Press, 1959).

(The basic rule is to extend *de facto* recognition when a new state is born; the fact of its existence is the key. But some states will extend recognition only *de jure*, that is, when they approve of the new government.) The United States was slow to recognize both the Soviet and the Chinese communist governments. Sometimes the situation becomes awkward when different states recognize rival governments of another state. During World War II the Germans established puppet governments in conquered lands, but the Western allies continued to recognize the former governments, which were usually quartered in exile in London. Poland at one time actually had three governments: one recognized by the West, one recognized by the Germans, and one (composed of pro-Moscow Communists) recognized by the Russians! Since World War II, Moscow and Washington have at times recognized rival governments: in East and West Germany, North and South Korea, North and South Vietnam, and Communist and Nationalist China. Both now recognize each of the Germanies. South Vietnam no longer exists, but the United States has not recognized the new unified Communist People's Republic of Vietnam, and Washington has finally withdrawn recognition from the nationalists on Taiwan. (Clearly, determining when to shift recognition from one government to another in a civil war or when to recognize a completely new state is a political issue.)

Nothing could have illustrated this truth in a more gruesome fashion than the bizarre instance of Cambodia (renamed Kampuchea). Its communist government, which, under Pol Pot, won power toward the end of the Vietnam war, reportedly killed an estimated 2 to 3 million of a total population of 8 million people between 1975 and 1978 (as estimated by the communists themselves). Pro-Chinese, anti-Russian, and anti-Vietnamese (Vietnam is a historical enemy), the regime provoked Vietnam into invading Cambodia and installing a new and friendly government, which was also pro-Russian and anti-Chinese. But the remnants of the Pol Pot regime continued to resist, and the fighting made growing food difficult, especially as each side deliberately destroyed crops so that the other side would not be able to feed itself. The result has been widespread starvation for many of the remaining 5 to 6 million people. Refugees have streamed into neighboring Thailand. Estimates of the number of Cambodians who have died from starvation range up to 2 million. The subsequent spectacle seems almost incredible: The Vietnamese-installed Cambodian government and the Vietnamese, who, given their ancient hatred, probably cared little for the fate of the starving Cambodians, refused to allow American food supplies into the country, while the United States was virtually insisting that it be permitted to feed Cambodia's people. Later, when some food was allowed in, it was either left in storage or used to feed the Vietnamese or the new Cambodian government's armies. Clearly, as most of the world reluctantly still recognized the predecessor government, which had initiated a policy of genocide toward its own people, the new Cambodian government, imposed by Vietnamese bayonets, was seeking to use its own starving people to gain diplomatic recognition and legitimacy from the United States and other foreign countries. Recognition was the price "for allowing the world to feed its starving people".[2] In

---

[2] *The New York Times*, October 25, 1979, and *Time*, November 12, 1979.

44 the meantime, Russia, defeated in its effort to substitute the new Cambodian regime for the old one in the United Nations, declared for all the world to hear that no one was dying of hunger in Cambodia, that the story of starvation was an invention of Western propaganda, and that the West's so-called humanitarian aid was in fact a cover to bring military help to the enemies of the new Cambodian government!

One final characteristic of states in the contemporary world is worth mentioning, if only because we often use the terms "state" and "nation-state" interchangeably. Before 1789 and the French Revolution, most states were ruled by kings, and most people living within the territorial confines of such dynastic states did not really identify with them. At times, kings traded people and lands. But the nationalism born in France and then stirred up in the rest of Europe in reaction to French conquest led people increasingly to identify with their nations. (It is difficult to define a nation exactly, but we can say that it is a collective identity shared by people living within certain frontiers as a result of their common history (plus a good deal of mythology dramatizing the past), expectations of remaining together in the future, and usually a common language that allows them to communicate more easily with one another than with the inhabitants of neighboring nations who speak different languages. Ernest Renan, a Frenchman, characterized a nation as "a daily plebiscite," a continuous emotional commitment to a group of people distinct from every other segment of humanity, celebrating their "nationhood" with anthems, poetry, statues of heroes who have defended it, and other symbols. But nationality and geographical boundaries do not always coincide in real life.) Russia is a multinational state; so are Belgium and Canada. Such multinationality can become divisive, leading to disintegration and civil war, as has happened frequently in the new LDCs, which are often composed of various ethnic or tribal groups that speak different languages and have little in common other than short periods of subjection to colonial rule. (Maintaining national unity remains the primary problem for many of these new states.)

CLASSIFICATION OF STATES

GREAT POWERS AND SMALL POWERS

(The most widespread and traditional means of distinguishing among states is in terms of the "power" they possess. The components of power include geographic location, size, population, industry, wealth, and so on (see Chapter 7). Most observers have long distinguished between "great powers" and "small powers." We can say, almost by definition, that the great powers have generally been considered the primary actors in the state system.)

Particularly striking is the remarkable stability in the ranking of great powers, despite vast geographic, industrial, and social changes in Europe during the nineteenth century. We need only list the great powers since the French Revolution and the Napoleonic wars.

	Napoleonic Wars	World War I	World War II	Cold War and Détente
Austria-Hungary	X	X	–	–
Britain	X	X	X	X
France	X	X	X	X
Italy	–	X	X	X
Japan	–	X	X	X
Prussia-Germany	X	X	X	X
Russia	X	X	X	X
United States	–	X	X	X

Stability in these rankings does not mean that changes in individual positions have not occurred. Prussia, which made its mark against Napoleon Bonaparte, became an enlarged and united Germany in 1870 after the defeat of France. Germany then replaced France as the Continent's preeminent power and became a rival to England, at that time the leading power in the world. Germany built a large navy, in addition to the sizable and highly efficient army that it already possessed. Austria-Hungary, by contrast, declined after the Napoleonic wars and lost its place as the primary power in central Europe to Prussia, which, to the astonishment of the rest of Europe, defeated Austria rapidly in six weeks in 1866. By the turn of the twentieth century, Japan and the United States had joined the other great powers and had transformed the Europe-centered system into a global system. Germany made its bid for European, if not Eurasian, dominance in 1914, but American intervention in 1917, after Russia's defeat, ensured the failure of this venture. American withdrawal into isolationism again meant that the postwar European balance remained fragile. Germany was too strong for Britain and France to contain by themselves. Again, American intervention was the key factor in the failure of Germany's second drive for domination. But two world wars in this century had exhausted Britain, France, and Germany. Only two powers emerged still strong: Russia, despite its enormous losses in World War II, and the United States. Both were continental powers with populations and resources to match, dwarfing the great powers of the past. Hence the term "superpowers."

The international system has always granted a special place to the great powers. During the nineteenth century the Concert of Europe was composed exclusively of the great powers; they were the self-appointed board of directors of the European "corporation," meeting from time to time to deal with significant political problems that affected the peace of Europe. This special great-power status and responsibility were reflected in the League of Nations Covenant, which gave such powers permanent membership on the Council; the Assembly, composed of the smaller nations, was expected to meet only every four or five years. In those

46 days, "the world seemed to be the oyster of the great powers."[3] After Germany's second defeat, their privileged status and obligations were again recognized in the United Nations Charter provision that conferred upon the United States, the Soviet Union, Britain, France, and China (which at the time was still controlled by the Nationalists) permanent membership on the Security Council. The General Assembly was not expected to play a major role in preserving the peace. These same five states were, by 1971, when Communist China was admitted to the United Nations, the only members of the nuclear club. After China, India was the first to explode a nuclear device; possible future nuclear powers may include such already highly industrialized states as Japan and such potential future powers as Brazil.

In contrast, small powers have often been less acting than "acted upon." Their security has often depended on the great powers. Even a state like Israel, which has fought its own wars, is very conscious of its dependence on the United States for modern weapons and money; it is also constantly concerned about American diplomatic pressure to compel concessions that it believes inimical to its interests but that Washington perceives as necessary to achieve an overall settlement in the Middle East. Even a greater sense of limited choice is felt by the states of eastern Europe. Although they are no longer completely subservient to Russia and cannot be called "satellites," Moscow has, through the Brezhnev Doctrine, claimed the right to determine when socialism is in danger of being subverted and to intervene militarily as it did in 1953 in East Germany, in 1956 in Hungary, and in 1968 in Czechoslovakia. The United States under the Monroe Doctrine has frequently intervened in Latin America. After Fidel Castro's assumption of power in Cuba, overt American intervention in the Dominican Republic in 1965 and covert intervention in Chile a few years later were carried out allegedly to protect this hemisphere from alien and subversive forces. Washington defined these forces as communist and asserted the right to intervene to prevent the establishment of other communist governments in this hemisphere. Not all small countries lie near enough to great powers to be subject to military intervention or political manipulation, but, in general, smaller and less powerful nations claim to be victims of international politics, exploited by the stronger powers for their own benefit. (The LDCs atribute their poverty and difficulties in modernizing to the alleged dominance of the West. The colonial powers first exploited the LDCs, and the great powers' international financial institutions continue to dominate them. The strong are favored by the laws of supply and demand in the international market. The LDCs therefore demand a new international economic order. Victims or not, small states have generally not been too influential.)

(Actually, the dichotomy between great and small powers, though useful, is rather unsophisticated. It is useful because it simplifies the analysis and conduct of international politics. It allows the scholar and diplomat to focus on demands and fulfillment of the great powers' national interests; the needs of the weak can either be ignored or receive negligible attention and satisfaction. Although obviously

---

[3.] Inis L. Claude, Jr., *Swords into Plowshares* (New York: Random House, 1956), p. 53.

oversimplified, the old axiom that the strong do as they please and the weak suffer as they must expresses a simple truth about the relations among nations. But the international hierarchy of states is more complex than the simple hierarchy of great and small powers.)

At the top of the hierarchy since World War II are the two superpowers, the United States and the Soviet Union. Clearly, the very term "superpower" suggests their preeminence in the state system and their superiority even to the traditional great powers. The United States and the Soviet Union are in a category all by themselves. Usually their status is equated with their vast nuclear forces; the small forces of other nuclear nations are not yet comparable. But, even if nuclear arms had never been invented, these two countries would be superpowers. As countries with populations of more than 200 million people and sizable industries, they have also been able to afford large conventional forces and to use their wealth and technology to advance their aims. (Their interactions at the top of the international "pecking order" have influenced, if not determined, the policies of more states than the interactions among lower-ranking members.[4] One of the paradoxes of the post-World War II state system has thus been that it has witnessed simultaneously a massive expansion of states—approximately 100 new states—and a significant contraction of primary actors, like the superpowers, in the system.)

Underneath these two powers are the second-rank powers, Britain, France, West Germany, China, and Japan, whose capacities to act in one or more of the regions beyond their own are relatively limited. The first three, pre-World War II members of the great-power club, have recovered from their collapse after 1945, but they can play a world role again only if collectively they succeed some day in extending the economic unity of the Common Market, whose leading members they are, to political and military unity in Europe. Individually, these nations will remain in their present status. One change especially can already be pointed out: The frequently held assertion in the late 1960s and early 1970s that Europe and Japan, economically recovered from World War II and very prosperous, would be able to use their economic power to attain great political influence has died with the rise of the Organization of Petroleum Exporting Countries (OPEC). The nine European states, which together have a population slightly larger and a productive capacity quite a bit larger than those of Russia, quickly folded before their former colonies and endorsed Arab aims in the 1973 war. So did Japan, often called an economic superpower in those days. (Great-power status without sufficient military power and some definition of the political role that the nation ought to play is not possible; economic capacity alone is not enough. Neither Europe nor Japan can defend itself without American power or exercise influence commensurate with its economic productivity and wealth. Similarly, China, weak economically and even militarily, remains only a potential superpower.)

From there on down we can divide nations into middle-rank powers like Italy and Spain in Europe, India in Asia, and Brazil in Latin America, the latters

---

[4] Steven L. Spiegel, *Dominance and Diversity* (Boston: Little, Brown, 1972), p. 19.

48 two potential superpowers; minor powers like Norway, Hungary, South Korea, and Colombia; and microstates like Grenada and the Bahamas.[5]

A closely related criterion for classifying states according to their power is the extent of their interest and capacity to intervene in affairs beyond their own frontiers. Power "makes ambitious projects feasible and increases . . . their chances of success; weakness constrains, restrains and limits choice and independence."[6] The superpowers thus have the capacity to project their power throughout the entire state system. The United States, with its navy and air-lift ability, has long had a global reach. (It could intervene overnight in Lebanon and fight a long war in Vietnam at the end of 10,000 miles of supply lines. The generals in Moscow must have been envious.) Russia, the Avis of the superpowers, was initially a Eurasian power (though control of foreign communist parties did extend its reach), but an enormous military build up, including a blue-sea fleet and airlift capacity, has given Moscow a system-wide capability as well. Under both tsars and commissars, Russian expansion has been concentrated on the nation's periphery. In the 1970s, for the first time it expanded its influence beyond Eurasia—to Angola, Ethiopia, and South Yemen.

The second-rank states are essentially regional powers. The former colonial powers have largely limited their roles to Europe. Britain's last foreign intervention came during the Suez war in 1956; it was a dismal failure, ending in the collapse of the British government. France, which had joined with Britain to intervene in Egypt, reacted by developing a nuclear bomb in order to recoup its prestige and to play an active role in Europe. In the 1970s, however, France increasingly used troops to support its interests, largely in former French Africa. In 1978, it intervened with small forces in Zaire, formerly the Belgian Congo, though it needed American planes to carry them. Middle-rank and minor powers have even less capacity to act beyond their regions or even their frontiers. Many of the smaller states have virtually no individual influence.

Nevertheless, if it were this easy to calculate power and predict who will influence whom and, in war, beat whom, it would have been difficult—if not impossible—to predict North Vietnam's victory over the United States in the Vietnam war or the quaking of the West European industrial countries before their former colonies in OPEC, most of whose member countries have tiny populations, no industry, and no military muscle. A ranking of states by power may thus give us an initial quick impression of which are likely to achieve their aims and which are not, but though such ranking is useful, even necessary, it is clearly not sufficient. States may be classified according to amounts of power, but power relations among states may be quite complex. The components of power, as we shall repeatedly emphasize in the next few chapters, are not automatically translated into equivalent influence or ability to achieve desired goals. Even rankings are difficult to establish below the level of the secondary powers. Is Cuba, which in 1978–1979 had more

---

[5] See *ibid.*, pp. 93–96, for a comprehensive list of states by rank.

[6] David O. Wilkinson, *Comparative Foreign Relations* (Belmont, Calif.: Dickensen, 1969), p. 27.

than twice the number of troops in Africa that France had, a minor power or a secondary power? Cuba with a population of almost 10 million has a military of 200,000 (for the American population, the equivalent would be 4-5 million, twice the size of current U.S. forces); 40,000 Cubans are reportedly serving overseas, 35,000 of them in Angola and Ethiopia.[7] And what about Saudi Arabia, a country even the United States fears to offend—is it a superpower, a secondary power, or on a level lower even than the minor powers like Yugoslavia, Pakistan and Israel? Rankings are too often impressionistic, not necessarily very accurate guides.

One final point should be noted. It has been suggested by some analysts that states may be differentiated not only by their power and the scope of their interests but also by differences of behavior.[8] States approximately equal in power—regardless of regime, according to Steven Spiegel—behave similarly; states very unequal in power act differently. Robert Rothstein has specifically warned that a small power is not a great power writ small, that its behavior is different in kind and not only in degree from that of its bigger brethren. A first-rank power can occasionally make a mistake without disastrous results, for it can, once it has recognized its error, exercise its great capability to correct the earlier blunders. At times it may even sustain setbacks, which are not fatal. But a small power does not usually have that luxury; a mistake may well be fatal. A great power can, more often than its small colleague, wait a little longer to see whether or not its adversary will really attack; its margin of safety—especially in the age before nuclear weapons—has been greater, and thus it has been less likely to be tempted to strike preemptively. But for small powers, "it means, in sum, that the margin of error is small or nonexistent: to choose incorrectly may end the possibility of free choice. A lapse in vigilance can be fatal. Procrastination or 'muddling through' appears to be ruled out."[9] We need only look at Israel's two preemptive strikes at Egypt and its allies in 1956 and 1967, as the Arab countries appeared to be ready to launch a war; this situation was in contrast to that of 1973, when for political reasons Israel decided not to strike first and, as a result, suffered heavy casualties and loss of prestige in the subsequent fighting, which, in turn, affected its negotiating strength in the subsequent diplomatic efforts to achieve a more lasting regional peace. In those negotiations Israel was constantly afraid of being betrayed by the United States, of being forced to make concessions that it did not want to make in order to ensure oil for the United States. Israeli suspicions, occasionally bordering on paranoia, were striking, considering the long history of American support for Israel and commitment to its existence. The difference reflected in good part the differences of power: The United States, as a relatively secure superpower, could suggest concessions that it felt sure would lead to a comprehensive peace; Israel was a small power, very insecure despite repeated military victories over hostile neighbors, and

---

[7] James C. Goldsborough, "Dateline Paris: Africa's Policeman," *Foreign Policy*, Winter 1978–1979, pp. 174–190; and F. Clifton Berry, "Cuba's Expanding Power Potential," *Air Force*, April 1980, pp. 43–47.

[8] Robert L. Rothstein, *Alliances and Small Powers* (New York: Columbia University Press, 1968).

[9] *Ibid*, p. 5.

50   apprehensive that every concession would weaken it, especially in relation to the Palestinians. An Israeli prime minister might well have uttered words similar to those spoken by Nguyen Van Thieu, the last President of South Vietnam, to Henry Kissinger, when he rejected the terms worked out by North Vietnam and the United States for ending the Vietnam war in late 1972:

> You are a giant, Dr. Kissinger. So you can probably afford the luxury of being easy in this agreement. I cannot. A bad agreement means nothing to you. What is the loss of South Vietnam if you look at the world's map? Just a speck. The loss of South Vietnam may even be good for you. It may be good to contain China, good for your world strategy. But a little Vietnamese doesn't play with a strategic map of the world. For us, it isn't a question of choosing between Moscow and Peking. It is a question of choosing between life and death. [10]

STATUS QUO STATE VERSUS REVISIONIST STATE

We can classify states according to their general aims in the state system: Are they willing to accept things as they generally are, or do they seek to change them? If they are largely willing to accept the existing situation, they are "status-quo powers." The status quo can, therefore, be identified with such words as "satisfied," defense," "preserve"; revisionism is associated with "expansion," "offense," and "change." These terms have been particularly useful in the past, when they have been associated with peace treaties concluded at the ends of wars. As territorial settlements have usually been involved, the victors have sought to preserve the status quo, which has generally benefited them; the vanquished states have wished to arrange changes to alleviate some of the grievances outstanding from the war. At the end of World War I, for example, the Versailles peace treaty included a number of provisions about Germany's frontiers with the new Poland and Czechoslovakia that were disliked by most Germans. France arranged for alliances with the countries to Germany's east in order to contain German power. It was thus committed to these countries and their frontiers with Germany; there were also other provisions, like limitations on the size of the German army and the kinds of weapons that it could have. Germany wanted some changes, even before the rise of Adolf Hitler.

After World War II there was no formal peace treaty with the two Germanys, then divided among the superpowers. The frontier in Europe was the line between the Soviet and Allied armies when Germany had surrendered. Over time this line between western and eastern Europe became accepted by both the United States and Russia. The nearest thing to a peace treaty was the Helsinki agreement in 1976, in which the *de facto* (existing) situation was mutually accepted and legally recognized. In general, the United States and the West have considered themselves the status-quo powers during the Cold War and détente; the Soviets are viewed as revisionist, constantly probing for weak spots into which Russian power can flow—

[10.] Quoted by John Stoessinger, *Henry Kissinger* (New York: Norton, 1976), p. 68. Reproduced by permission.

initially around their own periphery, now in Africa, the Arabian peninsula and Asia as well. The issue is less one of territorial changes than of spreading Soviet influence to strategically located nations; this effort is viewed as potentially damaging to American and Western interests. It ought to be added that the Soviet Union in return views the US as a status-quo power—the defender of world capitalism—while it associates itself with the historical change from capitalism to (Soviet-style) socialism, a change it seeks to speed up.)

(Designation of a state as favoring the status quo or as revisionist looks straightforward but it is often not simple.) Both Germany in the interwar years and Russia since 1945 have wished to overthrow the status quo, which each deemed unfavorable because it blocked the realization of vision of what the international system ought to be—a world order ruled by Germany or Russia in the name of either the German Aryan race or the world's proletariat. But to their later adversaries it was not so obvious. Germany in the 1930s claimed that it wished to restore the old pre-World War I Germany. Such revisionist aims would have been limited and would have constituted little danger to Europe: once satisfied, Germany would presumably have taken its place in the European subsystem as a status-quo power. London believed Germany's claim and thus misjudged Hitler's intentions. His appetite grew with the feeding. He was unappeasable, but that was easier to see in retrospect. With his predecessors, whose ambitions had been limited to the restoration of pre-1914 Germany, this appeasement policy might have worked. Under Hitler, whose ultimate ambitions were unlimited, the policy was doomed to fail.

One major reason for this was that the two status-quo powers, France and Britain, could not even agree on what the status quo was. For Paris, it was the Versailles settlement; any change in the settlement terms was viewed as undermining the status quo. In London, to enforce the Versailles status quo against a country as potentially powerful as Germany seemed provocative and self-defeating, for it would in the long run ensure war; it was better to allow some revision of the peace terms, including Germany's eastern frontiers, in order ultimately to strengthen the status quo. Second, as noted, there are different degrees of revisionism and this distinction is critical. A small amount may not be harmful and can be tolerated by neighboring states; sizable changes may not be acceptable. But this distinction may not be clear at the time. Hitler cleverly disguised the fact that he wanted a complete revision of the status quo; each time he made a demand, it was a limited one, and he claimed it was his last one. For a while his neighbors believed him.

During World War II, as we saw earlier, the United States thought Russia was basically a status-quo power. After the war, Russia was redefined as revisionist. Is Russia today still a revisionist state? Or has it become basically a status-quo power seeking primarily to protect its postwar domination over eastern and central Europe and its long frontier with China against Chinese claims for border changes? Do Moscow's rulers still seek to fulfill their ideological objective of world revolution? Or have they become more and more conservative as they have become older, as the revolutionary fervor of an earlier day has evaporated, and as Russia—seventy years after the revolution—has become a highly bureaucratic and industrialized nation with much to lose in a nuclear war? In short, the questions of how revisionist

52 a state is and on what issues, or to what extent it has become *in practice* a status-quo nation, even though it may still mouth revisionist purposes and slogans, are not easy to decide and become matters of controversy, if not confusion. What are the criteria of judgment—declaratory statements or acts and, if so, of what specific kind? How especially does the observer decide when a status quo power has become revisionist and the reverse? Nevertheless, for all of the ambiguities and difficulties involved in classifying states in this manner, it can be useful in analysis if used with care and awareness of the complexities involved.

WEST-EAST-NONALIGNED (FIRST, SECOND, AND THIRD WORLDS)

(A tripartite classification of states, unlike those already given, is more contemporary. It is based on neither power nor goals. Instead, it is based on states' relations with the superpowers—alignment with the United States (the West), with the Soviet Union (the East), or with neither (nonaligned). The three divisions are also known as the first, second, and third worlds. This categorization was especially useful during the Cold War years, when the Western alliance (the North Atlantic Treaty Organization, or NATO), and the Soviet Union and its allies in eastern Europe, as well as China, confonted each other in two solid blocs, often called in the West the Free World and the Communist World. In between were the new nations, former colonies, which organized themselves as a third bloc.

This threefold division is no longer quite so applicable. NATO, although it continues to exist and is likely to do so for a long time, can no longer be called a bloc, as if it were a cohesive unit with a single policy. Differences among Western allies means that we must also speak of French or West German policies, for example. Divisions also exist among Russia's allies in eastern Europe. Rumanian policy does not mirror Soviet policy. And the Sino-Soviet alliance has completely split: China now aligns itself with the United States, Europe, and Japan. China even briefly invaded Vietnam after Vietnam had invaded communist Cambodia to overthrow its pro-Chinese regime and replace it with a pro-Vietnamese and pro-Russian government. Despite China's move away from Russia toward the United States, China publicly identifies itself as a third-world state. Yet it does not belong to the third-world "Group of 77," originally composed of 77 LDCs—now 120 members—who push issues of interest to the LDCs. China is instead aligning itself with the West politically and economically as it seeks safety from Russian attacks and economic help to become a great power.

(The nonaligned states, too, have become increasingly divided. Composed as they are of more than 100 nations from different regions, of varying sizes, differing in history, ideology, political and economic systems, and divided between pro-American and pro-Soviet sentiments, they can no longer be considered a bloc. OPEC probably caused the sharpest division as it highlighted the enormous gap between the few resource-rich nations and the many poorer nations. The latter are increasingly called the "fourth world.")

(Yet, despite the divisions in each of the three blocs, the classification remains useful, for members of NATO remain opposed to the Soviet Union; the Soviet alliance with the states of eastern Europe survives as well; and the nonaligned states do still meet from time to time in special conferences and more regularly at the United Nations.)

RICH NATIONS AND POOR NATIONS

(Another axis of conflict beside East–West is rich–poor, or north–south. These terms are handy, even though also oversimplified; they are tags. Parallel sets of terms include "first world" (Western industrial states) and "third world" (non-Western, economically underdeveloped countries), on one hand, and "developed countries" (DCs) and "less developed countries" (LDCs), on the other. The first-world nations include the former colonial powers, and the third-world nations those that had been governed from London, Paris, Brussels, and other Western capitals.) During the Cold War, the third-world nations used their in-between status to enhance their bargaining strength and attract economic assistance from both East and West for their own development. But during détente, as their leverage declined, the poor countries increasingly focused their attention on the richer Western states, which supposedly dominated the international economy and exploited them. They demanded a new international economic order (NIEO). The Soviets, insisting that they had never been a colonial power and therefore were not accountable for the lot of the underdeveloped countries, refused to do much to help improve the conditions of the latter, on grounds that they were the West's responsibility. Yet, by the standards of most southern nations (in Africa, Latin America, and southeast Asia), Russia is also a rich nation, and it is therefore doubtful that Moscow can long refuse to upgrade its assistance. Nevertheless, since 1973 and OPEC's quadrupling of oil prices and the oil embargo against the United States, the conflict between rich and poor has shared center stage in the world arena with the older adversary relationship between East and West; the third-world nations' problems of population, food, and poverty are now very much part of the international agenda, and they are especially pressed through the United Nations Conference on Trade and Development (UNCTAD) which has been called a "trade union of the poor."[11] (Despite all the differences and conflicts among the third-world nations, the labels described here still serve as useful shorthand, immediately focusing the observer's thinking on the nature of the issues and the principal actors.)

INTERGOVERNMENTAL ACTORS

(Individual nation-states are complemented by other actors composed of groups of states: intergovernmental organizations (IGOs), or, as they were more commonly called in the past, international organizations. Decisions are negotiated among the

---

[11.] Robert L. Rothstein, *The Weak in the World of the Strong* (New York: Columbia University Press, 1977), p. 127.

54 governmental representatives assigned to the IGOs, including foreign and defense ministers, who attend specified meetings; the day-to-day business of each IGO is carried out by its bureaucracy. The institutional machinery of IGOs may be relatively small or large and complex, as in the European Economic Community (EEC).

IGOs may be classified in two ways. First, the organization may be global or regional. The United Nations includes most existing states and strives for universal membership. The British Commonwealth, by contrast, comprises states in almost every area of the world; far short of universal membership, it is nevertheless a global organization. Similarly, the Organization of Petroleum Exporting Countries (OPEC), the nucleus of which is Arab (Saudi Arabia, Algeria, Qatar, Kuwait, Libya, Iraq and the United Arab Emirates), has other members in the Middle East (Iran), Africa (Nigeria and Gabon), southeast Asia (Indonesia), and Latin America (Venezuela and Ecuador). Other producer cartels also have multiregional or global membership. Most IGOs, however, are regional. Many areas have organizations through which states may resolve common political problems or internal quarrels. The Organization of American States (OAS), the Organization for African Unity (OAU), and the Arab League are three examples. On the other hand, there are strictly military alliances like the North Atlantic Treaty Organization (NATO) and its Soviet counterpart, the Warsaw Treaty Organization (WTO), also known as the Warsaw Pact.

A second method of distinction is by function: political, military, economic, or social. The United Nations and Organization of African Unity are basically political organizations, even though they may carry out other tasks as well. NATO obviously has a primarily military purpose. The European Coal and Steel Community (ECSC) was established in 1950 to integrate these two sectors of the economies of West Germany, France, Italy, and the Benelux countries (Belgium, the Netherlands, and Luxembourg). Organizations dealing with health, education, communications, and food, like the World Health Organization (WHO) and the U.N. Educational, Scientific and Cultural Organization (UNESCO), focus on social purposes. It ought to be noted that, although it is not obvious from this short and random list of regional IGOs, relatively few of them are concerned with issues of peace and security; most IGOs have economic and social functions.

Membership in IGOs has been of particular value to some of the smaller states, which, though not too strong themselves, can gain extra leverage when they are involved in disputes with greater powers. Panama is tiny in comparison to the United States, the "colossus of the north." The canal running through Panama has long been a symbol of American colonialism to Panamanians and other Latin Americans. The Panamanians wanted to run the canal and to regain control of the territory that the United States had leased when it built the canal. All the Latin American states supported Panama's determination to reassert its sovereignty over a piece of territory that the United States treated as if it were American territory. Although it had long dominated the OAS, the United States could thus not expect much support in a meeting, but Panama shrewdly informed the United States that, if a satisfactory agreement could not be achieved, the issue of the canal would be taken to the United Nations. In the world forum, where LDCs are in the vast majority, the United States would have been on the defensive. Panama thus gained from membership in the regional and global IGO on this issue—from what might be called "group power."

(One final point: There is one significant exception to the rule that in IGOs the participating members maintain their autonomy. In western Europe since 1950 there has been a revolutionary attempt to move beyond the nation-state toward a supranational actor. The six members of ECSC had joined in an IGO to transfer the authority of their governments in specified economic sectors to a new federal authority, which was to be established above them. Decisions were to be made by this higher authority; they would no longer be arrived at by negotiations among the member governments. By 1958 the ECSC had been succeeded, owing to efforts to integrate the complete industrial and agricultural sectors of the same six states into a single European Economic Community (EEC). These efforts, joined later by Britain, Denmark, and Ireland, have had only partial success. A monetary union has been established, but the EEC has not made much progress in shifting from an economic to a political union, a United States of Europe, though cooperation on foreign policy and defense issues has increased. Still, the various European communities have moved beyond most of the more traditional IGOs in their decision-making processes.)

NONGOVERNMENTAL OR TRANSNATIONAL ACTORS

Increasingly visible since World War II has been the transnational actor that, unlike the IGO, is a(nongovernmental organization (NGO). It is characterized by headquarters in one country and centrally directed operations in two or more countries. The word "transnational" is appropriate because the NGO performs its functions not only across national frontiers but also often in disregard of them. The increase in the number, size, scope, and variety of NGOs since World War II has led observers to speak of a transnational organizational revolution in world politics.[12] NGOs differ from IGOs in a number of significant ways. The latter are composed of nation-states, and their actions depend upon their members' common interests; conflicting interests must first be reconciled through negotiations, which may not always be successful or rapid. The transnational organization represents its own interests and pursues them in many nations. "The international organization requires *accord* among nations; the transnational organization requires *access* to nations. . . . The restraints on an international organization are largely internal, stemming from the need to produce consensus among its members. The restraints on a transnational organization are largely external, stemming from its need to gain

---

[12] Samuel P. Huntington," Transnational Organizations in World Politics," *World Politics*, April 1973, p. 333.

56   operating authority in different sovereign states. International organizations embody
the principle of nationality; transnational organizations try to ignore it."[13])
(The most prominent contemporary NGO is the multinational corporation
(MNC), the usually huge firm that owns and controls plants and offices in many
countries and sells its goods and services there. MNCs may be classified according
to the kind of business activities they pursue:[14]

> extractive (resources)
>   oil (Exxon)
>   copper (Kennecot)
>
> agriculture (Standard Brands)
>
> industrial (manufacture)
>   capital equipment (International Harvester)
>   automobiles (General Motors)
>   consumer goods (Colgate-Palmolive)
>
> service
>   tourism (Hilton Hotels, Holiday Inn)
>   retail (Sears, Roebuck)
>   transportation (Hertz, Avis, Greyhound)
>   public utilities (General Telephone and Electronics)
>
> finance
>   banking (Chase Manhattan, Bank of America)
>
> conglomerates (International Telephone and Telegraph))

(The sheer size of these MNCs is one of the reasons they are now often
listed as actors of increasing importance internationally. Lester Brown, in ranking
nations and MNCs according to gross national product (the total worth of goods
and services produced) and gross annual sales respectively, found that in the early
1970s the first twenty-two entries were the twenty-two largest nations, ranging from
the United States to Argentina. Number 23 was General Motors, followed by
Switzerland and Pakistan; Standard Oil of New Jersey and Ford ranked 27 and 29.
Royal Dutch Shell was number 36, ahead of Iran and Venezuela; General Electric
and IBM were 43 and 45 respectively, ahead of Egypt, Nigeria, and Israel. Of the
top fifty, forty-one were nations, and nine were MNCs; of the second fifty, eighteen
were nations, and thirty-two were MNCs.[15] These rankings have changed somewhat
because OPEC nations have greatly increased their wealth, which has affected the
MNCs too. Exxon, for example, has replaced General Motors as the world's largest
corporation.
(Regardless of the actual rankings, the implications are obvious. One is the
strength of MNCs, compared to that of the weaker countries, and the influence

---

[13] *Ibid.*, p. 338.

[14] The following classification is based on the table in David H. Blake and Robert S. Walters,
The Politics of Global Economic Relations (Englewood Cliffs, N.J.: Prentice-Hall, 1976), p. 83.

[15] Lester R. Brown, *World without Frontiers* (New York: Vintage, 1973) pp. 213–215.

they can presumably exert within nations. The fear is that these "new sovereigns" will in fact become more powerful than the governments of many countries, gain control of their economies, and thus dictate their futures. Another—and of even greater significance—is their possible effects on the state system itself. Because of the MNCs' multinational production, distribution, and services—and the trend is toward attaining global reach but with planning still centralized—some observers have argued that they will make the nation-state irrelevant. The MNCs are viewed as ushering in a global economy, tying nations together with the cords of economic benefit. As the MNCs satisfy people's aspirations for higher standards of living, the territorial state will become outdated and irrelevant.[16]

(There are also other types of NGO. One of the oldest and most visible is the Roman Catholic Church, with a membership of approximately 560 million people in the early 1970s. To save souls, the Church has learned to coexist with all manner of governments, including that of Benito Mussolini in Italy and that of Hitler in Germany. The political influence of the Church can hardly be doubted, especially in relation to birth control in the LDCs. Even a communist government treats the Church with caution; Pope John Paul II's 1979 visit to his native Poland attracted huge crowds and was a matter of concern to the regime.)

(A final actor of increasing importance in the state system is the terrorist group, or "national liberation" organization, depending on who is naming it.) The Palestinian Liberation Organization (PLO) claims to speak for the Palestinian people and seeks the establishment of a Palestinian state, which its leaders would presumably govern. It has been recognized as the legitimate representative of the Palestinians by the Arab states, has been granted observer status at the United Nations, and attends the meetings of the nonaligned countries as a full-fledged member, even though it is not a state. Its leader has met with the Chancellor of Austria (who happens to be Jewish!) and the Prime Minister of Spain. The Common Market countries, including such pro-Israeli countries as Norway and the Netherlands, have issued a statement suggesting that the PLO must be involved in the Arab-Israeli peace talks and have called for Palestinian self-determination. Other such organizations include the Patriotic Front, which fought a guerrilla war against the government of Rhodesia, claiming that it represented the interests of the majority of black Rhodesians (it later won power in a free election and now controls the new state of Zimbabwe); the Southwest African People's Organization (SWAPO), which is seeking power in what it calls Namibia, a former German colony that has been administered by South Africa since the end of World War I; the Irish Republican Army (IRA); the Japanese Red Army (a kind of terrorist-for-hire organization), the Baader-Meinhoff gang in West Germany; and the Red Brigades in Italy.(Hijackings, assassinations, and random terror have drawn attention to the demands of these groups and have compelled governments to take notice and in some instances even to negotiate with them. The PLO exerts considerable leverage in international politics—more than many states—in its efforts to found a state of its own. Until these efforts definitively fail or succeed, such a "state in waiting," remains classified as a transnational actor.)

[16.] For elaboration of these themes, see Chapter 19.

4 States and Their Objectives

SECURITY, WELFARE, AND OTHER AIMS

Despite the proliferation of NGOs, the state remains—as it has remained for 300 years—the primary actor in the state system. The birth rate of new states has been high, and it continues. Nationalism seems especially rife in the LDCs. People can, of course, be loyal to more than one organization, but the nation-state remains for most people the object of their most intense loyalty. States also remain unique because of their control of territory. The MNCs need access to it to make profits, the Roman Catholic Church needs access to it to save souls, terrorists and national-liberation groups need access to bases from which to pursue their campaigns. The Palestine Liberation Organization is based in Lebanon; the former Patriotic Front conducted its war from the countries surrounding Zimbabwe. Such liberation groups cannot survive without the active support of states like Libya. Finally, the state remains the principal user of *legitimate* force. It can enforce decisions at home and can decide whether or not to go to war and when.

Two authors have commented about the MNC, which some observers regard as the strongest competitor of the state, if not indeed a threat to the future viability of the state system:

> [T]he MNCs lack a fundamental characteristic which will quite probably not permit them to challenge the nation-state. And this characteristic is "territoriality." Whether a multinational corporation executive works for IBM, Singer, Unilever, Volkswagen, or Hitachi, he lives in a nation-state which possesses some sover-

eignty, greater authority, and even greater control capacity over its environment. MNCs have no jails, no courts and executioners, no passports, no armies, and very, very few weapons. In the last analysis, national governments control an overwhelming concentration of power and authority that would allow them to break up any MNC, provided there were adequate cause for such an operation.[1])

(The state has survived since 1648, and throughout this period the state has *never* been the sole actor in the system. That system has long been defined by the major actors, however, rather than by all the types of actors within it.[2] The NGOs and their transnational activities are not unimportant, but they have not yet made the state system obsolete. It is clear that at present states remain the principal actors and interstate relations fundamental. Later (see Chapters 19 and 20) we shall analyze whether or not this primary role of the state is declining; whether or not the state system is being transformed into a new, more interdependent system in which the states may no longer play principal roles; and whether or not such a transformation is desirable and states ought to help make this goal more easily attainable. But, given the longevity of the state as principal actor, an analysis of international politics must start with the state, its motivations, objectives, and interaction with other states. Only then shall we also understand the role and impact of other actors.[3])

(First of all, the conditions that states seek to preserve or enhance for themselves may be divided between *possession* and *milieu* objectives.[4] The former are the objectives states seek for themselves in competitive situations; the latter are concerned with shaping the environment of the state system in which all states live. States tend to perceive possession objectives, like security, in finite terms, which means that more for an adversary means an equivalent reduction for oneself. Milieu objectives, by contrast, are viewed as a gain for all.) Arms-control negotiations between the United States and the Soviet Union involve the security of both superpowers, but, to the extent that they make the international environment safer, all states presumably benefit. If the first and third worlds could reconcile some of their differences, thus narrowing the gap between the rich and poor nations, the international environment would be both more stable and more conducive to the LDCs' economic growth and prosperity. As these two examples suggest, states may

---

[1] Theodore A. Couloumbis and Elias P. Georgiades, "The Impact of the Multinational Corporations on the Interventional System," in Abdul A. Said and Luiz R. Simmons, eds., The *New Sovereigns* (Englewood Cliffs, N.J.: Prentice-Hall, 1975), p. 164. Also see Hedley Bull, *The Anarchical Society* (New York: Columbia University Press, 1977), pp. 272–273.

[2] Kenneth N. Waltz, *Theory of International Politics* (Menlo Park, Calif.: Addison-Wesley, 1979), pp. 93-94.

[3] According to Waltz, "Two points should be made about latter-day transnational studies. First, students of transnational phenomena have developed no distinct theory of their subject matter or of international politics in general. They have drawn on existing theories, whether economic or political. Second, that they have developed no distinct theory is quite proper, for a theory that denies the central role of states will be needed only if nonstate actors develop to the point of rivaling or surpassing the great powers, not just a few of the minor ones. They show no sign of doing that." *Ibid.*, p. 95.

[4] Arnold Wolfers, *Discord and Collaboration* (Baltimore, Md.: The Johns Hopkins Press, 1965), pp. 73-74.

60   simultaneously advance their individual national security or prosperity and their milieu goals. (Conceptually, then, it may be difficult to distinguish between possession and milieu goals; yet, clearly, it remains an analytically useful distinction because a state, even if it has no immediate or short-range interests at stake, may still be greatly concerned about the systemic environment in which it lives and must by necessity operate.)

What are the most common objectives that states generally seek? The first and most basic is *security*. At the very minimum, this means simple physical survival. Israel, born in 1948, was surrounded by states which until 1973 at least, were sworn to her extinction. As Colonel Nasser, Egypt's leader during most of the 1950s and 1960s, once reportedly said, "Israel's existence is aggression." Israel had to fear for her survival if she lost one of the wars she fought with her Arab neighbors. A loss would not just entail some loss of territory; the Jews were to be "driven into the sea." The Arabs refused to recognize Israel's right to exist. Admittedly, this was an exceptional case, and now, under Sadat, Egypt has made peace with Israel. Jordan and perhaps Syria would probably also do so if mutually satisfactory terms could be negotiated. In the nuclear age, of course, even when adversaries like Russia and America recognize one another's right to exist, their physical survival is at stake. Nuclear proliferation is likely to increase that danger.

A second and more common meaning of security refers to the preservation of a state's territorial integrity. Because some frontiers do change over time, states may redefine the meaning of "territorial integrity" from time to time. Poland, for example, has shifted her eastern and western frontiers westward since World War II. By the same token, Russia's frontier has also moved westward. Communist China, on the other hand, frequently refers publicly to the Chinese territories seized by the Russian czars during the last century and wants to renegotiate the "unequal treaties" that compelled earlier Chinese rulers to accept those losses. Russia, however, claims that the present frontier between the two countries is final. The issue of frontiers is a particularly troublesome one among the LDCs, for their territorial integrity does not usually correspond to ethnic and linguistic divisions. The new nations inherited their boundaries from colonial rulers, and it is this territorial integrity some LDCs seek to defend. Others, however, claim pieces of their territory on the basis of reuniting ethnic groups separated by artificial boundaries drawn by foreigners. Somalia, for example, has claims against Ethiopia, which led to fighting in 1978 and to Soviet-Cuban intervention to defend Ethiopian territorial integrity.

A third meaning of security refers to a country's political independence, which, negatively, means its freedom from foreign control and, positively, means preservation of its domestic political and economic system or "way of life." Security, then, refers not merely to the maintenance of a state's physical survival and territorial security but also to the perpetuation of the values, patterns of social relations, life styles, and varied other elements that characterize its way of life.

This simple point is worth a little elaboration. Earlier we briefly analyzed how the United States became involved in the two world wars and the Cold War. We emphasized that the threat that precipitated American involvement on all three occasions was the possibility that one power—Germany or Russia—would come to dominate Europe. We should note two additional points. First, this threat had little to do with ideology; it was certainly not anticommunism that motivated the United States against Germany, first characterized by monarchical conservatism and then by fascism. Second, it was not related to physical danger, for neither Germany on either occasion nor Russia after 1945 had the air power to reach and destroy the United States, let alone to invade it across 3,000 miles of ocean. American intervention came because, on each occasion, American leaders saw the domination of Europe by a nondemocratic—indeed, *antidemocratic*—great power as a threat to the security of the United States as a particular kind of nation and as a threat to the kind of world environment in which the United States could most comfortably live. As President Franklin D. Roosevelt explained his decision to aid England in 1940–1941, the United States should not become a lone democratic island surrounded by totalitarian seas to its east and west (Roosevelt included Japan's threat in east Asia in his descriptive phrase). He meant that, to defend itself in such circumstances, the United States would have to turn itself into a "garrison state"; democracy would have to be dumped overboard. He also meant that, as a *democratic* state, the nation wished to preserve an international order in which democracy could flourish; committed to this milieu the United States could not stand by and watch one democracy after another snuffed out by antidemocratic regimes. The result would be a hostile external environment, incompatible with American conceptions of the just and the unjust, whether that threat came from the extreme right or the left. It was this same concern for a world in which democratic objectives would remain safe even when nondemocratic states were in a vast majority that led some people—including Zbigniew Brzezinski, President Carter's national-security assistant—during the 1970s to favor greater attention to bringing the democracies in the Western Hemisphere, Europe, and Japan closer together in trilateral cooperation, rather than focusing American policy on its principal adversaries, Russia and China.

(One additional point about security as an objective is worth repeating: We are speaking of a *degree* of security that allows a state to feel *relatively* safe; conversely, we accept as a fact of life that all states have to live with a degree of insecurity. (There is no such thing as absolute security in the state system, at least not short of universal conquest and the destruction of all other independent states, an unlikely possibility.) As all states have to "live dangerously," the question is how much security do they feel is essential to protect their "nonnegotiable" vital interests?)

(A second objective important to many states is *prestige*. Precisely because prestige is, as we shall see later, closely related to power, it may be defined as a nation's *reputation for power* among its fellow states. It is a reputation that, given the nature of the state system, is not to be sneered at and shrugged off as "mere prestige." For a nation's reputation for power may mean it will not be challenged and will thus avoid war; or it may gain compliance with its demands, again without having to threaten or fight. Prestige is thus of special concern to would-be great powers; they expend major resources and efforts in quest of it and often even more to avoid its loss.)When the Russians first put Sputnik into orbit and particularly

62   after they sent the first man into space in 1961, their achievements were widely interpreted as symptomatic of a changing distribution of power in favor of the Soviet Union. Within a short time of its first Sputnik, Moscow began a policy of intimidation, trying to pressure the West to leave West Berlin. Conversely, Russian achievements were seen throughout the world as a loss of prestige for the United States, for American power—especially in weaponry—was based to a very large extent on its technological ability and innovation, an area in which until then the United States was deemed far superior to Russia. President Kennedy reacted to the Soviets' man in space by setting the United States' goal as placing a man on the moon before the end of the 1960s in order to recoup American prestige. The effort cost more than $30 billion. But, by late 1962, after its success in compelling the Soviets to withdraw their missiles from Cuba, the United States had already largely recovered its prestige.

By contrast, the American intervention in Vietnam was a less successful and, at approximately $150 billion, more costly effort to prevent the loss of prestige that Washington thought would attend defeat of South Vietnam, a loss it was unwilling to entertain lest it erode the credibility of American power and commitments in other, perhaps more significant, areas than Vietnam. As one Pentagon memorandum written by an assistant secretary of defense assessed the reasons for American intervention:

> 70 percent—to avoid a humiliating American defeat
> 20 percent—to keep South Vietnamese territory out of Chinese hands
> 10 percent—to permit the people of South Vietnam to enjoy better, freer way of life.[5]

Most of the time, the prestige of a nation is reflected in the parading of military forces and elaborate diplomatic ceremonials. It is also associated with high technology and, more broadly, with a way of life that appears to much of the world to be successful in resolving the problems that all societies face. In the last century, Western democracy was admired throughout much of the world, including the non-Western world, not only because of the superior firepower that had allowed it to conquer colonies, but also because the firepower was an aspect of a technologically and politically superior society that was reflected in infant birth mortality, longer life, and higher standards of living, health, and education.

It is not the superpowers alone that are concerned with prestige. Countries like Britain and France, former great powers reluctant to accept their secondary status, and countries like China and India, striving to establish their status, have all become nuclear powers. Possession of "the bomb" is—and seems likely to remain—as much a symbol of prestige as empires were in an earlier age. Indeed, giving up the remnants of empire was sometimes painful just because it was equated with loss of prestige. France fought two wars, one in Indochina, another in Algeria, to prevent such a loss, and even Britain, which did not generally try to buck the

---

[5.] *The Pentagon Papers* (Chicago: Quadrangle, 1971) p. 432.

historic trend, reacted fiercely to Egypt's 1956 seizure of the Suez Canal. (Nor did the United States, with its Central American sphere of influence, find it easy to surrender its sole control over the Panama Canal, even though militarily and economically the canal had lost much of its former utility.) But even smaller countries that do not harbor memories of glory or entertain thoughts of future greatness are concerned about prestige. For them, it is less a sense of power than of simple dignity that is at stake; they wish to be treated with respect even though they are not strong countries.)

(*Economic wealth or prosperity* has also long ranked high as a goal for states. Wealth has been directly related to the military strength that a state can afford; only if it has a lot of "ploughshares" can it have a lot of "swords.") In an age before nationalism, the wealthy prince could buy a large army; since the French Revolution, with its mobilization of the masses, followed by the Industrial Revolution, states with sizable populations and industrial capacities have ranked at the top of the power hierarchy. But industry and technology involve more than "power"; they also involve "welfare," the desire of people in all societies for a better material life, and therefore demands that governments—even dictatorial ones—respond to their citizens' aspirations. The "revolution of rising expectations" is a universal one; if it is usually thought of in connection with underdeveloped countries, that is only because they are copying the large Western states, which as the first to industrialize, have provided their people with the world's highest standard of living.)

Indeed, in the West it may be said that until the recent concern with environmental problems, mostly the by-products of industrialization, economic growth was the chief, if not the sole, criterion for social policy. Raising everyone's living standards, including redistributing more of an ever-rising GNP among those who had previously been neglected or denied, was at the heart of all modern Western welfare states' social policies, including those of the United States. Attempts to redistribute existing or only slowly growing wealth among different classes or segments of society would have precipitated intense social conflict (for one class would have gained at the expense of another); rapidly expanding the "economic pie," so that everyone could have a larger share of it, made it possible to avoid such conflict and any possible political instability while satisfying the vast majority of groups and people. OPEC's short 1973–1974 embargo and its quadrupling of oil prices therefore demonstrated the vulnerability of Western industrial societies, with their dependence on economic growth and affluence for social peace, to supply interruptions and price increases. (The possibility of future "energy crises" and other deprivations of resources or of sharp price rises threatens that comfortable standard of living and exposes those countries to political pressures. What is clear in any event, is the degree to which the prosperity of Western economies—income, economic growth, employment, ability to afford social services—is entwined with the fortunes of the international economy and international politics.)

(The desire for the "good life" is not limited to Western states. The drive for even higher economic growth rates and increased gross national product (the value of a nation's total production and services) is shared by the Soviet Union as well. Every few years the Russian leaders promise their long-suffering compatriots

64   that, at the end of this or that five-year plan or decade, their standard of living will be comparable to that of the United States, the nation whose economic and social system they denounce as exploitative and inhumane. Precisely because in the Second Industrial Revolution of electronics, especially in computers, the Soviet Union was falling behind and because this lag affected all areas of its economy and not just the sector devoted to consumer-goods production, it needed access to Western trade and technology as a "fix" for its own overcentralized, overbureaucratized, and often ideologically hamstrung economy. Otherwise, it might suffer some social unrest; its attractiveness as a model of modernization for the underdeveloped countries would decline; and even its military capability could be affected. Therefore, détente was partly the political price the Soviet Union was willing to pay for the improvement of its industrial, as well as its agricultural, economy.)

But the LDCs are those that have been most bent on modernizing—industrializing and urbanizing—themselves. To attract assistance from the competing sides during the era of bipolarity (see Chapter 6), most of the formerly colonial states pursued a policy of nonalignment. When the Cold War turned into détente, they began to press their demands more assertively. OPEC, attempts to organize other producer cartels to control supplies and prices of resources, and demands in the United Nations for a "new international economic order" are all aimed at changing the distribution of wealth and power beween the first and third worlds. Whatever the ultimate outcome of these demands, they have already led to clashes; in any event, the confrontation between the first and third worlds is supplementing that between the first and second worlds. Future attempts to cut off resources needed by the Western industrial states may well lead to the use of force in some circumstances; certainly present and future differences of views between the "haves" and "have-nots" may produce a great deal more bitterness. (With a rapidly growing world population, and the third world's drive toward industrialization in an age of finite natural resources (especially oil), the desire of nations for economic growth and greater prosperity may well result in higher levels of conflict as economic issues rival political-military ones or, more accurately, as economic issues have become so heavily politicized that to refer to them as "economic" issues is a misnomer.)

(A fourth value, which some states pursue more than do others, is the *protection or promotion of ideology.* An ideology is a set of beliefs that intends to explain reality and to prescribe a desirable future existence for society and the world in general, as well as the roles of specific nations in bringing about this future condition. Revolutionary ideologies in particular are expressed in terms of long-range goals that amount to a universal transformation of the state system; they tend to impart to the revolutionary state a strong sense of mission and commitment to the achievement of its aim.)

In the nineteenth century, protected by the balance of power in Europe, the United States, regarding itself as the New World, with a political system morally superior to the regimes of the Old World, thus chose to isolate itself from possible contamination by the European nations. In the twentieth century, by contrast, it has increasingly been sucked into the Old World's quarrels as Britain's power has weakened. The United States has engaged Germany twice in hot wars and Russia once in a cold war as it has become involved in ideological crusades to repel the threat of despotism and defend democratic values. On the other hand, revolutionary regimes, like that of France after its democratic revolution, that of Russia after the Bolshevik revolution in 1917, and that of China after 1949, have energetically sought to expand their influence and power in the international system in order to convert it to their respective faiths. The initial expectation after revolution is that it will spread from one country to another by means of "spontaneous combustion." Leon Trotsky, the first Soviet People's Commissar for Foreign Affairs, did not expect his job to last long. "I will issue a few revolutionary proclamations to the peoples of the world and then shut up shop," he declared.[6] But the proclamations did not spark a global revolutionary fire. Later Soviet leaders preferred to ensure that history would march their way by helping it along wherever and whenever possible, if necessary by imposing upon reluctant people the faith that would make them free and ensure their secular salvation.

One critical problem that arises for states that harbor universal goals is that these goals are usually long-range ones and frequently conflict with shorter-term and immediate aims, like security; as a result, unlimited revolutionary goals tend to become subordinate to more limited national objectives and demands. China, for example, though born as a revolutionary state, proclaimed itself during the 1960s as the true inheritor of the revolutionary tradition of Marx and Lenin. It would spearhead the revolutionary struggle against American imperialism; Russia had already sold out the revolution by its increasing cooperation with the United States. But, when China was faced with possible Soviet military action, it turned to the world's most powerful "imperialist" state. Machiavelli became a more important guide to action than Marx.

(Note that, although we have emphasized that states pursue such values as security, prestige, wealth, welfare, and ideologies, two objectives have not been mentioned: peace and power. Both seem rather obvious, and there can be no doubt of their significance. All statesmen, indeed, constantly proclaim that their nations' goal is peace, and there is no reason to doubt their sincerity in most instances. No national leader would be so bold as to declare that he hated peace and wanted war, even if he agreed with Frederick Schuman that

> War is a habit men enjoy, as they enjoy drunkenness, gluttony, fornication, gambling and crime. Its vast superiority over all other forms of sin is that it embraces all the vices and casts over them the thrilling shadow of danger and the glittering cloak of honor, thereby making them "heroic" or at least permissible. This is so because all one's fellows, sharing vicariously in the experience of war, glorify and indulge those who bear the brunt of battle.[7])

---

[6] Quoted in E. H. Carr, *The Bolshevik Revolution 1917–1923* (London: Macmillan, 1953), p. 16.

[7] Frederick L. Schuman, *The Commonwealth of Man* (New York: Knopf, 1952), p. 49.

66 War in the twentieth century has become increasingly costly, and the nuclear bomb hangs over all civilization. Indeed, these weapons, the destructive potential of which exceeds that of all other weapons in prior history, both in the immensity and in the speed with which they can wipe out tens of millions of people, raise the central issue whether or not the nation-state system can survive a nuclear holocaust in the long run.

(Peace is a desirable aim for states, if not now a necessity. Rarely have statesmen gone to war lightly. Too many things can go wrong, so that few can feel certain of victory at the outset. Defeat may mean losing territory, having to pay reparations, loss of national honor—all in addition to losses during the fighting. As long as other objectives can be satisfied in peacetime, the peace will be kept, as the basic objective of states is to ensure their own security. Most states do feel secure when they are at peace, though clearly peace is the product of their sense of security. That is why historically their preferences for peace have not been unqualified and why, when they have believed their security endangered, they have sacrificed peace. No major nation has wanted "peace at any price," at least not before discovery of the atom bomb. Inasmuch as war was not tantamount to committing suicide before 1945, it was indeed a principal instrument for preserving the balance. Preventing the hegemony of any single power or coalition of powers took precedence over peace. If a nation forgot to distinguish between peace and security and gave a higher priority to peace, as did Britain in the 1930s, the end was likely to be disaster. In that decade memories of World War I were still so vivid and the losses suffered had been so enormous that anything appeared better than to fight. What possible goal was worth such a cost, short of a direct attack on the homeland? Another war like the Great War from 1914–1918, which had brought down four of Europe's great empires—the Ottoman Turkish, Austro-Hungarian, tsarist Russian, and even monarchical German empires—had left Britain exhausted. Another war, it was feared, would push the nation into the abyss. But, in seeking to preserve the peace by not responding to German expansionist moves, Britain allowed the distribution of power to shift against it, endangering its security and forcing it to go to war anyway in 1939. Had Britain kept its priorities straight, it might have resisted Hitler earlier, contained German power, and avoided major war.)

(We have also omitted power as an end or goal of states. Some analysts claim that the accumulation of power is a continuous concern of states. Whatever the ultimate aim, the immediate one is power. In this view power is seen as desirable in itself and may be pursued as a value desirable for its own sake. "Whatever preserves and enhances power must be cherished. Whatever leads to the enfeeblement of power must be avoided."[8] Yet to treat power as an end in itself is analogous to discussing the accumulation of money without any reference to the purposes for which it is spent. An analysis of power must, therefore, start with a "theory of ends."[9] States are not always preoccupied with enhancing power. Sometimes they

---

[8] *Ibid*, p. 38.

[9] Wolfers, *Discord and Collaboration*, pp. 89–90.

are; sometimes they are satisfied with the power they have; and sometimes they will even reduce it. It depends on the objectives they seek and how intensely these are pursued.)

THE COMPETITION OF OBJECTIVES

(If these are some—although by no means all—of the principal values states seek, the resulting conflict among these values within each state suggests that *the acquisition of more of one value often comes at the cost of another; values are frequently incompatible with one another.* One such conflict is between security and welfare or, in more colloquial language, "guns" and "butter." Realistically, the more a state spends on maintaining military forces, the less it can spend on foreign aid, on construction of schools, hospitals, and roads, on education, vocational training, and a "war on poverty." The more taxes it needs to buy bombs, the less the taxpayer has left to buy a new house or car, purchase family insurance, go to Europe on vacation, or send the children to college. Nations have limited resources, even if these are great, and they must make choices; and the choice is not usually *either* guns *or* butter but *how many* guns and *how much* butter. The question then becomes: how many more guns will yield how much of an increase in relative security—taking into account the fact that the opponent is also likely to increase the number of its guns to match our increase? Or conversely, how much *less* butter is a possibly small additional increase in security worth, assuming it is an increase? If such a reduction in butter, for instance, depresses the quality of life in the society and perhaps its cohesion as a functioning entity, will the extra arms have enhanced its security, even if the opponent does not or cannot match it in arms? These have been the kinds of questions widely and frequently asked in the United States since Vietnam.

This issue whether or not foreign policy, including defense spending, should have priority over domestic policy, it ought to be noted, aptly illustrates the emotional-moral context in which international politics issues are often phrased. Guns versus butter: How can one possibly be for guns and destruction and violence as opposed to greater prosperity and happiness and a better life for all? Yet to pose this issue as if it were a matter of military service versus social services is really false. Is buying guns by the government *not* a *social* service? Is not a government's first responsibility to its citizens to keep them alive and well and free?

(Another set of competing values for a country like the United States is that of security versus democracy. This has both domestic and external implications. If a democratic nation really sought to maximize its security, it could start at home by establishing a "garrison state": the young would be drafted into military service and the older people into work in factories producing war materials; all would be subjected to a strict discipline and orthodoxy that would squash diversity of opinion, and those who differed with the official viewpoint would be sent to prison camps as security and loyalty risks; all resources, except those used in producing the necessities of life, would be channeled into military production; and the power of the government would be centralized in the hands of a few leaders. Democratic values, competing political parties and opinions, the entire way of life would fall victim to the organization of the nation for maximum military security. It is to avoid this "garrison state" that American leaders have repeatedly felt it necessary to maintain a European balance.

This balance has in fact been kept, but the extensive, intensive, and lengthy American involvement in world affairs since World War II has led critics to feel that in trying to ensure the external safety of American democracy, democratic values have become endangered domestically. The constitutional balance has been upset as the presidency has become "imperial," going to war without congressional support or with support purportedly elicited by deceiving and lying to the legislature; the authority of Congress has been emasculated; the CIA, among other questionable activities, has helped to overthrow a legitimately elected government in Chile and planned a number of assassinations of leaders in other countries; the CIA and the FBI, in carrying out domestic surveillance, have broken various laws forbidding precisely such activities; indeed, it has been charged further, a "military-industrial complex" has come to dominate the American political process and has distorted the purposes of American society. Wrongly perceiving security threats almost every-where, the United States has become a weapons culture dedicated to the invention, production, and deployment of ever newer arms, the enrichment of the large corporations, and the subsidizing of its entire economy; in the process, it has neglected its poor, barely made an effort to resolve the nation's terrible racial problem, continued to ignore environmental, urban, and mass-transportation prob-lems, and alienated a sizable minority of its educated youth. Allegedly, the real interests of the vast majority of Americans have thus been deliberately neglected—indeed, sacrificed—for the enrichment of the few who benefit from war and in-ternational strife.

The external implications of the clash of security and democracy are starkly apparent when a democracy allies itself with undemocratic states. Can a democracy associate itself with dictatorial states without undermining its own cause? On the other hand, should it confine itself only to allies sharing the same political values, even to the point of jeopardizing its security by failing to take advantage of the strategic position, economic benefits, and added military strength that can be gained from alliance with certain undemocratic states? During World War II Winston Churchill had welcomed Russia as an ally after Hitler became the common enemy. Russia might not be a democracy, the prime minister said, but to beat Hitler he would eat supper with the devil—though he did admit that he would use a long spoon. But this alliance had been brought about by Germany's attack on Russia.

After 1945 and the outbreak of the Cold War, the United States made alliances with many undemocratic regimes—Turkey, Greece, Spain, Nationalist China, Brazil, and Portugal, to name some of the more prominent—in the pursuit of the containment of Russian and Chinese communist power. Indeed, contain-ment began with the Truman Doctrine, which somewhat ironically pictured the threat to Turkey and Greece from the Soviet Union as a conflict between democracy and totalitarianism. The Turkish and Greek regimes were hardly models of democratic purity. Were President Truman's declaration and American policy hypocritical because they were inconsistent with the values of American democracy, or was the United States acting as the bipolar distribution of power after World War II, obliged it to act? President Truman's action demonstrated clearly that he believed that a democracy can align itself with undemocratic governments in strategically located areas at moments of perceived danger to American security.

Only in western Europe did American leaders view national self-determination and national security as incompatible. In eastern Europe, they also found it safe to push the principle of self-determination, for success would mean the retraction of Soviet power. In the meantime, the United States could point out that the Russian-controlled people's democracies were a farce. But outside Europe, the choice appeared to be in favor of safety and equilibrium. In Korea, for instance, the United States defended a governing regime that was not stamped with the seal of good democratic housekeeping; the issue, however, as American policy makers saw it at the time of intervention, was American security vis-à-vis the Soviet Union or Communist China, not the democratic purity of the South Korean regime.

Nor was this view just a matter of simple cynicism or hypocrisy, though it may often have appeared that way. It was a matter of priorities. If the defense of the democracies of western Europe was judged to be a vital American interest and if bases in undemocratic Portugal and Spain would strengthen that defense during the 1950s and 1960s, then should the United States not have associated itself with the latter regimes? How can we "prove" that American air and sea bases on the Hispanic peninsula would contribute to deterrence of the Soviet Union? The answer is that we cannot. As the test of deterrence is that nothing happens, we can neither prove nor disprove the value of these bases. It becomes a matter of judgment.

The defense of South Korea can perhaps shed some light on the considerations involved. Japan is potentially very powerful; it has also been a democracy since World War II. Historically Japan has considered the southern half of the Korean peninsula vital to its security. That was one major reason for the American defense of South Korea when it was invaded by North Korea, a Soviet dependency at that time. That is also why American troops are still on the peninsula almost twenty-five years after the Korean war was ended and why they can be withdrawn only if the timetable of such a pullout does not leave the Japanese insecure or in doubt about American resolve and willingness to defend Japan from external threats. South Korea, then, like Portugal and Spain, has contributed to the security of a major democratic ally of the United States. Yet its government remains a repressive one.

This issue can also be applied to a related issue such as prosperity. In the 1970s, as the United States was becoming an oil importer and Europe and Japan's dependence on oil from the Persian Gulf area was also growing, the United States—in an increasingly isolationist mood after Vietnam—selected Iran as America's "policeman." If the United States was unable or unwilling to police the Persian Gulf, including the oil-rich sheikdoms on the Arabian peninsula, someone else must be found to do it, and Iran's Shah was willing. Presidents Nixon and Ford were, therefore, not willing to pressure the Shah for liberal domestic reforms, including greater respect for political and civil rights. The Shah, who did not participate in the 1973–1974 oil boycott against the United States, who supplied oil to Israel when the Arab members of OPEC refused to do so, and who supported Egyptian President Sadat's peace moves with Israel, ruled his country autocratically while supporting American policy objectives. In 1978, as his authority was eroding and it looked as if his days were numbered, the United States wavered. Should it give the Shah all-out support and encourage him to use force, if necessary, to quell disorders; or should it discourage him from violent reaction and seek what Washington appeared to (falsely) believe would be a more constitutional post-Shah regime? President Carter, who had proclaimed the promotion of human rights as the cornerstone of his foreign policy, could not decide whether to support the Shah, the despot who was a friend of the United States, or to seek reforms that might risk weakening or displacing him, which would make America's foreign policy more consistent with its democratic justifications.[10] American policy was thus ambiguous and fluctuated between the objectives of security and democracy.

(The crucial question is, therefore, whether or not these alignments given that they were organized to protect the world's principal democracies against the world's foremost totalitarian power, are morally justified. If we answer that some "unholy alliances" may in certain circumstances be morally justifiable (or at least morally ambiguous and tolerable), how can we justify American support of dictatorial regimes that are not strategically important to democracies—as, for example, in Latin America? If this time we say that such alignments are not moral, are we not then in fact demonstrating that morality is merely a function of political and strategic interests?)

(Clearly, in a world containing only a minority of democratic states, security and democracy are bound to be competing values on occasion; which value is to be granted priority in such circumstances often calls for a difficult and agonizing decision. If, in the name of security, a democracy somewhat indiscriminately supports a fairly large number of authoritarian allies to enhance its power, gain strategic position, ensure prosperity, or play off one country against another, it may indeed cast doubt on its purposes; on the other hand, if in the name of democracy it refuses or minimizes alignment with authoritarian regimes, it may remain pure but may ultimately weaken its cause against the principal enemies of democracy.)

In the wake of the Vietnam war, critics frequently said that the United States should not again fight for the defense of dictatorships, that it should commit its blood and treasure only for the cause of democracy, as in World War II. Yet the critics have forgotten that World War II broke out when Britain went to the rescue of Poland, an undemocratic country; Britain apparently did so (as the United States did in Greece and Turkey after that war) because it saw its own security linked to that of Poland, regardless of that country's government. And in 1980 the United States confronted a situation in which it had to decide whether or not to

---

[10] Michael A. Ledeen and William H. Lewis, "Carter and the Fall of the Shah: The Inside Story," *The Washington Quarterly*, Spring 1980, pp. 3–40.

send military aid to Pakistan after the Soviet invasion of Afghanistan had made Pakistan vunerable to possible Soviet incursions. The Pakistani military regime was no less repressive than that of South Vietnam had been. Yet, given its strategic position and its ties to the United States, could Washington write Pakistan off?

(The central question raised by all these examples of conflicting values is *What price security?* The means of securing a nation's territorial integrity may be incompatible with the values by which it lives. Should a nation root out all possible "security" risks and dissidents at home, even though under a broad definition of security innocent people may well be hurt and the fear of expressing any criticism of governmental actions may stifle free speech, perhaps even leading to the censorship of books and the banning of debates on "controversial" topics (as did occur in the United States in the 1950s)? Is a democratic nation, in allying itself with patently undemocratic countries, augmenting its own security? Or is it weakening itself by staining its own reputation and imparing the credibility of its claim to be a champion of democracy? Should a democracy committed to holding free elections and abiding by the results help to overthrow a freely elected government elsewhere, as the United States did in Chile because it perceived Chile's government as increasingly radical domestically and feared that it might align itself with Russia? Should a democracy intervene in the affairs of a major NATO member, financing anticommunist political parties in order to prevent the communist party from being included in a coalition government, thus weakening the alliance? Should a democracy attempt to "destabilize" a country like Italy in hopes that the communist party will be dismissed from office? Can a democracy launch a preventive war, firing the first shot? Obviously, security and other objectives may clash; so may the objectives and the methods by which states pursue their ends. For policy makers, deciding on the exact mix of objectives that the nation ought to pursue, the means by which to achieve them, and the level of commitment to them is controversial and difficult.)

(One conflict of values is continuous, however, regardless of the distribution of power—peace versus security. We said earlier that one of the purposes of the balance of power is to preserve each state's security, not to obtain peace *per se*. Although states generally prefer security *and* peace, they would sacrifice the latter if necessary for security. But, because peace is a dearly held value, policy makers, in fact, have on several occasions placed the cart of peace before the horse of security.) Britain and France in the 1930s were concerned for their security, but they also feared a repetition of the Great War, which could bring about their collapse. Security in those circumstances seemed to depend not upon going to war but upon preserving the peace at almost any price. But security and peace were in that instance incompatible goals. Britain and France, by identifying one with the other and making peace an exclusive priority, ended by appeasing Hitler and helping him upset the balance against themselves.

(In the nuclear age, however, peace and security have become inextricably intertwined. In a sense the dilemma has sharpened. To the extent that the balance of power still depends largely, if not primarily, upon the superpowers' military strength, it is maintained by the threat of total force, rather than by its actual use.)

72   The danger of total war does, however, remain. It may not come, as we shall see, through a coldly calculated premeditated attack; it may come instead through miscalculation as a result of rapid technological changes in weapons, inept "crisis management," or escalation of a limited war. But such a total war can hardly be fought for the enhancement of a nation's security; it will only doom the contestants to extinction. Britain and France during the interwar period had already sensed this danger and were therefore willing to go far—too far, it turned out—to avoid all-out war. Since World War II, both the United States and the Soviet Union have, as their past behavior has shown, ruled out total nuclear warfare as an instrument of policy. Both know that peace and security have become inseparable. The crucial question, however, is how national power can be used so that it can simultaneously preserve security *and* peace.

THE PRICE OF DÉTENTE AND HUMAN RIGHTS

In the nuclear age the need to remain secure yet maintain the peace poses the question of the price to be paid for what the Soviets call "peaceful coexistence." This issue came very much to the fore as Richard Nixon's administration moved, in the popular phrase, "from confrontation to negotiations." When the Republicans came into office in 1969, their purpose was, as Henry Kissinger explained it, the establishment of what "the President has called a structure of peace . . . an international system less geared to the management of crises, less conscious of constant eruptions of conflict, in which the principal participants operate with a consciousness of stability and permanence." Kissinger emphasized that this policy "puts a particular obligation on the two great nuclear powers that have the capacity to destroy mankind and whose conflicts have produced so many of the crises of the postwar period."[11] The new relationship sought by the administration, soon to become known as "détente," stressed the reduction of danger from a continuing arms race, which could be achieved only through more restrained competitive behavior. Détente thus meant a lower level of international tensions, even an attempt to codify the terms of competition; it meant not only continued rivalry but also superpower cooperation in the field of arms control, as well as in other political, economic, technical, and scientific areas.

Yet the improvement in American-Soviet relations raised the issue of the competing values that the United States seeks: Has détente been purchased at the cost of justice and the democratic values that this country has long professed proudly and defended in the world? In the days before détente, liberals used to advocate a thawing of Cold War tensions because they expected the vigilance of Soviet totalitarianism to relax, thus creating at least a degree of freedom for Soviet citizens. Instead détente produced a partial return to Stalinism. Ideological orthodoxy, censorship, and the squashing of dissent have increased as party ideologues, military

---

[11.] *The New York Times*, June 23, 1973.

conservatives, and especially the secret police have been concerned that American liberals could be right, that détente might create pressure for change and possible demands for fewer restrictions and less supervision. These groups in Russia fear that such change will threaten the foundations of the Soviet state.

In the United States the price of détente has come to be symbolized by the Soviet author Alexandr Solzhenitsyn and the issue of Soviet Jewish emigration to Israel. Solzhenitsyn, a severe critic of the Soviet system (and also of Western democracy: his solution for Russia is a return to the traditional paternalistic autocracy), also became a critic of détente, warning against the dangers of appeasement à la Chamberlain.[12] Nevertheless, his courage in speaking out, despite obvious personal danger, as well as the eloquence of his criticism of the Soviet regime, evoked worldwide sympathy. The Kremlin, instead of imprisoning him and creating a martyr, finally exiled him to the West. The Jewish-emigration issue arose because many Jews, discriminated against in Russia, wanted to go to Israel. The authorities made emigration extremely difficult by imposing a very high, often unpayable, tax on each émigré, as well as by taking other measures. Although the Russians suspended their restrictions on an informal basis and allowed many Jews to leave as part of an attempt to seek better relations with the United States, where Jewish groups were very aroused about this issue, some members of Congress sought to tie an improvement in American-Soviet commercial relations to a Soviet agreement permitting "the right to emigrate." The Nixon administration opposed this link in vain. The result was that the Soviets rejected the trade treaty, and Jewish emigration—which had substantially risen as a result of Kissinger's private diplomacy—fell precipitously. The Soviets obtained sizable credits in Europe, the United States lost business at a time of major recession, and the administration lost a major tool for seeking to influence Soviet behavior.

(The central issue of détente for many, including liberal intellectuals and hard-nosed senators, was the role of "human rights" in foreign policy. No issue could have struck more at the core of American policy.)The critics of the President and of Kissinger argued that their position was, at best, amoral. The United States, they said, being the kind of country it is, cannot close its eyes to injustice, whether in the Soviet Union or in Brazil. American foreign policy, they said further, must have a moral basis if it is to have any real meaning; the United States cannot pursue a foreign policy divorced from its democratic ideals. As playwright Arthur Miller has said, détente has been "sterilized of any human meaning," a "détente that suppresses human liberty is a travesty. It not only sells out American ideals but encourages the Kremlin to repress its critics and deny its people freedom and dignity."[13] The trouble was precisely that American policy did not concern itself—and had not concerned itself for a number of years— with issues of right and wrong, freedom and slavery.

Not that the critics of détente did not appreciate the administration's attempt to create a safer and stabler world, but the central question was whether or

---

[12] *Ibid.*, September 12, 1973.

[13] *Ibid.*, July 5, 1974.

not that end would justify any means. Was the basic aim of American foreign policy survival at any cost? If, by comparison, Britain's pre-World War II policy of appeasement had worked and a British-German détente had followed, could the British with good conscience have accepted a peace bought at the price of millions of Czechs, German Jews, and other persecuted groups? Can a democracy make peace with states whose principles and domestic organization are abhorrent to Western man? Could the United States, toward the end of World War II and right afterward, really have shown no concern about eastern Europe as a Soviet sphere of domination, despite all the atrocity stories about Russian behavior and the brutality with which the Soviets exerted their influence? Would the United States not have denied its very essence had it shown indifference to those events because good Soviet-American relations depended on remaining silent? (Some revisionist writers claim that American interference in eastern Europe brought on the Cold War, but they have never been willing to face the implications of noninterference, despite the fact that they profess to be democrats and humanitarians.) Solzhenitsyn has charged American supporters of détente with precisely such a contemporary betrayal of the nation's essential character and basic purposes. "Whole peoples are being suppressed, and yet there is talk of détente. . . . If the groans of millions cannot be heard, we think we can base some sort of détente on this. Thinking that they are strengthening the prospects for peace, the Western countries are instead conferring the enslavement of the countries of East Europe."[14]

(Does "moral" in the context mean that states with antithetical values cannot coexist in peace except at a cost of "selling their souls"? The principal danger to the world is the disaster of a nuclear holocaust; only one failure would be one too many. Therefore reducing tensions between the superpowers and attempting to regularize to a degree their continuing rivalry is imperative. Détente, Kissinger argued, "is a process of managing relations with potentially hostile countries in order to preserve peace while maintaining our vital interests. In a nuclear age, this is in itself an objective not without moral validity.[15] Détente does not, however, mean the end of American–Soviet political competition, a sharing of common values, or approval of each other. At most, the United States can expect Russia to keep agreements and to behave responsibly (as Washington tried to clarify to Moscow when it placed American forces on alert during the Middle East war of 1973, when the president and Kissinger thought the Russians might send troops in to prevent an Israeli rout of Egyptian forces). But, the proponents of détente argue, this state of relations cannot be made dependent upon a transformation of the Soviet domestic structure. Indeed, it was this very right that Soviet Russia had claimed since the Bolshevik revolution, and it was to deny this right to intervene in other states in order to impose ideology upon them that the Cold War had started. Furthermore, just as a practical matter, to put such public pressure on the Soviet rulers for domestic reforms is to encourage rejection, resistance, and bitterness (comparable to that which would be engendered in the United States if the

---

[14] *Ibid.*, July 1, 1975.

[15] *Ibid.*, March 8, 1974.

Soviets announced that the price of détente for us would be the immediate and full realization of equal opportunities for all blacks in education, housing, and employment. It may also endanger those leaders favoring détente, as well as détente itself, which remains in the long run the best hope for the emergence of forces for change in the Soviet Union. The United States does not have to condone what the Soviet Union does internally. But American policy does have to face the basic question, which, as Kissinger phrased it, is "whether and to what extent we can risk other objectives—and especially the building of a structure of peace—for these domestic changes."[16] President Nixon summed up the argument as follows:

> There are limits to what we can do, and we must ask ourselves some very hard questions. . . .
> What is our capability to change the domestic structure of other nations? Would a slowdown or reversal of détente help or hurt the positive evolution of other social systems? What price in terms of renewed conflict are we willing to pay to bring pressure to bear for humane causes?
> Not by our choice but by our capability, our primary concern in foreign policy must be to help influence the international conduct of nations in the world arena. We would not welcome the intervention of other countries in our domestic affairs and we cannot expect them to be cooperative when we seek to intervene directly in theirs. We cannot gear our foreign policy to transformation of other societies. In the nuclear age our first responsibility must be the prevention of a war that could destroy all society.
> Peace between nations with totally different systems is also a high moral objective.[17])

The Carter administration, however, came into office convinced that its Republican predecessors had shamefully neglected the moral values that are the basis of American foreign policy. The United States had long proclaimed itself the defender of democracy and individual liberty. "Human rights" were therefore to be a principal concern; individual freedom, after all, constitutes the very essence of American democracy. The liberal tradition, which Kissinger was accused of having abandoned, was to be reunited with American foreign policy. The nation, it was proclaimed, once more stood for something, having reclaimed its democratic heritage. Jimmy Carter, the born-again Christian, had become the redeemer of American tradition.

But the Carter policy ran into trouble almost immediately. The Soviets, as Kissinger had predicted, did not care for Carter's emphasis on human rights, which they saw as specifically directed against them. Furthermore, they interpreted calls for political opposition, freedom of assembly, and free speech as attacks upon the foundations of their system; a system that claims to be based upon exclusive

---

[16.] *Ibid.*

[17.] *Ibid.*, June 6, 1974.

knowledge of Truth is bound to regard those who disagree as "conterrevolutionary." The President's emphasis on human rights and his support for Russian dissidents—epitomized by his letter to Andrei Sakharov—were thus viewed in Moscow as serious attempts to undermine the Soviet system. Predictably, it led to a stiffening of Soviet diplomacy on strategic arms limitations; consequently an agreement on this issue was delayed to a time when there was increasing opposition in this country. The Soviet invasion of Afghanistan ensured postponement of a Senate vote on SALT II and probably has killed hopes for the agreement. The human rights emphasis also resulted in a further decline of Jewish emigration and crackdown on dissidents. It did not even help those whom it was intended to help.

Similarly, when early in his administration the president announced withdrawal of all American ground forces from its ally, South Korea, a move presumably heavily influenced by South Korea's poor human-rights record, Japan—the United States's main ally in Asia—felt much greater insecurity. The American army had been the principal deterrent to another possible North Korean attack on South Korea, which Japan considered vital to its security. In addition, the withdrawal, if it is carried out, will hardly help to improve South Korea's respect for human rights, for its own government, feeling abandoned by its protector, will be even more concerned about censorship and quelling dissent as its sense of insecurity rises. On grounds of both American security and the human rights of individuals living under despotic regimes, therefore, the wisdom of the Carter administration's strong emphasis on human rights can be questioned.

Another result of the emphasis on human rights has been stress on the United States's double standard of judgment, if not its hypocrisy. One of the early goals of the administration was to normalize relations with Cuba and Vietnam (shortly after the collapse of South Vietnam in 1975, North and South Vietnam became unified under Hanoi's control). How could that be consistent with "human rights"? And how could the President square his human-rights stand with normalizing American relations with the second most important communist country, China, whose government is one of the most repressive in the world?

Even in relations with noncommunist regimes, concern for human rights came to stand in the way of other objectives. One of the key Carter goals was to stop further proliferation of nuclear weapons. Brazil, for example, seeking to cut oil imports and to find other sources of energy, was buying a complete nuclear fuel cycle from West Germany. This would have given Brazil the capability of manufacturing nuclear weapons, for they could be built from the enriched uranium used to fuel the nuclear reactor or from plutonium reprocessed from the waste materials. American policy was vigorously opposed to the sale of the entire fuel cycle. But, instead of seeking to influence the Brazilian-West German deal, the Carter administration condemned the Brazilian government for its human-rights violations and further strained American-Brazilian relations. Similarly, when he placed a food-grain embargo on Russia after the invasion of Afghanistan, Carter hoped other grain exporters would not make up for the loss of American shipments. Argentina, however, did not agree, for the Carter administration had repeatedly criticized its human-rights record.

Finally, when in order to gain other objectives, the president had to tone down his human-rights declarations, he cast doubts on the credibility of his own commitment to human rights and his control of the policy process. The same doubt about Carter's sincerity was raised by his support for the Shah of Iran until his flight in 1979. The president publicly praised the man who, while ruling with an iron fist, had supplied both the West and Israel with oil and who, the United States hoped, would also help to stabilize the Persian Gulf area. No official word was heard about the Shah's human-rights violations. Nor did the administration dare to speak out on Saudi Arabia's human-rights record. Indeed, Carter even visited South Korea, despite his criticisms of that regime's authoritarian ways.

In all these instances, the problem for the administration was one of deciding priorities; its initial failure to decide whether to give priority to human rights or to security when these objectives clashed resulted in the pursuit of both and the enhancement of neither in the United States' relationship with Russia. Gradually, compelled by circumstances, the administration increased its emphasis on security in its day-to-day policy (with occasional verbal endorsements of general human rights). It is ironic that, as the 1980s opened, Carter, shocked by the Soviet use of force to consolidate its power in Afghanistan, committed this country to the defense of Pakistan, a corrupt military dictatorship, in order to contain the further expansion of Soviet influence. He also promised Iran, which was still holding American diplomatic personnel hostage after illegal seizure of the American embassy, aid in defending itself against the menacing Russian armies if it first released the hostages. Iran by then had a regime whose human-rights violations probably equaled or exceeded those of the Shah. Under its fanatical religious leader, the Ayatollah Khomeini, who held full power under the new Islamic constitution, the country had gained a despot to replace the one it had overthrown. Members of the old regime and those who opposed the Ayatollah were executed and imprisoned; the mass media were censored, and many marks of Western influence were banned, as the regime portrayed itself increasingly as conducting a "holy war" against atheism and satanic influences. No experience could more painfully have taught the lesson that a nation must choose its objectives carefully, clearly decide its priorities, and make sure that its various purposes are reasonably compatible with one another, or at least not incompatible.

In the final analysis, does not the advocacy of human rights smack of the missionary sense that only a few years ago was widely denounced as the cause for America's anticommunist crusade and "overinvolvement" in the world? Does it not reflect a kind of ethnocentrism and self-righteousness, asserting that our values and ways are best and that we also know what is best for other peoples? Said a third world representative a few years ago:

> Some political analysts go so far as to deny even the universality of *political* rights in the present world—arguing that Western-type freedoms of opposition and dissent may serve a constructive purpose in a well-established pluralistic society; but they may in fact result in disintegrative and separatist movements in countries which have only recently gained independence.

(Yet, even if one were to accept as a matter of faith the universal and inalienable nature of "human rights" . . . nearly a billion human beings in the third world lack minimum requirements of food, health care, housing and functional literacy. To the extent that the basic needs of these vast masses of human brings are unmet, their "human rights" in a larger context are certainly not adequately safe-guarded . . . as far as the third world is concerned, they are largely one-sided, passive and abstract. . . .

[Human rights] are silent about the society's obligation toward the individual; they say precious little about the right to economic opportunities, the right to employment, the right to obtain a meaningful education, the right to enjoy a minimum of life's amenities. These "active" and "positive" sides (that is, society's obligations) are either ignored or considered as secondary in the roster of Western "human rights."[18])

(In short, are Western notions of human rights applicable to nations still concerned with fundamental needs of food, jobs, and health? To sum up: the pursuit of human rights, even when desirable and applicable, conflicts with other, often more important, objectives. Policy remains the art of the possible and requires discriminating judgement between competing and equally legitimate aims.[19])

[18.] Jahangir Amuzegar (former Iranian representative to the International Monetary Fund and World Bank) Rights and Wrongs," *The New York Times*, January 29, 1978 (italics in original).

[19.] Ernst B. Haas, "Human Rights," in Kenneth A. Oye *et al.*, *Eagle Entangled* (New York: Longman, 1979), pp. 167–196; Arthur Schlesinger Jr., "Human Rights and the American Tradition," *Foreign Affairs (America and the World 1978)*, pp. 503–526.

The State System and the Security-Prosperity Game 5

THE ANARCHICAL NATURE OF THE STATE SYSTEM

International politics is the product of a state system that is characterized by the absence of a legitimate central government (whose policy decisions are accepted as binding by society), and the absence of a common political culture, a set of rules or norms that govern the way in which political conflicts can be resolved peacefully.) Their absence is indeed a primary reason why we so often hear it said that international conflicts are settled with bullets, whereas domestic differences—at least in democratic political systems—are resolved by means of the ballot. Admittedly, this distinction is oversimplified. Not all quarrels between states result in war; most are settled without even invoking the threat of violence. Nor are all domestic clashes of interest settled without force or violent disturbance, even within contemporary Western democratic political systems. Of the 278 wars fought between 1480 and 1941, 28 percent were civil wars.[1] (Since World War II political violence and disorder have been frequent among the new nations in formerly colonial areas of the world. The repetitiveness with which governments have been overthrown and the recurrence of civil wars and revolutions suggest that, where legitimate governmental institutions and commonly shared political culture have not yet been achieved, domestic politics tend to resemble international politics.)

[1] Hans J. Morgenthau, *Politics among Nations: The Struggle for Power and Peace* (4th ed.; New York: Knopf, 1967), p. 490.

Nevertheless, in some nations, especially the older, more settled Western nations, the role of violence in the settlement of disputes is considerably less important than that of international war in the state system. Why? What conditions and processes of conflict resolution exist within these nations to account for their greater capacity to solve inevitable domestic problems peacefully? One factor is the presence in Western systems of executive branches of government to administer and enforce the law. The executive normally holds a preponderance, if not a monopoly, of organized violence with which it can legitimately enforce the law, protect society, and discourage potential rebels. The executive controls the armed forces and the national police, and it disarms the citizens of the nation by regulating the ownership of arms and forbidding the existence of private or party paramilitary forces. Domestic peace is, therefore, always armed. If the executive ever loses this superiority of power, either because all or part of the army refuses to support it, as in Weimar Germany or pre-Franco Spain, or because of the rise of political parties that possess their own armed forces, as did the Nazis in Germany, the communist Chinese, and the Vietcong in South Vietnam, the government may be challenged and the nation plunged into civil war. In Lebanon in 1975–1976, a rare variation of this pattern occurred when the underprivileged Muslims in that country allied themselves with the Palestine Liberation Organization (PLO) against the Christian half of the population. The Lebanese army, weaker than the PLO, was paralyzed because its composition reflected the split among the country's religious groups. The result was bloody civil war. One section of the population had attracted the armed help of an extranational actor residing in its midst.

(Western political systems also have institutionalized legislative processes through which conflicts of interests within society, articulated by political parties and interest groups, have historically been channeled and resolved peacefully. The term "legislative process" is used, rather than "legislative branch," because the latter does not legislate by itself. In any Western political system, it is the leader of the majority party who, as president or prime minister, draws up the legislative program to be submitted for approval to the congress or parliament. In legislation, too, therefore, the executive plays the leading role. The significance of the process of legislation, however, is that lawmaking is essentially synonymous with the issue of domestic war and peace. The most controversial, significant, and bitter conflicts in society revolve around questions of what the law should be. The legislative process is thus focused on the basic issue of politics, which—as Harold Lasswell once summed it up—is "who gets what, when and how."

(Politics is thus a series of conflicts over the distribution of "goods" like wealth, status, and power in society. Other political scientists have used more formal terms, like "allocation of values."} Should there be a redistribution of wealth? Should blacks be granted full equality in American society, and should discrimination in interstate travel, housing, and employment be banned? Should the poor, the unemployed, the aged, the sick, and the hungry receive some kind of help and how much? If so, what kind of help? Should labor be permitted to bargain collectively? Should farmers be subsidized or rely on the free market? Should the country have a national health-insurance plan, and, if so, what type and at what cost?

(These questions pose major social issues and arouse strong passions. Yet they are unavoidable; in a pluralistic society new demands are continually being advanced, and men and women differ on how to resolve the many problems confronting society. A political system that is not very responsive to demands for change and does not provide for sufficient peaceful change will sooner or later erupt in revolution, the domestic equivalent of international war. A political system must either meet important aspirations of rising and discontented new social groups with sensitivity and sufficient speed or confront violent upheaval. If discontent is widespread enough, the executive's superior power cannot prevent the government's fall, because the army and police are largely recruited from the population. In the ultimate breakdown of society, many soldiers will refuse to fire on their own people; units of the armed forces will instead join the rebellion,) as in Iran in 1978–1979, and in Afghanistan, where many soldiers defected from the Soviet-imposed government and joined the rebels. (The ordinary soldier-citizen will have no more vested interest in maintaining the system than will most other citizens.)

(Finally, a judiciary, together with the executive and legislative institutions, helps to maintain expectations of individual and social justice. Violence, domestic or international, is normally an instrument of last resort. While hope remains that peaceful change is possible through existing political processes, rebellion can usually be avoided. But, just as there is no international executive with a monopoly of organized violence and no international legislative process to help provide for peaceful change, the state system lacks an international judiciary that, like the American judiciary, might have the authority to ensure this sense of justice and thus help to ensure peaceful change.)

(The state system, however, not only lacks effective central political institutions for preserving peace and regulating the behavior of its members; it also lacks an international political culture or consensus on political values comparable to those existing within most Western states. A state's political culture includes the shared political values and attitudes of its people related to the general purposes for which society exists and, even more important, the rules or norms by which the domestic "game" is played. The consensus thus comprises both substantive values (agreement on what the country stands for) and procedural values (agreement on how government should be conducted—for example, majority rule and the supremacy of law). As nondemocratic states can, after all, proclaim the same substantive goals as democracies (as, in fact, the Soviet Union does in its constitution), it is the way of governing or making political decisions that is critical. If policies were not made according to rules, they would be disregarded and disobeyed; they would lack moral sanction or legitimacy. People obey the law because they agree that the government has the right to govern, not because the government has at its command superior power and the individual is fearful of punishment.) "For, if force creates right," the French philosopher Jean Jacques Rousseau wrote in the eighteenth century, "the effect changes with the cause: Every force that is greater than the first succeeds to its right. As soon as it is possible to disobey with impunity, disobedience is legitimate and the strongest being always in the right, the only thing that matters is to act so as to become the strongest." But, Rousseau continued, "the strongest is never strong enough to be always the master, unless he transforms

82   strength into right and obedience into duty."[2] (If government is considered legitimate, even people who disagree with the content of a law will normally obey it because they will acknowledge that the government has the authority to decide policies for the entire society.)

(Politics, to sum up, deals with conflicts among groups whose objectives clash. The peaceful resolution of such differences depends on, first, an executive with superior power, which discourages potentially violent challenges and allows the government to enforce legitimate decisions (in Vernon Van Dyke's apt phrase, "A peaceful country is a policeful country"); second, a set of governing institutions, executive, legislative, and judicial, that provide for peaceful conflict resolution and allow most people and organizations to attain "justice" or what they themselves regard as fair shares of what society has to offer; third, and, perhaps most important, widespread agreement on common purposes and rules of the game so that, even in major disputes, the differing views and needs can be expressed through acceptable political channels, rather than leading to confrontation and violence; and, fourth, the fact that this consensus, which serves to legitimate the government, is reinforced by a deep emotional commitment embodied in nationalism and its various symbols: the flag, the national monuments, the national anthem, national institutions like the Congress and Supreme Court, and national celebrations and rituals like those connected with the Fourth of July. Such symbols are reminders of national history and the common beliefs and loyalty of a people, as well as of the supremacy of society and the common good.)

(Instead of such broad agreement, which can buffer and limit areas of conflict so that they do not shred the whole social fabric, the only common agreement on what may be called a minimal "international political culture" is the commitment to the existence of nation-states, their independence, and their security. But this commitment *maximizes* divisions and conflict among nations. The primary loyalty of the nation-state is to itself. The absence of the conditions for peaceful change and accommodation internationally means that the basic condition of the state system is one of potential warfare among its members; at least, there is a higher expectation of violence than in national political systems.[3])

INTERNATIONAL POLITICS AS SELF-HELP AND A "STATE OF POTENTIAL WAR"

(The primary distinguishing characteristic of the state system follows from its decentralized or anarchical nature. *Each state in this external environment can rely*

---

[2] Jean Jacques Rousseau, *The Social Contract* (New York: Dutton, 1947), p. 6.

[3] That the domestic system in the United States, for example, assumes people will generally obey the law voluntarily is clearly shown by the contrast between the limited number of police (national, state, and local)—certainly not enough to deal with massive resistance to the law—and the number of men in the armed forces to be employed outside the United States. For an interesting analysis in which the willingness of governments to use force against other governments is contrasted with their reluctance, if not unwillingness, to use it against their own populations, see E. E. Schattschneider, *Two Hundred Million Americans in Search of a Government* (New York: Holt, Rinehart and Winston, 1969), pp. 17–22.

upon itself, and only upon itself, for the protection of its political independence and territorial integrity and national prosperity. In a condition of what might also be called "politics without government"—perhaps the shortest way of summing up the distinction between international and domestic politics—the issue of who receives what, when, and how is decided, not by a national government recognized as legitimate, but by the interactions of states in a system whose basic rule is "every state for itself.") As a human being's highest secular loyalty is to the nation, policy makers of all states will be intensely committed to the maintenance of national security, the prerequisite for enjoyment of the nation's other values—its "way of life" or "core values." (If it is further correct that the external milieu is anarchical, posing a constant danger to this way of life, policy makers responsible for protecting the nation will react fearfully to perceived threats to their country.)

(More specifically, we may say that states living in an environment in which none can acquire absolute security are bound to feel insecure and are therefore driven to reduce their sense of insecurity by enhancing their power) As with human beings in the Hobbesian state of nature, so with states in the state system: They are haunted by continuous fear and danger of *violent* death.[4] (It is the resulting mutual fear and suspicion among states that produce "power politics.") When a nation sees its neighbor as a potential foe, it will try to deter potential attack by becoming a little stronger than the neighbor; the latter, in turn, will also fear an attack and will therefore feel that it too must be strong enough to deter one or, if deterrence should fail, to win the resulting conflict. (*The insecurity of all states in the system compels each to acquire greater security by engaging in a constant scramble for increased power.*) But, as each state watches its neighbor's power grow, its own sense of insecurity recurs; it then tries all the harder to gain even greater strength. (The result is that each state is continually faced with a "security dilemma."[5])

The nature of the state system thus conditions the behavior of its members, committing each state to a continuing concern with power because of its security dilemma. Nations therefore seek power not because simple maximization of power is their goal; they seek it because they wish to guard the security of their "core values," their territorial integrity, and political independence, as well as their prosperity. And they act aggressively because the system gives rise to mutual fear and suspicion: Each state regards its neighbor state as a potential Cain, so to speak.[6] The dilemma inherent in the state system is essentially "kill or be killed," strike first or risk destruction. In this context, it does not take much for one state to arouse and confirm another state's apprehensions and thus to stimulate the development of reciprocal images of hostility, each of which will be validated by the adversary's

---

[4] Thomas Hobbes, *Leviathan* (New York: Dutton, 1950), p. 104.

[5] Herz, *International Politics in the Atomic Age*, pp. 231–232.

[6] The "very realization that his own brother may play the role of a Cain makes his fellow men appear to him as potential foes. Realization of this fact by others, in turn, makes him appear to them as their potential mortal enemy. Thus there arises a fundamental social constellation, a mutual suspicion and a mutual dilemma: the dilemma of 'kill or perish,' of attacking first or running the risk of being destroyed. There is apparently no escape from this vicious circle. Whether man is 'by nature" peaceful and cooperative, or aggressive and domineering, is not the question." Herz, *Political Realism and Political Idealism* (Chicago: University of Chicago Press, 1951), pp. 2–3.

84 behavior. Conversely, these images will be hard to dislodge by means even of friendly acts; indeed, such acts may well be construed as indications of weakness and may therefore be exploited.

Perhaps a more apt way of defining this almost compulsive concern with power, which is shared by all states, is in terms of the high potential for violence in the anarchical state system. For, in its decentralized circumstances, threats of violence or actual resorts to violence are in the end the principal means by which one state can impose its demands on other states or, conversely, resist demands imposed on it by others. If we follow our earlier argument that in domestic politics government performs a distributive function, we may say that *in international politics force or coercion takes the place of government*. It is for this reason that the international system has frequently been characterized as being in a state of potential war; it is war, or the constant possibility of war, that all too frequently determines who receives what and when. In an environment of conflicting demands, in which there are no recognized and universally accepted supranational institutions to mediate differences and to provide for the nonviolent resolution of differences, it is the power of the respective adversaries—power to win a war should it erupt—that will settle who gains what and who loses what. Geoffrey Blainey has remarked that warfare has historically been a convincing way of measuring the actual ratio of power among contesting states. The end of a war, he says, produces a neat ledger of power, which has been duly audited and signed.[7] The actual strength of each party will be clear from the outcome: defeat, stalemate, compromise, peace, or victory. Not that wars are frequent or even the principal expressions of power. Persuasion, rewards, and coercion are other means and are more frequently used. War is the instrument of last resort, the ultimate test.

Yet the characterization of international politics as a state of potential war does not seem incorrect historically. For, even had there been far fewer wars, it remains true, as Hobbes suggested, that

> . . . war consists not in battle only, or the act of fighting but in a tract of time . . . as it is in the nature of weather. For as the nature of foul weather lies not in a shower or two of rain, but in an inclination thereto of many days together, so the nature of war consists not in actual fighting, but in the known disposition thereto.[8]

Coercion, or the threat of force, is always present in the background, affecting negotiations among conflicting states, just as the threat of domestic strikes always affects the bargaining between labor and management. A given strike does not *have* to occur to demonstrate the power of labor; management knows what the effects of a prolonged strike will be on corporate production and profits. On the other hand, management knows that the workers do not like to be laid off and jeopardize their earnings and that the union will eventually run out of strike funds. The desire

---

[7] Geoffrey Blainey, *The Causes of War* (New York: Free Press, 1973), p. 113.

[8] Quoted in William Ebenstein, *Great Political Thinkers* (3d ed; New York: Holt, Rinehart and Winston, 1960), p. 368.

to avoid a strike—a long one, anyway—is thus an incentive for both sides to compromise.

Similarly, the possibility of violence does not mean that it will occur immediately; war, as already noted, is usually considered the instrument of last resort. States do not go to war lightly, for the costs are high, and in the "fog of war" the outcome among evenly matched opponents can rarely be certain, no matter how carefully each has calculated its power and that of its adversary beforehand. The knowledge that war is a possibility is more likely to *moderate* demands and provide a *stimulus for other means of conflict resolution* like persuasion, rewards, and coercion. Renunciation of force, on the other hand, eliminates the penalty for an uncompromising attitude and gives the advantage to the party willing to invoke violence.

Although the structure of the state system, then, makes it necessary for states to be constantly concerned about the ratio of power between themselves and other states, it should nevertheless be stressed that coercion does not always mean the threat of violence; it may mean the use of nonmilitary, especially economic, sanctions that can also be effective, sometimes more effective than the threat of force. OPEC members have in recent years dramatically demonstrated this point to the world. In a system in which, according to all conventional calculations, great powers should be influencing small powers, the reverse seems to be happening. *One principal characteristic of power is the capacity to hurt.* A state that makes demands on another says in fact, "Give me what I want, or I will hurt you worse than compliance will hurt." If the other state's calculations agree that compliance will hurt less than resistance, it is likely to submit; if it calculates that the cost of resistance will be less than yielding what is demanded, it is likely to defy the demands made upon it. The threat of force is an obvious example of coercion matched by the "reward" of withholding it and not hurting the adversary; the threat of withholding resources vital to a nation's industry or of greatly raising the prices of these resources is also an effective form of coercion. Inflicting force or deprivation of needed resources are just two of the many strategies that can hurt an adversary severely. In the latter instance, a small, unindustrialized country can have great influence in its relations with far bigger and militarily stronger countries. As Sheik Yamani, the Saudi Arabian oil minister, told an American television audience in 1979: "If you think in the West that there will be no interruption in oil without a settlement of the Palestinian question, you are mistaken."[9] The late Mao Tsetung has often been quoted as having said that power grows out of the barrel of a gun; Yamani was saying that power grows out of a barrel of oil as well. The military weapon can thus be replaced by the "economic weapon." Karl Marx a long time ago called it the replacement of the cannon by capital.

Nor are such economic means used only to achieve national security objectives, often also called "high politics" goals. They may be invoked for such economic, or "low politics," purposes as achievement of national prosperity. Obviously, trade is a principal way of obtaining those goods, services, and other

---

[9.] "NBC White Paper," *The New York Times*, September 4, 1979.

86 resources that a country needs for economic growth, high employment, and a statisfactory standard of living. Oil, for example, can be bought on the international market. But, if it were deliberately withheld or if production were cut back to create short supplies, or if the price were deliberately raised to the point where it created ever higher unemployment and inflation in the Western industrial countries, possibly causing economic collapse, can it be doubted that, in the absence of any other solution, force would be used to prevent economic strangulation of the West and the collapse of the American economy? The nature of the state system, in which each member can in the end rely only on itself, is nowhere clearer than in relation to the oil issue. It is precisely in order not to become even more dependent on oil imports and to deny other states leverage over American foreign policy and the domestic economy that recent presidents have sought more energy conservation, higher domestic oil production, and development of alternative sources of energy. The aim has been to decrease dependence on OPEC, especially its Arab members, so that the United States can more effectively control its own political destiny and economic life. No state wants to become too dependent on other states, for that gives the latter leverage. But, if these domestic efforts to reduce dependence fail, oil may well be the cause of war.

In the meantime, as the 1980s began, the United States became increasingly involved politically and militarily in the Persian Gulf area in order to protect the West's oil lines, especially from Soviet interference. Indeed, as the tightness of oil supplies in the long run takes effect, and as rising oil prices increasingly face Western consumer nations with growing debts and possible bankruptcy, and non-Western non-oil nations with the end of their hopes for development and a better life for their peoples, "power politics" may well receive an added impetus. As the nations seek to enhance their living standards, or at least preserve their economic gains, in an era of greater scarcity at reasonable prices of oil and other resources, conflict over access to the resources needed to industrialize or maintain an industrial society will intensify—and this is likely to be true even if nations like America should lower their past expectations of rapid economic and personal income growth. Prosperity or bread-and-butter issues, in short, are less likely to result in greater economic interdependence and peaceful relations among nations, than in more strife. The world, instead of becoming less Hobbesian, will become more so.

The very terms that make up much of the language of international politics are indicative of the contentious nature of the state system and its proneness to coercion. We speak of war, economic warfare and aggression, diplomatic fronts, waging peace, cold wars, crusades for peace, war as the continuation of politics by other means, and peace as the continuation of the last war by other means. And, in the wake of OPEC actions, many Americans, recognizing that the United States had become the food basket of a hungry world, have begun to talk of "food as a weapon." In politics among nations, almost anything—oil, food, investments, technology, trade—can become a weapon, a means by which one state can seek leverage over other states. A 1975 Central Intelligence Agency research report, for example, concluded that world grain shortages "could give the United States a measure of power it had never had before—possibly an economic and political dominance greater than that of the immediate post-World War II years."[10] The implications of this statement, if true, are enormous, especially when we recall that in those years the United States possessed a monopoly of atomic power. Furthermore, the countries becoming partially dependent on American food imports are not just underdeveloped countries but also Russia and possibly China (especially, the CIA speculated, if the world climate continues to cool, which would reduce food production in both those countries). In a world of continued food shortages, occasional famine, and more widespread malnutrition, therefore, the United States would acquire virtual life-and-death power over needy countries without the use of a single bomb. Indeed, in 1979 a country-western song entitled "Cheaper Crude or No More Food" was popular; the target clearly was OPEC. Hobbes would have understood and not been surprised at the possibility of using food exports as a weapon in the self-help system that is the state system; nor would he have been surprised by the use of such terms as "investment wars" and "trade wars," which we shall come across later.

THE BALANCE OF POWER AS A SYSTEM

(The final characteristic of the state system that follows from the security and power problems confronted by all states is that, *if states wish to deter potential attackers and ensure their own independence and their ways of life, they will pursue "balance of power" policies.* The balance of power is sought because of fear that, if one nation gains predominant power, it may impose its will upon other states, either by the threat of violence or by actual use of violence.) In Arnold Wolfers' words:

> Under these conditions of anarchy the expectation of violence and even of annihilation is ever-present. To forget this and thus fail in the concern for enhanced power spells the doom of a state. This does not mean constant open warfare; expansion of power at the expense of others will not take place if there is enough counterpower to deter or to stop states from undertaking it. Although no state is interested in a mere balance of power, the efforts of all states to maximize power may lead to equilibrium. If and when that happens, there is "peace" or, more exactly, a condition of stalemate or truce. Under the conditions described here, this balancing of power process is the only available "peace" strategy.[11]

The term "balance of power" is often used in loose and contradictory ways. It may, for example, refer to any actually existing distribution of power between two states, whether it is an equilibrium, an approximate balance, or an imbalance

---

[10] *The New York Times*, March 17, 1975. This claim is examined further in Chapter 11.

[11] Arnold Wolfers, *Discord and Collaboration*, p. 83. For contrary interpretations correlating peace with a superiority of power and war with a balance, see A.F. K. Organski, *World Politics* (New York: Knopf, 1956), pp. 325-333; and Blainey, *op. cit.*, pp.. 112–114.

(meaning either superiority or inferiority of power, as in the sentences "the balance has shifted toward Egypt" and "the balance has shifted away from or against Israel)."[12] As we shall use the term here, however, it refers to a "balance-of-power system," in which any shift away from equilibrium in the state system leads to countershifts through mobilization of countervailing power. This definition suggests a mechanism, like the "invisible hand" in the classical free market, that preserves the equilibrium. The systemic nature of the balance of power is further explained by Wolfers in a passage that is worth quoting in full:

> While it makes little sense to use the term "automatic" literally, as if human choices and errors were irrelevant to the establishment, preservation, or destruction of a state of equilibrium, there nevertheless is a significant element of truth in the theory of "automatism" which is valid even today. If one may assume that any government in its senses will be deeply concerned with the relative power position of hostile countries, then one may conclude that efforts to keep in step in the competition for power with such opponents, or even to outdo them, will almost certainly be forthcoming. If most nations react in this way, a tendency towards equilibrium will follow it; will come into play whether both sides aim at equilibrium or whether the more aggressive side strives for superiority. In the latter case, the opposite side is likely to be provoked into matching these aggressive moves. Forces appear therefore to be working "behind the backs" of the human actors, pushing them in the direction of balanced power irrespective of their preferences.[13]

That is, states cannot be trusted with power, for they will be tempted to abuse it. *Unrestrained power in the system constitutes a menace to all other member states. Power is therefore the best antidote to power.* The fundamental assumption, of course, is that power will not be abolished, that it is inherent in a system characterized by competition and rivalry, and therefore that the principal task of the international system is the management of power.[14] Not that in "real life" all states—especially the great powers—have always and everywhere sought to expand their power. They have not, as the United States' return to isolationism after World War I and Japan's unwillingness to play a major and active political role even in Asia since World War II have demonstrated. Nevertheless, states have sought to enhance their power often enough so that we can say that not doing so is the exception and often a cause of wonderment, if not puzzlement, to other states, which may be tempted to exploit the situation. For this reason, even a state wishing to act with restraint will usually act preemptively, knowing that potential adversaries may seek such advantage and that it will then be compelled to react to the latter.

Power thus begets countervailing power. But note the twofold aim of countervailing power. The first aim is the *protection of the security of each state,*

---

[12] Discussions of the different meanings of "balance of power" can be found in Morgenthau, *op. cit.*, pp. 161–163; Ernst B. Haas, "The Balance of Power: Prescription, Concept, or Propaganda?" *World Politics*, July 1953, pp. 442–447; and Inis L. Claude, *Power in International Relations* (New York: Random House, 1962, Part I).

[13] Wolfers, *op. cit.*, p. 123.

[14] Claude, *op. cit.*, p. 6.

not the preservation of peace.) To be sure, most states normally feel secure when they are at peace, but peace is the product of a balance that is acceptable to the leading powers because it ensures their individual security. (Peace may be desirable in itself, but it is also only one of several objectives that states pursue. Security may easily be given priority over peace, especially when security is threatened. The second aim is the *protection of the state system as a whole.* The rationale underlying the balance of power is the protection of each participating state. The way to ensure this protection is to prevent the emergence of a preponderant state. States are therefore rarely eliminated by the great powers.) The most prominent recent exception is, of course, Poland. Having had the misfortune to be surrounded by Russia, Austria-Hungary, and Prussia—and later by Soviet Russia and Nazi Germany—Poland has been divided several times to permit a balance among its neighbors. More common is the behavior of the victors at the end of the Napoleonic war. Despite twenty-five years of fighting, the costliest that Europe had experienced since the Thirty Years' War, which had ended in 1648, France was neither eliminated nor punished. A lenient peace treaty was signed, so that France could once more take its place in the family of European states and contribute to preservation of the system. A vengeful France might have started another war, instead of contributing to the European system's peace and stability.

By contrast, the Treaty of Versailles ending World War I was a harsh one. At least, Germany considered it punitive, and many regard it as a central reason why that nation remained a threat to the stability and peace of post-1918 Europe. Had Britain and France signed a treaty of reconciliation or modified the Versailles pact in the 1920s, when Germany was still weak, the German Republic might have weathered the Depression and become a pillar of support for the European settlement. Instead, Hitler was able to exploit German nationalism to help him achieve power, mobilize support for his regime, and proceed to destroy the Europe of Versailles. Ironically, it was only when Germany threatened to use force that the Western powers sought to appease Hitler, but by then German ambitions and power had outgrown any possibility of being satisfied.

The United States learned from this interwar experience. It signed a generous peace treaty with Japan after World War II and treated West Germany in a spirit of reconciliation. In the subsequent postwar containment policy, in which its former enemies figure prominently, the United States accepted the premise that Russia is a *permanent fixture* on the international chessboard. The aim of containment was not to eliminate Russia. There was no reason to believe that eliminating Russia would end the United States' international involvements, any more than had the prior elimination of Hitler's Germany. The aim of containment was merely to prevent further Soviet expansion. The expectation was that, with time, the Soviet Union would "mellow" and become easier to coexist with. In the long run, there was even the possibility of another realignment as the distribution of power in the system changed again.

Let us reemphasize that this balancing operation is primarily carried out by the great powers. Historically, the actors "who count" have been relatively few. The state system, though characterized on one hand by anarchy, is, on the other,

90   also characterized by a hierarchy composed of the principal states, which, while seeking to preserve a distribution of power that protects the independence and security of member states, also provide the system with a degree of restraint or order. The balance among the great powers thus protects not only themselves but, in most instances, also the smaller members of the system. Such activity on the part of those states that compose the hierarchy and the passivity of those that do not should be noted, for in "real life," as distinct from our model, the latter feature appears to be changing dramatically during the temporary period and this will require us later to reexamine the model.[15]

(In any event, the rules of the balance of power remain the basic norms, or "rules of the game," for states. These norms may be ignored or forgotten only at a nation's peril. They are usually so "internalized" that those who conduct foreign policy think almost "automatically," as Wolfers has put it, in balance-of-power terms. Policy makers become "socialized" by the system; even revolutionary leaders learn quickly and follow the logic of the balance of power, rather than the dictates of ideology. In addition (as we shall see in Chapter 6 and throughout Part II), the norms of behavior vary with the structure of the system, that is, with the number of principal actors or great powers and the distribution of power among them. For the moment, however, we can state these rules in general terms:

1. Watch a potential adversary's power and match it. (The emphasis on power, rather than on intentions, suggests that a peaceful state today may become warlike tomorrow if it gains superior power.)

2. Ally oneself with a weaker state in order to restore the balance of power.

3. Abandon such alliances when balance has been restored and the common danger has passed.

4. Regard national-security interests as permanent; alliances must therefore change as new threats arise.

5. Do not treat defeated states harshly through punitive peace treaties. (Today's adversary may be tomorrow's ally.) ⏎

WAR AND PEACE AS A CONTINUUM

We usually think of war and peace as two quite distinct conditions, separated by a formal declaration of war. Our analysis should by now have shown this assumption to be incorrect. We have characterized the state system, in Stanley Hoffmann's phrase, as a "state of war" and then slightly amended it to a "state of potential war."[16] It is thus more accurate to think of war and peace as existing on a continuum

---

[15] See Chapter 12.

[16] Stanley Hoffmann, *The State of War* (New York: Praeger, 1965).

along which states have conflicting interests of increasing scope and intensity. Some of these conflicts will be resolvable by peaceful negotiations, but at some point one side will feel that the demands made upon it are excessive, that it can no longer offer concessions without endangering its own security. It may calculate that the distribution of power is sufficiently equitable so that it can reject the adversary's demands without war's resulting. But the opponent may not be willing to accept this rejection, estimating that the ratio of power favors it. The opponent therefore attempts to intimidate the adversary and, when intimidation proves ineffective, resorts to force. (War, then, begins when the contestants *disagree* on their relative power; it will end only when they *agree* on their relative strength.[17] That is, war erupts because one of the nations in an adversary relationship has miscalculated the power distribution. The fighting will clarify the actual ratio of power; war is thus a bitter teacher of "reality." The point is that one state finally decides, correctly or incorrectly, that peaceful bargaining will not resolve the dispute and decides to continue bargaining over the terms of coexistence—who receives what—by war, "the continuation of politics by other means."[18])

(Peace, in short, is not absolute but conditional. If a state can preserve its security in peacetime, it will do so, but, if it cannot, it will invoke force as the instrument of last resort) as Britain finally did when Hitler attacked Poland. (Once fighting erupts, and fighting is not as frequently preceded by an official declaration of war as may be thought,[19] it will continue until at least one side attains terms that it can live with peacefully (as in the two world wars, in which the vanquished parties had to surrender unconditionally) or, more frequently since 1945, until both sides reach a new set of mutually acceptable terms and conclude the war, an event often symbolized by an official peace conference in which the new postwar balance of power is registered.) At the end of World War II the conflict over this new balance began so quickly after the cessation of hostilities that no formal conference was ever held. But the key point is again that peace is conditional. Negotiations between North Vietnam and the United States in 1968–1973, for example, could have led to peace at any time, but neither side was willing to accept the other side's *terms of* peace. The fighting, and the bargaining, thus continued, for they held out the promise to each side of better or more acceptable terms later. (*The price of peace was of greater concern than peace itself*: the normal cause of war between states. War does not end, and peace is not restored, until the cost is, at the very minimum, tolerable.)

(War and peace are therefore hardly mutually exclusive conditions. Political conflict continues from one to the other; so does bargaining. The axiom "when diplomacy stops, war starts" is simply untrue. Bargaining, which in peacetime is called "diplomacy," continues after the shooting starts. War is not normally an

---

[17] Blainey, *op. cit.*, p. 122. Also see J. David Singer, *Explaining War* (Beverly Hills, Calif.: Sage, 1979) and Singer and Michael D. Wallace, *To Augur Well* (Beverly Hills, Calif.: Sage, 1979). They seek to find early warning indications forecasting war.

[18] Blainey, *op. cit.*, pp. 115–119.

[19] *Ibid.*, pp. 170–173.

alternative to negotiations; it is a *continuation* of them carried on violently. Power, especially military power, is always present. Although we talk of peaceful negotiations, power stands in the background—"on guard"—and, when needed, is brought to the fore. It is invoked as a threat, and, if that is insufficient, it will be used openly. Power is omnipresent. Peace and war therefore have much in common. "Diplomacy without armaments is like music without instruments."[20])

Peace becomes difficult, perhaps impossible, to define in this context, because it has so many different meanings. It may simply denote an absence of war (at least, of large-scale war, as distinct from more limited kinds). Another meaning is the absence of major political conflict and rivalry, like the intense form of competition that in our age has been called "cold war." It may even include a high degree of cooperation or rapprochement between states. A third meaning is more positive, emphasizing not what is missing but what is present, including global organizations like the United Nations, which provides an institutional setting in which most nations of the world meet. There they *should* resolve their differences in a spirit of concern for mankind as a whole, rather than with selfish regard only for their own national portions of mankind. Even this expectation of peaceful and orderly change is not quite satisfactory for some observers. Peace, they insist, cannot coexist with continued poverty throughout much of the world, even within the rich countries, and oppression of millions of people in many societies is still unacceptable. Peace in this interpretation must be not only the absence of warfare but also the presence of decent standards of living and social justice for all people. Such a "true peace" can occur only at a yet higher level, that of world government. Such a government would more fully institutionalize the processes of change than the United Nations ever could. A global community in which national differences and jealousies had disappeared would allow the institutions to work so that all humanity would share the blessings of peace, prosperity, freedom, and justice. Reasons for differences among men would have evaporated, and a lasting peace would exist for the first time in history. World politics in such a global order would be domestic politics.

Until that time comes, however, war—and certainly the threat of war—will continue to play its historical role. Are contemporary statesmen, like statesmen in the past, hypocrites when they profess their devotion to peace? Undoubtedly, some have used words of peace to disguise their militaristic and aggressive aims. But, for most, the gap between their desires for peace and preparations for war has been the product of the fundamental tragedy of the state system, which traps all states in a security dilemma and compels them to prepare for the possibility of war, however much they may prefer to avoid it. Wars have occurred frequently enough—even in our nuclear era—so that recurrence is to be expected. The possibility of war is a fundamental assumption that no statesman can afford to operate without; to do so might well be fatal. A national leader may thus be quite sincere in his or her desire for peace, but, by the very nature of his or her position as a guardian of national security, he or she may harbor suspicions about a traditional enemy

---

[20] Frederick the Great, quoted in *ibid.*, p. 108.

or a rising power—even when the latter publicly disavows hostile intentions and declares its desire for friendship. "Beware of Greeks bearing gifts" sums up the attitudes of states toward one another; "maybe that state is acting in a friendly manner in order to relax my guard just before it will attack me." It may be, of course, that the other state does have friendly intentions; a suspicious attitude may then result in conflict, even war. But if it does harbor unfriendly intentions, then "being on guard" may well help to avoid conflict. This dilemma clearly haunts policy makers. [21]

Furthermore, although peace may be desirable, it has not usually been the most important objective for a given state. When its security is endangered, any state may sacrifice peace and fight. Similarly, when other objectives, such as the defense of a nation's freedom or promotion of certain national or ideological views, are pursued, peace may be secondary. A state may be quite willing to forgo peace if it feels that it must help to achieve the "national liberation" of oppressed peoples. Wars have also been fought repeatedly because they have been effective instruments for achieving the objectives of states. War may be regarded as evil, a curse on mankind, and condemned as destructive and immoral, but the fact is that war has all too often been useful.)

Germany owed its unity after 1870 to war; Czechoslovakia and Poland owed their existence as states to World War I; Britain and Russia owed their survival to victory in World War II; more recently, the threat of violence has protected the Western democracies for more than three decades. The actual use of violence has brought the Chinese communists to power on the mainland and kept South Korea independent; has provided European Jews who survived the Nazi holocaust with a home in Israel; has allowed communist leaders to unify Vietnam; has provided Cuban forces serving as Soviet proxies in Africa with victories in Angola, Ethiopia, and Eritrea (with more perhaps still to come); and remains the principal hope of self-styled "national liberation" movements like the PLO and the Southwest African People's Organization (SWAPO) in Namibia for achieving statehood or seizing the governments of already existing states—as occurred in Zimbabwe in 1980, when the Patriotic Front won an election that the white minority agreed to after a long civil war.

(The idea that war is irrational or immoral or that it profits nobody except munitions makers is not particularly convincing to those who have benefited or hope to benefit from war. Even in this age of nuclear weapons, nonnuclear warfare is still widely regarded as a rational instrument of policy.) As James Shotwell wrote many years ago,

> War . . . has been the instrument by which most of the great facts of political national history have been established and maintained. It has played a dominant role in nearly all political crises; it has been used to achieve liberty, to secure democracy, and to attempt to make it secure against the menace of its use by other hands. The map of the world today has been largely determined upon the battle-field. The maintenance of civilization itself has been, and still continues to be,

---

[21.] See Chapter 7 for further analysis of states' intentions.

94

underwritten by the insurance of army and navy ready to strike at any time where danger threatens. Thus, even in peace, the war system has to a large degree determined not only international relationships but the character and history of the nations themselves.[22]

This remains true today. For coercion and force as principal characteristics of much of international politics spring from the basically anarchical nature of the state system and its fundamental rule of self-help. Nuclear weapons, for all their horror, have not changed either one of these features; they have affected the ways in which military power is used, but they have not yet led to a transformation of the current system to a new world order characterized by greater harmony and cooperation among states and the elimination of the uses of threats and force.

CONFLICTS AND THE LIMITS OF COOPERATION

In the state system, as we have emphasized, the struggle for security is basic. States perceive one another as adversaries. The insecurity of an anarchical system of multiple sovereignty places the actors under compulsion to seek maximum power even though this may run counter to their real desires."[23] The inherent fears and suspicions of states would be reflected even in a situation of general disarmament. States might well be better off if none were armed. But then one state might calculate that, if it armed, it would be able to gain an advantage; it could coerce unarmed opponents or go to war to impose its demands. Precisely because most states fear such a possibility, they will not disarm in the first place but will make sure that they are as strong as potential adversaries. States are enemies, then, not because they are necessarily aggressive or have ideological differences but because they see that they can harm one another and, being cautious, view one another as possible enemies. Note the following statement by former Secretary of Defense Robert McNamara:

> In 1961, when I became Secretary of Defense, the Soviet Union possessed a very small operational arsenal of intercontinental missiles. However, they did possess the technological and industrial capacity to enlarge that arsenal very substantially over the succeeding several years. Now, we had no evidence that the Soviets did in fact plan to fully use that capability. But as I have pointed out, a strategic planner must be "conservative" in his calculations; that is, he must prepare for the worst plausible case and not be content to hope and prepare merely for the most probable. . . .
>
> Since we could not be certain of Soviet intentions—since we could not be sure that they would not undertake a massive buildup—we had to insure against

---

[22.] James Shotwell, *War as an Instrument of National Policy* (New York: Harcourt, 1929), p. 15.

[23.] Wolfers, *op. cit.*, p. 84.

such an eventuality by undertaking ourselves a major buildup of the Minuteman and Polaris forces. . . .

Clearly, the [subsequent] Soviet buildup is in part a reaction to our own buildup since the beginning of this decade. Soviet strategic planners undoubtedly reasoned that if our buildup were to continue at its accelerated pace, we might conceivably reach, in time, a credible first-strike capability against the Soviet Union. This was not in fact our intention. Our intention was to assure that they—with their theoretical capacity to reach such a first-strike capability—would not in fact outdistance us.

But they could not read our intentions with any greater accuracy than we could read theirs. And thus the result has been that we have both built up our forces to a point that far exceeds a credible second-strike capability against the forces we each started with. . . .

It is futile for each of us to spend $4 billion, $40 billion, or $400 billion— and at the end of all the spending, and at the end of all the deployment, and at the end of all the effort, to be relatively at the same point of balance on the security scale that we are now.[24]

On one hand, then, the structure of the system traps states in adversary relationships. On the other, states cooperate with one another as well. In their competitive pursuits, states form alliances. Even enemies cooperate. McNamara, for example, convinced that the momentum of the arms race had to be slowed, was instrumental in proposing what are now called the strategic-arms limitation talks (SALT). Arms-control negotiations between the United States and the Soviet Union have become almost routine since the early 1960s. Trade negotiations are another symptom of collaboration. Even while a war is going on, there may be cooperation. If nuclear warfare is to be avoided when "limited wars" erupt, it becomes critical for both superpowers to work together to prevent the latter from escalating too far.

(International politics is thus a *mixture of conflict and cooperation*, though cooperation occurs *within the context of adversary relations*. A state wants to attract the strength of allies to enhance its power position in order to compete better; an arms-control agreement with an opponent may reduce the level of armaments, reduce international tensions, and make the world a slightly safer place to live in, but such agreements are signed, after all, by states whose weapons are aimed at each other because they are political rivals. Cooperation, in brief, is a subsidiary part of the conflict game) There are exceptions, as always, in the real world. Britain and the United States can hardly be called potential adversaries any more, though that has not always been true. The Common Market states are unlikely to go to war with one another; not long ago some of them were bitter enemies. Yet even these cooperative relations began in conflict. Early in this century, Britain recognized that Germany's growing power posed a possible threat and made it a deliberate

---

[24] Robert McNamara, Address to United Press International, San Francisco, *The New York Times*, September 19, 1967.

96   policy to improve relations with France, Russia, and the United States, as well as with Japan. Britain remained particularly anxious to maintain the American connection, for the United States was the most powerful country in the world, even though it did not exercise that power in the 1920s and 1930s. During World War II and most of the Cold War, the two nations had what was widely acknowledged as a "special relationship." Similarly, the Continental states that were the original members of the European Economic Community (EEC) decided to move toward what would one day be a powerful United States of Europe within the broader context of American-Soviet rivalry.

(Indeed, the structure of the state system limits cooperation among states in two significant ways.[25] States concerned about their security or wealth cannot let themselves become too dependent on other states, for then they might become vulnerable to threats to reduce or eliminate whatever exchange of goods and services has been occurring.) A Saudi oil embargo or reduction of oil production or the cutoff of exports of American high technology, including computers and oil-drilling equipment, to Russia can mean serious loss. To avoid such loss, a state may have to accept demands made upon it. A preferable strategy is to import from several countries or to export to several foreign markets, rather than to depend on only one, which might unexpectedly be closed to it.

Even when states cooperate on such critical issues as arms control, each worries about the distribution of benefits. Allowing another nation to gain a greater advantage might be potentially damaging. SALT II might thus have been defeated by the U.S. Senate had the President not withdrawn the treaty after the Soviet invasion of Afghanistan, because many senators thought it an unequal treaty advantageous to Russia and jeopardizing, rather than enhancing, American security. Even among Common Market countries, which have grown close during two decades of cooperation, there are setbacks, delays, and bitter disputes over the distribution of benefits. Is French agriculture benefiting more than West German agriculture? Are the Continental states gaining more from Britain's annual contribution to the EEC than Britain receives from the community?

(Each state thus continues to be concerned about its national security and welfare. The state system remains a model of a primitive political system the primary feature of which is anarchy moderated by a modicum of order imposed by the balance of power.[26] The fundamental assumptions are that nation-states place high value on national security in order to protect their "core values"; that states react fearfully to threats to their security and seek to enhance their own power; that states are responsible only to themselves; that self-help is the fundamental rule of the game; and that relations among states are determined by the interactions of their respective power.)

---

[25] Waltz, *Theory of International Politics*, pp. 105–106.

[26] Roger D. Masters, "World Politics as a Primitive Political System," *World Politics*, July 1964, pp. 595–619.

THE STATE SYSTEM

Primary actors	nation-states
	intergovernmental organizations
	universal: United Nations
	regional: Organization of African Unity
	special interest: producer cartel: OPEC, "Group of 77" (representing the third-world countries)
	supranational organization
	regional: Common Market
	nongovernmental or transnational organizations: multinational corporations, terrorist groups, churches
Characteristics	decentralized—composed of mainly sovereign and independent states
	anarchical—absence of commonly accepted political institutions and legitimate rules of the game for allocation of values and enforcement of decisions
	high expectation of violence—coercion and force as the principal allocative mechanism, or substitue for government
	balance of power—principal mechanism that provides systemic stability and individual national restraint
General rules	1. Protect and guard oneself.
	2. Be concerned with systemic power distribution.
	3. Calculate self-interest rationally on the basis of power, not ideology.

BALANCE-OF-POWER TECHNIQUES

Because the balance of power plays such a central role in international politics, we ought to look briefly at the principal techniques used in balancing power.

MOBILIZING POWER

The most obvious method, mobilizing power, usually involves rearmament. Given the key role that force has played historically, this reliance is not surprising. But mobilization comprises two other important components of power. One is the economy. Obviously, a rich economy can afford to support large military forces. But, equally important, it can also afford economic aid and can use its technological and scientific capabilities in industry and agriculture to advance its purposes. Computers and tractors may help technologically lagging nations, especially LDCs, to modernize. The other component is the psychological mobilization of a people, the arousal of popular support for government policy by means of appeals to patriotism and pride in their country.

98   ALLIANCES

(The formation of alliances is one of the time-honored techniques, whether the main purpose is to supplement the state's own power or to draw lines around its sphere of interest.) The only relatively new features of some contemporary key alliances are longevity—NATO is already more than thirty years old—and permanent headquarters. (The latter keeps the alliances functioning on a day-to-day basis and functions to organize the military forces of the various allies into unified forces. Alliances in the past have been shorter and planning for war has consisted mainly of coordinating separate military plans of the member states for such an eventuality.)

COMPENSATION

(Dividing a strategically located country in order to preserve a balance among the major states involves compensation.) Russia and Germany divided Poland in 1939. Russia would not have tolerated German occupation of all of Poland; similarly, Germany opposed Russia's taking all of Poland. So the two powers split this country located strategically between them, maintaining the balance that had existed before partition. At the end of World War II Russia became allied with North Korea, the United States with South Korea. Again, neither big-power bloc would have tolerated a united Korea under the other's control. The possibility of this in 1950 precipitated American intervention to preserve South Korea and later Chinese communist intervention to preserve North Korea.(As one side gains in power, the other seeks "compensation" in order to keep the preexisting balance.)

NEUTRALIZATION

(A technique opposite to compensation is neutralization. Instead of dividing a country in order to preserve the balance of power, no one is granted anything.) Switzerland is surrounded by Germany, Italy, and France. None of its neighbors could accept its addition to one or both of the other states; Switzerland is too strategically important. Therefore the agreement has been to accept Swiss neutrality and to keep "hands off," maintaining the country as a buffer zone between the other three. Similarly, Belgium, surrounded by Britain, France, and Germany, was neutralized in the nineteenth century. When Germany violated that neutrality at the beginning of World War I, the British government—until then divided over whether or not to come to France's aid—declared war on Germany. German conquest of the channel ports facing England had to be prevented. After the Soviet invasion of Afghanistan, the Common Market foreign ministers suggested neutralization as a means of resolving the problem. Soviet troops would be withdrawn and the West would pledge noninterference. Moscow rejected the idea because it knew that the collapse of its puppet regime was inevitable without Soviet troops. Western intervention was not the problem, the unpopularity of the pro-Soviet regime was.

INTERVENTION

(States have long intervened in the affairs of other states when events in the latter were perceived as threatening. Such interventions have been carried out primarily by the military or by intelligence organizations—that is, they have been either overt or covert.) The American record of intervention speaks for itself:

> Military intervention (including limited wars): Korea, 1950–1953;
> Lebanon 1958; Vietnam (including Laos and Cambodia), 1965–1973;
> Dominican Republic, 1965–1966

> CIA interventions (to overthrow or attempt to overthrow
> unfriendly governments): Iran, 1953; Guatemala, 1954; Cuba, 1961;
> Chile, 1970–1973.

(Another category could be included: intervention with military advisers,) as when the United States sent advisers to Greece in the late 1940s and to Vietnam in the early 1960s before the full-fledged military intervention. The Soviets have recently come up with a very visible and effective means of intervention by means of proxy forces—Cuban, in this instance—in Angola, Ethiopia, and reportedly South Yemen. Proxies are useful because, if the Soviet Union intervened directly, the risk of American countervention would arise(proxies may help to avoid this response and make the conflicts look more like struggles for "national liberation.")

DIVIDE AND RULE

(The principle of divide and rule is a time-honored one. There are two versions of it. In the first, the aim is to prevent two powers from forming an alliance. It may be called preemptive divide and rule.)In the months before World War II Winston Churchill, for example, exhorted the British government to form an alliance with Russia in order to contain Hitler and to deter a war. Similarly, many critics of American Cold War policy argued for the early normalization of relations with the People's Republic of China in order to exploit the potential differences between Russia and China. Neither of these proposed policies was pursued by the British and American governments at the time. Post-1945 American policy toward third-world nations was, however, launched to prevent their moving toward the Soviet bloc.

(A much more common version of divide and rule is the attempt to create or exploit differences among the adversary's allies.) The United States has, since 1972, exploited the Sino-Soviet schism. American moves, however, came after the schism already existed; whether or not American policy could have speeded this split earlier through a more receptive attitude toward Mao's China remains a matter of speculation. The United States has also improved its relations with some of Russia's eastern European allies, but it is cautious in this respect, lest the Soviets become so jittery abut their client states' loyalties that they invade them again. In

100   its turn, the Soviet Union tried frequently during the Cold War to play on western
Europe's memories of German aggression, conquests, and brutality to drive a wedge
between West Germany and the other members of NATO, the European Coal
and Steel Community, and EEC.

During World War II Britain and America agreed with Russia not to lay
down their arms until Germany had surrendered unconditionally. This approach
was intended to prevent the Germans from trying to divide and rule. The Western
allies were concerned that the Russians, who had suffered enormously, might be
offered a German withdrawal from Russian soil and might be tempted to accept
it, leaving the two Western states to fight Germany by themselves. They would
then have to land in France and confront the might of the entire German army,
and they might fail to defeat it. The Soviets, on the other hand, were fearful that
their allies might be tempted to accept a separate peace, leaving them to face the
German war machine by themselves. Moscow wanted the allies to draw off part
of the German army.

WAR

The final technique of balancing power is war. When the balance is about to be
upset or has been upset, the threat of war or an actual resort to war may provide
the only way in which a new equilibrium can be created. We have noted that, as
Britain's ability to keep the balance in Europe has weakened, the United States has
been drawn into two world wars to preserve that balance against Germany. Historically, the threat or actual use of violence has been "serious enough to stimulate
preventive measures, but mild enough to enable statesmen to invoke the threat,
and on occasion the actuality, of force in support of policy. War should be im-
aginable, controllable, usable."[27] Whether or not these three requirements can be
attached to warfare among the superpowers and their respective principal allies in
the contemporary world is a question. The emphasis has therefore shifted to deterrence and the threat of force; the *use* of force has largely been in "limited wars."
For nonnuclear countries not allied to any superpower war remains an option.

THE FOUR CHARACTERISTICS OF FIRST-LEVEL ANALYSIS

Analyzing the security–prosperity games that nations play on the level of the state
system will give us certain very specific notions of the behavior of states. First, the
interactions of states revolve around the axle of the balance of power. Systemic
change affects the behavior of all member states. Whenever the system becomes
unbalanced, trouble follows. When Britain weakens and can no longer contain a
Continental power seeking European hegemony, a previously isolationist power,

---

[27.] Claude, *op. cit.*, p. 91.

the United States, must step in to play Britain's role. When Germany, in the center of Europe, is defeated, a conflict erupts between two previous allies, both superpowers on the periphery of Europe. Eliminating a troublesome member does *not*, therefore, guarantee the end of trouble and conflict. Nor can it. (*To alter the structure of the system is to change everyone's behavior*; the new distribution of power merely leads to new alignments. But competition among states continues.)

(A second characteristic of international politics is that *the system imposes a high degree of uniformity of behavior upon states, regardless of their domestic complexion.* The same basic interests and motivations are ascribed to all members. The "necessity of state" overrides such different national attributes as political culture, economic organization, or class structure—or, at least, it is supposed to. The systems analyst will thus examine internal variables only if they seem to have interfered with how a state *ought* to have behaved.)

(In this connection, the systemic model also tends to minimize the importance of ideologies, which are generally considered as justifying whatever states do. States are motivated largely by their security interests and are therefore concerned with preserving or enhancing their power. Ideology is viewed as a function of this interest.[28])For example, despite its antifascist and anticapitalist ideology, communism did not prevent Russia from aligning itself with France in 1935, then with Nazi Germany in 1939, and, in 1941, with the United States and Britain against its previous ally. And after World War II Soviet Russia acted very much as czarist Russia had done, in expanding into eastern Europe and attempting to extend its power into the eastern Mediterranean area. Ideology did not prevent Moscow from behaving in typical balance-of-power terms, guided by *Russian* security interests. Indeed, the wide range of policies seemingly compatible with a specific ideology is generally cited as evidence that ideology is essentially a rationalization of policy, rather than a motivation for it.

This deemphasis on ideology, then, suggests that the analyst of world politics need pay little attention to what policy makers *say* about their policies. Clearly, they will say whatever will make their actions look good. They will talk about freedom, national self-determination, liberating peoples from communist or capitalist slavery, and bringing about a world of peace, law, order, and justice. But such concepts should not be confused with the concrete interests that are the real, underlying reasons for the state's behavior. Indeed, the analyst who assumes that state behavior is the product of an ever-changing distribution of power can, according to Hans Morgenthau,

> retrace and anticipate, as it were, the steps a statesman—past, present, or future—has taken or will take on the political scene. We can look over his shoulder when he writes his dispatches; we listen in on his conversation with other statesmen; we read and anticipate his very thoughts. . . . We think as he does, and as disinterested observers we understand his thoughts and actions *perhaps better than he*, the actor in the political scene, does himself.[29]

[28.] Morgenthau, *op. cit.*, pp. 83–86.

[29.] *Ibid.*, p. 5. Emphasis added.

102 Whether Morgenthau is correct or not, less emphasis on ideologies and statements of intentions does tend to reduce the probability that international politics will be viewed as a moral sphere, a conflict between good and evil, and it refocuses attention on the security dilemma shared by all states living in an anarchical environment in which they see other states as potential enemies and are therefore bound to be concerned with their power vis-à-vis one another.

Third, *the system places limits on the policy choices of states.* Some observers refer to "system-determined" behavior. Although this phrase may understate the degree of a state's "free will" or the actual range of its choices, it is a healthy reminder that, for states, as for individuals, the available options depend on external realities—in this instance, the distribution of power. "The choice with which governments are in fact confronted is not that between opting for the present structure of the world, and opting for some other structure, but between attempting to maintain a balance of power and failing to do so."[30]

Finally, and closely related, *continuity of policy is a characteristic of many nations.* The political complexion of a great power—like Russia—may change, as may its perception of its role in the world and its definition of objectives. But it still lives in a system in which neighbors to the east and west remain the same; so, therefore, does Russia's need to secure eastern Europe. Russia, czarist or communist, has no natural protective barrier, like the English Channel for Britain or mountain ranges for Italy and Spain. The system, in other words, places constraints upon its members and presents them with only a limited number of options or, in some situations, no options at all. The degree of constraint and the foreign-policy alternatives available to a state responding to the external environment, as we shall see, depend in large measure on the particular distribution of power.

Before analyzing the security game in detail we emphasize again that what we are examining is a *model* of the state system that our observations about state behavior are deductive. A model is just that, an ideal representation from which in practice—in "real life"—there will be varying degrees of deviation. Nevertheless, constructing such a model and deducing behavior patterns from it is a useful exercise; the conclusions can, after all, be checked empirically, and many of them will in all likelihood survive such checking. If this method of analysis improves the observer's capacity to understand real life, it justifies itself. Understanding is the key; whether or not the observer approves of the "logic of behavior" that a particular model seems to suggest is another matter. If not, he or she can, of course, propose changes in particular patterns of behavior. It is one thing to say, as we have done, that the state system condemns each state to be continuously concerned with its power relative to that of other states that, in an anarchical system, it regards as potential aggressors; it is quite another to approve such attitudes or the resulting actual conduct of international politics. The utility of the state-system model is that it points to the "essence" of state behavior; it does not pretend to account for all factors, such as moral norms, that motivate states (as, indeed, we shall see later).

---

[30] Hedley Bull, *The Control of the Arms Race* (New York: Holt, Rinehart and Winston, 1961), p. 49.

But as a necessarily simplified version of reality, it does highlight and clarify what most basically concerns and drives states and what kinds of behavior we may see in certain well-defined circumstances, such as bipolar or multipolar balances of power.)

6
Systemic Structure and Stability: From Bipolarity to Tripolarity

STRUCTURE AND STABILITY

Analysis at the state-system level, we have suggested, is focused upon the distribution of power as the key to explaining and understanding the behavior of states. More specifically, we can now add, first-level analysis is based on the assumption that the behavior of states depends upon the *structure* of the system in which it occurs. The structure of the state system is defined by the number of major actors, or *poles*, and the *distribution of power* among them. A pole, in turn, is what is popularly known as a "great power"; the standard of that greatness has in the past usually been military strength. State systems may vary in the number of poles they contain; whatever the number, however, when we speak of a polar system we refer "to the number of centers of military power (whether individual states or coalitions) which are capable of substantially affecting the balance of power in an extensive area of the world, which are independently committed to the support of vital interests distinct from the interests of other centers, and which therefore might go to war independently of other centers."[1]

In first-level analysis it is recognized that there is a relation between the structure of the international system and its *stability*. In this context stability is defined as absence of any nation's predominance, the survival of most member states, and the absence of a major war. This last point needs special stress, for the

---

[1] Robert E. Osgood and Robert W. Tucker, *Force, Order, and Justice* (Baltimore, Md.: Johns Hopkins Press, 1967), p. 170.

concept of balance of power is based on the assumption that war is an instrument that, as a last resort, may have to be invoked to preserve systemic equilibrium or to restore it if it has been upset. War, then is not *per se* destabilizing, especially on a limited scale. Major violence, like a war among superpowers, will certainly be destabilizing. Therefore a stable system may be said to be characterized by minimal violence and the generally peaceful settlement of differences among states, in order to retain the principal features of the system. An unstable system, by contrast, is prone to major violence that may result in the hegemony of one pole; such hegemony may be a threat to the survival of some major actors.[2]

BIPOLARITY

One possible distribution of power is *bipolar*. In this structure, two opposing states or coalitions are involved in preserving the balance of power. More specifically, we can say that a bipolar system is distinguished by the presence of two actors whose power is so far superior to that of other states that they are called "superpowers," several secondary powers, and a host of lesser states. Immediately after World War II such a pattern emerged, with the United States and Russia as superpowers and most of the prewar great powers reduced to secondary powers. In a bipolar structure each superpower regards the other as an adversary; in an anarchical system in which each state is its own protector, the other power is the only one in the system strong enough to threaten its security. Indeed, in this situation each feels such a high degree of insecurity that it may be said to be "driven" or "compelled" to react against the perceived potential threat from the other pole. The balance of power is continuously at stake, for each side fears that it will be upset, that the adversary will achieve hegemony, and that such hegemony will be irreversible—that "the game" will be over.

In a bipolar system, then, *friend and foe are clearly distinguished, and conflict is structurally determined.* Paul Seabury caught the quintessence of this absence of choice when he said that the Cold War was the result of historical circumstances that forced the United States and Russia "into a posture of confrontation neither had actually 'willed,' yet one from which extrication was difficult." To put it another way, *Bipolarity intensifies international conflict because each of the antagonists tends to see any gain of power and security for the other as a loss of power and security for itself and it is determined to prevent this consequence.* Both poles are hypersensitive to the slightest shifts of power. Neither, in the perception of the other, can make an "innocent move"; each will see any move by the other—even if defensively motivated—as a deliberate and hostile attempt to enhance its own position. Counteraction is thus inevitable. Even moves in areas not normally considered of vital interest to the other superpower will be opposed for symbolic and psychological reasons. Each fears a *domino effect*—if one of its allies, friends, protégés, or satellites falls, others will follow—thus upsetting the equilibrium.

---

[2] Joseph L. Nogee, "Polarity: An Ambiguous Concept," *Orbis*, Winter 1975, pp. 1211–1212.

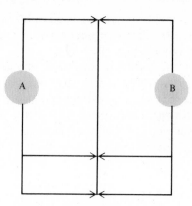

Figure 6.1 BIPOLAR ACTION AND REACTION

It is then not so much the single loss that is feared, for in itself it may not create a large deficit in the balance; it is, rather, a series of such smaller losses over a longer period that must be prevented, for together they could cause a sizable deficit. *When one superpower pushes, the other therefore feels compelled to push back* (see Figure 6.1). Each constantly watches the other and both are "trapped," in a real sense prisoners of the system. Neither can advance or retreat—at least in areas where it has some control. Positions must be held. In a bipolar system, states have few policy options. *Drawing lines, or "frontiers," between their respective spheres of influence and then preserving this territorial status quo becomes the heart of the bipolar struggle. Consequently, bipolar politics is the politics of confrontation.* When one side challenges the "frontier" at some spot, it is testing its adversary's will to maintain its own position. Crises involving serious threats of violence, and even the use of limited violence, with all the inherent possibilities of escalation into total war, thus recur continually. Furthermore, the possibility of a surprise attack by one side to eliminate the other can never be excluded. Because, by definition, the two major actors in a bipolar system cannot be effectively restrained by their far weaker allies or by a powerful third party, bipolarity is very dangerous.

Is a bipolar system which is both *simple* (because there are only two adversaries) and *rigid* (because most of the allies and friends of the two poles are tied to them and do not shift from one side to the other), stable or unstable? The answer seems clear from the basic rule for behavior in a bipolar structure: Oppose any unilateral attempt by the adversary to upset the balance of power. If the opponent pushes, push back. The almost frantic search for allies; the cohesiveness of the principal alliances; attempts to undermine the opposing "camp" while preventing defections from one's own through interventions; the attendant arms race, spurred by the constant fear that the opponent may achieve an irreversible power advantage—so that the "game" would be over—all mean frequent crises, occasional limited wars, and the persistent threat of general war. For these reasons, bipolarity has usually been judged an unstable system.[3]*)*

Let us now turn and clarify the way in which an abstract model like this can help us understand the real world and explain the events that occur—specifically, the early years of the American-Soviet conflict, usually called the Cold War, whose impact still affects us as the superpowers' competition for influence continues in a changing environment.

BIPOLARITY AND THE COLD WAR

THE GLOBAL NATURE OF THE CONFRONTATION

The Cold War was, in a sense, an accident of history.[4] Had the powers of central and western Europe—Germany, France, and England—not all collapsed, the bipolar conflict might never have emerged. Indeed, because the exhaustion of Britain's power was not immediately apparent after Germany's defeat, a prime American fear during the late stages of World War II was of a postwar British–Russian conflict! Washington initially saw itself as a mediator and tried to maintain some distance from London's position in some of its disputes with Moscow, in order to maintain friendly relations with the latter; siding with London, it was judged, would ensure Anglo-American conflict with Russia and make it impossible for the United States to use its restraining influence not only with the British government but with the Soviet government as well. Initial Western opposition to Russian power came from London, not from Washington.

But, as British power collapsed, the two major World War II allies stood face to face. Each perceived the other as the only power left in the entire system that could threaten its own security. Characteristically, then, in order to reestablish the balance of power, the wartime alliance against the common enemy fell apart, and the two victors came to view each other as menacing. Each therefore took the defensive measures necessary to strengthen itself for a potential future conflict, but perceived the adversary's similar measures as offensive. This perception validated its own defensive measures, enhanced concern for security, and ensured that additional steps would be taken to strengthen its own position. The structure of the system, in short, determined for each power whom it saw as an adversary.

[3.] There is considerable disagreement about the dangers and virtues of bipolarity. For the former, see Hans Morgenthau, *Politics Among Nations*, pp. 346–347; and for the latter, see Kenneth N. Waltz, "The Stability of a Bipolar World," *Daedalus*, Summer 1964, pp. 881–909. Our own assessment is given in Chapter 12, on multipolarity. For a suggestive comparative study of the bipolar struggle between Athens and Sparta, see Peter J. Fliess, *Thucydides and the Politics of Bipolarity* (Baton Rouge: Louisiana State University Press, 1966).

[4.] For broad analyses of the beginning of the Cold War and American foreign policy during the Cold War period, see Louis J. Halle, *The Cold War as History* (New York: Harper & Row, 1967), John Spanier, *American Foreign Policy since World War II*, 8th ed. (New York: Holt, Rinehart and Winston, 1980), and Seyom Brown, *The Faces of Power* (New York: Columbia University Press, 1968).

108   Russia, as noted earlier (pp. 14–16), first consolidated its position throughout eastern Europe and the eastern half of Germany. It then attempted to expand beyond this sphere along its southern perimeter, in Iran, Turkey, and Greece, but it met with resistance from Britain and increasingly from the United States. The Truman Doctrine, declared in early 1947, was the first American acknowledgment that the world had become bipolar and that the United States would exercise the responsibility of establishing and preserving balance in the system.[5] As it had done twice before when Germany threatened to attain superiority over Europe, Washington then undertook to strengthen its position in western Europe. Whereas on previous occasions, the United States had abstained during the early years of the European wars, only to be drawn in as Germany appeared about to attain hegemony by defeating France and England, this time it sought to avoid World War III by early involvement. It decided to rebuild exhausted western Europe and to make clear to Russia that the United States was committed to defense of that region.[6] Unlike Germany, then, Russia would not be tempted to miscalculate and go to war believing it could dominate western Europe without risking war with the United States. The first major measure was the Marshall Plan, a massive program of economic aid designed to restore Europe's economic viability and political vitality. The Marshall Plan was followed shortly afterward by the Berlin airlift and in 1949 by the North Atlantic Treaty Organization (NATO). These acts demonstrated that the United States considered western Europe an area of vital interest and was committed to its protection. The United States could no more have acquiesced in the Soviet domination of western Europe than Russia could have tolerated American domination of eastern Europe, especially the Polish corridor, through which the armies of Napoleon, Kaiser Wilhelm, and Hitler had all marched to invade and defeat or almost defeat Russia.

The United States thus transformed a situation of weakness in Europe into one of strength. It had drawn a "frontier" between the American and Russian spheres of influence and had demonstrated that it was in Europe to stay. By 1949 Europe no longer provided opportunities for the expansion of Soviet influence. To cross the demarcation line drawn by the United States was to risk total war, and this risk was one the Soviet Union was unwilling to assume. Asia was a more profitable area for political and military exploitation. Most countries there had only recently emerged from Western colonialism, and their nationalistic and anti-Western feelings were strong. In late 1949 Nationalist China collapsed, and a communist government was established on the mainland. It had been beyond the capacity of the United States to prevent this development, largely because Chiang Kai-Shek's regime had been corrupt, reactionary, and inefficient.[7] Aid to Europe had offered a good possibility of restoring the economic health and strength of Britain and the

---

[5] Joseph M. Jones, *The Fifteen Weeks* (New York: Viking, 1955); and Harry S. Truman, *Memoirs, II: Years of Trial and Hope* (Garden City: Doubleday, 1956), pp. 104-109.

[6] Theodore White, *Fire in the Ashes* (New York: William Sloane Associates, 1953).

[7] Tang Tsou, *America's Failure in China, 1941–50* (Chicago: University of Chicago Press, 1963).

Continental nations. On the other hand, the Truman administration believed that no reasonable amount of aid could restore a government that had lost the confidence of most of its own people. Chiang's fall, however, weakened the Western position in Asia, shifted the balance, and created a vacuum that attracted Russian attention.

In June 1950 the North Korean communists marched across the thirty-eighth parallel, which divided North Korea from South Korea, to attack the latter. At the end of World War II the Russians had occupied the northern half of Korea, in order to disarm the Japanese; they had stayed long enough to place a communist regime in power. The attack, which could not have been launched without Soviet knowledge, encouragement, and support, was seen by Washington as a move that had to be opposed; to permit it to go unchallenged would have endangered the entire policy of containment, or balance of power. The Korean conflict was the first American "limited war," a painful and frustrating three-year experience in defense of part of the "frontier" drawn around the periphery of the new and still cohesive Sino-Soviet bloc.[8] But South Korea was defended and the thirty-eighth parallel, like the frontier lines along Iran, Turkey, and Greece in the eastern Mediterranean and through Germany in central Europe, continued to mark the respective Western and communist spheres. The next frontier to be drawn, in Indochina, did not.

After Japan's surrender the French tried to reimpose colonial control on Indochina, only to find that, in an age of decolonization, such an attempt was doomed. Worse, all nationalists were driven into the arms of the communist-led Vietminh movement. A bitter guerrilla war lasted from 1946 to 1954. Although the United States was initially unsympathetic to France because of its refusal to grant Indochina independence, North Korea's aggression and China's intervention in that war caused this country to send large-scale military and economic aid to the French. American policy makers had come to view all communist states as part of a single cohesive bloc, led by Moscow and pursuing expansionist goals. When the French suffered defeat in Vietnam in 1954, the United States briefly considered intervention but finally decided against it. A negotiated peace at Geneva in 1954 resulted in the division of Vietnam at the seventeenth parallel. Another line, like the thirty-eighth parallel in Korea and the one drawn through the middle of Germany along the Elbe River, divided still another country.[9] Subsequent establishment of the Southeast Asia Treaty Organization (SEATO) was to ensure that the seventeenth parallel would become part of the extensive frontier dividing the communist from the noncommunist world. Russia and China, which had participated in the Geneva negotiations, presumably accepted the division of Vietnam. Twice in the late 1950's Moscow sponsored—unsuccessfully—the applications of both Vietnams to the United Nations.

Between 1946 and 1954 the challenges and responses centering on Iran, Greece, Turkey, Berlin and western Europe, Korea, and Indochina had resulted

---

[8] John W. Spanier, *The Truman-MacArthur Controversy and the Korean War*, rev. ed. (New York: Norton, 1965).

[9] Melvin Gurtov, *The First Vietnam Crisis* (New York: Columbia University Press, 1967).

110   in "hands off" or "cross at your own risk" signs all around the Eurasian continent. Transgressions of such lines might have ignited the highly combustible postwar bipolar system. Lines were also drawn off the Chinese coast, as the United States formalized its commitment to defend the Nationalist Chinese on Taiwan after two crises over the islands of Quemoy and Matsu in 1954–1955 and 1958. And, in the unprotected area between the nations of the North Atlantic Treaty Organization (NATO) and Southeast Asia, the United States sponsored a British-led alliance of Turkey, Iraq, Iran, and Pakistan, known initially as the Middle East Treaty Organization (METO) and, after Iraq pulled out in 1958, as the Central Treaty Organization (CENTO). This "northern tier," most of which ran along Russia's southern frontier, was organized by Britain, which still retained great influence in the Middle East. Washington also hoped to attract the leading Arab states, especially Egypt, a rival of Iraq. As this hope dimmed, the United States drew closer to CENTO. The only area of the world basically left outside this bipolar competition was sub-Sahara Africa, where the two superpowers clashed only briefly when Belgium granted independence to the Congo (now Zaire) in the early 1960s. (Bipolarity had, as the model predicts, led to an extensive, virtually global confrontation. A gain for one side was seen as a loss for oneself, one which had to be prevented if the balance were to be kept.)

ALLIANCES: FORMATION AND ROLES

Given the pattern of bipolar challenge and response, it is not surprising that the superpowers would search for allies. The United States in particular was often accused of suffering from "pactomania." There were many states around the Sino-Soviet periphery, and the United States signed up forty-three of them! The Soviet Union, itself spanning Europe and Asia, signed up only the states of eastern Europe and China. But it had no need to formalize its alliances because the primary relations among communist states were at the party rather than the state level. Although the Warsaw Treaty Organization (WTO) was not formalized until after West Germany joined NATO in 1955, there was no doubt of the close relations between Russia and its satellites—as they were then—or that the West risked war if it intruded into this clearly demarcated Soviet sphere.

      By 1954, the United States thus had four multilateral alliances (each composed of more than two states) and four bilateral alliances: the 1947 Rio Treaty with twenty-one Latin-American states; the NATO treaty (fifteen states), signed in 1949; the Anzus Treaty (three states), signed in 1951; the SEATO pact (eight states), signed in 1954 after the first Indochina war ended with the partition of Vietnam; the Philippine Treaty of the same year; the Japanese Treaty, signed in 1951; the pact with the Republic of Korea (or South Korea), signed in 1953 right after the Korean war was concluded; and the pact with the Republic of China (or Nationalist China), also signed in 1954 (see Figure 6.2).

      The Soviet Union set up the WTO, of seven nations, in 1955, and in the previous year signed the Sino-Soviet Treaty with China. (The Soviet Union has in recent years signed a number of treaties of friendship with Angola [1976],

Ethiopia [1978], Vietnam [1978], and Afghanistan [1978]. Although Moscow has emphasized that these treaties have only a consultatory function, by implication they involve defense commitments; one aim is certainly to deter the United States from any action against these nations and, if Afghanistan is an example, another is to grant the Soviet Union the right to intervene militarily.)

The numbers of these American- and Soviet-led alliances, however, are less important than their nature and roles.(The nature of bipolar alliances follows from the enormous disparity in power between the superpowers and their allies. The superpower is the *producer of security*; its partners are the *consumers* of that security. The latter cannot enhance their protector's security by significantly adding to its power; it supplies the bulk of the alliances's strength.) In NATO and the Warsaw Treaty Organization, the superpowers provide the strategic nuclear capability to keep the deterrent balance; they also furnish the conventional military backbones of both organizations. But the critical ingredient is the strategic nuclear protection that each extends to its allies. *A bipolar alliance, given the unequal internal power distribution, is in effect a unilateral guarantee extended by the superpower to its allies, which are really its protectorates.* The pledge of the allies to come to the superpower's assistance in the event of attack, a normal obligation for all coalition members when signing a treaty of alliance, is consequently a ritual. By contrast, the purpose of alliances in multipolar systems composed of at least five or six major actors is to *add the power of other states to one's own*. In these alliances, the mutual obligations of defense do matter. Indeed, as such an alliance cannot afford the defection of any great-power member without being seriously weakened in relation to the adversary alliance, constant attention must be paid to holding the coalition together. In a bipolar alliance, by contrast, one nation's defection normally would not seriously reduce the coalition's collective power.)

The principal function of a bipolar alliance in these circumstances is deterrence, to "draw lines" "or "frontiers" that leave no doubt about the areas that are considered vital and are to be left alone if war is to be avoided. The alliance thus clarifies the superpower's interests, as dictated by the systemic structure. Just as bipolarity determines who the rivals will be, it also greatly influences which states lying between them will align themselves with one or the other. In a highly sensitive bipolar structure in which each of the principal competitors is constantly fearful that the balance will be upset and, worse, that the resulting imbalance against it may be irreversible, it will at the very least seek to enhance its defense by extending its control over neighboring states in what one historian, noting Russia's establishment of the eastern European satellites after the war, has called "defensive expansionism.")After all, if Russia did not do so, would not a potential adversary try to extend its power to Russia's frontiers? But, given the nature of the state system, once one of the superpowers has expanded into contiguous areas, its rival views the move as offensive, and a countermove is inevitable.(The result is that each pole stakes its territorial claims, especially in the areas lying between the two, and warns the other pole not to intrude in those areas, at the risk of war. *A bipolar coalition does not, therefore, create new interests; it registers the interest of*

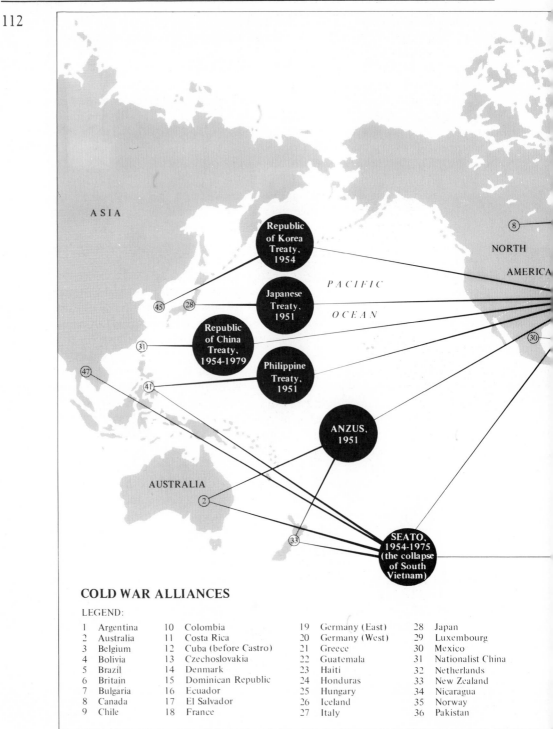

COLD WAR ALLIANCES

LEGEND:

1	Argentina	10	Colombia	19	Germany (East)	28	Japan
2	Australia	11	Costa Rica	20	Germany (West)	29	Luxembourg
3	Belgium	12	Cuba (before Castro)	21	Greece	30	Mexico
4	Bolivia	13	Czechoslovakia	22	Guatemala	31	Nationalist China
5	Brazil	14	Denmark	23	Haiti	32	Netherlands
6	Britain	15	Dominican Republic	24	Honduras	33	New Zealand
7	Bulgaria	16	Ecuador	25	Hungary	34	Nicaragua
8	Canada	17	El Salvador	26	Iceland	35	Norway
9	Chile	18	France	27	Italy	36	Pakistan

Figure 6.2

37	Panama	46	Soviet Union
38	Paraguay	47	Thailand
39	People's Republic of China	48	Turkey
40	Peru	49	United States
41	Philippines	50	Uruguay
42	Poland	51	Venezuela
43	Portugal		
44	Rumania		
45	South Korea		

U.S. Treaties

Soviet Treaties

114   *each superpower in the areas beyond those it already controls and seeks to dissuade the adversary from attempting to expand into them.*[10])

The United States and the Soviet Union, as already seen, both stood at the center of Europe at the end of World War II. The American army and the Russian army, by driving the German forces backward, had in fact already drawn the lines between the American and Russian spheres when the postwar bipolar conflict emerged. Shortly after the European war ended, a perceptive observer noted that "most of the lesser nations are being drawn by a sort of Law of Political Gravity into the orbit of one or the other Super-Power. So far neither Russia nor the United States has yet completed its protective belt of satellites. Some areas are being tugged both ways, like small planets caught between two stars."[11]

The resulting division of Europe, symbolized by the initials NATO and WTO, was thus a foregone conclusion. If bipolar alliances are in reality unilateral guarantees in the form of the superpowers' extension of deterrence to those areas that they wish to protect against hostile attack, another characteristic of such alliances is their *cohesiveness.* Britain provides a good illustration of the "tightness" of bipolarity. The Labour Party, which had been elected at the close of the war, came into power with certain ideological preconceptions. As a convinced democratic socialist party, it opposed capitalist foreign policy and was committed to international working-class solidarity and the repudiation of allegedly immoral "power politics," with its ultimate reliance upon armaments. Yet it was Britain that condemned Soviet actions in eastern Europe and initially helped Greece and Turkey. The Labour party leadership had adopted the historic British policy of opposing any nation seeking European hegemony. Furthermore, aware of Britain's weakness, the leadership tried from the beginning to enlist American support. Labour acted as any procapitalist Conservative government would have done, aligning socialist Britain with a capitalist nation that, by definition, should have been the enemy, against a socialist power that, by definition, should have been a peaceful and nonexpansionist state. The realities of the state system had rendered such slogans as "Left understands Left" and "no enemies to the left" obsolete and had underlined the continuity of foreign policy, despite ideological differences among policy makers. Labour leaders recognized the environmental restraints on postwar Britain and had made the necessary adjustments to them. This behavior testifies to the "socialization" of a nation's leadership, which may not perceive the external reality correctly but soon finds that it must adjust to environmental demands and pressures.[12] Bipolarity thus produced a close alignment of the United States with Britain,

---

[10] Glenn H. Snyder, "Conflict and Crisis in the International System," in James N. Rosenau, Kenneth W. Thompson, and Gavin Boyd, eds., *World Politics* (New York: Free Press, 1976), pp. 687–694, and Snyder and Paul Diesing, *Conflict among Nations* (Princeton: Princeton University Press, 1977), pp. 429–440.

[11] John Fischer, *Harper's*, August 1945, quoted by Norman A. Graebner, *Cold War Diplomacy* (2d ed.; New York: Van Nostrand, 1977), p. 23.

[12] Michael R. Gordon, *Conflict and Consensus in Labour's Foreign Policy* (Stanford: Stanford University Press, 1969), pp. 1–44, 102. Also see Leon D. Epstein, *Britain—Uneasy Alliance* (Chicago: University of Chicago Press, 1954).

as well as the other former great powers: France and Germany in Europe and Japan in Asia.

(The threat to the security of each bipolar alliance is considered so basic by all of its members that they subordinate their diverse interests to the common fear of the enemy. Differences within the coalition are essentially over the *means* of meeting their common danger.) Should West Germany be rearmed? Should the alliance negotiate Moscow's demands that it leave West Berlin? How can the allies stand firm without risking war? How accommodating can they be without undermining their interests? What issues should they emphasize in mutual negotiations with the Russians? Where, if challenged, should they stand firm? A tribute to the cohesion of NATO is its extraordinary longevity as a free association. (In the Warsaw Treaty Organization, or WTO, a Soviet-imposed alliance that because of Communist party ties, would exist *de facto* even if no interstate treaty had been signed, differences of views are only rarely aired.) Despite some subsequent loosening of its bonds, NATO, originally signed for a twenty-year term, is already more than thirty years old. Given the geographical fact that Europe, eastern and western, fills the space between the two superpowers, and given the likelihood that their rivalry will continue—moderated mainly by a common desire to avoid nuclear warfare and mutual suicide—there is no reason not to expect the continued existence of NATO, as well as of WTO.

(One final point about alliances in a bipolar system is that the superpowers tend to perceive their commitments as linked.[13] In a structure in which each pole sees a gain of power for the adversary as a loss of power for itself, any attempt at incursion by either pole anywhere will be resisted. Objectively, not all countries protected by either superpower are equally important; some presumably will warrant a greater risk of war in their defense than will others. But subjectively any single loss, even if not significant in itself, is like the fall of the first domino, expected to lead to the collapse of a series of others, and an eventual power deficit.) Why should the loss of one domino lead to a loss of others? (Because the failure to honor a commitment in one area may be seen by both the adversary and allies as an indication that other commitments also may not be honored. In a bipolar structure each pole thus tends to emphasize the *interdependence of commitments.*)

For example, the United States fought in Korea in 1950 to preserve the credibility of the NATO commitments that it had accepted in Europe, as well as to prove its fidelity as a friend to Japan, which was about to be signed up as the linchpin of American policy in Asia. American policy makers calculated that a refusal to help South Korea could only whet Russia's appetite and tempt it to devour other areas. Failure to meet the Soviet challenge was seen as likely to affect not only Soviet behavior but also that of NATO. The United States' European allies might conclude that they, too, would be abandoned in a similar crisis. The Europeans might dismiss as valueless Washington's treaty pledge to protect them, and

---

[13] Thomas C. Schelling, *Arms and Influence* (New Haven, Conn.; Yale University Press, 1966), and Alexander L. George and Richard Smoke, *Deterrence in American Foreign Policy* (New York: Columbia University Press, 1974), pp. 552–553.

116 turn to neutralism. They would then be subject to increasing pressure and eventual domination by the Soviets. As mainland China had just fallen to the communists, the United States wished to rearm Japan and to create a new situation of strength in the Pacific, but the precondition for transforming Japan into an American ally was the protection of Japanese security. A noncommunist South Korea was critical to that security. All frontiers were thus thought to be interrelated.

DEFECTIONS AND INTERVENTIONS

Another index of each superpower's sensitivity to changes in the bipolar balance was its sensitivity to any actual or attempted defection from its respective bloc or sphere of influence. Each bloc was to be guarded from within as a fortress would be guarded; bloc loyalty had to be ensured. Changes in alignments were not to be allowed. Simultaneously, each superpower suspected the other of intending to undermine its own sphere.[14] For example, over a period of twenty years in Latin America the United States helped (by means of the Central Intelligence Agency) to overthrow what it deemed to be a procommunist Guatemalan government, which had received weapons from the East; sought unsucessfully to topple Fidel Castro's regime after the Cuban leader had tied his island politically and economically to the Soviet Union; sent troops to prevent the victory of alleged pro-Castro, procommunist elements in the Dominican Republic; in the early 1970s, financed opposition to the Marxist government of Salvador Allende in Chile and thus helped to topple it. It frequently "interfered" in European and other elections to the extent of making it clear which party it favored (sometimes going beyond public declarations to secret financial assistance of parties and politicians) and which it opposed (particularly the communist parties and any possibility that they might be included in coalition governments in Italy and France). The United States defended South Korea when North Korea crossed the dividing line between them; favored and supported South Vietnam's refusal to participate in the nationwide election stipulated in the 1954 Geneva agreements because it seemed likely that the election would be won by Ho Chi Minh's North Vietnamese regime, rather than the American-supported Ngo Din Diem regime in the South; and intervened militarily when it appeared that South Vietnam might collapse completely in 1965.

On the other side, the Soviets seized power in Czechoslovakia in 1948 to "fill out" their eastern zone; suppressed the East German revolt in 1953; threatened to crush the Polish uprising and did crush both the Hungarian revolution in 1956, as well as the Czech experiment in "communism with a human face"in 1968—a loosening of some of the restrictions and orthodoxies of communism. Similarly, they have refused to allow the East Germans to express their views on the issue of reunification with West Germany through free elections and have ignored the obligation set forth in the postwar Yalta agreement with the Western allies to permit free elections in Eastern Europe, in which all parties (except those that collaborated

---

[14.] Thomas M. Franck and Edward Wiesband, *World Politics* (New York: Oxford University Press, 1972).

with Nazi Germany) would participate. Finally, when American forces crossed the thirty-eighth parallel and advanced into North Korea during the Korean war, China intervened—both to guard its security and to preserve a communist regime; similarly, the North Vietnamese increasingly intervened in support of the Vietcong, the arm of the North Vietnamese Communist party in South Vietnam, after the American military intervention in 1965.

Each superpower had staked out or strengthened its claim to its own sphere of influence. (Historically, such spheres encompass areas lying near the great powers and defined by them as vital to their interests. Whether or not such spheres will remain as important in a changing world is debatable.) Russia has long defined eastern Europe, an area through which invading armies have marched on the way to Russian soil, as essential to its security. After 1945 Moscow imposed total control on the area. But the enemy this time was not, as in the past, another European land power; rather it was a transoceanic power capable of an intercontinental air attack. Domination of eastern Europe is hardly relevant strategically to this completely new circumstance for Russia. Even though Russian power grew enormously in the three decades after the Cold War erupted, the government never wavered in its anxiety over the area contiguous to its western frontier. Somewhat similarly, the United States has for over a century defined Latin America as a sphere of American influence; actually this definition has been applied primarily to the Caribbean-Central American area. Concern about the area continued after 1945, was embodied in the Rio Treaty, and was not reassessed until the 1970s, when more and more Latin American countries, feeling strongly nationalistic, asserted themselves vigorously against the United States (more strongly than the states of eastern Europe did against Russia, which was less willing to tolerate a considerable reduction of its control). American adjustment to this development is symbolized by the Panama canal treaties which will turn the canal over completely to the Panamanians by the end of the century.

The reason for concern by Russia and the United States, beside historic interests, is easy to understand. (Bipolarity encouraged each great power to suspect its opponent when trouble broke out within its own sphere (even when, in fact, this was not justified). As each believed in the domino effect, it had to prevent such a result by defending its entire sphere. It therefore intervened whenever it suspected that a particular country, in league with the adversary, might defect. It tried to prevent such loss, which would presumably stimulate the adversary to intrude elsewhere and would be reflected in the overall distribution of power. In any event, permitting the other superpower to establish bases in one's own sphere could not be allowed.) That is why the United States did not attempt to exploit Russia's troubles in eastern Europe in 1953, 1956, and 1968. It is also why Washington, havng failed in 1961 to remove Castro and having reluctantly learned to live with the new Cuba, vehemently opposed Moscow's attempt to place offensive missles on the island and precipitated the most dangerous crisis of the Cold War in order to compel their withdrawal. Cuba was not to become a strategic Soviet base. During the early 1970s, the United States srongly and successfully opposed the building of a Soviet nuclear-submarine base in Cuba through quiet diplomacy.

118   In the late 1970s it opposed the presence of a Soviet combat brigade on the island. Although President Carter was willing to accept the Soviet explanation that these forces had been in Cuba since the early 1960s and that their function was to train Cuban forces, the Senate's lesser willingness to believe this explanation was a factor in its opposition to the second strategic-arms limitation treaty (SALT II). In any event, to tamper with the other superpower's sphere of influence is dangerous, a threat to peace and to the establishment of more amicable American-Soviet relations.

THE ARMS RACE

The bipolar balance was perhaps most clearly symbolized by the "arms race," but the focus on the military balance was more than symbolic, for military power was the central ingredient. In a bipolar system, as we have seen, each superpower has its allies. They do not, however, shift from one alliance to the counteralliance, but even if one or two were to do so, it would not matter much. The difference in power between the superpower and one of its allies is so enormous that even if the ally shifted to the adversary superpower, it would not significantly affect the power balance (China was a major exception, at least in the long run). The counterbalancing mechanisms that exist in multipolar systems, especially the shifting of allies and the acquisition of new territories, are thus ruled out; adding strength through alliance building is one of the remaining techniques, but the relatively small amounts of power that allies can contribute reduce the importance of alliances for balancing purposes. *The bipolar balance is thus more dependent on military power for its preservation than is a multipolar balance.* The reason is that the attempt of one side to achieve a superiority of power and efforts by the other to maintain the equilibrium are in these circumstances most likely to be achieved through mobilizing each superpower's vast domestic resources—that is, by converting its "plowshares" into "swords." In addition, given the precariousness of the bipolar balance, resulting from the fear that a major addition of power to one side might be irreversible and give that side the superiority it needs to become the dominant power, each superpower is bound to be hypersensitive to possible changes in the military equilibrium.

(Indeed, the development of nuclear technology increased this hypersensitivity because it fundamentally changed the manner in which military strength could be used.) Historically, force has been used either to deter wars or, once wars have erupted, to win them. In prenuclear times, when no weapons were so destructive that their employment threatened their *users* with extinction, the critical test of military policy was not the prevention of hostilities but the ability to attain victory once they had broken out. The gains to be won seemed to outweigh the costs of fighting. War was therefore considered a rational instrument of national policy. (Nuclear arms, however, threatened the very substance of life that military force was supposed to protect. Total war thus became suicidal and irrational.[15])

[15.] Bernard Brodie, *Strategy in the Missile Age* (Princeton: Princeton University Press, 1959), remains the finest introductory analysis of the changing nature of warfare in the twentieth century.

(The result was paradoxical. On one hand, the chief threat to the state system has always been the possibility of dominance by one power or bloc; to prevent such dominance, war has been the principal and ultimate instrument. On the other hand, war—total war—had come to threaten the very existence of the state system; the "instrument of last resort" to ensure the security of all members now threatened them, if used, with extinction. The principal remaining utility of all-out warfare as an instrument of policy lay in the threat of its use precisely in order to assure its *nonuse* —in short, deterrence. Deterrence, in turn, required that the enemy must at all times be convinced that the costs of a first strike would be its own virtually total destruction. Only in this way could deterrence be made permanent and that one mistake too many avoided.)

Each of the two superpowers must therefore constantly concern itself with maintaining its offensive superiority, for its adversary must never doubt that it could be destroyed in a retaliatory blow should it be tempted to strike. In his circumstance, however, each power tends to be consumed by the constant fear that a technological breakthrough may grant its opponent a temporary advantage that could result in a first strike to end the conflict on the enemy's terms. Both superpowers are highly industrialized nations with sophisticated technological knowledge, so the possibility of an offensive breakthrough that would give one side the capacity to destroy the other's retaliatory capability is seen as a very real threat by each protagonist. And rightly so. For the marriage of such knowledge to intense mutual fear leads to a fantastically large investment of resources and skills in the development of ever-newer arms, in order that the offense be kept ahead of the defense and, on the other hand, that the defense catch up with the offense. The perennial arms race thus becomes a *series* of arms races, as technology constantly produces new weapons.

> As the United States and the Soviet Union throw one weapons system after another into the effort to maintain at least a balance of terror, neither dares fall behind in either the discovery of new physical relationships or in the application of scientific knowledge to military hardware and political-military strategy. Thus, by the end of the first decade of the Cold War, about 50 percent of the engineers in the United States and 25 per cent of the scientists were employed by the federal government, either directly or on contract, and about 65 per cent of the scientific research in universities and 57 per cent of that in private industry were government-financed.[16]

The result has been an intensive effort to design delivery systems with high performance characteristics. Because of the rapidity of technological change in delivery systems, this effort has required constant attention. The bomber, which came into its own during World War II, was already on the way out less than two decades after the end of the war. No sooner had one bomber been designed, produced, and placed in service and crews trained, than the bomber became obsolescent. The Flying Fortress, the workhorse of the U.S. Army Air Corps, had been in use before the nation entered World War II, and it was still being flown

---

[16] Warner R. Schilling, "Scientists, Foreign Policy, and Politics," *The American Political Science Review*, June 1962, p. 288.

120   at the end of the war in Europe. Only in the last stage of the air war against Japan was it replaced by the Superfortress. In the nuclear age, it was soon outmoded, as the intercontinental bomber was developed. The B-36, with its six-piston motors, four jet engines, and a range of 10,000 miles, filled this need, but its slow top speed of just over 400 miles per hour (mph) soon made it vulnerable to fighter attack, and it had to be replaced by the B-47, a pure jet bomber with a speed of more than 600 mph. But, because the B-47 was a medium-range bomber, it could operate from the United States only if it was refueled in the air, so it flew mostly from overseas bases in Europe, North Africa, the Middle East, and the Far East. Overseas bases were within range of the Soviet Union's sizable force of medium-range bombers; continental American bases were still beyond the range of Soviet bombers in the early and middle 1950s. Consequently, still another intercontinental bomber was necessary. The United States therefore developed the B-52, whose eight jet engines gave it a speed of more than 650 mph and a range exceeding 6,000 miles. This bomber subsequently became the backbone of the Strategic Air Command (SAC). The B-47 was retired after about a decade; the B-52 survived in dwindling numbers into the 1980s.

By the late 1960s, however, the backbone of deterrence was the intercontinental ballistic missile flying at 18,000 mph. It, too, went through several technological changes during the next decade: from land-based intercontinental ballistic missile (ICBM) to submarine-launched ballistic missile (SLBM); from liquid fuel to solid fuel and instant firing; from a single warhead to multiple warhead; from reasonable accuracy to pinpoint accuracy. Each new weapon, of course, cost more than its predecessor, with the result that financing the arms race became increasingly burdensome for both superpowers. Yet, in the bipolar system, the superpowers felt they had little, if any, choice if they were to preserve the balance of power. Furthermore, they were not really races in the sense that each built all the weapons it could; Russia did not build a large intercontinental-bomber force, and the United States did not add a new missile after it completed its quantitative buildup in the mid-1960s. The race took on a more *qualitative* nature, reflecting the continuing technological advances in weapons systems, advances that both strengthened and simultaneously threatened to undermine the deterrent balance.

THE ROLE OF NEW NATIONS

Postwar bipolarity was also evident in the increasingly important role of the new, ex-colonial, non-Western nations. These nations could not escape the Cold War, once the focus of American-Soviet conflict had shifted from Europe to the underdeveloped world. The superpowers, reluctant to engage in direct conflict, channeled their rivalry into "safer" competition for the loyalty and support of these new nations. The third world, between the American-led first world and Soviet-led second world, thus acted as a kind of safety valve. Not only was the superpowers' confrontation diverted from Europe, the area where their respective vital interests were greatest and the possibility of hostilities were thus equally great, but also among the principal instruments of this new competition outside of Europe were economic aid and technical assistance.

(It was the systemic distribution of power that made nonalignment not only feasible but also attractive for states that wished to maintain their freedom of choice in foreign policy. In a bipolar structure, they become major stakes for the superpowers. The desire of the less developed countries (LDCs) to modernize themselves, whether they chose to do so by dictatorial or by democratic means, would profoundly affect whether communism would find new adherents or whether the world would become safer for democracy. Their choice of one or the other was considered critical.) For example, the author of an influential American study on the future of the LDCs said.

> Whether most of these countries take a democratic or a Communist or other totalitarian path in their development is likely to determine the course of civilization on our planet.
> Should that large majority of the human race which lives in underdeveloped countries turn to totalitarian ways for meeting its problems, the blow to the prestige of free institutions could not fail to affect the outlook for freedom in the United States itself. Americans have long believed, and with more reason today than ever, that our own institutions are in danger in a world where freedom does not flourish.
> . . . The Communists offer a competing system which borrows the industrial technology of the West but repudiates Western political freedom and the dignity of the individual. Communism now directs its main drive toward the underdeveloped countries. The choice of these countries between taking the Communist path or modernizing with Western aid and friendship will probably determine whether the totalitarian or the democratic way of life eventually acquires throughout the world a preponderance of economic, psychological, and military power. In other words, it will probably determine our own security and the course of world civilization.[17]

The Soviets, in their turn, talked of a vast "peace zone" to encompass the majority of the world's population and to include the socialist states (the Soviets use the term "socialism," rather than "communism") plus the "nonsocialist" but "peace-loving" underdeveloped states. These states had achieved political independence but, though they were not members of the socialist world, they did not belong to the aggressive imperialist bloc either; indeed, they were highly nationalistic and anti-imperialist or anti-Western. Economic aid to the new states, which still had to break their economic links with the West, would strengthen their independence, attract them to the socialist bloc, and fatally weaken the Western capitalist economies. The Soviet political offensive in the West's European front yard had been stalemated by the Marshall Plan, NATO, and the Berlin airlift; the Russians then switched direction and initiated an attack on the West through its back yard—the former colonies. By the middle 1950s, the Soviets had recognized the importance of the third world, which had risen out of the crumbling Western empires and had separated itself from the capitalist bloc but had not yet joined the socialist camp.

[17.] Eugene Staley, *The Future of Underdeveloped Countries* (rev. ed., New York: Holt, Rinehart and Winston, 1961), pp. 3, 15, 37.

122   The stakes were high: Both superpowers, having drawn clear lines between their respective spheres in Europe and protected them with their deterrent capability, extended their competition to this third world between them. To enhance their individual strengths, each sought as its maximum objective the territory, population, and resources of the new nations, or at least, the potentially stronger and politically more important of them. The minimum aim was to prevent these states from joining the adversary's bloc.

For the new states, all of which were militarily weak and economically and politically underdeveloped, nonalignment made tactical sense in the context of this postwar distribution of power. An "in-between," or third-world, posture presumably allowed them to maximize their bargaining influence, which was significant in at least two respects. First, the new nations needed economic aid and technical assistance. Second, nations that had long been controlled by the West could reduce their political and economic dependence by means of such aid. When a nation moved away from the West, the communist states would offer it aid. Conversely, when it became too dependent on the communists or when it resisted them, an American loan would most likely be forthcoming. The middle position in the Cold War was therefore politically and economically very useful, permitting maximum economic assistance and minimum dependence on the principal donors.

> The possibility of "blackmail" is built into the very structure of Cold War competition. But from the point of view of the excessively dependent, relatively impotent new state, this is not blackmail. It is the equally ancient but more honorable art of maintaining political equilibrium through the diversification of dependence, the balancing of weakness—in short, the creation of an "alternative" lest the influence of one side or the other become too imposing.[18]

Bipolarity was thus conducive to a policy of nonalignment and enhanced the bargaining capacity of the new states.

MULTIPOLARITY

A *multipolar* system is, according to most theorists, composed of at least five approximately equal great powers.[19] Such a system, it is usually claimed, is characterized by more restrained national behavior and is generally more conducive to preserving the peace. The reason is that, compared to the *simple* and *rigid* bipolar division, multipolarity is *complex* and *flexible*. When the division is simple and the major actors aligned on one side or the other, friend and foe are easy to discover; this division is rigid because no realignment is possible. But *a multipolar structure does not by itself distinguish between friends and foes*; each pole views all other major actors as potential adversaries—and potential allies. *Among a larger number*

[18.] Robert C. Good, "State-building as a Determinant of Foreign Policy in the New States," in Laurence W. Martin, ed., *Neutralism and Nonalignment* ((New York: Holt, Rinehart and Winston, 1962), p. 11.

[19.] Morton Kaplan, *System and Process in International Politics* ((New York: Wiley, 1957).

of great powers, each state has the mobility to align and realign itself. Alliances are created as specific conflicts arise, and they usually last for only short periods, as the equilibrium shifts and alignments change. In contrast to bipolarity's confrontations and crises, in which antagonisms are constantly reinforced, *the greater opportunity for shifting combinations under multipolarity reduces the risk of mutually reinforcing hostilities between various "players."* Allies of today may be tomorrow's adversaries—and allies once more the day after. As a state may need its present opponent as an ally in the future, hostilities cannot be allowed to become too intense—because individual states have changing relations with so many other states, their loyalties will cut across one another.[20] A member of one alliance will have interests in common, as well as in conflict, with those of its partners, but some interests are also likely to overlap with interests of members in the opposing coalition. When the enemy of today may become the ally of tomorrow, it is a bit more difficult to become aroused about any specific state or cause.)

(In a particular dispute, for instance, the possibility that an ally may defect is claimed to be a restraining factor on the other members of the alliance. A multipolar alliance is an alliance in the sense that most of us use that term: a collection of states, most of approximately equal power, who by joining together strengthen themselves versus a potential enemy. The possible loss of one partner is, therefore, a serious matter because it will weaken the alliance against the adversary. If one member of an alliance formed to preserve the status quo should, therefore, decide to try instead to sway the membership to support changing that status quo, another member's threat of "de-alignment" is likely to block those efforts. The coalition cannot afford such a loss. Because the state threatening to defect might move into a nonaligned position or even join the opposition, members of the coalition will bring collective pressure to bear on the dissenter to moderate its aims. Furthermore, if one state should enhance its power—for example, by increasing its armed forces or by seizing territory—another previously unaligned state may throw its weight onto the scales for the weaker side. In a multipolar structure, with its inherent flexibility, not only are friends and foes more difficult to distinguish than in a bipolar structure, but also the balance is not nearly as sensitive to changes in the power distribution. Changes do not seem irreversible, for imbalances can be remedied. A multipolar system is thus inherently more stable than a bipolar one. If one of the two superpowers in the latter type of system wishes to act in a manner not supported by its allies, they cannot inhibit it. Because of the enormous difference in power between the superpower and its allies, the threat of defection cannot work; defection cannot appreciably reduce the superpower's power. In any event, the far weaker ally needs the superpower's protection more than the latter needs its support.)

(One additional argument has been advanced to explain the restraining and peace-preserving characteristics of multipolarity. The more numerous the actors, it has been claimed, the less attention any single actor can give to any other. This

---

[20.] Karl W. Deutsch and J. David Singer, "Multipolar Power Systems and International Stability," *World Politics*, April 1964, pp. 392–396.

124   is beneficial because "the average share of available attention for any one conflict drops sharply as soon as there are more than three power centers in the system, and more gently after there are more than five such centers." More specifically, it has been suggested that, if a conflict requires at least 10 percent of a government's critical attention before armed conflict can result, then the "minimal attention ratio for an escalating conflict would have to be 1 : 9, since it does not seem likely that any country could be provoked very far into an escalating conflict with less than 10 percent of the foreign policy attention of its government devoted to the matter."[21] Whereas in a bipolar system the contestants watch each other unceasingly and are able to devote themselves fully to their quarrels, a multipolar system with as many as eleven approximately equal great powers would be able to avoid major conflicts. To sum up, we can say that, whereas bipolar systems are prone to crises and the eruption of war, multipolar systems, because of their flexibility, are more likely to maintain peace.)

TABLE 6.1

TWO TYPES OF STATE SYSTEMS

	Bipolar System	*Multipolar System*
Number of Powers	Two superior states	Many (usually cited as 5 to 10) approximately equal states
Nature of System	Simple and rigid	Complex and flexible
Principal Characteristics	Confrontation, crisis, arms competition, preoccupation with adversary's preemptive or first-strike capability, search for allies	Self-restraint and emphasis on negotiating major political differences
Alliance Relationship	Cohesive	Rapidly changing

TRIPOLARITY

(As may be apparent, the understanding and even the prediction of the ways in which states will behave in various kinds of polar systems are logical exercises. We deduce the behavior patterns from a model with two or more poles.) Because of the increasing importance of China in contemporary superpower relations, tripolarity

---

[21.] *Ibid.*, pp. 396–400.

is well worth analyzing. The relations among the United States, the Soviet Union, and China do not constitute a genuine tripolar system, for China does not possess material and military power equal to that of the other two. But the exercise is worthwhile in order to show how analysts derive their models. Furthermore, tripolarity raises a basic question. Is behavior in a tripolar system closer to that under a bipolar system or that under a multipolar system? Some analysts suggest the latter because each pole will have at least two incentives for self-restraint and moderation in its behavior. The first is that total nuclear warfare between any two poles would weaken the participants so catastrophically that the third pole would attain a dominant systemic position. The "victorious power," if there were one, would confront a third power still untouched by nuclear havoc; and, even if that third power were to possess only an inferior strategic nuclear capability, it could still dictate the terms of peace. Second, not only would each pole be opposed to such an outcome, but each would also wish to prevent the emergence of a dominant coalition composed of the other two poles. Such a coalition could result only if any of the three exhibited unduly aggressive behavior. Self-restraint would thus be a wise policy for each pole.[22] It is probable that, *whereas in a bipolar system each power most fears becoming militarily inferior, lest the opponent achieve a dominance that may not be reversible, in a tripolar system each pole most fears diplomatic isolation.*

In a tripolar structure, system-maintenance demands abstention from the kinds of confrontation and lower-level military engagements that may escalate into a nuclear conflagration, nonintervention in one another's spheres of influence, and relative moderation in each pole's demands and behavior. Each pole is also likely to concentrate its attention and energies on its relations with its two rivals, for to become too involved outside the triangular structure and to neglect relations with the other two poles may be disadvantageous to any of the actors.

The basic rules of behavior are as follows:

1. The existence of "adversary number one" leads to "objective collusion" with "number two."

2. Each of the three players aims to reduce collusion between the others to a minimum.

3. At the same time, it is in the interest of each to bluff or blackmail the chief adversary by threatening collusion with the other.

4. The surest way for any of the three to provoke the other two into collusion is to display undue aggressiveness.[23]

[22] Ronald Yalem, "Tripolarity and the International System," *Orbis*, Winter 1972, pp. 1051 ff.; and "Tripolarity and World Politics," *The Yearbook of World Affairs 1974* (London: Institute of World Affairs, 1974), pp. 23 ff.

[23] Michel Tatu, *International Negotiation: The Great Power Triangle, Selected Comment* (Subcommittee on National Security and International Operations of the Committee on Government Operations, U.S. Senate, 92d Congress, 1st session; Washington, D.C.: Government Printing Office, 1971), p. 11.

Figure 6.3 DIFFERENT INTERACTIONS IN BIPOLAR AND TRIPOLAR SYSTEMS

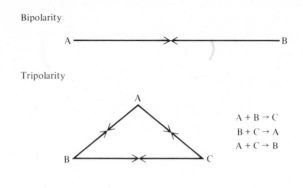

Notice the use of the word "collusion." Although the term connotes an underhanded intention, such an implication is not necessarily present. Two powers may well seek a *rapprochement* on some particular issue for reasons having little or nothing to do with power number three. Nevertheless, the latter is likely to be suspicious of the motives of the other powers and therefore to perceive "collusion," whether it exists or not.

A tripolar system, then, promises to be stable, perhaps more stable than a bipolar system for—as already noted in a multipolar system—it need not be quite so sensitive to slight increments of power by any pole as the emphasis shifts from continual crises toward maneuver and from rigid confrontation toward flexibility. Whereas in a bipolar system each state thinks that it must match the other, in a tripolar system some gain in power can be permitted because, if the increase should become too threatening to the other two poles, they are likely to combine their power. If one of the poles has been aligned with the expansionist pole it will shift toward the third pole. Or the third pole, because it can throw its power in the scales on the side of the weaker opponent, may be in a position to act as moderator in the dispute. *Rational calculations of power and self-interest, not ideology, will be the basis of each pole's foreign policy.*

There is an opposing view; some analysts argue that tripolarity is closer to bipolarity than multipolarity and is unstable. Again, there are two main reasons. First, precisely because tripolarity is bipolarity plus one, it may revert to bipolarity if two powers align themselves against the third pole on more than just a temporary basis. Each pole greatly fears a long-term alliance or collusion of the other two, and this fear is bound to raise tensions. Second, even when tripolarity does not revert to bipolarity, the addition of one pole triples the number of possible interactions from the single pattern possible under bipolarity (see Figure 6.3). These patterns may be cooperative, but the likelihood of conflict is even greater as each strives for superiority in a three-way competitive system. Although the number of interactions increases, the flexibility of tripolarity is far more limited than that of a multipolar system, in which several great powers may maneuver to maintain the equilibrium. Tripolarity may therefore be somewhat unstable.

III

THE NATURE OF POWER: NEW ROLES AND LIMITATIONS

Of Power, Relationships, and Intentions

7

POWER: A DEFINITION

P ower," "great power," "superpower," "balance of power"—we have used these terms repeatedly. Yet at no point have we stopped to inquire into the nature of power. In one sense, there hardly seems reason to do so, for power is a term with which we are all familiar; it seems so "obvious" what power is. When the United States lands soldiers in the Dominican Republic to prevent a political faction judged by Washington to have been infiltrated by "pro-Castro communists" from capturing the government; when the Red Army invades Czechoslovakia to throw out a government whose communist sympathies are suspect in Moscow; when the United States demands the withdrawal of Soviet missiles from Cuba; when the Soviet Union demands that West Berlin be turned into a "free city" (free of the Western allies, that is); when Soviet advisors and Cuban troops intervene in African nations, and Soviet troops intervene in Afghanistan; when Saudi Arabia threatens an oil embargo unless there is progress on Palestinian self-determinination—we all know that power is being exercised.

It is a fact of life that some nations are more powerful than others and that international politics has generally been the story of the games played by the stronger members of the state system.[1] When we use adjectives like "more powerful" and

---

[1] Only recently has this assumption that the great states are the primary actors been questioned by some analysts. See Stanley Hoffmann, *Gulliver's Troubles or the Setting of American Foreign Policy* (New York: McGraw-Hill, 1968), pp. 26–43. For a response to Hoffmann, see Kenneth N. Waltz, "International Structure, National Force, and the Balance of World Power," *Journal of International Affairs* 21 (1967), 220–228; and Waltz, *Theory of International Politics*, pp. 161–193.

132   "stronger," we are usually referring to military capacity. No one thinks of Belgium or Burma as "powers"; their military strength, by either conventional or nuclear standards, is puny. (The label "power" has historically been awarded to states that have won successful military victories.) Until such a victory who could have known of the victor's "power"? In the absence of the successful exercise of a state's power, that power is in abeyance. But military victory confers a reputation for power or prestige. In the ninteenth century Prussia's two rapid victories, the first over the ancient and redoubtable Austro-Hungarian Empire in 1866, and the second over Europe's strongest power, France, in 1870, left no doubt that the newly unified Prussia had become not only *a* power to be reckoned with but, in Europe, also *the* power. The United States' defeat of Spain in Cuba in 1898 and Japan's defeat of Russia in 1904–1905 similarly conferred great-power status on these newcomers to the international stage. World War I confirmed these rankings.

Conversely, a military defeat like the one suffered in 1940 by France, which had already been bled white during the 1914–1918 war, puts a nation's reputation for power in jeopardy. (There may not even have to be a defeat; the mere fact that a great power is unable to win a conflict with a lesser power will hurt its prestige.) Perhaps the great power should not have indulged in such a conflict in the first place, but, once it has done so, its ability to exercise power effectively is one of the issues at stake. Britain's inept use of force against Egypt during the Suez war in 1956, for example, made it plain to Conservative party leaders that Britain was no longer a first-rank power and that, as a nation-state, its status and influence could become great once more only if it joined Europe in its efforts to become a United States of Europe. A few years after Suez, therefore, Britain, a country that had long regarded a divided Europe as prerequisite for its own security, first applied to join the European Common Market. Just as Britain might have been better off had it not intervened in Egypt, so might the United States have better avoided entanglement in Vietnam. Once this country was ensnared, Presidents Johnson and Nixon found it difficult to disentangle it from the war, largely because of the high priority they gave to the *"credibility* of American power."

There are, of course, variations on this theme of victory and defeat. During the 1960s, when all-out war was no longer viewed as a true test of a nation's power, the "space race" replaced the test of battle. In 1960 Kennedy pounded home the message that this country's second-rate performance in space during Eisenhower's years as president meant that we were not yet aware of the global political and psychological impact of the bipolar competition in space. The first manned Soviet satellite to orbit the earth in April of Kennedy's first year as president convinced him that a second-rate effort was not consistent with his country's role as a world leader and a great power whose reputation was based to a very large extent on its industrial-technological capabilities. The technology in this new sphere had come to symbolize the power, as well as the way of life, of the United States and the Soviet Union. Kennedy immediately ordered a review of various space projects in which the United States could surpass Russia.[2] The most promising was the landing

---

[2.] Theodore C. Sorensen, *Kennedy* (New York: Bantam, 1966), pp. 589–592.

of a man on the moon, and, in May, the President announced that this objective would be achieved before the end of the decade. In July 1969, indeed, the first men stood on the moon and, though they talked of having come on behalf of all mankind, their shoulder patches read "U.S.A."

An image of international power may also change as a result of policy decisions taken primarily for internal reasons. Stalin's massive purge of the Soviet general staff in the late 1930s was thought by Western observers to have left the Soviet military weak to the point of ineffectiveness, with the result that Russian influence on the world scene plummeted. The French then estimated Poland to be stronger than Russia, and later, when France and Britain were already at war with Germany, they almost took on Russia as well when they decided to help Finland in its courageous defense against a Red Army attack.

(Three points are very important. The first, generally shared by many citizens and policy makers, is the popular *identification of power with military capacity*—regardless of whether the estimate is based on power overtly applied, peacefully demonstrated (as in parades, maneuvers, and space shots), or held in check during bargaining.) When books are written on power, they bear such titles as *The War Potential of Nations*.[3] Because war has historically been the *ultima ratio* of power in interstate politics, the emphasis on military strength is hardly surprising. (The Prussian general Karl von Clausewitz, in a classic definition, called war the continuation of political relations by other means; turning this phrase around, peace may be called the continuation of the last war by other means.) Earlier, we suggested that the state system, unlike most modern Western domestic political systems, is characterized by a condition of potential warfare. Each state's concern with its military power has thus historically set an acceptable standard of behavior. And it is military power that today, because of its enormous destructive ability, we most need to control and manage. To be sure, there are—as we shall see—other ways of exercising power, especially by economic means. (But coercion and the use of violence to achieve state ends in a system of politics without government has long substituted for governmental allocation of values.)

(The second point is that *power is what people think it is*. A distinction must thus be drawn between subjective, or perceived, power and objective, or actual, power.) For example, the United States retired into isolationism after World War I. It did not participate actively in the state system, and its power was by and large discounted by other states. It pursued no political objectives outside the Western Hemisphere; it wished only to be left alone. It ranked low in the great-power hierarchy, behind France, Britain, Germany, Russia, and Japan—yet, objectively, the United States remained the world's number-one power, far stronger than Germany or its Western adversaries.

(Third, *a reputation for power will confer power*, whether others' estimates of a nation's power are correct or not. If a nation or its leadership has prestige, it is less likely to be challenged; if its prestige is declining, challenges, not only from

[3] Klaus Knorr, *The War Potential of Nations* (Princeton: Princeton University Press, 1955); and Knorr, *Military Power and Potential* (Lexington, Mass.: Heath, 1970).

134   powers of equal strength but also from less powerful states, are likely.)These challengers will think that they can defy that nation's policies with impunity. Mussolini said, after Britain's appeasement of Hitler at Munich in 1938 over the issue of the Sudetenland: "These men [the British and French leaders] are not made of the same stuff as Francis Drake and the other magnificent adventurers who created the Empire. They are after all the tired sons of a long line of rich men."[4] Shortly afterward, Hitler seized the rest of Czechoslovakia and began to look hungrily at Poland. Having challenged Britain repeatedly without response, except for verbal protest, Hitler thought that it was safe to try again. The British would back down as usual. But that time the British government stood firm, and the result was World War II.

Twenty-three years later, in 1962, Soviet missile installations in Cuba precipitated the most dangerous crisis of the Cold War. President Kennedy demanded their removal, believing that what was at stake was the United States' reputation for power. The Soviets apparently thought little of it; otherwise, how could they have believed that they could place strategic weapons in the United States' historic sphere of influence and so close to its shores? They had to be disabused of this notion before they mounted an even more dangerous challenge to American interests, which would have precipitated a nuclear war. For a great power to be viewed by its adversaries, its allies, or even nonaligned countries, as weak is to court disaster.

Whether or not a nation's leaders know that their nation's reputation is at stake is not always clear. They cannot know precisely what their adversaries are thinking, and the latter may publicly deny holding low estimates of their prestige, even when such estimates actually motivate them. This key issue is thus a matter of judgment and often of controversy among policy makers. It poses a major problem because leaders must always be aware of the impact of their policies on other states. How do the latter perceive these policies? This issue is critical in policy making. The policy makers may come up with the best of all policies, but, if it is not correctly perceived in the affected states, it may fail.

(Power may often be identified with military power and may exist only "within the mind,"—but what *is* power? The most common definition of power is probably the capacity to influence the behavior of other states in accordance with one's own objectives. Implicit in this definition is the understanding that, without the exercise of power, the other states will not accede to the demands made upon them. Power, then, is several things. It is something that a state *has*; the exact amount or quantity depends on measurement of each of the various components of power (as we shall see later in this chapter). It is also a *means* to achieve the state's various ends, or goals. Finally, and most important, it is a reciprocal *relationship* among two or more states. A influences B, and B influences A, but the amount of influence that each possesses is not necessarily the same; A's ability to influence B may be much greater than the reverse. Power relationships, though reciprocal, are not necessarily symmetrical.)

---

[4] Quoted by Winston Churchill, *The Gathering Storm* (Boston: Houghton Mifflin, 1948), p. 341.

It has been argued that power relations exist when three factors are present.[5] First, there must be a conflict of values or interests. If A and B agree on objectives, B will consent freely to A's demands or proposed course of action. Power is not used. One state may be stronger than the other, but, as there is *agreement* on what to do, power remains latent. Even when there are relatively small differences among states, as perceived by the parties to a dispute, *persuasion* is very likely all that is necessary to resolve the differences. There is an appeal to common interests, principles, and values; there may be attempts to introduce facts new to one party or interpretations of the situation that have not yet been considered; and the consequences of different courses of action may be pointed out.

Second, for a power relationship to exist, *B must accede, however unwillingly, to A's demands*. Accession is necessary because, though the two may be involved in a conflict of interest, B may simply stand its ground and not comply. Then A must either give up its demands or resort to force. Third, *in a power relationship one of the parties invokes sanctions that the other regards as likely to inflict "severe deprivations" or pain upon itself*. The cost of noncompliance for B must be greater than the cost of compliance. The threatened state B must believe that the adversary A's threat of sanctions is credible and not a bluff.

This emphasis on sanctions is not meant to imply neglect of *rewards* that A may offer B to promote resolution of their differences. When these differences are too large to be settled by persuasion but not of such magnitude that sanctions must be invoked, the granting or withholding of rewards may be the most effective way of exercising power. Such grants may involve economic rewards of some kind: for example, aid, lowered tariff barriers, or high-technology products. These grants can, of course, be cut off. But a conflict involving deep disagreement may lead one party to invoke sanctions against the other. *Punishment*, or *coercion*, comprises a wide variety of measures the purpose of which is to inflict "pain": reduction of imports, imposition of embargoes, raising of prices, withholding of arms (in peace or war), breaking off of diplomatic relations, threats of the use of force, deployment of naval units, and so on. American-Soviet relations during much of the Cold War involved little economic intercourse, but they did involve the very visible presence of military forces and frequent threats of their deployment.

Finally, when differences between states are extreme, *force* is most likely to be used. If B complies when A exercises coercion, the use of force is, of course, unnecessary; A must resort to force only if B does *not* comply with A's demands. When A does resort to force it admits failure to attain its objectives by threats of punishment. Using force does not, however, guarantee attainment of these objectives. American involvements in two limited wars in Asia came after American help to protégé governments had failed to deter a direct, overt attack in Korea and the organization of a revolutionary war in South Vietnam. American interventions were intended to prevent losses of "dominoes" and resulting imbalances. Britain's

---

[5.] Peter Bachrach and Morton S. Baratz, *Power and Poverty* (New York: Oxford University Press, 1970), pp. 17–38. Also see Charles A. McClelland, *Theory and the International System* (New York: Macmillan, 1966), pp. 68–88, and K. J. Holsti, *International Politics: A Framework for Analysis* (Englewood Cliffs, N.J.: Prentice-Hall, 1967), pp. 191–209.

136   declaration of war in 1939, on the other hand, had been intended to restore an equilibrium upset by Hitler's succession of military moves. But one important point should be emphasized:(*The use of force may at times result in loss of one's reputation for power.*[6])If the sanctions, once applied, do not inflict as severe a deprivation as A's threat has implied, B's future compliance with A's demands is less likely. Other states may not comply with A's demands either—until, at some point, A insists on compliance and is willing to enforce its demands to restore its prestige.

    We shall analyze power relations in detail later, but it is well to remember now that the different scopes of disagreement that lead states to use persuasion, rewards, coercion, and force depend on the parties involved, their demands, their disinclination to comply with demands, and their perceptions of the stakes involved. Furthermore, these methods of exercising influence may in practice be mixed: If persuasion cannot quite resolve differences, rewards may be held out; rewards may be enticing, but hints of threats for noncompliance may be useful; and a threat may well be more effective if the belief is strong that force will be used unless agreement can be reached. Combinations of carrots *and* sticks may be more useful in resolving differences than either carrots *or* sticks. Carrying a "big stick" but "speaking softly" may be more fruitful than swinging the stick. Finally, coercion and force are more likely to be used against adversaries than against friendly states, but rewards may accompany such threats. Let us look now at some of the main components of power and how they are measured.

POWER CALCULATIONS

    Most readers will have an idea of the principal components of power. They probably include most of the following:

geography	economic capacity
population	military strength
natural resources	political system and leadership
	national morale

    Let us make several preliminary points before taking a brief look at each of these elements separately. First, any calculation of a nation's power and the power balance must include a mix of *tangible* components, like population, men in uniform, and numbers of tanks and missiles, and *intangible* components, like morale, efficiency and effectiveness of political systems, and quality of political leadership. The intangible components do not lend themselves to accurate calculations; they are matters of judgment. Second, we must always remain aware, when doing such calculations, of the distinction between *potential power* and *actual*

---

6. See "American Power and the 'Rules of the Game' in Vietnam," in Chapter 10.

capability—that is, power that has been mobilized. Short of total war, states do not completely transform their economies into "war economies" or maximize their military strength. There is thus always a gap between potential and actual power.)

(Third, when we look at each component individually, we see that accurate assessment of even the tangible ones is not at all easy.)Population figures for different states, for example, can be readily compared, and the rule of thumb "the bigger, the better" tends to favor the more powerful states—the United States and the Soviet Union, for instance. The trouble is that sometimes a large population may be a liability, rather than an asset. For China and India, the enormous size of populations and high birth rates that have led to anticipated populations of 1.5 billion and 1 billion respectively by the turn of the twenty-first century, make modernization and economic development difficult. Progress is eaten up by the need to feed, clothe, and educate millions of new people. The problem of over-population in the LDCs, many of which are already overpopulated, is likely to place major stress on the international system in the future.

For all countries, with large populations or small, developed or under-developed, other factors must be taken into account: age distribution, educational and skill patterns, and ethnic composition, for example. Any one of these factors can complicate the calculation of a single component. For countries deeply divided by various nationalities and religious and racial factions, we would surely have to "substract" from the calculation, for in crisis or war such states may demonstrate low morale or even disintegrate. The LDCs are particularly subject to political fragmentation because of such problems.

(A fourth and final preliminary point: Calculations of any single component of power make sense only when linked with those of other components.) Large populations by themselves can ensure great-power status only when there is also industry. It is the marriage of a large population with an industrialized economy that constitutes "power." The power rating of a nation characterized by poverty, a largely agrarian and unskilled population, a high birth rate, and great difficulties in urbanizing and industrializing is certain to be low.

GEOGRAPHY

(The location and size of a nation are clearly very important.)The United States and Britain have long been protected from invasions by bodies of water too wide for their enemies to cross easily. The United States, indeed, was even able to isolate itself from the international political system for more than a century. Similarly, states like Italy and Spain have been well protected by high mountain ranges—the Alps and the Pyrenees respectively. Indeed, little of western Europe's modern culture seems to have crossed the Pyrenees until late in this century! But the countries on the axis from France to Russia all lie on a plain. The Rhine, separating Germany and France, was of little help in halting repeated German invasions of France; Russia has no natural protection at all and has been repeatedly invaded

138   from the West and defeated. Note the correlation between the world's leading democracies and geographic protection: The United States, Britain, and the northern Scandinavian countries lie off the axis of repeated invasions. The states lying on the axis—France, Prussia/Germany, and Russia—know war well, and not surprisingly they have developed large bureaucracies and standing armies to guard themselves. Notions of individual freedom, the rights of opposition, and criticism are in such circumstances luxuries subordinate to security and physical survival. Highly centralized governments and authoritarian politics have become the pattern. Even in France, the westernmost of these states, bounded by both the Atlantic Ocean and the Mediterranean Sea, the home of nationalism and democracy since the revolution of 1789, democracy continues to face challenges from the authoritarian tradition. But democracy was foreign to Prussia and Germany (Prussia unified Germany in 1870) until after World War II, when it was imposed upon the country by its conquerors; it was also foreign to czarist and Soviet Russia. And, though there is no suggestion that the reason these countries have long been authoritarian is primarily owing to geography, geography surely has been a major contributing factor. The farther east one goes in Europe, the more authoritarian it becomes; the farther west, the more democratic.

The United States, the power lying farthest west of all and until recently isolated from the rest of the world, survived with only a small navy and had plenty of time to nurture its democratic roots. Not until modern technology made the long-range bomber and flying missile possible was the United States drawn into the daily rough-and-tumble of international politics. (Note, by the way, how many critics of American foreign policy have argued that, in the name of security, the United States has too often forgotten its democratic principles, even forfeited its democratic "souls" to imperial presidents, immoral and illegal intelligence practices, and authoritarian right-wing allies.) Had the United States been geographically nearer to other great powers, isolationism would have been impossible. Instead, like Russia (against Napoleon and Hitler) and China (against Japan), this country would have had to make shrewd use of its vast interior space to neutralize an attack. It could have drawn the enemy in, so that it would have been exhausted in the attempt to conquer such a vast territory, maintaining long supply lines and attempting to pacify and control a large and hostile population. (In Russia, of course, there was a long and icy winter as well.)

Today location and size are no longer of such benefit in an all-out war because modern weapons can fly far and fast and are amazingly accurate over long ranges. More broadly, technology has reduced the significance of geography. Not that it no longer has any significance. On the contrary the Russians have always been driven to expand around their periphery because they can bring their influence to bear more easily there than on a distant adversary. Yet until recently the few supply lines running from European Russia to Central Asia and the Far East hampered the application of power in Asian Russia. Since the recent Sino-Soviet schism, transportation and communications have been greatly improved. Still, the long 4,150-mile Russian frontier with China obviously gives even the powerful Soviet Union a sense of insecurity, a feeling intensified by the Sino-American alignment. Geography, should a war between Russia and China erupt, would certainly make it extremely difficult, if not impossible, for the Red Army to occupy, pacify, and govern a country as vast as China, with a population of more than 1 billion. Probably these considerations are among the factors preventing a possible large-scale Soviet invasion.

Geography certainly continues to affect the sense of insecurity of small states, perhaps more so because they possess little room to maneuver in wartime. Negotiations in the Middle East since 1973 have foundered continually on the issue of the right of the Palestinians to a state of their own on the West Bank. Apart from any alleged Biblical claims to that land and refusal to negotiate with the Palestinian Liberation Organization (PLO) Israel wanted to keep control of the West Bank because otherwise Arab guns could fire into Israel, a long, narrow state. Israel's great insecurity is closely tied to geography, though in fact, even if Israel controlled or annexed the West Bank, it could easily be hit by modern, medium-range missiles from Jordan, Syria, or even farther away. Objectively, Israel would be no more secure, but subjectively—in its feelings of security—it apparently would be.

In the United States, it is not always easy to understand other nations' feelings of insecurity, despite great intermittent concern about Soviet forces in Cuba. Historically, isolationism ensured the United States' security; this country has never had to worry that Canada or Mexico would become a great power itself and align itself with American enemies, who would then send the United States' neighbors modern arms. Empathizing thus with Russia's fears of China or Israel's fears of its Arab neighbors and the PLO is very difficult. The United States' principal adversaries remain thousands of miles away across the Pacific and Atlantic oceans and the problem is how to apply American power effectively over such long distances.

POPULATION

(Population figures are good initial indicators of a nation's power ranking and of possible changes in its ranking) In Table 7.1, we can immediately see how Prussia's unification of Germany in 1870 changed the map of Europe and finally brought the United States out of its isolation. Except for Russia in the east, the Continent's traditional great powers, Austria-Hungary and France, had been displaced by Germany. France, which had the largest population in 1850 (36 million) was by 1910 just ahead of Italy, the least populous country in Europe. Germany's top ranking was underscored by its large-scale industrialization. Britain had become the world's greatest power in the nineteenth century. Steel production was usually the major indicator of industrial strength because of its association with the production of modern arms. In the first decade of this century Germany overtook Britain in steel production (and, by using much of that steel to build a sizable navy, obviously challenged the British navy and drove England closer to France and Russia).

TABLE 7.1

POPULATION OF MAJOR EUROPEAN POWERS, 1870–1910
(in millions)

Year	Austria-Hungary	France	Germany	Britain	Italy	Russia
1870	36	36	40	31	27	82
1890	41	38	49	38	30	110
1900	45	39	56	41	32	133
1910	50	39	64	45	35	163
1914	52	39	65	45	37	171

Adapted from Quincy Wright, A *Study of War*, I (Chicago: University of Chicago Press, 1942), 670–671; and A.J.P. Taylor, *The Struggle for Mastery in Europe* (London: Oxford University Press, 1954), p. xxv.

Only the United States was a match for Germany. With a population of 76 million in 1900 and 92 million in 1910 and with steel production more than twice that of Germany, the United States clearly would be compelled eventually to abandon its isolationism. In the words of A. J. P. Taylor: "By 1914 she was not merely an economic Power on the European level; she was a rival continent. Her coal production equalled that of Great Britain and Germany put together; her iron and steel production surpassed that of all Europe. This was the writing on the wall: economically Europe no longer had a monopoly—she was not even the centre of the world."[7] In Europe, however, Germany was becoming too powerful for its neighbors. It was acquiring the capability to become the dominant power and thus a threat to the independence of the other European great powers. World War I and the United States' participation in it were predictable from population and industrial figures alone. The fact that, without continued American political involvement, no lasting peace in Europe was feasible even after Germany's defeat, was also clear. For Germany was left intact and not broken up into separate states, as the French had wanted. Unified Germany therefore remained potentially Europe's most powerful state, despite some restriction on its armed forces. The United States' return to isolationism was certainly one factor responsible for World War II, which again required American intervention.

At the same time, the deceptiveness of population figures by themselves is revealed in the example of Russia, France's ally. It had a population two and a half times that of Germany, but these statistics hid more than they revealed. Czarist society was in the throes of revolution. The giant Russia, as it was thought of, had been defeated by that "small upstart," Japan just a few years earlier, in 1904–1905. Defeat was followed by widespread peasant revolts, which revealed inner social rot. The largest population in Europe did not therefore prevent Russia's basic weakness: Not only was its industry small—about the size of that of Austria–Hungary—but also much of the population was disenchanted with the regime.

---

[7] A. J. P. Taylor, *The Struggle for Mastery in Europe* (London: Oxford University Press), p. xxxi.

The peasantry, which constituted the bulk of Russia's population, as well as the small working class and the industrial middle class, all wished to be rid of the czar. Morale—popular support for a government—was low; Russia in 1914 already stood on the brink of revolution.

Even more revealing was the situation of Germany's ally Austria-Hungary; the latter's population was larger than that of either France or Britain. Composed of a multitude of different nationalities who hated one another, disintegrating as these various ethnic groups became more nationalistically self-conscious and demanded self-determination, Austria-Hungary was determined to crush Serbia, a Slav state that fanned the flames of nationalism in Austria-Hungary in order to destroy it. And so, on the brink of dissolution, Vienna decided that it could avoid death only by risking suicide in a war to eliminate Serbia. Because Russia supported Serbia, Germany Austria, and France Russia, the result of Austria-Hungary's ethnic composition was World War I.

If the coming of World War I provides a good illustration of the value of changing population figures, as well as the limitations of looking only at such figures, it remains true nonetheless that basically a large population in a developed nation clearly confers an advantage for several reasons. First, it translates into a big army, especially if the age distribution is such that the country has a sizable percentage of youth. Second, a large population means that the industries which develop to serve so many consumers tend to be large-scale and the country is likely to be very productive. This translates into large numbers of guns, as well as butter. In Sherman Kent's words, such a nation has a lot of fat in the economy, a lot of slack and flexibility. Fat refers to the economy's great productivity and wealth, so that a significant amount of butter can be converted into guns and yet leave the population with enough butter. Slack refers to unused productivity because of such factors as unemployment, the small proportion of women in the labor force, and the forty-hour week. Flexibility refers to the ability to turn the economy quickly from the production of peacetime goods to weapons.)

The American economy has in the past possessed all of these. In the future, the amount of fat may however be more sparse. A greater percentage of Americans will be over the age of 65; the increasing amounts of social security payments required may well cut into the military budget. Indeed, welfare payments in general (which may in the future include an expensive national health program) in an era of high inflation are bound to raise the issue of guns (whose costs are also going up) versus butter as a major political issue. By contrast, a state like Israel with its small population has never been able to afford both guns and butter and needs foreign military and economic assistance. Israel cannot fight long wars because her armed forces are recruited from the civilian population; long absence from work therefore means the collaspse of the economy. Israel has to fight short wars and this may well be a powerful incentive to preempt when she believes the Arabs will attack in the immediate future.

(Three, a large economy with many consumers means that many nations will want access to that nation's economy to sell their products. This gives that nation leverage. Four, it also means that the latter can use its wealth as an instrument of foreign policy—foreign aid, for example—and because large population with

TABLE 7.2

LARGEST COUNTRIES BY POPULATION*
(in millions)

Country	1979 Population
China	958
India	653
Soviet Union	261
United States	220
Indonesia	151
Japan	116
Brazil	120
Bangladesh	84
Pakistan	80
Nigeria	70
Germany (West)	62
Italy	57
England	56
France	54

*The World Almanac and Book of Facts (1979), pp. 513ff.

many scientists and engineers is also likely to produce high technology, this too can be employed to advance the nation's purposes internationally.)

Two final points are worth noting. One is how few nations have populations over 50 million and how many of these—eight (including China) are already classified among the major actors or potential great powers of the future (India, Indonesia, Brazil, and Nigeria). Indeed, China's population may already exceed 1 billion; by the year 2000 its population may reach 1.5 billion, with India following at 1 billion.

The second point is the population forecast by region. National population-growth figures reveal that Europe and the United States will contain a minority of the world's population (see Table 7.3). When these figures are combined with productivity data, the trend toward a *division of the* world between a minority of states that are rich and a growing majority that are poor becomes clear. This trend is obviously potentially very dangerous and is one reason for growing concern about the North-South confrontation. By the year 2000, Western men and women may constitute only 15–20 percent of the world's population. The LDCs will have 80–85 percent!

NATURAL RESOURCES

(As must be clear by now, industrialization married to population gives birth to power. But industrialization cannot occur or continue to produce a nation's guns and butter without natural resources.) Britain, Germany, and the United States

142

TABLE 7.3

ESTIMATED POPULATION BY REGION FOR THE YEAR 2000*
(in millions)

Developed areas	
North America	296
Europe	540
USSR	315
Less-developed areas	
Latin America	620
Africa	813
East Asia	1,369
South Asia	2,267
Oceania	33

U.N. Demographic Yearbook, 1978, p. 137.

were all able to industrialize because of plentiful supplies of coal. Coal is, in fact, being thought of today as the major alternative source of energy for oil in the production of electricity, safer than nuclear energy, though coal does have environmental effects that make its social costs high. The United States has enormous reserves of coal, far more than Saudi Arabia has of oil. The index of economic development in the earlier stage of industrialization was steel—which was used for everything from railroad tracks to cannons to machinery. Iron and coal were thus key resources. The Soviet Union, it may be noted in passing, overtook the United States in steel production in 1974, about the same time that the number of Soviet missiles exceeded the American total. Was this change symptomatic, like the shift between Britain and Germany seventy years earlier?

After World War II, oil replaced coal, because oil was cheap. One has to wonder whether or not the oil companies, often accused now of jacking up oil prices and earning "obscene" profits, did the West a favor by keeping oil so inexpensive for so long. Had oil always been more expensive, especially in the United States, the industrial nations might have kept a better balance between oil and coal and become less vulnerable to OPEC and its continual price increases.[8] Not only bombers and tanks, but also the whole Western industrial structure and high standard of living have been based on oil. (Would southern cities like Houston and Atlanta have become great cities and commercial and cultural centers without oil and air conditioning?) The United States, once an oil exporter, now imports almost half its oil. Our allies in the North Atlantic Treaty Organization (NATO), import about 85 percent of their oil (though Britain is becoming self-sufficient thanks to its North Sea reserves) and Japan 90 percent of its oil. The Central Intelligence Agency has estimated that in the 1980s even Russia will begin to import oil, thus straining the world's reserves even more (and naturally raising prices higher). It is fair to say that energy production and consumption from all sources—coal, oil,

---

[8.] Alan L. Madian, "Oil Is Still Too Cheap," *Foreign Policy*, Summer 1979, pp. 170–179.

TABLE 7.4

PERCENTAGE DEPENDENCE ON IMPORTS*

Import	European Economic Community	Japan
aluminum	61	100
chromium	100	100
cobalt	100	—
copper	81	90
iron ore	79	94
lead	53	76
manganese	100	90
nickel	100	100
phosphate	99	100
platinum group	100	—
tin	87	97
tungsten	99	—
uranium	59	—
vanadium	99	—
zinc	68	80

*Amos A. Jordan, Robert A. Kolmarx, and Dan Haendel, "The U. S. Strategic Minerals Stockpile: Remedy for Increasing Vulnerability?" *Comparative Strategy* (1979), 1:307.

natural gas, nuclear power, and the sun—are signs of modern and technologically advanced economies. What will replace oil tomorrow as the principal energy source remains unclear.

Other imported resources on which the United States is becoming increasingly dependent are shown in Figure 7.1. Of all these imports, petroleum is the fastest growing. But American access to some of these and other resources may be endangered by nearby Cuban forces (e.g., cobalt in Zaire, Angola's neighbor), the control of resources by unfriendly governments, and—in the future—by the Soviet Union's growing naval power. Europe and Japan are even more dependent upon imports (see Table 7.4).

One result of the resource problem has been a search for replacements on or under the seabeds. Drilling for oil in the world's oceans is now commonplace. At least 20 percent of the world's oil comes from offshore wells, and the energy crisis is likely to cause a significant jump in this percentage. Oil companies estimate that offshore reserves are greater than those on land. There are also coal and iron, tin, limestone, sulphur, diamonds, and barium ore in the seas. Contemporary interest is focused on potatolike manganese nodules, that lie on deep seabeds and contain nickel, copper, cobalt, and manganese as well, all important industrial metals. With western technology nodule mining is feasible; it "has given man the keys to a storehouse of treasures in the oceans undreamt of even 50 years ago."[9] The oceans hold perhaps the greatest reservoir of untapped resources, both oil and minerals. But this very wealth increases the possibility of national claims over

---

[9.] U.S. Department of State, A *Constitution for the Sea* (Washington, D.C.: U.S. Government Printing Office, 1976), p. 5.

FIGURE 7.1.

U.S. IMPORT DEPENDENCE AND IMPORT SOURCES
(1977 estimates, except where noted.)

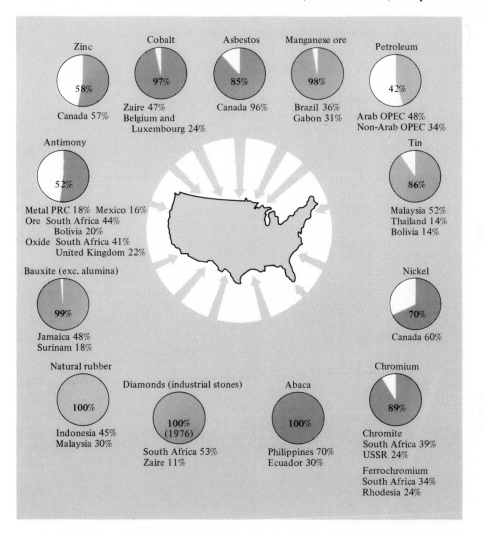

formerly international seabeds, straits, and fishing grounds. The potential for tension is high, as conflicting national claims are put forth. Access to these resources may produce rivalries of a kind that have already been major causes of conflict on land. That competition may lead to more than fiction. If Russia does become an oil importer in the 1980s, American-Russian rivalry in the Persian Gulf area will become intense and might even lead to a spark which will ignite a holocaust.

145

ECONOMIC CAPACITY

(A common standard for comparison of national power, probably more reliable than population in this industrial age, is wealth or degree of economic development. Wealth is obviously related to military power, for the richest states presumably can afford to buy the most military power. Indeed, wealth can buy power of all kinds, which remains important for distinguishing the superpowers from the secondary powers.) Britain, for example, cannot afford to build a sizable nuclear force or to keep up with the ever-changing state of the art in delivery systems and warheads. It must make a choice between trying to keep up with the leading members of the nuclear club, the United States and Russia, and developing sufficient conventional capacity to defend its many other interests. Its failure to make this choice, its decision instead to have some of each, meant that in the 1956 Suez war, for instance, it did not have a nuclear force to deter Soviet threats of rocket attacks against London (Washington had to tell Moscow not to try that one) or the conventional capabilities to occupy the Suez Canal and defeat Egyptian forces. The United States and the Soviet Union can mobilize both kinds of forces in sizable quantities, plus other kinds of power, like economic and technical assistance, if they wish to use those means as diplomatic tools. A nation's gross national product—the total value of its production and services measured in its currency—has thus frequently been used as a relatively accurate and measurable standard for comparing the power of different states.

A glance at Table 7.5 shows, first, the clear-cut distinction between the superpowers and the secondary powers over two decades; second, the ranking of the principal and secondary actors listed, which are pretty much as most observers would guess without knowing the GNP figures; and, third, the wide gap between the Soviet Union and the United States. Japan is closest to the United States but still far behind. The figures for the LDCs with the largest populations are far lower: India ($106 billion), Indonesia ($23 billion), Brazil ($202 billion), Bangladesh ($8 billion), Pakistan ($18.5 billion), and Nigeria $34 billion). For many smaller LDCs, the figures are even lower.

Still the GNP figure is not completely reliable. For one thing, in the United States at least, it reflects the production not only of steel but also of nineteen varieties of cat food and billions of hamburgers sold through fast-food chains. The Soviet Union, with a GNP less than half that of the United States in the mid-1960s launched a massive arms program; it can compete with the United States in arms and aerospace manufacturing because it devotes less of its wealth to consumer goods. Russian cats, no doubt, do not eat as well as American cats. At the official rate of exchange between the dollar and the ruble in the fall of 1979, the American GNP was almost two and a half times as great as that of the Soviet Union. Yet, whereas American military spending was about 5 percent of GNP—the lowest percentage since before the Korean war in 1950—Moscow was spending an estimated steady 12–14 percent of its GNP. In 1978, that meant that Russia

TABLE 7.5

RANKING OF ECONOMIC CAPACITY AMONG GREAT POWERS

Country	Estimated 1978 GNP (billions)
United States	$2,107
Soviet Union	781[a]
Japan	930
Germany (West)	634
France	463
Britain	302
China	373[b]
Italy	259

[a]At official exchange rates.
[b]China does not issue official statistics on GNP; this figure is taken from a CIA estimate for 1977.

These figures are taken from The International Institute for Strategic Studies, *The Military Balance, 1979–1980* (Dorking: Bartholomew Press, 1979).

spent about $44 billion more than the United States, and the momentum of its military growth was threatening to shift the distribution of power toward Russia.[10]

GNP also does not reflect total production and services. The American figure would be even higher if it reflected the billions of dollars earned in the drug business—the cocaine trade among middle- and upper-income groups alone is estimated to be in excess of $15 billion a year[11]—and Mafia activities; nor does it reflect volunteer work or women's household duties, for which wages are not paid.

In any event, GNP, however calculated, does not always lend itself to ready comparison. Take for example, Japan's GNP, which at the end of the 1970s was about two and a half times that of China, forty times that of Indonesia and almost 70 percent of that of the entire region, composed of fourteen other nations, including China. (China's GNP, however, was approximately twice that of all the thirteen other countries put together, excluding Japan.) This comparison demonstrates at the same time the limits to the reliability of GNP figures as measures of power—indeed, how misleading they can be. China possesses nuclear weapons and, as a totalitarian state, controls the allocation of resources in order to concentrate on whatever objectives it chooses—for example, a nuclear capability at the cost of larger domestic investments. Japan is economically far superior and is likely to enhance its economic lead over China. Japan, however, has no nuclear forces and only a small conventional self-defense force; whatever influence it has is based solely on its economic strength. Indeed, Japan is probably the first major power— by all the indexes of population, industry, education, technical skills, and so forth— in history to attempt to project influence as an industrial power only, rather than

---

[10.] William G. Hyland, "Brezhnev and Beyond," *Foreign Affairs*, Fall 1979, p. 61.

[11.] *The New York Times*, September 9, 1979.

148 as a military power with a self-defined political role[12] Japan is not so much a nation as a large trading company—or, as some wag has called it, Sony Incorporated. Japan has therefore been called an *economic* superpower, but 1973 demonstrated that its vaunted economic power was not enough to allow it to face up to Saudi Arabia. Politically and militarily it was only a potentially great power, still searching—and not too hard at that—for a role after years of American tutelage. More broadly, GNP reveals little about a nation's unity, the stability of its government, popular morale, military doctrine, and quality of diplomacy, which are relevant to analysis of a nation's power and foreign policy. At best, then, economic productivity—like population and military power—remains a crude indicator of power and a convenient shorthand means of comparison.

Sometimes per capita incomes are used as a standard of wealth. Again, the assumption is that individual income is highest in the most economically advanced nations. The figures for the United States, western Europe, and Japan are indeed the highest, although the United States—which long enjoyed the highest standard of living in the world—has slipped below Sweden, Switzerland, and West Germany since the oil crisis while Britain has slipped to a level just ahead of Italy, which has the lowest per capita income of the larger European states. In a way, per capita income figures are more accurate indicators than GNP figures. The Soviet GNP may be second to that of the United States, but Soviet per capita income is below that of any major Western country, indicating a much lower standard of living. The United States could, at least until the inflation of the 1970s, afford substantial amounts of guns *and* butter, whereas Russia built its guns at the expense of butter. The per capita incomes of the LDCs are the lowest. Actually, these figures can also be misleading on occasion. In 1979 Kuwait's per capita income was $15,000, twice that of the United States, fifty times that of Egypt, and one hundred fifty times that of Ethiopia.[13] Libya's per capita income was $6,250, which places it among the world's fifteen richest countries.[14] These nations have enormous oil incomes, but the incomes are not widely distributed, so that in fact the majority of their peoples remain poor.

Two final points must be emphasized. First, a nation's economic capability is enhanced if it possesses strength in the scientific and technological arenas. American technology is widely sought throughout the world—as are European and Japanese technologies—not only by LDCs but also by Russia and China. China is looking to the United States and Japan for economic assistance and to Europe for military hardware. American computer technology is so advanced that it is even sought in Europe. "Whereas, beginning in the latter part of the nineteenth century, control over petroleum resources became essential once naval ships shifted from sail to diesel, so today an independent aerospace and electronics industry, along

---

[12] See Robert E. Osgood, *The Weary and the Wary* (Baltimore: Johns Hopkins University Press, 1972), and Kunio Muraoka, *Japanese Security and the United States* (Adelphi Paper 95; London: International Institute for Strategic Studies, 1973); and Maratako Kosaka, *Options for Japan's Foreign Policy* (Adelphi Paper 97; London: International Institute for Strategic Studies, 1973).

[13] *The New York Times*, September 9, 1979.

[14] *The New York Times*, October 20, 1979.

with the supporting sciences, has become crucial for a nation to enjoy diplomatic and military freedom of action."[15]

(Second, the importance of agriculture is often underrated.) A country like England, which neglected agriculture while it industrialized, has confronted the possibility of starvation during wars in this century. Germany almost succeeded twice in blockading the British isles during the world wars. Today the LDCs, in their eagerness to modernize—by which they mean industrialize—have tended to neglect agriculture, with devastating results for their rapidly growing populations: widespread malnutrition and occasional starvation. Although most of their populations live on the land, agricultural production is inefficient and unscientific. By contrast, the United States, with only 5 percent of its population employed in agriculture, has become the breadbasket for the world. A balance between the agricultural and industrial sectors of the economy is clearly desirable and, indeed, necessary for economic growth and modernization.

MILITARY STRENGTH

As international politics does resemble a state of potential war, military power has become a recognized standard of measurement. Every new great power in the past proclaimed its appearance by a feat of arms, and the decline of a great power is equally signaled by defeat at arms, or what other states interpret as a defeat.)

(A nation's military power is usually measured by the number of men in uniform and by the number of different weapons that it has. As might be expected, the countries with the largest populations have the largest armed forces, though not necessarily in proportion to their populations) Table 7.6 shows the military strength of the fourteen largest countries and the sizes of their armed forces in 1978. These figures do not include reserves, nor do they tell us much about the training, morale, and discipline of these forces. The American army in Europe, for example, is often reported to be suffering from a lack of discipline, widespread drug use, and racial strife. Israel, with its population of slightly fewer than 4 million, is obviously not in the same league with the countries listed in Table 7.6, yet in twenty-four hours it can mobilize 400,000 soldiers to supplement its permanent army of 164,000, and these forces are highly trained and well led, as four victories in four wars have shown. (Reportedly there have also been several successful air encounters against Russian-piloted planes over Egypt; several MIGs were shot down by the well-trained Israeli pilots in the early 1970s.) Switzerland, with slightly more than 8 million people, can mobilize 625,000 troops in forty-eight hours; Swiss reservists train three weeks each summer. Sweden, with roughly the same population, can mobilize 750,000 troops within seventy-two hours. These countries can

---

15. Robert Gilpin, *France in the Age of the Scientific State* (Princeton: Princeton University Press, 1968), p. 76.

TABLE 7.6

COMPARATIVE MILITARY STRENGTH IN 1978*

Country	Population (in millions)	Size of Armed Force (ten thousand) (to nearest)
China	958	4.4 million
India	653	1.1 million
Soviet Union	261	3.6 million
United States	220	2 million
Indonesia	151	250,000
Brazil	120	270,000
Japan	116	240,000
Bangladesh	84	73,000
Pakistan	80	430,000
Nigeria	70	230,000
Germany (West)	62	490,000
Italy	57	360,000
England	56	310,000
France	54	500,000

*The figures are from The International Institute for Strategic Studies, *The Military Balance, 1979–1980.*

thus almost overnight raise forces as large as the standing armies of Britain, France, or West Germany!

The heavily populated industrial powers are also the nations with the largest nuclear arsenals. The United States and the Soviet Union are, of course, in a class by themselves, for they can wipe each other, as well as any other country, off the face of the earth. It is significant that the first five nuclear states were the five great powers whose status was reflected in permanent U.N. Security Council member-ship. India has since joined this nuclear club. Possible future members include Brazil, Pakistan, and Japan; West Germany has forsworn acquisition of nuclear weapons. China (Communist) and India both have great-power aspirations, and Brazil is said to share them. Pakistan is fearful of India, and Japan could be a great power if it ever decided to play that role again.

The two superpowers are, of course, also producers of huge quantities of conventional arms, as are the Western allies. These nations are the world's largest arms suppliers. Furthermore arms, including nuclear weapons, are becoming con-stantly more destructive and technologically sophisticated. The adjective "conven-tional" hardly does them justice. For one thing, they are becoming ever more accurate, so that opposing forces use war matériel at an ever-faster clip. A war can last only a few days under these conditions; a steady stream of new supplies is needed to continue hostilities. In such circumstances, a superpower's client state cannot be defeated. If defeat appears likely, the allied superpower must send more arms to avert it. As Russia poured in arms for the Arabs in the 1973 Yom Kippur war, the United States poured in even more arms for the Israelis, who were badly mauled in the opening phase of the war. When later Egypt stood on the verge of defeat, Mocow threatened intervention. Indeed, in Korea and Vietnam the United

States did intervene to prevent defeat of its friends and protégés, but American intervention was matched by help from the Soviets and the Chinese. Only countries with no superpower friends can still win wars! "[W]ars between small countries with big friends are likely to be inconclusive and interminable; hence, decisive war in our time has become the privilege of the impotent."[16]

Weapons balances are not easy to calculate.[17] How do we compare an ICBM (with a single warhead) and a MIRV, with multiple warheads; or a missile with a megaton (million-ton) warhead to one with a 200,000-ton warhead but with extreme accuracy? How do we compare bombers having quite different characteristics or compare tanks with antitank guns? It is also difficult to compare divisions of different sizes and compositions. In every war Israel's enemies have had more men, guns, tanks, and fighter planes, but the smaller Israeli forces have consistently outfought their enemies. Better leadership, training, discipline, motivation, and tactics have helped to beat numerically superior forces. In 1940 the stunning German defeat of France was accomplished, not by a much larger German army, as has usually been thought, but by forces of about the same size as those of the Allies. One-hundred thirty-four German divisions beat 135 French, British, Belgian, and Dutch divisions; the numbers of tanks on each side were about the same. The German army won because of its better leadership, its mobility, and its unique tactical combination of tanks and fighter planes (in which the German air force was superior).

In the 1960s a proud American army of half a million men equipped with all the latest equipment that American technology could invent was unable to defeat the Vietcong and the North Vietnamese army. American military leaders thought that they were fighting a miniature World War II and used orthodox military tactics. But the North Vietnamese military leaders were fighting an unorthodox war. It helps to understand the kind of war one is fighting; weapons are not everything, and wars are not all the same.[18] The key ingredients may well be the quality of the officer corps, high morale, strategic doctrine, and tactical adaptability to the nature of the war and conditions of the battlefield.

THE POLITICAL SYSTEM AND LEADERSHIP

It is one thing for nations to "have" power. But how is that power used and for what purposes? These issues must be decided by the political system. What role does the nation decide to play in the world? What are its objectives and the priorities among them? Can its leaders make decisions with reasonable speed, gain popular approval for their policies, and then carry them out with reasonable effectiveness?

---

[16] John G. Stoessinger, *Why Nations Go to War* (New York: St. Martin's, 1974), p. 220.

[17] For the problems involved in comparing weapons systems and defining the meaning of a balance, see Chapter 8.

[18] For further analysis, see Chapter 10.

152   Are their policies appropriate to the circumstances? What methods are used to achieve the nation's various aims, and are they compatible with its values? Is overall foreign policy steady, or does it change from one administration to the next? Are governments stable, or do they fall frequently, to be replaced by new ones (as in Italy and in France before Charles de Gaulle established the Fifth Republic)?

(These questions can be asked about any political system, although we shall not even attempt to deal with all of them here. Often the issue of the effectiveness of different types of governments in dealing with the outside world is presented as an issue between dictatorship, authoritarianism, or totalitarianism, on one hand, and democracy on the other. Frequently the superior effectiveness of dictatorship is assumed. The reasons are obvious: First, decisions can be taken relatively quickly; second, there are no leaks or attempts to head off or dilute that policy while it is being formulated; and third, once the decision has been taken by the top officials, it can be executed immediately—there are no independent parliaments, parties, or interest groups and no free press or organized public opinion to question, criticize, or oppose it. On the other hand, making foreign policy in a democracy is like running an obstacle course without any certainty of reaching the end. The policy process is usually slow, and the result usually embodies a compromise among many conflicting points of view, which may weaken its effectiveness in alleviating the problem at which it is aimed. And, given ultimate dependence on public opinion and support, a democratic foreign policy may—as George Kennan has pointed out—be either too little or too much for the issues the nation confronts.)

But are totalitarian governments in fact more effective in making policy on issues of war and peace? Not necessarily. Neither Hitler nor Mussolini nor the Japanese militarists who were responsible for World War II succeeded; their regimes were all defeated. This point raises a fundamental question about the wisdom of their policies: They started a war they could not win. Miscalculation, admittedly, is not a vice peculiar to undemocratic regimes; democratic governments miscalculate as well, but, perhaps, in systems in which policy is debated and criticism must be answered the substance of policy may more often be wiser and more balanced. Dictatorships may have the advantage of being able to make more rapid decisions and to seize the initiative, but this freedom is no guarantee that they will give sufficient consideration to their moves. Democracies appear to be a bit slow because often so many decision makers are involved and all interested parties have the right to be heard; it takes time to win legislative and public approval. Undemocratic states can act more quickly because relatively few policy makers are involved, and they need no one's approval except their own.

Actually, the dichotomy between democracy and totalitarianism on such issues is probably exaggerated. Obviously, both types of governments have at times acted successfully, at other times with folly. Even undemocratic regimes, unrestrained by democratic politics, can act slowly and hesitantly, and democratic governments can on occasion act speedily with the full support of public opinion. It may be fair to say that the former can usually move more decisively and exploit unexpected opportunities more freely than democracies, but not always. It took the Soviet government eighteen months to reply to President Johnson's invitation to start the strategic-arms limitation talks; presumably conflicting views in the Soviet bureaucracy, behind the facade of totalitarian unity, took that long to resolve. It took the American government eighteen months to reevaluate the World War II policy of cooperation with Moscow; only gradually did the latter's actions lead Washington and the nation to debate American policy toward the Soviet Union and to initiate the policy of containment. A sudden switch of policy—as when in 1939 the Soviets shifted overnight from alliance with France against Nazi Germany to alliance with Germany against France—is probably impossible for a democracy. Yet the Truman Doctrine in support of Greece and Turkey, as well as the Marshall Plan for the economic recovery of Europe, took only fifteen weeks to decide in 1946–1947. The decision to demand the withdrawal of Soviet missiles from Cuba in 1962 took less than a week; the entire crisis lasted only thirteen days!

Whatever the differences in effectiveness between democracies and totalitarian regimes, there are also differences among democratic governments. American political scientists after 1945 worried that, as the United States became a world power, the constitutional separation of powers would make it very difficult to conduct a coherent, responsible, and steady foreign policy. Quarrels between the president and Congress, lack of party loyalty, and the influence of pressure groups exploiting this political fragmentation were expected to result in a paralysis of policy or at best slow decision making, a change of policies with every administration, and constant pressure reflecting electioneering and the disproportionate influence of all types of interests seeking to impose their narrow demands. The British parliamentary system, with its unity of executive and legislative branch and its strong party discipline, appeared more likely to meet the requirements of the Cold War. But the structure of the American government could not be transformed. Friction between president and Congress has frequently occurred, especially in the years since the Vietnam war. Often the United States has spoken to the world with (at least) two voices. Executive policies have been weakened, undermined, or rejected by the Congress, especially the Senate, and interest-group pressures, especially from ethnic groups (Jewish, Greek, black, and so on), have been effective in constraining the president's freedom in negotiations and the conduct of foreign policy. Conflicts over priorities (for example, human rights versus arms control, détente with Russia versus opposition to Russia in Africa) have often remained unresolved because administrations could not make up their minds exactly what to do.

What is the overall record of recent American foreign policy, and is it primarily owing to the constitutional organization of the government? To be sure, there have been some first-class errors: the thirty years of nonrecognition of mainland China, the costly war in Vietnam, and frequent support of right-wing authoritarian regimes abroad. But American policy has also helped to preserve the general peace for almost forty years; has protected the security and democratic values of western Europe and North America, while their material standards of living rose to new heights; and has bought the time for at least three right-wing regimes (in Portugal, Spain, and Greece) to make the transition to democracy. Enemies of the United States have sought to emulate its productivity and have relied on its grain to feed their own peoples and on its technology to improve their factories; at the same time

154   the third world has turned to the United States for economic aid, technology, and cooperation in their own modernization. The United States has even protected communist states—Yugoslavia initially and China later. The American role has expanded from containment of Russian communism and preservation of Western security and democracy to the additional task of protecting communism from Russia. In Yugoslavia, China, and western Europe the Communist parties have become increasingly independent of Moscow's control.

Judgments about a nation's foreign-policy record are necessarily subjective, but it is probably safe to say that American policy has generally been steadfast, that decisions have been made with sufficient speed when necessary, and that they have been sufficiently flexible to fit changing circumstances, with a few major and costly exceptions. These characteristics, desirable for the conduct of any nation's foreign policy, might have been more completely realized under a parliamentary system— but perhaps not. Britain's record in postwar foreign policy has hardly been outstanding; rather, it has been characterized by indecision, procrastination, and mistaken choices (its slowness to join the European community and its maintenance of an "independent" nuclear force).[19]

By contrast, the Soviet Union built unprecedented military power and attained global status. But, as it entered the 1980s, its policies had driven virtually all the world's great powers together—the United States, Europe, China, and Japan—in an anti-Soviet alliance. Russian industry has lagged technologically, and its agriculture remains troublesome. After six decades of communism, Russia's principal achievement has been the relatively efficient and massive production of arms. The proletariat and peasantry in whose name the revolution had been made remained without political or civil rights or the higher standard of living they had been promised for so long.

It may appear that the differences in decision making, continuity of policy, and flexibility between totalitarian and democratic regimes, as well as among the latter, are not very great. Furthermore, the wisdom of policy or lack of it can surely be attributed as much to the intelligence, ability, and drive of specific national leaders as to governmental structure and processes. We need only mention the names of some twentieth-century leaders whose special qualities have shaped history: Lenin, Stalin, Hitler, Woodrow Wilson, Franklin D. Roosevelt, Churchill, and de Gaulle. Others, perhaps not quite of the same stature, are Truman and Kennedy, who did not have sufficient time to demonstrate great leadership. These men had impact because they could articulate their nation's purposes, make significant domestic- and foreign-policy decisions—sometimes changing drastically their nations' directions—pursue their goals with vigor and flair, mobilize support for their courses of action at home, and even inspire their peoples to sacrifice and discipline. Some of these men reshaped history. How can we compare the current

---

[19.] Waltz, *Foreign Policy and Democratic Politics* (Boston: Little, Brown, 1967). Also see William Wallace, *The Foreign Policy Process in Britain*, p. 275. Wallace concludes that if "government is the exercise of choice over strategic decisions, then the record of British foreign policy since the war must be adjudged a poor one. At times, the process of government has seemed to be dedicated to the avoidance of choice."

aging and stodgy leaders of Russia with Lenin or even Stalin? Contemporary leaders in the West seem colorless compared to such giants of yesteryear as Roosevelt, Churchill, and de Gaulle. Yet the perceived need of societies for leadership remains. In the United States in 1979 and 1980 the challenge to President Carter's hopes for renomination as the Democratic presidential candidate by two other leading figures in his own party occurred precisely because of the sense that Carter was not a leader, that he was floundering at home and abroad, and that the Democrats would be defeated in the 1980 Presidential election without a more charismatic figure heading the ticket. All nations, democratic and otherwise, require leadership.

Still, the nature of the political system must be kept in perspective, regardless of who its leaders are at the moment. We noted earlier that, at the end of the Napoleonic wars, France was not heavily punished, despite twenty-five years of destruction all over Europe. Instead, France was welcomed back as a great European power and expected to play a role in preserving this system; this surprising lack of vengeance meant that France accepted the system and its responsibility to help maintain it. At the end of World War I, the attitude toward Germany was quite different. After four years of enormous bloodletting and destruction, the allies were in a vengeful mood. They tried to put Kaiser Wihelm and some military leaders on trial for war crimes and imposed on Germany punitive measures like astronomical reparations and limits to the size and character of German armed forces. It is easy to understand this mood and the hatred for the Germans, with their love of militarism, aggressive attitude, and strutting; the desire to make them pay for the devastation they had caused seemed natural, and it was supposed to "teach them a lesson."

Unlike the earlier Napoleonic wars, World War I was a war among states in which the people played active roles; instead of being passive subjects, they were citizens of nations. The length of the war and the endless killing aroused intense passions of patriotism and desires to punish the enemy. The war became a crusade against evil. These moods were reflected in the Versailles peace treaty. Germany was not reaccepted into the European state system; it was not to be allowed to become a menace to its neighbors again as it had been in 1862, 1866, 1870, and 1914. The result, even before the rise of Hitler, was that Germany wanted to overthrow the Versailles settlement. Hitler was later able to mobilize German nationalism to help him gain power, by arousing German pride and patriotism against the treaty and for his regime. Had France and Britain not been democracies, their leaders might have been able to draw up a peace treaty less spiteful, less insulting, and less harmful to the Germans; they might have been able to arrange a settlement acceptable to all parties and allowed Germany to take its place in the European system again. Perhaps another war could then have been avoided because Germany would have been a member of the system with a vested interest in its preservation, instead of an outcast seeking its destruction. But the days of monarchical rule were over. The age of democracy—and punitive crusades—had dawned.

A more contemporary example can be cited in the Middle East, and perhaps all we can do is ask questions. Would President Anwar Sadat, surely a leader in his own right, have been able to hold out the hand of peace and accept

156 the legitimacy of Israel's existence had Egypt been a democracy? Despite popular yearnings for peace, would there not have been opposition party leaders, possibly men in Sadat's own party, newspapers, and other segments of Egyptian society who would have opposed his moves, perhaps successfully? If Israel, on the other hand, were an authoritarian state, as Egypt in fact is, would it not be easier for an Israeli leader to make greater concessions on the West Bank and Gaza Strip in order to resolve the Palestinian problem, which is the key to a comprehensive peace for that area of the world? For, quite apart from genuine Israeli fears of a Palestinian state governed by the PLO, how can a government composed of a coalition of parties, many of whose supporters deeply believe that the West Bank rightfully belongs to Israel by Biblical inheritance and who wish to settle on the West Bank, give it up? How can they work out security arrangements that would enable Israel and a Palestinian state to live without constant fear of each other? These questions, like the earlier example, are not meant to suggest that democracies are obstacles to peace—probably because of their nature, they find it harder to go to war than do undemocratic states—but only to suggest that differences in political regimes do matter and that some institutional arrangements are probably more effective than others in permitting policy making and execution.

NATIONAL MORALE

(National morale is such an elusive concept that it is easier to illustrate than to analyze. It can perhaps best be defined as popular dedication to the nation and support for its policies, even when that support involves sacrifice) Examples abound, and most of them have occurred in wartime, when identification with one's country is intense. The government cannot do without mass support even in undemocratic states, and public acceptance of military service, separation of families, and possible death measures a people's commitment to the nation. Indeed, whether or not morale in democracies is higher, more intense, or longer lasting is debatable. The German armies fought very well in two wars, despite the Allied blockade of World War I and the heavy bombing of World War II; widespread support for Germany's government lasted until near the end in each instance. Japanese soldiers demonstrated a tenacious fanaticism during World War II, which led them to fight hard for every inch of territory, to sacrifice their own lives freely in the process, and to impose heavy casualties on American marines.

Examples since 1945 are numerous; we shall mention only two. The Chinese Nationalist armies after World War II were all too often led by incompetent officers, who treated their men as animals, stole their pay, even sold their American equipment to the Chinese communists whom they were supposedly fighting, avoided battles, and retreated whenever possible. Discipline and morale were obviously low, and the armies' looting and raping hardly endeared the regime to its people. Similarly, the South Vietnamese army, with the exception of some élite units, fought poorly when it fought at all. The reasons included poor pay, no recreational leaves (one reason for the high desertion rate), knowledge that the rich could buy their sons' way out of military service, limiting of officers' commissions to the well-to-do and the educated, a government that seemed to care little for the poor or for ending social abuses.

Bombing, which is frequently favored as a way of beating an enemy into submission, appears to be a positive factor in preserving and even raising morale. Before World War II, it was widely believed that bombing cities would not only destroy the war industries supporting the front-line soldiers but would also break civilian morale. Civilians were not expected to be as tough as soldiers. The Battle of Britain after the German defeat of France proved otherwise. The German bombing of Britain, whose prime minister by then was the eloquent Winston Churchill, probably did more to raise British morale than any other single factor. The American bombing of North Vietnam probably helped to maintain support for the Hanoi government. North Vietnamese General Giap, the mastermind behind his nation's strategy, predicted victory against the United States because he believed that democracies lose patience in long, drawn-out wars and will finally quit. The war did, as Giap had forecast, cause immense domestic turmoil in the United States, which in the end had no choice but to disengage from the conflict.

It is difficult to make definitive statements about American morale. The two world wars were fought far away, and there was no physical damage to this country through invasion or sustained bombing. The loss of American life was very small compared to that of the other combatants. Standards of living were maintained at a fairly high level at home. Sacrifices were minimal and lasted for just over a year in one instance and a bit over three and a half years in the other—compared to four years for Britain and France in World War I and six years for Britain in World War II. The Vietnamese war, because it was considered a "limited war"— in response presumably to a limited threat—was never popularly perceived as a major threat to American security, and life went on pretty much as usual here. There was little willingness to sacrifice butter for guns, as in the world wars. The draft of college students was resented, and there was quite a bit of resistance to it; many youths emigrated to Canada and elsewhere. Perhaps it was the nature of that particular war only; there is still no record of how the national morale will hold up when sacrifice is demanded in a real crisis. The peacetime domestic "gas crisis" of the 1970s has not shown that Americans like to do with less. The overall twentieth-century evidence remains fragmentary and ambiguous. American society has not really yet been tested.

What seem to be critical components in upholding national morale are patriotic feelings that can be rallied when the nation is attacked or insulted, even when the government may not be particularly popular (as in Russia during World War II), and a belief that the government places the nation's welfare first and pursues policies compatible with the nation's historic role. Many patriotic Americans felt that Presidents Johnson and Nixon were betraying the American heritage by fighting on the side of an authoritarian South Vietnamese regime against a North Vietnamese regime that, though communist, was nationalistic and committed to unifying Vietnam.

158   In this context, two categories of problems should be mentioned. One is the Soviet-dominated states of eastern Europe. In any war with NATO, could Moscow really count on the Polish or Czech armies? The other is the deep internal divisions of many nations, rent by quarrels among ethnic, tribal, racial, or religious groups who do not see each other as "fellow countrymen" but only as enemies and rivals, even as pctential persecutors if once in power. In the early phase of the Germany invasion of Russia in World War II, many Russians, especially the Ukrainians, rallied to the German side until Hitler's secret police, the Gestapo, began large-scale massacres of the population. This killing drove all Russians to unite behind Stalin, who became during the war a symbol of traditional Russian nationalism. Russia remains a country composed of many nationality groups, many of whom detest their subordination to the Great Russians. In the postwar world, especially among the LDCs, this phenomenon of strong ethnic loyalties in competition with national loyalties has been remarkably widespread. It is even present in such Western nations as Canada, Belgium, England, and Spain.

POWER CALCULATIONS AND WAR

Even this brief discussion of a few of the components of power should suggest some of the difficulties in calculating power and its exact distribution. Not only are there many components, so that the calculation requires addition of tangible and intangible factors, but these various components also change over time, sometimes rather rapidly. The balance is rarely static. Weapons technology, as we shall see repeatedly, changes quickly, and the nuclear balance between the United States and the Soviet Union is continually having to be recalculated. Furthermore, policy makers are not concerned only about the current balance; they have to think about future relation and foreign-policy needs, which means they have to project their calculations ahead for five, perhaps even ten, years. A weapon, for example, is not invented, produced, and deployed overnight; it takes years in the planning, testing, and manufacturing. Men must also be trained to service and use it. Whether or not a particular weapon is required, what kind, for what purposes, and how many cannot be decided without some notion of the possible strength of potential adversaries.

        Such calculations have influenced decisions to go to war in two ways. The power of the adversary has either been underestimated or overestimated. The result is that, on one hand, the state that has underestimated its opponent's power may be emboldened to make reckless decisions leading to war. On the other, the state that has overestimated its opponent's power may become so fearful or cautious that it makes unnecessary concessions, weakening its own position and giving its adversary an incentive to push again—or, in order to avoid later disaster, it may strike preventively before the enemy has grown too strong.

        Examples are unfortunately plentiful. Hitler, believing that Russia would collapse quickly and confident of German power, invaded Russia before he had eliminated England, thus creating a two-front situation for Germany. Then, after Japan had attacked Pearl Harbor, the Nazi dictator declared war on the United States as well. He had contempt for the United States, a racially mixed society.

In Korea the United States advanced northward to China's frontier, despite Chinese warnings that it would not tolerate American troops on its frontier. General MacArthur disregarded these warnings because he had a rather low opinion of the Chinese forces.

In Vietnam a few years later the Joint Chiefs of Staff failed President Johnson badly when they predicted that 200,000 men could win that conflict in a reasonable amount of time—about two years. But few Americans rated North Vietnam highly. Presidential candidate Nixon expressed a widely shared view when he called the communist state a fourth-rate power. Who, before 1965 and the large-scale American military intervention in South Vietnam, would have doubted that it was but a matter of weeks, at most months, before the world's greatest military power would clobber North Vietnam, one of the world's smallest powers, a "half-country" with less than 10 percent of the American population and virtually no industry—"a bunch of peasants"? Yet those peasants fought one of the finest and best-equipped American armies of all time to a stalemate.

Quite the contrary occurred just before World War II. The French and the British, remembering German military prowess in World War I and impressed by Hitler's aggressive speeches and bold international moves, consistently exaggerated German power on land and in the air and were therefore never sure that they could resist him without precipitating war and perhaps being defeated. But, after Hitler had made several advances—in the Rhineland, Austria, the Sudetenland, and the rest of Czechoslovakia—the British finally said that they would defend Poland, against which Hitler also had claims. But the German leader dismissed London's pledge of defense for Poland as mere words; in the crisis over his demands he believed that the British would retreat, as before. But the British leaders meant what what they said. World War II thus began as a result of Hitler's miscalculations, calculations that to him seemed rational in view of past British policy. In a sense, Britain was responsible for Hitler's miscalculation.

Israeli policy makers, too, have consistently overestimated Arab power. Given the history of persecution of Jews and Hitler's more recent policy of extermination, the leaders of the new Jewish state felt highly insecure among hostile neighbors who had tried to strangle Israel at birth. In 1956 and 1967, when these neighbors were forming joint commands, talking of war and of "driving the Jews into the sea," boasting of their imminent victories, and parading their Soviet weapons, Israel struck preemptively. Power seemed to be shifting to its enemies. Why leave them the initiative to strike? Why not hit them before they were completely ready? Overestimating an opponent's power can thus also result in war.

In the final analysis, even if power were easier to calculate accurately, the calculation would still be gross. In this respect, such devices are handy for obtaining a quick initial picture of the power ratios and rankings among states. They can tell us that a nation like Canada, with a population of 24 million, cannot attain more than middle ranking, despite its large territory, modern economy, natural resources

160   (including oil), and productive agriculture. They can tell us that Communist China will not achieve superpower status, despite its enormous population, territory, and potential oil reserves, until it has extensively industrialized.

Such calculations could also have told American policy makers, before the fall of the Shah of Iran in 1979, that their hopes of devolving some of the United States' guardianship role around the world on so-called regional superpowers were unrealistic.[20] The idea of transferring some "policing" duties to third-world states in strategic positions and with populations, wealth, and military potential great enough may have seemed sound as the United States sought to reduce its "global policemanship." Iran was to police the vital Persian Gulf, through which passes most of the West's oil. India as the guardian of the Indian Ocean, as well as other countries like Brazil in Latin America, Nigeria in Africa, and Indonesia in southeast Asia were all potential candidates for similar roles.

The problem was that the calculations of these nations' power potential did not include their general internal weaknesses. Their governments were often unpopular, repressive, corrupt, and authoritarian; they also suffered from lack of national cohesion and massive poverty. These characteristics would seem to disqualify them as leading regional actors, at least for the present. The Shah's overthrow by means of mass demonstrations organized largely by Muslim religious leaders and work stoppages should be a lesson; not even his large, modern armed forces rallied to his cause. The political instability and social conflicts of many new nations are too great to impose this extra burden on them. They may look like regional superpowers, with all their modern weapons, but these warriors stand on the proverbial "feet of clay."

Gross assessment of nations' power is also misleading in another way. Implicit in the "adding up" of the various components of power is the conclusion that, once the total figure is reached, it may be assumed that this much power is available and usable across the board. If state A, for example, is a superpower because of its continental size, population, economic capacity, and military strength, then logically it follows that it can have its way on most issues, except when confronting the other superpowers. But the fact is that A may be able to deter superpower B from an attack on its homeland, be unable to compel small nation C to halt an attempt to take over a country friendly to A, be able to mobilize some states to pass a resolution in the United Nations but unable to win the votes for another resolution, be able successfully to negotiate a tariff reduction with some second-rank allies but fail to prevent one of those allies from pulling its forces out of the integrated military structure of the alliance and so on.

An evaluation of why A is successful in some instances and unsuccessful in others may suggest one of two answers.[21] First, it may be that A did not try hard enough or was not sufficiently skillful. For example, it has been claimed that the United States did not win the war in Vietnam because political restraints were

---

[20.] Henry Bienen, "Little, But Made Mighty," *The New York Times*, January 15, 1979.

[21.] David A. Baldwin, "Power Analysis and World Politics: New Trends Versus Old Tendencies," *World Politics*, January 1979, pp. 163–164.

placed on the military. Had we bombed North Vietnam very hard from the beginning and made the war unbearably painful for the North Vietnamese, they would have had reason to sue for peace. No doubt there are occasions when such explanations of diplomatic failure are correct. But more often they are misleading and prevent our drawing the correct lessons from an experience like the Vietnam war.

A second explanation of why a state may achieve success in one situation and encounter failure in another is that a state may have the right *kind* of power for the former but not for the latter. The variables are the *kind* of power being used or not, the *purposes* for which it is used, and the *situations* in which it is used. These three factors account for the American failure to win in Vietnam or its helplessness to prevent OPEC from raising oil prices and damaging it far more seriously than the loss of South Vietnam ever did. A gross assessment of American power cannot explain such instances.

The difference is between power as a *possession*—involving quantitative measurement of the components of national power—and power as a set of *relations* among states. James Rosenau has put this difference this way:

> . . . for reasons having to do with the structure of language, the concept of "power" does *not* lend itself to comprehension in relational terms. Without undue violation of language, the word "power" cannot be used as a verb. It is rather a noun, highlighting "things" possessed instead of processes of interaction. Nations influence each other; they exercise control over each other; they alter, maintain, subvert, enhance, deter, or otherwise affect each other, but they do not "powerize" each other. Hence, no matter how sensitive analysts may be to the question of how the resources used by one actor serve to modify or preserve the behavior of another, once they cast their assessment in terms of the "power" employed they are led— if not inevitably, then almost invariably—to focus on the resources themselves rather than on the relationship they may or may not underlie.[22]

THE MISSING LINK: INTENTIONS

The second major problem with the traditional type of power analysis is the glaring omission from these calculations of other states' intentions. In a way, this omission is understandable. Intentions are unstable; friendly intentions today may change tomorrow, as leaders' views change or as the leaders themselves change. Capabilities may also vary, but they are not as likely to fluctuate dramatically from one day to the next. The underlying tangible components do not alter overnight; mobilizing them usually takes a few months, if not a year or more. "Playing it safe"—and what else should a state in the international environment do?—thus suggests that keeping up with a potential adversary's capabilities, even to anticipating a buildup

---

[22] James N. Rosenau, "Capabilities and Control in an Interdependent World," *International Security*, Fall 1976, p. 34.

162   in order not to be caught napping, is the safest course. Conversely, it seems wise
to play down intentions as unreliable. The balance of power is capabilities, and
they can be measured to a degree, whereas intentions cannot. The rule is "Never
estimate intentions, only capabilities.")

(In addition, many calculations of capabilities are "worst-case" analyses.
As power calculations are not *that* accurate and leaders cannot be sure of the extent
of an adversary's buildup, rule number two slips in almost unnoticed: "When in
doubt, assume the worst."[23] The potential or actual buildup will then be assumed
to be extensive, and the presumed threat to security will seem all the more grave.
It makes eminent good sense in an anarchical environment, then, to assume the
worst: "Better be safe than sorry.")

In real political life, however, policy makers do make judgments about
intentions. Indeed, so do those whose advice is to ignore intentions, for, implicit
in their concern with capabilities—especially in "worst cases"—is an unspoken
estimate of the adversary's intentions: that they are unfriendly, indeed very unfriendly, and that the buildup had better be matched if not exceeded, in order to
serve as a deterrent. Capability analysis cannot be divorced from some sort of view
of intentions.)

Ironically, despite the quantifiable nature of weapons, calculations may
not tell us much more than that they exist. What does their existence *mean*? That
is a question of intentions. Judgments of an opponent's intentions may, of course,
vary. Its leaders know the reasons for the buildup, but they may prefer to keep them
to themselves: "Keep them guessing." If they do reveal their reasons publicly, the
first state may fear that they are telling only part of the truth or lying outright. Its
own leaders are still left with the task of divining "the truth."

Was the purpose of the enormous Soviet strategic and conventional military
buildup during the late 1960s and throughout the 1970s to catch up with the
United States, behind which it had so long lagged? Was it to achieve parity militarily, as well as psychologically, in order to attain recognition that it is equal to
the United States? Or was it undertaken because Russia needed larger forces than
the United States in order to confront both NATO to the west and China to the
east? Was defense the primary motive for Russia, a country that had repeatedly
been invaded throughout history? Or was the widespread Western impression that
Russia's new arsenal, including its airlift and sealift capabilities, which had been
developed over a decade and at huge cost, is offensive and far larger than anything
required for defense, correct? This power may not be used to attack anybody, but
its very existence must be taken into account in Washington and other capitals.
Its primary effect, then, is political because it is available underpinning for the
Soviet Union's efforts to expand its influence in areas possibly vital to Western
interests. Counting weapons, therefore, is not enough; obviously more important
is what people believe the weapons mean.

(The lesson to be learned from this illustration is that, when a state seeks

---

[23.] Raymond L. Garthoff, "On Estimating and Imputing Intentions," *International Security*,
Winter 1978, pp. 22–32.

to preserve the balance of power with another state, it takes into account both the perceived power of that other state and its intentions, which are presumed to be potentially or actually hostile.) After all, the United States does not increase the numbers of its weapons when Britain, France, or West Germany builds up its military strength; these countries are allies, and their intentions are friendly. A threat to a nation's vital interests is perceived when another nation's intentions are seen as threatening; the other nation's capabilities simply confirm that it can carry out such intentions. The capabilities *per se* are not menacing. If they were, the United States would have been considered a major menace in the interwar years. It was *potentially* the most powerful country in the world, but it was isolationist and clearly had no intention of playing a political rule in the world. Neither Germany nor Japan took much notice of the United States before World War II, and France and Britain knew that they could not count on help from the United States. Similarly, today Japan and western Europe have great potential power, but neither has yet defined its political role and its aims beyond the minimum objective of defense—which is being mainly left to the United States.

Judging intentions is not easy, as the current controversy over the meaning and consequences of the Soviet arms buildup shows. It is easy to make definitive judgments *after* events have supported a particular interpretation. Often there is evidence for each of the alternative interpretations of an adversary's intentions, and there may well be as much evidence for the wrong version as for the correct one. The proponents of each interpretation will see either the same evidence or "facts" and interpret them differently, or they will select different facts from the all too many that are available. Implicit in each interpretation of the recent Soviet military buildup is a specific view of the Soviet Union, of its roles and goals, and especially of whether it is a status-quo or revisionist state and, if the latter, willing to run only minor risks to expand Soviet influence or willing to take bigger risks for high stakes.

Let us take a look at one example that, in retrospect, seems so clear to everyone that, even after four decades, people still wonder how anyone could possibly have misunderstood: the rise of Hitler. In fact, a strong case can be made for Britain's appeasement policy ("Appeasement" was until that time a respectable word, not a word of accusation synonymous with cowardice. It meant satisfying those who had grievances partially in order to avoid otherwise inevitable conflict. Appeasement is in many ways the heart of democratic politics.)

Nations never resort to war lightly, and, after the bloodletting that France and Britain had sustained during World War I, it is not surprising that there were strong antiwar feelings in both countries. Neither could bear such losses again. But there was also a sizable guilt complex about the Versailles peace settlement, which had concluded a war that had brought down four of Europe's mightiest states and left England and France barely standing. The victors who had drawn up the settlement began to feel that they had wronged Germany and therefore that Hitler was a spokesman for legitimate German grievances. For instance, at Versailles the Allies had said that Germany's military limitation was only the first step toward a more general reduction of armaments. But after two wars with Germany—that of 1870 and the 1914–1918 conflict—France was actually more concerned about

164   maintaining its military strength than about disarmament. Hitler could therefore pose as the spokesman of an aggrieved Germany that had, in good faith, "accepted" a large measure of disarmament, whereas its former enemies, despite their avowals, had not. A great power, the equal of France and England, Germany was being treated as a second-class state; all it supposedly asked was to be treated fairly. Hitler's other claims were advanced in the context of the democratic principle of national self-determination, the very basis of the Treaty of Versailles. This principle had not been implemented fully; like other principles, when applied, it clashed with competing principles. National self-determination had been violated in the Rhineland, the Sudetenland, and the Polish Corridor, primarily for security reasons. Hitler could thus invoke a fundamental Western principle against the West in order to undermine the post-World War I settlement.

On what basis could France and England deny him any of these claims? Were equality and national self-determination all right for themselves but not for anyone else? Hitler's claims were recognized as just. Who could really say that he was insincere and that he was using the Versailles principles cynically? Had not the West—as Hitler repeatedly pointed out—violated its own principles? Was not the German leader therefore justified in demanding that the two Western powers correct the inequalities they had written into the peace treaty? No wonder the Western powers felt guilty about Versailles! They had preached one thing and practiced another; they had thus placed the moral validity of the Versailles settlement in jeopardy. France and especially Britain felt that, if war were to erupt, it would be *their* fault for clinging too stubbornly to the territorial settlement defined by Versailles. Hitler's bold speeches could be explained by the vigorous German resentment at the unjust treatment dealt it by France and England.

In other words, Hitler shrewdly disguised his ultimate intention of making Germany the world's dominant power and paralyzed the will of his opponents to act against him. Each challenge confronted them with the question of whether or not they wanted to fight to preserve a morally dubious status quo. After the horrors of World War I, the answer was obvious. Why should a war be fought to defend unjust positions, especially if it could be avoided? If Hitler was a nationalist who only wanted the return of German territory, would not the satisfaction of his demands for national self-determination end his claims and gain his support for the preservation of the European balance of power? The Nazi leader might be a repulsive person, but his personality was not the issue; peace was. He did, of course, also arrest those who opposed him, and he was a militant anti-Semite, sworn to the destruction of world Jewry. What he did within Germany, however, was a German affair; Germany was a sovereign state. Besides, who could really believe that any man would really kill millions of innocent people just because they had been born Jewish? Such monstrosity was simply unbelievable, beyond the imagination of decent people. It was all talk—"politics."

A post-World War II generation that thinks of Hitler as a warmonger has forgotten that, to their predecessors of the 1930s, his character was not so apparent. He could announce German rearmament while pledging Germany's willingness to renounce all offensive weapons or disband its entire military establishment—if only other nations would pledge to do the same. He could denounce a treaty with a neighbor while simultaneously issuing assurances that it was his own fondest hope to sign a nonaggression pact with that same neighbor. He "solemnly" guaranteed other countries' frontiers, promising not to interfere in their internal affairs, and he never tired of declaring that his present claim was the last one he would ever make. Ironically, Hitler became a most effective spokesman for "peace." To his contemporaries, Hitler often appeared to be sincerely and honestly dedicated to resolving all problems that might stand in the way of peace in Europe. His constant refrain was that Germany would never break the peace. The real question is thus not why appeasement was attempted but why it should *not* have been attempted. Only in 1939 did it become clear that Hitler's ambitions were not limited by the principle of national self-determination. Britain then committed itself to Poland's defense, but it was too late.

The dilemma for a great power like Britain in the 1930s is clear, and such dilemmas still occur. If it is assumed too early that a potential adversary's intentions are expansionist when in reality they may not be, policy may create an enemy where otherwise there would have been none. On the other hand, as the revelation of a nation's "real" intentions can come about only over a longer period of time, of watching for emerging patterns over a series of issues, it may be too late to act once it becomes clear that this pattern is expansionist. Remember that, if a state is genuinely revisionist, it is most likely to test its adversary on small issues, none of them too important in themselves to the defender of the status quo, certainly not important enough to risk war over. Quick recognition of another state's intentions is thus difficult. What to do thus remains a problem for the policy maker, who frequently has to make decisions in an environment of uncertainty; the temptation is to wait and see, as Chamberlain, the British Prime Minister in the late 1930s, did. The consequence of a mistaken assessment may, however, be war. Only when it was too late did Chamberlain understand that Hitler's aims were unlimited and that Britain had to oppose them. He then committed Britain to Poland's defense.

Not only did Britain mistake German intentions, but Hitler also made a grave mistake. He did not believe that the British would keep their commitment to Poland. They had not opposed him before, despite occasional threatening noises. So he invaded Poland, expecting Britain to do nothing.

This historical experience has influenced policy makers since that time. The memories of Hitler and "Munich," the symbol of appeasement, have had enormous influence, especially on American leaders after World War II. The lesson appeared crystal clear: Dictators are expansionist; attempts to appease them only whet their appetites for more, instead of satisfying them, and their demands have thus to be opposed from the beginning—if necessary, by force. It was only too easy after 1945 to think of Stalin as a left-wing resurrection of Hitler; of communist Russia as comparable to Nazi Germany, a totalitarian state; of Soviet expansion in eastern Europe and Soviet pressure on Iran and Turkey as emulating Berlin's expansionist course. Such analogies can be very useful; they may immediately highlight what the stakes really are in a conflict. But analogies must be treated with

166   great care, lest they be applied in the wrong circumstances. The contemporary analogy influencing American policy makers is the Vietnam war. "No more Vietnams" is the cry. But is the Vietnam experience at all relevant to most of the challenges that the United States has had to face in the world since 1975? The usefulness of analogies is to help avoid repeating past mistakes; but what if they only lead to new ones?[24]

[24.] Ernest R. May, *"Lessons" of the Past* (New York: Oxford University Press, 1973).

The Strategic Balance and The Role of Coercion

8

BARGAINING AND CONFLICT RESOLUTION

The importance of the balance of power in the state system and the effects of different distributions of power on state behavior should by now be clear. The difficulties involved in calculating power and the dangerous consequences of miscalculating an adversary's capability and neglecting its intentions should also be clear. But, assuming that states act upon correct calculations, (how do they use their power to protect or advance objectives they deem important?) We shall deal with these issues in the next three chapters (the protection of security interests by means of coercion (deterrence and crisis diplomacy), defense of those interests by force (limited war), and the defense of both security and welfare interests by various economic means, particularly economic coercion. We note that, on different types of issues, or as they are sometimes called, "issue-areas" (for example, security and welfare), different actors are involved, and different kinds of power are exercised in different ways for different purposes.)

(The essence of relations among the actors involved however, lies in bargaining. We noted earlier that, when force is used between states, the outcome on the battlefield usually decides the ratio of power, and the peace treaty reflects which won or lost what and how much. Whether force, the threat of force, or economic pressure ranging from tariffs to resource production and pricing is used, we are talking of diplomacy. We shall use the term "diplomacy" simply to mean negotiations; bargaining is the centerpiece of relations among nations, for it is through

167

168 bargaining that the distribution of the values or goods over which nations differ is decided. The leverage that each nation has in negotiations reflects its power, the ways in which that power is used, and the nation's willingness to use it.)

(Our use of the word "diplomacy" differs somewhat from common usage, which implies officials ("diplomats") seated around a table in rather formal negotiations to arrange some compromise between conflicting positions and thus to avoid more serious conflict. We shall use the term, regardless of who conducts negotiations—indeed, regardless of whether formal negotiations occur or not. Bargaining is going on between states not only when diplomats gather and talk but also when no such formal activity takes place. Much of diplomacy, admittedly, is explicit, but in the next few chapters we shall focus on *tacit negotiations.*[1])

When the United States intervened with its military forces in Vietnam in 1965, it did so in order to avoid the loss of South Vietnam to the North Vietnamese. By destroying enemy forces, or at least by inflicting heavy and sustained casualties on the enemy, the United States hoped to weaken the communist side and to strengthen South Vietnam. Either the North Vietnamese would then finally call off the war, or, if negotiations did occur, the United States and South Vietnam would have more leverage. The fighting itself was thus the bargaining. There was no visible or explicit negotiating: American diplomats did not meet with North Vietnamese diplomats at some neutral spot in Switzerland. Nevertheless, "negotiations" were going on constantly. North Vietnam had already stated its expectation of unifying Vietnam. Any solution short of taking over the South was unacceptable. The United States rejected that solution, intervened massively to prevent it from occurring as the South Vietnamese army failed, and attempted to improve on the battlefield the terms of any final settlement. Actual formal talking is only a minor part of such tacit negotiations, if it occurs at all.

A domestic analogy can be found in a strike. The fact that formal talks have been broken off between labor and industry does not mean that negotiations are not going on. Usually they are. Labor is staying off the job and waiting to see how long industry can hold out against its demands; management, in turn, is waiting to see how long the union's strike fund will last. The two parties are testing each other's power and determination to "win." From time to time, a formal bargaining session may be called, and the old terms may be altered in order to test whether or not either party is ready to accept some form of compromise. If so, the strike will be over; but, if one side hopes that, by waiting longer, it can further weaken the opponent, then the strike will continue. The strike itself is the means of bargaining.

(Whether diplomacy is explicit or tacit, resolution of conflict does not necessarily always take the form of compromise. There are at least four different kinds of conflict resolution: those in which both states lose, in which neither state

---

[1.] The emphasis on tacit bargaining, as distinct from traditional diplomatic negotiations, was introduced by Thomas C. Schelling, *The Strategy of Conflict* (New York: Oxford University Press, 1963); and Schelling, *Arms and Influence* (New Haven: Yale University Press, 1966).

wins, in which one state wins everything, and in which both states are partial winners and partial losers in a compromise agreement.[2])

LOSS BY BOTH STATES

(The first mode of conflict resolution is the essence of strategic deterrence. One side prevents the other from achieving its aim of defeating or eliminating the first by announcing, in effect, "You may kill me if you strike me, but I will kill you before I die." The deterrent is based on the first nation's ability to retaliate even after the enemy's first strike. Mutual deterrence is therefore frequently said to be equivalent to mutual suicide. Indeed the United States calls its capacity to destroy the Soviet Union an "assured destruction" capability. The reciprocal capacity is called "mutual assured destruction," or MAD—probably not a bad name for a strategy in which "everyone loses.")

VICTORY FOR NEITHER STATE

(When neither party can win, the conflict resolution is called a "stalemate." It can occur under a variety of conditions: when both parties have exhausted themselves in struggle, when both are unwilling to invest greater resources in a struggle that is not *that* important, when both are unwilling to escalate because the risks are too great, when a third party (perhaps one or both of the superpowers or the United Nations) intervenes and calls a halt to the conflict, or when new problems and priorities arise.) In the Korean war, the United States, unwilling to risk attacking China and escalating the war, sought instead to exhaust the Chinese through a war of attrition. In Vietnam the American strategy of physical attrition was designed to exact such a heavy price—in bomb damage in North Vietnam and in soldiers killed in battle—that at some point the North Vietnamese would supposedly stop trying to take over South Vietnam and leave it alone. In Korea a stalemate did result, when the battle lines were drawn at about the same place as when the war had started, along the thirty-eighth parallel; in Vietnam, however, American strategy failed. A variation on this strategy occurred in some of the Arab-Israeli wars. Through the United Nations, the superpowers called for cease-fires and placed United Nation forces between the combatants preventing a complete Israeli victory and total Arab defeat and surrender. Although Israel did win territory in 1967, it had to withdraw to behind its frontiers in 1956. In 1973, it lost some land battles and did surrender some of the territory conquered in the Sinai six years earlier.

VICTORY FOR ONE STATE

(Probably the most obvious form of conflict resolution is a clear-cut victory for one side. It occurs when one side is much stronger than the other or the issue no longer

---

[2.] A similar typology may be found in Keith Legg and James Morrison, *Politics and the International System* (New York: Harper & Row, 1971), pp. 69–70, 280–284.

170   seems important enough to cause the other side to take great risks and pay a high price. The Allied victory over Germany, Italy, and Japan in World War II is one illustration; the America victory over Russia in the Cuban missile crisis in 1962 is another. The Soviet interventions to crush the Hungarian rebellion in 1956 and the Czechoslovakian uprisings in 1968 are others, as are the Vietnamese communist defeat of France in 1954 and of the United States two decades later.

COMPROMISE

Conflict resolution through compromise is probably the most common. Both states win part of what they want and give up part of what they want. The two sides may "split the difference," or one side may gain more than the other. The settlement is likely to reflect the perceived power relationship of the two states; their respective willingness to run risks and make sacrifices; or the importance each attaches to the issue in dispute. A compromise may be easier to achieve among allies or states friendly to one another than among adversaries; a higher degree of mutual trust may be the critical ingredient.

The search for compromise, especially among adversaries, may be promoted by the use of force (like the Egyptian-Syrian attack on Israel in 1973), the threat of force (as in the conflict between the United States and the Soviet Union over Berlin in 1948–1949), the offer of rewards (as when the United States offered North Vietnam the withdrawal of American forces, continued communist control of captured South Vietnamese areas, and American economic aid in 1973), or a mixture of the proverbial sticks and carrots (most agreements).

ECONOMIC RESOLUTION

Actually, for economic issues, there is another method of resolving conflict, one that we have not mentioned before: reliance on the free market and the "laws" of supply and demand. If there are plentiful supplies of a resource, greater than the demand, the price will be low; if the supply is tight, the price will be high. The third world, however, complains that such "laws" have benefitted the West and kept its own members poor. The market, these nations insist, is not free or neutral; it is biased in favor of the strong, that is, the Western industrial powers. These laws have become a major source of contention between the first and third worlds, with the latter seeking to change them through political intervention. The goal is a more equitable distribution of wealth. For example, because the Organization of Petroleum Exporting Countries (OPEC) has been an effective cartel, it has managed to raise oil prices far in excess of the original market price of $3 a barrel to over $32 a barrel in the six-year period between late 1973 and December 1980.

THE NUCLEAR REVOLUTION AND THE BALANCE OF POWER

The military component of national power has always been important, for, as E. H. Carr wrote, "war lurks in the background of international politics just as a revolution lurks in the background of domestic politics."[3] Ironically, it is democracy, which was expected to abolish war, that has multiplied the importance of this component many times over. One democratic assumption used to be that only irresponsible rulers are belligerent, that wars are for them merely an enjoyable— and quite profitable—"blood sport." In this view, it is the people who pay the price of wars with their lives and taxes. If peace-loving people can hold their rulers accountable, wars should be eliminated and peace secured. Democracy would then bring an era of good will—of individual freedom and social justice at home, of peace and harmony abroad. The world would be safe for democracy—because it would be democratic. Government by the people, of the people, and for the people would ensure perpetual peace.[4]

Instead, democracy became tied to nationalism, and the two gave birth to the "nation in arms." Once men were freed from feudal bondage and granted the right to some form of self-government, they were thrust into close identification with their nations. They came to equate their own well-being with that of their nations and it seemed only reasonable that the nations should be able to call on them—the citizens—for defense. Not surprisingly, it was the French Revolution, which broke the intermediary bonds of traditional society and brought men into immediate contact with the nation-state and whose leaders revered the norms (if not the forms) of democracy, which led directly to the first system of universal military service. When men's supreme loyalty was to the nation, the "nation in arms" followed logically. Democracy and nationalism thus enabled France to mobilize fully for total war—and to fight a war to destroy its opponents completely.

This change was one reason why the Congress of Vienna reacted with such horror to the revolution, which had unleashed mass passions and all-out war. Previous wars had been restrained because men had identified not with nations but with smaller units, like towns or manors, or with universal ties as embodied in the Church. The armies of the *ancien régime* were composed largely of mercenaries and such lowly elements of society as debtors, vagrants, and criminals—men who were animated neither by love of country nor by hatred of the enemy but who fought because they were paid or compelled to do so. States lacked sufficient economic resources to maintain sizable armies. Indeed, their tactics were determined by the need to limit expenses; the emphasis was on maneuver, rather than on pitched battle, in order to keep casualties low. But the revolution enlisted

---

[3] Edward Hallet Carr, *The Twenty Years Crisis* (London: Macmillan, 1951), p. 109.

[4] See, for example, Immanuel Kant, *Perpetual Peace*, trans. by Carl J. Friedrich in *Inevitable Peace* (Cambridge, Mass.: Harvard University Press, 1948), pp. 251–252.

172　popular support, and mass armies aroused by nationalism began to fight in defense of their countries. "A new era in military history now opened, the era of cannon fodder."[5]

It remained only for the Industrial Revolution to produce the instruments enabling men to kill one another in greater numbers. Modern military technology brought total war to its fullest realization.[6] Mass armies could be equipped with ever more destructive arms, and nations could therefore inflict progressively greater damage on one another in shorter and shorter periods. It took thirty years for the states of Europe to slaughter half the population of central Europe in the seventeenth century. In the second decade of the twentieth century it took only four years for the European nations to bleed one another into a state of exhaustion and, for some, collapse. "Mankind," Winston Churchill wrote after 1918,

> has got into its hands for the first time the tools by which it can unfailingly accomplish its own extermination. . . . Death stands at attention, obedient, expectant, ready, if called on, to pulverise, without hope of repair, what is left of civilization. He awaits only the word of command. He awaits it from a frail, bewildered being, long his victim, now—for one occasion only—his Master.[7]

It was not until the ascendancy of strategic air power and the development of atomic and hydrogen weapons that human beings found the means with which to accomplish their own extermination. Cities—indeed, whole nations—could now be laid waste in a matter of hours, if not minutes. The effectiveness of that kind of strategic air power against a highly urbanized and industrialized society is no longer a matter of dispute. Nuclear bombs have the capacity to impose destruction that would make World War II bombing attacks appear trivial by comparison. The atomic bombs dropped on Hiroshima and Nagasaki (each equivalent to 20 kilotons, or 20,000 tons, of TNT) were within a few years surpassed in destructive power by new weapons produced by both the United States and the Soviet Union. Kilotons were replaced by megatons (1 megaton = 1 million tons of TNT). A single U.S. Strategic Air Command B-52 bomber can carry 25 megatons of explosive power— which represents 12.5 times the entire explosive power of all bombs dropped during World War II, including the two atomic bombs![8]

A nuclear explosion has three effects: blast, thermal, and radiation effects. The blast, or shock wave—the almost solid wall of air pressure produced by an

---

[5] Bertrand de Jouvenel, *On Power*, trans. by J.F. Huntington (Boston: Beacon, 1962), p. 148.

[6] The interrelations between war and industrial power are well treated in John U. Nef, *War and Human Progress* (Cambridge, Mass.: Harvard University Press, 1950); and Richard A. Preston and Sidney F. Wise, *Men in Arms: A History of Warfare and its Interrelationships with Western Society* (rev. ed; New York: Praeger, 1970), pp. 176ff. For the impact of democratization and industralization on American military performance, see Walter Millis, *Arms and Men* (New York: New American Library, 1956).

[7] Winson S. Churchill, *The Second World War, I. The Gathering Storm* (Boston: Houghton Mifflin, 1948), p. 40.

[8] Arthur T. Hadley, *The Nation's Safety and Arms Control* (New York: Viking, 1961), p. 4.

explosion—resulting from a low-altitude bomb exploding in a city will collapse all wooden buildings within six miles of ground zero for a one-megaton bomb, within fourteen miles for a ten-megaton bomb, and within thirty miles for a one-hundred-megaton bomb. For brick buildings, the figures for the same bombs are four, nine, and eighteen miles; and, for sturdier buildings, the distance ranges from three to twelve miles.

(The thermal impact is even more devastating. The heat generated by a one-megaton bomb is tremendous, producing second-degree burns of the skin up to nine miles from ground zero; a ten-megaton bomb has the same effect up to twenty-four miles, a one-hundred-megaton bomb up to seventy miles.[9] Furthermore, the heat would in most instances ignite wooden houses—as in many suburbs—and other combustible objects over about the same range.) World War II demonstrated that the real danger from fire, even when started with ordinary incendiary bombs, is the "fire storm."[10] In a fire storm, the intense heat from the fire rises, heating the air in turn. The pressure differential between the hot and colder air sucks in fresh oxygen to feed the hungry flames, and the process builds in intensity. Air rushes in at ever greater speeds until wind velocity surpasses gale force. The flames, whipped by the wind and fed further by the gas, oil, and other incendiary materials of the homes and streets of the burning city, leap upward, stabbing high into the air, enveloping the stricken area. Everything burns in this tomb of heat and flame. There is no escape. Those who have not yet been crushed in their shelters are asphyxiated by lack of oxygen or by carbon monoxide poisoning; if they seek to escape into the burning streets, their lungs are seared, and their bodies, exposed to the intense heat, burst into flame. During the attack on Hamburg, the fire storm caused a ground temperature of 1,400 degrees F. Indeed, near the center of the fire storm the temperature exceeded 2,200 degrees F. A 100-megaton bomb could cause fire storms up to seventy-five miles from the point of explosion; woods, trash, and dry leaves all provide kindling.

(The third effect of a nuclear explosion, the radiation impact, can be maximized by a ground burst or low-altitude explosion. The resulting fireball—a large, rapidly expanding sphere of hot gases that produces intense heat—scoops up the debris and converts it into radioactive material. The fireball of a ten-megaton bomb has a diameter of six miles. The heavier particles of debris fall back to earth within the first few hours. The lighter particles "fall out" during the following days over an area the size of which depends on the magnitude of the explosion, the

---

[9.] Ralph E. Lapp, *Kill and Overkill* (New York: Basic Books, 1962), p. 37; and Scientists' Committee for Radiation Information, "Effects of Nuclear Explosives," in Seymour Melman, ed., *No Place to Hide* (New York: Grove Press, 1962), pp. 98–107.

[10.] A vivid account of a fire storm is given in Martin Caidin, *The Night Hamburg Died* (New York: Ballantine, 1960), pp. 80–105, 129–141. The German estimate of those killed in Hamburg was 60,000. The American B-29 attack on Tokyo on March 9–10, 1945, burned up 16 square miles and killed 84,000 people, most of whom were burned to death or died from wounds caused by fire. In contrast, the Hiroshima atom bomb killed 72,000 people. The most destructive attack ever, however, was the two-day Anglo-American bombing of Dresden in February 1945, in which 135,000 people were killed. On this attack, see David Irving, *The Destruction of Dresden* (New York: Holt, Rinehart and Winston, 1964).

174   surface over which the explosion occurs, and meteorological conditions.) The American fifteen-megaton thermonuclear explosion of 1954 in the Pacific Ocean caused substantial contamination over an area of 7,000 square miles (equivalent to the size of New Jersey). Under more "favorable" conditions, the fallout could have covered an area of 100,000 square miles (equivalent to the areas of New Jersey, New York, and Pennsylvania).(Such fallout, furthermore, can emit radiation for days, months, even years. The power of this radiation to kill depends on the amount absorbed.[11] A dose of 100 to 200 roentgens causes radiation sickness—a combination of weakness, nausea, and vomiting; it is not fatal, though it can result in disability. At 200 roentgens, radiation becomes very dangerous: Disability is certain, and death can come within a month. The possibility of death increases until, at 500 roentgens, it is certain for 50 percent of those exposed to the radiation. Above 600 roentgens, the number of deaths continues to mount, and deaths occur more rapidly.[12] Radiation also has two other effects: It can cause cancer, and it can cause genetic transmutations that may affect following generations.)

It therefore appears that, in an era of nuclear weapons, the World War II problems of failing to hit a target industry and of damaging only the buildings but not the machinery inside no longer exist. An entire city can now be eliminated with a single bomb. A coordinated nuclear attack on a nation's major urban and industrial centers would be catastrophic, reducing everything to rubble and leaving the population dead or injured, with little hope of help. Most hospitals, doctors, nurses, drugs, and blood plasma would be destroyed; so would the machinery for the processing and refrigeration of food and the purification of water. There would be no transportation left to take survivors out of the smoldering ruins and into the countryside; most, if not all, of the fuel would also have burned. Estimates of those likely to be killed in such a coordinated urban strike range from 30 to 90 percent of the population, depending upon the yield of the bombs, the heights at which they were exploded, weather conditions, civilian protection, and preparations for coping with the aftermath of such an attack.

The psychological impact upon the survivors would be as devastating as the physical destruction. The elimination of a nation's larger cities; the deaths of more than 100 million countrymen, the wrecking of industries, communications, and transportation—all would be bound to undermine the confidence of those who survived. A nation in ruins is not likely to retain its *élan vital* or entertain optimistic expectations for the future. It took Europe, and especially France, more than forty years to recover from the psychological wounds of World War I and the loss of a generation on the battlefields. Recovery after World War II was made possible primarily by extensive infusions of American economic aid, yet European wounds and losses were minor compared with those that would be suffered during a nuclear attack. In the latter instance, the result would be not only the destruction of cities but also the disorganization of all social life.

---

[11] Lapp, *Kill and Overkill*, pp. 53–54.
[12] *Ibid.*, p. 77.

Any society operates through confidence in an orderly succession of events, either natural or social. A catastrophe is an interruption in what has come to be considered natural. The panic it often produces is the reflection of an inability to react to an unexpected situation and attempt to flee as rapidly as possible into a familiar and, therefore, predictable environment. If a familiar environment remains, some confidence can be restored. Most natural catastrophes can be dealt with, because they affect only a very small geographic area or a very small proportion of the population. The remainder of the society can utilize its machinery or cooperative effort to come to the assistance of the stricken area. Indeed, such action tends to reinforce the cohesiveness of a society, because it becomes a symbol of its value and efficiency. The essence of the catastrophe produced by an all-out thermonuclear war, however, is the depth of the dislocation it produces and the consequent impossibility of escaping into familiar relationships. When all relationships, or even most relationships, have to be reconstituted, society as we know it today will have been fundamentally transformed.[13]

Indeed, it may be even worse than Henry Kissinger has suggested. In 1974 it became known that nuclear war can possibly destroy the ozone layer in the stratosphere. This layer protects all living things from ultraviolet solar radiation that destroys protein molecules. In addition to death, destruction, and radiation, therefore, extensive ozone depletion could destroy the food chain of plants and animals upon which humankind depends for survival.

The impact of this awesome power on the conduct of international politics has been revolutionary; it has changed the manner in which military strength can be used either to attain superior power or to maintain a balance and to prevent an adversary from achieving dominance.[14] Before 1945 war was still considered a rational instrument of policy, despite the rapidly increasing costs of modern warfare. States usually preferred these costs to that of submission. Nuclear weapons, however, mean that the very substance of national life is at risk. Rather than helping to preserve civilization, the new instruments of violence threaten to destroy it. What possible goal could be "worth" the cost of self-immolation? How could a nation defend its political independence and territorial integrity if, in the very act of defense, it might well have to sacrifice itself? Nuclear war can know no victors; all the contestants must be losers. Total wars may *thus be suitable when weapons are of limited destructive capacity, but they are incompatible with "absolute weapons."*

The conclusion to be drawn from this general principle is that the main function of strategic military strength in the nuclear age is *deterrence* of all-out attack. The purpose is to protect a nation's security by preventing an attack from occurring, rather than by defending the nation after an attack. The opponent is

---

[13.] Henry A. Kissinger, *Nuclear Weapons and Foreign Policy* (New York: Harper & Row, 1957), p. 79. Also Office of Technology Assessment, *The Effects of Nuclear War* (Montclair, N.J.: Allenheld, Osmun & Co., 1979).

[14.] Glenn H. Snyder, "Balance of Power in the Missile Age," *Journal of International Affairs*, 14 (1960), 21–34.

176   threatened with such massive retaliation that it dare not attack. The assumption is that, faced with the risk of virtual suicide, the enemy will desist. The price of attack would be excessive. Mutual deterrence between two states, each seeking to protect its own security interests, thus becomes a matter of "conflict resolution." "I won't destroy you, if you don't destroy me" is the offer of each side to the other. "We shall both lose if you attack me because I shall always retaliate" is the answer.

In this extraordinary situation military capacity must be great, so that it will *not* have to be used. Its primary value is in its peacetime impact; if war erupts, it will have failed. The decisive test of arms is no longer the vanquishing of the enemy in battle, it is not having to fight at all. Furthermore, deterrence must be perpetual. There can be no margin for error. In previous periods of history, when deterrence failed, war resulted. Because no weapon was so destructive that failure spelled extinction, such mistakes were not irreparable. The critical issue for the military was not whether or not it could prevent the outbreak of hostilities. This is no longer true. The superpowers today, on the one hand, possess overwhelming power and, on the other, are completely vulnerable to attack and destruction. We must logically conclude that modern nuclear warfare would be irrational. Nuclear technology has so vastly augmented the scope of violence and destruction that total war can destroy the very nation that wages it and can do so in a matter of hours, not years.

To sum up: the balancing of power has historically had two purposes: protection of individual states and protection of the state system as a whole. Peace has not been the chief aim. When states have been secure, peace has followed; when states have not been secure, they have gone to war. The philosophy of "peace at any price" has been rejected by states. But nuclear weapons have changed all that; security can no longer be given priority over peace. Security and peace have become virtually identical. The deterrent function of the balance has therefore become supreme; war—a total war—to restore a balance that has been lost, is no longer feasible.

DETERRENCE, THE STATUS QUO, AND RATIONALITY

Bipolarity, as we noted earlier, requires the drawing of clear lines around each superpower's sphere of influence and the preservation of this status quo. Deterrence is based upon the acceptance of the territorial status quo, which, it is assumed, the opponent seeks to change. This acceptance, in turn, is founded upon either a belief in the justice of the general international settlement or, if not in its justice, in the virtue of stability. Deterrence thus could not have worked in the 1930s—and, as we know, it did not, in fact, work.[15] The Versailles peace treaty was widely regarded

15. Evan Luard, "Conciliation and Deterrence: A Comparison of Political Strategies in the Interwar and Postwar Periods," *World Politics*, January 1967, pp. 167–189; Alan Alexandroff and Richard Rosecrance, "Deterrence in 1939," *World Politics*, April 1974, pp. 404–424. Also see Arnold Wolfers, *Britain and France between Two Wars* (New York: Norton, 1966); and John Wheeler-Bennett, *Munich: Prologue to Tragedy* (London: Macmillan, 1948).

as unjust, even by the dominant powers. The result was that they did not enforce it. In the postwar period, however, memories of Adolf Hitler and of the appeasement policy that has been held responsible for World War II tended to reinforce Western determination to defend the status quo. The failure of appeasement was attributed to the insatiable appetites of dictators; feeding them a few choice morsels would merely whet their appetite for more. For those confronting Josef Stalin, it was all too easy to think of him as the Russian Hitler. In more impersonal terms, both men were regarded as leaders of totalitarian regimes the very dynamic of which was "permanent revolution." In the first comparative scholarly analysis of totalitarianism, Sigmund Neumann concluded in 1942 that totalitarian dictatorships were "governments for war. The analysis of their inner structure . . . has proved conclusively that the permanent evolution of perpetual motion is the driving force of totalitarianism. Expansion is of its essence. The rise, development, and survival of modern dictatorships are inextricably tied up with continuous dynamics."[16] Russia's postwar behavior seemed only to confirm this conclusion. Soviet intentions were viewed by the United States as expansionist.

The first requirement of American policy under these circumstances was to hold fast. Changing frontiers was considered appeasement that could only undermine the peace, whereas in the 1930s changing frontiers and appeasement had been expected to build a more solid foundation for peace. Conversely, preserving the territorial status quo had been considered the sure way to war because Germany had legitimate grievances against this status quo. After 1945, the division of Germany, for instance, had not been "just," but both superpowers could live with it. At least it provided for a degree of stability in central Europe. When a challenge to the status quo occurred, the response was to demonstrate firmness, rather than to make concessions. To give in would only make the situation worse.

In this way "all the most important issues in dispute—Berlin, Germany, Formosa, the offshore islands—have remained in dispute even twenty years after the end of the war. There have been no 'betrayals.' But there have been no settlements either."[17] The challenge of the postwar world has often been just learning how to live with problems and how to defuse them in order to avoid nuclear catastrophe. Once asked whether or not he hoped to be remembered for having achieved a settlement of the Berlin problem by the end of his time as secretary of state, Dean Rusk answered that he was not so vain. His ambition was to be remembered in history for having succeeded in passing the Berlin problems he found upon entering office down to his successor intact.[18] But, even without the vivid memories of the 1930s, the bipolarity of the postwar period would have led the United States to fear the loss of "dominoes" and to support the frontiers between the respective spheres of influence. The Soviet fear was equally great. The government in Moscow was constantly concerned about eastern Europe and prepared

---

[16.] Sigmund Neumann, *Permanent Revolution* 2d ed; New York: (Holt, Rinehart, and Winston, 1965), p. 257.

[17.] Luard, *op. cit.*, pp. 174–175.

[18.] Roger Hilsman, *To Move a Nation* (Garden City, N.Y.: Doubleday, 1967), p. 41.

178 to use force to preserve hegemony there. Both superpowers carefully guarded against defections. Force was used mainly to preserve or to restore the status quo, not to transform it. History and the nature of the world after 1945 thus combined to produce a policy of preserving lines and demonstrating firmness. (This capacity to prevent changes in the status quo ought perhaps to be called *negative power*. Its purpose is to prevent expansion and to deny territorial changes.

(A second assumption on which deterrence is based, an assumption independent of political conditions, is that the policy makers on both sides are *rational*—that is, that they can calculate the costs and gains of any moves they contemplate and can keep a situation from getting out of control. In the nuclear era especially, this assumption implies that they can recognize that the gains to be had from destroying the adversary are completely disproportionate to the costs.) "It is sometimes stated," writes Herman Kahn,

> that even an adequate . . . deterrent would not deter an irrational enemy. This might be true if irrationality were an all-or-nothing proposition. Actually, irrationality is a matter of degree, and if the irrationality is sufficiently bizarre, the irrational decision-maker's subordinates are likely to step in. As a result, we should want a safety factor in . . . deterrence systems so large as to impress even the irrational and irresponsible with the degree of their irrationality and therefore the need for caution.[19]

In the 1930s, in contrast, the British were not so sure. On one hand, they thought of Hitler as rational, believing that he would settle down once he had been appeased; on the other hand, they thought of him as irrational—that is, reckless enough to engulf Europe in flames. If the Nazi leader was really such a raving maniac, it seemed the better part of valor to satisfy his demand for national self-determination and to give him his "last territorial demand in Europe." Schelling has compared political leaders who either are or feign to be irrational with some inmates of mental institutions. He has noted that the inmates "are either very crazy or very wise, or both, [because they] make clear to the attendants that they may slit their own veins or light their clothes on fire if they don't have their way"—and so may have their way.[20] When this suicidal technique is used politically, it is intended to suggest that the "fire" will also burn those who are threatened, as when Arab terrorists, for example, hijack and threaten to blow up an airplane unless the pilot does what he is told. Surely this behavior is irrational in the sense that blowing up the plane will kill them too. But, as fanatics, they are credible in their threats.

No American policy maker in the postwar period thought of Stalin or his

---

[19.] Herman Kahn, *Thinking about the Unthinkable* (New York: Horizon, 1962), pp. 111–112; and Schelling, *Arms and Influence*, pp. 229–230. It may be added that by "irrationality" Kahn means more than "craziness" and presumably, therefore, "recklessness"; his definition of the term also includes panic, nervousness, and fear rather than cool-headed calculation, at a moment of crisis.

For a further critical analysis of the themes of "rationality" and deterrence, see Patrick M. Morgan, *Deterrence* (Beverly Hills: Sage, 1977); and John Steinbruner, "Beyond Rational Deterrence: The Struggle for New Concepts," *World Politics*, January 1976, pp. 223–245.

[20.] Schelling, *Arms And Influence*, pp. 37–38; and *Strategy of Conflict*, p. 17.

various successors as irrational. Quite the contrary. George Kennan, in analyzing the sources of Soviet conduct during the period of containment, spoke of the impact on Russian behavior of both communist ideological perception and Russian history:

> The Kremlin is under no ideological compulsion to accomplish its purposes in a hurry. Like the Church, it is dealing in ideological concepts which are of long-term validity, and it can afford to be patient. It has no right to risk the existing achievements of the revolution for the sake of vain baubles of the future. The very teachings of Lenin himself require great caution and flexibility in the pursuit of Communist purposes. Again, these precepts are fortified by the lessons of Russian history: of centuries of obscure battles between nomadic forces over the stretches of a vast unfortified plain. Here caution, circumspection, flexibility and deception are the valuable qualities; and their value finds natural appreciation in the Russian or the oriental mind. Thus the Kremlin has no compunction about retreating in the face of superior force. And being under the compulsion of no timetable, it does not get panicky under the necessity for such retreat. Its main concern is to make sure that it has filled every nook and cranny available to it in the basin of world power. But if it finds unassailable barriers in its path, it accepts these philosophically and accommodates itself to them. The main thing is that there should always be pressure, increasing constant pressure, toward the desired goal. There is no trace of any feeling in Soviet psychology that that goal must be reached at any given time.[21]

Studies of the "operational code of the Politburo" have confirmed this appraisal.[22] The Kremlin leaders did not believe in "adventurism" or "romanticism." They counseled against being "provoked" by the enemy into an untimely or unwise advance and suggested that, with every plan for advance, there must be a provision for retreat. Communist China's foreign-policy behavior has been equally cautious—as distinct from the Peking leaders' verbal militancy.

Conversely the Russians, first by their actions and later by their words, demonstrated that they believed American policy makers to be rational as well. The early years of the Cold War, when the United States held an atomic monopoly, were also the years of pressure in Iran and Turkey, of the Greek civil war, the coup d'état in Czechoslovakia, the use of Communist parties and communist-controlled unions to try to undermine the Marshall Plan, and, of course, North Korean aggression. The last element in particular showed that the Russians did not fear a retaliatory attack on Moscow. Even in 1957–1962, when massive retaliation had become possible for the Soviet Union as well, though Soviet leaders *knew* that American strategic power remained vastly more destructive than their own, they were confident that they could raise tensions *without* provoking the United States to war. As long as tensions were not raised too high, the Soviet leaders felt able to control the risk of war. To ensure that tensions would not go out of control,

---

[21.] George F. Kennan, *American Diplomacy 1900–1950* (Chicago: University of Chicago Press, 1951), p. 118.

[22.] Nathan Leites, *The Operational Code of the Politburo* (New York: McGraw-Hill, 1951); and Leites, *A Study of Bolshevism* (New York: Free Press, 1953), pp. 27–63.

180   they either left themselves diplomatic escape hatches or were willing to make timely withdrawals whenever they underestimated American reactions. The Cuban missile crisis of 1962 attests to the Soviets' confidence that, short of major provocation—from which they carefully abstained—they could challenge the United States without fear of nuclear response. Nikita Khrushchev later distinguished between American "madmen" and "realists" in Washington, the former allegedly believing that communism must be eliminated by military force, the latter committed to coexistence and arms control. It was the latter group that was in power in Washington.

COERCION AND DIPLOMACY

Deterrence equals diplomacy. It is not a military concept. The soldier's primary test has always been on the battlefield, and his primary professional concern has been with weapons and the exercise of violence. Deterrence, if it is to be successful, obviously is based on weapons, but the test is not in the use of force but in the *threat* of force, or in *coercion* to dissuade an adversary from attacking.[23] The purpose is to influence the adversary's intentions. Such manipulation of the threat of violence is one aspect of diplomacy.[24] As already noted, a state's capacity to use nuclear arms to inflict enormous destruction upon an adversary or destroy it if deemed necessary —or to reward it by refraining from such destruction—ensures the capacity to bargain.[25] The promise of not having to suffer immense pain is an offer that B can extend to A even in peacetime, for nuclear weapons no longer make it necessary to defeat A in war first. A knows that it can be immensely hurt; and does not have to engage in war to make this discovery. Indeed, A shares a *common interest* with B in avoiding war. The ability to inflict great damage can thus be exploited diplomatically *before* the eruption of war.[26] Modern technology has enhanced the importance of "threats of war as techniques of influence, not of destruction; of coercion and deterrence, not of conquest and defense; of bargaining and intimidation."[27]

---

[23]. Schelling, *Strategy of Conflict*, pp. 3–10.

[24]. Symptomatic of the fundamental change from the conduct of war to the implementation of deterrence through exploitation of coercion is that virtually all the seminal thinking on military force has been by civilian intellectuals. The student interested in what is usually called national-security affairs does not go to works written by generals and admirals; he or she turns to the civilian experts, mostly academicians. Those political scientists, historians, mathematicians, and physicists have concerned themselves with issues of strategy. As the word "strategy," historically meaning the use of battles to achieve the objectives of war, is now applied more to what Schelling has called "the manipulation of risk," it is to their writings that we turn. By taking the mystery out of a subject that civilians have usually thought only professional soldiers understood, analysts like Bernard Brodie and Henry Kissinger have transformed the interested layman into an expert and permitted him or her to question the soldier's judgment on matters of strategy, force levels, and weapons.

[25]. Schelling, *Arms and Influence*, pp. 1–34.

[26]. *Ibid.*, p. 22.

[27]. *Ibid.*, p. 33.

But how does B persuade A not to attack when A can threaten B in the same manner? Surely B's attempt at intimidation is less believable or credible; A knows that if B resorts to war it risks suicide. It is one thing to try to influence an opponent not to resort to violence but quite another to make the opponent believe that war will result, considering the price of such war. More bluntly, how can the opponent be made to believe that a threat is *credible?* (The principal answer: by means of a *credible commitment*[28] But how? (The answer has two parts. Credibility is, first, a product of the nation's interests.) Clearly a nuclear power is most likely to go to war and to risk enormous losses if its home territory is attacked; it is also more likely to take this risk if its more important allies are attacked than it is when lesser allies or friends in areas of secondary importance are attacked. The potential attacker will understand this set of priorities, as historical experience confirms. Moscow's leaders can have little doubt that an attack upon the United States will lead to a retaliatory strike. From time to time there may be some question in the Kremlin whether or not the United States will come to the defense of its North Atlantic Treaty Organization (NATO) allies in Europe, but the precedent of two interventions in two world wars suggests that the United States does take its NATO obligations seriously and that a Soviet attack upon western Europe would be extremely risky. In non-Western areas, however, American commitments may be perceived as less credible, and limited probes may be made to test such commitments. (Credibility is therefore largely the reflection of a nation's interests and the priorities among those interests.) Not all areas or countries are of equal value in this sense. Nations may have great power, but none is omnipotent. Each has only so much power with which to achieve many different aims. This limitation is reminiscent of the old saw about having "champagne taste on a beer income." Choices must be made and priorities arranged.

(Second, credibility can be achieved by means of certain techniques. They are intended to reinforce the adversary's perception of the nation's interests and their intensity, thus strengthening the deterrent. A number of different techniques —like *staking one's reputation* and making *automatic commitments*—may be used to communicate this credibility to an opponent. The former technique consists of making a commitment that involves a nation's honor and prestige, its bargaining reputation, and the confidence of its own public and allies. Once having made a threat involving these values in public, it will be difficult not to carry it out. Staking a reputation is particularly important when a nation is involved in both continuous and intersecting negotiations. In continuous negotiation any issue will probably be in negotiation with the same country over a long period of time; in intersecting negotiation issues will be negotiated with several counties simultaneously. In both instances, staking a reputation is intended to persuade the adversary:) "If I make a concession, it will lower my bargaining reputation with you (or other countries), and you (or they) will expect me to concede in future negotiations. Therefore, even if I would like to satisfy you, I cannot retreat." In the repeated Berlin crises during the Cold War, the United States has always believed its reputation to be at stake;

[28.] *Ibid.*, pp. 43–55; and Schelling, *Strategy of Conflict*, pp. 21–28.

182 if it withdrew from West Berlin the Russians would, in the American view, demand further concessions, and the NATO allies would be discouraged and demoralized.

(Staking one's reputation, then, is a commitment from which there can be no retreat; it is too costly not to honor such a commitment. An automatic commitment, on the other hand, is one from which it is physically impossible to retreat.) This kind of commitment has been likened to "burning one's bridges." An opponent may not find the commitment credible if it can be withdrawn. But, if there is no bridge across which to retreat and no choice but to fight, the adversary may find the commitment credible. There is a story that before World War I, during staff talks between the British and the French military, a French officer was asked by a British colleague how many British soldiers would be needed in France. The Frenchman replied that he needed only one. This soldier would then be placed so that on the first day of a war with Germany he would be killed, thus ensuring Britain's entry into the war. One of the purposes of stationing an American army in post-World War II Europe has been to serve this "tripwire" function; loss of American lives in a Red Army attack would leave this country no choice but to fight. The forewarned enemy will thus presumably be deterred. The ultimate but imaginary automatic commitment is Kahn's fantastic "doomsday machine," which would blow up the whole world if the enemy fired its nuclear weapons—even if the defender were caught by surprise. In contrast, we need only note that the Korean war erupted after the United States had withdrawn its forces without leaving a specific commitment to defense. Indeed, the officially announced American defense perimeter excluded the Korean peninsula[29] The main point remains: The "power to bind oneself" is the crucial factor in any bargaining situation.

(Two other important points should be underscored with respect to bargaining by means of credible commitments. First, these and other tactics are intended to support commitments that presumably leave the defender no choice as to a course of action should the opponent move despite the warnings and threats. The deterrer *relinquishes the initiative*; it has made known that it will stand firm, regardless of costs, and the responsibility for the next move and the responsibility therefore for precipitating a conflict rest with the other side. The deterrer's "initiative that forces the opponent to initiate" thus becomes the crucial coercive instrument. But in real political life irrevocable commitments are rare, for states seldom deliberately take inflexible stands from which they cannot retreat if their adversaries stand firm and hostilities appear to be both imminent and undesirable. Threats are usually more ambiguous and commitments somewhat looser. Irrevocable commitments may indeed place the choice of war or peace on the adversary, but they also mean surrender of the defender's control over events. A mixture of firmness and flexibility is therefore a more normal pattern of interaction.[30])

(The second point is that the concept of balance of power would be more

---

[29] John W. Spanier, *The Truman–MacArthur Controversy and the Korean War* (rev. ed.; (New York: Norton, 1965), pp. 16–21.

[30] See particularly the two chapters entitled "Resolve and Prudence" and "Freedom of Choice" in Oran R. Young, *The Politics of Force: Bargaining during International Crises* (Princeton: Princeton University Press, 1968), pp. 177–265.

useful analytically if it were subdivided into a *balance of resolve* and a *balance of capability*.[31] For bargaining purposes, the deterrer's requirements are threefold: possession of military capability, willingness to use it, and evaluation of both by the potential attacker. Power, however massive, is ineffective without the disposition to use it, and, even when these first two factors are present, deterrence will still fail unless the adversary perceives their presence.

$$\text{deterrence} = \text{capability} \times \text{perceived resolve}$$

Why, we asked earlier, did World War II erupt? We saw that the answer revolved around Britain's policy of appeasement. The German–Allied military balance was not as lopsided throughout the late 1930s as the swift German victory in the spring of 1940 suggests.[32] What was more significant was the balance of resolve. Even after Britain had publicly pledged assistance to Poland in the event of a German attack, Hitler continued to perceive a lack of British determination. After years of appeasement, this perception was not surprising. Perhaps it is more surprising that British leaders thought the Nazi leader would see their commitment as credible. In the deterrent equation, if either capability or political will is low (or perceived as low), ability to deter declines.

The intangible element of resolve is particularly difficult to evaluate. Each power's perception of the other's resolve is likely to fluctuate with time and specific occurrences. Khrushchev's image of American determination was apparently sufficiently lowered by John Kennedy's early policies—acceptance of a neutralist coalition, including communists, in Laos; failure to support with American forces the abortive Bay of Pigs landing by anti-Castro Cuban refugees in 1961; inaction at the time of the building of the Berlin Wall—so that he was tempted in 1962 to establish a missile base close to American shores, despite the Monroe Doctrine and Kennedy's own warning against establishment by another power of a base in the Western Hemisphere.[33] After 1962 American resolve was once again clearly established.

The danger is that, if A acts—or does not act—consistently with B's image of the way A should act, B may push, expecting A to retreat. A may do so, and its resolve may then decline further. But, if at some point A vows to stand firm instead of retreating but fails to make that vow credible to B, war will erupt because of miscalculation. The balance of resolve may therefore be unstable in two respects: first, inclination by one side to retreat and, second, a propensity to produce hostilities when one side fails to communicate its genuine resolve to the opponent.

---

[31] Glenn H. Snyder, "Crisis Bargaining," in Charles F. Hermann, ed., *International Crises* (New York: Free Press, 1972), p. 232.

[32] This point is well documented by Newman, *Balance of Power in the Interwar Years, 1919–1939* (New York: Random House, 1967), pp. 112–122, 131–146.

[33] Elie Abel, *The Missile Crisis* (New York: Bantam, 1966), pp. 24–26, 28; and Young, *op. cit.*, pp. 79–80, 87. Khrushchev's explanation in his "memoirs" emphasizes only his desire to defend Cuba from an alleged American invasion. For an evaluation of this motivation, see Arnold Horelick, "The Cuban Missile Crisis: An Analysis of Soviet Calculations and Behavior," *World Politics*, April 1964, pp. 365–369.

184   It is not surprising, therefore, that both nuclear giants have been continuously concerned about the credibility of their commitments and have tended to see their commitments as interdependent.[34] For it follows that, if a specific commitment to preserve a particular line, or "frontier," is no longer credible, regardless of how distant or unimportant that line may seem, B may then come to believe that other commitments made by A are also no longer credible, which may tempt B to seek further expansion of its own power. It is, of course, true—as critics of the disastrous American commitment in Vietnam have repeatedly stressed—that a nation's interests and commitments are not all equally important and that they are scaled hierarchically according to criteria of security. A country's defaulting on some commitments that are of lower priority does *not*, therefore, automatically signal to the adversary that there is a lack of resolve to honor more important commitments. Had South Vietnam not been defended, according to this line of argument, it would not have meant that West Berlin would not be defended. In the abstract, this qualification of the "interdependence of commitments" is correct. But two key questions remain: First, how can B always be sure of A's ranking of priorities, and, second, even if B can make some pretty good guesses, will A's yielding of a lower-priority commitment not tempt B to test A's resolve in an area of greater importance? After all, without testing, B cannot really know whether or not A's determination is indeed stronger. (The failure of A to honor a commitment in one area may thus be viewed by the potential attacker as an indication that other commitments will also not be honored because *states generally think that their overall reputation is more important than, and relatively independent of, the specific interest and commitment being challenged.*[35]) "Weakness is weakness."

(One final point should be repeated in connection with this intangible aspect of power. Deterrence is tested by what does *not* occur. Precisely because it is impossible ever to say with absolute certainty why an event did not occur— or even that it might have and did not—and because we cannot prove that "nonevents" result either from specific weapons systems or from resolute support of specific commitments, both issues have, in an open society, increasingly given rise to differing evaluations. As the price—in money and in lives—for preserving deterrence has become increasingly taxing and agonizing, these questions have generated intense debate.)

AMERICAN ARMS CONTROL AND THE STABILITY OF MUTUAL DETERRENCE

There is a need for tangible *forces* that can implement the "massive retaliation" with which the deterrer threatens its opponent should it be tempted to strike. Before World War II states normally had military forces with which they hoped to prevent enemy attack; but these forces were never near to the strength of the forces that

---

[34.] Schelling, *Arms and Influence*, p. 56.

[35.] Snyder, *op. cit.*, pp. 232–233.

could be mobilized after war actually broke out. As war was not invariably fatal, there was no reason to keep large and expensive forces continuously at the ready. Plowshares were to be converted into swords *after* the attack. This attitude was particularly prevalent in the United States. Protected by two oceans and thus not subject to invasion or even air attack, it had time to mobilize its vast power after it became involved in war. But nuclear deterrence requires peacetime readiness of *all* the forces that would be required for retaliation if an enemy attack occurred. For the enemy must never doubt for even a moment—if deterrence is to be permanent—that it would be committing suicide should it strike first.

The need for offensive superiority is thus constant and requires unfailing concern with effective delivery systems. The difficulty arises from the rapid technological changes that have occurred every few years since 1945. Like the factor of resolve, they have become critical in determining the stability of the nuclear balance of power. Even the early nuclear delivery systems tended to destabilize the postwar equilibrium because of the ability of fast bombers to execute surprise attacks. It is true, of course, that even before the development of high-speed bombers surprise attack had been possible. The Germans had achieved it against the Russians in 1941, despite the large-scale movement of troops to Poland that it had necessitated, and the Japanese had been highly successful at Pearl Harbor a few months later. The speed of postwar bombers, however, made surprise attack even more feasible, particularly as it would no longer have to be preceded by massive troop or ship movements. Although the United States, for instance, during the first two decades of the Cold War, sought to deter a Soviet attack by threatening to drop enough bombs virtually to wipe the Soviet Union off the map, its threat would have been meaningless if most American bombers could have been destroyed in a surprise attack. The surviving bombers would then not have been able to retaliate with sufficient destructiveness. Not all of them would have had enough fuel to reach their targets. Soviet fighters and ground-to-air missiles, alerted for the arrival of those bombers that did reach Soviet territory, would have been able to shoot down many, if not most. The few that did manage to penetrate Soviet defenses might no longer have been able to wreak catastrophic damage. The level of damage might indeed have been acceptable to Soviet leaders if it meant the elimination once and for all of their deadliest enemy and its ability to destroy the Soviet Union.

The vulnerability of bombers to a nuclear Pearl Harbor thus rendered the balance of power very unstable because of the high dividends likely to accrue to the side that struck the initial blow. Possessing bombs was insufficient to ensure that war would not result. The possibility of eliminating the opponent's retaliatory bombers—bombers above ground being considered "soft" targets—constituted a powerful incentive to attack. The consequent balance was therefore "delicate." What conditions might instigate an opponent's first strike against one's own retaliatory force? And what could be done to prevent such attack and "stabilize" mutual deterrence?[36] These questions preoccupied students of "arms control" in the late

---

[36.] This continuing concern with different strategies and changing weapon systems is discussed by William W. Kaufmann, *The McNamara Strategy* (New York: Harper & Row, 1964).

186   1950s and 1960s. Proponents of arms control rejected the feasibility of general disarmament and assumed that neither conflicts among states nor nuclear weapons would be abolished.[37] Instead, the best hope for earthly salvation seemed to them to lie in the "control" of armaments. In a competitive state system deterrence was recognized as the only feasible policy. It had to be improved, however, to be made "safe."

(Arms control thus supplemented the more traditional defense policies, as its aim was identical: to protect the national security by deterring war. Whereas disarmament stressed the reduction of a nation's military *capability*, either completely or partially, arms control emphasized the elimination of American and Soviet *incentives* to strike first. *Two presuppositions underlay arms control: first that, despite the continuation of their political conflict, both nuclear powers shared a common interest in avoiding nuclear war and, second, that, though the basic tensions arose from political antagonism, the nature of the delivery systems exacerbated them by providing a strong and independent incentive for a first strike.*[38] This incentive was simply the paramount importance of hitting first, for in the nuclear age to come in second is to lose; to be caught off guard can be fatal. Policy makers might thus be tempted to launch a first strike. Remember the first law of preservation in the state system: Be suspicious. One side's gain—and any proposal by a potential adversary is assumed to incorporate advantages for itself— is usually considered the other side's loss. The fear of loss is particularly acute in the military sphere, where each party is hypersensitive to the possibility of being inferior. Few arms agreements have existed in history precisely because states, driven by their sense of insecurity, prefer to *add* arms to their already existing arsenals, to ensure that they will not find themselves lacking. But *arms-control thinking is based on the assumption that one side's gain is not necessarily the other's loss; both sides can gain simultaneously.*)

(If the only defense is indeed an offense, then a *preemptive strike* is a particular danger during crisis periods. It differs from a *preventive strike*, in which the aggressor coolly plans the strike beforehand with confidence that it can obliterate the opponent; the attacker picks a specific date and then sends its forces on their way, regardless of possible provocation. In a preemptive strike, however, the attack is launched in order to forestall a strike by the enemy. In this instance the aggressor believes that the opponent is about to strike; it therefore strikes first in order to destroy the enemy's forces before they take off. The attack results from moves on the *other side* that are interpreted as menacing.[39])

---

[37] See Chapter 17, section on disarmament.

[38] Fine introductions to the field of arms control can be found in Hedley Bull, *The Control of the Arms Race* (2d ed.; New York: Holt, Rinehart and Winston, 1965); and Schelling and Morton H. Halperin, *Strategy and Arms Control* (New York: Twentieth Century Fund, 1961).

[39] In Schelling's words: "The 'equalizer' of the Old West [the pistol] made it possible for *either* man to kill the other; it did not assure that *both* would be killed. . . . The advantage of shooting first aggravates any incentive to shoot. As the survivor might put it, 'He was about to kill me in self-defense.' Or, 'He, thinking I was about to kill him in self-defense, was about to kill me in self-defense, so I had to kill him in self-defense.' But if both were assured of living long enough to shoot back with unimpaired aim, there would be no advantage in jumping the gun and little reason to fear that the other would try it." Schelling, *Strategy of Conflict*, pp. 232–233, (Emphasis in original.)

The role of possible miscalculation in precipitating a preemptive strike is clear. The sign that an opponent is about to launch an attack is likely to be ambiguous. The opponent may simply be taking measures to render its own strategic force less vulnerable and thus to enhance its deterrent stance. For instance, during the bomber era, it might have sent many of its bombers into the air in order to avoid having them caught on the ground; by rendering them less vulnerable to sudden destruction, it was trying to prevent the other side from launching an attack. But the action itself could easily have been misinterpreted as the prelude to an attack. In a situation of mutual vulnerability, in which the "nice guy" finishes last, delay can prove fatal. Offensive action may therefore be the only wise course: " 'Self-defense' becomes peculiarly compounded if we have to worry about his striking us to keep us from striking him to keep him from striking us."[40] What is important, therefore, is not what A *intends* to do but B's *perception* of A's intentions. In this type of hair-trigger situation, the interpretation can not be conservative. Because the survival of the nation is at stake, it is necessary to assume the worst. The strategic bombers of both sides were, of course, ready at all times to take off on their missions. When one side places a large number of them in the air, the possibility of a sudden attack increases. Even defensive actions, intended merely to enhance one's deterrent power, may thus serve to intensify international tensions and perhaps to touch off nuclear conflagration. Paradoxically, then, the very weapons intended to deter nuclear war may well precipitate it.

The crucial problem is how a preventive war and a preemptive strike can be forestalled. The remedy, as already suggested, is to render each side's retaliatory or second-strike forces invulnerable. (A *second-strike force is one that can absorb an initial blow and still effectively perform its retaliatory task.*) The deterrent force that matters is, then, that part likely to be left after an initial enemy attack; the size of the force before the attack is less relevant. In the bomber era, the solution was to develop a well-protected retaliatory force composed primarily of solid-fuel missiles that can be fired instantly. They can be *dispersed* more easily than bombers, which are generally concentrated at a relatively small number of bases, the location of which is easily discoverable. Missiles can also be *hardened*—that is, buried in concrete silos that can withstand great pressure. Finally, and most important, missiles can be made *mobile*, so that the enemy never knows their exact locations. Mobile missiles, like the Polaris missiles, which are carried underwater on nuclear-powered submarines, are virtually impossible to hit. To the extent that an enemy might seek to destroy mobile missiles, the underwater system has the additional advantage of moving an initial strike—or at least a good part of that strike—away from the land, or the "zone of the interior." In the words of a navy jingle:

> Move deterrence out to sea
> Where real estate is free
> And where it's far away from me.

(The importance of the dispersal, hardening, and mobility of missiles lies in the fact that they deprive a surprise attack of its rationale. The entire justification

---

[40.] *Ibid.*, p. 231.

FIGURE 8.1
THE AMERICAN DETERRENT TRIAD

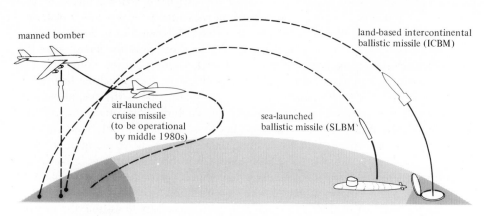

By the late 1980s a mobile land-based missile, the MX, will have been added.

for a first strike had been to surprise the opponent with its bombers on the ground and to destroy them. But, when the opponent's retaliatory power is basically invulnerable, obliterating the enemy's cities will benefit the aggressor very little. Surprise no longer confers any significant advantage to the side that hits first. The enemy's first strike cannot destroy the ability to strike back. The fact that a second-strike force will remain is the best guarantee against war. *Invulnerable deterrents thus stabilize mutual deterrence.*[41] Once the advantage of an initial attack has been greatly reduced, if not eliminated, the incentive to strike at all, and therefore the possibility of war, also disappears.)

There are three critical elements of American arms-control thinking: First, the numbers of weapons needed to achieve "assured destruction" of the other society is the criterion, not the number of weapons the opponent has; second, the deterrent requires willingness to permit urban areas to remain vulnerable, as "hostages"; third, the second-strike forces must be invulnerable, so that the enemy can never believe that it can destroy enough forces to survive retaliation intact.)

(These points are worth some elaboration First, *the balance of capability does not necessarily require equality in numbers of bombers and missiles.* A balance is achieved when each side has a second-strike force able to destroy the opponent's homeland after absorbing an initial blow) The optimum size second-strike force may vary quite a bit in the views of American and Soviet leaders. For example, the first agreement on offensive arms to come out of the strategic-arms limitation talks (SALT), a five-year interim agreement, froze the strategic missiles of the United States at 1054 intercontinental ballistic missiles (ICBMs), plus 656 more missiles on nuclear submarines, and the Soviet Union to 1618 ICBMs, plus 740

[41.] *Ibid.*, p. 232.

missiles on nuclear submarines. The treaty seems to have been very unequal and to have given the Soviets a hefty advantage of 2,358 to 1,710 missiles, but the proportions seem less unequal when we note that approximately 450 American bombers (as opposed to 150 Soviet bombers) were also allowed.

According to American arms-control thinking, even if most American land-based missiles were destroyed in their silos by Soviet ICBMs, a sizable bomber fleet plus forty-one nuclear submarines, each one of which carries sixteen missiles, would remain. Indeed, thirty-one of these submarines carry missiles which are armed with ten warheads each, for a total of 4,960. Could Moscow's leaders, therefore, really risk initiating a strike on the assumption that they might be able to destroy enough of the American second-strike force to prevent the latter from inflicting overwhelming damage on Russia? Would such a move not represent a reckless gamble—a "cosmic roll of the dice," as Carter's Secretary of Defense Brown called it—even if the total Soviet strike force is larger than that of the United States by several hundred missles?[42]

The conclusion drawn from this logic is that the superpowers can inflict unacceptable damage on each other, that they long ago reached a plateau—variously called "parity," "sufficiency," "mutual deterrence," "nuclear stalemate," and "balance of terror"—in their capability to destroy each other. The nuclear balance, or mutual deterrence, is not sensitive to numerical variations as long as each side retains an invulnerable deterrent force capable of the "assured destruction" of the enemy's society.

Second, *urban industrial areas are deliberately left unprotected, as hostages.* In 1964, the Soviets had begun to deploy an antiballistic-missile (ABM) system around Moscow. By itself, the Soviet ABM constituted no problem; the problem lay in the possibility of the deployment of an extensive ABM system to protect the Soviet urban population. If such a system were capable of shooting down a large percentage of missiles in a retaliatory strike—or if the Soviets believed it could—it might weaken the American deterrent. If deterrence depends upon the ability to hold the adversary's population hostage, then Soviet ability to weaken an American second strike and greatly reduce American capacity to inflict catastrophic urban population losses might be a temptation to the Soviets to launch a preventive or preemptive first strike. Anything that detracts from the superiority of the offense tends to "destabilize" mutual deterrence, which is based on a vulnerable population and invulnerable offensive forces. An ABM is a bad weapon in the sense that it can endanger nuclear deterrence.[43] In the SALT I treaty, the ABM was, for all practical purposes, abandoned and cities left correspondingly vulnerable.

Third, as invulnerable second-strike forces are the key to the stability of mutual deterrence, *it is imperative that the weapons produced and deployed be the*

---

[42] For a discussion of the lack of any payoff from a position of strategic superiority that the Soviet Union might achieve, see Benjamin S. Lambeth, "Deterrence in the MIRV Era," *World Politics*, January 1972, pp. 221 ff.

[43] Jerome B. Wiesner *et al.*, *ABM: An Evaluation of the Decision to Employ an Antiballistic Missile System* (New York: Signet, 1969); and Johan J. Holst and William Schneider, Jr., eds., *Why ABM? Policy Issues in the Missile Defense Controversy* (New York: Pergamon, 1969).

190   *"right" kind*. Whether a weapon is "right" or "wrong," "good" or "bad," depends
on whether it will help to stabilize the balance or to destabilize it; these terms have
no moral connotations in this context.)Bombers, when they constituted the backbone of deterrence, were bad because they were vulnerable to attack. Missiles,
because they can be dispersed, protected in silos, and moved around, are good;
surprise attack cannot so easily then destroy retaliatory capacity. The problem,
however, is that some weapons can be either good or bad. A missile with a single
warhead may be good but a missile with multiple warheads (multiple independant
reentry vehicles, or MIRVs), each of which can be fired at a separate target as the
missile keeps changing its trajectory, may be a good or a bad weapon. The MIRV
was originally invented to counter an antiballistic missile system by overwhelming
it with more missiles than it could handle; it was intended to help preserve an
offensive edge and thus to preserve the credibility of deterrence. The first generation
of American MIRVs were, by thermonuclear standards, relatively small—a Minuteman carrying three 200-kiloton (200,000-ton) warheads and a Poseidon submarine missile carrying ten 40-kiloton warheads (each missile thus armed with a
smaller total megatonnage than when it had carried only a single warhead). One
of these warheads was not powerful enough to destroy a missile in a silo, but it
could destroy a city. Even if cities were defended by ABMs, MIRVs could still
pose the threat of devastation and therefore act as a deterrent. Such MIRVs, because
their warheads were not "too large," lacked pinpoint accuracy, and were targeted
against cities and populations, were good MIRVs.

By contrast, Soviet missiles, generally considerably larger than American
ones, have far more and bigger warheads in the multimegaton range (the SS-9
carried three five-megaton warheads, the SS-18 ten one-to-two megaton warheads).
Why such huge warheads? They are far bigger than necessary to destroy the largest
city. American belief has been that they are first-strike weapons; they are big enough
to destroy missiles in silos, even if they land a quarter of a mile from the target.[44]
With improving technology, all MIRVs, Soviet and American alike, including the
American MX to be deployed in the 1980s, are increasingly perceived as bad.(Even
if the explosive yield of each warhead were to be reduced, the increasing accuracy
of the guidance systems means that silos of land-based missiles are increasingly
vulnerable to destruction and that the possible incentive to risk a first strike is
higher.)

SOVIET MILITARY DOCTRINE AND TECHNOLOG-
ICAL INNOVATION

American arms-control doctrine came increasingly into question in the late 1970s,
as SALT II was being negotiated and debated in the U.S. Senate. Critics of the
agreement charged that the Soviets do not accept the elements that we have out-

---

[44.] R. J. Rummel, *Peace Endangered* (Beverly Hills: Sage, 1976).

lined. SALT II therefore looked like an agreement that, instead of enhancing American security, would reduce it.[46] First, the massive Soviet growth of military power—both strategic and conventional—since 1964 suggests that the aim was not merely to catch up with the United States and to achieve parity, but also to gain superiority. Second, the Soviets are said to have taken extensive civilian-defense measures in order to protect much of their population. Third, Soviet ICBMs, including the 308 SS-18 missiles, each with its ten multimegaton warheads (as specified by SALT II but estimated to be able to carry thirty-five smaller warheads), are said to constitute a first-strike force. The 820 land-based missiles allowed under SALT II, when fully equipped, will make it possible for the Soviet Union to destroy most of the American ICBMs.

The Soviet Union has thus been building a first-strike or counterforce capability, rather than a second-strike, or retaliatory, counter-city (or economy) force. Its leaders had adopted a "war fighting" strategy while the United States was thinking only of deterrence. The result is that, instead of war being "unthinkable," as Americans proclaimed, it has become "thinkable" and will be a genuine option for Soviet policy makers by the middle 1980s. They can destroy most of the American ICBM force and limit the damage from any retaliatory blow because of their extensive air defenses against bombers and the smaller submarine-launched warheads, as well as large-scale civil-defense preparations. Most of the Russian population can be saved; some American estimates set the figure at about 90 percent.

But even if this percentage were lower, the Soviets could deter an American second strike. The reason is that it would not have used all its ICBMs or most of its submarine-launched missiles in the first strike, and it could therefore warn the American government that a second strike against Soviet cities would elicit a third strike against those American cities that had been spared the first strike. An American second strike would thus be deterred by the threat of a Soviet third strike! Even if this scenario—which may sound bizarre—were never enacted, the fact that the Soviets have the forces to destroy many of the United States' ICBMs may be used to intimidate the United States, as the Soviet Union becomes more active in seeking to expand its influence and more confident that it can face down the United States. Meanwhile, the United States, aware of its new vulnerability, will become more cautious about reacting to Soviet moves. It is not the chances of war so much as the possibility of political exploitation of Soviet military power that worry the critics of SALT II and American arms-control doctrine.

The differences between the American arms-control doctrine and the Soviet military doctrine are summed up in Table 8.1. If it is correct that, for the Soviets, nuclear warfare does remain a rational instrument of policy, mutual deterrence may fail, despite strategic-arms limitation talks and agreements. It is for this reason that, despite equal ceilings on delivery systems specified in SALT II,

---

[45.] Richard Pipes, "Why the Soviet Union Thinks It Could Fight and Win a Nuclear War," *Commentary*, July 1977, pp. 21–34; Roger W. Barnett, "Trans-SALT: Soviet Strategic Doctrine," *Orbis*, Summer 1975, pp. 533–561; Fritz W. Ermath, "Contrasts in American and Soviet Strategic Thought," *International Security*, Fall 1978, pp. 138–155; and Joseph D. Douglas, Jr., and Amoretta M. Hoeber, *Soviet Strategy for Nuclear War* (Stanford: Hoover Press, 1979).

TABLE 8.1

COMPARISON OF AMERICAN AND SOVIET NUCLEAR DOCTRINES*

American Arms-Control Doctrine	Alleged Soviet Military Doctrine
Deterrence and mutual assured destruction	war and victory
retaliatory, or second strike	first strike
countercity, or economy, targeting	counterforce
cities as hostages	civil defense
strategic parity	strategic superiority
stability	no references to stability

*This table is based on recent statements by American leaders and critics, as well as on Soviet writings on strategy and arms control, included in Robert J. Pranger and Roger P. Labrie, eds., *Nuclear Strategy and National Security* (Washington, D.C.: American Enterprise Institute, 1977).

the Senate Armed Services Committee reported that the treaty is not in the national-security interest of the United States. The committee differed from the more favorably inclined Senate Foreign Relations Committee. The Soviets, of course, deny that they would ever launch a first strike or are seeking strategic superiority.[46] Nevertheless, American doctrine has recently shifted to incorporate greater counterforce targeting, so that the United States can avoid a situation in which it can only retaliate against Soviet cities—at a risk of a Soviet third strike against American cities.

Doctrine apart, the other—and perhaps greater—danger to a stable balance is technology. When missiles first replaced bombers as the backbone of the superpowers' strategic forces, they were believed to be invulnerable and mutual deterrence appeared sure. Technology did not, however, stand still. The development of MIRVs and greater accuracy in guidance systems has once again altered the situation. Regardless of Soviet thinking about issues of war and peace, the United States must be concerned about the vulnerability of its ICBMs. The Soviets, too, will have cause for concern when 200 large American MX mobile missiles with ten very accurate warheads apiece are deployed; nor can they disregard the American cruise missile launched from bombers. Although its speed is subsonic, this missile comes in low and is extremely accurate. Indeed, the Soviets will have even more cause for concern, for 70 percent of their warheads and 80 percent of their megatonnage are in silos, compared to only 25 percent of American warheads and 40 percent of United States megatonnage.[47] Technological advances may also occur in other fields that can endanger the strategic balance: laser beams to shoot down missiles, antisatellite satellites (by means of which the superpowers can watch each

---

[46.] For the view that the Soviet leaders think of nuclear war and deterrence in very similar terms to those of American leaders, see Raymond L. Garthoff, "Mutual Deterrence and Strategic Arms Limitation in Soviet Policy," *International Security*, Summer 1978, pp. 111–147; and Garthoff, "SALT I: An Evaluation," *World Politics*, October 1978, pp. 1–25. For a view that American strategy is moving toward the Soviet view, see Leon V. Sigal, "Rethinking the Unthinkable," *Foreign Policy*, Spring 1979, pp. 35–51.

[47.] John M. Lee, "An Opening 'Window' for Arms Control," *Foreign Affairs*, Fall 1979, p. 129.

FIGURE 8.2

THE PROVISIONS OF SALT I AND SALT II.

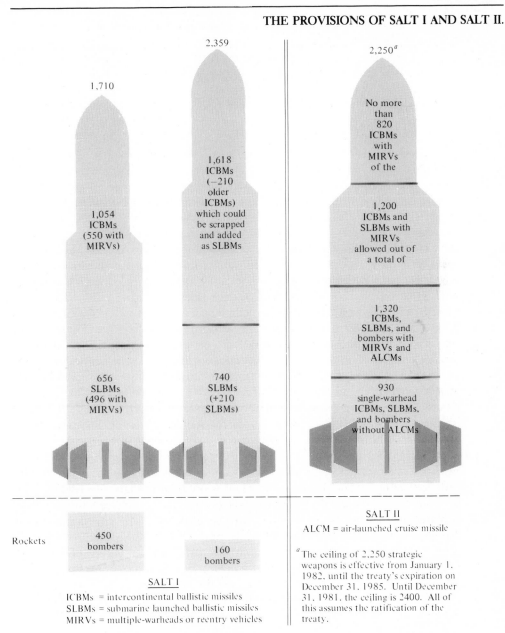

2,359

1,710

2,250[a]

No more than 820 ICBMs with MIRVs of the

1,054 ICBMs (550 with MIRVs)

1,618 ICBMs (−210 older ICBMs) which could be scrapped and added as SLBMs

1,200 ICBMs and SLBMs with MIRVs allowed out of a total of

1,320 ICBMs, SLBMs, and bombers with MIRVs and ALCMs

656 SLBMs (496 with MIRVs)

740 SLBMs (+210 SLBMs)

930 single-warhead ICBMs, SLBMs, and bombers without ALCMs

Rockets

450 bombers

160 bombers

SALT II

ALCM = air-launched cruise missile

SALT I

ICBMs = intercontinental ballistic missiles
SLBMs = submarine launched ballistic missiles
MIRVs = multiple-warheads or reentry vehicles

[a]The ceiling of 2,250 strategic weapons is effective from January 1, 1982, until the treaty's expiration on December 31, 1985. Until December 31, 1981, the ceiling is 2400. All of this assumes the ratification of the treaty.

other, monitor the SALT agreements, and communicate to their forces around the world), and devises for antisubmarine warfare, among others.

Because of doctrinal differences and constant technological change in weapons systems, it is difficult to "count" and evaluate the military and strategic balance (see Figure 8.2). Did SALT I, in which the Soviets were allowed to have

193

194   40 percent more missiles on land and water than the United States, achieve a balance? The American bomber advantage was 3:1, and the United States was already well ahead of the Soviets in placing MIRVs on its missiles. Was the Soviet quantitative advantage offset by the American qualitative superiority? Or was there an imbalance? Was the SALT II agreement—even if it is not ratified—equitable just because both sides had the same ceilings on all strategic delivery systems—2,400 (including bombers this time), to be reduced by 1981 to 2,250, and 1,320 MIRVs?[48] Or was it inequitable because the American land-based missiles, of which 550 at present have MIRVs with three "small" warheads of "only" 200,000 tons TNT each (though this load is to be doubled), were not comparable to the potentially larger number of much bigger Soviet MIRVs allegedly designed for greater counterforce capability? Under the treaty, both sides were allowed 820 land-based MIRVs out of a total of 1,200 land- and sea-based MIRVs.[49] Did the United States lead in extremely accurate, subsonic, cruise missiles, twenty of which can be placed on each of 120 bombers for a total of about 2,400 (or twenty-eight on each aircraft designed for carrying cruise missiles), constitute an advantage over the Soviet Union, which did not have comparable cruise missiles? (Bombers carrying cruise missiles were to be counted as MIRVs, and, as each side could have 1,200 ICBMs and SLBMs, the 120 extra MIRVs were the bombers themselves.)

Our analysis of deterrence, then, brings us back to the issue of the numbers of weapons. Whether American leaders are correct in arguing that the strategic balance does not require equality in the *numbers* of arms or whether Soviet leaders are correct in their alleged faith in superior numbers of weapons, *numbers do appear to be critical to the balance of resolve.*[50] It is understandable that weapons are usually assessed in the context of war and that analyses of military strength focus on the numbers needed to destroy an enemy should war erupt. Presumably, according to this thinking, if each nation has enough weapons, deterrence will work. Yet *the emphasis on quantities calculated according to how many are required to fight is misplaced*, especially when war is unthinkable and must be avoided. The really crucial point about strategic weapons is not their military effect on day one of a war but their political and psychological impact on the continuing daily relations between the superpowers *before* war breaks out. The critical question is how many weapons are needed for bargaining purposes in "peacetime," to help gain and maintain at least tolerable, if not favorable, terms of peaceful coexistence in the continuing competition of the two nuclear giants. What counts is each side's perception of the other's power. In this sense the number of weapons may become critical, for it is likely to affect profoundly the balance of resolve. Indeed, imbalances in *this* area tend to produce crises which can be ended only by restoration of this

---

[48] On the SALT II agreement, see Thomas W. Wolfe, *The SALT Experience* (Cambridge, Mass.: Ballinger, 1979), and Strobe Talbott, *Endgame* (New York: Harper & Row, 1979).

[49] For an informed critical view of the changing balance in favor of the Soviet Union, see John M. Collins, *American and Soviet Military Trends Since the Cuban Missile Crisis* (Washington, D.C.: Center for Strategic and International Studies, Georgetown University, 1978).

[50] Jerome H. Kahan, *Security in the Nuclear Age* (Washington, D.C.: Brookings, 1975), pp. 237–240.

balance. *The balance of resolve may thus be more important than the balance of capability in precipitating crises, which, in the nuclear age, have displaced war as the ultimate test of strengh in conflicts between superpowers and in settling the terms of coexistence.*

9
Crises as Substitutes for War

CRISES AND THE BALANCE OF RESOLVE

The postwar bipolar world was characterized not only by deterrence but also by frequent crises. Situations of intense confrontation, usually of short duration, in which the perceived possibility of war rises significantly, crises are probably unavoidable in any international system characterized by anarchy. In a bipolar system, however, the insecurity, fear, and suspicion of both superpowers make avoidance of crises particularly difficult. It may thus be correct to conclude, as Kenneth Waltz has suggested, that in a bipolar distribution of power "a large crisis now [is better] than a small war later."[1] A crisis is evidence that the balance is being kept.

Crises, then, serve a purpose when war is no longer the instrument of last resort. Earlier we characterized the state system as a state of potential war; war is the medium for either demanding or resisting change. In a system in which no legitimate means for achieving change exist, conflicting demands, if they cannot be resolved peacefully, must be settled by force. War often decides who gets what; the power ratio when the shooting ends settles whatever issue is at stake. *But war is no longer the ultima ratio in the nuclear age. Crisis is now the substitute for war as the "continuation of politics by other means"* (as Clausewitz defined war).[2] Coercion now takes the place of all-out force as the means of deciding who gets

---

[1] Kenneth N. Waltz, "The Stability of a Bipolar World," *Daedalus*, Summer 1964, p. 884.

[2] Glenn H. Snyder, "Crisis Bargaining," pp. 685, 709. Also see Snyder and Paul Diesing, *Conflict among Nations* (Princeton: Princeton University Press, 1977).

what in a crisis, which may be defined as a situation in which one state demands a change in the status quo and the other resists, creating a heightened perception of the possibility of war. In such a confrontation, each party tests the other, takes the measure of its adversary (including its firmness in defending its interests and its willingness to accept risks on behalf of these interests) by means of what Schelling has called the "manipulation of risk." Successes or setbacks in individual tests are equivalent to victories and defeats in war. *In direct bipolar confrontation, in which it is too dangerous to fight and maneuver becomes a surrogate for actual hostilities, each country's perception of the other's resolve is central. At stake is its reputation for power as judged by its adversary.* This perception, rather than the specific tangible issue at hand, is the axis around which the crisis revolves. On a nation's reputation for power rests the credibility of its commitments. If this reputation is intact, the nation is not likely to be challenged. If it is in doubt, challenge is likely to follow, and, unless the reputation is restored, the crisis cannot be ended.[3]

(The very eruption of a crisis suggests that the existing pattern of power has been "significantly disturbed" and that the relationship between the adversaries has become "politically fluid."[4] Two kinds of change are particularly significant. One is a change in capability.) For example, in 1958—the year of the first space shot, and of the first test of an ICBM (both Soviet "firsts")—Soviet leaders, believing that the balance was changing, attempted to exploit diplomatically what they considered to be a military advantage. Khrushchev and his defense minister repeatedly proclaimed that the Soviet Union was producing ICBMs "on the assembly line" and threatened the United States with annihilating defeat. "We now have stockpiled so many rockets [ICBMs], so many atomic and hydrogen warheads," Khrushchev said, "that, if we were attacked, we could wipe from the face of the earth all of our probable opponents."[5] They shrewdly exploited resulting American uncertainty about actual Soviet strategic strength.[6] By 1960 thirty Soviet ICBM tests had been reported in the American press, the Soviets had launched six successful space shots, and Americans informed about this nation's defense efforts forecast a sizable "missile gap" lasting until the year 1964. Suddenly, Americans were startled by their new vulnerability to nuclear attack. The Strategic Air Command was said to be particularly vulnerable to a surprise missile strike, and its credibility as a deterrent was in some doubt both in the United States and among the NATO allies.

As if to demonstrate their claimed new strength and the weakened position of the West, in 1958 the Soviets suddenly demanded that West Berlin be "demilitarized" and turned into a "free city," with the withdrawal of Western troops.

---

[3] For a somewhat different analysis, see the excellent and detailed analysis of crises that result from deterrence failures in Alexander L. George and Richard Smoke, *Deterrence in American Foreign Policy* (New York: Columbia University Press, 1974).

[4] Young, *The Politics of Force*, pp. 63–95.

[5] Arnold L. Horelick and Myron Rush, *Strategic Power and Soviet Policy* (Chicago: University of Chicago Press, 1966), pp. 50, 58.

[6] The forecast of Soviet and American strength in ICBMs was 1960, 100 to 30; 1961, 500 to 70; 1962, 1,000 to 130; 1963, 1,500 to 130; 1964, 2,000 to 130. This forecast was based on interviews with persons presumably knowledgeable about the defense effort. The gap would be closed after 1964. Quoted from *The New York Times* in *ibid.*, p. 51.

198   What was significant was that the Russians made the demand at all. It was the most serious challenge to Washington leaders since 1948–1949. The Truman Doctrine, the Marshall Plan, the Berlin airlift, and NATO had made it very plain to the Soviets that Western Europe is an area of vital American interest and that Soviet domination over this margin of the Eurasian continent is no more tolerable to the United States than German control had been twice before. Presumably this knowledge had deterred the Russians in the late 1940s, and it was fear of war that had led them to redirect their challenges to areas outside Europe. But ten years after the first Berlin crisis the Soviets once more challenged the West in Europe. Indeed, the fact that, for the first time in the postwar era, they were publicly demanding that the Western powers abandon territory and were threatening them with an ultimatum suggested a new Soviet confidence in their own power to achieve their stated political aim of converting the western half of Germany's former capital into a "free city."

(The other kind of change is in the balance of resolve.) By 1962 Khrushchev had apparently become convinced that the United States would not use force to defend its vital interests. He talked openly of the American failure of nerve and the West's passive acceptance of the Berlin Wall in 1961 was seen by him as one indication. Another was the debacle of the Cuban invasion of the Bay of Pigs sponsored by the Central Intelligence Agency in 1962.[7] If eliminating Castro was a vital American interest, then, once the Cuban exile force had been defeated, American forces should have been committed to accomplish that goal; on the other hand, if eliminating Castro was not important, then the Bay of Pigs operation should never have been launched. Khrushchev, who had used the Red Army to crush the Hungarian revolution in 1956, read Kennedy's unwillingness to follow through on his action in Cuba as a sign of inexperience and weakness; it therefore did not seem that the installation of Soviet missiles in Cuba would involve great risk. The Soviet Union merely had to confront the United States with a *fait accompli*, and the latter would then retreat, rather than face a test of will. Past American inactions or ineffective reactions seem to have encouraged the Soviets to continue their probes—and, in the instance of the missile installations, the probe reached within ninety miles from the American shore.

Note that the Cuban missile challenge occurred even while the balance of capability favored the United States. Spurred by Khrushchev's statements about large-scale production of missiles and his threats, the Kennedy administration, upon coming into office in 1961, launched the massive buildup of Minuteman and Polaris missiles, which by 1966 were to total 1,000 and 656 respectively. It also soon discovered that Russian claims about rocket production were greatly exaggerated. Furthermore, Khrushchev was aware that the Americans knew of this exaggeration. The Russian medium- and intermediate-range missile installation in Cuba could therefore be interpreted partly as a technological shortcut to enhance Soviet strength. Obviously, the imbalance of strategic capabilities did not deter the

[7] Theodore C. Sorensen, *Kennedy* (New York: Harper & Row, 1965), pp. 326–346; Arthur M. Schlesinger, Jr., *A Thousand Days* (Boston: Houghton Mifflin, 1965), pp. 219–250; and Tad Szulc and Karl E. Meyer, *The Cuban Invasion: The Chronicle of a Disaster* (New York: Ballantine, 1962).

Soviets from placing missiles so near to American territory; equally obviously, the Soviet leadership thought that the imbalance of resolve favored Russia and that this imbalance was more important than the strictly military one.

CRISIS MANAGEMENT

(We have argued that in the nuclear era crisis is a substitute for war. Two contradictory sets of motives are at work.[8] One is winning . The aim is to compel the opponent to retreat and to make concessions. The emphasis is on competition and conflict. In this sense, a crisis reflects the general nature of international politics painted in very bold colors. The contrary motive is to avoid war. Given the characteristics of a crisis—perception of a grave threat to the security of at least the challenged party, the suddenness and unexpected nature of this threat, the "players' " sense that they must act quickly, and their heightened expectation of violence—it is obviously highly dangerous. The alternative to some sort of settlement, however, is so catastrophic in our nuclear age that restraint becomes imperative. Given the unpredictability inherent in a crisis, the possibility that this "substitute for war" can get out of hand and blow up under certain circumstances places a premium on "crisis management.")

(The Cuban missile, or October, crisis provides a textbook example, partly because the unexpected discovery of the Soviet installations allowed the United States a week for debating the meaning of the buildup, what Soviet purposes might be, how these purposes would affect American interests, the future of American-Russian relations, and the alternative ways of getting the missiles removed. (There was virtually no debate on whether or not removal was necessary.) In a sense, the October crisis was unique; usually the surprised party is not afforded the luxury of time for debate and careful consideration of options. In any event, several factors favored the Americans' ability to "manage" the crisis and to achieve their objective: to persuade Moscow's leaders to undo what they had already done—not simply to stop further activities—and simultaneously to avoid nuclear war.)

Note these aims because they may be critical in resolving a crisis without resorting to violence. For, in seeking to coerce a challenger, there is a difference between a demand that the challenging activities be stopped (as in Berlin) and a demand that whatever gains have already been made be given up (as in Cuba). An adversary may be more inclined to accept the former than the latter.[9] If the challenger is unwilling to "stop and undo," the only way to gain compliance is to

---

[8] Phil Williams, *Crisis Management* (New York: Wiley, 1976), pp. 27–31. This book is an excellent summary of the crisis literature.

[9] The whole strategy of coercion to "asymmetry of motivation" and balance of power is explored in greater detail in the excellent analysis of the Cuban missile crisis in Alexander L. George, David K. Hall, and William E. Simons, *The Limits of Coercive Diplomacy: Laos, Cuba, Vietnam* (Boston: Little, Brown, 1971), pp. 23–24.

200   escalate the pressures. But such stronger threats also enhance the risks and possibility of war. ⌠One perhaps fundamental reason why the United States was successful in achieving its purpose in this particular crisis was that American motivation to succeed in Cuba was far stronger than that of Russia; the "asymmetry of motivation" favored the United States.[10] Passivity in the face of such a clear menace—underlined by both the stealth and the speed of the Soviet missile buildup—was perceived by Washington's leaders as humiliating to the United States, lending credence to repeated Soviet claims that communism was the wave of the future and that the Soviet Union was becoming the world's foremost power. To have acceded to it would have demonstrated American impotence to a watching world; a United States unable or unwilling to prevent the installation of Soviet missiles in its traditional sphere of influence—as Ronald Steel has observed, the Monroe Doctrine was really a Caribbean Doctrine[11]—would obviously also be thought too weak or fearful to defend vital interests farther away. Soviet medium-range ballistic missiles (MRBMs) in Cuba would to some degree have enhanced the Soviet capacity for a first strike, for the American early-warning lines were all positioned in the north to detect a strike across the North Pole. Furthermore, when confronted by American inaction, the Soviets might well have shipped many more such missiles to Cuba.

Nonetheless, as President Kennedy recognized, it was less the balance of capability that was affected than the balance of resolve. Not the strategic balance but the *appearance* of the balance, as he worded it, would be substantially altered.[12] In these circumstanes, the Soviets would undoubtedly have renewed their pressure on Berlin; they had already announced that they wished to resume "negotiations" on this subject after the American midterm election in November. They would also have furnished "proof" that the United States' allies in Europe, the Middle East, and Asia could not rely upon the United States in any major crisis. The future existence of these alliances would thus have been seriously jeopardized. And, in the Western Hemisphere, this evidence of American impotence would have encouraged Castro and other leaders of anti-American movements by sharply reducing the authority of the "colossus of the North" in Latin America.

All in all, Kennedy thought that the Russians had broken a fundamental "rule of the game" in Cuba. The United States had not established bases in eastern Europe; it had not aided anti-Russian revolts. In return, the Russians were not to encroach militarily in America's own sphere of influence. Castro's takeover of power, which resulted from internal Cuban conditions and despite the opposition

---

[10] *Ibid.*, pp. 86–136.

[11] Ronald Steel, *Pax Americana* (New York: Viking, 1967), p. 195.

[12] The best accounts of the missile crisis can be found in Sorensen, *op. cit.*, pp. 752–809; Schlesinger, *op. cit.*, pp. 726–749; and Elie Abel, *The Missile Crisis* (Philadelphia; Lippincott, 1966). The most detailed analysis of American policy may be found in Graham T. Allison, *Essence of Decision* (Boston: Little, Brown, 1971). For an analysis of Soviet motivations, see Horelick, "The Cuban Missile Crisis: An Analysis of Soviet Calculations," pp. 363–370. For a more recent, although considerably less important, crisis see Richard G. Head, Frisco W. Short, and Robert C. McFarlane, *Crisis Resolution* (Boulder: Westview, 1978), primarily an account of the rescue of the merchant ship *Mayaguez* from the Cambodians in 1975.

of the Cuban Communist party, had not represented such an encroachment. Soviet missiles did. If the Soviet action were to pass with impunity, the terms of bipolar coexistence and competition would have been redefined. There were, of course, major risks in demanding the withdrawal of the Soviet missiles, but the consequences of *inaction* were, despite the United States' greater strategic striking capability, perceived to be disastrous. The Russians had much to gain; because potential American losses were seen to be vastly greater, Kennedy saw no choice but to react in Cuba and to demand the withdrawal of Soviet missiles. The asymmetry of motivation thus favored the United States.

Second, the balance of capabilities also favored the United States, and the president could be reasonably confident and resolute. Kennedy made his demand for the withdrawal of the Soviet missiles in a public speech, thus committing the country to this course of action. There could be no compromise or retraction of this demand without humiliation and a loss of national prestige. The president had staked his own and the nation's reputations. Establishment of a blockade was evidence of this determination to succeed. American warships on the high seas were to stop Soviet missile-carrying vessels, and SAC was on a state of alert. Both measures were part of a show of force, a substitute for actual fighting, which lent Kennedy's demand credibility. If Khrushchev thought of the president as an inexperienced and bumbling young man, he had to be disabused of this notion if war were to be avoided. Kennedy himself wanted to lower American-Soviet tensions, but détente was impossible if Khrushchev continued to push and push, creating dangerous crises to enhance Soviet influence because he thought that Kennedy had—as Theodore Roosevelt once said of William McKinley—a chocolate éclair for a backbone. The minimal condition for negotiations was Soviet respect for American power.

Given American strategic strength, Kennedy could slowly pressure the Russians while avoiding any dangerously quick resort to an ultimatum. He remained cautious until just before Russian missiles were to become operational. Once he did deliver the ultimatum, Khrushchev assumed a conciliatory tone and promised to dismantle the missiles in Cuba and ship them back to Russia. The Russian leader did not, as some expected, take any retaliatory action in Berlin, where conventional Soviet power was dominant. Quite the reverse: Khrushchev followed his Cuban surrender by speaking more reasonably about Berlin too. The balance of resolve and capability, which had been placed in some doubt by the Berlin crises from 1958 to 1962, had once more become settled. American-Soviet relations were no longer "politically fluid."

The outcome reflected the strategic balance at the time. But we must ask whether, had that balance been reversed, Kennedy could have made his demand at all, even though, from his perspective, the pullout of Soviet missiles was a must. Did the favorable balance of capability strengthen his resolve? Would a balance favoring the Soviet Union have made him more hesitant in responding to the challenge confronting him, reinforcing Khrushchev's conviction that Kennedy "could be pushed around?"

It is striking that shortly after stepping into the presidency, Kennedy, having

202   watched Khrushchev's behavior in Berlin in the late 1950s, speeded up the American missile buildup and raised the levels of land-based and sea-launched missiles substantially over those maintained by his predecessor. If the Soviets could demand that the West leave West Berlin and precipitate a series of crises over this issue at a time when the balance of capability did not even favor Russia, what demands would they make—and how far would they then push—when they did acquire strategic parity? It should also be noted that after the Cuban crisis and the fall of Khrushchev, partly as a result of the Soviet "defeat," his successors, at great detriment to the rest of the economy (especially the consumer-oriented section), began the enormous strategic growth that resulted in the 1970s in a larger number of Russian land- and sea-based missiles whose combined total yield or payload greatly exceeded that of the American deterrent. If in the 1980s it were discovered that the Soviets stationed nuclear submarines in Cuba, thus violating the 1962 agreement that no Soviet missiles were to be placed in Cuba (including presumably its territorial waters), would the United States face the Russians down as it had in 1962?

(A third reason for Kennedy's success was the way in which the pressure was exerted on the Russians.)To the extent that crises are substitutes for a war that the contestants wish to avoid, the nuclear threshold has to be raised, allowing for a wide range of physical maneuvers to test each other's will or nerve. It becomes important in this context that coercive moves start on a low rung of what has been called an "escalation ladder"; and that the pressure be raised only after careful observation of the adversary's response and full consideration of how it is likely to react to one's own moves. Ultimatums should be delivered only when absolutely required by the situation. Between the lower and higher rungs of the escalation ladder there must be an extensive series of possible steps to increase the pressure short of war. This requirement is critical for the contestants, who must preserve some freedom of maneuver. On the one hand, they make commitments and appear to surrender their initiative in order to impress their opponents with the credibility of their demands; on the other, they cannot afford to be caught out on a limb. Each therefore must preserve a degree of freedom in its course of action. It can state its basic aim, sound menacing, keep up the pressure—but, in order to maintain tactical flexibility, it can at first take only small upward steps. If these steps elicit no resistance and if demands remain unmet, it can then take a few more steps upward.

Commitments to physical moves are taken only gradually and at low levels of pressure. That is how the Soviets sought to erode the Wetern position in Berlin between 1955 and 1958, when they demanded it be made a "free city." For three years they had watched the Allies' response to their declarations and moves in Berlin, assessing their own possible responses if publicly challenged. In 1961, construction of the Berlin Wall was preceded by placement of barbed wire and establishment of numerous crossing points between East and West Berlin, to see whether the allies would do more than protest feebly; when no demands or moves were made for its removal, the barbed wire was replaced by a massive brick wall. Although all these moves were clearly Soviet-designed, the Russians shrewdly let their East German proxies make the moves, in order to avoid a direct confrontation with the United States and its allies.

Similarly, Kennedy began his solution to the Cuban crisis with a blockade. He did have other options: a private warning to Khrushchev, a protest at the United Nations, an air strike on the missile sites, or a full-fledged invasion. But the blockade was selected. Kennedy realized, of course, that, though it might prevent more Russian missiles from entering Cuba, it would not rid the island of the ones already there. The blockade was intended as a signal of American determination (which a private warning or protest might not have accomplished so successfully); if Khrushchev then failed to remove his rockets, the pressure could be stepped up. In the meantime, Khrushchev would have to decide his response, while Kennedy could delay the even more agonizing decision on what he would do if missile construction continued. No great power presents an ultimatum to another lightly.

It is revealing that Khrushchev was not so afraid of war that, when the president announced the blockade, he immediately desisted. The Soviet leader was not a man to panic easily. He accepted the blockade, and Soviet missile-carrying ships did not try to run it, but he ordered the acceleration of efforts to make the missiles in place operational. In the midst of the crisis, Khrushchev thus confronted Kennedy with a new and much more difficult challenge. American warships could keep more missiles from coming into Cuba, but, short of an ultimatum, how could the president have the ones already on the island removed?

It was the ultimate test. Kennedy responded with the same steel nerves he had shown throughout: at the end of the week of crisis, he escalated the challenge by intensifying the pressure. He informed the Russian leadership that, if the missiles, which were about to become operational, were not removed immediately, the United States would remove them.[13] But he presented this ultimatum not publicly but privately, through his brother Robert, to the Russian ambassador in Washington; simultaneously, he gave his personal assurance of the removal of the few American missiles in Turkey, which were supposed to have been removed before the Cuban crisis erupted and whose removal the Russians had publicly suggested, quite late in the course of the crisis, as a quid pro quo for the removal of their own missiles from Cuba.

A fourth reason why the American threat of coercion was successful was the careful handling of the details of the crisis. Leaders in Washington seized and held the tactical advantage, fully exploiting the "initiative that forces the opponent to initiate."[14] The blockade of offensive missiles left it to Khrushchev to decide whether or not to break this quarantine and, if so, how. Kennedy, however, managed the details of the blockade shrewdly. Khrushchev had to make the key decisions, but he was not to be affronted in such a way that he would have no alternative but to respond militarily. He was also to be given time to think over what he should do; he was not to be forced into hasty and ill-considered actions.

---

[13] Robert F. Kennedy, *Thirteen Days: A Memoir of the Cuban Missile Crisis* (New York: Signet, 1969), pp. 107–109; and George *et al.*, *op. cit.*, pp. 115–134.

[14] Young, *op. cit.*, pp. 348–361.

Although the U.S. Navy wished to intercept Russian ships 800 miles from Cuba, so as to be out of range of the MIG fighters based on the island, the president reduced the distance to 500 miles.[15] Furthermore, the first ship to be boarded and searched was not to be one owned and manned by the Soviets. A Russian tanker, which had identified itself and its cargo to American navy ships, was allowed to pass because it was unlikely to be carrying missiles. An East German passenger ship was also cleared. The first ship that was finally halted and searched was an American-built Liberty ship, Panamanian-owned, registered in Lebanon, captained by a Greek, and bound for Cuba under a Soviet charter.[16] It is vital in a crisis—one of the chief characteristics of which is the perceived need for quick decisions, which, in turn, can easily result in miscalculation and accident—to slow the momentum of interaction and to introduce "pauses" for careful reflection and calculation. The way Kennedy managed the details of the blockade was characteristic of his careful attention to every detail of the crisis, no matter how small, and his control over all phases of the operation, especially those involving military forces.

All the moves and countermoves during the days of crisis were part of the opponents' testing of each other's resolve and willingness to run risks and of the strength of their respective interests in Cuba. No words were exchanged between official representatives of the two governments at a diplomatic table, yet the moves were all part of the bargaining process. In a crisis words are not enough. Diplomacy also involves action. The antagonists communicate their intentions, expectations, attitudes, and determination by means of the moves that they make. The bargaining is tacit, not verbal. Yet, though words alone are not sufficient, they are nevertheless indispensable. Terms must be outlined, possible compromises must be explored, time limits may be set, and the order of the steps in deescalating the crisis should be agreed upon. Explicit negotiations are thus necessary as well. But how are they to be conducted? The "hot line" between Moscow and Washington was not established until a year after the Cuban missile crisis. There was no quick, informal way to make contact; these were only the slower official channels. The two leaders improvised. Messages were passed between President Kennedy and Khrushchev, as well as between Robert Kennedy and the Soviet ambassador in Washington, D.C. Perhaps most important were the meetings of a Soviet embassy official and an ABC television reporter, in which the Russian unofficially proposed the bargain that ended the crisis—removal of the missiles in exchange for an American pledge of noninvasion.

When the crisis was over and the Russians had acknowledged defeat by withdrawing their missiles, Kennedy refused to humiliate Khrushchev. With the United States' reputation for power restored, he did not have to gloat over his victory; instead he praised Khrushchev's "statesmanlike decision to stop building bases in Cuba [and dismantle] offensive weapons. . . . This is an important and constructive contribution to peace."[17] This is the reason that he gave the Russian

---

[15.] Kennedy, *op. cit.*, p. 67.

[16.] *Ibid.*, p. 82.

[17.] Quoted in Abel, *op. cit.*, p. 183.

leader a pledge not to invade Cuba, which he had no intention of doing anyway. As a result, Khrushchev had his own loophole: the claim that he had sent the missiles to Cuba to defend Castro from an American invasion and that, having received a pledge of noninvasion, he could bring them home.

Note that Kennedy's demand at the end was the same as at the beginning: withdrawal of Soviet missiles. Castro and communism in Cuba were not made additional issues. The Russians were not asked to pull their missiles out and also to stab Castro in the back as they left (as the North Vietnamese for years had insisted that the United States do to the Saigon government). The greater the demand, the greater the disinclination to comply and the riskier the confrontation. Had the United States added the downfall of Castro to its demands, the Soviets would surely have thought that they had to respond either in Cuba or, more dangerously, in Berlin. But Kennedy kept the agenda of demands limited to the Soviet missiles, and he "won." The crisis started because Khrushchev had misread American resolve; the crisis ended when the balance of resolve was restored.[18] Other terms than victory for one side and defeat for the other are, however, possible (however much it is dressed up cosmetically to avoid imposing the final humiliation on an enemy, which can hardly be in doubt of its "defeat"). Conflict can be resolved by means of compromise, stalemate, even war.

COERCION AND THE NATURE OF POWER

What can be learned about the nature and role of power from this analysis of deterrence and crisis? First, it is probably not very useful to draw general conclusions such as "A is the most powerful country in the world" and "B is more powerful than C." Conceptually more useful conclusions can be drawn when the focus is limited to a *specific power relationship*, to *the specific kind of power* used to influence the behavior of another state, the *specific components of power actually involved*, and, finally, to the *type of objective sought*. In the deterrent/crisis relationship between the two superpowers, military power, especially strategic nuclear power, is central. Historically, examination of a military relationship between two great powers would have highlighted each state's economic capacity, as measured by its gross national product (GNP). Before the nuclear era that figure was considered a better indicator of a state's strength, of its ability to convert its plowshares into swords. The defense budget reflected only the size of the peacetime forces; such actual capability, it was recognized, was not the same as potential capability, which could be mobilized only when the shooting was about to start or had already started.

Since 1945, however, a total war has threatened to destroy industry in the opening hour of hostilities; hence the current emphasis on standing forces. There can be no potential forces because no additional bombers or missiles are likely to

---

[18.] For analysis of Chinese-American crises, see J. H. Kalichi, *The Pattern of Chinese-American Crises* (Cambridge,: Cambridge University Press, 1975).

206   be built once the first strike has occurred. Any general assessment of the superpower balance must thus include the economic component, but it is irrelevant in reckoning wartime strength; only in peacetime is the economic element still important, for, among other things, it provides the basis for developing strategic strength. When calculating a specific balance like the deterrent balance, there is no point in including components of power that are not relevant.

(A second lesson involves the difficulty of calculating that balance even when the components have been carefully sorted out. The word "balance" does not mean an equal number of weapons on both sides. Historically, we can say—admittedly, at the cost of simplification—that one-to-one relations prevailed in calculating the military balance. But in the nuclear balance, if arms-control doctrine is correct, equal numbers of bombers or missiles are not as militarily critical as the deployment of the right kinds of weapons; the decision whether a strategic weapon is of the "right" or "wrong" kind is a function of what provides stability to mutual deterrence.)

(A closely related third lesson is that technology is of key significance. If one tangible component of the strategic equation is more important than any other—the industrial economy, the number of missiles, the size of the population, for example—it is technology, which can either stabilize the balance or destabilize it.) Unfortunately, some weapons do contribute to stability whereas others detract from it; some have both effects. Missiles, because they can be dispersed and hardened, are relatively invulnerable and therefore help to stabilize the balance; but a MIRV, with either a very large silo-destroying warhead or a smaller but very accurate warhead, jeopardizes the land-based ICBM and is therefore destabilizing.

(Fourth is the critical importance of the perception of power and the intangible factor of resolve. Why should either superpower believe the other's deterrent threats, considering that failure to heed means possible suicide? On the one hand, because the adversary's vital interests are perceived as at stake and the adversary possesses the determination to defend those interests. On the other hand, should one side doubt the other's determination, the deterrent will be weakened. This "balance of resolve" is equally critical in a crisis, in the willingness of one side to challenge the other or pressure it and in the subsequent conduct of the crisis. Indeed, this intangible balance, as we have suggested, may be more significant than the tangible one. *In a condition of equilibrium in which the balance of capabilities is considered equal (as each side possesses invulnerable second-strike capabilities), the balance of will may constitute the crucial difference.* If deterrence = capability × political resolve (as viewed by the adversary), possessing enough weapons will not be enough; the opponent will be calculating not only the balance of capability but also the balance of will. If it seems that will is lacking, the opponent may risk a challenge—as the Soviets did in Cuba in 1962—even when its capability is inferior. The challenger can always retreat in order to avoid catastrophe if the challenge is resisted. The point is the inevitability of the probe.)

(Fifth, it is nevertheless an error to conclude from inability to use strategic weapons that force is of declining utility. Absolute power, it is frequently said, equals absolute impotence. In the prevailing situation of mutual deterrence strategic power is useful as a means of denial but not of positive gain. Sometimes critics suggest that strategic military power, no longer equatable with "positive power" or capacity to achieve gains, ought to be discounted as an instrument of national policy. It is almost as if deterrence of war were not of primary significance or as if the balance were eternal and could never be upset by technological breakthrough, developments of asymmetries in deployment of weapons systems, or vulnerabilities in one side's forces.)

The Soviets do not accept the view that strategic nuclear arms are weapons only of denial or deterrence. As they have achieved parity with the United States, they have increasingly stressed the *political* utility of these weapons.[19] Specifically, they have made three claims. First, the attainment of parity has forced the United States to take Soviet positions on international issues into account and to accommodate itself to these positions. As Soviet Foreign Minister Andrei Gromoyko has stated the issue:

> The Soviet Union is a great power situated on two continents, Europe and Asia, but the range of our country's international interests is not determined by its geographic position alone. . . . The Soviet people do not plead with anybody to be allowed to have their say in the solution of any question concerning the maintenance of international peace, concerning the freedom and independence of the peoples and our country's extensive interests. This is our right, due to the Soviet Union's position as a great power. During any acute situation, however far away it appears from our country, the Soviet Union's reaction is to be expected in all capitals of the world.[20]

In addition, the Soviets assert, the loss of American strategic superiority has been *the* principal factor restraining the United States from taking action to stop or reverse the undermining of American interests. The United States, as Moscow views it, disengaged from Vietnam in 1973, accepted total defeat of South Vietnam in 1975, changed its mind and desisted after initially intervening covertly in Angola in 1975–1976, accepted the establishment of Soviet influence in Ethiopia and South Yemen in 1977–1978, failed to intervene in Iran when the Shah was overthrown and an Islamic republic established in 1979, and failed to counter the Soviet intervention in Afghanistan during the coup in 1978 or military invasion in 1979–1980. Conversely, the Soviet Union has felt able to expand its influence, supporting with its own and East German military advisors, billions of dollars worth of military equipment, and Cuban proxy forces what it has defined as a progressive "national liberation" movement in Africa; and in Afghanistan Soviet troops were used for the first time since World War II outside of the Soviet sphere of influence

---

[19.] Daniel S. Papp, "Soviet Perceptions of the Strategic Balance," paper delivered at the annual meeting of the International Studies Association, Toronto, March 21–24, 1979; and Papp, "Nuclear Weapons and the Soviet World View," paper delivered at the annual meeting of the Southern Political Science Convention, Gatlinburg, Tenn., November1–3, 1979.

[20.] Quoted by Herbert Block, "Value and Burden of Soviet Defense," in Joint Economic Committee, eds., *Soviet Economic Prospects for the Seventies* (Washington, D.C.: U.S. Goverment Printing Office, 1973), p. 201.

208   to suppress the opponents of the Soviet-supported government. More menacing yet, the Soviet ambassador to France in 1980 gave a speech in which he seemed to be asserting that Moscow would support any pro-Soviet regime in the world and "repel . . . the threat of a counterrevolution or a foreign intervention." Appearing to extend the right the Soviet Union had long claimed to intervene in Eastern Europe in order to defend its friends, to areas beyond these neighboring countries, the ambassador said that his country would "not permit another Chile."[21]

(To sum up: the Soviet Union views the utility of strategic nuclear weapons as not only—or even primarily—a military matter, but as political. Not that Russian conventional military forces have not previously counted, but their usefulness has grown now that the Soviet Union is no longer strategically inferior and can prevent the United States from restraining it and undertaking expansive initiatives of its own.)

(It is therefore an error to confuse *nonuse of strategic power with lack of usefulness*. As Kenneth Waltz has suggested, such confusion is tantamount to saying that the police force that seldom if ever employs violence is weak or that a police force is strong only when policemen are swinging their clubs. To vary the image, it is comparable to saying that a man with large assets is not rich if he spends little money or that a man is rich only if he spends a lot of it.[22] Power is what people think it is; weapons deployment, numbers of weapons, innovations in weaponry, and the momentum of the growth of military power can therefore have major effects on the willingness of one party to risk challenging the other and on the determination of the challenged party to resist) Robert Osgood perceptively noted many years ago that

> . . . the most important consequence of a stable or unstable, credible or incredible, posture of deterrence may be, not the prevention or outbreak of overt aggression, but rather the maintenance or loss of prestige and morale, the strength or weakness of political positions and diplomatic maneuvers, or the consolidation or disintegration of the alliance itself. For expectations about the circumstances and consequences of war in the minds of nations and statesmen—Americans, adversaries, allies and the non-aligned—may affect the fortunes of the cold war [and détente] no less decisively than war itself.[23]

(As long as conflict and bargaining over the terms of coexistence between the two superpowers continue against a background of *beliefs* about their relative power the importance of strategic military power is clear. The Berlin crises after 1958 and the Cuban missile crisis of 1962 occurred precisely in circumstances in which the perceptions of power by adversaries, allies, and nonaligned countries were changing. Under these conditions, strategic weapons furnish *diplomatic leverage*. They are

---

[21] *The New York Times*, April 22, 1980.

[22] Kenneth Waltz, "International Structure, National Force, and the Balance of World Power," *Journal of International Affairs*, 2 (1967), 224.

[23] Charles Osgood, *NATO: The Entangling Alliance* (Chicago: University of Chicago Press, 1962), p. 116.

not, then, "good for nothing but deterrence;" they may rather confer the capacity to intimidate in order to extract concessions. Conflict does not necessarily have to be resolved by reaffirmation of the status quo.)

(Sixth, the adversaries may hold diverse views of the desirability of use of nuclear force and may therefore perceive the balance quite differently. Until the Soviets gained nuclear parity, the strategic balance had been measured between the SAC, which held Russia's population hostage, and the Red Army, which held Europe's population and American servicemen in Europe hostage. The balance was thus asymmetrical. Now it is symmetrical. The question is whether or not the Soviets have drawn the same set of conclusions from possession of nuclear weapons that United States has drawn: Deterrence, open cities, parity, and stability are preferable. Can reasoning about nuclear arms lead to only one set of conclusions? Or can a nation with a different set of historical experiences, political attitudes, and military traditions look at the same "facts" but arrive at a quite different set of conclusions? Whether or not the Soviets do think of nuclear war as feasible and winnable with Soviet society left intact is much debated in the West. The lesson for us, however, is that power calculations and the dangers and restraints they impose, on one hand, and the opportunities for expanding influence, on the other, reflect different perceptions of the ways in which power can be used and for what purposes.)

10 Force and the Limits of Its Utility

LIMITED WAR

Nuclear weapons, to paraphrase President Woodrow Wilson, have made the world "safe" only for limited wars.[1] Although the use of total force may be irrational, it does not follow that the use of *any* violence is irrational. If one of the major adversaries or one of its allies can pose a limited challenge to which the opponent can respond *only* with all-out war, the latter confronts an agonizing dilemma: to risk suicide or to surrender because the cost of resistance is far too great. It is one thing for a nuclear giant to threaten its adversary with all-out war in response to an attack on its own homeland. Such a threat is credible. The same type of threat is credible when protection of key allies is involved. But the same threat is not credible as a deterrent to attacks on less important allies or friends. The ability to drop "the bomb" on Moscow is less than useless in deterring limited incursions into areas of less than vital interest.)

Following World War II the United States enjoyed virtual immunity from attack until the mid-1950s, for the Soviets did not explode their first atomic bomb until late 1949, and the Soviet long-range air force did not undergo major development until 1954. Conversely, the Soviet Union was vulnerable to SAC bombers, whose American bases were supplemented by a global string of bases around the periphery of the Sino-Soviet bloc. Yet, even under such favorable conditions, it

---

[1.] The two best introductory books on limited war are Henry A. Kissinger, *Nuclear Weapons and Foreign Policy* (New York: Harper & Row, 1957); and Robert E. Osgood, *Limited War: The Challenge to American Strategy* (Chicago: University of Chicago Press, 1957).

was not rational for the United States to fight a total war in response to limited provocation. (The credibility of commitments, as we know, is related to the importance of the interests at stake. A power may risk a major war in defense of itself and its principal allies but not of lesser states in areas of secondary concern.) The ineffectiveness of threats of all-out war in deterring limited Soviet probes was in no way more clearly demonstrated than in the North Korean attack on South Korea in June 1950. The Soviets were apparently quite willing to resort to force by proxy, despite the United States' overwhelming strategic superiority. Obviously, the Soviets did not expect direct retaliation for a limited challenge on the Korean peninsula.)

("Limited war" may be defned as war fought for limited political purposes.[2] In contrast to the aims of total war, which generally include the complete destruction of the enemy's military forces and its government, the aims of limited war fall far short of total victory and unconditional surrender. Perhaps the most obvious goal is the capture of strategically located or economically important territory.) In the Korean war, the North Korean army sought to capture South Korea and to establish communist control over the entire Korean peninsula; it would then, in the deadly metaphor used by the Japanese, have "pointed the Korean dagger straight at Japan's heart." It helps to recall that the precipitating cause of the Russo-Japanese War of 1904–1905 was Russia's penetration of Korea from Manchuria. Japan at that time offered to divide Korea at the thirty-eighth parallel, but the czarist government refused. As a result, Japan attacked Siberia. Japanese security demanded that the southern half of Korea remain free of Russian control. In June 1950, when Japan served as a base for American forces, the United States' reaction was similar.

(But territory is not necessarily the principal aim of a limited challenge. More often, in a bipolar system a challenge is viewed as a test of the will and determination of the power defending the status quo.) President Truman and his advisers certainly saw the North Korean attack in that way, for they compared it with Nazi aggression during the 1930s. A failure to meet the communist challenge in Korea was regarded as affecting both Soviet behavior and that of America's allies. If the United States had not measured up to the test, the leaders in the Kremlin would have succeeded in demonstrating their own strength and resolution, as well as American weakness, fear, and unreliability.[3] It was expected that the allies and Japan—a much sought-after ally once Nationalist China had disintegrated—would in such circumstances seek safety in a neutral position. Commitments in the bipolar world were viewed by American policy makers as interdependent. (The consequences of inaction would be intangible, related more closely to political and psychological than to strictly territorial factors. For the defender of the status quo, therefore, compelling the attacker to desist or denying an enemy victory became the key objective.)

(If limited war is an alternative to fighting all-out nuclear war, while preserving the balance of power, the very existence of the opponent's state cannot

---

2. Kissinger, *op. cit.*, p. 140.

3. See Harry S. Truman, *Memoirs, I. Years of Trial and Hope* (Garden City, N.Y.: Doubleday, 1958), pp. 332–333.

212   become the issue. Halting the opponents' violations of one's own interests is the issue. Unconditional surrender or total victory cannot be the goal. The "winner" on the battlefield is especially responsible for forgoing complete victory; the "loser" will then not be compelled to escalate the conflict by, for example, calling on friends to intervene.) The Korean war again provides a good example of this situation. The United States first merely sought to restore the status quo. But, once the North Korean forces had been driven back to the thirty-eighth parallel, the United States, seeing an opportunity to unify all Korea and to destroy a communist satellite government, changed its objective. By turning the "dagger" once aimed at Japan around and thus endangering the political survival of the North Korean regime, the United States provoked Chinese intervention.[4] China's entry into the conflict intensified the fighting and brought the risk of an even greater escalation of the war. But leaders in Washington, afraid that striking back against China *in* China would trap the United States into a full-scale war on the Asian mainland or precipitate World War III, reverted to their original aim.

This result was exactly the opposite of that in Vietnam. The first Indochina war had been fought after World War II between the French, who were trying to reassert their colonial control over the country, and the communist-led Vietminh nationalist movement. It had been concluded at Geneva in 1954 with the partition of Vietnam at the seventeenth parallel. All the principal parties had seemed to gain in Geneva—except for the Vietminh. The Russians, helping the French out of a bad situation, were rewarded by France's scuttling of the European Defense Community, an organization within which West Germany was to rearm; the Chinese, by having been included in a major international conference, enhanced their claim to great-power status; and both communist powers avoided having to decide what to do if the Geneva accords failed and the United States should intervene and if the war resumed.[5] This did not occur and the United States avoided having to fight another limited war, and managed to see to it that half the country was salvaged from communism.[6] But the communist leadership could not be persuaded to settle for half of Vietnam for very long. Seeing itself as the legitimate heir to French rule in Vietnam, if not the whole of Indochina, the Hanoi government was absolutely determined to unify Vietnam.

(In addition to this basic political constraint, American, Russian, and

---

[4.] See John W. Spanier, *The Truman-MacArthur Controversy and the Korean War* (Cambridge, Mass.: Harvard University Press, 1959), pp. 84–134; and Allen S. Whiting, *China Crosses the Yalu: The Decision to Enter the Korean War* (New York: Macmillan, 1960).

[5.] Gurtov, *First Vietnam Crisis*, pp. 152–153.

[6.] Reunification was supposed to come after elections two years later. But this goal was unrealistic: the election stipulation in the Geneva agreements went unsigned. In Saigon, Ngo Dinh Diem's new government, which had not been a party to the agreement, denounced it immediately—the regime was unlikely to acquiesce in its own extinction. In the context of intense international bipolarity of the period, there was also no reason to expect American leaders to preside over Diem's political elimination. The seventeenth parallel thus became part of the international frontier. Nor could Ho Chi Minh really have believed that elections would be held; he was not that naive. More probably, he expected South Vietnam to collapse, which would enable him to pick up the pieces. The Saigon "government" was hardly in control of its half of the country in 1954. See Bernard B. Fall, *Viet-Nam Witness: 1953–66* (New York: Holt, Rinehart and Winston, 1966), pp. 75–76.

Chinese troops must remain uninvolved if war is to be limited.) Not that, if these forces were to clash, total war would be inevitable. But their involvement would increase the difficulty of limiting conflict. The great powers seem to be well aware of this second constraint, and the United States and the Soviet Union have been careful to avoid any embroilment in which they might confront each other directly. One of the purposes of stationing American troops in Europe has been to let the Soviets know that any attack there would inevitably involve the United States in war. In the ground and air corridors to West Berlin, as well as within the city itself, incidents involving direct clashes between American and Russian forces have been scrupulously avoided. (It is significant that limited wars have not occurred in Europe, an area of vital interest to both superpowers. Clearly, each fears that such conflicts could not be limited; the momentum to escalate in order to protect each power's sphere would perhaps be too great.)

Significantly, the Soviets have risked conflict only in a situation in which American forces had been withdrawn—in South Korea, an area of secondary American interest at that time. After the commitment of American forces, the fighting was between troops of North Korea, the Soviet Union's proxy, and troops fighting under the flag of the United Nations. The Communist Chinese troops that later intervened were not sent officially by the Chinese government. The government in Peking never declared war and never accepted responsibility for the Chinese troops in Korea, which were declared to be "volunteers." Nor did the United States declare war on North Korea or on Communist China. American troops were regarded as part of the U.N. force fighting a "police action." The absence of a declaration of war and the use of volunteers may well seem rather obvious fictions, yet such fictions help to keep wars limited.

(A third constraint is geographical—that is, limited wars have generally been confined to territory of a single nation.) The Yalu river served as the frontier between North Korea and China in the Korean war, and even after the Chinese intervention the war was not extended beyond it. Bombers were not sent to hit factories, railroads, and military supply depots in Manchuria. In fact, even the bombing of bridges crossing the Yalu into China was restricted to the North Korean side. The Korean war was thus fought in Korea. Similarly, the second Indochina war was confined to Indochina. More specifically, it was fought in North and South Vietnam, though the North used Laos and Cambodia as routes for sending troops and supplies southward, and these trails were also bombed regularly. In Laos, American aid was essentially limited to providing the neutralist government with air support against the communist Pathet Lao and North Vietnamese forces on its soil. In early 1971 the United States temporarily intervened more visibly with air support for South Vietnamese ground forces attempting to cut the Ho Chi Minh trail. The United States was also heavily bombing certain areas of Cambodia, where, in 1970, five years after the American intervention had secretly begun, the Nixon administration sent ground forces for an eight-week period in an unsuccesful and widely opposed effort to clean out North Vietnamese sanctuaries.

(The precedent of Korea, by contrast, suggested that in a limited war each side usually acknowledges that it must allow the other some clearly demarcated

214 "privileged sanctuaries"—inviolable areas for reserve troops, supplies, and air and naval bases. To attack these areas is to risk removing one of the constraints on the scope of the conflict.) Manchuria was such a sanctuary for the communists during the Korean war. Although its use as a sanctuary was known in the United States, especially by those who demanded that Manchuria be bombed, it was less well known that the United States, too, possessed privileged sanctuaries within the actual area of the fighting. No air attacks were launched on either Pusan or Inchon, the two largest ports through which most of the supplies for the U.N. forces were channeled. If either port had been subjected to frequent bombing, U.N. operations might have been seriously hampered. Similarly, Communist Chinese jet fighters did not attack U.N. troops in the field, American air bases in South Korea, or aircraft carriers lying off the coast; instead, they were limited to the Yalu river area, defending the bridges.

(A final constraint on limited wars is refusal to use tactical nuclear weapons.[7]) These weapons, which did not become available until the mid-1950s, do not necessarily favor the defending side. A conventional defense is generally calculated to hold an offense three times its size, but tactical nuclear weapons eliminate this advantage. Given the use of such weapons, if both sides are equally matched in numbers, there is no reason why the defender should hold its ground, let alone advance. More important, though, tactical nuclear weapons are a political liability. Few nations want to be "saved from communism" by means of nuclear weapons, which could devastate them.)

(If these principal constraints are present wars can be limited. *Tacit* bargaining between the participants is required. However ridiculous these restrictions may appear from the military point of view, their principal aim is to provide some incentive for the enemy to accept similar restraints. The limitations must be clearly drawn: Precisely because they are *not* formally negotiated but tacitly agreed upon, it is necessary that the terms be qualitatively distinguishable from possible alternatives. Frontiers and the distinction between conventional and nuclear weapons are so crystal clear that it is relatively easy to "agree" on them tacitly; once these limits have been violated, however, it is far more difficult to draw new lines. If small nuclear weapons should be used, for example, will the momentum of battle not lead to the employment of ever larger nuclear weapons until escalation finally results in the use of strategic arms? Nonuse of tactical nuclear arms is simple and unambiguous, easily understood and observed.[8])

(In addition, the restraints tend to reinforce one another; conversely, the more they are violated, the more tenuous the limitation. No single step in escalation will lead immediately and automatically to total war.) There are different gradations

---

[7] Arguments to the contrary are presented in Kissinger, *op. cit.*, pp. 174–202, though Kissinger had changed his mind by the time he wrote *The Necessity for Choice* (New York: Harper & Row, 1961, pp. 75–86); *see also* Oskar Morgenstern, *The Question of National Defense* (New York: Random House, 1959), pp. 145–154; and Osgood, *op. cit.*, pp. 251–259.

[8] Thomas C. Schelling, *Strategy and Conflict*, (Cambridge, Mass.: Harvard University Press, 1960), p. 75; and Schelling, *Arms and Influence*, (New Haven: Yale University Press, 1966), pp. 137–141.

or levels of violence among the landing of American marines in Lebanon in 1956, the crises over Quemoy and Matsu, Korean or Indochinese wars, and all-out nuclear conflict between the United States and the Soviet Union. Because the removal of each constraint tends to weaken the capacity to limit the conflict, when one side does escalate, the step must be taken carefully and slowly. After each step upward on the ladder, careful leaders pause to see whether or not the opponent will desist as a result of this escalation and fear of greater risks and costs. If the leaders have succeeded in arousing this fear, there may be no need for further escalation; if not, escalation may be necessary.[9] The important point is that at each rung of the "escalation ladder"[10] there be time for either tacit or explicit bargaining. The side against which the escalation is directed must have time to evaluate its next move, and it can do so only after it has decided what the escalation signifies about the opponent's intentions. It is thus very important to "slow down" the momentum of military operations in order to maintain political control and keep the war limited.

But, if one side persists in its original goal and refuses any concessions to end the war, the conflict becomes more difficult to restrain, for in such circumstances escalation appears necessary. Only by imposing more severe sanctions and by exacting a greater price for "victory"—and simultaneously risking the greater possibility of a rapid escalation into a far larger and more expensive war—can the "escalator" hope that the opponent will back down and give up some of its objectives. The result is a paradox. On one hand, limited goals are established in order to avoid escalation. On the other, if one belligerent goes beyond these goals, escalation is expected to compel self-restraint. Escalation, by bringing the hostilities one step nearer to all-out war, is supposed to underline the fact that the price of complete victory is far too high. The paradox becomes painful, however, when, despite escalation, the adversary persists in seeking total victory (which, as we shall see, happened in Vietnam).

REVOLUTIONARY WARFARE

Revolutionary, or guerrilla, conflict even more than conventional limited war, reflects the restraints imposed upon the use of force by nuclear weapons. The Soviets and the Chinese communists, who used it to come into power, call them "wars of national liberation." In the less-developed countries (LDCs), the aim of guerrillas is to capture state power *in order to transform completely the social-*

---

[9] For a critical view of American escalation, suggesting that the steps taken from late 1963 to 1966 were designed to prevent negotiations, presumably in order to avoid an unfavorable political settlement while the military situation was unfavorable, see Franz Schurmann *et al.*, *The Politics of the Escalation in Vietnam* (New York: Fawcett, 1966).

[10] Hermann Kahn, *On Escalation* (New York: Holt, Rinehart, Winston 1965), pp. 38–41. Also see Richard Smoke, *War* (Cambridge, Mass.: Harvard University Press, 1978) on controlling escalation.

216   *political structures and economic organizations of these nations.* That is why guerrilla warfare is often also called revolutionary warfare.⟩

⟨One advantage of such wars is that they do not raise the issue of aggression as clearly as do conventional limited attacks; the initiators thus remain free of the stigma "aggressor." There is no single moment when a major attack across a well-defined frontier occurs.⟩

⟨In the conventional war, the aggressor who has prepared for it within the confines of his national territory, channeling his resources into the preparation, has much to gain by attacking suddenly with all his forces. The transition from peace to war is as abrupt as the state of the art allows; the first shock may be decisive. This is hardly possible in the revolutionary war because the aggressor—the insurgent—lacks sufficient strength at the outset. Indeed, years may sometimes pass before he has built up significant political, let alone military, power. So there is usually little or no first shock, little or no surprise, no possibility of an early decisive battle. In fact, the insurgent has no interest in producing a shock until he feels fully able to withstand the enemy's expected reaction.[11]⟩

⟨Furthermore, because guerrilla forces generally are preponderantly native, a guerrilla war has the appearance of being a "domestic" conflict. Finally, guerrilla wars tend to be lengthy. If the guerrillas were as strong as or stronger than their opponents, they would seek quick victory in conventional battle. But their very weakness compels them to whittle away at their enemies' strength bit by bit. This process of attrition can go almost unnoticed in the outside world until the last stage of the war, when the guerrillas are poised to defeat their weakened and demoralized opponents. By then, it is usually too late for effective countermeasures. Waging guerrilla warfare is thus considerably safer than fighting a regular war in the nuclear age.⟩

⟨In the initial phase of a revolutionary war, the weaker guerrillas are strategically on the defensive; tactically, though, they are always on the offensive. In order to wear down the enemy, they adopt hit-and-run tactics. Mobility, surprise, and rapid military decisions are characteristic of their operations. They fight only when there is a good chance of victory; otherwise, they do not attack and, if engaged, quickly disengage. Their attacks are swift, sudden, and relentless. There is no front line in such a war. The front is everywhere, and the guerrillas can strike anywhere. Guerrilla tactical doctrine is perhaps most aptly summed up in Mao Tse-tung's well-known formula: "Enemy advances, we retreat; enemy halts, we harass; enemy tires, we attack; enemy retreats, we pursue."[12]⟩

Rather than inflicting major defeats on the enemy, these tactics result in harassment, confusion, and frustration. The guerrillas do not engage in conven-

---

[11] David Galula, *Counterinsurgency Warfare* (New York: Holt, Rinehart and Winston, 1964), pp. 9–10.

[12] *Mao Tse-tung on Guerrilla Warfare*, trans. by Samuel B. Griffith (New York: Holt, Rinehart and Winston, 1961), pp. 103–104. For the Vietminh's seven rules for the conduct of guerrilla warfare, see Otto Heilbrunn, *Partisan Warfare* (New York: Holt, Rinehart and Winston, 1962), pp. 78–79.

tional battle until the last stage of the war because they are too weak throughout most of the hostilities. Physical violence is important, but it is the *psychological* impact of the war that is decisive. Although the enemy cannot be beaten physically, its *will to fight* can still be eroded, in two ways. Basically, the regular army can be demoralized. Suffering one minor defeat after another, rarely engaging the enemy directly in battle, forced increasingly on the defensive by the guerrillas' tactics, the army loses its offensive spirit as it finds its conventional tactics useless. Determination to stay and fight decline and stamina is sapped.

Even more important in undermining the enemy's will to fight is to isolate it either by capturing the support of most of the population or by neutralizing it. Control of the population is essential if the guerrillas are to achieve their objective of "internal conquest." The populace provides them with recruits, food, shelter, and, above all, intelligence. If the guerrillas are to surprise the enemy, they must know where to strike and when. They must know all the opponent's moves in order to be able to choose favorable moments at which to fight and in order to be able to escape when government reinforcements suddenly arrive.

Victory is naturally one way of impressing the people, who at the beginning of a revolutionary war are likely to be divided into three groups: a fervent minority favoring the guerrillas, a militant minority favoring the government, and a majority of the population—between 50 and 70 percent—who are neutral. This last group will remain passive until it is clear which side will win. Its neutrality, of course, favors the guerrillas, because it hampers government forces; the people will not provide the latter with the information necessary to locate the guerrillas. As the government's troops become demoralized and defensive, as increasingly they appear unable to provide the population with elementary security in daily life, the government loses whatever allegiance it has had. It is the peasants, generally removed from any contact with their government, who are most concerned about their own future. If they think the guerrillas will win the war, they are unlikely to antagonize them but will instead cooperate.

Terrorism also helps to elicit cooperation. This kind of terrorism is usually selective, and its aim is to reaffirm the weakness of the government; in the main it is therefore applied to local government officials. Obviously, wholesale and indiscriminate terrorism would only alienate the very people whose support the guerrillas seek to win, though on occasion wholesale execution or the burning of a village is used to influence other villages and towns. The guerrillas have made their point vividly when they can show the peasants that the government is not able even to protect its own officials.[13] Furthermore, by eliminating these officials, the guerrillas break the link between the government and the majority of the people, thus restricting the government's authority mainly to the cities.

Even in the cities, this authority may not go uncontested. In the Tet offensive of 1968 the Vietcong infiltrated major South Vietnamese cities and district capitals. The populations were shocked into recognition that they were not safe

---

[13.] In South Vietnam, for instance, more than 15,000 village officials were murdered between 1957 and 1965. Fall, *op. cit.*, p. 293.

218   either. Just as Vietcong control of a village and executions of some villagers who cooperated with, or were on the side of, the government conveyed to the peasants the message that they had better support the guerrillas—or at least remain "neutral"—so the attacks on cities were intended to warn their inhabitants that they had better be careful about which side they supported. These attacks further undermined confidence in the Saigon government, as well as in the United States; if, after three years of intensive warfare, apparently neither could so much as guarantee the safety of the cities they were supposed to control, why should the population expect any better in the future?

(Guerrillas, however, achieve popular support mainly because of an effective *social strategy* in which they are identified with a popular cause or grievance.[14]) Communist guerrillas do not usually present themselves as communists, nor do the people support them because they are communists or desire the establishment of a communist state. The guerrillas present themselves simply as spokesmen for existing social causes and aspirations. If the people are resentful of continued colonial rule or of a despotic native government, the guerrillas take up the cry. If certain classes seek social and economic justice, the guerrillas demand it on their behalf. The guerrillas identify themselves as "liberators" and "reformers," promising that they can satisfy rising expectations. In South Vietnam the Vietcong appealed to the peasants by pointing out that they were working in the landowners' rice fields for the landowners' benefit. When the landlords fled to the cities, the Vietcong told the peasants that they no longer had to pay exorbitant and exploitative rents (or taxes); the peasants owned the land, and the Vietcong would protect them if anyone sought to take it away. The result was a deep schism between the government in Saigon and the peasantry.

(This social strategy, as Jeffrey Race has called it, is basic to the guerrillas' revolutionary warfare; important as the military component of this warfare is, it is neither the most significant nor the distinguishing characteristic of this particular kind of war, especially as it is waged by communist parties whose entire social outlook is based on a class analysis and class struggle. Indeed, the struggle begins *before* the military phase of the war begins, as in each village and hamlet the revolutionary party establishes its cells, seeks local control and support, and thus diminishes the base of popular support for the government. The fact that a large proportion of the population tends to be neutral in the war, waiting to see who is likely to win, is partly the result of this *preemptive* social strategy. Whereas the revolutionaries' maximum goal is to mobilize the population to fight with them against the government, their minimum aim is to prevent the population from fighting on the government's side.)

When the war has gone on long enough for the revolutionaries to have won widespread popular support, the government will have become increasingly isolated socially and weakened militarily, so that only a final blow is needed to

---

[14] Jeffrey Race, *War Comes to Long An* (Berkeley: University of California Press, 1972), pp. 141 ff; Heilbrunn, *op. cit.*, pp. 145–146; and George K. Tanham, *Communist Revolutionary Warfare* (New York: Holt, Rinehart, and Winston, 1961), p. 143. On the different components of strategy, see Michael Howard, "The Forgotten Dimensions of Strategy," *Foreign Affairs*, Summer 1979, pp. 975–986.

topple it. This last step involves resort to conventional battle—*unless*, as in Cuba and South Vietnam before the American intervention, the entire governmental structure and authority have already disintegrated. The guerrillas must, of course, be extremely careful in their timing. If they engage in conventional fighting too early, before the enemy army has lost most of its will to fight and before they themselves are properly trained and equipped, they may be badly defeated. But, if they have the patience and are able to calculate correctly the moment of transition, the war will end in victory for them. The defeat of the French forces at Dienbienphu in Indochina broke France's determination to hold onto its old colony, yet the French garrison at Dienbienphu consisted of only one fifteenth of the total number of French troops in Indochina; though the French suffered 12,000 casualties, including prisoners, the estimated Vietminh casualties were 15,000. As its total force was not as large as that of the French, the Vietminh clearly had been badly hurt. Nonetheless, this single battle sapped France's will to resist.[15] The French decided to end the long and—for them—futile fighting.[16]

Guerrilla warfare may at times seem militarily primitive, for guerrilla weapons do not begin to compare with the highly intricate weapons in Western arsenals. Guerrillas may, of course, receive sophisticated weapons, but their success does not depend upon them.(Politically, however, guerrilla warfare is "more sophisticated than nuclear war or atomic war or war as it was waged by conventional armies, navies, and air forces."[17])

(No counterrevolutionary war can be won by conventional military means alone: A *purely military solution is impossible*. It is interesting to note in this connection that the successful guerrilla and counterguerrilla leaders of the past two decades have usually not been military men.[18]) In China, Mao, a student, a librarian, and subsequently a professionally trained revolutionary, defeated Chiang Kai-shek, a professionally trained soldier. In Indochina, Ho Chi Minh, a socialist agitator, and General Giap, a French-trained history teacher, defeated four of France's senior generals, including a marshal. Castro was a lawyer, and Magsaysay, who led the counterguerrilla war in the Philippines, was an automotive mechanic who became a politician. In short, the orthodox military officer has generally been unable to cope with the unorthodox nature of guerrilla warfare.

(In the final analysis, the government can win its war against the revolutionaries only if it alleviates the conditions that have led the peasantry to support the revolutionary party in the first place.) For example, in Malaya the British

---

[15.] Tanham, *op.cit.*, pp. 32, 97.

[16.] In the final phase, according to some experts, guerrilla forces need an external source of support and supply. Bernard Fall held external sanctuary to be decisive: "The success or failure of *all* rebellions since World War II depended on whether the active sanctuary was willing and able to perform its expected role." Yet he himself admitted that "the French were definitely the 'aliens' and the Communist-led Viet-Minh forces could count on the instinctive support of the native population." The French were therefore unable to build antiguerrilla forces, and their intelligence was often faulty because they were isolated from the population. See Fall, *Street without Joy* (rev. ed.; Harrisburg: Stackpole, 1966), p. 16.

[17.] Griffith, in Introduction to *Mao Tse-tung on Guerilla Warfare*, p. 7.

[18.] Charles W. Thayer, *Guerrilla* (New York: Harper & Row, 1963), pp. 42–60.

220   promised independence during the war there from 1946 to 1960; because they had already granted independence to India, Pakistan, and Burma, their word was credible, and the Malayans had a stake in the government's struggle. The communists were thus stripped of their guise as liberators from colonialism. Many Malays fought alongside British troops. The contrast with the situation in Vietnam is striking. In the first Indochina war, the people supported the Vietminh as national liberators because the French refused to grant them full independence. Ho Chi Minh thus became a symbol of Vietnamese nationalism. Anticommunist Vietnamese who had fought with the French against the Vietminh (as anticommunist Malays had fought with the British) were never able to compete with Ho for this nationalist identity. After 1954 they appeared to many—including many in the West—as puppets of France. This image was reinforced by their lack of social conscience and concern. Indeed, the government's suppression of political opponents, critics of the war, and advocates of settlement with the Vietcong only fortified this image.

Popular confidence, then, is the *indispensable* condition for successful antirevolutionary warfare. Military countermeasures alone can never be adequate; troops trained in the tactics of unconventional warfare must be supported by political, social, and economic reforms. It was this kind of combination that defeated the communist-led Huks in the Philippines during the 1950s. The government won the allegiance of the peasantry by instituting reforms to improve their lives; the communist appeal was weakened, and the Huks lost their support.[19] A British colonel summed up the essence of counterguerrilla warfare: "There has never been a successful guerrilla war conducted in an area where the populace is hostile to the guerrillas. . . . The art of defeating the guerrillas is therefore the art of turning the populace against them."[20]

(The major task of antirevolutionary warfare, then, is fundamentally *political.*) Guerrillas are a barometer of discontent. This discontent must be ameliorated, for it is the decisive element in bringing about victory or failure. Perhaps the French experience in Algeria offers the clearest evidence. The French actually won the military war against the Algerian guerrillas. By 1960 the Algerian National Liberation Army no longer possessed even a battalion-size unit. By the end of the war in 1962, the Algerian guerrillas had, according to French army sources, fewer than 4,000 troops left (10,000 according to other, more sympathetic French sources) out of a total of almost 60,000 three years earlier.[21] French military tactics had been as effective in Algeria as they had been ineffective in Indochina. Nevertheless, the French lost the war because it was *politically* "unwinnable." The Algerian

---

[19] See Frances L. Starner, *Magsaysay and the Philippine Peasantry: The Agrarian Impact on Philippine Politics, 1953–1956* (Berkeley and Los Angeles: University of California Press, 1961). For views of the contrasting situation in South Vietnam, see Fall, *The Two Viet-Nams: A Political and Military Analysis* (rev. ed.; New York: Holt, Rinehart and Winston, 1964); and Denis Warner, *The Last Confucian* (New York: Macmillan, 1963).

[20] Quoted in Heilbrunn, *op. cit.*, p. 34. On the decisiveness of civilian loyalties, see Chalmers A. Johnson, "Civilian Loyalties and Guerrilla Conflict," *World Politics*, July 1962, pp. 646–661. Also see Johnson, *Autopsy on People's War* (Berkeley: University of California Press, 1973).

[21] Fall, *Two Viet-Nams*, pp. 346–347. The Algerian example also clearly demonstrates that counterterror is not effective in ending guerilla warfare.

population was hostile; so were France's NATO allies and the nonaligned states. The suppression of a nationalist movement was politically unpalatable and unfeasible in an age when the right of all former colonies to rule themselves was almost universally recognized and asserted.(*Understanding that, in certain circumstances, war is revolution allows us to understand why conventional military force often tends to be self-defeating.*)

AMERICAN POWER AND THE "RULES OF THE GAME" IN VIETNAM[22]

We might suspect from the preceding analysis that it would have been difficult for the United States to counter guerrilla warfare in Vietnam. American military leaders had been, first of all, trained in military orthodoxy. They saw this war like other wars, as essentially a military undertaking, not as a political one.[23] All that was necessary, they believed, was to apply American technology and "know-how" to the problem. It was difficult to conceive of the world's mightiest nation, with its huge army led by well-trained officers and supported by the might and knowledge of American industry, as unable to defeat a few thousand black-clad Asain guerrillas. It was easy to indulge in the "illusion of omnipotence." The United States had, after all, beaten far greater powers. France's earlier failure was judged as owing to alienation of the Vietnamese nationalists and an army that was not well equipped or led and had poor air support. None of these factors, presumably, would hamper the United States.

(*Hubris* (the Greek word for overweening pride) proved a great impediment, however. In effect, the United States was so powerful and so sure of success that it believed it could fight a guerrilla war simply by *changing the rules* and fighting

---

[22] We are not concerned in this section with judgments on whether or not the United States should have intervened in Vietnam. We focus only on the manner in which force was used. Judgment is, of course, implicit in such an analysis. Ultimately, it reflects on the issue of the original intervention, for, if the conculsion is that force was exercised ineffectively—indeed, counterproductively—it may also be deduced that the intervention should have been avoided in the first place. This judgment, to be sure, is pragmatic, not moral. For moral and legal judgments on the war, see, among others, Telford Taylor, *Nuremberg and Vietnam: An American Tragedy* (New York: Bantam, 1971); and Richard A. Falk, Gabriel Kolko, and Robert J. Lifton, eds., *Crimes of War* (New York: Vintage, 1971). For a contrary pont of view, defending the war's legality, see Guenter Lewy, *America in Vietnam* (New York: Oxford University Press, 1978), pp. 223–270, 343–373.

This writer's final pragmatic judgment on Vietnam is much the same as that of Donald Zagoria in *Vietnam Triangle: Moscow, Peking, Hanoi* (New York: Pegasus, 1967); p. xiii: that American strategy and tactics raise "serious doubts in my mind whether we as a nation have the wisdom, the skills and the manpower to cope with civil wars."

[23] General Lewis W. Walt, assistant commandant of the U.S. Marine Corps, confessed in 1970 that, when he visited Vietnam in 1965, he did not understand that the war was primarily a guerrilla war. Rather, he thought of it as a more conventional war like World War II and the Korean war; *The New York Times*, November 18, 1970. General Earle Wheeler, chairman of the Joint Chiefs of Staff, held the same opinion, as reported by Hilsman, *To Move a Nation*, p. 426.

222   according to the American concept of war.)[24] This concept emphasized the achievement of victory through attrition of the enemy's forces. The soldier's concern was
"strictly military"; politics was not his business. This division of labor suggests that
the crucial political war was going to be ignored until after the achievement of
military triumph. Then, and then only, would the Saigon government carry out
the necessary political and social reforms. (Of course, if the guerrillas could be
destroyed by purely military means, reforms would be unnecessary later. Then why
should the Saigon government bother?) The additional advantage that the military
saw was that the United States would be fighting the war, thus avoiding the difficulties and frustrations of cooperating with the ineffective South Vietnamese army,
which was expected only to stay out of the way. This policy and ordering of priorities
guaranteed failure. Surely the war could not be won *primarily* by foreign troops;
rather an indigenous army with a will to fight and support from a sizable portion
of its people was required.

In any event, the American strategy in South Vietnam from 1965 to 1968
was one of "search and destroy" in order to defeat the North Vietnamese forces.
Translated into daily operations, this strategy allocated 80 percent of American
forces to the central highlands and frontier areas, in which only 4 percent of the
population resided. More than 90 percent of the people lived in the Mekong delta
and coastal plain, and it was in those areas that the actual guerrilla war was being
fought.[25] As the United States sent in more troops to decimate the North Vietnamese
forces, the Hanoi government matched the buildup.(The American aim was *physical* attrition; that of the North Vietnamese was *psychological* exhaustion.[26])The
American victories in battle and the heavy casualties among the Vietnamese could
not, as a result, be transformed into lasting political success.

The United States was therefore irrevocably committed to a seemingly
interminable war that would eventually erode the patience of the American public.
Indeed, the search-and-destroy strategy, by leaving the cities essentially undefended,
was an invitation to Vietcong attack. The dramatic Tet offensive of 1968 not only
revealed the folly of American strategy but also forced Americans to ask whether
or not the war could be brought to a successful political and military conclusion
at all.[27] Psychologically, the Tet offensive was the beginning of the end for the
United States in Vietnam, as the American public, already beset by doubts about
the wisdom and costs of the war, became increasingly disillusioned. It was the
United States' Dienbienphu, sapping American will and determination. It was not
a military defeat. Quite the contrary: the Vietcong lost most of its elite forces.

(The core of revolutionary warfare—gaining control of the population—
was rejected as an objective by the American command as requiring too defensive
a strategy. Not only does counterrevolutionary war necessitate gradual clearance

---

[24] Robert Thompson, *No Exit from Vietnam* (New York: McKay, 1969), pp. 13–17; and
Lewy, *op. cit.* Both authors stress American misconduct of the war.

[25] Kissinger, *American Foreign Policy* (New York: Norton, 1969), p. 102.

[26] *Ibid.*, p. 104.

[27] Thompson, *op. cit.*, pp. 40–74.

of guerrillas from one zone after another; it also requires providing continuing security in the cleared zones, which means keeping troops there. The population can then be separated from the guerrillas, the guerrilla political cell structure flushed out, and necessary reforms carried out to win the people's allegiance. Such a "clear-and-hold" strategy is, of course, slow. It is not dramatic and yields no big body counts or weapons captures; by subordinating military to political and psychological considerations, it contradicts the aggressive self-image of the military establishment. Had American forces been able to start destroying the Vietcong infrastructure in South Vietnamese villages, the Vietcong and the Hanoi government would have seen their control begin to wither, which would have increased their incentive to accept a political settlement of the war before their village cells were destroyed. The casualties they suffered provided no comparable incentive.[28] Manpower was the price the guerrillas expected to pay for success; as harsh as it sounds, the dead were replaceable. The cells, built up over twenty-five years, were not easily replaceable.

Orthodox military doctrine thus led to the adoption of an irrelevant strategy. American officers apparently had not heard the axiom that a conventional army in a guerrilla war loses if it does not win, whereas guerrrillas win if they do not lose. But winning this kind of war demands a strategy that gives priority to political and psychological factors. Instead, the United States selected a strategy guaranteed to lose. Characteristically, however, the military blamed its lack of success on the flow of men and weapons from North Vietnam. In this way, military leaders could avoid acknowledging their faulty strategy in the South, the only place where the war could be won.

In the United States political leaders also focused on North Vietnam, believing that it too had to be defeated if the war was to be won. They knew that counterguerrilla wars could be lengthy affairs. In Malaya, where the communist terrorists had almost no outside help and little or no suport from the Malays or wealthier Chinese, it had taken 80,000 British and Commonwealth troops, plus 180,000 Malay special police, constables, and village militia members, twelve years (from 1948 to 1960) to defeat only 8,000 guerrillas.[29] In the Philippines it took five years (from 1947 to 1952) to defeat the Huks. And after President Magsaysay died, the succeeding corrupt Garcia administration faced a revival of Huk activities; when President Macapagal took office in 1962, he had therefore to order mop-up operations.

But Americans like to win their wars quickly. President Johnson could recall the more direct challenge in Korea. Within one year Americans had been fed up with "Truman's war" and the continuing, apparently futile loss of American lives. This mood contributed to the defeat of the Democrats in the 1952 presidential election. A long-drawn-out, indecisive engagement does not fit the traditional American all-or-nothing approach, and guerrillas can exploit this impatience. Not permitting the enemy to take shelter within its main sanctuary seemed one possible

[28] *Ibid.*, pp. 51, 57–58.
[29] Fall, *Two Viet-Nams*, p. 341.

224 way of ending the hostilities reasonably quickly, a justifiable reason for disregarding one of the principal constraints on limited warfare.)

(The concept of graduated escalation in limited wars was viewed as a means of influencing the adversary's will through a process of bargaining on ascending levels of violence in order to provide an incentive to agree to acceptable terms and conclude hostilities.[30])North Vietnam was to be punished for its role in the war and made to pay an ever-increasing price until it had suffered enough to quit. The air force was to be the instrument for administering this punishment. But the task was beyond the ability of the air force; indeed, the political consequences of the limited air war against North Vietnam have to be judged as disastrous.

For one thing, an air force's ability to affect the enemy's capacity to fight lies in its ability to attack the sources of enemy supplies and the enemy supply lines; it requires that the army then engage the enemy on the battlefield.[31] The Vietnamese sources of supplies, however, were Russia and China; furthermore, it was the North Vietnamese who generally chose the times and lengths of engagements in this unconventional war. Only the trails running to South Vietnam and, of course, roads, rivers, and a few factories in North Vietnam were left to attack. The trails through the jungle, however, were difficult to find and ran mostly through Laos and Cambodia; long periods of bad weather and the lack of an all-weather fighter-bomber (except for the F-111, which came into service late and was plagued wth problems) only added to the difficulties. As for bombing the North, it could

> succeed in wiping out all North Viet-Nam's conventional industrial and military targets, but it would probably have little immediate effect on its armed forces. After all, they [the guerrillas] successfully fought the French for eight years from hidden guerrilla bases and without making use of electric-power plants and rail-roads. . . . Lest it be forgotten, the United States Air Force was unable successfully to interdict Communist supply operations in Korea despite the fact that all conventional targets had been effectively destroyed.[32]

In Vietnam, as in Korea, supplies kept on coming. Indeed, the flow of men and ammunition increased, and the trails were not even used to full capacity.

(The real difficulty with the bombing campaign of 1965–1968, however, seems to have been the concept of graduated escalation itself. It is perhaps doubtful that it can be made to work against an underdeveloped country; an industrial state simply has more to lose.)No doubt, there must be some level of punishment that would affect even an underdeveloped nation's will. But in Hanoi the motivation to succeed the French in all of Indochina was so tenacious, had been held so long, had been fought and sacrificed for during so many years, and had been so near to fulfillment on more than one occasion—only to be repeatedly betrayed—that the

---

[30.] The attempts to force the Hanoi government to cease operations in South Vietnam before the large commitment of ground forces in July 1965 are catalogued in the Pentagon study of the intervention. See *The Pentagon Papers* (New York: Quadrangle, 1971).

[31.] Townsend Hoopes, *The Limits of Intervention* (New York: McKay, 1969), pp. 75–79.

[32.] Fall, *Two Viet-Nams*, p. 402.

will to fight on was intense. By contrast General Giap, the victor of Dienbienphu and strategist of the war in the South, had a shrewd political estimate of the Western democracies' determination to continue fighting an inconclusive war for very long: "The enemy will pass slowly from the offensive to the defensive. The blitzkrieg will transform itself into a war of long duration. (Thus, the enemy will be caught in a dilemma: He has to drag out the war in order to win it and does not possess, on the other hand, the psychological and political means to fight a long-drawn-out war."[33])

Whereas in Cuba in 1962 the Soviets calculated that the cost of noncompliance with the American demand to pull out Soviet missiles was greater than the cost of complying, in Vietnam, the Hanoi government calculated that the cost of noncompliance with the Johnson administration's demands—to desist in military activities in the South and to pull its troops back to the North—was less than the cost of complying. The North Vietnamese were willing to pay the price of bomb damage, civilian casualties, and heavy losses in military manpower for their fundamental belief that they were the rightful heirs of French power throughout all of Vietnam, if not all of Indochina.

(It can be argued that more bombing and quicker escalation would have raised the price of noncompliance higher than that for compliance. Perhaps. What we do know is that, in the three years of air war against North and South Vietnam, the air force dropped three times the total tonnage dropped in Europe and the Pacific area during World War II (at a cost of 50 cents per pound of bomb, a total cost of $3 billion!).[34])We also know that, for North Vietnam, as for any other country, there must have been a level of pain at which the government in Hanoi would "break" and give up its attempt to expand its control into South Vietnam. Nevertheless, the enormous casualties accepted by the Hanoi government suggests that that level had not yet been reached. John Mueller has argued that the military costs suffered by the North Vietnamese were "virtually unprecedented historically," even though the North Vietnamese—unlike the combatants of World Wars I and II—were not fighting for their survival.[35] The American goal was to deny them victory in the South, not to eliminate Vietnam altogether. Estimating communist battle deaths at 500,000–600,000, a figure that Hanoi leaders have admitted to, Mueller notes that it is equivalent to 2.5–3 percent of the prewar population of Vietnam, a percentage twice that suffered by the fanatical Japanese during World War II. In the last 160 years only a few of the participants in more than 100 wars have lost as much as 2 percent of their prewar populations (in World War I Germany lost 2.7 percent, Austria-Hungary 2.3 percent, France 3.3 percent, and England 2 percent; in World War II, Russia and Germany each lost 4.4 percent). The North Koreans had given up continuing to fight in 1953, after far fewer casualties; the Vietminh had done the same in 1954. Under "normal" conditions, the expectation

---

[33.] Quoted in *ibid.*, p. 113.

[34.] Raphael Littauer and Norman Uphoff, eds., *The Air War in Indochina* (Boston: Beacon, 1972); Lewy, *op. cit.*

[35.] John E. Mueller," The Search for the 'Breaking Point' in Vietnam: The Statistics of a Deadly Quarrel," unpublished paper.

226   that the government in Hanoi would desist if punished heavily was, therefore, a rational one. But, clearly, its willingness to suffer immense physical losses while psychologically wearing out the United States gave it the upper hand; its determination to succeed was greater than the American will to continue. The bombing of North Vietnam, then, had little effect on North Vietnamese determination or ability to infiltrate. Quite the contrary. The government benefited through bombing! It undoubtedly received greater domestic support for its efforts in the South because, as the Battle of Britain had already epically demonstrated in World War II, people who are bombarded daily are strengthened in their resolve; without the bombing, Ho might not have been able quite so easily to rally his people to support a long war with a high casualty rate. [36]

(Worse, the bombing, more than any other issue, deeply divided the American population and aroused widespread antagonism in even friendly Western nations.) To have bombed Hanoi "back to the Stone Age," as one air-force general summed up his recipe for victory, would have aroused even greater political hostility. As it was, the bombing made the United States appear a bully and North Vietnam the underdog. It aroused international sympathy and support for the Hanoi government, and it stirred many an American conscience. The fact that the bombing brought many people out for anti-American demonstrations all over the world was as significant as the actual battles—and seemingly more decisive; it made it more difficult to handle the war "politically at home and diplomatically abroad." [37] It shifted the onus of the war from Hanoi to Washington. The bombing, to put it bluntly, was politically counterproductive.

(It was not really until after Tet and Nixon's assumption of power that the conduct of the war changed in significant respects and that the *political context* within which the war was fought changed dramatically. For Tet was a turning point not only psychologically within the United States but also militarily in South Vietnam. The North Vietnamese surprise attack, though contributing to American public disillusionment with the nation's involvement in the war, nevertheless resulted in extremely heavy casualties for the Vietcong; many of their best-trained and most experienced military cadres were killed, so that by 1970 most of the combat had to be carried on by the North Vietnamese army instead of by indigenous forces.) The replacement of both the American field commander and the President resulted in greater adaptation to classical counterinsurgency operations in South Vietnam. Vietcong capabilities were gradually reduced, though not eliminated. Politically, the president sought to preserve—as his predecessors had done—an anticommunist government in Saigon, but he needed time at home. He proceeded to withdraw American troops gradually in order to cut casualties, reduce the draft, and thus lessen domestic opposition; South Vietnamese forces, closely supported by American air power, were to foreclose the Vietcong's taking over of the government in Saigon—the objective of the revolutionary war.

[36.] Thompson, *op. cit.*, pp. 139–140.

[37.] Hoopes, *op. cit.*, p. 82.

The result was that in spring 1972 the North Vietnamese launched a large-scale conventional attack across the so-called demilitarized zone separating North and South Vietnam, presumably in order to administer the coup de grâce at a time when few American combat troops were left and the president was about to visit Moscow. This attack was heavily supported by tanks and artillery, which came primarily from Russia. It proved successful at first against some of South Vietnam's worst troops (an offensive had been expected elsewhere), though, when reinforced, they rallied. Very heavy American air support probably won the day; the North Vietnamese, exposing themselves to conventional warfare with modern weapons, with all the logistical needs the latter involve (bringing up gasoline, artillery shells, and so forth), provided American planes for the first time in seven years with destructible targets moving in open country.

In addition, President Nixon, in retaliation for what he called a full-scale invasion and a clear-cut instance of aggression, decided to commence the bombing of North Vietnam—including the use of B-52s against urban and industrial targets, which had been off limits during the Johnson years—and to mine the harbor of Haiphong in order to stop all incoming supplies. This latter step was one that President Johnson had continually rejected, partly because the Vietcong, being a guerrilla force, was less dependent on modern weapons and, more important, because he feared that such a blockade of North Vietnam's principal harbor might precipitate Chinese military intervention. But Nixon's new bombing campaign took place in politically quite different circumstances.

Whereas Johnson had tried primarily to persuade the Russians to put pressure on the government in Hanoi, which generally received support from Peking, to help him find a settlement, Nixon used both Russia's and China's needs for a détente with the United States to isolate North Vietnam. Nixon offered both communist countries carrots. Although his retaliation invoked the risk that the Moscow summit meeting would be called off, the President took the gamble, hoping that the Soviets needed the SALT agreement and modern technology to help their sagging economy enough not to jeopardize the summit conference. He also gave Peking's leaders an opportunity to concentrate on what they perceived to be the greater and more immediate Russian threat without simultaneously confronting the United States.

Even North Vietnam, suddenly subjected to a heavy beating with a stick, was offered some carrots. In 1965–1968, when North Vietnam had been offered only a cease-fire and peace if it pulled out of South Vietnam altogether, it was now offered complete withdrawal of American forces, including air forces, an opportunity to retain control of those southern areas that it controlled, as well as a possible place in a coalition government to be arranged through negotiations among the various parties in South Vietnam after a cease-fire and return of American prisoners of war. The isolated Hanoi government was willing to accept a settlement that would ensure no further direct American participation in the war and would leave future opportunities to capture partial or full control in the South. But South Vietnam, itself isolated now, collapsed two years later. Saigon's leaders,

228 for too long too concerned only with holding onto their power, too dependent on external military and economic support, and too little concerned about developing a social strategy to mobilize the support and morale of the population, reaped their reward.

POWER AND THE USE OF FORCE

(Limited war is a reminder that in the nuclear era the superpowers have to be disciplined in their use of power. It is not coincidental that the age of absolute weapons is the age of limited wars. First of all, this type of warfare reflects the gap between a nation's existing capability and its potential power if all of its resources are mobilized.)In neither the Korean nor the Vietnamese war did the United States mobilize fully; the objective was not the total defeat of the enemy, as it had been in the wars against Germany, and therefore full mobilization was not required. The United States did not feel its security threatened in any immediate sense; its interventions in Korea and Vietnam were intended to forestall a perceived long-run danger arising from the fall of a series of dominoes. Most men were not drafted, and industry was not converted from automobile to tank production; for most Americans, daily life and concerns went on much as before. In total war "butter" was immediately subordinated to "guns" until victory was achieved; in limited war, however, guns still must compete with butter, as most individuals and groups in society continue to pursue the same goals as before. Was the United States not basically at peace? There were no attacks on American shipping on the high seas or in a harbor to spur the country to unite or to elicit a presidential declaration of war.(In such a clear-cut transition from peace to war, it would be "natural"—and, in a democracy, politically feasible—to give priority to the nation's needs and the common danger.\

In these circumstances, it is worth repeating, generalizations about the United States as "the most powerful country in the world" are hardly helpful. Even if accurate, they imply a fully mobilized country, not a nation fighting a limited conflict while conducting other "business as usual." A nation that does not convert much of its economy to war production cannot count its gross national product (GNP) as an indicator of strength and possible victory; nor can it add in a population of more than 200 million. At the height of the Vietnam war American troops constituted less than one-quarter of 1 percent of the American population.(In the future, the cost of oil may mean that even "the most powerful country in the world" will not be able to afford war at all, no matter how many men are called up! The country might go bankrupt before it won its victory or settled for a stalemate.)

(Second, given the need for restraint in the conduct of limited war, certain components—even if mobilized—are simply irrelevant to power relations and predictions of who will "win." The nuclear armory, both strategic and tactical, which is such a major part of American military strength, cannot be included in such calculations. Such power is either politically (and perhaps a Westerner should add "morally") unusable, especially against a nonnuclear adversary, or irrelevant to the type of hostilities being waged. This element of American capability is thus of no use in limited war.) Neither North Korea nor North Vietnam was deterred from attempting to take over South Korea and South Vietnam—both American protégés. They could regard the possibilities of war with the United States quite differently because, for both political and military reasons, the latter could not use nuclear weapons. (Indeed, *this American inhibition enhanced the utility of the enemy military forces (whether used conventionally or unconventionally)*) Those two wars thus seemed to be fought between equals, rather than between a giant and a dwarf. (Indeed, was the United States not perhaps the dwarf in Vietnam?)

On the other hand, to pick an intangible and ever-present component, how could analysts in Washington just before the American intervention have calculated North Vietnamese or American morale, an intangible component? Would it not seem that increasing pressure on North Vietnam through bombings would hurt the regime and undermine its willingness to continue directing and organizing the conflict in the South? Would anyone have questioned the willingness of the American public to support its government in a war that would presumably compel the Hanoi government to desist in the South within approximately two years? In fact, it was American morale that was eroded during the war while North Vietnamese morale remained high despite enormous losses. The "asymmetry of motivation" clearly favored the North Vietnamese.

(Third, Vietnam will long stand as another reminder that power, in order to be effective, must not only be mobilized but must also be of the right kind, applicable to the prevailing conditions. The power that was applied in Vietnam was not really useful because it was applied without much regard for the political context of revolutionary warfare.[38]) The United States thought of power in quantitative and military terms, rather than in qualitative and political-psychological ones. The guerrillas, on the other hand, linked their inferior military strength from the outset of the struggle to such fundamental attitudes and social forces as the appeal of nationalism and the desire for political, social, and economic changes within Vietnam. These forces, which would have existed even in the absence of the guerrillas, were shrewdly exploited by them as "multipliers" of their own power. At least of equal importance were attitudes generated by the war itself; such attitudes within the United States were of critical importance.

(The Vietnam war attests to the grave limitations, if not the outright uselessness, of force in unfavorable political circumstances.) The fact that, toward the end of his own days, President Kennedy acquiesced in the South Vietnamese military's overthrow of Diem is evidence, in Theodore Draper's words, of the political bankruptcy and catastrophic failure of American policy. "Kennedy's decision in 1963 to back Diem's overthrow was the most deadly criticism of Kennedy's decision in 1961 to back Diem to the hilt."[39] Long before Johnson's massive escalation in 1965, the situation in South Vietnam had thus clearly become un-

---

[38.] For post-Vietnam limited war strategy, see Robert E. Osgood, *Limited War Revisited* (Boulder, Colo.: Westview, 1979).

[39.] Theodore Draper, *Abuse of Power* (New York: Viking, 1967), p. 59; *The Pentagon Papers*.

230 promising. General Walter Bedell Smith, head of the American delegation to the 1954 Geneva conference, reportedly once said that any second-rate general should be able to win in Indochina if there were a correct political atmosphere. Without such an atmosphere, not even a first-rate general could win. Draper was obviously correct when he concluded from this remark that ("sound politics in Vietnam was the precondition of military victory, not that military victory was the precondition of sound politics."[40] *Resort to force in unfavorable political circumstances can result only in political failure and the loss of a state's reputation for power.*)

(Fourth, the record of the Vietnam war underscores the distinction between negative and positive power. Negative power, the capacity to prevent unfavorable changes in a nation's perceived security interests, seems to be the kind of power that the superpowers wield most effectively. Both have managed to prevent total war and to forestall any major changes in the territorial division drawn in World War II. The international status quo has, on the whole, been frozen since 1945. Historically, most major territorial changes have resulted from the threat or the use of force. But, as the costs of warfare have risen out of all proportion to the objectives that might be achieved, most conflicts have been perpetuated rather than resolved. Preventing change has become the principal purpose of threatening or using force in a bipolar system. In contrast, positive power, the capacity to compel favorable alterations in the status quo, seems less common in the postwar period. Although the United States succeeded in compelling the Soviets to pull their missiles out of Cuba in 1962, it clearly failed to force the Vietcong and the Hanoi government to desist in South Vietnam. The contrast between the American ability to preserve the status quo vis-à-vis the powerful Soviet Union and the inability to compel relatively small and puny North Vietnam to comply with its demands is startling.)

IS THE USE OF FORCE DECLINING?

(The failure of a superpower to coerce such a minor country as North Vietnam was owing to two factors: calculations of cost effectiveness and national self-determination. The insurgents obviously represented no physical threat to the home country for they were in no position to invade it, nor did they possess the sophisticated weapons of the intervening industrial power. To win, therefore, the weaker side had to wear out the stronger adversary, to sap the latter's will to continue fighting. And the way to accomplish this goal was to develop the capacity to resist pacification.) Ever since the French Revolution the growth of nationalism has made it increasingly difficult to conquer *and* pacify foreign territories and populations. The conquered peoples of Europe resisted their Nazi oppressors. If Britain had toppled Nasser of Egypt in 1956 or if the United States had successfully overthrown Castro in 1961, each would have found itself confronting a lengthy and (for democracies) morally

---

[40] Draper, *op. cit.*, pp. 29, 30.

repugnant task of pacification.(A weak country with a strong sense of national identity—and foreign attack can be a powerful stimulant to nationalism—can make the use of force against itself most unattractive because of its capacity for resistance.) American forces were involved in fighting in Vietnam for eight years, and by the time they disengaged in 1973, the costs were regarded as far in excess of any conceivable gains. The loss of 50,000 American lives, thousands of injuries, a total cost of an estmated $150 billion, the use of overwhelming firepower on behalf of an authoritarian government, were too costly in terms of the nation's self-image. (The army, which suffered from discipline, drug, and racial problems, paid the price in low morale and was saved from collapse only by the ending of the war; the political turmoil and social divisions within the United States were a heavy additional price. To be sure, the strong could probably still have prevailed over the weak in the long run, but the price of victory would have been so high that it did not seem worth it. Pacification can thus be made so costly and difficult for a foreign intruder that it will give up the effort. The costs of such wars in both lives and material will, in the future, be enhanced even further as LDCs acquire the new generation of cheaper, highly accurate or precision-guided weapons so that even smaller countries can pose high costs for a great-power invader.)

(Segments of democratic public opinion in the interventionist power, as well as in other countries, also tend to inhibit the use of force and, if force is employed, to make victory difficult, if not impossible.)For an established Western nation with a predominantly white population and a colonial past to attempt to coerce one of the non-Western, largely nonwhite former colonies in an age of national self-determination arouses guilt and moral repugnance in democratic societies. One need but note the opposition within Britain and the Commonwealth countries to the Suez war in 1956, the internal American resistance to the Vietnam war (as well as criticism in allied countries), and President Kennedy's apprehension that the use of American forces in Cuba in 1961 would alienate the very progressive elements in Latin America whose support was necessary to the success of the Alliance for Progress.[41]

In such circumstances, the differences in power between David and Goliath are, if not neutralized, certainly reduced, for(*domestic political conditions*—not just external ones—may make it impossible to mobilize power or to use existing capabilities as the policymakers may wish.)Nothing stimulated domestic protest more effectively than the air war against North Vietnam. The Johnson administration felt so vulnerable on this issue that, for example, it limited its attacks to certain kinds of targets, like bridges and railroad lines, that would not involve extensive civilian damage and loss of life. Nixon, when he became president, was unable to use ground forces because of the uproar about American casualties, and he gradually withdrew them. When he blockaded North Vietnam and began massive heavy bombing in 1972, he precipitated an uproar among influential segments of congressional, journalistic, and public opinion. The Christmas bombing, which Nixon claimed would compel the Hanoi government to accept a cease-fire (which

---

[41.] For an elaboration of this theme, see Chapter 17.

232   it did do shortly afterward, whether because of the bombing or not), was especially
criticized.

Goliath, therefore, beset by inner doubts about the merits of his cause and
accused of ruthlessness, finally gives up, because he calculates that the costs—
physical, economic, and moral—of continuing his attempts to coerce David are
no longer acceptable. They are disproportionate to the end to be achieved. David,
on the other hand, highly motivated by strong nationalism and determined to win,
is encouraged by his enemy's problems, which, he expects, will sooner or later
force Goliath to quit. David calculates that the cost of complying with Goliath's
demands is far greater than that of not complying.

The balance of resolve is, in short, as critical in the conduct of revolutionary
warfare as it is in crisis management. Military defeat in the field is not the decisive
issue. In fact, although external forces supporting the government do not win
militarily (the French came near to doing so in Algeria, however), neither are they
defeated. It is the decline of resolve at home that is decisive. In a revolutionary war
two fronts exist: the traditional battleground, on which men are killed, and the
domestic one, usually nonviolent but, in the end, decisive. If a country's will to
keep on fighting can be eroded, its superior military capability can be neutralized;
indeed, the capability may as well not exist. An English scholar has said that, for
this reason,

> . . . the [Chinese Communist] slogan "imperialism is a paper tiger" is by no means
> inaccurate. It is not that the material resources of the metropolitan power are in
> themselves underestimated by the revolutionaries; rather, there is an acute aware-
> ness that the political constraints on their maximum deployment are as real as if
> those resources did not exist, and that these constraints become more rather than
> less powerful as the war escalates.[42]

Therefore, adding up the components of power—even the conventional ones—
would not have resulted in an accurate prediction of the outcome of the Vietnam
war. So much for addition! (*Big Western democratic nations lose small wars.*)

The American experience in Vietnam has tended to reinforce the widely
accepted thesis that the political utility of force is declining. Originally based on
the development of nuclear weapons, which were said to make war "unthinkable,"
this thesis gained confirmation from the fear that even conventional limited war
is dangerous because of the possibilities of escalation; the Vietnam war also showed
that very high costs relative to benefits make force less useful. But it is probably
an error to draw such a sweeping conclusion about the role of force. The evidence
suggests that the declining utility of force is not a global phenomenon but a Western
one.

It is the industrial and democratic states—Western Europe, Japan, and
increasingly the United States—that find it harder and harder to resort to force.

[42.] Andrew J. R. Mack, "Why Big Nations Lose Small Wars: The Politics of Asymmetric
Conflict," *World Politics*, January 1975, pp. 187–188. Also see Mueller, *War, Presidents and Public
Opinion* (New York: Wiley, 1973); and Larry Elowitz and Spanier, "Korea and Vietnam: Limited War
and the American Political System," *Orbis*, Summer 1974, pp. 510–534.

The issues likely to compel them to do so are becoming more and more narrowly defined—essentially as issues of self-defense. War or even the threat of force for coercive purposes is increasingly considered illegitimate. Indeed, since the ill-fated Suez invasion of 1956, European military forces have had little capacity to project their power beyond western Europe. Even European defense seems a growing burden on the United States, as the states of Europe, with their large combined pool of manpower, great industrial and technological strength, and potential military power, continue to rely on this country for their defense to a far greater degree than their resources suggest they need to. In the era since the Vietnam war, American vital interests have also been defined more and more selectively. In the abstract, refusal to commit power indiscriminately and to squander it in unnecessary causes is, of course, highly desirable, but, when it means paralysis of will and inability to decide when and where key interests are at stake, it can damage a nation's security interests. The memory of the Vietnam war will probably continue to haunt American policy makers and will probably lead to intervention in the third world only in the most extreme circumstances: when American honor and prestige are at stake or vital political and economic issues are so endangered that the United States has little choice but to resort to military power.

(Communist and third-world states are not similarly constrained by the principle of national self-determination and calculations of costs and gains. Whereas the United States tends to accept national self-determination as almost absolute, the Soviet Union interprets it in the light of its own struggle against the West. Self-determination *against* the Soviet Union is regarded as illegitimate, and therefore the Soviet Union has used force several times in eastern Europe; opposition to Soviet domination is defined as "counterrevolutionary" and "reactionary," rather than as a legitimate attempt by Hungary, Czechoslovakia, or another nation to gain control of its own destiny. The Soviet government regards the existing regimes throughout eastern Europe, and the Marxist government installed by a coup in Afghanistan in 1978, as legitimate. On the other hand, in the non-Western world, the Soviet Union regards activities to reduce or eliminate Western influence as legitimate. The governments or movements that Russia supports are defined as movements of "national liberation," and those who oppose them are condemned as "reactionary" and "imperialist.")

(The LDCs themselves strongly support national self-determination, the legitimizing principle on which rest their claims to independence from colonial masters, but they interpret it in two ways: against the West and also against one another, for many of the former colonies lay claim to people and territory of neighboring states on the basis of ethnic identification. For the LDCs the principle of self-determination can thus also justify intervention.) The absence of open societies is beneficial to the Soviet Union, other communist states like Cuba, and most LDCs, for they can more easily sustain the costs of intervention. Public opinion does not play a strong role and cannot therefore exert a restraining or inhibiting influence on governmental leaders. The Soviet Union has not only repeatedly intervened in eastern Europe, as well as Afghanistan, but, together with Cuba, it has also intervened in Angola, Ethiopia, and South Yemen. North Viet-

234 nam intervened in South Vietnam, and later reunited Vietnam invaded Cambodia. China, in turn, temporarily invaded Vietnam. Egypt intervened in Yemen; and North and South Yemen clashed in the late 1970s. Syria sent its forces into Lebanon during the latter's civil war; and since the early 1950s, India has seized the Portuguese colony of Goa on the Indian subcontinent, intervened in East Pakistan during the Pakistani civil war, and was intrumental in depriving Pakistan of its eastern territory and destroying it as a rival. In addition, Tanzania invaded Uganda to overthrow its dictator, Iraq attacked Iran, and Somalia invaded Ethiopia. Rather than a decline in the use of conventional force, there has been a global shift in attitudes toward the utility of force.[43]

---

[43] A similar thesis has been suggested in Klaus Knorr, "Is International Coercion Waning or Rising?" *International Security*, Spring 1977, pp. 92–110; and Knorr, "On the International Uses of Military Force in the Contemporary World," *Orbis*, Spring 1977, pp. 5–27. Also see Chapter 17 for a further analysis of this theme.

Economics as an Instrument of Policy **11**

THE REDISCOVERY OF ECONOMIC POWER

U ntil 1973, the year of the oil embargo against the United States and the quadrupling of oil prices by the Organization of Petroleum Exporting Countries (OPEC), analysts of international politics had largely ignored the economic dimensions of relations among states. Security considerations were primary, and, not unnaturally, the shadow of the bomb had led to an emphasis on deterrence, crisis management, and limited warfare. The behavior of states was explained primarily in terms of the state system. Economics was relegated to a subordinate, indeed peripheral position. It was not that such issues seemed unimportant or to have no political effects. They clearly did on occasions. When the United States raised tariffs on cheese imports from Denmark or France in order to protect the Wisconsin dairy industry; asked Japan to limit its steel exports to the United States in order to protect an American steel industry that had failed to modernize; or taxed textiles and shoes from Japan and Taiwan to protect corresponding industries (and jobs) in this country, it stirred up anger, even bitterness, among allies and friends. But economics did not seem central to international politics; scholarly attention was not unnaturally focused on the management of military power in the nuclear age.

This neglect of economics as an instrument of international politics for security or high political purposes has come to an end. OPEC's use of oil as a stick against the United States and Henry Kissinger's attempt to use American technology as a carrot to encourage Soviet restraint in foreign policy are but two examples of

236 the attention now being paid to economics as an instrument of national power. A dramatic illustration of "economic warfare" came in November 1979, when American embassy personnel were taken hostages in Teheran, Iran, in total violation of international law, which recognized the immunity of embassies and diplomatic personnel. Ayatollah Khomeini, the fanatical religious leader who had only a few months earlier overthrown the Shah, denounced President Carter as "an enemy of humanity" and the United States as "satanic." He gave his blessing to the so-called "students" who had invaded the American embassy and to their demands for the return of the shah, who was at that time in the United States for cancer treatment, to face trial (and certain death) in Iran. A long stalemate resulted, while mobs daily reviled the United States in the streets of Teheran and burned American flags. In retaliation the United States halted all oil imports from Iran (accounting for a mere 4 percent of total American daily consumption), and then, when the Iranians sought to retaliate by withdrawing several billion dollars in oil earnings held by American banks, President Carter froze all Iranian assets in this country. That is, no Iranian money could be taken out of the United States. Oil and money were used as means of bringing pressure for release of the hostages on one hand, and for the return of the shah, on the other. We shall focus here on the uses of economic leverage to achieve critical high politics goals—with the major exception of oil which clearly affects low politics goals or the welfare of entire societies, developed and underdeveloped, as well as security issues.[1]

FROM COLD-WAR EMBARGO TO INTERDEPENDENCE UNDER DÉTENTE?

One of the economic tools more frequently used by states in conflict is the embargo, which is intended to prevent the shipment of certain specific products or even all products to the targeted country. During the Cold War, in what might be called economic warfare or a strategy of denial, the United States regulated exports to the Soviet Union. All products that might have had some sort of military application or could have contributed to the economic strength of the communist state were placed on the embargo list. One of the problems in implementing the embargo was coordination with the North Atlantic Treaty Organization (NATO) allies, whose definition of items to be included was less restrictive than that of the United

---

[1.] The books in which the impact of economics on international politics and the uses of economic means for political ends were first explored are Walters and Blake, *The Politics of Global Economic Relations*; and Joan Edelman Spero, *The Politics of International Economic Relations* (New York: St. Martin's, 1977); and C. Fred Bergsten, *The Future of the International Economic Order* (Lexington, Mass.: Heath, 1973). See also various articles by Bergsten: "The Threat from the Third World," *Foreign Policy*, Summer 1973, pp. 102—134, and "The Responses to the Third World," *Foreign Policy*, Winter, 1974–1975, pp. 3–34; and "Coming Investment Wars?" *Foreign Affairs*, October 1974, pp. 153–175. Finally, see Bergsten and Lawrence B. Krause, eds., *World Politics and International Economics* (Washington, D.C.: Brookings, 1975).

States; their economic stake in trade with the East was greater than that of the United States. As we shall note repeatedly, this kind of problem constitutes a major constraint on the effective exercise of coercive devices. In addition, the United States and its allies made it very difficult for the Soviet Union to sell in Western markets. As a consequence, the West and East remained two separate economic systems, each independent of the other. There is no evidence, however, that these Western attempts at coercion achieved Soviet political compliance; the cold-war years until 1962 were among the most tense and conflict-filled years of the post-war era.

It was part of Kissinger's diplomatic strategy to bridge this gap and to make the American and Soviet economic systems more *interdependent* or, perhaps more accurately, to make the Soviet economy more dependent upon that of the United States. It should be recalled that, when Kissinger became President Nixon's national-security adviser, he recognized two opposite forces at work internationally. The first was a tired and disillusioned United States, weary of the burden of its many cold-war commitments—which had ended so frustratingly in the quagmire of Vietnam—and wary of new obligations. The mood of the country was pseudo-isolationist. In a poll taken at the time, more than 50 percent of the people said that the United States should defend only one foreign country—Canada! The percentages favoring defense of Europe, Israel, and Japan were far lower.

This popular desire to limit American involvement in the world coincided with the emergence of strategic parity between the United States and the Soviet Union. But the Soviet Union had not only caught up with the United States in strategic weapons; it had also considerably upgraded its conventional capabilities, developing a sizable suface fleet plus airlift capability. Czarist and Soviet Russia had always been essentially a Eurasion, or continental, power. Now, for the first time in its history, it had become a global power. As Soviet ability to neutralize American nuclear power grew, its capacity to project its power beyond Eurasia thus grew as well. Would the Soviet Union, in these new circumstances, continue to expand its influence only on land and in territory contiguous to its own? Or would it feel a new confidence and take greater risks, challenging the United States in new areas farther away from Russia? Would the United States, on the other hand, having lost its strategic superiority, be more cautious and hesitant to react? In any situation involving American interests, American leaders had to calculate whether or not the Soviet Union would also intervene and, if so, what the risks and costs would be.

Kissinger compared the emergence of the Soviet Union as a world power to Germany's development at the turn of the century. Both were land powers, and the symbols of their aspirations were the navies that they built; nothing could have been more challenging to Great Britain and the United States, the two greatest naval powers in their times. Germany's determination to be a world power led to World War I. How could Soviet expansionist aspirations be managed peacefully while American security interests were simultaneously safeguarded? At the very moment when the United States was experiencing its greatest doubts about its own international role and when the strategic superiority that had allowed it to "contain"

238   the Soviet Union with the threat of force had eroded, the Soviets were probably feeling more self-assured than ever before and continuing to search for opportunities to expand their influence. If this analysis is correct, then the question was how to prevent the Soviet Union from challenging the United States. How could the Soviets be induced to follow a path of self-restraint? Was there a nonmilitary lever to supplement and even to replace the military one?[2]

One tactic was to offer "carrots." The Soviet economy was, to put it simply, stagnating in both the industrial and the agricultural sectors. During the 1950s the Soviet economy had grown at a rate of 6 percent a year; during the 1960s this rate declined to 5 percent, and by the middle 1970s it had fallen to 3.5 percent. The Central Intelligence Agency forecast for the 1980s is 2.5 percent.[3] Stagnation was especially serious in the electronic, computer, and petrochemical industries. The Soviet Union was falling behind in the Second Industrial Revolution: The implications for its military power, for its ability to satisfy the cravings of its own people for more consumer goods, and for the attraction of Russian communism as a model for the less-developed countries (LDCs) were serious. Because they judged fundamental structural reforms of their centrally controlled and directed economy as politically too risky, it was logical for Soviet leaders to turn to the West for modern technology and credits with which to buy what they needed. Kissinger was quite willing to offer them American technology in return for restraint in the conduct of their foreign policy.

(By extending to the Soviet Union the most-favored nation (MFN) agreement—which is misnamed; its purpose is not to grant special favors but to remove cold-war discriminatory tariffs so that Russian imports can be treated as are those of other states—Kissinger hoped that more and more branches of Russian industry and agriculture would gradually become more dependent on good relations with the United States and its industrial allies) The pressures from the different sectors of the Soviet bureaucracy to maintain the supply lines of Western technology, spare parts, and credit (with which to pay for these American imports) would compel the political leaders to act with restraint in order not to jeopardize these economic links. Restoring MFN status, which Russia had lost in 1947, was thus important for commercial—and especially symbolic and political—purposes. The Senate, however, decided to link this issue with that of Jewish emigration from the Soviet Union. The Soviets then turned down the trade agreement. Nevertheless, the idea had been a shrewd one: As the military stick with which to restrain Russia might be less politically and militarily usable, economic carrots should be substituted.

Actually, some trade has occurred, despite the rejection of the MFN agreement, and the real question is whether or not trade can create such dependence. During the 1920s and 1930s, as Stalin embarked on his intense drive to modernize Russia, American corporations became actively involved. This involve-

---

[2] For analyses of the feasibility of economic leverage, see Samuel P. Huntington, *et al.*, "Trade, Technology and Leverage," *Foreign Policy*, Fall 1978, pp. 63–106; and Herbert S. Levine, Francis W. Rushing, and Charles M. Movit, "The Potential for U.S. Economic Leverage on the USSR," *Comparative Strategy*, I (1979), 371–404.

[3] *The New York Times*, June 29, 1979.

ment did not, however, create dependence on the United States or alter Soviet leaders' anticapitalist impulses. In the mid-1930s, this phase ended abruptly. Marshall Goldman, an expert on the Soviet economy, thinks that contemporary trade may, however, entangle Russia so deeply in the world economy that the cost of disruption would be very high and would serve as a deterrent.[4] Technology was simpler before World War II, he argues: the Russians could manufacture their own spare parts. Today, in electronics and in petroleum and mineral extracting, for example, technology is highly sophisticated and requires continuous servicing and upgrading if productivity is to be increased. In agriculture, furthermore, the Soviets may no longer be self-sufficient, especially as they want to upgrade their diet to include more meat. This step requires more feed grain for cattle. Given Russian climatic conditions, the nation must depend heavily on imports. The United States produces large surpluses, which can be sold for export. A degree of interdependence with the United States and the rest of the capitalist world can thus perhaps be generated.

But a note of caution should be sounded. One limiting factor to trade as a means of leverage is whether or not the United States would in fact cut off profitable trade with the Soviets if the latter sought to exploit political opportunities unilaterally.[5] American farmers let President Ford know in 1975 that, if he expected their votes, he had better not try another grain embargo against Russia. He did not. In 1979, when a Soviet armed-combat brigade was discovered in Cuba and President Carter declared the situation unacceptable, several million tons of grain continued to be shipped to Russia. Only after the Soviet invasion of Afghanistan in December 1979, in what the president called the most serious crisis since World War II, did he put an embargo on 17 million tons of grain, most of it earmarked for livestock feed. Simultaneously, to cushion the fall of prices and lessen the farmers' protests, the government took a series of remedial measures. Patriotism also stilled farmer protests—but not for long. Given the eagerness of American banks, corporations, and farmers to trade with the Soviet Union and the pressures that they can exert on the U.S. government, this kind of leverage is not likely to be used frequently. We cannot, in fact, dismiss the possibility that the Soviets may manipulate economic interests more often than American leaders, because American economic interests will seek to avoid confrontation and "unpleasantness" in order to protect their profits. (So much for capitalist enmity toward communism!)

A second limiting factor is that the Soviets can buy technology and obtain credit from western Europe and Japan as well. Trade and credits are satisfactory bargaining tools only when the items that an adversary needs cannot be obtained elsewhere. Even if the American government were to stand firm, businessmen and farmers overseas would be happy to receive the contracts instead. The Soviet Union could, in fact, play off one Western country against another and gain economic benefits without becoming deeply enmeshed in a web of economic interdependence

---

[4] Marshall I. Goldman, *International Security*, spring 1979, pp. 18–37.

[5] See Walter C. Clemens, Jr., *The U.S.S.R. and Global Interdependence* (Washington, D.C.: American Enterprise Institute, 1978) for a more skeptical interpretation of the likely impact of "interdependence" on the Soviet Union.

240   with the United States. Indeed, the Western countries might become *doubly* dependent on the Soviet Union: for debt repayment (either in cash or in Russia's abundant natural resources) and for markets for specific American and European industrial, consumer, and agricultural products. Yet, should American-Soviet trade blossom, could the United States and it allies not use the availability of credit, supplies of spare parts, and the latest technology effectively to induce more acceptable Soviet foreign-policy behavior?

THE SUPERPOWERS AND THEIR ALLIES

The United States resorted to economic means to advance its foreign-policy goals from the very beginning of the Cold War. It was, in fact, western Europe's economic collapse that finally made it impossible for the United States to return to isolationism, as it had done after World War I. Just as Britain's weakening position had brought the United States into World War I in 1917 and brought her close to World War II in 1941 even before Pearl Harbor, so its postwar collapse left the United States no alternative but to commit itself first in the eastern Mediterranean area and then in western Europe.

On the surface, Britain's crisis was an economic one. As an island nation, it depended for survival on international trade. It had to export or die, for during the Industrial Revolution in the nineteenth century it had become almost completely urbanized. By World War II, less than 5 percent of the population was engaged in agriculture, which meant that the nation had to import much of its food. Before the war, for instance, Britain had bought 55 percent of its meat; 75 percent of its wheat; 85 percent of its butter; all its tea, cocoa, and coffee; and 75 percent of its sugar. Except for coal, it also had to import most of the raw materials for its industries: cotton, rubber, wool, iron ore, timber, and oil, upon which it was becoming increasingly dependent for the fueling of factories.

Before 1939 Britain had paid for these foods and raw materials by three means: in such services as shipping, in income from foreign investments, and in manufactured exports. But the war had crippled the British merchant marine, liquidated most of the nation's foreign investments, and destroyed many of its factories. Britain thus had to increase its exports to an enormous extent. Simply to regain its 1939 standard of living, it had to raise them by 75 percent. By December 1946, despite an American loan and a severe austerity program that included rationing bread, Britain had only reached its prewar level of production. In those circumstances nature delivered almost a knockout blow: In the winter of 1946–1947 Europe suffered one of its severest cold spells in history, with temperatures below zero. In Britain the transportation system came to a virtual standstill; trucks and trains could not move, barges were frozen in rivers, and ships could not leave their moorings. Industry could not be supplied with fuel, and factories were closed. By February 1947, more than half of Britain's factories lay idle. Coal was not even being mined any longer, and gas and electricity were in short supply. Electricity to industrial consumers was cut off for several days, and domestic consumers had to do without electricity for three hours every day. When the thaw finally arrived, Britain was beset by floods. It took months to recover.

In the meantime, the export drive had completely collapsed. Britain had come to the end of its economic rope. The financial editor of Reuter's press service saw the true dimensions of the winter disaster: "The biggest crash since the fall of Constantinople—the collapse of the heart of an Empire—impends. This is not the story of a couple of snowstorms. It is the story of the awful debility in which a couple of snowstorms could have such effects."[6] The future looked bleak: Millions of Britons were unemployed, cold, hungry—and worn out by the long years of war and determined efforts to recover. Despite all the sacrifices they had made, their efforts had come to nothing. Britain's fate could have been worse only if it had lost the war.

Germany, which had been defeated, and France, which had never recovered from its defeat in 1940 and the years of German occupation, were in no better shape. All Europe stood on the verge of collapse, and everything appeared to compel dependence upon the United States. Most of the items necessary for reconstruction—wheat, cotton, sulphur, sugar, machinery, trucks, and coal—could be obtained in sufficient quantities only from the United States. Yet Europe, with a stagnating economy, was in no position to earn the dollars to pay for these goods. Furthermore, the United States was so well supplied with everything that it did not have to buy much from abroad. European countries were thus unable to obtain enough dollars to buy the commodities required for their recovery. The result was the ominous "dollar gap"—a term that frightened Europeans as much as "cold war."[7]

In former times, the closing of this gap would have been left to the mechanism of the international market. The European states, unable to pay for the machinery or the raw materials they needed, would simply not have bought them. Although this alternative would have meant the closing of factories, large-scale unemployment, millions of hungry and cold citizens, and widespread social discontent, that would have been merely unfortunate. In the long run, though, it would have brought about the desired result: The unemployed would have no money with which to buy goods manufactured with imported resources or machinery, and demand would therefore be driven down to the point at which trade would once more be in balance.

This "remedy" could hardly be adopted in the mid-twentieth century. The Europeans had not fought the war and suffered so much in order to face that kind of future. The war had been fought for a *better* future, in which men could live decently. In addition, the old-fashioned way of closing the dollar gap simply seemed incompatible with the humanitarian basis of Western civilization. It was no longer politically possible. When people elect their representatives, governments can hardly allow them to remain unemployed, to live in cold homes, or to starve.

The European collapse thus posed a fundamental question to the United

---

[6] Quoted in Joseph M. Jones, *The Fifteen Weeks* (New York: Viking, 1955), p. 80.

[7] An excellent book that conveys the "feelings" of this period in both Europe and the United States is Theodore H. White, *Fire in the Ashes* (New York: Sloane, 1953). See also White, *In Search of History* (New York: Warner Books, 1979), pp. 263–306.

242   States: Is Europe vital to American security? The answer was never in doubt. Two
world wars had demonstrated it, and the collapse simply reaffirmed it. The American commitment was demonstrated by the grant of billions of dollars in Marshall
Plan funds to stimulate economic recovery and in the establishment of the NATO
military alliance. The American role in Europe was akin to that of a doctor in
relation to a patient—the prescribed cure was a massive injection of dollars. This
large-scale program of economic aid was to be administered in the form of grants,
rather than loans, which would only have intensified Europe's dollar problems.
Only such a grant program could restore and even surpass Europe's prewar agricultural and industrial production, close the dollar gap, and stimulate revival of
European *élan vital*, political stability, economic prosperity, and military strength.

This infusion of dollars was imaginative, but the French use of economics
was revolutionary. France, after the experiences of 1870, 1914, and 1939, suffered
a natural fear of Germany. American plans for the revival of the German economy
in order to help revive that of all western Europe aroused the French. For them,
the question was how to contain Germany's great power. Since unification of
Germany in 1870, France had attempted to deal with the greater inherent strength
of this aggressive and militaristic neighbor by forming alliances to balance German
power. Before World War I, France had found an ally in czarist Russia; in the
interwar years Poland, Czechoslovakia, Rumania, and Yugoslavia had all been
allied with France. Yet none of these alliances had been enough to save France
from attack. British and especially American power had been more important. As
World War II was coming to a close, the French responded as they had traditionally
done. For France, Germany was still enemy number one. Hence the French-
Russian Treaty of Mutual Assistance of 1944, which was quickly rendered obsolete
by the Cold War.

The failure of the traditional balance-of-power technique, by which an
inferior power seeks to balance a stronger one, led France to seek a new way of
exerting some control over German power. French statesmen found a revolutionary
means: European integration. It was through the creation of a supranational community, to which Germany would transfer certain sovereign rights, that German
power was to be controlled. Only in this manner would German strength be
prevented from harming the rest of Europe and channeled instead into support for
European welfare and security.

France made its first move in the direction of a united Europe in May
1950, when it proposed the formation of the European Coal and Steel Community
(ECSC), to be composed of "Little Europe" (France, Germany, Italy, Belgium,
the Netherlands and Luxembourg). The aim was to entwine German and French
heavy industry, so that it would become impossible ever to separate them again.
Germany would never again be able to use its coal and steel for nationalistic and
militaristic purposes. The German use of political and military power derived from
the industrial Ruhr area was to be eliminated for all time. War between Germany
and France would become not only unthinkable but even impossible.

The French idea was not, however, based on emotional appeals for a
united Europe or a call to discard narrow nationalitic loyalties in favor of a broader

European allegiance. A united Europe could not be created out of sentiment alone. The French rejected "the rosy mists of idealism" and determined to erect the new Europe upon a solid foundation, building from the bottom upward. A united Europe, they knew, could be forged only by binding together the interests of politically powerful and economically important groups across national boundaries. For instance, the removal of all trade barriers in the coal and steel sector of the economy would encourage modernization of mines and plants, as well as elimination of those that continued to operate inefficiently. Once the efficient producers had adjusted to the wider market and its opportunities, leaders would want to remove national barriers in other areas. Furthermore, as production increased, Europe's standard of living would rise, French and Italian workers would receive what they believed to be their fair share of income, and labor in general would recognize that the goal of a welfare state could be achieved only at the European level.

The French also showed great political astuteness in their selection of heavy industry as the first to be integrated. Coal and steel are the basis of the entire industrial structure, a sector that cannot possibly be separated from the overall economy. Success of the ECSC would thus exert pressure on the unintegrated sectors of the economy, and, as the benefits of pooling heavy industry became clear, other sectors would follow suit. ECSC was thus viewed as the first stage of an attempt to create a wider market in one particular area of the economy, and it was expected that this approach would be gradually extended to other areas, like agriculture, transportation, and electricity. Eventually it would lead to the creation of a single European market and efficient mass-producing industries. Clearly, the basis for this shrewd plan was material. Industry, labor, and agriculture would all benefit. ECSC. was thus the forerunner of the European Common Market (The European Economic Community, or EEC), the express purpose of which was to integrate the entire economies of its members and eventually to transform the separate nations into a United States of Europe, in which countries like France and West Germany would become states in a federal union.

The Common Market was formed in 1958. Apart from its integrative function (to be discussed in Chapter 19), it adopted a new goal in the late 1970s. With a membership already expanded from the original "inner six" to nine (including Britain, Denmark, and Ireland), the EEC elected to enlarge its eventual membership to twelve to include Greece, Portugal, and Spain. The last became associate, rather than full-fledged, members at first. The inclusion of these three semi-developed countries in a community of industrialized states was significant—and to some people disturbing. It was disturbing because earlier additions, especially of England, had already complicated the integration process. The addition of three more states, all on the periphery of Europe and among the continent's less developed states, will place even greater strains on the EEC's institutions, policies, and distribution of resources. The reason why the members of EEC proceeded with this enlargement is that the community now aims also to support democracy.

The three new members had been ruled for long periods by authoritarian right-wing regimes, and their new democratic governments remained fragile. Many

244 of their people came to western Europe seeking jobs. EEC employed millions of foreign workers, including Yugoslavs and Turks. A new fascist regime in Spain or Portugal or another colonels' coup in Greece would seriously affect the security and democratic basis of the EEC. It is for this reason that the community decided to help these nations lay the social and economic foundations for stable democracies and thus to ensure the security of all the democracies in Europe. This new role was prefigured when, after the collapse of Portugal's right-wing government and subsequent turmoil between the democratic parties, on the one hand, and the communist party and radical military officers, on the other, the EEC offered help in rebuilding Portugal's shattered economy—but only in a "democratic" Portugal. This offer provided one incentive for those Portuguese who sought democracy; they struggled harder and won the government.

The Soviets had a different way of organizing the economies of eastern Europe after World War II. After initially forming mixed companies, in which the Soviet Union held a 50 percent interest but wielded total control, the Soviets founded the Council for Mutual Economic Aid (known in the West as Comecon). After Stalin's death, his successors decided to treat all of eastern Europe as a single economic region, in which each country would produce certain items for the whole region. Poland would mine bituminous coal, East Germany would produce lignite and chemicals, and Czechoslovakia would manufacture automobiles. If each country was specialized, all countries would have to cooperate. The aim was to link the political and economic interests of the communist countries and to create a high degree of interdependence among them. Economic specialization was to be the instrument of political union.

Whatever the underlying political purposes, neither Comecon nor the national planning of any of the individual eastern European countries could quite meet national aims, especially providing populations with a much higher standard of living. Clearly, there has been economic progress among Comecon members, and living conditions are generally higher in eastern Europe than in Russia itself. The Soviet allies are also secure, for the Red Army defends them, and the nationalistic outlook of most eastern European regimes confers a degree of legitimacy. Economic improvements have helped to strengthen this legitimacy. It is in this connection that the proximity of the Western economies is so important, providing as they do a standard of comparison and a constant reminder to the peoples of eastern Europe of their lower living standards. The success of EEC puts pressure on these regimes to do better.

East European trade with the West, including the United States, did in fact rise rapidly during the 1970s, so that, from 1974 to 1978, eastern European debt rose from $13 billion to $55 billion! The political implications of this debt, owed primarily to Western banks, must be a matter of concern to Moscow. Eastern European economies may become more dependent on the capitalist countries of the West, as trade, technological, and financial relations increase. Furthermore, Western nations may gain some control of eastern European nations' domestic policies. In 1979 Poland, in order to obtain a new loan, permitted Western banks to monitor its economic policies! It was made clear to the Poles that, if they were to meet their payments on the $15 billion they owed in the West, they would have to adopt policy of austerity. Such belt tightening meant slowing down Poland's rate of economic growth and freezing the military budget, despite Soviet pressures to increase military spending. The Poles also provided their private creditors with comprehensive financial information, including figures on the country's total foreign debt and debt-repayment schedules. The resulting austerity, however, spilled over in 1980 into widespread workers' strikes and demands not only for higher pay but also independent trade unions. Whether such unions, claiming to represent the workers' interests against the ruling Communist party that claims the same thing, will threaten the partys' monopoly of power (and whether the Soviets will tolerate this) remains to be seen. In the meantime, Poland's actions represent a marked change of policy for a communist state and attest to the enormous influence not only of official Western foreign-aid programs—from which Poland has also benefited—but also of Western economies in general, both public and private.[8] As a competing trading system, the Soviets cannot match the appeal of the West and what the West can offer.

THE SUPERPOWERS AND SECONDARY ADVERSARIES

Economic means are, however, not only means of advancing the common purposes of the superpowers and their allies. They are also frequently used in conflict situations. Two prominent American examples have involved Cuba and Chile. After Castro assumed power in Havana, friction with the United States grew. The signing of the Soviet-Cuban trade agreement in 1960 was symptomatic of Cuba's shift toward the Soviet bloc. When Castro demanded that several American- and British-owned oil refineries process Soviet imported crude oil and they refused, the refineries were expropriated. All this evidence of Cuban alignment with the United States' principal enemy led the Eisenhower administration to try both to punish and to warn Castro. The United States suspended imports of 700,000 tons of sugar that remained unshipped out of Cuba's total 1960 quota of approximately 3 million tons. For Cuba, whose entire economy was based on sugar production, this suspension was a form of pressure. A quota is an import level for a particular product established by the importing government for a specific time period. This amount can be sold at a good price, above the international market price. But, despite the potentially painful loss of an ensured market, Cuba was not deterred from re-orienting itself politically and economically toward the Soviet bloc, even after the United States put an embargo on all exports to the island (except food and medicine) and put a stop to its own citizens' traveling there. Havana had been a great tourist center.

---

[8] William P. Bundy, "Elements of Power," *Foreign Affairs*, October 1977, p. 10.

246   A decade later in Chile Salvador Allende came to power, despite American attempts to prevent his doing so because of his radical left-wing views. The Nixon administration then cut off all American short-term bank credits for Chile. Actually, this loss did not prove too painful to Chile because Allende obtained even more credits from Russia, China, a number of eastern European countries, Argentina, Brazil, Mexico, Finland, France, West Germany, the Netherlands, Spain, Sweden, and Japan. Most of these credits, however, were tied to purchases in the creditor countries, in order to boost their own exports. Chile therefore could find no substitutes or spare parts for its American machinery and no comparable industrial technology. The transportation system (cars, buses, diesel trucks) and the copper industry, the source of Chile's international earnings, were seriously affected. Only massive Soviet financial support could have saved Allende's regime. Russia did extend considerable aid, but after spending more than $4 billion to support the Cuban economy from 1967 to 1972, Moscow was not prepared to underwrite the runaway inflation and socially divisive domestic policies, which resulted from Allende's own policies rather than from American pressure.[9]

What conclusions can be drawn from these two examples? In the Cuban example, American economic pressure was unsuccessful. In fact, the elimination of the sugar quota strengthened Castro's popularity at home, diverted Cuban attention from the regime's failures, and allowed Castro to use the United States as his scapegoat while simultaneously urging his people to work harder and rally to his cause. Attempted economic coercion also brought him admiration throughout Latin America, precisely because of successful defiance of the United States. It probably also strengthened his determination to continue playing David against the North American Goliath, because "he might have overestimated the enemy and . . . it might be worth while to see whether history had destined him to play the role of liberator of the entire continent."[10] Probably no amount of American economic aid could have dissuaded Castro from enacting his role as a revolutionary leader. In any event, the economic sanctions served only to arouse Cuban nationalism and to rally public support for Castro's regime. They had the opposite effect from the one sought.[11]

A second lesson to be drawn from the Cuban experience is that sanctions will inflict only temporary pain if alternative sources of supplies and export markets are available. A nation is vulnerable only if it is largely dependent on one product and trades mainly with one country. Castro was able simply to switch markets. Cuban sugar was sold to the Soviet bloc, which also became the source of products that Cuba had previously imported from the United States. Given the diversity of available markets, any targeted regime can survive.

The Allende example confirms these lessons, although at first the collapse

---

[9] Joseph L. Nogee and John W. Sloan, "Allende's Chile and the Soviet Union," *Journal of Interamerican Studies and World Affairs*, August 1979, pp. 339–365.

[10] Andrés Suarez, *Cuba* (Cambridge, Mass.: M.I.T. Press, 1967), p. 86.

[11] Richard S. Olson, "Economic Coercion in World Politics: With a Focus on North–South Relations," *World Politics*, July 1979, pp. 472–479. Also Otto Wolff von Ameringen; "Commentary: Economic Sanctions as a Foreign Policy Tool?," *International Security*, Fall 1980, pp. 159–167.

of his regime suggested the opposite, that is, that American economic pressures abetted by CIA activities can subvert a regime. Allende's government could have survived—if Allende, like Castro, had presented himself as the leader of all his own people. Instead, he declared, "I am not President of all Chileans"; that is, he saw himself as president of some Chileans—the poorest segments of society—and not of the others. The latter included not only the rich but also the middle classes, even the *petit bourgeoisie*. Allende deliberately relinquished the possibility of arousing nationalist sentiment in support of his policies. Instead, he divided Chileans among themselves and pursued a highly inflationary policy to satisfy "his" Chileans.

> . . . Defiance of international corporations and foreign governments need not lead to economic or political collapse. The Allende policy, however, which combined inflation with deliberate class polarization, was a formula for disaster.
>
> The lesson, if there is one, in the relations between the United States and the Allende government is that a government which is determined to nationalize US companies without compensation and to carry out an internal program which effectively destroys its ability to earn foreign exchange cannot expect to receive a subsidy to do so from either the US government or from US private banks. It may, however, receive some assistance from other countries either for political (aid to a fellow "socialist" country) or economic (encouragement of exports) reasons—at least for a time. What it cannot do is blame all its problems on foreign imperialists and their domestic allies, and ignore elementary principles of economic rationality and effective political legitimacy in its internal plolicies. No amount of foreign assistance can be a substitute for these, and *no amount of foreign subversion or economic pressure can destroy them if they exist.*[12]

(A government that is legitimate and enjoys widespread domestic support can successfully resist attempts at economic coercion and subversion.)

The weakness of the embargo as a coercive device was dramatically illustrated after Iranian "students" seized the American embassy in Teheran in 1979 and took its personnel hostage. Supported by the Ayatollah Khomeini, they demanded the return of the shah for trial and presumably execution for what they charged had been unusually oppressive and despotic rule. The Carter administration was in no position to fulfill this demand. In the first place, the shah was in this country for medical treatment. Second, if the United States had met Iranian demands it would have provided an incentive for other seizures of American embassies and diplomatic personnel. The resulting situation would be intolerable; the principal victim would be diplomacy itself, for this tactic would surely encourage its use against other countries as well.

American reaction was initially limited to cutting off Iranian oil imports to the United States and freezing Iranian assets in the United States; the latter are estimated at $6 billion. Neither measure gained the hostages their freedom; rather, each elicited threats to put them on trial as "spies." Concerned about the possible outcomes of such trials and the potential application of "Islamic justice," American

---

[12.] Paul E. Sigmund, "The 'Invisible Blockade' and the Overthrow of Allende," *Foreign Affairs*, January 1974, pp. 339–340 (emphasis added).

248   leaders began to think of tightening the economic screws. The United States asked
the U.N. Security Council to impose an economic embargo. The Soviets vetoed
the resolution. For a while nothing happened as hopes for the hostages' release
went up and down. But by the spring of 1980 after the shah, now in Panama, had
moved once again, this time to Egypt, the negotiations over the hostages continued
to be unproductive. Not even a transfer from the militants to the custody of the
newly elected government could be arranged. Economic sanctions were the obvious
next step—indeed the only step since a U.S. rescue mission failed and the hostages
were reportedly dispersed throughout Iran to render a second rescue effort futile.

    The effect of the sanctions were, as our other examples would have led
us to expect, limited. The initial cut-off of Iranian oil constituted only a small
percentage of American oil imports and was easily replaceable. Iran sold most of
it to Japan at twice the price, thus gaining a handsome profit from the American
action until Washington protested to Tokyo. But America's allies initially resisted
applying economic sanctions; to a degree that reluctance was understandable since
Europe and Japan imported more oil than America from Iran. Later, to forestall
American military action, they agreed to sanctions, including the termination of
oil imports. After the rescue mission, they dragged their feet again. Only contracts
signed since the day the hostages were seized on November 4, 1979, would be
canceled; all prior contracts would be honored. Britain diluted even these limited
sanctions further by saying the ban on commerce with Iran applied only to new
contracts; all contracts already signed would be carried out. In short, after promising
full sanctions, all the allies defaulted, with Britain, which had issued strong verbal
declarations of support for the United States after the initial seizure of the hostages,
retreating completely from any meaningful sanctions. The American position was
that the Iranians must be increasingly isolated and pressured. Iran had to be shown
that it had nothing to gain by continuing to hold the hostages and much to lose.
The allied position was that sanctions would be counterproductive. A country that
had oil could sell it elsewhere for $70–80 million a day and would attract plenty
of suppliers to fill its need. (So why should they give up lucrative contracts, they
appeared to be saying.) It would also strengthen Iran's resistance. Both positions
were persuasive but one thing was clear: such sanctions could work only if collectively applied. By itself or with only partial allied support, the United States could
not apply sufficient pressure (assuming that there was a level of pressure that would
suffice to persuade a fanatical, even irrational, leader like the Ayatollah Khomeini
to release the hostages). The sanctions were, therefore, very "leaky."

    They might also be leaky for a second reason. Iran could arrange for
overland routes via Russia should her harbors be mined and blockaded. Indeed,
one of the ironic results of Western sanctions might be to drive the allegedly
religious Iranian leadership into the arms of its antireligious neighbor, maybe even
lead it to request Moscow's assistance in case of U.S. military action. Such an
extension of Soviet influence to just north of the Arabian peninsula, following the
earlier advance of Soviet influence toward the Arabian peninsula from the south,
was obviously contrary to American interests. Thus even "leak-proof" sanctions,

applied to gain one objective, might result in greater danger to other—and possibly more vital—interests.

In the end, release of the hostages may come about through internal factors in Iran. Iran actually hurt itself when it raised oil prices so high that some of the allies such as Japan stopped buying its oil. Lack of maintenance and unrest in the oil fields by the Arab working minorities reduced oil production. Other ethnic minorities, like the Kurds and Baluchis, were also seeking greater autonomy while Islamic militants and secular leftists, largely Marxist, clashed on the streets of Teheran. Even Khomeini finally publicly called for an end to "chaos" in Iran, a chaos hardly rendered less severe by the subsequent Iraqi-Iranian war. When the nation decides to concentrate on rebuilding Iran's economy and turns to pragmatism again to run its society, the hostages and fanaticism are likely to be of lesser concern.

The failure of such *public* and highly visible attempts at economic coercion reflects recognition by the leaders and populations of the target nations that the stakes are high. Compliance is considered a surrender of the nation's dignity and freedom to decide its own future. The Russians learned this lesson in the late 1940s, when Stalin cut off all trade and aid to Yugoslavia after his quarrel with Marshal Tito. The Yugoslav leader simply shifted to American and western European markets, while the people rallied to his support. Indeed, as leader of the Yugoslav guerrilla movement against the occupying Nazi armies in World War II, Tito had come to symbolize Yugoslav nationalism. The Chinese taught this same lesson to the Soviets in the late 1950s. Despite the damaging withdrawal of all Soviet advisers and technical experts, the Peking government refused to follow Soviet policies. The Chinese "decided to go it alone, whatever the problems and costs, determined to end their economic dependency and vulnerability."[13] They repaid Soviet loans, so that they would not be financially indebted to Moscow. "[W]hereas in the mid-1950's China had seemed well on its way toward full incorporation into a Moscow-dominated 'Communist world system,' by the end of the 1960's it had nothing more than minimal diplomatic contact with Russia."[14] Ironically, perhaps, it is a lesson that the Soviets in turn taught the United States, when they rejected the MFN agreement because of American demands that they change their policy on emigration, especially Jewish emigration. No power, and certainly not a great power, will admit publicly that it has mistreated its own citizens; none will promise to improve its behavior under pressure and in return for certain material goods. Domestic affairs are considered the business of the national government and of no one else. To insist on domestic changes is thus an affront. The Soviets, therefore, turned down the treaty. (In contrast, quiet behind-the-scenes diplomacy had gained the release of 35,000 Soviet Jews in 1973.) Even after the Soviet invasion of Afghanistan, the grain embargo and other economic measures, though communicating to Moscow the message that such actions cannot be taken with impunity, did not compel Soviet withdrawal. Nor should they

---

[13] A. Doak Barnett, *China and the Major Powers in East Asia* (Washington, D.C.: Brookings, 1977), p. 41.

[14] *Ibid.*, pp. 41–42.

250 have been expected to. In a clash between a nation's vital interests and economic benefits, the former are likely to be chosen. (To sum up, then, attempts at economic coercion are generally self-defeating because they strengthen the morale of the targeted nation and stiffen its resistance to negotiations.)

THE SUPERPOWERS, THE THIRD WORLD, AND ECONOMIC AID

(The very distribution of power in the immediate postwar world enhanced the ability of the LDCs to attract the funds needed for their development. Furthermore, since during the days of bipolarity the superpowers were unwilling to risk total war, and each hoped to defeat its opponent in the developing areas, foreign aid thus became an instrument of policy. In a sense, in the nuclear age aid was a substitute for arms: "In our times, economic acitivities are not an alternative [to war]; they are a substitute. They are no longer a preferable alternative to clearly feasible war and to equally despicable but apparently dispensable power politics. They are instead a substitute for practically self-defeating major war, and they are more than ever an instrument of the again respectable politics of power."[15] Foreign aid thus became for a while an instrument of economic warfare.

The Soviet aid program began in 1954–1955 and, until approximately 1964,[16] was concentrated in just a few countries. Aid was given to states that were either politically vital (like India) or strategically located (like Afghanistan). In particular, aid was given to those states that were perceived by the West as "troublemakers"—Egypt, Iraq, Algeria, and Cuba, for example. Furthermore, the Soviets did not necessarily demand economic justification of a project as a condition for aid. They furnished aid to build the Aswan dam in Egypt and a steel mill in India, in each instance responding to a request by the host country for such support, rather than initiating the program. They were not especially concerned with how a particular project fitted into a country's overall plan for development. If it served Soviet purposes, it received support. One such purpose was public relations, or prestige; they therefore spent their money on highly visible projects like the high dam at Aswan, the paving of Kabul's main street, buses for the Afghans, and sports stadiums in Rangoon, Burma, and Jakarta, Indonesia. They were quite willing to send modern weapons to the new states, providing the recipients with the symbols of modern nationhood and the illusion of national strength. During the Cold War they entered into close alliances with Arab states in a joint effort to eliminate Western influence from the Middle East.

The Soviets relied heavily on credits, whereas the United States relied

---

[15] George Liska, *The New Statecraft* (Chicago: University of Chicago Press, 1960), p. 3.

[16] See Joseph S. Berliner, *Soviet Economic Aid* (New York: Holt, Rinehart and Winston, 1958), pp. 179–180; and Hans Heymann, Jr., "Soviet Foreign Aid as a Problem for U.S. Policy," *World Politics*, July 1960, pp. 525–540. Also see Wynfred Joshua and Stephen P. Gibert, *Arms for the Third World* (Baltimore: Johns Hopkins Press, 1969).

largely on grants. It was often argued that the former offered a distinct psychological advantage over the latter. Unlike grants, which supposedly made the recipients feel they were accepting charity, credits, it was claimed, enabled borrowers to retain their dignity. Because they would pay for loans, they could perceive themselves as engaged in normal business transactions of mutual benefit. Furthermore, the Soviet loans were extended at interest rates of 2–2.5 percent, whereas American loans were generally carried at 4–5 percent. The Russians could thus accuse the West of exploiting the developing countries in typical capitalist fashion and stress the advantage to a developing country of receiving Soviet aid. The Soviets also seemed more willing to accept repayment in local currencies or in exports, which often helped to relieve surpluses of cotton, rice, fish, or sugar and to preserve a country's slim dollar or sterling reserves. Yet, though the Soviet loan policy may have had many advantages for the developing nation, it was also geared to specific Soviet purposes, which actually had little to do with the recipient's well-being. The Soviets used loans not to preserve the recipient's self-respect but to keep down costs; a loan is always less expensive than an outright grant. Furthermore, because loans must be repaid, the number of applications is limited. Equally important, loans help to establish bilateral trading relations with the recipients; the Soviet Union thus obtained commodities that it needed.

The Soviet Union's aid program was not as successful as we might expect. The results speak for themselves. Soviet aid to a particular country has often been initiated at a point when relations between the recipient and the West have been poor. Aid to Iraq was begun after that nation's pro-Western government had been overthrown by a new nationalist government, which, having denounced Western "imperialism" and withdrawn from the Middle East Treaty Organization (METO), was very much "open" to new sources of support. When Guinea left the newly formed French Commonwealth and France accordingly withdrew all its aid, Soviet rubles began to pour into the former colony. As Egypt grew increasingly anti-Western in the mid-1950s, opposed CENTO, and sought to overthrow pro-Western governments thoughout the Arab world, the Soviet bloc offered it a huge supply of modern weapons. When the United States then retracted its offer to build the Aswan dam, partly because of Egypt's new ties with the Soviet Union, the Soviets took over the financing of that project.

Yet Iraqi did not go communist, and the new government eventually arrested the Iraqi communist leaders. Sékou Touré of Guinea sent the Russian ambassador home for allegedly plotting to overthrow his government and then began to reestablish relations with France. And Nasser arrested Egyptian communists and denounced Russia on several occasions, while his successor shifted toward closer relations with the United States. Indonesia aligned itself with China against Russia. In no developing nation has Soviet aid resulted in the acceptance by national leaders of Soviet dictation on domestic or foreign policy—except in Cuba, where the communists were already in power *before* the Soviet aid program began. Even Castro, who initially received about $1 million a day (by 1979, the estimated figure had risen to $8 million a day), has criticized the Soviet regime for

252   refusing to support revolutionary action in Latin America. The Soviet leaders presumably do not want a dangerous confrontation with the United States in an area of traditional American dominance.

Why has the Soviet Union had such limited success with its aid program? One reason is Soviet performance. The Soviets have at times failed to deliver the quantities of goods promised; have engaged in questionable practices (like reselling Egyptian cotton at lower than world market prices and thus underselling Egypt's own cotton);[17] have delivered poor-quality crude oil, wormy wheat, and unsatisfactory machinery; and have indulged in shoddy construction. The Aswan dam, for instance, had all sorts of unanticipated ecological effects. Some of these failures might, indeed, have been expected. The Soviets generally perform best in the area of heavy industry, where they have considerable experience, rather than in light industry and production of consumer items. Soviet experience in agriculture, the Achilles' heel of the Soviet economy anyway, has little applicability to the tropical farming that characterizes most of the underdeveloped areas.

Yet the defects of the Soviet aid program should not be overstressed. The American program has suffered similar failures and has been inferior to the Soviet program in certain respects.[18] Not needing congressional approval of annual foreign-aid appropriations, the Soviets have been able to commit themselves for years in advance, thus allowing the recipient nation to plan a long-range economic program. They have also had the flexibility to exploit favorable new situations as they have arisen; no legislature must be persuaded to allocate aid money for specific projects. The Soviet government can also mobilize its best engineers and technicians if it so desires, for there are no private Russian corporations whose higher wages attract top talent away from government-sponsored aid projects. Finally, no citizen, official, ethnic group, or farm lobby in the Soviet Union embarrasses the government by denouncing the recipient country or by attempting to block payment through the sale of products in competition with Soviet products.

The fundamental reason why Soviet aid during the cold-war years did not achieve more is that Soviet long-range political aims did not coincide with the aspirations of the LDCs. Short-range Soviet goals were often compatible with national independence and nonalignment in foreign policy. Indeed, one of the attractions of Soviet aid was that it strengthened the newly independent nation by lessening its otherwise exclusive dependence on the former mother country or on the United States. But ultimate Soviet aims diverged sharply from the objectives of the new states.

The people of most of these nations have keen memories of their long colonial subjugation; they are not about to substitute Soviet colonialism for the Western variety. Their nationalism is directed against *any* foreign control, which poses a real dilemma for the Soviets. When the Soviets have not interfered in domestic politics, they have enjoyed good relations with the recipient nations—as with India. But when they have sought to pressure a government to support Soviet

---

[17.] Berliner, *op. cit.*, pp. 171–177.

[18.] Heymann, *op. cit.*, pp. 538–539.

positions, attempted to overthrow governments, or refused to support governmental goals, they have alienated friendly states—like the Sudan, Egypt, and Somalia. Even Angola and Mozambique are beginning to look westward as well.

For the United States, the principal purpose of an aid program—after emphasis had shifted from Europe to the LDCs—was to help stop communism. Indeed, the term "economic aid" is actually something of a misnomer,[19] as the giant portion of American aid since the Korean war has been *military aid* to support mainly the armies of allied nations around the Sino-Soviet periphery: Nationalist China, South Korea, South Vietnam, Pakistan, and Turkey. Such military assistance may be viewed as a form of economic aid, for the recipient nation spends less of its own resources on military forces and can instead invest more heavily in economic development, assuming it would invest in a military force without aid.

Another form of aid may—for want of a better term—be called "bribery" aid. Much if the aid extended to Latin American republics before the formation of President Kennedy's Alliance for Progress could be included in this category. Dollars, as well as military equipment, sent to these countries supposedly for economic development or collective hemispheric defense, were actually intended to "buy" the support of the ruling classes and the military, neither of which was particularly interested in modernization. The United States was preoccupied in Europe, Asia, and the Middle East—that is, outside Latin America, whose grave social, political, and economic problems it ignored until Castro suddenly and dramatically drew attention to the vulnerability of the United States in its own backyard. Up to that point, the United States had been interested primarily in preserving hemispheric stability and securing votes in the United Nations. Latin American armies, hardly threatened by the Russian or Chinese military and useless as fighting machines anyway, could nevertheless be strengthened to deal with unrest at home. Outside Latin America, "bribery" money was from time to time given to key leaders to help them maintain "stability" in their countries.

But the most significant form of aid, in view of the almost global scope of the "revolution of rising expectations," has been the *development* loan.[20] American policy makers were eager to promote economic growth. They feared that some of the more important new nations, should they fail to transform themselves into unified, urban, industrialized societies, might adopt communism in order to organize themselves for modernization more effectively. In nations with ineffective political institutions, the appeal of communism is that it makes government possible. "They may not provide liberty, but they do provide authority; they do create governments that can govern."[21] Implicit in American promotion of economic growth was the assumption that poverty would benefit the communist cause.

[19] For the classification of aid generally followed here, see the excellent article by Hans J. Morgenthau, "A Political Theory of Foreign Aid," *American Political Science Review*, June 1962, pp. 301–309.

[20] For an excellent study of Cold War American aid programs, see Joan M. Nelson, *Aid, Influence and Foreign Policy* (New York: Macmillan, 1968).

[21] Samuel P. Huntington, *Political Order in Changing Societies* (New Haven: Yale University Press, 1968) p. 8.

254   (Conversely, it was frequently assumed that economic development would nurture more open societies and democratic institutions,[22] which would in turn ensure peaceful international behavior. Although these assumptions are questionable, it is true that democracy cannot develop amid conditions of poverty. Aristotle pointed out that "Poverty is the parent of revolution and crime. . . . When there is no middle class, and the poor greatly exceed in number, troubles arise, and the state soon comes to an end." Aristotle believed that political stability depends upon the absence of extreme wealth and poverty:

> Thus it is manifest that the best political community is formed by citizens of the middle class, and that those states are likely to be well-administered, in which the middle class is large, and stronger if possible than both the other classes, or at any rate than either singly; for the addition of the middle class turns the scale, and prevents either of the extremes from being dominant.[23]

That is, widespread moderate affluence is a prerequisite for democratic government. When the majority of men live in dire need—and, though aware that a better life is possible, see no signs of improvement—democratic government will not establish roots. A higher national income and a more equitable distribution of that income are more likely in a developed economy, and such an economy does tend to promote democracy. The society that can afford to "deal everyone in" can afford to be democratic.[24] Economic growth does not, of course, automatically produce a democratic society—Germany and Japan in the 1930s and the Soviet Union today being obvious examples. In each of these instances an economically developed nation has been controlled by an authoritarian or totalitarian regime bent on regional or global expansion. Freedom and democracy are not the necessary results of economic development. But, if economic development is not a *sufficient* condition to ensure the maturation of a democratic society, it nevertheless remains a *necessary* condition.[25]

American promotion of domestic development in the new nations was, of course, clearly related to the hope that conflict between the older and newer states is avoidable. American policy makers generally assumed that a world divided between rich and poor nations is incompatible with American interests.) It was about nineteenth-century Western society, divided between the wealthy few and the destitute masses, that Karl Marx wrote in *The Communist Manifesto*. He projected this social division into the future and prophesied the demise of capitalism.

---

[22] This assumption was never made explicit in the doctrine of foreign aid, for reasons analyzed in Robert A. Packenham, "Developmental Doctrines in Foreign Aid," *World Politics*, January 1966, pp. 194–225; and Packenham, *Liberal America and the Third World* (Princeton: Princeton University Press, 1973).

[23] William Ebenstein, ed., *Great Political Thinkers* (3d ed.; New York: Holt, Rinehart and Winton, 1960), p. 105.

[24] David M. Potter, *People of Plenty* (Chicago: University of Chicago Press, 1954), pp. 118–119.

[25] See Black, *Diplomacy of Economic Development*, pp. 19, 23. For a general analysis of the conditions necessary for democracy to flourish, see Seymour M. Lipset, *Political Man* (Garden City, N.Y.: Doubleday, 1959), pp. 45–67.

Most of the Western nations, however, managed to avoid the "inevitable" proletarian revolution by redistributing their national incomes, stabilizing their economies, and regulating their large industrial corporations. Democracy, by reforming capitalism, "derevolutionized" labor and ensured its allegiance to a form of welfare capitalism, or social democracy, in which labor shares in the general improvement of living standards. Now maldistribution of income plagues the underdeveloped world. The question is whether or not what Marx called "the specter of Communism" has been defeated domestically in the West only to reappear and defeat the West internationally.[26] (American policy makers preferred to promote peaceful evolution, economic development, and even political democracy, thus building an environment in which Western democracy could continue to flourish.)

Since the middle 1960s, however, there have been significant changes in both American and Soviet aid policies, for a number of reasons. Briefly, both of the superpowers have become increasingly aware that "instant development" is an unrealistic expectation. Modernization is a very long and very complex process, not to be achieved in a "Decade of Development" (as the 1960s were designated by the United Nations) or by simple transfer of factories and machinery to a cultural environment unable to cope with modern industry and accompanying social, political, and psychological demands. The enormous efforts already made and the disappointing results have both tired and disenchanted the two principal competitors. Both have also recognized that aid does not necessarily buy allies or votes. The Soviet Union, specifically, became increasingly disillusioned with the more radical leaders it had once sought as partners against the West. Several of them, had, by 1965, been deposed; but, in addition, in each instance the successor regime had claimed that a principal reason for the coup d'état had been economic stagnation and domestic chaos. Furthermore, the recipients of Soviet aid often did not repay their loans. The United States, on the other hand, grew more sophisticated; while coming around to accepting nonalignment even before the fall of such radicals as Ben Bella in Algeria, Nkrumah in Ghana, and Sukarno in Indonesia, it has been disenchanted with those who had bitten the hand that was feeding them. Finally, now that bipolarity has passed and negotiations between the superpowers on issues dividing them occurred more frequently, competition for most third world nations seems less urgent, particularly as other external and domestic commitments and demands on resources become more pressing.

American aid has, as a result, declined, in relation to rising GNP. In the late 1940s Marshall Plan aid totaled 2.75 percent of GNP. By the beginning of the 1970s nonmilitary aid had reached a low of 0.29 percent of GNP, the lowest of all major donor countries. In 1980, Ameican aid constituted 0.18 of 1 percent of GNP! Comparison of American aid with that of other countries at the height of the Vietnam war in 1968 is striking. Between 1956 and 1961, total combined development aid had been increasing rapidly; it increased more slowly up to 1967 and then in 1968 began to decline. In that year, the total foreign-aid bill was

---

[26.] This thesis has been reexamined in a general reevaluation of the American foreign-aid program by Huntington in "Foreign Aid for What and for Whom?" *Foreign Policy*, Winter 1970, pp. 161–189; and Huntington, "Does Foreign Policy Have a Future?" *Foreign Policy*, Spring 1971, pp. 114–134.

TABLE 11.1.

OFFICIAL DEVELOPMENT AID AS A PERCENTAGE OF THE GNP OF MAJOR COUNTRIES (1968)*

France	0.72	United States	0.38
Australia	0.57	Canada	0.28
Netherlands	0.54	Sweden	0.28
Britain	0.42	Japan	0.25
West Germany	0.42	Italy	0.23
Belgium	0.42		

*Organization for Economic Cooperation and Development and the Development Assistance Committee, from Lester B. Pearson, *Partners in Development: Report of the Commission on International Development* (New York: Holt, Rinehart and Winston, 1969), p. 148.

approximately $5 billion. After military aid and a few lesser programs were deducted, only $309 million was left for development purposes. This amount was equivalent to the cost of six days of fighting in Vietnam. In contrast, the Western industrial nations together that year spent $35 billion on liquor and $15 billion on cigarettes, a figure much higher than the aid they gave as a percentage of their combined GNP (see Table 11.1).[27]

As Robert Rothstein has noted, American aid has been extended to seventy counties, but eight of them received 75 percent of the total up to the late 1970s since aid for LDCs was initiated. Seven of those eight—South Korea, Taiwan, South Vietnam, Pakistan, Turkey, Jordan, and Brazil—are either formal allies or generally closely aligned with the United States. The eighth country is India, in the 1950s and early 1960s a leader of the nonaligned movement and one of the few democracies in the non-Western world (indeed, India has often been called "the world's biggest democracy"). In contrast, most LDCs receive "so little aid that it is difficult to see why aid became so controversial an issue".[28]

Aid was increasingly shifted from development programs to *technical assistance*, with emphasis on teaching skills and knowledge in areas like health, education, and food production. Furthermore, American military aid and economic aid have been separated, and development loans have increasingly been channeled through international institutions like the World Bank, the various regional banks, and the U.N. Conference on Trade and Development (UNCTAD). This approach, it was hoped, would leave the United States less vulnerable to charges of using aid to advance American political and strategic aims, and perhaps it would also satisfy those senators who argued after the Vietnam war that bilateral aid had involved this country too deeply in the affairs of too many other countries. But no effort has been made to increase aid funds—even to the 0.7 percent of GNP recommended in 1969 by the Commission on International Development, headed by former Canadian Prime Minister Lester Pearson. Greater emphasis was to be placed on technical assistance and on a larger role for American private enterprise.

[27.] Robert Rothstein, *The Weak in the World of the Strong*, p. 160
[28.] *Ibid.*

One main criterion for future aid was to be economic, rather than political: Could the recipient mobilize its resources and adopt policies to make sound use of the proffered funds? There were, of course, exceptions: for example, exerting pressure on international institutions to withhold loans from Allende's Chile and commitments to aid Egypt as it became more accommodating toward a settlement with Israel after 1973.

The Soviet Union has followed suit. Indeed, ideologically, the shift in attitudes toward foreign aid since 1964 has been startling.[29] In the early 1960s Soviet advice to new states was drawn straight from Marxism-Leninist theory: Expand the public sector of the economy in order to gain control over the economy; expropriate and nationalize private foreign and domestic firms, in order to keep profits for reinvestment, rather than letting them go into private hands at home or abroad; and orient economic relations toward Russia and its friends in order to break Western imperialist economic chains that have kept small nations underdeveloped. This approach has changed. Soviet aid policy now also emphasizes economic criteria more heavily than political ones. Soviet leaders have deemphasized—in very un-Marxist fashion—state control and nationalization of industry and have suggested that private capital, even *Western* capital, can play an important role in the modernization of new nations. They have also pointed out the need for more balance between industrial and agrarian development. And, of course, the amount of Soviet aid has declined.

> Khrushchev's successors have adopted more conservative foreign aid policies. The practice of making lavish expenditures for largely political purposes is now abandoned. Commitments made by the Brezhnev administration now require careful study and are made for economically viable projects. Futhermore, an increasingly important consideration is the compatibility of aid programs with domestic economic plans. Almost all Soviet aid is tied to the purchase of Soviet equipment or services. Approximately 95 percent of all aid consists of credits which must be repaid. Thus there is an integral link between aid and trade.[30]

For both superpowers, then, economic effectiveness has become more important. The United States has usually been somewhat concerned with economic rationalism, but for the Soviets this shift in emphasis is a real departure. Not that political considerations are now insignificant. But both superpowers wish the recipients of their aid to place greater emphasis on putting their economic houses in order. Presumably each expects political benefits from such improvements: neither will be pleased if reforms are accompanied by shifts from friendly to hostile postures in the recipient countries. Clearly, both now use economic aid, as did the great powers before them, to keep or to gain influence, rather than to bring about radical changes in the new nations' domestic structures. It has been said of the Russian program that the effort to make aid economically more telling is "not in

---

[29.] Elizabeth Kridl Valkenier, "New Trends in Soviet Economic Relations with the Third World," *World Politics*, April 1970, pp. 415–432; and Valkenier, "New Soviet Views on Economic Aid," *Survey*, Summer 1970, pp. 17–29.

[30.] Nogee and Sloan, *op. cit.*, p. 358.

258   order to lessen the influence of 'socialist' economies [or of mixed economies, as in the United States] but to improve its chances and popularity."[31] The same can be said of the American program. Nevertheless, the amounts of economic aid spent on this goal are smaller than at any time since World War II. Indeed, foreign aid does not even cover the extra costs of oil that many underdeveloped nations have had to pay since OPEC began raising prices in 1973.

OPEC, THE WEST, AND THE NON-USE OF FORCE

The year 1973 was the year of the Yom Kippur war in the Middle East and the year in which OPEC's Arab members, which held the world's largest oil reserves, instituted an embargo against the United States and the Netherlands to protest their political support of Israel. They also planned monthly production cutbacks for the other noncommunist industrial states and raised oil prices from $3 to $12 a barrel. The impact upon the Western industrial countries, as well as upon many LDCs, was devastating. OPEC's actions caused not only minor inconveniences to consumers who had to pay more for gasoline and other oil-based products, but also profound upheaval in entire economies, life styles, and standards of living. They also upset the plans for economic growth of many states, developed and undeveloped alike. Governments and citizens the world over learned the true meaning of the word "interdependence" (see Chapter 20 for further analysis of interdependence). Economic issues rose to the top of the international agenda and became intensely politicized.

More specifically, in the Western industrial nations and Japan, the quadrupling of oil prices—and later raises, especially in 1979—meant a permanent lowering of living standards. Families could no longer buy as much because gasoline, heating oil, plastics, and other oil-based materials like clothing had become much more expensive. Food prices also rose, for cultivation and distribution depended upon energy. The price rises stoked Western inflation, already high, and simultaneously precipitated the worst recession since the Great Depression of the 1930s, with very high unemployment rates. This "stagflation" in turn made recovery more difficult. The economic growth rates of all industrial countries were set back. Western Europe and Japan, the United States' principal allies in the security game, were hit much harder than the United States, for they were almost completely dependent upon OPEC oil.

The fragility of all Western economies, including America's, however, was starkly demonstrated. They were dependent on oil. Relatively inexpensive oil had led to neglect of enormous coal deposits in the West. As Alan Madian has pointed out:

> The artifically low prices from 1945 to 1973—in the late 1960s oil was priced at under $2 a barrel—turned the industrialized countries into petroleum junkies. Had oil been priced with due respect for the scarcity value of supplies, the present price might well be lower. Producers would have far less market power,

---

[31.] Valkenier, "New Soviet Views," p. 29.

since oil would have a significantly lower market share. There would be both less demand and more supply under U.S. control, and probably a more developed synthetic crude oil industry and other substitutes.

The major oil companies are now accused of creating artificial shortages. Yet for 28 years they were responsible for producing capacity surpluses in what are now the OPEC countries. Low prices subsidized the development of the industrialized nations and contributed to unprecedented growth rates. Cheap petroleum kept other energy prices low and eroded their market share. This bargain led to distortions in the industrial economies, and petroleum use doubled each decade. Investments in plant and equipment were based on the assumption that petroleum and other energy alternatives would remain cheap.[32]

It was this oil-hungry world that OPEC faced when it broke the cartel of Western oil companies. The extent of OPEC power, directly reflecting Western dependence on oil, is very clear from the American example. Beginning as self-sufficient in oil and an oil exporter, the United States became an importer in the 1970s. By 1976 it was importing 42 percent of its oil—7.3 million barrels per day (b.p.d.) of 17.4 million b.p.d.—at a cost of $35 billion a year. Almost 40 percent of this imported oil came from the Arab members of OPEC (AOPEC), four of which—Saudi Arabia, Kuwait, Iraq, and the United Arab Emirates—with Iran possess more than 50 percent of the world's known reserves and produce 40 percent of its supplies.

In 1977 American oil imports cost more than $40 billion. The major suppliers were, in order, Saudi Arabia, Venezuela, Nigeria, Libya, and Iran. In the summer of 1979, the United States was importing 9 million barrels *each day* out of a total of 21 million barrels used *each day*. From 1973 to 1979, American oil imports had increased more than 40 percent. The nation was as dependent on oil as a drug addict on heroin, and like the addict, it was inviting disaster. Yet after the clear warnings of 1973–1974, it continued to increase its dependence. In 1979, disaster struck. The Iranian cutback in oil production after the collapse of the shah stretched supplies so tightly that prices increased almost 100 percent in less than one year![33] By December 1979, the price of oil stood at $24 a barrel, up from about $13 a barrel in January, 1979. (Some countries, however were already selling for up to $40 a barrel in the tight oil market.) American oil costs for that one year alone rose $28 billion! By early 1980, the average price had risen to over $32 a barrel, a 150 percent increase in just over a year. At the current rate of increasing dependence on oil the United States could be paying over $100 billion a year by 1980 and over $200 billion by 1995, a sum the nation could hardly afford.[34] As it is, the ever greater outflow of funds to pay for oil is reducing the value of the dollar and increasing domestic inflation. If the oil producers ever decide to abandon the dollar as the medium of payment, it may collapse.

---

[32] Alan L. Madian," "Oil is Still Too Cheap," *Foreign Policy*, Summer 1979, pp. 173–174.

[33] On the collapse of the shah, see George Lenczowski, "The Arc of Crisis," *Foreign Affairs*, Spring 1979, pp. 796–820; and Richard Cottam, David Schoenbaum, Shahram Chubin, Theodore H. Moran, and Richard A. Falk, "The United States and Iran's Revolution," *Foreign Policy*, Spring 1979, pp. 3–34.

[34] *Ibid.*

There is an irony in this situation. None of the oil-producing states can be considered a major power, not even Iran with its substantial population. Most of these states have small populations, little industry, and virtually no military muscle. All they have is oil! But that really is "all," and they have been able to influence profoundly not only the domestic affairs but also the Middle Eastern policies of the noncommunist industrial states. Japan first, then western Europe acceded to Arab demands to show more sympathy for the Palestinian cause. Even the United States, long a major supporter of Israel, decided to play a more even-handed role, and shortly after the 1973 war Kissinger began trying to bring about a more lasting peace in the region. The weak have come to seem omnipotent, the strong impotent. It appears that the world has turned upside down, as, one by one, the Western states, former rulers of these small countries and still military giants relative to OPEC's members, have complied with some Arab wishes. Nothing could more vividly and dramatically illustrate that power relations do not always follow the rule that the nation that can produce "more bang for a buck" or "more rubble per ruble" can achieve its demands and successfully resist the demands of others.

Some OPEC members' highly public and dramatic use of their economic power seems to contradict our earlier conclusion that the exercise of economic sanctions is counterproductive. The most powerful military states in the world have passively accepted high rates of inflation, recession, the declining value of the dollar, and continual oil-price increases. How can we account for the success of these military "minipowers" against the leading industrial nations of the West?

A preliminary comment about this success is in order. Even before the 1973 war Europeans had been leaning toward the acceptance of U.N. resolution 242, which called on Israel to withdraw from the Arab territories conquered in 1967, in return for Arab recognition of the state of Israel and an end to hostilities. The cost of compliance with initial Arab demands in 1973 was thus not painful. The United States would have sought a comprehensive peace in the Middle East even without the Arab oil producers' actions. From the outbreak of the 1973 war, Kissinger had been determined to make such an effort, in order to win for Israel the security it had long sought, improve American relations with the Arabs, and displace Soviet influence in the Arab world. The cycle of Arab-Israeli wars had to be ended. Each conflict brought the superpowers closer to intervention and total war. A Soviet threat to intervene and an American global military alert averted that danger in 1973. But would nuclear holocaust erupt from a subsequent Arab-Israeli war? The degree of the Arab petroleum states' initial success, then, was probably somewhat less than it appears at first.

Still, embargo, restricted supplies, and higher prices hovered in the background as reminders of OPEC's power and the pain that its Arab members could inflict if their legitimate interests remained unsatisfied. The oil barrel could exert more leverage in the West than the gun barrel could in OPEC countries. In any event, force was not used. This refusal to use force on issues of vital interest was new.[35] Admittedly, Secretary of State Kissinger did threaten the use of force if

OPEC attempted to "strangle" the United States. But, of course, when a nation's survival is at stake, it is unlikely to submit without resisting. Kissinger's threat also was related to a security issue, but the oil issue is generally viewed in the West as a welfare, or bread-and-butter, issue, which presumably does not require the use of force.

OPEC has, in any event, claimed *the right to determine prices for its oil and to deny that oil to Western nations, through an embargo or reduced production.* The West, by its acceptance of such measures has, in a sense, legitimated this claim. It has interpreted the principle of national self-determination to mean that, if another country owns resources it can do with them what it pleases, regardless of the difficulties inflicted on themselves and the rest of the world.

Indeed, this interpretation of this principle by the West has led it to acquiesce in the virtual disregard by some OPEC nations of their contracts. As Walter Levy, a noted oil expert, has stated:

> The producing countries . . . in fact do not recognize as binding supply or price arrangements even if freely concluded by them. Recently they have gone so far as to change agreed-upon prices retroactively. This, they argue, they are entitled to do under the doctrine of sovereign control by producing countries over their natural resources. . . .
>
> Because of the fear of being arbitrarily cut off from supplies, Western nations and their [oil] companies now accept within a wide range practically any economic or political terms that a producing country may impose upon them.[36]

This subservience can only serve to encourage OPEC to raise prices further and/or limit production. In Levy's words, "We have thus entered a period in international oil of near 'lawlessness' in the relationship between producing countries, the oil companies and the importing countries."[37]

Can it be doubted that OPEC's past price increases have been far more damaging to the West than the loss of West Berlin, the placement of Soviet missiles in Cuba, or the loss of South Vietnam could ever have been? Among the major effects have been the weakening of the Western alliance and the undermining of the social and economic health, as well as the political stability, of Western democracies. Can the oil issue still be defined primarily as a welfare issue? Can we disagree with Robert Tucker's conclusion that "a persuasive case may be made to the effect that it is the oil cartel, and not the rising military power of the Soviet Union, that has formed the greatest threat in the 1970s and 1980s to the structure of American interests and commitments in the world"?[38]

---

[35] See Louis J. Halle, "Does War Have a Future?" *Foreign Affairs*, October 1973, pp. 20–34; and Klaus Knorr, "On the Uses of Military Power in the Nuclear Age" and Knorr, "The Limits of Power," in Raymond Vernon, ed., *The Oil Crisis* (New York: Norton, 1976), pp. 229–43.

[36] Walter J. Levy, "Oil and the Decline of the West," *Foreign Affairs*, Summer 1980, pp. 1003–1004.

[37] *Ibid.*, p. 1004.

[38] Robert W. Tucker, "Oil and American Power," *Commentary*, September 1979, p. 39.

TABLE 11.2

AMERICAN IMPORTS OF CRUDE AND REFINED OIL (IN THOUSANDS OF BARRELS DAILY)*

1970	1971	1972	1973	1974	1975	1976	1977	1978	1979
3,418	3,923	4,739	6,201	6,088	6,056	7,295	8,744	8,044	8,157

*These figures have been calculated from *The Oil and Gas Journal*, January 29, 1979, p. 124; and Bureau of Economic Analysis, Department of Commerce, *Survey of Current Business* for the respective years.

TABLE 11.3

AMERICAN PETROLEUM IMPORTS (in millions of dollars*)

1970	1971	1972	1973	1974	1975	1976	1977	1978	1979
2,764.3	3,323.3	4,299.6	7,614.2	24,269.5	24,814.3	31,794.5	41,526.1	39,108.9	56,046.0

*These figures have been calculated from *The Oil and Gas Journal*, January 28, 1980, pp. 119, 124 and Bureau of Economic Analysis, Department of Commerce, *Survey of Current Business* for the respective years.

Even if world demand for oil falls, which theoretically should lead to a reduction of prices since supply would be greater than demand, oil is not like other commodities and does not, therefore, behave in terms of the laws of supply and demand. Even with an excess of oil, the price remains upward-bound.[39] OPEC simply cuts production back to the level of demand and keeps world supplies tight. There is no way for the consumer countries to win this game. They are no longer fully in control of their economies; an anti-inflationary policy pushing a nation deeper into hopefully only a short but deep recession cannot work if oil prices continue to rise sharply. They remain at OPEC's mercy. Indeed, the rapidly escalating oil prices since the shah's fall have stoked chronic Western and world inflation and brought the global economy and financial system to the brink of major disaster, possibly collapse. In the spring of 1980, the Western industrial countries had 18 million unemployed and the figure was still going up. An estimated 250–450 billions worth of industrial capacity lay idle. Not only did other major sources of oil supply seem more unstable all of a sudden—even Saudi Arabia had to worry about internal security—but OPEC was jeopardizing the economic growth—in fact, economic viability—of the Western consumer nations. It was also leading them into increasing debt, since few could earn enough money through exports. But as trade deficits grew by leaps and bounds, they tried more energetically to expand their foreign trade while seeking protection from imports to protect their workers from unemployment and keep their foreign earnings up. The 1980s may under these circumstances see the industrial countries pursue "beggar my neighbor" policies or "trade wars" as one state seeks to increase its earnings at the cost of its neighbor. The alliances the United States has with Japan and the European NATO nations might well be further weakened. In the meantime, the oil imports, paid for in dollars, led to a flood of dollars on the international market; the United

---

39. In June 1980, with an excess of oil available and 5 billion barrels of oil stored in the West, whose recession-hit economies were demanding less oil, OPEC raised prices again.

FIGURE 11.1

ESTIMATED OPEC 1979 EXPORTS AND EARNINGS

Consuming countries buy this much oil from abroad . . .		. . . and OPEC collects this much in return	
Estimated 1979 oil imports	Billions of U.S. dollars	Projected 1979 revenues*	Billions of U.S. dollars
United States	$ 61	Saudi Arabia	$ 62.3
Japan	40	Kuwait	21.0
Germany	22	Iraq	20.6
France	19	Iran	20.5
Italy	18	Nigeria	16.7
Netherlands	14	Venezuela	14.7
Britain	12	United Arab Emirates	13.6
Other industrial countries	16	Libya	13.1
Brazil	7	Indonesia	12.0
India	4	Algeria	10.5
South Korea	3	Qatar	3.6
Other developing countries	26	Ecuador	2.4
		Gabon	1.7
Total	$242	Total	$212.7
Data: Central Intelligence Agency and *Business Week* estimates		Data: Chase Manhattan Bank and *Business Week* estimates	

*Includes oil exports plus investment income.

Business Week, November 19, 1979, p. 176.

States, with its thirst for oil, contributed enormously to this flood, the end result of which was to cheapen the United States currency's value and increase oil prices further as the dollars paid to OPEC continued to be worth less, which in turn fed the fires of inflation.

Can OPEC's actions in these circumstances not be considered "economic aggression" because they affect the essential security of the Western states? Has the price of oil not become extortionate to the point that it threatens international economic collapse (see Tables 11.2 and 11.3)? And will the present Western response of acquiescence and talk of accommodation not lead to a domino effect more damaging than that feared during the Cold War—because passive submission to each price increase only leads to the next round of increases? Will that not happen, as surely as day follows night, precisely because the OPEC nations do not have to fear any sanctions, let alone violent reprisal? Are the Western democracies really going to let a handful of basically small, undemocratic states, which count on the democracies' refusal to use force as an instrument of national *economic* policy, dictate their futures? (See Figure 11.1.)

263

264   ⎰ Regardless of the answers to these questions, a resort to force on the oil issue or other "interdependence" issues is unlikely (for reasons elaborated in Chapter 20). OPEC will therefore remain in a very strong bargaining position as long as the following conditions remain:[40]

> Substantial Western dependence on imported oil, so that even sharp price increases do not result in a major reduction in demand
>
> A small number of producers, which control most international trade in this commodity.
>
> Limited possibilities of substituting other energy sources for oil in the short or medium run
>
> Common political or economic goals among the exporting nations
>
> Producers' invulnerability to embargo by consumer nations ⎱

One other condition is worth mentioning: OPEC deals with private American oil companies, which are primarily interested in maintaining their rights to market and distribute OPEC oil, not in price restraint. In fact, OPEC price increases enhance company profits. Neither the OPEC nations nor most western European states leave decisions about buying and selling oil in private hands. Decisions that so profoundly affect national economies are considered to fall within the sphere of government, as do decisions about war and peace and the export of nuclear technology. A national purchasing organization, which would be the sole buyer of OPEC oil, would perhaps be able to face OPEC's sales monopoly more evenly; such an agency could trade off American oil needs against OPEC nations' desires for American arms, technology, and food. The major obstacle to the formation of such an agency is the commitment to private enterprise, which is interpreted more broadly in the United States than in western Europe.

ECONOMICS, POWER, AND MORALITY

⎰ Our first lesson about the use of economic power may be somewhat surprising—that, with the admittedly major single exception of OPEC, the use of the "economic weapon" as a substitute for the "military weapon" to advance a state's purposes is an indicator of a nation's strength.⎱ All our examples have involved the traditionally great powers, and OPEC's success, it must be emphasized, results from the consumer nations' having allowed themselves to become "hooked" on oil. Because the Western states are "powerful"—especially in technology, industry, and other resources—new sources of oil, as well as coal, synthetic fuel, nuclear power, and solar energy are all possible in the future. Eventually they may be able to reduce their vulnerability to OPEC.

[40.] See Chapters 12 and 20 for further analysis of OPEC "power."

In any event, powerful states—in terms of the usual criteria of population, GNP, and military strength—have historically been able to afford all sorts of power instruments. Today the United States can afford strategic nuclear weapons, sizable conventional capabilities that are becoming increasingly more sophisticated and expensive, and economic power. Britain, formerly the world's greatest military and economic power, can afford only relatively small conventional forces, which in 1956 could not even quickly defeat Egypt; unable to afford to keep up with rapidly changing military technology, Britain has based its small "independent" nuclear force on American weapons. In 1979, American military transport planes had to carry the British peace-keeping force to Rhodesia (now Zimbabwe); Britain did not have planes that could carry helicopters and jeeps. The nations that have been able to afford the whole range of power instruments have not had to resort to force in the pursuit of their objectives as often as weaker states. "Economic weapons" have provided their leverage. As Waltz has reminded us, 'non-recourse to force' is the doctrine of the strong."[41] E.H. Carr wrote long ago: "Great Britain's unchallenged naval and economic supremacy throughout the nineteenth century enabled her to establish a commanding position in China with a minimum of military force and of economic discrimination. A relatively weak power like Russia could only hope to achieve a comparable result by naked aggression and annexation."[42]

(It is, of course, this issue of the superior economic power of the West that is at the heart of third-world complaints about continued poverty and lack of modernization. The LDCs perceive the international political and economic order as grossly unfair, dominated by the first world, which makes the economic rules, receives the giant share of economic and political benefits, and keeps the poor countries poor and subordinate. With a few exceptions, the poor countries seem unable to develop.) During the Cold War the United States and the Soviet Union competed for the allegiance and support of the third world with foreign aid; but détente has led to reductions in aid. The problem is that the majority of the former colonies are unable to earn enough to pay their way. They face immense difficulties (which will be discussed in detail in Chapter 14) because they see the laws of supply and demand as "stacking the deck" against them. Any one of these countries is likely to have one, perhaps two, raw materials to sell for foreign exchange with which to buy machinery and food. But this situation means that its income depends upon the health of the Western economies; its earnings fluctuate with the swings of the business cycle.(In addition, competition among raw-materials producers means that, as each nation works harder to produce more and raise its income, it merely succeeds in lowering the price through oversupply and driving its income down.)The increasing use of synthetic materials in Western states has made the situation even worse.(Finally, the underdeveloped countries claim that what they buy in the West costs them more because of inflation. The "terms of trade" in the so-called free market favor the economically powerful over the economically weak. Indeed, to sum up the third world's case succinctly, the rich have become rich by

---

[41] Waltz, *op. cit.*, p. 185.

[42] E.H. Carr, *The Twenty Year Crisis 1919–1939* (London: Macmillan, 1951), p. 130.

266   "plundering" the poor; Western industrialization, prosperity, and power have been built on the LDCs' cheap resources. Even with foreign aid and increased export at world market prices, the third-world countries have not been able to earn sufficient revenues to modernize by organizing cartels and raising their own prices, as OPEC has done; they could perhaps do so. The present rules of the economic game have not so far benefited them.) Why not write their own rules? The third-world countries in the U.N. General Assembly have therefore demanded a fairer international distribution of wealth, a new international economic order (NIEO). Underlying their demands is a sense of deep frustration and anger at their past subordinate status and exploitation, as well as a determination that their fates will now be in their own hands. They intend no longer to be the pawns in the international economy. The issue is again one of power. The LDCs are no longer colonies, but they claim that they are still pseudocolonies, for they have not yet gained control over their own economic destinies. Their economies remain tied to Western industry and are dependent on exports and foreign markets, rather than on domestic consumption, for prosperity.

These complaints would not have surprised Friedrich List, a nineteenth-century German political economist, who, after studying the economy of England, the world's first industrial state to champion free trade, advised Germany against free trade.

> I saw clearly that free competition between two nations which are highly civilized can only be mutually beneficial in case both of them are in a nearly equal position of industrial development, and that any nation which owing to misfortunes is behind others in industry, commerce, and navigation . . . must first of all strengthen her own individual powers, in order to fit herself to enter into free competition with more advanced nations.[43]

The free market may well be a superior mechanism for allocating goods, when those competing and exchanging goods are of approximately equal power. When one nation is clearly more advanced economically, however, free trade benefits it more because it is able to penetrate the markets of weaker countries; if the latter do not protect themselves with tariffs to keep cheaper foreign imports out, home industries can never develop. During the initial stages of development, new industries are bound to be more expensive. Free trade is thus the weapon of the strong; tariffs to protect "infant industries" while they grow to efficiency are the weapon of the weak. The laws of the free market are *not* neutral. Power is the "invisible hand" determining the distribution of wealth. Among nations that are equal in economic power, economic relations may well breed interdependence, as in the EEC, and between them and the United States. But between the economically strong and the economically weak, the inevitable result is dependence

---

[43] Quoted in Edward Mead Earle, "Adam Smith, Alexander Hamilton, Friedrich List: The Economic Foundations of Military Power," in *Makers of Modern Strategy* (Princeton: Princeton University Press, 1943), p. 140.

of the latter. Economic weapons, then, remain "pre-eminently the weapons of strong Powers."[44])

(One special characteristic of the use of economic power is worth noting at this point: The exercise of the economic weapon appears more "moral" than the military one. Perhaps we should say "less immoral." In reality, it may be no more or less immoral.) A wartime blockade may cause just as many—or more—people to starve to death as are killed by high explosives in a series of air raids. Similarly, granting a nation political independence even though economically it is dependent on foreign markets and thus not in control of its own destiny, generally seems less immoral than direct political control by a foreign occupying power. Such appearances of morality are not unimportant in the relations among nations and national reputations. Carr has called this popular distinction between dollars and bullets an illusion. Power, he argues is "one and indivisible."

> It uses military and economic weapons for the same ends. The strong will tend to prefer the minor and more "civilised" weapon because it will generally suffice to achieve his purposes; and as long as it will suffice, he is under no temptation to resort to the more hazardous military weapon. But military power cannot be isolated from military power, nor military from economic. They are both integral parts of political power; and in the long run one is helpless without the other. . . . But generally speaking, there is a sense in which dollars are humaner than bullets even if the end pursued be the same.[45]

THE VISIBLE AND "INVISIBLE" USES OF REWARDS AND COERCION

(States have been more successful in attaining their aims by means of economic rewards than by means of depriving target nations of economic products and services. Rewards promise economic improvement, higher standards of living, and better life styles.) Such rewards led to western Europe's economic recovery after World War II and to the strengthening of NATO; provided the foundation upon which European nations have integrated their economies and laid the basis for possible political union and status as a third superpower; and attracted Russia to détente. They hold some promise of more restrained American-Soviet political relations. And, although economic aid in its various forms may not have given either superpower control over the LDC recipients or helped the latter to develop, it has attracted supporters, helped stabilize regimes (at least in the short run), and enhanced the independence of some new nations, allowing them to resist seduction or pressure from the other superpower. Nor have all economic projects and technical-assistance programs been failures.

[44.] Carr, *op. cit.*, p. 131.

[45.] *Ibid.*, pp. 131, 132.

268 (Whereas rewards can help to cement relations, economic punishment has generally proved ineffective in achieving high political purposes. That should not be surprising. Economic coercion cannot be successful if other markets or sources of supply are available to the target nations or if the latter's leaders and people perceive the demands as affecting national integrity, pride, and independence) Richard Olsen has suggested, however, that the instances of failure described here are all examples of publicly visible coercion. Economic coercion, he claims, can also be exerted "invisibly"—and more effectively:

> In most cases of economic coercion, the sanctions are more subtle; they are applied in areas in which the target is the solicitor: aid, investment, finance, and technology. Trade sanctions are usually highly visible. . . . Furthermore, trade, however, unequal the terms, is a partnership in which groups in both the sender- and target-countries stand to lose when sanctions are applied. This is much less the case in the more subtle and complex areas of international technology transfers, finance, investment, and aid. Ours is a capital- and technique-scarce world, with keen competition among LDCs for what is available. . . .
>
> First World governments, their aid agencies, international financial institutions such as the World Bank or the regional development banks, private bank consortia, and multinational corporations are, for many LDCs, integral and influential parts of the domestic economy and policy-making apparatus. Dependency is indeed vulnerability; as George Ball has asked in apparent commiseration: "How can a national government make an economic plan with any confidence if a board of directors meeting 5,000 miles away can by altering its pattern of purchasing and production affect in a major way the country's economic life?"[46]

Publicly applied economic sanctions tend to fail to achieve high political goals, but "relatively covert, subtle economic sanctions will ultimately be *politically* effective with only moderate, purely *economic* effects."[47] Dependence thus allows for the exercise of economic coercion without publicity and patriotic rallying around the flag in the target state. Not publicly announced cuts in quotas or embargoes but delays in delivery of spare parts, drying up of credit, decline in value of investments, reduction of multilateral and bilateral loans, and refusal to refinance debts are more effective though less visible means of coercion. Kissinger's détente policy, with its emphasis on trade, technology, and credits, fits this mold; the Soviets would pay both a financial price for American products and services and a political price.

PETROPOWER (OIL) VERSUS AGRIPOWER (FOOD)

Among the chief reasons OPEC has achieved leverage is that the consumer countries have no item to withhold which is as critical to the OPEC nations' daily existence

---

[46] Olsen, *op. cit.*, pp. 477, 481.

[47] *Ibid.*, p. 485.

as oil is to the Western consumer nations. Even if the United States and the other industrial states were not competitors in the sale of industrial technology and weapons, OPEC would retain the upper hand because, without millions of barrels of imported oil each day, Western industries would have to stop functioning, and their economies would collapse. One exception to this outline is often mentioned: food. In 1979 a country-western song entitled "Cheaper Crude or No More Food" became quite popular. According to the lyrics, the United States would "lower the boom," "forget the Golden Rule," and "cut off the food." "Let'em make a loaf of bread out of a gallon of crude" was the refrain. We could last longer without oil than they could without food was the underlying theme. But could we? Is food a coercive tool to match oil, and would it give the United States, the world's bread-basket, a power greater than that of Saudi Arabia with its oil? Can "agripower" match "petropower"? Can the United States put an embargo on grain and trade a "bushel for a barrel"? The answer to all these questions has to be "no."

Analysis will reveal why one critical resource or commodity cannot be used to exert influence but another can.[48] For one thing, an oil producer can bring oil to the surface, leave it in the well, or store it without deterioration. Its value is likely to rise nevertheless. Food is produced in the United States by hundreds of thousands of individual farmers, and its availability depends very much upon weather conditions. Crops, if not harvested or if stored too long, lose their value. Furthermore, in a democracy the government rarely exercises sufficient control over farmers to plan the harvest, and it is subject to considerable political pressure should it attempt to use food as a weapon. American farmers stand to lose a lot of money, and they do vote in presidential primaries and elections. "Cold cash" comes before "cold war." Food exports, in fact, are managed almost entirely by private firms, as the nation learned to its horror in 1972, when the "great [Russian] grain robbery" sent domestic food prices soaring.

In the target nations the interruption of the food trade is not nearly as serious as a break in oil deliveries in the West. Most countries import only 5–10 percent of their food; western Europe imports approximately 90 percent of its oil, and Japan imports even more. The OPEC countries also import food, but many of the Arab members, have only small populations. The OPEC nations' purchase of American food in 1978 accounted for less than 10 percent of American food exports. Even a larger country like Iran, with a population of almost 40 million, can find other sources of food if American sales are cut off. Food can be used effectively as a weapon only against a very large importer, as happened in 1980, when, after the invasion of Afghanistan, President Carter put an embargo on 17 million tons of feed grain intended for the Soviet Union. But the possiblility of such an embargo had not deterred the Soviets; even in that instance, agripower was of limited utility as a means of coercion. The greater effectiveness of petropower is hardly surprising. "More than half of the world's oil consumption is satisfied through imports, compared to only one-eighth of all consumption of the world's

---

[48.] Robert L. Paarlberg, "Food, Oil, and Coercive Resource Diplomacy," *International Security*, Fall 1978, pp. 3–19 and "Lessons of the Grain Embargo," *Foreign Affairs*, Fall 1980, pp. 144–162. Also see Emma Rothschild, "Food Politics," *ibid.*, January 1976, pp. 285–307.

270 most traded food source, grain. A large export share in the world oil market is more likely, as a result, to translate into real political power."[49]

There are also other suppliers of food for the approximately 120 importing nations. Canada, Australia, and Argentina, for instance, are quite willing to ship food to countries that the United States places under embargo. And in good years Russia and India themselves sell surplus crops. The food market is competitive; there is no grain cartel and, for all the reasons mentioned, it appears impossible to organize one. Finally, the condition of this food market is normally one of abundance, rather than of scarcity. Food is therefore not a likely bargaining device for dealing with the oil producers. "Cheaper" energy will be produced only when more oil reserves are found and developed or when other sources of energy become feasible, thus reducing Western vulnerability to oil embargoes, production cutbacks, and price rises.

Petropower remains a more effective lever than agripower. We need only examine some of the events of 1979. Britain's new prime minister, Margaret Thatcher, after hinting that she would recognize the new government of Zimbabwe-Rhodesia, backed down before a Nigerian threat of reduction in oil supplies to the British Petroleum Company. A similar threat was made against the United States, though President Carter denies that it was this threat that led him to maintain sanctions against Zimbabwe-Rhodesia (now Zimbabwe) that the Senate had wanted him to lift.[50] Lately, in 1980, Nigeria's President threatened to use oil to pressure the United States to oppose South Africa's apartheid policy. Canadian Prime Minister Joseph Clark, in response to Arab pressures, did not keep his campaign pledge to move the Candian embassy in Israel from Tel Aviv to Jerusalem. Mexico, thanks to its petropower, was able to protect its vegetable exports, prevent a real crackdown on illegal immigration into the United States, and even snub an American President publicly. And Saudi Arabia's Sheik Ahmad Zaki Yamani said aloud what many American policy makers aleady know, that further oil interruptions may occur if there is no progress on the Palestinian issue.

The problem, however, is not just one of interruption in Saudi deliveries. As Iran lowers its daily output, Kuwait announces that it will do the same, and Libya threatens to export no oil at all for several years, the West must rely on Saudi Arabia to *increase* its production. OAPEC is building a tanker fleet, so that by 1985 Arab vessels can carry as much as 40 percent of their own oil exports. And Arab technicians are being trained in other phases of the oil business, from exploration to refining. "This is not a commercial venture as such," said a consultant to the new shipping company. "This is a strategic situation. We must have our own ships to strengthen our hand to resist pressure from the oil companies or anyone else who seeks to dilute our control of our national assets."[51]

Not surprisingly, the Palestinian Liberation Organization (PLO) is gaining increasing recognition from those who are dependent on Arab oil. Yasir Arafat, its

---

[49.] Paarlberg, *op. cit.*, p. 15.

[50.] *The New York Times*, September 27, 1979.

[51.] *Ibid.*, Octobr 27, 1979.

leader, has paid an official visit to Spain and an unofficial one to Austria. His "foreign minister" won "political recognition" (the next best thing to full recognition, which can be given only to a government) for the PLO from Italy; while in Brussels, he met a senior Common Market official, as well as the Belgian foreign minister, who agreed that the visit constituted *de facto* recognition.[52] Later, Arafat said western Europe would "be made to pay dearly" if it continued its "pro-Zionist policies." He demanded that France invite him officially and recognize the PLO as "the sole legitimate voice" of the Palestinians.[53] As Egyptian-Israeli talks on Palestinian autonomy got nowhere while Israel built more settlements on the West Bank, the Common Market countries moved closer to a European initiative on this matter by calling for Palestinian self-determination, the end of Israel's "territorial occupation" of the West Bank, and for PLO "association" with the peace process.[54] While these may well be part of a formula for a peace in the Middle East, the European declaration and its timing clearly reflect the enormous influence of the oil lever. Yet the PLO complained that the Europeans had not gone far enough because they had stopped short of official recognition of the PLO and a call for a Palestinian state.[55] As one American official was quoted in 1979 as saying: "The taut situation gives blackmail ability to everybody. It requires strong nerves to do what you would otherwise do."[56] The power to blackmail hardly provides much support for the views of those who foresee a new era of economic interdependence in which every state's well-being will be dependent on all other states and in which sanctions, especially force, will no longer play a role in conflict resolution and allocation of resources.

---

[52] *Ibid.*, October 30, 1979.

[53] *Ibid.*, May 19, 1980.

[54] *Ibid.*, June 14, 1980.

[55] *Ibid.*, June 15, 1980.

[56] Quoted by Steven Rattner, "Oil Guns Get a Bigger Bang for the Barrel," *The New York Times*, July 15, 1979.

Multipolarity and Future International Politics

12

STABLE NUCLEAR BIPOLARITY—AND BEYOND

Our analysis of bipolar international politics has revealed two main powers, watching each other's every move and drawing lines around their respective spheres of influence. Fearful of falling dominoes, each power has devoted itself to preserving these lines. As a consequence, the bipolar system has been characterized by numerous confrontations and crises, as each nation has anticipated a preventive or preemptive strike by its opponent. Such a bipolar structure, it is easy to understand, is to be feared because it encourages violence. Yet, if the world has been existing in an atmosphere of impending violence for thirty-five years, how can we explain the fact that total war has not occurred? Theoretically it ought to have occurred.

The answer is that, since 1945, one tangible component of power has become decisive: technology. The existence of nuclear arms provides the key to the two superpowers' success in preserving peace, despite the scope and intensity of their rivalry. The two powers have repeatedly tested each other, just as the model predicts, but the fear of nuclear suicide has imposed some restraint that they might not have exercised had they had no reason to fear total destruction. Before nuclear times, overestimating one's own power and underestimating that of the adversary were frequent causes of war; in the nuclear age, policymakers have had to be more careful. The result has been an emphasis on deterrence, crisis management, and limited war. Total war no longer seems a rational instrument of national policy; crises have become the ultimate instrument, the substitute for war, as each state has attempted to shift the status quo and the other has resisted. Crises have become the testing grounds, as the balance of resolve has become critical. Even though historically a bipolar balance has been unstable, the post-1945 *nuclear* bipolar balance has, on the whole been stable.

The rules that kept it stable were as follows:

1. Preserve "essential equivalence" in strategic nuclear weapons.

2. Use nuclear weapons as deterrents, but not militarily.

3. Use nuclear arms principally for political advantages, especially for purposes of bargaining in crises.

4. Oppose acquisition of nuclear weapons by other countries. (Britain was the exception.)

5. Stake out a sphere of influence and most of the time—but not always—respect the adversary's claims to its own sphere.

6. Avoid direct conflict with the other superpower, for the danger of escalation is too geat.

7. Indirect conflict through allies, friends, and satellites is acceptable. The principal arena of such indirect conflict is the third world.

Some, if not most, of these "rules" have developed through trial and error over many years, but some have been negotiated explicity. Negotiation has particularly characterized efforts at arms control; the superpowers, through basically adversaries, have found it necessary to cooperate on this issue. It is instructive simply to list some of the many agreements that they have worked out, especially since the Cuban missile crisis of 1962 (see Table 12.1).

The passing of the bipolar system is not likely to produce genuine multipolarity—in which half a dozen or more powers have approximately equal capability. Nothing even close to such a system can develop until countries like China and possibly Brazil become full-fledged powers, with sizable populations, large-scale industries, and military strength to match the capabilities of the present superpowers, and until the EEC countries can unite politically to form a United States of Europe. None of these events is likely to occur in the next decade or two.

Thus the system might be called *bipolycentric*. As awkward as that term is, it aptly represents the two elements of the contemporary international system. The "bi" refers to the continuing superpower status of the United States and the Soviet Union. Their relationship is still critical. Since the dangerous confrontation of the Cuban missile crisis, this relationship has become more complex, mixing elements of conflict and cooperation. The superpowers remain adversaries; but they are also partners sharing common interests, especially in arms control. Given the stark alternatives of coexistence or nonexistence, the recognition that their fate is inextricably bound together if they wish to avoid committing suicide, the need to negotiate and lower tensions, if possible, is obvious. Hence the two powers, who

TABLE 12.1

ARMS CONTROL

Objective	Agreement	Year
Quantitative and qualitative limits strategic delivery systems	SALT I. A.B.M. treaty	1972
	SALT I interim agreement on offensive arms	1972
	Vladivostok guidelines	1974
	SALT II treaty[b]	1980
Direct communication between American and Soviet leaders during crises	Hot-line agreement	1963
	Hot-line modernization agreement	1971
Barring nuclear-weapons from specific regions	Antartica treaty[a]	1959
	Outer-space treaty[a]	1967
	Seabed treaty[a]	1971
Discouragement of nuclear proliferation	International Atomic Energy Authority[a]	1954
	Nonproliferation treaty[a]	1968
	Nuclear Supplier's Club[a]	1975
Limiting of nuclear tests	Limited test-ban treaty[a]	1963
	Threshold test ban treaty	1974[b]
	Peaceful nuclear-explosion treaty	1976[b]
Banning nonnuclear weapons of mass destruction	Biological-weapons convention	1972

[a.] Multilaterial agreements.
[b.] Signed but not yet in force.

would be superpowers even if they possessed no nuclear weapons at all, have become locked in an "adversary partnership," combining a changing mix of cold war and détente, competition and accommodation over time.)

("The "polycentric" in bipolycentric refers primarily to the many new state actors or centers of foreign policy. In a multipolar system, there are a number of roughly equal great powers; in a polycentric system, there are numerous actors whose "power" varies considerably, although none of them is the equal of the superpowers who remain at the top of the state hierarchy. But weak or relatively powerful, their actions affect events in the international system and the consequences of their behavior may be dangerous,)whether it is an Egypt and Syria going to war with Israel, a Bangladesh seceding from Pakistan, an Iran seizing American hostages or an Iraq going to war with Iran. The world is no longer as dominated or controlled by the superpowers as in the bipolar days; even their allies who continue to rely upon them for their security have regained a considerable measure of diplomatic freedom. In a sense, it is precisely because the superpowers are stalemated while continuing to be the producers of their allies' security—they are mainly its consumers—that the latter have been able to take advantage of this stalemate to become once more independent centers of foreign policy decisions.

(This system will not enjoy the stability that generally characterizes a multipolar system, partly because nuclear weapons have tended to reverse the characteristics of bipolarity and multipolarity. That is, *nuclear* bipolarity tends to be stable, and *nuclear* multipolarity will tend to be unstable. The reasons for the probable instability of a postnuclear bipolar polycentric system are complex and numerous.)

THE MULTIPLICATION OF STATES

In 1939, on the eve of World War II, there were only sixty states in the world. Thirty-five years later, in 1974, Guinea, a Portuguese colony, became the Republic of Guinea-Bissau, the 150th state; by 1977 there were 156 states, and this birth rate may continue. Whether there are 175, 200, or even more states in another decade or two, the number will be unprecedented. Furthermore, this proliferation of states poses unprecedented problems. In the year 2000 many of the existing states will have tiny populations if U.S. State Department estimates are reasonably accurate. About 60 percent of them will be smaller than metropolitan Chicago; about fifty of them would be unable alone to fill the Super Bowl. The increasing number of microstates, like the Cape Verde Islands, the Seychelles, and the Maldives (each of which has a population of fewer than 300,000), and submicrostates, like Grenada, Nauru, Ifni, and Tonga (with fewer than 100,000 people) which may join the United Nations and vote in the General Assembly, raises basic questions about the legal fiction and international practice of equality among states. Quite apart from the likelihood that many small states may join anti-Western majorities, their proliferation raises the issue whether or not, in spite of the right of peoples to be politically independent and to manage their own affairs, such states "irrespective of their size and ability to fulfill their responsibilities . . . should also be entitled to sovereign equality in the affairs of the community of nations."[1] Does the right to self-determination justify the equal participation of such Lilliputian states in the affairs of the state system? Should eighty member states of the United Nations, each paying 0.02 percent of the organization's budget—for a total of 1.6 percent—be able to impose their views on a country like the United States, which pays 25 percent of the budget but has only one vote? With a few other small states, which together contribute 2.5 percent of the United Nations' budget, these ministates

---

[1.] Elmer Plischke, *Microstates in World Affairs* (Washington, D.C.: American Enterprise Institute, 1977), pp. 9, 23.

276   would actually be able to mobilize two thirds of the vote in the General Assembly. Are the richer nations, including the Soviet Union, obligated politically and morally to support these wards of the system because it is the "democratic" thing to do? Does the system have to be fragmented, or decentralized, even further for the sake of national self-determination, a principle that is being invoked increasingly on behalf of secessionist movements in existing states (many of which are new states)? Who is supposed to take care of these states? Many of them do not meet any but legal criteria of statehood; they usually do not have viable economies or the capability to defend themselves. Because states have equal votes in the General Assembly, a majority of such states can vote to demand that the wealthier states take care of them. Does the rule of one vote for one state have to be abolished? The possible increase of 50–100 microstates thus raises some fundamental issues, particularly for the more fortunate democratic states.

THE PROLIFERATION OF CONFLICT

Another reason for the instability of a polycentric system follows from the multiplication of third-world states in the wake of the collapse of European colonialism: The more states there are, the greater is the scope for conflict. The logic of earlier forms of multipolarity does not apply. For example, it has been claimed that a major cause of multipolar stability is that each state must divide its attention among many other states. It is unable to concentrate on any single state, thus reducing the possibility of the intense interaction, confrontation, and enmity associated with bipolarity (see Chapter 6). In a system of more than 150 states, it may be that each will be compelled to divide its attention among several possible adversaries, but it is also true that the number of potential occasions for friction among states will vastly increase. Furthermore, the attention of involved states will not be divided equally. Some conflicts will clearly attract more attention than others because the perceived interests and stakes will be higher. It can be predicted that the amount of strife and the passions aroused will surely make the system increasingly dangerous.) Stanley Hoffmann has said rather pessimistically:

> An elementary rule of the game is this: every player, from the lowliest to the most-eminent, will try to find, develop, and exploit some asset in order either to maximize his influence or to ensure his security. But when all do this simultaneously, the outcome on the chessboard, inevitably, may be frustration for many and a threat of chaos for all.[2]

More specifically, conflict among the many new states will arise from a variety of causes, particularly the continuing ethnic, religious, racial, and linguistic divisions among the highly nationalistic less developed countries (LDCs). The basic

---

[2] Stanley Hoffmann, "Notes in the Elusiveness of Modern Power," *International Journal*, Spring 1975, p. 191.

problem, inherited from the colonial rulers who drew the frontiers of these "nations," is that many ethnic groups were at that time divided between two or more colonies and at the same time other ethnic groups suddenly found themselves lumped together in the new colonial country. The postcolonial states have inherited these boundaries, and the results have been, on one hand, irredentism and, on the other, separatism. (*Irredentism* is the movement by one state to incorporate within its boundaries the portion of its predominant ethnic group that has been separated and also the territory on which that portion lives. Political borders, it is claimed, should coincide with ethnic and regional boundaries.) In the drive to reunite divided "peoples," frontiers thus become objects of conflict among the LDCs. (For example, Somalia claimed the right to portions of Ethiopia and Kenya; the claim against Ethiopia led to an undeclared war, in which Soviet and Cuban intervention prevented Somalia from taking part of Ethiopia and incorporating it into Somalia.) (*Separatism* is a movement for self-determination. The new LDCs have invoked this principle to legitimate their claims to independence from colonial rulers.) But now it is being invoked against them by ethnic groups in their own populations, which could lead to national disintegration. An attempt to secede may lead to civil war as the government resists (as in Zaïre after it became independent from Belgium, or in Nigeria). It can even lead to international war if another state becomes involved. For example, when East Pakistan sought to secede from Pakistan, its people were brutally dealt with by the Pakistani army; millions fled to India. The cost of feeding and caring for all these refugees was so high that war seemed cheaper. India therefore fought and defeated Pakistan and established the state of Bangladesh in what had formerly been East Pakistan. This move also weakened Pakistan so that it could no longer seriously rival India on the subcontinent. Some secessionist movements are successful, as in the instance of Bangladesh; others, like those in Nigeria and Ethiopia, fail; and still others smolder and flare up once in a while. In 1979, during the period after the American hostages had been seized in Iran, the Kurdish, Azerbaijani, and Baluchi minorities all tried to gain greater autonomy. The last group, for example, boycotted a referendum on the proposed Islamic constitution, which was to invest in the Ayatollah Khomeini supreme spiritual and political leadership in Iran. Indeed, it is very likely that one reason for Soviet military intervention in Afghanistan was fear that the Muslim rebels against the Soviet-supported Marxist regime might win and follow Iran's example in setting up a militant state. Such an event might very well stir up the 40 million Russian Muslims—one sixth of the Russian population. (It should be noted that, if most separatist movements were successful, the number of states would multiply even more, though few of the new ones would be economically viable. The dismantlement of former states is likely to increase regional instabilities.) For example, the Soviets, controlling Afghanistan, could encourage the Baluchis, who live in Iran, Afghanistan, and Pakistan, to secede to form a new state of Baluchistan. This state would be indebted to Russia, bring Soviet influence to the Persian Gulf, and would be the final blow to Pakistan's survival.

(Another reason for more frequent conflict in a polycentric system is that, among the many member states, some will seek to become more influential than

278 others, generating further friction.) Sometimes such nations are called regional powers; some examples are India, Brazil, Nigeria, and Iran before the fall of the shah, and since Iraq. The term "new influentials" may be more accurate, for some of these states may not only be leading regional powers but may also wield influence in other areas, as do oil-rich states like Nigeria and Saudi Arabia. Their influence may even be global. Whatever strengths and weaknesses such states bring to the exercise of regional or global influence; their mere presence is likely to create jealousies and conflicts and to rekindle historic rivalries in their regions. A vivid example is notable in the Middle East; the Arab-Israeli problem has been complicated by competition among Arab states for leadership of the Arab world. Egypt, Syria, and Iraq especially have competed at different times for this leadership role and have generally claimed to represent overall Arab interests aganst Israel. A premium has thus been placed on intense Arab nationalism and extremist rhetoric and policies. The state that most actively opposes Israel—that most militantly calls for war, that most adamantly refuses to recognize Israel, and that most eagerly seeks to "drive Israel into the sea"—seems most genuinely Arab. Peace with Israel has thus been impossible. Arab political leaders willing to live with Israel have been assassinated, isolated, or silent. Egyptian President Sadat, unlike his predecessor, Nasser, has rejected the role of a new Saladin come to lead the Arabs in holy war; his policies have led to a new round of competition for Arab leadership. Egypt has been isolated in the Arab world since the peace treaty with Isreal was signed in 1978. Syria, Iraq, and even the Palestine Liberation Organization (PLO)—actually not a state—compete for this leadership role. Israeli claims to the West Bank and Gaza, areas that the PLO claims for a Palestinian state, encourage both Egyptian isolation and the competition for leadership among Arab states. The point is that, even though Israel is only a Middle Eastern state, rival claims for regional primacy— which exist in other areas as well—enhance the possibilities of conflict. India and Pakistan have fought several wars already, and the government of what is left of Pakistan since the secession of Bangladesh is now seeking an atomic bomb to match the one that India has developed. In Southeast Asia, a new, strong, and self-confident Vietnam dominates Laos and Cambodia, and Vietnam's neighbors, especially Thailand, watch it apprehensively. Both Russia and China have been drawn into this friction-prone area. To sum up, the result of internal problems of the LDCs, regional rivalries in a world of many states, and an increasing trend toward "regionalization," is more—not less—conflict.

DECLINING CONTROL OF THE SUPERPOWERS

A third reason why a nuclear polycentric system is likely to be unstable is that the great powers can no longer exercise the degree of influence over many weaker states that they once could exercise among fewer states. In past multipolar systems, the great powers, because of their superior capabilities, provided a degree of stability in the anarchical order. In Robert Tucker's words, "The history of the international system is a history of inequality par excellence . . . states are, as it were, born unequal."[3] This inequality owing to differences in geographical position, size, population, and natural resources, was accentuated by the Industrial Revolution in the nineteenth century.(But the great powers' capacity to impose some degree of order has declined as the number of lesser

> . . . states has thus been steadily increasing throughout the twentieth century. In 1910 there was one great power for about every five and a half states; one for about eight in 1930; one for about fourteen in 1950; and one for over every eighteen by 1970. Since there was a closer degree of parity among the great powers in 1910 and 1930, in 1950 and 1970 it would perhaps be more accurate to include only superpowers, which makes the ratio one for about every 37.5 states in 1950 and one for every 63.5 in 1970. The relevance of these figures is that each great power had to deal with a progressively larger number of independent governments, no matter how weak, as the twentieth century progressed.[4])

In 1950 the United States and the Soviet Union were still able to preserve a high degree of control. In the bipolar system their allies were subject to the respective superpowers. The American alliance admittedly permitted some give and take among the allies and some respect for national independence and sensitivity. In contrast, Stalin managed his allies in eastern Europe as he did his own people— with total control. Yet both alliances were called blocs because they behaved as if they were single actors. Differences in points of view, which were at least expressed in the North Atlantic Treaty Organization (NATO), centered on means of achieving collective goals. On the goals themselves there was a large measure of genuine agreement.

By 1970, when the 1950 ratio of 1:37.5 had changed to 1:63.5 (by 1979 it was 1:77.5), the fragmentation of the first and second worlds was well advanced. Of the Western alliances, the Southeast Asia Treaty Organization (SEATO) in 1975, and the Central Treaty Organization (CENTO) died when the shah of Iran was overthrown. On the other hand, the Sino-Soviet alliance was also not renewed in 1980. The NATO alliance was in visible disarray, and the communist world was also showing signs of disintegration. In eastern Europe most states were successfully seeking greater freedom from Soviet direction; and in Asia, China and Russia were not only expressing harsh sentiments about each other, but Vietnam invaded Cambodia in order to overthrow a pro-Chinese regime and replace it with a pro-Soviet one; China then "punished" Vietnam with a short and limited invasion of its territory, and Russia threatened to "punish" China in a similar manner. The effects of nationalism were not, however, limited to the weakening of once-cohesive first- and second-world alliances; LDCs were affected as well. Despite a common anticolonial attitude, which was reinforced in the 1970s by bitter resentment of what was perceived as Western control of the world economy and Western responsibility for their continued poverty, the third world also showed signs of frag-

---

[3.] Robert W. Tucker, *The Inequality of Nations* (New York: Basic Books, 1977), p. 3.

[4.] Spiegel, *Dominance and Diversity*, pp. 120–121.

280   mentation. Different stages of development, political systems, economies, ideologies, and sympathies for the West or the Soviet Union all constituted divisive factors. Even issues on which there appeared to be unity—like demands for higher and stable guaranteed prices for natural resources—were divisive because such prices would benefit some considerably more than others. In addition, there was potential for the emergence of profoundly different views of the effects of the continued price rises by the Oil Producing and Exporting Countries (OPEC) on the LDCs; the first impact on the majority of them was even greater than on the industrial nations, for their hopes for economic growth were seriously jeopardized.

(The measure of the superpowers' declining control was apparent to any observer: they were unable even to manage their major alliances. The superpowers' search for friends and allies during the 1970s was itself a symptom of their declining influence. In the bipolar system, alliances were primarily means of designating areas of vital interest clearly.) But in the 1970s the Soviets *needed* the alliance of Vietnam against China; they *needed* friendship with Ethiopia to help them establish their influence (and military installations) on the African continent directly across the Red Sea from Saudi Arabia. The Soviets have signed a number of so-called "friendship treaties" with Vietnam and Ethiopia, as well as with states like Angola, South Yemen, Afghanistan and Syria. All are governed by pro-Soviet Marxist parties, and Russia's purpose may have been to "establish a new alliance system . . . in Africa and Asia, a looser eastern version of the Warsaw Pact." Yet these states are hardly satellites. Nationalism has engendered the same weakness that it had in Yugoslavia and China earlier. "The history of the modern world demonstrates that in the radical mixture we call national communism, the nationalistic ingredient is far more powerful than the Marxist."[5]

Similarly, the American search for friends who could help to ensure oil supplies, to restrain price hikes, and to support the United States on certain political issues, is evidence of reduced influence. Until his fall, the United States had courted, the shah of Iran with billions of dollars worth of modern arms, which he did pay for, in order to build up Iran as the guardian of the Persian Gulf, the oil lifeline of the West. It was hoped that Saudi Arabia would support American attempts to negotiate a Middle East peace acceptable to both Israel and the Arabs; the Saudis could buy off the radicals and persuade the reluctant with promises of help for their development plans.

SMALLER STATES' GREATER BARGAINING LEVERAGE

(Polycentric instability also reflects the fact that the weaker states are no longer as subservient or passive as they once were. The system increasingly appears to favor the weaker countries, most of which are not in the West.)

[5] Donald Zagoria, "Into the Breach: New Soviet Alliances in the Third World," *Foreign Affairs*, Spring 1979, p. 748.

(How do the weak gain leverage in "the world of the strong"? How do they exert pressure on the stronger Western states? Resource-rich LDCs that remain unaligned with either of the superpowers can form a coalition, pooling their collective bargaining power. One such coalition is the producer cartel OPEC; the strategy involves withholding needed resources, raising or threatening to raise prices, and keeping production at a level close to that of demand, so that consumers are in a constant state of fear that supplies will be unavailable.)

(The OPEC states claim to have learned a lesson from the overthrow of the shah: that rapid modernization may cause so much social instability as to threaten the political leadership. If the rate of development is too fast, the enormous inflow of money will cause social problems. Traditional values, industries, and agricutural patterns will be disrupted. Construction will boom and lead to urban sprawl. Finally, inequitable distribution of the new wealth will increase. A slower rate of development, for which less money is needed, may be safer politically, especially for the ruling Arab sheiks in some OPEC countries. For this reason, less oil needs to be sold. Their profits will nonetheless increase as the value of the dollar declines and oil prices soar.)

Price rises are more subtle and, at least superficially, less threatening weapons than public embargoes. Just as the possibility of a strike—plus perhaps a "wildcat" strike or two—serves to remind industry of the power of labor, and just as the mere possibility of war confers bargaining power, so the possibility of either a *cut* in oil production or an unwillingness to *increase* oil production to keep up with growing demand hovers over the consumer nations and reminds them of their vulnerability. Even the most powerful military states quake before the small states that possess one single component of power that gives them enormous leverage. Power genuinely grows out of a barrel of oil.)

And this leverage will continue to grow as long as the American thirst for oil remains and this country imports about 45 percent of that oil. But only so much money can be paid out before the overabundance of dollars on the international market will bring down their value; already the prices of imported goods have soared, and the United States has suffered double-digit inflation. In 1973, before the Arab embargo, the price of oil was $3 a barrel; by the summer of 1980 the minimum price was $32, and some was selling for more than $40! About $60 *billion* was paid out by the United States for oil in 1979; this figure could be $90 billion in 1980— equilavent to the total assets of I.B.M., General Motors, Ford, and General Electric! The revolution in Iran and the cutback of production to about half that under the shah underscored Western vulnerability. Until there is a serious effort at conservation and development of alternative energy sources— none of them likely to be cheap or without negative environmental impact—and a lessening of dependence on OPEC, the United States and the West in general will remain hostage to every price rise, production cutback, accident (like the 1979 fire in the Saudi oil fields), or unexpected political event (like the fall of the shah or the Iraqi-Irani war of 1980). Even though in 1979 the non-Arab OPEC members produced about 40 percent of the cartel's oil and 25 percent of the world supply and even though non-OPEC states (the United States, the Soviet Union, Canada,

282   Britain, Norway, and Mexico) produced 36 percent of the world supply, OPEC continued in a position to exercise major impact on the fragile global oil-supply system.

(Whether or not such "resource diplomacy" will be effective with other commodities depends partly on whether or not the West becomes more dependent on imported resources. Even though the United States is the least vulnerable of Western societies, it, too appears to be increasingly dependent on imported resources and therefore subject to external pressures. In 1950 the United States depended for only 15 percent of its resource needs (as measured in dollars) on imports; by 1970 the figure had reached 25 percent, and the projection for the year 2000 is 60–70 percent. Simultaneously, the United States' population, which constituted only 6 percent of the world's population, consumed 30–35 percent of the world's petroleum, 55–60 percent of its natural gas, 15 percent of its coal, 20 percent of its steel, 35 percent of its aluminum, and 30 percent of its copper.[6]

Nevertheless, LDC producer cartels for nonfuel resources are unlikely to achieve as much bargaining power as OPEC. The consumer countries have become immensely dependent on oil imports because they have neglected other sources of energy. A limited number of producers account for most of the world's oil trade and share common political and economic goals. Oil cannot be recycled, and substitutes are not easily found. Even a price rise therefore does not result in significant reduction of demand, and it takes many years and enormous capital to develop either new sources of oil or alternative sources of energy. The consumer countries have little retaliatory economic capacity because the producer states are relatively small and therefore less dependent on imports.

Other producer cartels will probably have less clout. Stockpiles against short-term disruptions can be built up; substitutes can be found somewhat more easily and synthetics developed; recycling can reduce the need for imports; resources that become too costly may in the future be extracted at less expense from the sea beds. At the same time, producer countries with large populations will be more dependent on imports from the consumer nations. The Western states appear to have more leverage—including the ability to resist LDC demands—when commodities other than oil are in question. This leverage is, furthermore, enhanced by two other factors. One is that the industrial countries possess about 60 percent of the nonfuel, nonfood raw materials and the underdeveloped countries only 30 percent (the communist countries account for 10 percent). As for food, Western countries, especially the United States, constitute the world's breadbasket. Second, many of the third-world countries want Western technology, machinery, and know-how (as well as arms) for their modernization. Still, the United States—and Western Europe and Japan even more so—will become more dependent on imports of some raw materials and this will enhance the leverage of those LDCs producing them (see Chapter 7).

A form of third-world coalition strategy is also reflected in the U.N. General Assembly and the U.N. Conference on Trade and Development (UNCTAD).

[6.] Zbigniew Brzezinski, "American in a Hostile World," *Foreign Policy*, Summer 1976, p. 78.

Outside the United Nations it is represented at annual meetings of the nonaligned nations and specially organized conferences on population, environment, food, and laws of the seas. All these conferences, attended by members from all regions, have essentially symbolic "public relations" functions as the participants seek to affect attitudes toward the distribution of wealth in the world.[7] The size of the third-world majority in the United Nations, the 120 or so members of UNCTAD (from which the "group of 77" emerged, as an informal working coalition within the U.N. to coordinate and push issues of interest to the LDCs) and other conferences, which are becoming more frequent, keep the international spotlight focused on this relationship of rich and poor, of "haves" and "have nots." The LDCs thus have several forums in which, in full view of the world (including the ever-present Western press), they can dramatize their grievances, express their anger and resentment, blame the West for their continued underdevelopment, and push for "equality" and "justice."

The purposes of this campaign are several: to enhance third-world leaders' awareness of their common interests and to bring them closer to one another, to convince Western leaders and their peoples that they cannot ignore the "poor of the world" any longer, and, most of all, to persuade the West to formulate plans to remedy their grievances. Howard Wriggins has considered these activities as a kind of "consciousness raising," an unrelenting effort to change the "symbolic environment" of North-South negotiations by influencing the agenda of these negotiations—that is, which issues are discussed—and by trying to influence the outcomes of specific issues. The third world has thus seized the initiative and has placed the Western powers on the defensive in negotiations over these problems. Many Westerners do believe that the West exploited the LDCs during the colonial period and that Western nations still take advantage of LDCs' generally cheap resources whenever they can. The related sense of shame and guilt probably strengthens the LDCs' hand.

Anyway, the general relations between Western initiative and non-Western defensiveness and dependence that prevailed before 1973 has been reversed. Not that the West has capitulated or even acknowledged officially that it is responsible for the poverty of the LDCs. In fact, Western leaders frequently claim the opposite. Whatever progress the LDCs have made, even their demands for progress, is said to reflect Western influence and ingenuity. Furthermore, in specific bargaining sessions on concrete issues, short-term national interests often erode the united front of the third-world participants, based mainly on common resentment and aspiration. The material welfare of each state usually outweighs the symbolic common front. Yet clearly the LDCs have done quite a lot with very little, by forming their coalitions for a seeming poor/rich confrontation and threatening the kind of international war that Marx predicted would occur domestically between the poor and the rich.

The LDCs have of course, one very strong bargaining chip: OPEC. In a way, it is amazing that this coalition has held together since 1973, for many of the

---

[7] W. Howard Wriggins and Gunnar Adler-Karlsson, *Reducing Global Inequities* (New York: McGraw-Hill, 1978), pp. 43–76.

284   LDCs have been hurt far more than have the developed nations! This impact has in fact, given rise to a distinction between the third world, composed of resource-rich countries and the fourth world, composed of resource-poor countries. The rise in oil prices threatens the latter nations' development plans in several ways. Obviously they can afford less oil. But, because the first world is suffering recession, it will buy fewer natural resources, which will lower the prices and LDC revenues as well. Foreign-aid funds from the first world will also fall (already in 1974, the oil bill for the LDCs had jumped more than $10 billion, a figure that exceeded the total foreign-aid funds they had acquired in 1973).[8] Tragically, then, reduced ability to buy oil gravely hampers the capacity of fourth-world countries to grow or even to buy enough food for their rapidly growing populations.

By and large, the LDCs had been giving a low priority to agricultural growth because their model was urbanized and industrialized Western society. In bad years—for example, years of drought—the United States, with its huge surpluses of grain, had been able to ship enough food to prevent large-scale starvation. Those surpluses were, however, sold off in the early 1970s, partly to eliminate several billion dollars worth of storage costs and partly because of enormous grain sales to the Soviet Union, which had also suffered repeated poor agricultural yields during the same period. Although the United States and Canada have restocked since then, LDCs can expect not only less of that food but also, because of the great demand for American grain, higher prices for it. With the increased cost of oil and the new demand for food, the United States now prefers to sell food, rather than to give it away, for such sales help maintain the balance of payments at a time of a huge outflow of funds for oil. Countries like India, which had been able to grow almost enough food to keep up with their rapidly multiplying populations because of new high-yield seeds ("miracle wheat" and "miracle rice"), may now face difficulties because they are heavily dependent on energy to grow sizable crops. The "green revolution" has demanded large amounts of oil for fertilizer, insecticides, and irrigation, and distribution of the harvest requires an extensive transportation system. The LDCs' expanding populations and high-technology farming methods and other countries' need for food, plus increased Western consumption of meat (fattening cattle demands considerable amounts of grain), all have given rise to fears of widespread starvation and malnutrition. They also mean that the new nations must spend more of their hard-earned funds for food. And, to the extent that they buy food, their orders for machinery decline. They might, of course, ask for more Western aid to buy the food they need—or decide to accept hunger for their peoples. The 1979 increases in oil prices only intensified this predicament, increasing inflation, retarding economic growth rates, and straining fragile political systems even more. Oil-import costs jumped in 1979, as they had in 1974, by more than $10 billion. India estimated that half its $7 billion foreign debt would go for oil payments. The Dominican Republic's annual exports barely covered the $300 million its imported oil cost.

Objectively, the plight of the fourth world should have led to alignment with the first world in an attempt to break up OPEC. But that did not occur because

---

[8.] Walter. J. Levy, "World Oil Cooperation or International Chaos," *Foreign Affairs*, July 1974, p. 696.

the fourth-world countries identify themselves with OPEC! The principal reason is their sheer delight at seeing the rich countries "get theirs"; considering themselves downtrodden, they feel exhilarated that some of their members have turned the tables on the privileged and powerful states, which suddenly no longer appear so powerful. The image of the former imperial states now quaking before those "lesser breeds" that they had once governed and humiliated, is so heart-warming and delicious that emotional identification has taken priority over economic calculations. While OPEC received immense financial rewards, the rest of the LDCs received an immense and gratifying "psychological income," to use Klaus Knorr's felicitous phrase.[9] As the North–South confrontation has emerged on the international scene and as the "revolution of rising expectations" has turned into the "revolution of rising frustrations" for many, this attitude is understandable. And it offers a plain lesson for the West: The LDCs are so angry that they will even support, at great economic cost to themselves, those who are impoverishing them now, in order to get even with those they believe have long exploited them. Material considerations, which may be rationally discussed and subject to compromise, do not necessarily outweigh psychological ones. The conflict between first and third (and fourth) worlds involves intense emotions. Yet, unless the nonoil-producing LDCs can persuade OPEC to agree to stabilize its prices to protect their development funds or unless they decide to surrender their "psychological income" and to align themselves with the West, their future looks grim.

The result is bound to be an intensification of the conflict between the Western industrial nations and LDCs. The rich nations, faced with insecure oil supplies and constantly rising oil prices, confront declining, or at best slowly rising standards of living. The poorer LDCs, however, face a possible end to their hopes for industrialization and growing agricultural productivity, since both depend on readily available and affordable energy—especially oil—prices. Thus the rich/poor or have/have-not division among the world's nations will be deepened. Instead of steady economic growth among the LDCs narrowing this gap, the lower global growth rates will intensify it.

Indeed, this division of the world may be overlaid with additional tension and probable conflict between the rich and *nouveau riches* or oil-producing nations to whom much of the world's wealth (and power) is flowing. As asked earlier, how much longer will the West tolerate a situation in which oil, the life-blood of their civilization, will be controlled by a handful of mainly small, undemocratic countries, some of whom are intensely anti-Western in their political sentiments? Surely, it is possible to envisage the day when the Western states may in desperation resort even to military measures if their economies threaten to break down and the future seems to hold only high unemployment, galloping inflation, and lower living standards and expectations. In short, the polarization between rich and poor nations may become a more complicated threefold division between rich, hopelessly poor, and *nouveau riches*, a division which is by its very nature bound to lead to international tensions and strife, even to violence.[10]

[9.] Klaus Knorr, *Toward a U.S. Energy Policy* (New York: National Strategy Information Center, 1975), p. 7.

[10.] William Ophuls, *Ecology and the Politics of Scarcity* (New York: Freeman, 1977), pp. 212–213.

THE DIFFUSION OF NUCLEAR ARMS

Hovering over the entire polycentric system is the threat of diffusion of nuclear weapons. Before elaborating the most likely consequences of such diffusion, we must understand why states seek nuclear arms. Do potential nuclear states not know that a few bombs or missiles constitute neither an effective deterrent nor a credible retaliatory force? Are they unaware that the extremely high cost of the crucial delivery system adds enormously to the estimated cost of obtaining a minimal nuclear strike force? The United States could afford to go through five stages—from subsonic bombers to supersonic bombers to stationary missiles (powered by liquid and solid fuels) to mobile missiles with single warheads to those with multiple warheads. But Britain could not. The cost could perhaps be reduced if national deterrents could be based on missiles from the start and if the rate of technological change in delivery systems could be slowed or stabilized by agreement among the major powers. Yet the costs would remain immense. Are the potential aspirants not aware that the costs far outweigh the potential benefits of weapons that may not be usable without staking one's very existence? If nuclear power is basically "negative power," conferring upon its possessor the capacity to deny demands made upon it, why seek such dangerous power?[11]

One answer is that, despite the costs and the sacrifice of other needs, national-security considerations remain foremost. Allies of the United States have become increasingly concerned about the credibility of American defense commitments made in a period when the United States had an atomic monopoly and vast strategic superiority but that now have to be carried out in an era of parity. The United States could easily honor its pledge of protection when it was essentially immune from destruction, but can it afford to do so when keeping its word may spell its own destruction? First Britain and then France have acquired small nuclear capabilities because they have been unsure, in view of the growing numbers of Soviet intercontinental ballistic missiles (ICBMs) that the United States would always and in all circumstances unhesitatingly come to their defense. Doubts arising from the changing strategic balance have, since the Vietnam war, been reinforced by concern that the United States has experienced a mood of withdrawal and is retracting its overseas commitments; at least, it is doubted that Washington leaders will fulfill commitments undertaken before the Vietnam war.

[11.] See Leonard Beaton and John Maddox, *The Spread of Nuclear Weapons* (New York: Holt, Rinehart and Winston, 1962); Beaton, *Must the Bomb Spread?* (Baltimore: Penguin, 1966); Raymond Aron, "Spread of Nuclear Weapons," *The Atlantic Monthly*, January 1965, pp. 44–50; George Liska, *Nations in Alliance* (Baltimore: Johns Hopkins Press, 1962), pp. 269–284; George H. Quester, *The Politics of Nuclear Proliferation* (Baltimore: Johns Hopkins Press, 1973); Quester, "Can Proliferation Now Be Stopped?" *Foreign Affairs, October* 1974, pp. 77 ff.; Lincoln Bloomfield, "Nuclear Spread and World Order," *Foreign Affairs*, July 1975, pp. 743h; Daniel Yergin, "Terrifying Prospect: Atomic Bombs Everywhere," *Atlantic*, April 1977, pp. 47–65; Richard K. Betts, "Paranoids, Pygmies, Pariahs and Nonproliferation," *Foreign Policy*, Spring 1977, pp. 157–183; Lewis A. Dunn, "Half Past India's Bang," *Foreign Policy*, Fall 1979, pp. 71–88; Dunn and William H. Overholt, "The Next Phase in Nuclear Proiferation Research," *Orbis*, Summer 1976, pp. 497–524; and Ernest W. Lefever, *Nuclear Arms in the Third World* (Washington, D.C.: Brookings Institution, 1979).

TABLE 12.2

NATIONS SEEKING THE BOMB

Latin America	Middle East	Asia	Africa
Brazil, Argentina	Israel,[a] Egypt	China,[b] Russia	South Africa,[d] Nigeria
	Israel, Iraq	China, Taiwan	
	Libya, Egypt	China, Japan	
		India,[c] Pakistan	

[a.] Reportedly has a dozen or so nuclear devices.
[b.] First exploded a bomb in 1964.
[c.] First exploded a bomb in 1974.
[d.] See *The New York Times*, October 26, 1979, for a story on possible South African nuclear detonations.

We need ask only one question: What would West Germany, South Korea, and Israel do if they felt unprotected? The first two states are American allies (West Germany was forbidden to produce and deploy nuclear arms in the treaty admitting it to NATO). Yet can it be doubted that, under circumstances in which they felt isolated or vulnerable to external pressures from a hostile state (Russia or North Korea), both countries would seek nuclear arms? And, although Israel is not formally an American ally, it is so in all but name. Can it be questioned that, without American diplomatic support and extensive military assistance, Israel might already have declared itself a nuclear power? It is widely believed that Israel already has such arms and that it developed them because it is surrounded by neighbors that had openly announced their intention to destroy it and because it could not be sure that friendly and helpful countries would always remain so. Perhaps its friends would change their minds, as France did after Charles de Gaulle became president. When some countries believe that the protection of a nuclear superpower is no longer credible or is suspect, they may feel compelled to seek nuclear weapons.

A state like Israel, increasingly isolated politically and pressured by friends to settle conflicts with its neighbors, is particularly likely to try to enhance its security by acquiring nuclear arms; another such state is Taiwan (the United States dropped its security treaty with the Nationalist Chinese government when it recognized the Peking government in 1979). South Korea could be another if American troops were withdrawn from the peninsula. More broadly, if other countries should feel that the United States was reducing its role in the world, the possibility of nuclear diffusion would increase. The United States cannot have it both ways: It cannot reduce its global security role and simultaneously expect its allies and friends to accept nonproliferation. There is a political cost to be paid, whatever the choice; and the choice is basically political. Should the American-Japanese security treaty lose credibility in Tokyo, will Japan not cast off the "nuclear allergy" that has characterized it since the bombing of Hiroshima? Since India exploded its first nuclear device, its bitterest enemy on the subcontinent, Pakistan, has reportedly moved closer to acquiring the bomb itself. Indeed, quests for "the bomb" often appear to come in pairs. The United States and the Soviet Union both exploded

288   their first bombs during the 1940s. Regionally, the pattern shown in Table 12.2 is likely to emerge.

Prestige is another potent consideration for states seeking to become nuclear powers. "Nukes" have become status symbols. Just as a great power once demonstrated its primacy by acquiring colonies and a strong navy, so, after World War II, it had to acquire nuclear weapons. For nations that were once great powers and continue to harbor the "great-power syndrome" and for nations determined to become great powers, nuclear weapons are symbols they must acquire. In their view, not to possess such weapons is to retreat from greatness and to abandon power and international respect—and therefore self-respect. For, in the nuclear age, is a nation not impotent if it does not own such arms? Can a nation still claim authority to make its own decisions on vital issues if it is dependent on another power's nuclear protection? National pride has been a powerful incentive to the development of national nuclear deterrents.

For Great Britain, nukes became a desperate matter of keeping the "great" in its name, despite its rapid decline in power after 1945. These weapons also fitted its image of itself as the United States' junior partner. For France, defeated during World War II by Germany and then suffering the loss of Indochina, humiliation at Suez in 1956, the lost war in Algeria, and a status in Europe second to that of England and later of West Germany as well, the nuclear bomb became a means of seeking to regain international respect and self-respect. For China, carved up by the European powers, including Russia, in the nineteenth century, the bomb is a symbol of great-power status and national dignity as well as a weapon for protection. It is, indeed, difficult not to associate such status and influence with possession of nuclear weapons because the United States, the Soviet Union, Britain, France, and China are also all permanent members of the U.N. Security Council. The bomb seems to be the "admission fee" to a rather exclusive club that discriminates against nonnuclear states.

India is an antagonist of China, its competitor for leading power in Asia; it is also the leading power on the subcontinent. And it was the first nation to break the "membership barrier" in 1974. Other aspirants for at least regional influence include Brazil and Argentina. Before 1979 Iran was another. The shah had spoken publicly of turning Iran into the Germany of the Persian Gulf area; presumably he dreamed of reestablishing the ancient Persian empire. Brazil, which is poor in coal but rich in uranium, seeks both abundant energy and political greatness as the number-one power in Latin America, but Brazil and Argentina are jealous rivals. If such states should acquire nuclear arms—let alone even smaller states like Saudi Arabia and Libya—can countries like West Germany and Italy forgo them? Can Japan continue without them if South Korea and Taiwan achieve them? The desire for nuclear arms as symbols of status and modernity, especially in third-world countries, is also reflected in the huge purchases of the most sophisticated conventional arms by countries like Iran and Saudi Arabia. The "have not" states not only want to become "haves"; they want all the symbols too—airlines, computers, and arms, both conventional and nuclear.

A third and final reason why states seek to acquire nuclear arms is related

FIGURE 12.1

THE NUCLEAR FUEL CYCLE
(Copyright © 1976 by The New York Times Company. Reprinted by permission.)

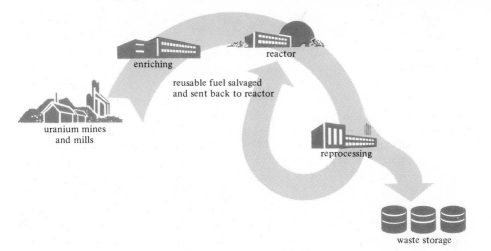

enriching

reusable fuel salvaged
and sent back to reactor

reactor

uranium mines
and mills

reprocessing

waste storage

to domestic politics. Such considerations may reinforce the other two reasons. A nation beset by economic and social problems and low morale may—if it possesses the technological capability—seek the bomb to boost morale, restore national confidence, divert attention from domestic problems, and, of course, mobilize popular support for the government.) Great powers have traditionally held military parades to stimulate nationalist feelings, and Indira Gandhi of India benefited politically from national pride in the first Indian nuclear explosion. The benefit may be only temporary for it does not alter the domestic conditions that may underlie political unpopularity, but that possibility does not lessen the incentive to join the nuclear club.

(Security, status and domestic politics are three major reasons for diffusion of nuclear arms.) The worldwide search for nuclear energy as an alternative to oil will provide many nations with the opportunity to acquire such arms. The United States is no longer the only nation exporting nuclear reactors to produce this energy. Such plants are very expensive, which means sizable profits, jobs, and improved balances of payment for the exporter, which must itself pay already high and continually rising prices for oil imports. The United States had sixty-two nuclear power plants in 1977. More than 233 commercial reactors are operating around the world and 323 more are on order for thirty countries. While countries like the United States, Denmark, and the Netherlands have halted or slowed down plans for nuclear expansion, others, like Japan and Brazil, continue to invest in nuclear energy.(But reactors that produce the energy to meet legitimate and growing economic and industrial needs also yield the by-product from which bombs can be built. There are three ways of recovering this material: First, the spent fuel from a nuclear power plant can be reprocessed and the critical plutonium extracted;

289

290   second, the uranium burned in these power plants can be enriched; and third, through a plutonium-fueled breeder reactor, which produces more fuel than it consumes (see Figure 12.1).)Britain, France, and Russia are actively pushing this reactor. Multiplying the number of reprocessing and enrichment facilities and the proliferation of breeder reactors greatly enhances the likelihood that nuclear material will be diverted to the manufacture of weapons.

> . . . civilian nuclear energy programs now under way assure that many new countries will have travelled a long distance down the path leading to a nuclear weapons capability. The distance remaining will be shorter, less arduous, and much more rapidly covered. It need take only a smaller impulse to carry them the rest of the way. There is a kind of Damoclean overhang of countries increasingly near the edge of making bombs.[12]

The diffusion of nuclear power may thus endanger the peace achieved with such difficulty, hazard, and diligence by the United States and the Soviet Union. Admittedly, the possibility that more nations may acquire reactors does not mean that they will necessarily seek nuclear weapons. Whether or not they do involves *political* decisions and depends on each particular nation's political circumstances and objectives. There is *no* technological momentum that automatically requires nuclear reactors to be followed by nuclear bombs. Several European states, as well as Japan and Canada, have both reactors and the requisite nuclear skills, but have not decided to build bombs.

Nor would diffusion have equal impact throughout the world. A Japanese decision to go nuclear would have profound effects, a Swedish decision little. A small Indian nuclear force may frighten Pakistan, but it is not likely to intimidate China. An Israeli nuclear force may overwhelm Israel's neighbors, but it would not be effective against the Soviet Union. Indeed, one nuclear explosion does not turn a country into a nuclear power. A token nuclear force does not constitute a militarily significant force, which requires a credible delivery system and a much larger investment of economic and technological resources than do conventional military forces. In Table 12.3 the various steps toward a nuclear capability are outlined; clearly, many must be taken to achieve a sophisticated strike force.[13]

Nonetheless, in a system of approximately 150 nations, the diffusion of nuclear weapons to perhaps twenty or thirty nations will considerably raise the statistical odds of nuclear conflict. It may be unfair to think of non-Western nuclear states as "juvenile delinquents" of some sort, but such thoughts are generated by the instability of some governments and the fanaticism of some leaders, which raise the specter of irresponsible behavior. Imagine what might have happened had Castro been in charge of Soviet missiles in 1962 or what Libyan ruler Colonel Qaddafi might do with a few nuclear bombs. But, even if all leaders were stable,

---

[12] Albert Wolhstetter, "Spreading the Bomb without Quite Breaking the Rules," *Foreign Policy*, Winter 1976–1977, pp. 148–149.

[13] Ernest W. Lefever, *Nuclear Arms in the Third World* (Washington, D.C.: Brookings Institution, 1979), pp. 9–11.

TABLE 12.3

PROLIFERATION IN LEVELS AND SCOPE OF NUCLEAR CAPABILITIES*

A. *Two Dimensions of Nuclear Proliferation*

1. Scope: the number of countries to which a given level of nuclear capability has spread
2. Depth: the level of nuclear capability achieved by a given country as measured by the ladder below (B)

B. *One Tentative Ladder Measuring Levels of Nuclear Capability*

1. Possession of basic nuclear knowledge
2. Possession of nuclear research or power reactors, followed in most cases by growth of a civilian nuclear-power industry dependent upon foreign-supplied nuclear inputs and in some cases by eventual acquisition of nuclear self-sufficiency
3. Access to fissionable material that conceivably could be diverted for weapon purposes
4. Possession of rudimentary weapon-design "know-how"; chemical, metallurgical and electronics industries; and some experience in managing large projects requisite to development of nuclear weapons
5. Possession of nuclear-weapon option, differentiated in terms of time necessary to build a bomb (1 year? 1 month?)
6. Possession of unassembled, untested "bomb(s) in the basement"
7. Explosion of nuclear device allegedly for peaceful purposes
8. Overt nuclear-weapon development program based upon either abrogation of safeguards or indigenous production of fissile material
9. Possession of a growing stockpile of more or less sophisticated fission weapons
10. Reliance upon "off-the-shelf" delivery systems such as nuclear-capable aircraft
11. Relatively unsophisticated command, control and communication systems and modes of protection against surprise attack
12. Initial articulation of strategic doctrine
13. Efforts to develop safe, reliable and well-packaged fission weapons; sophisticated missile delivery systems; more reliable and redundant C^3; more sophisticated strategic doctrine and posture
14. Possession of fusion weapons

*Based on Dunn and Overholt, *op. cit.*, p. 499.; (By permission of *Orbis.*)

wise, and careful in their calculations, there are so many of them that we must wonder whether or not they would be able to avoid accidents or miscalculations in every single confrontation that might occur. Will some nuclear states not be tempted to strike at their enemies before the latter also acquire nuclear arms? Will even the superpowers be safe then? The relatively tiny forces that most potential nuclear states might muster do not appear to threaten the superpowers. Yet could not some of them perhaps "rip off an arm," to use de Gaulle's vivid term for what he thought his small French force could do to Russia? Most disturbing is the vulnerability of many of these states to coups d'état. Among potential nuclear states that have experienced coups or civil wars since 1958 are Argentina, Brazil, Chile, Greece, Indonesia, Iraq, Libya, Nigeria, Pakistan, South Korea, Syria, and Turkey.[14] Let us take the example of the Lebanese civil war during 1975–1976 and consider what might have happened

---

[14.] *Ibid.*, p. 500.

292

. . . if that country had had an indigenous capacity to reprocess reactor fuel and to extract plutonium, even a small pilot plant. Who would have guarded the facilities? Who would have destroyed them, from nearby or from afar, at the risk of spreading deadly plutonium locally to keep bomb material from falling into mischievous hands? What outside country might have invaded if the spoils of war would have included a nuclear-weapon capability, even only to deny that capability to some other greedy neighbor? What neutral outsiders might have been invited in by the President or the Prime Minister, to guard or to abduct the dangerous stuff; and would all parties have willingly cooperated with the removal of such an awful prize, or would that have added merely one more armed group fighting its way to the cache? There may be some useful international understandings and procedures to be worked out for that kind of emergency. One thing is certain: in years to come there will be military violence in countries that have sizable nuclear power industies.[15]

(What can be done to slow down or halt nuclear proliferation? One possibility is to use a technological strategy.)The United States now refuses to export plutonium-reprocessing and uranium-enrichment facilities.)Indeed, in order to set an example for other nations, President Carter announced in 1977 that the United States would not use plutonium as a commercial-reactor fuel in this country. (In contrast, Russia, in the same year, declared that the Soviet bloc would proceed with "plutonium technology," without misgivings about the use of plutonium as a nuclear fuel.)[16] Congress, in fact, has approved a law banning economic or military aid to any country that sells or receives such facilities not subjected to adequate safeguards.[17] West Germany and France, however, have been willing to sell nuclear-fuel cycles,[18] though both have declared that they will not export reprocessing plants in the future. The pressure to sell, however, remains. It is a profitable business; but there are other reasons besides profits. For example, France and especially Italy are providing nuclear assistance to Iraq, a radical and militant anti-American and anti-Israeli state; Italy, importing one-third of its oil from Iraq, can thereby presumably gain long-term access to Iraqi oil.[19] West Germany and Switzerland have agreed to sell Argentina the facilities which could provide her with the components needed to produce nuclear weapons.

(The basic approach, however, has been multilateral. The United States, the Soviet Union, Britain, West Germany, France, Japan, and Canada have jointly

---

[15.] Thomas C. Schelling, "Who Will Have the Bomb?" *International Security*, Summer 1976, p. 89 (by permission of *International Security*.)

[16.] *New York Times*, May 10, 1977. Apparently the Soviets are planning a ten-fold increase in their output of nuclear power in the 1980s. The oil, coal, and gas deposits of Siberia are thousands of miles from industrial centers.

[17.] In 1979, it appeared that the United States might be relaxing its opposition to the use of plutonium by its principal allies. *The New York Times*, October 25, 1979. See Michael Brenner, "Carter's Bungled Promise," *Foreign Policy*, Fall 1979, pp. 89ff.

[18.] For discussion of West Germany's plan to sell such a cycle to Brazil, see Norman Gall, "Atoms for Brazil, Dangers for All," *Foreign Policy*, Summer 1976, p p. 155–201; and Steven J. Baker, "Monopoly or Cartel?", *Foreign Policy*, Summer 1976, pp. 202–220.

[19.] *The New York Times* , March 18, 1980.

devised a series of principles for regulating their nuclear exports.) The seven members of this "suppliers' club" (Belgium, the Netherlands, Sweden, Italy, Switzerland, East Germany, Poland, and Czechoslovakia have since joined) agreed upon the following guidelines: Recipients of nuclear technology must apply internationally accepted safeguards drawn up by the International Atomic Energy Agency (IAEA), and they must give assurances that they will not use these imports for making nuclear explosives, even for such peaceful purposes as excavation.[20] President Carter has been particularly insistent on tighter safeguards and controls. He has proposed that IAEA inspect "all nuclear materials and equipment" of countries receiving nuclear fuel from the United States for their reactors, so that closer supervision can be exercised over their nuclear-energy programs.[21] (India, however, has been a major exception.)

But the IAEA is grossly understaffed and can only report violations; it cannot apply sanctions. This loophole is significant. Should West Germany or France wish to increase nuclear sales or decide once more to export reprocessing facilities, it could do so. Indeed, the technological strategy may be deficient even if all members of the suppliers' club do cooperate. For the club may find itself outflanked by the club of "nuclear outcasts," composed of states that are very insecure—like Israel, South Africa, and Taiwan. These states can help one another while evading international restrictions. In return for uranium from South Africa, Israel has reportedly shared its nuclear expertise with the latter.

It may in fact be too late to turn back the technological clock. In early 1980, nuclear experts from 66 countries which had participated in the International Nuclear Fuel Cycle Evaluation concluded after two years of study that the American strategy for curbing nuclear weapons' diffusion by banning the manufacture and use of plutonium was too late. A country could not be stopped from building a bomb by outlawing plutonium-based technology; too much scientific knowledge and explosive material were already available.

In addition to the technological strategy, there is a legal one. Under the Treaty for the Non-Proliferation of Nuclear Weapons (NPT), for example, the signatories agree that, if they are already nuclear powers, they will not provide nuclear weapons to other countries and that, if they are not nuclear powers, they will not try to manufacture nuclear devices. They will also accept IAEA-administered safeguards for their peaceful nuclear activities; this will ensure that nuclear materials are not diverted into weapons making. The legal strategy for halting proliferation involves gaining maximum adherence to NPT. All Warsaw Pact countries are NPT signatories, reflecting Soviet concern about nuclear diffusion. The weakness of this approach is that any country can terminate its adherence to NPT with only ninety days notice. Furthermore, Argentina, Brazil, the People's Republic of China, Cuba, France, India, Israel, North Korea, Pakistan, Saudi Arabia, and South Africa have not signed the pact. The largest number of NPT members would not be able to build nuclear weapons anyway; of those capable of producing such weapons eventually, only a small number have signed. There are also other weak-

[20] *The New York Times*, February 24, 1976.

[21] *The New York Times*, April 28, 1977.

294   nesses. IAEA amounts to a monitoring agency for verifying national accounting systems for nuclear materials; it is also an agency very dependent upon the good will of the nations whose facilities it is inspecting. In these circumstances, it is not surprising that Taiwan may already have circumvented the IAEA inspection system. American intelligence has reported that Taiwan has secretly built a plutonium-reprocessing plant. If so, the prospects for the future are grim. Some experts have suggested either a multilateral agreement banning the export of enrichment and reprocessing plants or a market-sharing agreement guaranteeing each supplier country a minimum number of reactor sales a year as a solution.[22] This approach might at least reduce commercial competition and permit greater control by Western suppliers.

Finally, there is a political strategy, based on ensuring the security of nonnuclear states. The question asked by such states is "If we forgo becoming nuclear states, who will defend us against possible nuclear threat or attack by neighboring states?" The answer is "We (the United States or the Soviet Union) will." But neither superpower is in fact willing to make such a definite commitment; vague pledges at the time that NPT was signed have not been convincing enough. American and Soviet reluctance to tie their futures to states that they do not control and over which they may have little influence is understandable. But, as already stressed, so is the motivation of these insecure states to acquire nuclear arms. The United States cannot expect to play a lesser role in the world and also expect smaller states to forgo nuclear weapons. Nor can it withdraw its remaining 40,000 American troops from South Korea because of human-rights violations and expect a jittery regime not to contemplate the possibility of acquiring "extra insurance" against attack by North Korea.

The choices, as Richard Betts has properly emphasized, are fundamentally political, rather than technical, as in the refusal to sell nuclear-power facilities; and they are agonizing political choices because conflicting values and consequences are at stake.[23] For example, one frequently suggested way of protecting the security interests of small countries while avoiding nuclear diffusion is through supplying nonnuclear conventional weapons as substitutes for nuclear arms. Large-scale conventional arms for some states may, however, induce potential adversaries to acquire nuclear weapons; and a conventional arms race is very risky in its own right.

(In the final analysis, then, we return to the state system, its anarchical nature, and the security problem that it poses for all member states: "There are no simple solutions that are feasible, no feasible solutions that are simple, and no solutions at all that are applicable across the board."[24] Or, as two physicists and one political scientist have said:

> In the final analysis, it would be illusory to think that nuclear weapons proliferation could be severely limited by imposing controls on the sale of nuclear power

---

[22] Abraham A. Ribicoff, "A Market-Sharing Approach to the Nuclear Sales Problem," *Foreign Affairs*, July 1976, pp. 763–787.

[23] Betts, *op. cit.*; and Lefever, *op. cit.*

[24] Betts, *op. cit.*, p. 178.

facilities. The fundamental problem remains: minimizing the motivation nations have to acquire nuclear weapons altogether. This involves issues far beyond the realm of a nation's interests and involvement in the development of nuclear power to generate electricity.[25]

The central question is, then, Will man soon be an endangered species?

POLYCENTRISM: SUPERPOWER INTERVENTION IN QUARRELS BETWEEN WEAK POWERS

The real danger in the multiplication of states and interstate conflicts in the bi-polycentric system is the presence of two superpowers. Militarily, they remain in a class by themselves. No state, including China and a potential united Europe, can match them. The United States and Russia would still be superpowers, even without nuclear weapons; the latter only symbolize their superiority. The only military threat that each one has to fear to his physical survival is from the other. Their competition for influence, however, continues; it is no more likely to be abandoned than previous historic great power struggles.

A serious question is how the changing balance of power is likely to affect this competition. The Soviet Union's enormous strategic arsenal can now neutralize American strategic forces, for American land-based intercontinental ballistic missiles (ICBMs) are becoming more vulnerable to a first strike. American strategic superiority allowed the United States to respond to Soviet challenges during the Cold War and to compel Russia either to desist or retreat, but this no longer exists. In these changed circumstances, the Soviet Union may be emboldened to use its conventional forces or proxy forces to expand Soviet influence in the world's trouble spots. Russia has built a sizable sea- and airlift capability and can now for the first time in its long history send its forces to other continents. Previously, it had been limited to expanding around its own frontiers. Essentially, Russia was a Eurasian power. Under Brezhnev, it has become a global power, matching its aspirations as a communist state and its perception of itself as a great power equal to the United States.

Although Soviet Russia may feel a new self-confidence and expansiveness, the United States, shorn of its strategic superiority and psychologically traumatized by the Vietnam war, may be more hesitant and cautious. Less assured in this new strategic situation and more concerned about avoiding new "adventures," than stopping "communist aggression," will this country react to new Soviet challenges? *Should* it respond? Or will it retreat or not intervene at all as the risks and costs of confrontation rise with the growth of Soviet strategic and conventional power?

[25.] Ted Greenwood, George W. Rathjens, and Jack Ruina, *Nuclear Power and Weapons Proliferation* (London: International Institute of Strategic Studies, 1977), p. 32. Also see William Epstein, *The Last Chance* (New York: Free Press, 1977).

296   (In these circumstances, American-Soviet competition will in all likelihood not only continue but will probably also be intensified owing to increased opportunities in the bipolycentric system. Extended into the third world, this competition is potentially very dangerous because of the many local conflicts that may draw the superpowers in and produce explosive confrontations.) The best model for understanding and explaining the future is, surprisingly, the situation before 1914, which led to World War I.

The war began as a quarrel between Austria-Hungary and Serbia. Austria-Hungary was one of Europe's oldest empires, composed of many different ethnic groups. In an age of European nationalism and the desire of various nationalities for self-determination, Austria-Hungary was therefore on the verge of disintegration. Serbia, a Slavic state, was encouraging this disintegration, which would have left it as a leading Balkan state. When, on a visit to Serbia, Austrian Archduke Francis Ferdinand was assassinated, Austria-Hungary was determined to punish Serbia. The government in Vienna thought that, once Serbia had been crushed, Austria-Hungary might survive and that internal dissolution could somehow be avoided.

The problem was that all of Europe's great powers were allied with one or the other of these two countries. As a Slavic state Serbia was bound by culture and religion to czarist Russia. Furthermore, Russia could not afford to let Serbia be crushed, lest Austria-Hungary become predominant in the Balkans and thus pose a threat to Russia. At the same time, Russia was allied with France. After having been defeated by Germany in 1870, France found it natural to form an alliance with the largest country lying to the east of Germany. The common French-Russian interest was to contain German power. If Russia went to war, then France would back it up. It could not afford not to, for, if Germany defeated Russia, France would have to face Germany alone. Clearly, it would then have to comply with German demands.

On the other hand, Germany was not about to let Austria-Hungary be humiliated or dissolved; Austria-Hungary was Germany's major ally. In addition, Germany was ambitious. As the strongest nation in continental Europe, it was in an expansive mood. It was quite willing to take advantage of the Balkan crisis to fulfill its ambition to become the dominant European power. It had defeated France before and thought it could do so again quickly, in the opening stages of hostilities; then it could shift its armies eastward and defeat Russia, already weakened by defeat at the hands of Japan in 1904–1905 and by domestic revolutionary conditions. A local conflict in the Balkans, on the periphery of Europe, thus broadened into a European war because of rivalry among the great powers. This rivalry had existed before the Balkan crisis erupted, but it had remained quiescent until events in an area of secondary importance triggered war.

(A similar danger that regional conflicts will embroil the two superpowers is inherent in the contemporary emerging bipolycentric system.) In the Middle East the United States and the Soviet Union have actively competed for influence since 1956, when the Soviets and the Egyptians concluded an arms deal. The rivalry of the superpowers was superimposed on Arab-Israeli hostility and intra-Arab competition. Diplomatic support, economic aid, and military assistance from the two superpowers fueled the Arab-Israeli conflict through several wars. Without this competition for influence, the fundamental struggle could not have continued. From whom would the Arab armies and the Israeli army have received their equipment?

In any event, with each war, the possibility of superpower involvement has become greater. In 1956, when the British, French, and Israelis captured the Suez Canal, the Soviets threatened to send volunteers and rain rockets on Paris, London, and Tel Aviv. The Soviets were putting on a show, but a good show. The hostilities had already ceased, thanks to American pressure on its allies, but the Arabs, apparently believing that Soviet threats had led to the cease-fire, were grateful to the Soviets. The latter were probably primarily responsible for precipitating the 1967 war, for they deliberately floated false rumors of an Israeli force poised to invade Syria. The Syrians reacted immediately; what could Egypt, then the acknowledged leader of the Arab world, do but mobilize its forces and send them into the desert? For the first time also the Soviet fleet appeared in the Mediterreanean, presumably as a symbol of Soviet commitment to the Arabs and as a warning to the United States not to interfere while the Arabs defeated the Israelis with their enormous amounts of Soviet military equipment and training. Israel won again, even more quickly than in 1956. This time it kept the territories that it had captured; they were to be traded for genuine peace and recognition by the Arabs of Israel's right to exist. But no Arab leader would even sit down with Israeli representatives to talk.

In 1973 Egypt and Syria launched still another attack to recapture the "1967 territories." Despite initial successes, their armies were finally thrown back. As Egypt's armies stood on the verge of defeat, the Soviets mobilized paratroopers and threatened unilateral intervention if American forces would not join Russian troops to enforce the cease-fire that the two superpowers had agreed upon. The United States placed its forces throughout the world on alert as a warning to the Moscow government in such intervention. The crisis passed as the United States pressured Israeli to obey the cease-fire. The Nixon administration was also seeking to avoid Egyptian defeat and complete Israeli victory; a total humiliation for one side and total victory for the other were not judged conducive to persuading the two sides to sit down together and talk about troop disengagement and a possible peace settlement.

Another Arab-Israeli war, Washington leaders feared, might precipitate the dreaded superpower clash, a possibility perhaps even more frightening than the oil embargo by Arab members of OPEC. Each Arab-Israeli war had brought the two superpowers closer to conflict. How many wars can the Middle East sustain without engulfing the world in nuclear flames? For both superpowers the stakes in the area are enormous. Each therefore has its "client" states, which depend upon it for political, military, and economic support. If a client state does not behave itself, the sanction supposedly will be withdrawal of part or all of this support. Yet the danger is that no client is fully controllable; it has its own interests and ambitions and in pursuit of them may draw its "patron" into the conflict. Who really manipulates whom? The patron may be able to cut off aid, but the client is not really

298   helpless, for its leaders know that the patron is supporting them to advance its own interests. The client can threaten to find another patron, thus negating years of investment and support from the current patron and undermining all the political benefits the patron has enjoyed in that time.

In 1967, after Egypt had felt compelled to respond to the Soviet-inspired rumor of a threatened Israeli invasion of Syria, the Egyptians made a series of military moves that the Soviets had not expected and apparently did not like because they increased the risk of war. The Soviets lost control of the crisis as tensions between Israel and Egypt rose. The initial Soviet error had been the assumption that the Soviets could control Syria. Syria, a small and highly unstable country that was nevertheless attempting to challenge Egypt's primacy in the Arab world, ran with the rumor, taunting Egypt and suggesting that it was not fit to be the defender of Arab honor and standard bearer of the Arab cause if it sat passively by. Similarly, in 1972, when the Soviets apparently refused to supply Egypt with offensive arms to launch a war to recapture the territories lost in 1967, Egypt sent its Soviet advisers home. For the men in the Kremlin the possible defection of Egypt from the Soviet camp would have been a serious blow, jeopardizing all Russia's political gains in the area. So, in 1973, the Soviets supplied Egypt with the arms it wanted, and the Yom Kippur war was the result. Who manipulated whom? It appears that the tail wagged the dog. (The so-called client state appeared to dictate its patron's policy. A great power is not necessarily in complete control and cannot necessarily fully restrain its client (even if it so desires). The crisis therefore may balloon beyond its control.)

(In a bipolar crisis, only two states are involved, and that is a major reason why crises can be "managed" and war avoided. In a multipolar alliance in which the allies are of approximately equal strength, or even in an alliance between superpower and client in which the former is eager not to lose the latter, attention is focused not on the opponent but on holding the alliance together. Quite apart from the fact that the less attention given to the adversary, the greater the opportunities for miscalculation, the desire of the superpower to preserve the coalition gives the advantage to the weakest and less responsible party, provided that the latter is willing to defect if its demands are not met.) Egypt thus received the Soviet weapons that it wanted and went to war; and, once that war had begun to go against Egypt, President Sadat appealed to the Soviets to rescue it. The global alert of American strategic forces deterred Russia in 1973, but will Russia, with its more powerful current strategic forces, be deterred in similar situations in the future?

Why should the United States and the Soviet Union become involved when two smaller states, whether they possess nuclear weapons or not, engage in conflict? Would not both superpowers have every reason to dissociate themselves from the belligerents? Past behavior suggests that neither the United States nor Russia will permit any other country to involve it in a conflict in which its survival is at risk. For example, Russia would not let China involve it in its quarrel with the United States over Formosa in 1958, for that might have precipitated a nuclear confrontation. But can we be sure? Political interest may incite one superpower to intervene, leading the other to intervene as well, if shifts in regional balances are perceived to affect the central balance as in October 1973, when the United States and Russia appeared to stand on the brink of a duel. But, quite apart from the question of whether or not the two can avoid a showdown in the next war in the Middle East, the stakes may be even higher in other areas.

Since 1973 the Soviets have found opportunities to expand their influence in sub-Saharan African. Owing to their new sea- and airlift capabilities, they were able to intervene in Angola, Ethiopia, and South Yemen (on the Arabian peninsula across from Ethiopia). In Angola in 1975–1976 Russia supported one of the three ethnic factions struggling to control the country as Portuguese colonialism came to an end. Russia organized a large-scale airlift. More than 10,000 Cuban forces, as well as automatic weapons, armored vehicles, mortars, rockets, antiaircraft guns, jet fighters, and surface-to-surface missiles were transported into Angola to defeat the two opposing factions (ineffectively supported for a time by the United States, before Congress, afraid lest Angola become "another Vietnam," cut off the small amount of assistance). In Ethiopia in 1977–1978 the Soviets and Cubans intervened in another indigenous struggle. Somalia, ironically a pro-Soviet Marxist state that had received extensive Soviet military aid in return for allowing Russia to establish naval and air bases on its territory, turned on Ethiopia, in order to fulfill its irredentist ambitions and to incorporate the Ethiopians of Somali origin to Somalia. Ethiopia, a much larger country that had recently fallen under control of pro-Soviet military officers, was facing disintegration as a result of numerous rebellions, secessionist movements, and civil war. This time the Soviets supplied several Soviet generals to work out the battle strategy, 3,000 Soviet military technicians, 20,000 Cuban troops, and an estimated $2 billion worth of weapons, including 300 tanks.[26] A Somali attack on the Ogaden area was repulsed and the Ethiopian regime was helped at this time to crush the ethnic Eritreans' long-standing attempt to achieve self-determination. In South Yemen the Soviets, Cubans (reportedly 6,000–7,000 troops), and East Germans are also involved.[27] In Afghanistan the Soviets intervened with their own troops to consolidate a pro-Soviet Marxist regime. The Soviet aim appears to have been to achieve a series of Marxist states along the strategic sea lanes of the Indian Ocean, Persian Gulf, and the mouth of the Red Sea. The new Soviet naval base in Eritrea on the Red Sea looks across at Saudi Arabia, the capital of which is only 800 miles away.

In a sense, the Soviets have found a new and perhaps "safer" type of warfare, involving diplomatic and military moves in areas far beyond their periphery. (In neighboring states, like those in eastern Europe and Afghanistan, they have consistently used the Red Army.) In an age in which force must be restrained or at least disciplined, in which the world has witnessed a resurgence of "limited warfare," the Soviet combination of military advisers (including East German advisers), large-scale transfer of military equipment, and Cuban troops may constitute "sublimited warfare," though the term "proxy warfare" has already caught on in the mass media. The use of proxies is considered less provocative and dan-

---

[26.] Zagoria, *op. cit.*, p. 734.

[27.] *Ibid.*, p. 735.

gerous by Russia's leaders; Soviet troops are far more likely to stimulate an American political or military response. (In Afghanistan, for instance, the United States exacted a series of political and economic reprisals.) Clearly, political circumstances in Africa during the 1970s encouraged Soviet exploitation of regional conflicts, and the Soviets gained widespread African approval because they helped to defend national frontiers (in Ethiopia) and supported the cause of black majority rule (in Zimbabwe-Rhodesia, Namibia, and South Africa). In such favorable conditions for intervention, a few thousand soldiers make all the difference, and Russia's leaders have skillfully established Soviet influence. This new form of sublimited warfare is a formidable instrument of political and military policy.

The United States virtually failed to react, except for verbal protestations. Angola was not considered an area of vital interest. In Ethiopia, the government had a right to invite Soviet help, and the United States could hardly support Somalia, which was seeking to incorporate an area of a neighboring state on the basis of an ethnic claim. Virtually every state in Africa is liable to similar claims, and therefore supported Ethiopia's fight to maintain its territorial integrity. In the early 1960s, the United States itself had intervened, through the United Nations, in the Belgian Congo (now Zaïre) to guard its territorial integrity against the secession of Katanga province. Had the United States intervened on behalf of Somalia, the Organization for African Unity (OAU) would have been alienated. Only if Ethiopian forces had crossed over the legally recognized frontier into Somalia could the United States have intervened. Only when fighting did erupt between South and North Yemen in 1979 did the United States send some military equipment to North Yemen, because the Saudis felt insecure and had begun to question whether or not the United States knew where its vital interests lay and would defend them.

Whether American restraint resulted from disillusionment after the Vietnam war and weariness with commitments in faraway places or from indigenous political conditions, Soviet leaders presumably calculated that they could expand their influence with impunity. The American government each time denounced the Soviet and Cuban intervention, pointing out that such unilateral exploitation of political opportunities was a violation of détente, which presumably obliged both superpowers to restrain themselves in order not to jeopardize their more important direct relationship. The Soviet leaders rejected these charges; détente did not commit them to the status quo and would not prevent them from supporting "national liberation" movements against Western imperialism. This perception of the Soviet Union's historically appointed task of championing national-liberation movements, combined with American weakness, even paralysis, does not bode well for the future, as Soviet influence creeps nearer to the Persian Gulf.

But at some point presumably a political situation in which vital American interests are at stake may arise, and the United States may have to risk intervention. There has been talk of forming a quick-strike force composed of men from either the three main services or the marine corps in order to protect American interests around the Indian Ocean. Local conflicts arising from indigenous ethnic, racial, religious, and linguistic issues may well draw in both superpowers and escalate into war. This danger could be increased several times if the Central Intelligence Agency (CIA) is correct in its forecast that, by the middle 1980s, the Soviet Union, which has so far been self-sufficient in oil, will become an oil importer from the Middle East. Incentives to enhance Soviet influence in that region will then be even stronger. Control over the Persian Gulf may become a matter of life and death for both Russia and the West. Russia is in an excellent position for such a struggle. It borders on several Gulf states, and its invasion of Afghanistan has brought it even closer. The Russians are also in a position to exploit regional ethnic conflicts. The Baluchis, who straddle the borders of Iran, Afghanistan, and Pakistan, have a rebellious history, and Russian help for the Baluchis in Pakistan may help to unsettle that country even further. Should a People's Republic of Baluchistan ever be established, the Soviets could establish a naval base near the entrance to the Persian Gulf, through which most Western oil from this area passes.

Nor are other areas immune: In East Asia, for example, the adversary nature of relations among communist states may draw the United States into the conflicts between China, Russia, and Vietnam, and in southern Africa, conflicts between whites and blacks and among blacks have already led to diplomatic involvement. The world has become more inflammable than ever.

TERRORISM AS A FORM OF WAR

Along with concern about the diffusion of nuclear arms and superpower involvement in regional quarrels, there is also increasing concern about widespread use of terrorism. We have repeatedly noted that in the nuclear age the superpowers have shown great restraint in the use of violence: Their emphasis has been on deterrence, crisis management, limited war (including guerrilla war), and use of proxy forces. The common trend has been toward minimizing the possibility of a clash that might escalate into a nuclear confrontation.

Modern conventional warfare, as vividly demonstrated in the Indian invasion of Pakistan in 1971 and the Arab-Israeli war in 1973, has also become terribly expensive. Modern armaments have become so accurate that they destroy each other at rates unknown even in the 1960s. Few nations can afford to buy sufficiently large quantities of weapons, including antitank and antiaircraft missiles, to conduct war for more than a few days. Once they run out of weapons, the combatants have to be resupplied by the United States or the Soviet Union; the superpowers can use this need for more arms to end the conflict, as the United States did in 1973, when it threatened to cut off all arms deliveries to Israel unless it ended the fighting. The increasing dependence of many states on external funds and war material and the resulting constraints mean that

> A nation planning to wage a modern conventional war must, therefore, plan to achieve its military objectives quickly, before it runs out of tanks, before the cost of the war seriously disrupts its economy, before world opinion can be mobilized

302

to condemn the aggression or support a ceasefire, before the superpowers decide between themselves that the fighting should end, before the public at home turns off and domestic opposition to the fighting mounts. Blitzkrieg, always militarily attractive, has become an economic and political necessity.[28]

In this context the world has witnessed an increase in terrorism as a means of achieving objectives. Until now this weapon has been used most often by the most significant type of nonstate actors next to the multinational corporations (MNCs): the self-proclaimed liberation groups like the various Palestinian organizations, which have hijacked planes, assassinated individuals, and murdered groups like the Israeli Olympic team in Munich in 1972 and school children at Maalot in 1974; the Irish Republican Army (IRA), which has exploded bombs and letter bombs in London; the "urban guerrillas" in Argentina and West Germany; and the Japanese Red Army Group, which hires itself out as a killer group (for instance, to the Palestinians, for whom it committed mass murder at Israel's Lod Airport in1972; the victims were mainly Puerto Rican Roman Catholic pilgrims). All these groups and many others have shown that they cannot be ignored. They have clearly become prominent and may become more so if the state system cannot satisfy their grievances and claims.[29] As long as there are "just" causes—and in the world of multiplying ethnic and religious divisions, such causes seem to be multiplying too—there will be groups who believe that there are no legitimate ways to redress their grievances and therefore resort to terrorism.

Because television covers terrorist acts—whether the seizure of an airliner, the kidnapping of government or corporate personnel, the murder of an individual, or the occupation of an embassy—they are viewed by millions, some of whom will conclude that the acts have been successful, if not justified, and will perceive them as models to be emulated. Television does indeed provide an incentive for such acts, for it provides a world stage on which terrorists can publicize their causes; and the jet airplane allows them to strike quickly anywhere in the world and then fly to safety. Terrorism is theater in which there are no innocent bystanders. For the terrorists, everyone is a player. A small group of men and women can profoundly affect international politics, as the Palestine Liberation Organization (PLO) has demonstrated by acquiring legitimation as representative of the Palestinian people. What is especially frightening is that some fanatical group may in the future steal or divert nuclear materials or sabotage a nuclear facility.

What makes terrorist groups so dangerous is precisely the differences between them and constituted states. One difference involves the nature of a state system composed of actors whose basic concern is their security; they restrain the actual use of violence among themselves primarily by threatening one another with military power. States do not sacrifice themselves. Many of the more militant terrorist groups, sometimes called freedom fighters, clearly do not place primary

[28.] Brian M. Jenkins, "High Technology Terrorism and Surrogate War: The Impact of New Technology on Low-Level Violence," in Geoffrey Kemp, Robert L. Pfaltzgraff, Jr., and Uri Ra'anan eds., *The Other Arms Race* (Lexington, Mass.: Lexington, 1975), p. 102.

[29.] W. Laqueur, *Terrorism* (Boston: Little, Brown, 1977).

emphasis on their own survival; although their claims of being willing "to die for their cause" have not always been borne out, their fervor on behalf of their conceptions of justice, their dedication to their causes, and their occasional willingness to sacrifice their lives lend credibility to their threats. Terrorists have thus been quite successful. In fact, a study of seventy-five kidnapings shows that potential kidnappers have a high probability not only of survival but also of success:

- an 86 percent probability of actually seizing hostages

- a 77 percent chance that *all* members of a kidnaping team will escape punishment or death, whether or not they are successful in seizing hostages

- a 39 percent chance that at least some demands will be met when more than just safe passage or exit permission is demanded

- a 26 percent chance of full compliance with such demands

- an 86 percent chance of success when safe passage or exit for themselves or others is the sole demand

- a 60 percent chance that, if the principal demands are rejected, all or nearly all the kidnapers can still escape by going underground, accepting safe passage, or surrendering to a sympathetic government

- almost a 100 percent chance of gaining major publicity.[30]

Governments do not take terrorist threats lightly for another reason as well—namely that deterrence of terrorists is extremely difficult. Deterrence depends upon punishment. But who are the members of such groups? Where are they? How can they be seized and punished? The difficulties are increased if such groups live within state borders. This problem is also compounded when terrorists are granted shelter and protection by sympathetic governments (like Libya, Iraq, South Yemen, and Somalia)[31] or establish themselves in countries too weak to eject them, as the PLO did in Lebanon before the civil war in the mid-1970s. When the target state, Israel, retaliated, the situation in Lebanon deteriorated. In Lebanon, divided between Christians and Muslims, the army reflected this division and, because many Muslims were sympathetic to the PLO, the military was paralyzed. When the Christians then sought to eliminate the PLO, as Jordan had done (barely) a few years earlier, Lebanon was split and became consumed by civil war. But for Syria's military intervention, the Muslim coalition would have won and captured the government. Indeed, for a time the PLO was the strongest military power, a state within a state, taking over the functions of government in the areas of Lebanon that it controlled. The problem is: What if a terrorist group, equipped with sufficient

---

[30.] Brian Jenkins, Janera Johnson, and David Ronfeldt," Numbered Lives: Some Statistical Observations from 75 International Hostage Episodes," *Conflict* 1, 2 (1978), 92.

[31.] These countries have been accused of actively supporting terrorist groups by the U.S. State Department: *The New York Times*, May 9, 1977.

304   modern arms—perhaps even a "bomb"—establishes itself on the soil of a government too weak to control it? This situation may become a reality in the future.

(The second distinction between terrorist groups and states is that states become socialized by the system and learn "the rules of the game" by which nations play—as is clear in the manner in which the two nuclear superpowers have managed their adversary relationship. The leaders of the two nuclear giants and their respective top-level bureaucracies have *learned* through trial and error enough about each other's behavior so that they almost trust each other, if not each other's intentions, at least to the extent of expecting "responsible behavior" in moments of confrontation. Just as both fear the diffusion of nuclear arms because they believe that some nuclear newcomers may be "irresponsible" and may introduce all sorts of misperceptions, misunderstandings, and miscalculations, so terrorists, as nonstate actors, immensely complicate the calculations of statesmen and enhance the likelihood that violence will occur.)

The appearance, growth, and increasing significance of nonstate actors may thus have a profound impact on the state system, already extremely difficult to manage because of the constant possibility that the instrument of its preservation—war—may, paradoxically, be the instrument of its destruction. Can such a system cope with the possibility that someday revolutionary groups will even acquire and use relatively light, portable, surface-to-surface missiles that can zero in on airplane engines? (The British army turned out in force to patrol London's main civilian airport when it was rumored that some Arab guerrillas had obtained Russian-made portable missiles from a sympathetic Arab state and intended to shoot down a few jetliners.) In the future will revolutionaries even obtain nuclear devices, in order to have their way? Because of the trend toward lighter, smaller, more accurate, and cheaper weapons, a small number of men can today inflict an enormous amount of damage, which in previous times could have been inflicted only by large military units. These arms can now be acquired relatively easily by terrorists. Modern industrial society is very complex and integrated, its fragile technology very susceptible to breakdown and failure. If "natural" failures (like the great northeastern power blackout in the United States in 1965 or the breakdowns caused by severe winter weather in 1977), labor strikes, and even peaceful demonstrations can cause major disruptions, the potential for sabotage and terrorism—from bombs in buildings to the destruction of industrial plants, hydroelectric stations, and nuclear reactors, to the poisoning of urban water supplies—is frightening. So is the blackmail of society by groups that contest the state's monopoly of legitimate force. Yet, as the failure of United Nations attempts to curb the hijacking of airplanes and their innocent passengers has demonstrated, the use by nonstate actors of violence on behalf of their goals—expressed in terms of national self-determination and the struggle against racism or colonialism—is widely accepted as legitimate by people in many countries. Indeed, many such groups, like the PLO and the IRA have gained widespread sympathy because their aims have been expressed as desires for independent statehood. Ironically, if successful, these terrorist groups are likely to reinforce the state system.

In the meantime, though, prevailing conditions are likely to following terrorist tactics:

- the political fragmentation of states in all areas and groups holding grievances against the established order

- modern, light but lethal weapons, that are easily transportable and confer great destructive power to a small group of men

- commercial jets that provide both hostages and the means to transport them and their captors

- states that are sympathetic to the terrorists and provide them training, money and sanctuary

- mass media, especially television, that provide instant coverage and publicity for the terrorists' demands and cause.[32]

What may be new in the future is that states may resort to the use of terror. Given the dependence of smaller states upon external supplies of arms, the constraints that this dependence imposes upon their freedom of action, the new technologies of destruction, and the growing vulnerability of modern society, terrorist tactics may seem increasingly attractive to some states. Brian Jenkins has depicted terrorism as a form of "surrogate warfare":

> Finding modern conventional war an increasingly unattractive mode of conflict, some nations may try to exploit the demonstrated possibilities and greater potential of terrorist groups, and employ them as a means of *surrogate warfare against another nation*. A government could subsidize an existing terrorist group or create its own band of terrorists to disrupt, cause alarm, and create political and economic instability in another country. It requires only a small investment, certainly far less than what it costs to wage a conventional war, it is debilitating to the enemy, and it is deniable . . .
>
> We are likely to see more examples of war being waged by groups that do not openly represent the government of a recognized state: revolutionaries, political extremists, lunatics, or criminals professing political aims, those we call terrorists, perhaps the surrogate soldiers of another state. Increasingly, there will be war without declaration, war without authorization or even admission by any national government, war without invasions by armies as we now know them, war without front lines, war waged without regard to national borders or neutral countries, war without civilians, war without innocent bystanders.[33]

---

[32] John E. Karkashian, Acting Director, Office for Combatting Terrorism before the Subcommittee on Foreign Assistance of the Senate Committee on Foreign Relations, "Problems of International Terrorism," Washington, D.C.: The Department of State, Bureau of Public Affairs, September 14, 1977, p. 3.

[33] Jenkins, *op. cit.*, pp. 103–104 (emphasis added).

Indeed, one such instance occurred in late 1979, when the new religious regime in Iran encouraged and supported—perhaps even initiated—the seizure of the American embassy by a so-called "student" mob, who seized the embassy personnel as hostages in total violation of international law. This unprecedented action, which not even the United States and Russia had resorted to in the worst days of the Cold War, was carried out in order to compel the United States to send the shah back to Iran to stand trial and receive "Islamic justice" (undoubtedly death). The secular government of Iran resigned in protest at this seizure, but it had been impotent from the beginning of the revolution. Real power had been invested in an Islamic religious leader, Ayatollah Khomeini, who not only gave his blessing to the seizure of the embassy, which he claimed was legitimate because the embassy had been a nest of spies, but also escalated the confrontation with the United States by denouncing President Carter and the United States as satanic, the enemies of mankind. He called for a general Islamic uprising against Western civilization.

The militant "students" from time to time held press conferences and showed off some of their hostages in front of the television cameras; they also constantly paraded mobs chanting anti-American slogans before the cameras at the embassy. The three American television networks, in competition with one another, provided the Iranians—the Ayatollah, "students," and foreign minister—with access to every American living room and allowed them to vent their hatreds, demands, and resentments against the shah. This "terrorist theater," carefully staged for the cameras, was an effective weapon; for several months the "students" held the United States at bay, as the latter remained fearful of acting, lest the hostages be killed. Whether or not this form of surrogate warfare will be used by other governments remains to be seen. What cannot be doubted is that the state system of the future will hold many dangers.

IV

NATIONAL SYSTEMS AND FOREIGN POLICY

National and Elite Styles in Foreign Policy: American and Soviet Perceptions and Behavior

FROM INTERNATIONAL POLITICS TO FOREIGN POLICY

The utility of analyzing international politics in terms of poles and the distribution of power among them is by now clear. We have seen how helpful it was in explaining the behavior of states in a bipolar system, particularly the virtually global nature of the two-pole confrontation, the hypersensitive nature of the balance, and the particular preoccupation with military power. We noted that the nature and function of alliances differ in bipolar and multipolar systems and that, as a result of these differences, for example, crises are more likely to be successfully "managed" in a bipolar balance than in a multipolar one.

But knowledge of the power hierarchy can only be a starting point for analysis of the relations among states. Measuring power by adding up the various tangible and intangible components, even with great care and sophistication, all too often does not allow the analyst to predict the outcome of a specific set of interstate negotiations.

Far more attention must be paid to *the actual bargaining process that translates the components of power that a state has mobilized into influence that produces certain outcomes.* The mere addition of components is not a particularly useful exercise; when, however, the analyst isolates specific states, the kinds of issues they are involved in, the types of power applicable to these issues, and how they can be managed, the exercise can be very enlightening. Then power resources

310 that cannot be mobilized, or elements that can be mobilized but are inapplicable for political or military reasons, can be eliminated from the bargaining equation; and it is possible to evaluate the utility, as well as the limits to the utility, of the conditions under which power is applied and how that power is to be employed. (An examination of actual power relations has shown us that the bargaining relations between big and small states are far more equitable than mere addition of population, natural resources, industrial capacity, and military strength suggest. Indeed, one is sometimes tempted to say—admittedly, with some exaggeration—that the postbipolar era is the age of small and assertive powers that act as if they were great powers, and of great powers that frequently act as if they were minor.)

(This observation certainly raises the question whether or not the concept of "pole" still makes sense. The world is no longer the great powers' oyster; to switch metaphors, *the giants must increasingly share the global stage with the pygmies. This fact certainly appears to limit the usefulness of any analysis based on the number of poles.*)

(The principal focus of our first-level analysis has been on the relation between the structure and the stability of the system.)Theorists in the past have generally concluded that bipolar systems are unstable and that multipolar systems are stable; but, in our lengthy analysis of these different structures, we have concluded that these propositions ought to be reversed. The principal reason is the impact of nuclear weapons. This conclusion, in turn, suggests a deficiency in the models. If multipolarity is stable because of its inherent flexibility and the diffusion of attention, the nature of weapons should not matter. However, if despite the ability of states to shift from alliance to counteralliance, as well as the inability of states to become preoccupied with any single conflict, multipolarity's more numerous conflicts do arouse concern in the nuclear era, the traditional model is no longer valid. The logic of "the more states, the better for peace," which suggests that, as states pay relatively little attention to one another, the proliferation of nuclear weapons should not be a matter of great concern, is obviously faulty. Similarly, if bipolarity is unstable because of the continual confrontation and the frequent crises resulting from each pole's sensitivity to defections from its bloc and to the adversary's temptation to launch preventive and preemptive strikes, war should erupt sooner or later, especially as a result of one of these crises, regardless of the nature of the weapons that each possesses. The fact that this has not occurred suggests that nuclear bipolarity provides stability.)

(As one analyst has perceptively remarked, stability may in fact be independent of polarity. Peace or war, stability or instability, seems less a matter of the number of poles *per se* than of poles plus a combination of other factors like the actors' objectives, the domestic sources of international behavior, policy makers' perceptions of the nature of the state system, and the threats and opportunities posed for their countries.[1])

The United States, for example, would undoubtedly have been the world's greatest power from 1919 to 1939—had it been willing to mobilize its power and

[1] Joseph L. Nogee, "Polarity: An Ambiguous Concept," *Orbis*, Winter 1975, pp. 1219–1220; and Nogee and John W. Spanier, "The Politics of Tripolarity," *World Affairs*, Spring 1977, pp. 319–333.

use it. But it was not willing, preferring to return to an earlier isolationist position made temporarily possible again by Germany's defeat and the absence of external threats to France and Britain until the late 1930s. The United States, refusing to be a political and military player, thus ranked behind the various Europan powers, including Russia, and Japan in that period. The question was one of motivation. That is also what differentiates contemporary China from Japan and the European Common Market. China has the determination to play a primary role in Asia, as well as in other geographical and ideological (communist) subsystems. Neither Japan nor Europe has yet been able to define for itself the political roles that it wishes to play; both are still dependent upon the United States for their defense, though they possess the industrial strength, technological and scientific skills, and manpower to develop great power and to defend themselves.

In the early 1970s there was a great deal of talk of Japan and Europe as economic superpowers and of Japan's becoming the first great power to wield influence by economic means alone; it could be a superpower yet forgo the political will necessary to define and assert Japanese interests and at least a credible military force. The Oil Producing and Exporting Countries (OPEC) destroyed that belief, as Japan, followed closely by Europe (except for the Netherlands), bowed to Arab demands for support of Arab peace terms in the Middle East. Being an economic superpower is thus insufficient *unless* this economic potential is married to political will, for it is this will that converts potential into actual power. In the absence of such a determination to play a political role, a potential pole like Western Europe, with a population larger than that of Russia or the United States, remains a stake over which the superpowers contest, rather than an influential actor in itself.[2]

The most significant factor in what Steven Spiegel has called "motivational power" is the nature of the regime, as has been apparent in the change of regimes from czarist Russia to Soviet Russia, from Weimar (democratic) Germany to Nazi Germany, and from Nationalist China to Communist China.[3] Such transformations are, in general, more significant in their impact upon national goals than are changes in leadership within a single regime. This motivation in foreign policy may be measured crudely by such indicators as the percentage of gross national product (GNP) spent on such areas as defense and foreign aid, the percentage of the population serving in the armed forces, the number of diplomats and other foreign-policy and defense officials sent to other countries, the number and rank of official visitors sent abroad, the number and rank of visitors, and official radio broadcasts beamed to foreign countries. David Wilkinson has specifically distinguished between two broad classes of states, one characterized by the presence of a conscious, policy-controlling will, the other by its absence. He has suggested that

> The more one finds of this kind of hostile, dynamic leadership, the more its nature and peculiarities explain policy, while the less one finds of such "will," the more

2. George F. Kennan, "Europe's Problems, Europe's Choices," *Foreign Policy*, Spring 1974, pp. 13–14.

3. Steven L. Spiegel, *Dominance and Diversity: The International Hierarchy* (Boston: Little, Brown, 1972), pp. 71–78.

312

one will be able to explain policy by referring to traditions, history, and stable bureaucratic habit. Conversely, abrupt shifts of policy should more often than not coincide with the presence or appearance of a leadership of this kind.[4]

/This will to play an active and major role in the international system is therefore a prerequisite to becoming deeply involved in both the competitive and the co-operative relations that characterize the power struggles in the state system.)

First-level analysis, as this example suggests, must be supplemented by second- and third-level analysis. In Joseph Nogee's words:

> In short, it is highly plausible to view the number of polar actors as an indeterminant variable. No single structure can guarantee stability, yet all have a potentiality for it. Polarity relates to stability only when combined with other variables, but the nature of that relationship changes with circumstances and cannot be specified in advance. . . . The object of this critique is not to suggest the abandonment of bipolar and multipolar models. It is simply to stress their limitations for both policymaker and theorist. Polar concepts can provide useful descriptive labels for different historical periods. One step in the right direction might be to develop a more refined concept of an international "pole." We must, of course, have knowledge of the international hierarchy, including a description of its essential actors, in order to understand the international system. That must be determined empirically and can only be the starting point of analysis. To know which are the great powers of the moment is important but not enough. Power relationships are enormously complex and always changing. The great difficulty is that power, which is such a central variable, is an illusive one, difficult to measure. This is particularly true of those ingredients related to motivation and those which have a nonmaterial basis. That in part explains why the study of international relations has a greater tentativeness than most of the other social sciences. Theoretical models (especially polar ones) may have limited utility for predictive purposes, but we can, as Stanley Hoffmann reminded us, "project into the future a limited number of possible trends and rank them conditionally." If we cannot eliminate uncertainty, it is not a small thing to reduce it.[5]

THE CONCEPT OF STYLE

Therefore we now turn away from the game of intenational politics analyzed in terms of the interactions among the states. We have up to this point assumed that states are similar in interests, motivations, and internal structure and that their behavior is the product of systemic structure. In using the first level of analysis, we have therefore had no reason to look inward—except in those instances in which states have not done what they would have been expected to do. (Although assuming the identical nature of states is conceptually useful, it clearly does not suffice. If

---

[4] David Wilkinson, *Comparative Foreign Relations* (Belmont, Calif.: Dickenson, 1969), p. 27.

[5] Nogee, *op. cit.*, pp. 1219, 1223–1224.

we wish to analyze and more fully understand the actual behavior of states, we must look not only at their interactions but also at individual states and their foreign policies—that is, at their perceptions of themselves, their roles in the world, and their decisions and actions—as influenced by domestic factors. States do differ, and their behavior therefore also differs. They have their own particular economic systems, political systems, and manner of making decisions, and they are at particular stages of development. The foreign policies of countries reflect internal or domestic factors.

It is our claim that nations and elites have certain "styles," which affect the manner in which they conduct themselves in the international arena, whether they initiate action or react to what other states are doing.[6] Each state has a picture of the world "in its head." Each wears "colored glasses," because it possesses a repertory of acts and responses derived from its domestic and foreign experiences. Each perceives "reality" selectively because of its particular *Weltanschauung* (world view) or "cognitive map"; in practice, each has a corresponding "operational code" or "national style."

This method of analyzing foreign policy is based on the assumption that the manner in which a policy-making elite sees the world and defines its aims is decided within the framework of the nation's political culture. American policy, like Russian policy, derives from a set of attitudes toward politics and political conflict in general and toward international politics in particular, conceptions of how and to what extent historical development can be molded, and ideas of methods for advancing national objectives. But, whereas the Kremlin leaders' perceptions and behavior arise from the revolutionary framework within which they have been trained, American leaders have been influenced by nationally shared values and beliefs and the historical experience of American democracy. The concept of style can thus assist an analyst in clarifying the ways in which a nation and its policy makers are likely to view a specific situation, alternative courses of action, and the course selected. It can therefore be very helpful in analyzing a particular situation, though institutional and other pressures that help to shape the final decision also cannot be ignored.[7]

In a way, the idea of style is familiar to the reader from stereotypes about certain categories of perople—like capitalists, trade-union leaders, military men, Germans, Englishmen, and the Irish. Such stereotypes are often crude and impressionistic, and sometimes they are gross distortions in order to justify prejudices (about blacks or Jews, for example). But the fact that stereotypes may sometimes be misleading or false does not mean that they have to be. They are of course likely to be simplifications of reality. All concepts, however sophisticated and however

---

[6.] An exhaustive analysis of the American "style" may be found in Stanley Hoffmann, *Gulliver's Troubles, or The Setting of America's Foreign Policy* (New York: McGraw-Hill, 1968), pp. 87–213. See also Hans J. Morgenthau, *In Defense of the National Interest* (New York: Knopf, 1951) Robert E. Osgood, *Ideals and Self-Interest in America's Foreign Relations* (Chicago: University of Chicago Press, 1953); Kennan, *American Diplomacy 1900–1950* (Chicago: University of Chicago Press, 1951); and Spanier, *American Foreign Policy since World War II* (8th ed.; New York: Holt, Rinehart and Winston, 1980).

[7.] Alexander L. George, "The 'Operational Code'; A Neglected Approach to the Study of Political Leaders and Decision-Making," *International Studies Quarterly*, June 1969, pp. 190 ff.

314   careful the researcher, are distorted to a degree, for they are means of organizing, and therefore of imposing some sort of order, on masses of existing data. They always involve selection, inclusion of some facts and exclusion of other information. But selection is necessary if we are to gain some insight into and understanding of what is going on. With some care we can see, for example, that a certain nation or elite has repeatedly behaved in a particular fashion in similar situations and can then suggest that it has demonstrated certain distinctive characteristics in its foreign policy.

THE AMERICAN NATIONAL STYLE

In turning to the United States and suggesting that it reveals particular characteristics in its external behavior that are uniquely "American," we start with the recognition that fundamental to American experience is the nation's lengthy isolation from the quarrels of the great European powers. For almost a century the United States was able to devote itself to domestic tasks: strengthening the bonds of national unity, westward expansion, absorbing the millions of immigrants attracted by the opportunities of the country, and industrializing and urbanizing an entire continent. This freedom to concentrate on internal affairs cannot be explained entirely by the presence of the Atlantic Ocean and weaker neighbors to the north and south. As a democratic nation, the United States and its internal orientation must also be explained by the preferences of the electorate. Citizens in a democracy are concerned primarily with their individual and family well-being. All Western democracies, responding to public demands, have become welfare states to some degree.[8] Demands for service in the armed forces or for higher taxes to finance international obligations are bound to be viewed as burdens. And foreign policy will, on the whole, be considered a distraction from primary domestic tasks. The American citizen's intense concern with private and material welfare and almost compulsive striving for economic success—the measure of individual self-esteem—have been noted since the days of Alexis de Tocqueville. (If, in an egalitarian society, a citizen is judged primarily by his or her material achievements, which indicate his or her ability and therefore bring varying degrees of respect, he or she will concentrate on "getting ahead." Money becomes the symbol of status and prestige; it is a sign of success, just as failure to earn enough money is considered a token of personal failure.)

Given such a profound inward orientation, it is not surprising that the United States turned its attention to the outside world only when provoked. First there had to be a danger so clear that it could no longer be ignored. This point cannot be overemphasized: The United States rarely inititated policy; the stimuli

---

[8.] The hypothesis about democratic behavior offered by Klaus Knorr and others and discussed in Chapter 2, is generally supported by Gabriel A. Almond, who, in *The American People and Foreign Policy* (New York: Holt, Rinehart and Winston 1960), strongly emphasizes the "extraordinary pull of domestic and private affairs even in periods of international crises." See particularly Chapter 3, with Almond's summation of the American value orientation.

responsible for its foreign policy usually came from beyond its frontiers(Historically the result was that American foreign policy was essentially both reactive and discontinuous, a series of impatient responses to external pressures whenever there was "clear and present danger" and of returns to more important domestic affairs as soon as danger had passed. Long-range commitments and foreign-policy planning thus tended to be rare.)

(The American attitude was further characterized by a high degree of moralism and missionary zeal arising from the nation's perception of itself as a unique and morally superior society.)The United States was the world's first democracy, committed to improvement of the lot of the common man. Americans regarded themselves as the "chosen people." The new world stood for opportunity, democracy, and peace; the old world for poverty, exploitation, and war. Abraham Lincoln phrased the point aptly when he said that the United States was "the last best hope on earth." Woodrow Wilson in World War I and Franklin Roosevelt in World War II expressed much the same view. Just as in 1862 the United States had not been able to remain half free and half slave, so in 1917 and again in 1941 Americans thought that the world could not continue half free and half slave. Each war was considered an apocalyptic struggle between the forces of darkness and the forces of light.[9](Moralism in foreign policy reflected the awareness and pride of a society that believed it had carved out a better domestic order, free of oppression and injustice. It truly viewed itself as a society in which the *vox populi* was equivalent to the *vox dei*.)

(Isolationism from European "power politics"—not isolationsim from Latin America or Asia—was therefore basically a means of safeguarding American morality and purity.)Quarantining itself was the best way to prevent the nation from being soiled and tainted by the undemocratic domestic institutions and foreign-policy behavior of European States. The American experiment had to be safeguarded against the corruption of power politics, and withdrawing from the state system and providing the world with an example were therefore the only correct course. On the other hand, once it became impossible to remain aloof, in this century, the country went to the other extreme and launched crusades. As a self-proclaimed superior country—morally and politically—the United States could remain uncontaminated only by eliminating those that might infect it. Once the nation had been provoked, it tended to act as a missionary power and sought to make the world safe for American democracy by democratizing or Americanizing it as a series of peaceful facsimiles of the United States. American crusading and American isolationism sprang from a single source.

(A third characteristic follows from the liberal democratic values upon which the nation was founded and the resulting high moralism: a depreciation of power politics, with its connotations of conflict, destruction, and death.[10])Strife was con-

---

[9.] Paul Seabury, *The Rise and Decline of Cold War* (New York: Basic Books, 1967), pp. 39–45, offers some fitting quotations, especially a poem by Archibald MacLeish celebrating the *pax americana* as a preamble to the *pax humana* during World War II. The moralism of postwar Secretary of State John Foster Dulles is discussed by William L. Miller, "The "Moral Force" Behind Dulles' Diplomacy," *The Reporter*, August 9, 1956.

[10.] Osgood, *Limited War* (Chicago: University of Chicago Press, 1957), pp. 28–45, focuses on this point in explaining the difficulties that the nation experiences in conducting limited wars.

316   sidered abnormal and only transitory; harmony was viewed as the normal condtion among states. The use of power within the national political system is legitimate only in the service of democratic purposes; its employment in the state system can be justified only in the service of a moral cause. Specifically, in the state system power cannot be employed, at least without arousing guilt feelings, unless the nation confronts a morally unambiguous instance of foreign aggression. And, when that happens, the United States must completely eradicate the immoral enemy that threatens the nation and its democratic principles. The presumption is that democracies are peaceful states because people who elect their rulers and suffer the hardships of war are peaceloving; therefore the eruption of hostilities is attributable to authoritarian and totalitarian states whose rulers, unrestrained by democratic public opnion, wield power for their own personal aggrandizement. Their removal becomes therefore a condition of peace and the end of power politics itself.

(Arising from both this moralism and the depreciation of power is a fourth characteristic: the tendency to draw a clear-cut distinction between peace and war, peace being characterized by harmony among nations and war and power politics in general being considered atypical. In peacetime, little or no attention need be paid to foreign problems; indeed, such problems would divert people from their individual, materialistic concerns and upset the whole scale of social values.)

Once Americans are angry, and the United States has to resort to force, however, the use of force can be justified only in terms of the universal moral principles with which the United States, as a democratic country, identifies itself. Resort to the evil instrument of war can be justified only by noble purposes and the goal of complete destruction of the immoral enemy that threatens the integrity, if not the existence, of these principles. American power must be "righteous" power; only its full exercise can ensure salvation or the absolution of sin. The national aversion to violence thus becomes transformed into national glorification of violence, and wars become ideological crusades to make the world safe for democracy— by converting authoritarian adversaries into peaceful, democratic states and thus banishing power politics for all time. Once that aim has been achieved, the United States can again withdraw into itself.(Although foreign affairs are thus annoying diversions from more important domestic matters, such diversions are only temporary; maximum force is applied to aggressors or warmongers in order to punish them for provocation and to teach them that aggression is immoral and will not be rewarded. As a result, American wars are total wars, and, for all their fantastic destructiveness and loss of life, raise few moral qualms.)

Not only does the United States consider peace and war two mutually exclusive conditions, but it also divorces diplomacy from force, so that in wartime political considerations are subordinated to military considerations. Once the diplomats have failed to keep the peace through appeals to morality and reason, military considerations become primary. During wartime, the soldier is in charge. Just as the professional medical practitioner has the responsibility for curing his or her patients of their several maladies, so the military "doctor" must control the treatment of international society when it is infected with the disease of power politics.(The United States, then, has traditionally rejected the concept of war as a political instrument; war has not been viewed as the continuation of politics by other means. Instead, it has been regarded as a politically neutral operation that should be conducted according to its own professional rules and imperatives. The military officer is a nonpolitical technician who conducts the campaign in a strictly military, efficient manner. And war is a purely military instrument the sole aim of which is the destruction of the enemy's forces and its despotic regime, so that its people can be democratized.)

The same moralistic attitude that is responsible for the American all-or-nothing approach to war also militates against the use of diplomacy, in its classic sense: to compromise interests, to conciliate differences, and to moderate and isolate conflicts. Whereas, on one hand, Americans regard diplomacy as a rational process for straightening out misunderstandings among nations, on the other, they have also been extremely suspicious of diplomacy. If the United States is by definition moral, it obviously cannot compromise, for a nation endowed with a moral mission can hardly violate its own principles. That would constitute appeasement and national humiliation. National principles would be violated, national interests undermined, and national honor stained. To compromise with the immoral enemy is to be contaminated with evil. Furthermore, to reach a settlement with the enemy, rather than wiping it out in order to safeguard those principles, is to acknowledge American weakness. This attitude toward diplomacy, viewed as an instrument of compromise, thus reinforces the American predilection for violence as a means of settling international problems. War allows the nation to destroy its evil opponent, while permitting it to pursue its moral mission uncompromised.

(The fact that twice in this century the United States has successfully dealt its enemies total defeat has highlighted yet a fifth characteristic: the belief that the United States is omnipotent and, once engaged in a conflict, can "lick anyone in the system."[11]) Indeed, even in the earlier history of this country, American actions had met with quick success whenever the United States had been drawn into the international arena. At one time or another, it had beaten the British, the Mexicans, the Spaniards, the Germans, and the Japanese. Furthermore, the United States had never been invaded, defeated, or occupied (as most other nations had been); it had, to be sure, made mistakes, but with its great power it had usually been able to rectify them. To a nation one of whose popular slogans expressed confidence in doing "the difficult today, the impossible tomorrow"—a nation that, after all, could even turn Jesus into a superstar—failure would be a new experience. American history had included only victories; the unbroken string of successes seemed evidence of national omnipotence. This belief in American invincibility tended, of course, to be reinforced by domestic successes. Historically, the United States was unique for, with the single exception of the Civil War, it had never experienced national tragedy. Few other states have managed to avoid defeat and conquest. American policy makers have usually not been deterred by thoughts of failure, but, had failure in fact occurred, they could have expected a major political reaction. For in a country that is believed to be all-powerful, the public will understand

---

[11.] Denis W. Brogan, "The Illusion of Omnipotence," *Harper's*, December 1952, pp. 21–28.

318   failure or defeat only as the result of governmental incompetence or treason. The nation cannot admit that its situation may not be resolvable through the proper application of force.

A sixth and final characteristic is generally known as pragmatism. Again, it has been part of the nation's experience that when problems have arisen, they have been solved with whatever means were at hand. Americans have always been a "how to do it" people and have prided themselves on their problem-solving abilities. Europeans invented radar and the jet engine, but it was Americans who refined and developed these inventions, produced them on a large scale, and marketed them more effectively than the countries of origin. All problems have seemed solvable; they are only matters of "know-how." The question is not *whether or not* but *how*—and how quickly at that. This approach to foreign policy may be called the engineering approach:

> A pragmatic or instrumental approach to world problems typifies the Western policy-maker. Not theoretical conceptions enabling him to relate policy to the general trends of events, but know-how in the face of concrete problem-situations is what he typically emphasizes. He wants to "solve" the immediate, given concrete problem that is causing "trouble," and be done with it. Accordingly, diplomatic experience—always of great importance, of course—is exalted as the supreme qualification for leadership in foreign policy. For experience is the royal road to know-how. It teaches the statesman how to negotiate with the Russians, how to coordinate policy with the allies, how to respond to emergencies, and so on.
>
> In facing foreign-policy problems it is not the Western habit to attempt first of all to form a valid general picture of the world-setting events in which the problems have arisen. The tendency is rather to isolate the given problem-situation from the larger movement of history and ask: what can and should we do about it?[12]

More specifically, the United States tackles each problem as it arises. In the abstract, this approach may make sense. After all, until a situation has occurred and the "facts" are in, how can one react? The trouble is that, by the time sufficient facts are in, the situation may well be so far developed that it is too late to do much about it or, if one does try, the difficulties abound. The American quest for certainty is usually carried too far. Policy making should involve tackling problems early enough so that influence can still be usefully brought to bear; but usually it can only be brought to bear when there is still insufficient information. By the time the situation is clear, a crisis may be near or at hand, and it may be too late for any effective action short of applying military power; it may even be too late for that. Pragmatism thus reinforces the reactive and discontinuous nature of the American conduct of foreign policy, along with the emphasis on the immediate and short run to the detriment of longer-run policy considerations.[13]

---

[12] Robert C. Tucker, *The Soviet Political Mind* (New York: Holt, Rinehart and Winston, 1963), pp. 181–182.

[13] There is, in fact, a very important seventh characteristic: The belief that political problems can be solved through economic means. For an elaboration of this characteristic, see Chapter 20.

AMERICAN POLICY SINCE WORLD WAR II

The American approach to international politics reflects a series of simple dichotomies: domestic policy versus foreign policy, good nations versus bad nations, isolationism versus crusading, war versus peace, force versus diplomacy. But fundamental to all of them is the self-image of the United States as the epitome of democracy and the defender of the democratic faith. The United States, the shining "beacon lighting for all the world the paths of human destiny" in peacetime (in the words of Ralph Waldo Emerson) has been like a democratic St. George battling against evil aggressors. Kaiser Wilhelm in World War I, Adolf Hitler in World War II, and Josef Stalin after World War II all perfectly fitted and reinforced this set of perceptions. The first was an authoritarian monarch, and the other two were among the greatest tyrants of all time; all three threatened the survival of democracy.

During World War II this moral attitude led the United States to divide nations between those that were "peace-loving" (the United States, the Soviet Union, and Great Britain) and those that were "aggressors" (Germany, Italy, and Japan). The former had to destroy the latter and thus sought unconditional surrender. The Western democracies crusaded for total victory. Once that objective had been achieved, the aggressors were to be entirely disarmed and peace preserved through the cooperation of peace-loving nations within the new United Nations. Power politics would be ended; alliances, spheres of influence, and balances of power, said President Roosevelt shortly before his death, were to be replaced by international organization, which would furnish an alternative and better means for preserving peace. As the evil nations had been defeated, no new aggressors were expected. Russia, an ally, was certainly not expected to become an adversary.

Although Soviet behavior had already changed by the time hostilities ceased, a period of eighteen months was to elapse before American policy toward Russia was reassessed. The American public attitude toward the Soviet Union was still generally friendly and hopeful for peaceful postwar cooperation. The United States wished to be left alone to occupy itself once more with domestic affairs and the fulfillment of American social values. The end of the war presumably signaled the end of power politics and the restoration of harmony among nations. The emphasis was therefore on rapid demobilization. Only when Britain pulled out of the eastern Mediterranean and there was no longer any countervailing power on the European continent—and only after continued Soviet denunciation and vilifications of the United States and Britain—did America's leaders again commit themselves. For this commitment to be made, a major external stimulus was needed.

American identification of Russia as an enemy and aggressor was therefore the result of Russian actions in eastern Europe, Iran, and Turkey. Once the United States had responded to what it regarded as Soviet challenges, however, American moralism was transformed into militant anticommunism. This change was hardly surprising during the bipolar era. The antithesis between American democratic values and Soviet Communist values was striking; it was a clear instance of good against bad, and it fitted the traditional dichotomy of New World democracy versus Old World autocracy. The impact on policy was readily visible. American policy makers, for instance, put off any political settlement with Russia until after communism had "mellowed"—that is, changed its character. Until then, negotiations were thought to be useless not only because of the expansionist aims of the Soviet leadership but also because such diplomatic dealings with the devil in the Kremlin would be immoral. Recognition of Communist China became impossible, and China's intervention in Korea only confirmed the American appraisal of communist regimes as evil, even though the United States had itself precipitated this intervention with its march up to the Chinese frontier with North Korea.

Similarly, if communism *per se* were the aggressor, then the United States had to oppose it everywhere or at least wherever it seemed that counterbalancing American power could be effectively applied. The United States also supported any anticommunist regime, regardless of whether or not it was democratic—including the regimes of Franco, Chiang Kai-shek, Diem, and Thieu, to name only a few. Viewing communism as truly wicked, Americans counted all communist states as uniformly evil. The recognition of differences among communist states—and the exploitation of these divisions—was therefore delayed. Nationalism as a divisive factor within the communist world was played down because of the belief that all communist states are equally immoral. Above all, issues of foreign policy tended to be framed as part of a universal struggle between democracy and totalitarianism, freedom and slavery. At the beginning of the Cold War, President Truman stated the issue of Greece as follows—"Totalitarian regimes imposed on free people, by direct or indirect agression, undermine the foundations of international peace and hence the security of the United States"[14]—although Greece, for all its political and strategic significance, could hardly be classified as a democracy. Presidents since Truman have followed his precedent, as American commitments have become virtually global.

Because this anticommunist justification for American foreign policy was unaffected by time, place, or circumstance, anticommunism came back to haunt the policy makers, especially Democratic ones, as they found that, regardless of preference, they were committed to "tough" policies; in a two-party system, the "in" party is always fearful of being charged with failing to protect American interests and "coddling communism." In the wake of Nationalist China's collapse, the Truman administration thus found itself attacked as "soft on communism." Indeed, the unquestioned assumption that the United States was omnipotent suggested that the American failure in China had been caused by treason within the American government. If the nation was supposed to be omnipotent, then it could not be lack of strength that accounted for its "defeat."

It could not be that there was a limit to the nation's ability to influence events far away from its shores. Such setbacks seemed to have resulted from American policies: It was argued that China had fallen because the "pro-communist" administrations of Roosevelt and Truman had either deliberately or unwittingly

---

[14.] Quoted in Joseph M. Jones, *The Fifteen Weeks* (New York: Viking, 1955), p. 272.

"sold China down the river." This charge, which came primarily from the strong conservative wing of the Republic party (including Joseph McCarthy and Richard Nixon), was simplicity itself. American China policy had ended in communist control of the mainland. Administration leaders and the State Department were responsible for this policy. The government must, therefore, harbor communists and communist sympathizers who were "tailoring" American policy to advance the global aims of the Soviet Union.[15] Disloyal American statesmen were thought to be responsible for the "loss" of China; it was to them, not to China, that the collapse of Nationalist China was due. Low Nationalist morale, administrative and military ineptitude, and repressive policies that had alienated mass support were ignored, as were superior Communist organization, direction, morale, and ability to identify with popular aspirations. When supposed omnipotence failed, conspiratorial interpretations were the result.[16]

(The subsequent conduct of the Korean war provides a good example of the impact of anticommunism upon foreign policy. The Truman administration's decision to advance into North Korea was undoubtedly influenced by the fact that a midterm congressional election was coming up; a victory in Korea could deflect accusations of "softness" on communism and permit the Democrats to present themselves as vigorous anticommunist crusaders and defenders of the United States.) The subsequent Chinese intervention, which produced a stalemate at the thirty-eighth parallel—the line at which the war had started—certainly led to a renewal of these charges. One consequence was that Truman could not sign an armistice based on the prewar partition of Korea, for those boundaries would allegedly represent peace without victory and would mean risking a Democratic defeat in the 1952 presidential election. Truman was trapped. He could not extend the war without risking greater escalation, casualties, and cost, nor could he end the war. The continuing and frustrating stalemate was a major factor in the Republican victory in 1952. Only President Dwight D. Eisenhower, a war hero who could hardly be accused of being an appeaser, could sign a peace treaty embodying the division of Korea.

Similarly, when in 1960 it became popular "to stand up to Castro," presidential candidate John F. Kennedy dramatized his anticommunism by means of vigorous attacks on Castro and suggestions that the Cuban "freedom fighters" be allowed to invade Cuba. When he came into office, he found that the Eisenhower administration had been planning what he had suggested. Despite his own later uneasy feelings about the invasion planned and sponsored by the Central Intelligence Agency (CIA), he thought that he could not call it off. If the operation were canceled and the news were leaked by its proponents in the government, as well as by the Cuban exiles who had been trained for this invasion and would, in the event of cancellation, be returning to the United States from their overseas training

---

[15] Tang Tsou, *America's Failure in China* (Chicago: University of Chicago Press, 1963), pp. 538–541. For a study of the accusation of a leading State Department figure by Senator McCarthy, see McGeorge Bundy, *The Pattern of Responsiblity* (Boston: Houghton Mifflin, 1952), pp. 201–220.

[16] The repetitious pattern of charges of conspiracy in American political life has been explored in Richard Hofstadter, *The Paranoid Style in American Politics* (New York: Vintage, 1967).

322 camp, he would stand exposed as less anticommunist than his predecessor, as a president who lacked nerve.[17] So, with some changes, he permitted the operation to proceed, despite misgivings that turned out to be justified. The Bay of Pigs invasion was a humiliating personal and national experience and, ironically, left Kennedy vulnerable to the accusation that he was unwilling to stand up to the communists because he would not use American forces to eliminate Castro.

As the situation in Vietnam proceeded to disintegrate in late 1961, it is not therefore surprising that the president introduced American military "advisers," particularly after the Bay of Pigs fiasco and American inaction at the time of the erection of the Berlin Wall. Kennedy did not want the Democrats accused of being the party that had "lost" Indochina, as it had "lost" China. The military advisers kept the situation in Vietnam from deteriorating— temporarily. Kennedy's successor, however, had to deal with a defeat of the South Vietnamese. He therefore intervened with American forces, the logical culmination of his predecessor's actions. From Truman on, each president had done just enough to prevent the loss of South Vietnam.

For each postwar president, increasing involvement in Indochina led to a final military intervention calculated as *less costly* than doing nothing and disengaging from Vietnam. In the context of American politics acquiescence in defeat was believed to be unacceptable. The costs of nonintervention in the loss of congressional and public support was considered to outweigh the costs of intervention several times.[18] The basic rule was "Don't lose Indochina." As Daniel Ellsberg summed up this imperative for each White House incumbent, "This is a bad year for me to lose Vietnam to Communism."[19] Each time the possibility of disaster stared an American administration in the face, the latter escalated the involvement and commitment to not losing Vietnam. Note the negative nature of the goal: to prevent a disaster. It was hoped that, if they could not win, the North Vietnamese would finally just give up.

The United States was reasonably optimistic, seduced by its "illusion of omnipotence." After all, where had American power ever failed? Such optimism was expressed most strongly by the civilian policy makers. When a leading civilian government official was told that eliminating the guerrillas in Vietnam might take as long as it had in Malaya, he curtly responded, "We are *not* the British."[20] Indeed, the assumption was that Hanoi was fearful that the United States would use its power and that, should the United States indicate its willingness to do so, Hanoi would desist from directing and helping the Vietcong. The Saigon and Washington authorities would have only to mop up. A major war to prevent the loss of South Vietnam and, in the administration's opinion, the consequent loss of Southeast Asia, might therefore be averted if North Vietnam could be convinced

---

[17] Theodore C. Sorensen, *Kennedy* (New York: Harper & Row, 1965), pp. 330–332.

[18] Leslie H. Gelb, *The Irony of Vietnam* (Washington, D.C.: Brookings, 1979), pp. 220–226.

[19] Daniel Ellsberg, *Papers on the War* (New York: Simon & Schuster, 1972), pp. 101–102.

[20] Bill Moyers, President Johnson's special assistant from 1963 to 1966, reports this comment in an interview with *The Atlantic* reprinted in Robert Manning and Michael Janeway, eds., *Who We Are* (Boston: Little, Brown, 1969), p. 262.

of American determination; in the event of noncompliance, the Hanoi government would be subjected to ever-increasing force. A slow squeeze on the North Vietnamese thus began in 1964, and the administration started contingency planning for American air strikes to begin in early 1965.[21]

In Vietnam American pragmatism was combined with the belief that the proper techniques can solve all problems. The result was a resort to force. Policy makers characteristically regarded the subsequent war as essentially a "military" war, in which superior fire power and helicopter mobility would enable the United States to destroy enemy forces. The political aspects of the war, above all the basic land reforms necessary to capture the support of the peasantry, were by and large ignored, and therefore no South Vietnamese goverment could win popular support. Indeed, the unpopular successive regimes in Saigon seemed almost irrelevant. The fact that counterguerrilla warfare can be conducted successfully only if political conditions are ripe was ignored. The war in South Vietnam could not therefore be won. Instead of seeking the political reasons for this paradox in South Vietnam, the policy makers told themselves that the reason the war could not be won was primarily military: the infiltration of North Vietnamese troops and weapons. The bombing of the North was expected to remedy this problem by pounding the enemy into submission. The bombing did not, however, decrease the volume of men and supplies flowing southward, nor did it destroy the North Vietnamese people's morale or pressure the government into ending the war. Quite the contrary: Techniques employed in a political vacuum were bound to fail.

As hostilities in Vietnam therefore dragged on and as American casualties and impatience grew,[22] American political observers witnessed the reappearance of a characteristic dichotomy between those who advocated further escalation in the hope of attaining a clear-cut military victory and those who proposed withdrawal because victory seemed elusive. Indeed, these alternative responses were frequently put forth by the same people. President Johnson thus found himself increasingly subject to opposing political pressures. One was to escalate the war; to appease this pressure, which came mainly, as during the Korean war, from conservative and hawkish elements in the Congress, he did in fact escalate. This decision tended to be temporarily popular, but eventually it rebounded when it failed to achieve victory. On the other hand, to choose withdrawal was to risk the charge of "appeasement." If he chose the middle course of neither expansion nor retreat, domestic opinion would split further, leaving the center weaker than ever. Whatever he did, the president was trapped, and he could count on little aid from his deeply divided party.

---

[21] For details, see the inside account revealed in *The Pentagon Papers* Also see the careful reconstruction of the beginning of the 1965 bombing campaign in George *et. al.*, *The Limits of Coercive Diplomacy* (Boston: Little, Brown, 1971), pp. 144–200.

[22] Larry Elowitz and Spanier, "Korea and Vietnam: Limited War and the American Political System," *Orbis*, Summer 1974, pp. 510–534; and John E. Mueller, *War, Presidents and Public Opinion* (New York: Wiley, 1973). Mueller comes to the startling conclusion that the war had no *independent* impact on President Lyndon B. Johnson's declining popularity, though the rate of the decline was the same as that for Truman during the Korean war. See also Milton J. Rosenberg *et al.*, *Vietnam and the Silent Majority* (New York: Harper & Row, 1970).

　　　　　Not only did this all-or-nothing attitude erode President Johnson's support, leading him to withdraw from seeking a second term of office and producing a Republican victory in the 1968 presidential election; it also led to widespread American disillusionment with foreign policy and the use of power, especially the use of force. Power politics, it has been suggested, has historically been considered wicked, to be engaged in only by the states of the Old World. American power was supposed to be righteous power. The Vietnam war, which could be watched nightly on television in "living color," seemed to prove only that, in the exercise of power, the nation had been carried away and had forsaken its moral tradition. Driven by anticommunism, which exaggerated the cohesiveness and threat of the "Sino-Soviet bloc"; tempted to intervene in many places and to make widespread commitments in the name of anticommunism; and aligning itself with many a disreputable reactionary regime in the name of freedom, the United States appeared to have violated its own democratic and liberal professions. The use of power in Vietnam thus reawakened guilt feelings. Power was viewed as a corrupting factor. It seemed better to concentrate on domestic affairs and to return to a historic duty, that is to complete the unfinished tasks of American society, create a truly democratic nation in which the gap between profession and performance would be minimal and serve as an example for all mankind.

Whereas power is viewed as evil and its exercise as tantamount to abuse, providing an example of a just and democratic society to the world is considered the moral thing to do. In the words of former Senator William Fulbright, Chairman of the Senate Foreign Relations Committee until 1974, power had made the United Sates "arrogant;" he counseled that the United States should therefore focus its attention and resources in order "to serve as an example of democracy to the world" and to "overcome the dangers of the arrogance of power." More specifically, "the nation performs its essential function not in its capacity as a *power* but in its capacity as a *society*."[23] Ronald Steel, in criticizing the *pax americana*, has said the same thing more eloquently:

> It is now time for us to turn away from global fantasies and begin our perfection of the human race within our own frontiers. There is a great deal to do at home within a society which a century after the liberation of the slaves still has not been able to grant the Negro full equality, a society which has been plagued with violence in the streets and guilt in the heart, which has achieved unprecedented material riches and yet is sick from a debilitating alienation, where the ideals of American democracy are mocked by the reality of racial prejudice, where individual decency is in constant conflict with social irresponsibility, where prosperity has assured neither justice nor tolerance, where private affluence dramatizes the shame of public squalor, where wealth has brought psychoanalysis, and where power has bred anxiety and fear. This is a society whose extraordinary achievements are now being overshadowed by the urgency of its unfulfilled promises and by dangerous strains in its social fabric.
>
> America's worth to the world will be measured not by the solutions she seeks to impose on others, but by the degree to which she achieves her own ideals

---

[23.] William Fulbright, *Arrogance of Power*, pp. 256–258.

NATIONAL AND ELITE STYLES IN FOREIGN POLICY

at home. That is a fitting measure, and an arduous test, of America's greatness.[24]   325

The optimistic faith that the United States, with its power and missionary zeal, can improve the world was thus replaced by a mood of disillusionment as, in the wake of the Vietnam war, it appeared that the wicked world outside could not be quickly or totally reformed and that the attempt would corrupt the nation. The characteristic cycle seems to begin with commitment and an attempt to reform the world, which are eventually replaced by a mood of cynicism about whether or not the world is worth being saved, fear the nation will forfeit its soul in the effort, and renewed determination to concentrate on the United States, in order to improve national life so that the presumed American superiority and greater morality can once more spread to the world and be worthy of imitation. Setting an example for the rest of the world, instead of adulterating its own purity with power politics, is said to be the American task.

In reality, such a policy is a "copout." It implies that, before the United States can play a large role in the world and lead a coalition against an antidemocratic or immoral power, it must first purify itself and be fully democratic and moral itself. It must no longer be plagued by racial strife, crime, a wasteful life style, or political hypocrisy. The United States must be perfect. Corrupted by power politics and deeply immersed in international politics, which drains its resources, and diverts its attention from improving the quality of domestic life, the nation must no longer expend its energies on "foreign adventures" while its domestic base deteriorates; it must renew itself by withdrawing from "power politics" and devoting itself to "social politics," building the shining society promised by the Founding Fathers and, if realized, certain to be the envy of and model for the world. Fulbright and Steel were thus arguing for the same policy that isolationists had formerly favored.

Most societies throughout history have not believed that they could achieve perfection. Mortals have hoped for this state of grace in the next world. It is possible, of course to aspire to a better life and to create it here on earth. But it is quite another thing for critics of American foreign policy, as they have become disillusioned with the Cold War, to compare *actual* conditions of society with some *imaginary* state of perfection and then to draw the conclusion from the rather obvious gap that the United States is not worthy to participate in international political life, especially to champion the cause of democracy against totalitarian regimes that deny the values the democracies represent. In the critics' view, foreign policy is thus replaced by domestic policy, and virtue, not power, becomes the key. American influence should be derived solely from the United States' moral standing as a good and just society. Arms, alliances, and spheres of influence are not the answer. A redistribution of income, racial justice, environmental concerns—worthy ends in themselves—are favored as *substitutes* for a foreign policy that demands an extensive role in the world; the shift from military services to social services will presumably bring happiness to the United States and protect the peace of the world. The American approach to foreign policy thus still seems to be one of dichotomies:

[24.] Steel, *Pax Americana*, pp. 353–354.

326 (between peace and war, abstention and total commitment, no force and maximum force, and passionate crusading and disillusioned withdrawal.)

The moralistic gladiator of today can be converted into the repentant sinner of tomorrow and then back again the day after. But, as gladiator or repentant sinner, as defender of orthodoxy or as critic of official policy, the moralism of the political thinker remains constant; so does the expectation that this country can regenerate mankind—by force or by example. Only the American passion for victory remains constant. The right and left both share it. Both march for victory and peace, one seeking to Americanize the world and thus to redeem a wicked planet from aggressors, the other withdrawing as much as possible from the universe of power politics—and then resurrecting "globalism" in terms of a postpower politics era of interdependence in which the United States, having cleansed itself, will once more perform "good works" by creating a more harmonious, peaceful world dedicated to such humanitarian and moral tasks as erasing poverty in the LDCs. The right and left both assume that it is within the power of the United States to defeat the enemy or to bring about harmony among nations all by itself. One asks *why not victory?*; the other suggests *the peace race*. Both are committed to the proposition that what the United States wills, it can attain; it needs only the will to achieve its aim. (This testimony to American omnipotence, impatience, and moralism suggests that old, deep-lying attitudes and values—*especially* basic emotions and nostalgia for a simpler and morally less ambiguous past—continue to exercise profound impact upon American foreign policy.)

THE SOVIET ELITE STYLE

(Because foreign-policy decisions are made not by nations but by a few decision makers, some analysts have suggested that perhaps the styles or operational codes of the political elite, the small group that makes policy, may be analytically more useful.)The United States has frequently been called a one-class society; the basic values of American society have been essentially those of the middle class. De Tocqueville said that the United States was born middle-class. For this country, it can be argued, the policy elite and the masses do share a fundamental set of beliefs, values, and attitudes. But in other countries, where class differences are more obvious and the political elites clearly separated from the mass of the population, the beliefs and values of the elites are usually easily identifiable. Even in countries like the Soviet Union, which reject class distinctions and claim to be classless societies, the political elites are much more visible and far smaller in size than in Western societies, even those with clear class structures. For Lenin, who led the revolution in 1917, and his successors, the desire to overthrow czarism and capture power and the goals that they have sought internationally since that time have been shaped by ideology. Indeed, Marxist-Leninist ideology has legitimated the authority of these leaders and has sanctioned their actions in fulfilling their objectives.

Almost all debates over Soviet foreign policy revolve around this fundamental issue of the Soviet leaders' self-proclaimed adherence to the official ideology. Are they really motivated by communist ideology, or do they merely use it to justify and expand their power? Are they seriously bent on fomenting world revolution, or are they trying to increase the strength of Russia as a nation? That is, are the men in the Kremlin fundamentally revolutionaries or nationalists? We saw earlier, in our first-level analysis, that ideologies are viewed as justifications for what leaders believe they must do to preserve and enhance their security interests in the state system. Ideologies are instruments for rationalizing what would have been done anyway. Ideology, therefore, is not a motivating force. All leaders, including Soviet leaders, think in terms of "national interest"; it is this interest that motivates the behavior of nation-states. Ideology, it is said, has not led the Soviets to adopt any policy that Russian "national interest" has not demanded. It has been merely a means of promoting that interest. The manipulation of ideology in order to justify any and every change of foreign and domestic policy only "proves" that it is too flexible to be a guide to action.

The opposing arguments have been stated by Zbigniew Brzezinski, President Carter's national security adviser:

> To dismiss ideology as an irrelevant criterion to an understanding of the political conduct of Soviet leaders . . . would be to assume that it is possible to build up a large organization ostensibly dedicated to certain explicit objectives, in which individuals are promoted on the basis both of their professional ability and their demonstrable ideological dedication, but in which an inner sanctum operates, makes decisions with a complete disregard of the ideological principles of the movement, indeed remains immune to the constant pressures for ideological justification, and cynically disregards the official creed.[25]

(If this view is correct, then ideology first of all provides Soviet leaders with "a comprehensive, consistent, closed system of knowledge, to which its adherents turn to get answers to all questions, solutions to all their problems."[26] Marxism-Leninism is such a system of knowledge, what the Germans more accurately call a *Weltanschauung* (world-view), an all-encompassing picture, a complete explanation of man, society, and history. As a *total conceptual framework*, it embraces not only economics and politics, but also philosophy, science, the arts, and even spiritual matters. No sphere of life is exempt. The ideology is also *official*, and its interpretation is the task of communist-party leaders, who regard their reading as embodying the only true view of society and history; as "true believers," such ideologues have been quite dogmatic. Finally, it follows that this kind of ideology and any other are *mutually exclusive*. By its very nature, Marxism-Leninism is intolerant of contrary beliefs—even when different interpretations of the Truth have been offered by fellow believers. These dissidents, as we already know, are dismissed as heretics who have deserted "the faith.")

[25] Zbigniew K. Brzezinski, *The Soviet Bloc* (Cambridge, Mass.: Harvard University Press, 1967), pp. 388 ff.

[26] Herbert J. Spiro, *Government by Constitution* (New York: Random House, 1959), p. 180.

328 ⟨This stress on ideology as the key factor influencing foreign policies of the Soviet Union does *not* mean that, in a specific situation, Soviet leaders go to the library and find a statement of what to do clearly spelled out in Karl Marx's *Das Kapital*. It means only that the ideology provides them with a way of perceiving and interpreting "reality"—with *their* model of the world. Ideology in this context is what earlier we called an analytical framework that "organizes reality" for its devotees. It is through ideological lenses that the latter selectively perceive the world, define and understand it, and decide how to act in it. The basic characteristics of this Marxist-Leninist ideology will be elaborated in Chapter 15. We shall only summarize them briefly here:

> Economic forces are fundamental. The organization of the production and the distribution of wealth is the foundation, or "substructure," upon which society is built.

> The capitalist "superstructure" consists of the owners of the "means of production" and wealth and of those who work for them and are "exploited" by them. Class relations are essentially based on opposing interests and conflict. According to Marx, all history is the history of class struggle between the rich and the poor—between the slave owners and the slaves, the feudal land-owning nobility and the peasantry, the capitalist owners of industry (the bourgeoisie) and the working class (the proletariat).

> The capitalist political system, like the class structure, reflects the nature of the economic system. The owners of wealth control the state and use its instruments—the army, the police and other levers of governmental power—to keep control. They can also manipulate other means of control, like the legal and educational systems and religion, to maintain their power.

> This type of system cannot be reformed. Superficial, or cosmetic, changes may be attempted in order to "buy off" the underprivileged and the exploited, but they cannot save the system. Contemporary capitalism is based upon private property and the profit motive. Their abolition is the prerequisite for productive use of industry for the benefit of the many, rather than for the luxury of the few. But the nature of capitalism cannot be changed; attempts to create a socialist society will be resisted.

> The injustices of capitalism will, however, come to an end with the proletarian revolution. This revolution will occur when the proletariat has become the majority and politically conscious of its own exploitation. This day of reckoning is historically inevitable.

> Lenin explained the failure of this "inevitable" revolution to occur in the Western industrial countries by imperialism and the massive capitalist exploitation of non-Western, or colonial, peoples. This global exploitation was so profitable that some of the profits trickled down to the industrial proletariat, so that its standard of living was improved, its revolutionary

consciousness eroded, and its vested interest in capitalism strengthened. Domestic revolution was thus avoided by means of a policy of imperialism.

The Marxian class struggle within the capitalist states was thus projected onto the global plane. The rich are now defined as the Western industrial states, the poor and exploited as the LDCs. This worldwide "class struggle" has thus become the critical conflict in the world.

Only when the industrial states lose the cheap raw materials previously provided by the LDCs and their economic growth rate slows, so that unemployment increases and the standard of living declines, will the domestic proletariat again recognize that its interests clash with those of the bourgeoisie. Then the class conflict will resume and will end in the proletarian revolution. ⌡

Inherent in this general analytical framework is a critique of contemporary society, which is condemned as utterly sinful and beyond redemption. Marxism-Leninism is deeply rooted in the belief that social relations in capitalist societies are evil, the products of the private ownership of property and the profit motive. It is the prevailing capitalist order that is responsible for the fact that the mass of human beings live in poverty, ill health, and ignorance. And it is capitalism that is the main reason why humanity is cursed with war. People can be freed from economic exploitation, political subjugation, and international violence only through the destruction of capitalism. According to the laws of economics discovered by Marx, history had doomed capitalism; the proletarian revolution, which will usher in a better and more peaceful world, is inevitable.)

The other key element inherent in Marxist-Leninist ideology is the task it assigns to Soviet leaders: the historically appointed task of helping to bring about the new, postcapitalist order. The ideology does not merely embody a critique of contemporary capitalist society. It also projects communism as the desired state of existence for humanity; if justice is to be realized in this world, poverty erased, discrimination eliminated, and people to be truly free in brotherhood, communist values will have to be universal. The ideology thus dictates extensive economic and social changes. As Marx said, his purpose was not merely to philosophize about the world but also to change it. His followers therefore feel compelled to give history a helping hand, to speed it up a bit in order to liberate people from their capitalist chains and ensure their secular salvation. Ideology is thus a motivating force and not merely a rationalization. It provides its "true believers" with both a conceptual framework *and* a long-range aim.)

The Bolshevik revolution of 1917 brought to power in a major country a group of men who were convinced that domestic justice and international peace could be realized only if the old capitalist order were swept away throughout the entire state system; all people were to be liberated from the social tyranny of capitalism and the scourge of war. This purpose transformed Russia, a traditional great power, into *Soviet* Russia, a revolutionary state, committed to the secular

330

mission of eliminating world capitalism. (The Soviet leaders denied the legitimacy of what they regarded as the prevailing international capitalistic order and the right of noncommunist states—which, by definition, were called capitalist—to exist. This ideology is contrary to the basic assumption of the balance of power: that each state has the right to exist, regardless of its domestic structure. The balance is supposed to protect all members of the state system. But the revolutionary state is revolutionary just because it *claims universal applicability for its values and ways of organizing domestic society and thus makes the domestic structures of all other states the central issue of international politics*. It seeks to extend the revolution to all other states and to convert their peoples to the faith "that makes men free"; this mission becomes its historic *duty*. Only the worldwide victory of the "new order" can lead to the establishment of a universal society in which human beings will be for the first time in history genuinely free from oppression, need, and war.)

No state in a pluralistic system, obviously, can feel absolutely secure; yet each, though greatly concerned with its security, normally does not feel *so* insecure that it becomes completely preoccupied with its survival, seeking universal domination in order to eliminate threats from all other states. It seeks security within a balance-of-power system that provides for its survival, as well as for the survival of other states. Conflicts are therefore *limited* and *pragmatic*; no state seeks another's elimination. Each recognizes the right of the others to exist. Communist ideology, by repudiating the legitimacy of capitalist states, however, transforms the international struggle between the revolutionary power and its adversaries into a *total* and *ideological* conflict. If one state feels compelled to destroy the domestic structures of other states and to transform them according to its own ideological values, that state must seek dominance or hegemony so that it can impose its will on them. It seeks to overthrow the balance as a prerequisite to remaking the system in its own image.

In a brilliant and eloquent passage, George Kennan has described how this revolutionary approach to foreign policy has made a "mockery of the entire Western theory of international relationships, as it evolved in the period from the seventeenth to the nineteenth centuries":

> The national state of modern Europe, bitterly as it might feud with its neighbors over the questions of *relative* advantage, was distinguished from the older forms of state power by its abandonment of universalistic and messianic pretensions, by its general readiness to recognize the equality of existence of other sovereign authorities, to accept their legitimacy and independence, and to concede the principle of live and let live as a basic rule in the determination of international relationships. . . .
>
> It was this theory that the Bolsheviki challenged on their assumption of power in Russia. They challenged it by the universality of their own ideological pretensions—by the claim, that is, to an unlimited universal validity of their own ideas as to how society ought to be socially and politically organized. They challenged it by their insistence that the laws governing the operation of human society demanded the violent overthrow everywhere of governments which did not accept the ideological tenets of Russian Communism, and the replacement of these governments by ones that did. . . .

The significance of this situation has been somewhat obscured by those Western historians and commentators who have been unable to perceive any difference in principle between the attitude of the Soviet union toward the Western countries and that of the Western countries toward the Soviet Union. After all, they have said, were not the Western governments equally hostile to Russia? Did they not attempt to overthrow the Soviet regime by their intervention in 1918–1919? Could the challenge to existing concepts of international relations properly be laid only at the Soviet door? Was not the Western rejection of socialism as a conceivable governmental system just as important in the breakdown of the established theory of international life as the Soviet rejection of capitalism?

It is my belief that the answer to these questions is "No." Any unclarity on this point can lead to a grievous misunderstanding of some of the basic elements of Soviet-Western relations. There were, in those initial years of Soviet power, some very significant differences between anti-Sovietism in the West and the hostility which the Soviet leaders entertained for the Western powers. This hostility from the Communist side is preconceived, ideological, deductive. In the minds of the Soviet leaders, it long predated the Communist seizure of power in Russia. Anti-Sovietism in the West, on the other hand, was largely a confused, astonished, and indignant reaction to the first acts of the Soviet regime. Many people in the Western governments came to hate the Soviet leaders for what they *did*. The Communists, on the other hand, hated the Western governments for what they *were*, regardless of what they did. They entertained this feeling long before there was even any socialistic state for the capitalists to do anything to. Their hatred did not vary according to the complexion or policies or actions of the individual noncommunist governments. It never has. . . .

Surely, this approach cannot be equated with that of the pragmatic West, where for forty years the argument over the attitude to be taken toward Soviet power has revolved around the questions of interpretation of the behavior of the Soviet regime. There have undoubtedly been individuals here and there in the Western countries whose hatred of what they understood to be socialism has been so great that they have felt it should be rooted out with fire and sword, on straight ideological grounds, wherever it raised its head. But such people, surely, have been few; and I do not think that their views have ever been dominant in any of the major Western governments. . . . Had the Soviet leaders contented themselves from the outset with saying that they felt that they knew what was good for Russia, and refrained from taking positions on what was good for other countries, Western hostility to the Soviet Union would never have been what it has been. The issue has never been, and is not today, the right of the Russian people to have a socialistic ordering of society if they so wish; the issue is how a government which happens to be socialistic is going to behave in relation to its world environment.[27]

Marxism-Leninism, then, provided the new rulers of *Soviet* Russia with a comprehensive analytical framework; it presented them with a way of perceiving the world; it defined the principal operational economic and social forces; it helped them to discriminate between friend and foe; it established Soviet long-range pur-

---

[27.] Kennan, *Russia and the West under Lenin and Stalin* (Boston: Little, Brown, 1961), pp. 179–183 (emphasis in original). Used by permission of the publisher.

332   poses; and it provided for continuing commitment to these purposes. (Soviet policy makers perceive national security in the context of world revolution) a goal that the czars had never adopted.

    Marxism-Leninism also provides the Soviet leaders with more than a broad *Weltanschauung* and a definition of ultimate purpose as a guide to policy; it also provides a method of analysis that makes it possible to identify, explain, and comprehend the particular historical era that the world is passing through on the way to postcapitalism. In contrast to the more pragmatic American approach, in which leaders tend to react to each problem as it arises and to deal with each on its "merits," the Soviet approach is based on a type of broad conceptual approach that is rare in the United States. This conceptual approach means that the men in the Kremlin start with a broad picture of the world, the principal forces at work in it, and the direction of contemporary history.

    For example, Lenin, asserting that capitalism had used imperialism to avoid domestic revolution, claimed that the basic struggle between capitalism and communism had become worldwide and that revolution would begin in what we now call the third world. Instead of starting in the most highly industrialized nations, as Marx had predicted, the revolution would erupt in less economically developed nations, where the majority of the population are peasants, not proletarians. From the beginning, the Soviet leaders have seen their own revolution not as simply a single event in one country but as part of a larger, continuing historical process.[28] Unitl 1917 the international system had been controlled by the West; European colonial rule had spread to all parts of the globe, and by the beginning of the century the United States, already dominant over Latin America, had begun to play a role in the Pacific area. The Russian revolution signaled the first defection from this Western-dominated international capitalist system. Furthermore, the revolution was the beginning of the end of this basically European-centered world order; the defection of Russia was only the first one.

    The projected decline of Europe was to be paralleled by the emergence of a new world order, the nucleus of which would be postcapitalist Soviet Russia. As the West's "raw-materials appendages" in the third world became increasingly conscious of their subordinate status, their exploitation, and their poverty, they would become more and more resentful. In their "proletarian revolution" against the West, they would be drawn to the Soviet Union. In stage one—World War I—the defection of Russia had occurred; in stage two—beginning after World War II—the "peoples' democracies" of eastern Europe and China defected from the weakening world capitalist order. Initially Soviet Russia had been alone, confronted by "capitalist encirclement"; after 1945 it was no longer alone, and the conflict became one between the capitalist and communist worlds. As a greater number of Arab, Asian, and African nations became independent from colonial rule, Moscow leaders saw "the breakdown of the structure of Western dominion in the non-European parts of the world, the disappearance of most of what remained in the interwar periods (1919–39) of the great European colonial empires."[29] "Nonalign-

---

[28.] Tucker, *op. cit.*, pp. 185–189.

[29.] *Ibid.*, p. 190

ment" was defined as nonalignment with the West and was perceived as a radical shift in world affairs. "In an important sense . . . the nineteenth century finally came to an end in the aftermath of World War II."[30]

It is hardly surprising, then, given this interpretation of contemporary history, that the Soviet Union is committed to what is now called "national liberation." It sees its support for national-liberation movements, on the one hand, as helping to administer the final blow to the old international order, propped up by the United States since 1945, and, on the other, as promoting the creation of a new postcapitalist system centered on Russia. Even during the period of détente, Moscow thus always openly declared that détente did not mean the end of the "ideological struggle" and the abandonment of support for "national liberation." The Soviet-Cuban-East German interventions in Afghanistan, Angola, Ethiopia, and South Yemen during the 1970s were consistent with this perspective. That the Soviets' interventions undermined American influence and enhanced their own in the strategically vital Indian Ocean-Persian Gulf area was an extra incentive to support "the struggle against imperialism." An ideology that provides its leaders with a general world-view, an understanding of the principal social and political forces at work in the world, and sufficient insight into history to grasp the "essence" of contemporary international politics is obviously not meaningless, a mere rationalization of policies that would have been pursued even if the ideology had never existed.

Indeed, once Marxism-Leninism had committed the Soviet leadership to elimination of the old order, the conflict between the Soviet Union and the Western industrial states, all of which are regarded as capitalist, became total and irreconcilable. The basic "fact" of history is the condition of continuing and unending conflict between classes or, more specifically, between states controlled by antagonistic classes, until the moment of victory. Politics is no longer a means of reconciliation. It is instead an unending series of "campaigns," the aim of which is to defeat the capitalist enemy. The only question is *kto, kovo?* ("Who, whom?", meaning "Who will destroy whom?"),[31] though history has already predicted the outcome. But this formula is symptomatic of a basic outlook. Between adversaries, one of which has been condemned to extinction by history and the other one selected to triumph, there can be no final agreement or settlement. A genuine lasting peace can come only after the elimination of capitalism and the victory of communism. Until then, agreements can be only temporary, each only a tactical move in the struggle, and real peace remains impossible while the conflict between the two social systems continues.

The struggle to achieve this goal must be prosecuted with vigor and persistence; to relax from the historical struggle would be tantamount to betrayal of the revolutionary mission. Victory over capitalism is the raison d'être of the movement—which does not mean that "peaceful coexistence" until the moment of

---

[30.] *Ibid.*, pp. 190–191.

[31.] Nathan Leites, A *Study of Bolshevism* (New York: Free Press, 1953), pp. 27–63, and Robert Strausz-Hupé *et al.*, *Protracted Conflict* (New York: Harper & Row, 1959), pp. 21–22.

334   victory is impossible. There is no special emphasis in communist doctrine on the use of force, as there was in Nazi doctrine.

> The Kremlin is under no ideological compulsion to accomplish its purpose in a hurry. Like the Church, it is dealing in ideological concepts which are of long term validity, and it can afford to be patient. It has no right to risk the existing achievements of the revolution for the sake of vain baubles of the future.[32]

Soviet doctrine does not, therefore, reject temporary relaxation of tensions or détente when time is needed to recoup the nation's strength or build greater strength; nor does it reject accords with adversaries. Such tactical moves are required by the ebb and flow of circumstances, but the ultimate objectives remain constant. The scope for accommodation is thus clearly limited. The question is not whether or not ultimate objectives are to be abandoned but only how they can best be realized. The struggle must go on, for the long-range aims are unchangeable; only the methods to be employed are flexible. Cooperation and negotiations do not mean the end of conflict; rather, they are ways of conducting it. Even high-risk methods are not foreclosed if circumstances favor them. The only qualification is that the risks not be so high that they might endanger the "bastion of the revolution." Marxism-Leninism has thus infused Soviet policy with a compulsion to expand Soviet influence whenever and wherever the opportunity presents itself and does not endanger the home base of the revolution. It is virtually treason not to take advantage of favorable circumstances when they arise; equally it is tantamount to treason to allow "adventurism" or "romanticism" to lead to unnecessary risks that might threaten Soviet Russia itself.

Not surprisingly, the impact of this ideological image has greatly enhanced the degree of suspicion and fear among existing states in the anarchical system. This additional measure of skepticism and apprehension, for example, made it impossible to achieve after World War II the kind of *modus vivendi* arrived at after 1815. Perhaps the most significant characteristic of the Soviet leaders' thinking is their distinction between objective and subjective factors. The former are those fundamentally economic, *objectively existing forces* that determine the social structures and political behavior of any state. Any group of Soviet leaders, who are convinced that they have superior insight into history, is bound to see the international environment as *extremely* hostile and to regard with deep distrust any Western state, however benevolent its expressed intentions; indeed, as the Soviets have assumed that the Western states are out to destroy Russia—as they are bent on destroying the Western states—their attitude toward what they regard as a capitalist-dominated system borders on paranoia. Consequently, it was immaterial during World War II whether or not Stalin personally liked Roosevelt. Stalin *knew* that the deeper objective forces of the economic substructure, upon which the prevailing social and political superstructure rested, would determine Roosevelt's actions: In his view, the American President was merely a puppet—though perhaps a likable puppet—of Wall Street interests; governmental decisions thus simply

---

[32.] Kennan, *American Diplomacy 1900–1950*, p. 118.

reflected the "law" of capitalism. How could anyone have persuaded Stalin otherwise, when he, like other Soviet leaders before him and since, was absolutely convinced of his deeper insight into history, arising from his Marxist-Leninist training? Roosevelt's expressions of hope for peace and cooperation after the defeat of Germany were dismissed as "sentimental gestures," not reflecting "reality."

This suspicion of capitalist states was hardly new. After all, when any state defines another state as an enemy long enough and acts upon that assumption, it will come to see in the reactions of the other state confirmation for its suspicions, regardless of whether or not that reaction is firm or conciliatory. Toughness will be viewed as confirmation of the other state's enmity; conciliation will be seen as an attempt to soften, in order to strike when vigilance has been relaxed. All actions by capitalist states are thus regarded as reflecting only their hostility toward Soviet Russia; their behavior is never attributed to friendly motives or mistaken but correctable policies. Enmity toward the Soviet Union is always present, though perhaps carefully camouflaged; the capitalist states *always* know exactly what they are doing. Errors and misperceptions are not the causes of conflict.

The allied intervention in Russia after the Bolshevik capture of power in 1917 was thus seen as an attempt to restore the Czar and the old order. The French attempt to contain Germany between the two world wars by means of an alliance with Poland and several other eastern European countries was viewed as an effort to keep the Russians out of Europe. The appeasement of Hitler was perceived as designed to turn Nazi Germany away from attacking the Western states to an attack on Russia; appeasement "opened the gates to the East" by letting Hitler swallow Austria, the Sudentenland, then the rest of Czechoslovakia. In order to avoid further Western appeasement of Germany, Stalin made his own deal with Hitler, dividing Poland with him and turning Hitler's attention back toward France and Britain; he thus gained some time before Hitler once more moved to attack Russia.

During World War II, from 1941 to 1945, Moscow's leaders therefore saw the United States as a temporary ally only; once Germany had been defeated, the United States, the strongest Western capitalist power, would become Russia's principal enemy in the continuing struggle against capitalism. Leaders in the United States, thinking in terms of the country's historic approach to international politics, saw World War II as a temporary dislocation of the normal, peaceful condition among nations. After the conclusion of hostilities, American policy makers expected to live in harmony and friendship with the Soviet Union. The chief American objective in Europe in 1941–1945 was strictly military: the unconditional surrender of Germany in the quickest possible time, total victory, and the elimination of Hitler. A postwar balance of power against Russia played no role in the formulation of American wartime planning and strategy. Soviet policy makers, however, foresaw the postwar conflict and remained highly suspicious of the West.

To cite only one of many examples, the Soviets not unnaturally wanted the Western allies to invade western Europe to relieve the pressure on the eastern front. They did not believe any of the Western explanations of why that could not be done in 1942 or 1943, especially the claim that the West lacked sufficient landing craft for an operation of such magnitude or that the United States and

336   Britain were unwilling to risk cross-channel invasion of France unless there were assurances that the invading forces would not be driven back into the water with enormous loss of life. The Soviets dismissed these reasons as mere excuses. Why should the Western allies delay? Because they were waiting to invade the continent until Germany and Russia had bled each other white. Then they could administer the final blow to Gemany and dictate postwar terms to Russia as well. In the wake of the retreating German armies, Russia thus consolidated its hold on eastern Europe as a buffer zone to give it greater protection in the postwar conflict.

Ironically, given Stalin's expectations, the war years had created a great reservoir of good will toward the Soviet Union both in the United States and in western Europe. Russia had borne the brunt of the German armies, and the heroism of the Red Army and the Russian people was acclaimed everywhere. Stalin, the dictator who had collaborated with Hitler in 1939–1941, became "Uncle Joe," as American leaders spoke of a new era of good relations with Russia. In the United States and Britain, hopes for the postwar period were high; in France, where commmunists had played a leading role in the resistance movement, Russia was also much admired. By and large, the Soviet Union was described in glowing terms—virtually as a democracy—just as it was later depicted in almost satanic terms. Concerned as Russia was about its security in eastern Europe, in this atmosphere it should have been easily reassured.

Had the Soviet Union left Poland, Hungary, Rumania, and Bulgaria to govern themselves domestically while securing influence over their foreign policies, as it did in postwar Czechoslovakia, it could have avoided arousing and alienating the United States and Britain. The Western states accepted the Soviet contention that eastern Europe was Russia's security belt, but they argued that freely elected coalition governments that included communists could be friendly to both the Russians *and* the West. President Eduard Beneš in Czechoslovakia seemed a symbol of this model for eastern Europe, for the Czech communists had, in a free election, won a plurality of the vote and were therefore the dominant partner in the coalition government. But even that kind of coexistence was unacceptable to Russia. Noncommunist parties were regarded by nature as anticommunist because they allegedly represented class enemies; they were therefore to be eliminated from the Czech government, as they already had been in the rest of eastern Europe. The Soviets overthrew the coalition government in Prague.

The Soviet Union thus quickly emptied the reservoir of good will that would have guaranteed its minimum objective, Russian security. Why? No doubt one reason lay in the fact that their exclusive and intolerant ideology was incompatible with, and hostile toward, an open society and multiple competing groups. But this explanation accounts only for the Soviets' wholesale conversion of the eastern European states into satellites. What about the *timing* of the Soviet moves? This issue cannot be explained solely by the presence of the Red Army throughout most of the area; above all, it was the result of the ideologically induced expectation that the immediate postwar period would bring social and political upheaval and therefore would present an opportunity for the extension of Soviet power. It was anticipated that the United States would suffer another depression once war production had ceased and that, as a result, it would withdraw once more into its traditional isolationist posture. During the war Roosevelt had told Stalin that American troops would be withdrawn from Europe within two years of Germany's surrender. At the same time, Russia knew that the instability of Europe after a German defeat would not last forever and that American capitalism would eventually recover. The opportunity brought on by the fluidity of the immediate postwar situation thus had to be seized.[33]

It may be that much of Russian expansionist policy in the wake of the retreating German armies can actually be explained in systemic terms. But it can hardly be doubted that the Soviet leaders' perception of the capitalist states as permanently hostile made it impossible for them to believe in the professions of good will and friendly intentions by President Roosevelt. And their perception of the Soviet Union's role in the world made it impossible for them to abstain from exploiting weakness to the south and west of Russia in an effort to extend socialism from one country to a larger area. The relative security that the Soviet leaders could have gained for Russia by acting more cautiously was squandered because of their own ideological thinking and behavior. They aroused British and then American opposition; high international tension was in good part due to ideology, rather than to the mere distribution of power.

Communist ideology has also influenced Soviet ability to form alliances with noncommunist states, as for instance against Germany in the 1930s. France in the middle 1930s had signed a treaty with Russia; Russia in turn had signed one with Czechoslovakia. But the French were never to implement their own alliance. The French were highly suspicious of communist Russia, partly because of the sizable French Communist party and the French bourgeoisie's fear of social revolution and partly because of the government's fear that, if it aided Czechoslovakia, the Soviets would stand by until France and Germany had weakened each other sufficiently to leave Russia in the predominant position on the continent. Yet France and czarist Russia had been allies before World War I. It was only after that conflict and the ensuing Bolshevik revolution that French-Soviet relations became so loaded with mutual suspicion that no meaningful alliance was possible.

In Great Britain as well, behavior between the war was influenced by strong suspicions of Russian motives. When, after the Munich conference, Neville Chamberlain's British government responded to pressures from Winston Churchill and other antiappeasement conservatives and sought an alliance with Russia, it was so suspicious of Soviet revolutionary aims that it moved at a snail's pace; probably to British relief, Hitler signed up Stalin first. During World War II these suspicions were reduced because Roosevelt and Churchill tended to view Russia as primarily a czarist state. Various factors influenced this assessment: the apparent identity of Soviet aims with traditional Russian foreign-policy objectives (for example, concern for the security of eastern Europe and the search for a warm-water port); the Soviet stress on the "Great Fatherland War," which highlighted Russian nationalism and

---

[33.] Adam B. Ulam, *Expansion and Coexistence* (New York: Holt, Rinehart and Winston, 1968), p. 410; and Paul E. Zinner, "The Ideological Bases of Soviet Foreign Policy," *World Politics*, July 1952, pp. 497–498.

tended to obscure Soviet Communism; the dissolution of the Comintern; the replacement of the *Internationale* with a specifically Russian national anthem; relaxation of restrictions upon religion; and the West's own hope that wartime cooperation would mitigate, if not remove, Soviet suspicions of the West—particularly if the West proved its sincerity by recognizing Russia's historic security interests. Even the anticommunist Churchill of the prewar period spoke of a postwar peace guarded by the "Four Policemen"—the United States, Britain, Russia, and China: "I wished to meet the Russian grievance, because the government of the world must be entrusted to satisfied nations, who wished nothing more for themselves than what they had. If the world government were in the hands of hungry nations, there would always be danger."[35] If they were jointly to preserve the peace, all four states would have to be satisfied. Churchill's assumption was that, though Stalin might be hungry, his appetite was limited and an appropriate meal could therefore be served to satisfy him. Uncle Joe was viewed merely as an heir to Nicholas II. This assumption was, to be sure, based more on hope than on reality. But it was based on genuine hope. Perhaps wartime cooperation would erode Soviet suspicions and fear of Western intentions; in any event, the attempt to win Russian friendship had to be made if a major postwar conflict was to be avoided.

Not until the Allied invasion of France in June 1944 were Churchill's apprehensions about communist policy reawakened by Russian behavior in eastern Europe. But it was the postwar Labour government in Britain that took the initiative in mobilizing opposition to Soviet moves in Europe (though revisionists tend to forget this point). Even then, Washington's leaders were still hopeful. Indeed, throughout the war years and immediately thereafter, they thought of themselves as mediators between the Soviets and the British. Assuming that Russia and Britain would police the continent, the United States preferred to act as the impartial referee between two friends whose ambitions clashed in eastern Europe and the eastern Mediterranean. Not until the Truman Doctrine in 1947 were wartime assumptions about Russia as a state with legitimate and moderate aims replaced by recognition that Soviet aims were of a greater scope and that the United States would have to take the initiative in organizing the West to contain Russian power.

While communist ideology intensified the suspicions which already existed in the state system and hindered the establishment of alliances with Western states, they also impeded the formation of smoothly working alliances wth communist states.[36] The Soviet Union was also suspicious of other communist states,[37] as was revealed when, right after the war, Stalin expelled Yugoslavia's Marshall Tito—a loyal Stalinist until then—from the Soviet bloc. Soviet suspicion was revealed even more dramatically in Russia's relationship with Communist China; it simply proved impossible for these two giants of the communist world to maintain a long-term mutually beneficial alliance. Conflicts among communist nations were supposed to be nonexistent, for antagonism among states was ostensibly the result of the

---

[35] Winston S. Churchill, *The Second World War*, V: *Closing the Ring* (Boston: Houghton Mifflin, 1948), pp. 363, 382.

[36] Ulam, *op. cit.*, pp. 398–402.

[37] *The New York Times*, July 14, 1964.

competing interests of their dominant classes. Communist states professed to be classless societies, and no strife between them should have occurred. The problem was that the Soviet Union was no longer the only powerful communist state and that its monopoly of "truth"—that is, its total control of decision making—was being challenged. In part the Kremlin leaders had only themselves to blame for this undermining of their authority. One of the functions of communist ideology is to legitimate those who hold authority. Communist ideology was therefore designed to legitimate the Soviet leaders both as the rulers of the Soviet Union and—when the Soviet Union was the only socialist state—as directors of the international communist movement. Just as there can be only one pope, there can be only one source of ideological pronouncements in a secular movement like communism. Moscow was this infallible source. But Peking leaders challenged this authority and the Soviet monopoly of political wisdom. In the resulting interparty conflict, each contender claimed the correct interpretation of history and the true interpretation of party theology. Within years of Stalin's death, each country was denouncing the other for heresy. Claiming to be fundamentalists, the Chinese saw themselves as remaining true to Marxism-Leninism, which they believed the Soviets had betrayed. Moscow, the communist Rome, and Khrushchev, the new communist pope (and later Brezhnev), were thus challenged by Mao Tse-tung's Eastern Orthodox Church. How could China possibly follow a nation whose communism was "phony," whose revisionist domestic policies were "rapidly swelling the forces of capitalism" inside Russia,[37] and whose foreign policy was aligning it with the United States against China?[38]

Compromise on common policies between *communist* Russia and *communist* China was to pose an insuperable obstacle. In matters of doctrine, when the purity of ideology is at stake, does not a policy of give-and-take represent contamination? How can mutual adjustments be made between two members of a movement in which differences of emphasis become issues of loyalty to the faith? How could the primacy, infallibility, and doctrinal purity of the Kremlin leaders be reconciled with Chinese claims to an equal voice, Maoist infallibility, and ideological fundamentalism? The Western allies, themselves pluralistic societies, can cope with pluralism and diversity. Communist states cannot, for their parties impose uniform domestic patterns in accordance with their ideological interpretations. Each is a totalitarian society precisely because the Communist party claims to be the bearer of revealed "truth," which must be imposed upon society because "the truth will make men free." Heresy must be ruthlessly eliminated. How can two such states, each convinced that its interpretation of the truth is the only correct one, coexist? Nonrevolutionary great powers at least share a degree of toleration. If they are allies, as are France and the United States, they can resolve differences as mere conflicts of interest without the additional burden of a superimposed conflict between "good" and "evil." When differences of interest continue to exist, they do not necessarily lead to complete rupture. The self-righteous—for the righteous always tend to become self-righteous—exhibit no such tolerance, however. When ideology is so intimately linked with power, as it is in communist policy and

---

[38.] *The New York Times*, February 6, 1966.

340   decision making, then there are can be only one "correct" answer. Divergent policies cannot be compromised, and these differences affect the entire range of relations. The resulting bitterness between Moscow and Peking leaders over who is orthodox and who is heretical can be appreciated best through their own exchanges:

> After Stalin's death [say the Chinese] Khrushchev, a capitalist-roader in power hiding in the Soviet Communist party . . . usurped party and government power in the Soviet Union. This was a counterrevolutionary *coup d'état* which turned the dictatorship of the proletariat into the dictatorship of the bourgeoisie and which overthrew socialism and restored capitalism. [The Soviet Union is] a dictatorship of the German fascist type, a dictatorship of the Hitler type.[39]

> Matters have gone so far [replied the Soviets] that Hitler's raving about the need to "save" the people from the "Slav threat" has been taken out of the mothballs. The people in Peking emulate the ring-leaders of the Nazi Reich in attempting to portray the Soviet Union as a "colossus with feet of clay. . . ."

> By their action the Peking leaders leave no doubt that they strive to use the heroic freedom struggle of the peoples in their global intrigues that stem from the Great Han dreams of becoming the new emperors of "The Great China" that would rule at least Asia, if not the whole world.[40]

In these circumstances, it is clear that the essence of any give-and-take is blocked by the instance on doctrinal purity. One "correct" answer demands a single center of political authority and ideological orthodoxy. *Any relationship between communist states must therefore be hierarchical in nature; it cannot be one of equality.* Either Moscow or Peking must be the center of communist theological interpretation *and* the source of policy in most, if not all, issue areas.

A COMPARISON OF AMERICAN AND SOVIET STYLES

★ Final

On the eve of the Cold War, it should be clear by now, the styles of the two superpowers contrasted sharply. In their perception of the nature of politics— especially in their image of conflict—the Americans emphasized an international harmony of interests, which stood in stark contrast to the emphasis in the state system on the inevitability of conflict and differences of interests among states. The American view was that conflict is an abnormal condition, whereas the Soviets viewed harmony as an illusion. The United States, long isolated from Europe and therefore not socialized in the state system, did not accept the reality and perma-

---

[39.] *The New York Times*, May 3, 1970.
[40.] *Ibid.*

nence of conflicts among members of that system. Differences between states were not considered natural and certainly not deep or long-lasting; rather, they were attributed to wicked leaders (who could be eliminated), authoritarian political systems (which could be reformed), and misunderstandings (which could be straightened out if the adversaries approached each other with sincerity and empathy). Once these obstacles had been removed, peace, harmony, and good will would reign supreme.)

The Soviet emphasis, on the other hand, was on the inevitable conflict with capitalist states. Conflict was viewed not as the result of wicked capitalist political leaders—they might be very decent and likable men—but as the inevitable result of the system that they represented. There was nothing accidental about conflict. Genuine peace and harmony could come only after capitalism, the real cause of rivalry between states, had been eliminated and replaced by world communism; until then, it was only natural, indeed imperative, to exploit existing competition and conflict to advance Soviet Russia's cause.)

Whereas Americans in the early days of détente believed that an era of negotiation, rather than confrontation, was dawning, the Soviets never believed or said that détente was incompatible with continued struggle. Americans thus became disillusioned with détente as Soviet leaders exploited a number of opportunities—in Egypt in 1973 and in Africa later. Cynicism about Soviet intentions replaced initial confidence. At the same time, the Soviets claimed not to be able to understand why Americans should be so disappointed in détente. They were not doing anything very different from what they had been doing all along. The United States seemed to be overreacting. There had been no understanding between the two powers on freezing the status quo, and there had therefore been no violations. The United States and Russia clearly perceived détente differently and had quite different expectations.

(Above all, the United States has always considered itself a morally and politically superior society because of its democratic culture. Its attitude toward the use of international power has therefore been dominated by the belief that the struggle for power need not exist, can be avoided through isolation, or can be eliminated. Moralism in foreign policy had proscribed the use of power in peacetime; power was to be employed only in confrontation with unambiguous aggressors, at which point the United States would be obliged to fight on behalf of a righteous cause. Power, internationally, just as domestically, can be legitimated only by democratic purposes; otherwise, its exercise is evil and necessarily arouses guilt.)

(The Soviet belief in unceasing and irreconcilable conflict means acceptance of power as an instrument of policy, dedicated to the pursuit of communist ends. But this power is used with care and restraint:)

> [The Kremlin] has no compunction about retreating in the face of superior force. And being under the compulsion of no timetable, it does not get panicky under the necessity for such retreat. Its political action is a fluid stream whch moves constantly, wherever it is permitted to move, toward a given goal. . . . But if it finds unassailable barriers in its path, it accepts these philosophically and accom-

modates itself to them. The main thing is that there should always be pressure, increasing constant pressure, toward the desired goal. There is no trace of any feeling in Soviet psychology that that goal must be reached at any given time.[41]

(The Soviet use of power is not therefore subject to cyclical swings from isolationism to crusading and back again, as the American pattern used to be. Power is the raw material of international politics, to be applied discriminatingly and cautiously in the effort to achieve specific objectives. Its use arouses no guilt; the issue is whether or not it can be successfully employed to advance Soviet goals. It is used to probe for soft spots in the adversary's positions; on the other hand, "adventurism" and "romanticism," which might provoke the enemy and endanger the base of the world revolution, are to be avoided.)

(Americans, believing that peace is a natural condition and that differences between states can usually be dissolved through demonstrations of sincerity and good will, cannot comprehend an attitude so dedicated to struggle.) Soviet leaders because of this commitment, never hesitate to sacrifice opportunities to win good will in exchange for strategic gains. The expansion and consolidation of Soviet power in eastern Europe, which helped to undermine the wartime alliance, was not the only time that the Soviets torpedoed good relations with the West. In 1955 the summit conference and the "spirit of Geneva" quickly fell before the Soviet arms deal with Egypt, which helped to precipitate the Suez war a year later. More recently, the ink was hardly dry on the first strategic arms-limitation treaty (SALT I) when the Soviets supplied Egypt with the offensive arms that led to the Yom Kippur war in 1973 and almost to a military confrontation with the United States. During all the years of negotiations on SALT II, the Soviets never hesitated to extend their influence in Africa. Even while the Senate was debating SALT II and the survival of the treaty was in doubt, the Soviets expanded their influence to the Indian Ocean and Persian Gulf areas, even intervening with their own troops in Afghanistan. Believing in economic determinism and irreconcilable class struggle, they rejected the idea that opportunities for advancing their cause should be passed up; good will among enemies locked in a deadly struggle seemed to them an illusion anyway.

(In contrast, perhaps the most telling symptom of the American national style in conducting foreign policy is the reinterpretation, after every major war, of the country's participation. The *revisionist* histories have certain common themes: the conflicts in which the nation had been entangled had not in fact threatened its security interests. The politicians had seen a menace where none existed, and this illusion had been promoted by propagandists, who had aroused and manipulated public opinion; by soldiers with bureaucratic motives; and, above all, by bankers and industrialists— the "merchants of death" of the 1930s, the "military-industrial complex" of the 1960s—who expected to benefit from the struggle.) The United States' engagement in two world wars in this century (and in the Cold War) was mistaken; these wars had really been unnecessary, immoral or both. Yesterdays apparent aggressor and *provocateur* thus had not represented a threat to American

---

[41] Kennan, *American Diplomacy*, p. 118.

security after all; on the contrary, the threat turns out really to have come from within. Except for certain *domestic forces*, the United States could have continued to isolate itself from international politics.

(Such revisionism is perhaps the deepest symptom of the American aversion to "power politics.") As the distinguished American diplomatic historian Dexter Perkins has written, revisionists always seek to convince the public that "every war in which this country has been engaged was really quite unnecessary or immoral or both; and that it behooves us in the future to pursue policies very different from those pursued in the past."[42] What is most striking about the revisionists' claim that the Cold War was avoidable (based on second-level analysis) is that they really believe that, but for the United States' purported anticommunism and lack of sensitivity to Russian interests, the conflict between the superpowers would not have erupted. They are unaware that in the state system, according to first-level analysis, conflict is inherent, *regardless* of the nature of the states and that, after World War II, a new distribution of power had to be arranged in order to provide a modicum of safety and stability in an anarchical international system.[43] The revisionists have written the new "guilt" literature. Just as in the 1930s British and French revisionist historians suggested that, but for the harsh Versailles peace treaty imposed upon Germany in 1919, Germany would not again be threatening the peace of the world, so contemporary revisionists have sugested that the Cold War was totally the United States' fault. But for the Versailles treaty, the argument goes, there would have been no Hitler, and, because of the injustice of the treaty, Britain and France should have felt guilty and without any *moral* right to deny Nazi Germany its "legitimate claims." Similarly it is argued that, but for American anticommunism, Stalin's fears and suspicions would not have been aroused,and there would have been no need for the Soviet-American clash of interests; Stalin had only Russia's limited and legitimate interests in mind.

[42.] Dexter Perkins, "American Wars and Critical History," *Yale Review*, summer 1951, pp. 682–695.

[43.] For some of the revisionist histories that place the responsibility for beginning the Cold War upon the United States, see D. F. Fleming, *The Cold War and Its Origins* (2 vols.; Garden City, N. Y.: Doubleday, 1961); Gar Alperovitz, *Atomic Diplomacy: Hiroshima and Potsdam* (New York: Vintage, 1967); William A. Williams, *The Tragedy of American Diplomacy* (Cleveland: World, 1959); Gabriel Kolko, *The Politics of War: The World and United States Foreign Policy, 1943–1945* (New York: Random House, 1968); and Thomas G. Paterson, *Soviet American Confrontation* (Baltimore: Johns Hopkins Press, 1973).

Evaluations of the Fleming-Alperovitz thesis, in which American anticommunism is blamed directly, may be found in Arthur Schlesinger, Jr., "The Origins of the Cold War," *Foreign Affairs*, October 1967, pp. 22–52; J. L. Richardson, "Cold War Revisionism: A Critique," *World Politics*, July 1972, pp. 579 ff.; and Spanier, "The Choices We Did Not Have: In Defense of Containment," in Charles Gati, ed., *Caging the Bear* (New York: Bobbs-Merrill, 1974), pp. 128 ff. The Gati book provides a discussion of Kennan's analysis and the policy of containment twenty-five years after the latter's anonymous article "The Sources of Soviet Conduct" in *Foreign Affairs*, July 1947, pp. 566–582, later republished in *American Diplomacy 1900–1950*, pp. 107–128. In that article Kennan had provided the Truman administration with a rationale for its containment policy. Finally, for an assessment of economic interpretations of American policy, see Tucker, *The Radical Left and American Foreign Policy* (Baltimore: Johns Hopkins Press, 1971). For an analysis that suggests either poor scholarship or deliberate distortion of the documents, see Robert J. Maddox, *The New Left and the Origins of the Cold War* (Princeton: Princeton University Press, 1973).

344 (A change in *American* behavior is thus seen as the remedy. If Americans abandoned their anticommunism, there would be no need for cold wars, interventions, or large military budgets. Instead, they could build a truly just society at home, a wiser and more moral goal.)

> The reluctance, or the inability, to face the humiliating facts of international life is as noticeable in America as it was in the Britain of 30 years ago (wrote an observer in the late 1960s)—at least among the young and the intellectuals. When they could no longer see their country as the noble, disinterested guardian on the ramparts of freedom, when the competitive pursuit of security could no longer be glamorized as a fight for the highest values, many sought refuge in the old illusion that one only has to recognize the beam in one's own eye to remove the splinter from that of one's opponent and thus live happily together forever after.[44]

(Such an attitude, which seeks to deny the reality of international struggle and suggests that it can be avoided, is not to be found among the characteristics of Soviet style.)

A CRITIQUE OF NATIONAL AND ELITE STYLES

Finally, there remains the basic question: Is there really such a thing as national style? How can we be sure that when a decision is made, it is the result of a national style? Can we even distinguish between the style of a single nation and those of several nations whose governments and political systems are similar? Robert Tucker spoke of pragmatism in policy making as Western, not just American; the British have long been proud of what they call their pragmatism in foreign affairs. George Kennan has always focused on the international behavior of democracies, not merely on the United States' crusading style. Fred Iklé, in comparing Western and Soviet negotiating techniques, notes certain distinctively Western features: letting the opponent determine the issues to be negotiated; being shy about making counterdemands; fear of offering unacceptable proposals; and forswearing the use of threats. Why? Because the Western leaders, experienced in compromise and conciliation at home, believe in meeting opponents halfway, in splitting the difference; not to do so is considered improper, and to make counterdemands or invoke threats seems immoral. Good will and a sincere commitment to settle are believed to be desirable—though not exploiting a particular threat may leave one's own interests unsatisfied. Reluctance to put forth an unacceptable demand will encourage the opponent, fortify its commitments, and narrow the parameters of the Western diplomatic position. In Berlin after 1958, the refusal to state counterdemands left only Soviet demands on the books, which meant that any compromise would have undermined the West's own position. Luckily, it was part of the Russian style to "ask for a whole loaf where they could get a half loaf—and end up with nothing".[45]

[44] J. H. Huizinga, "America's Lost Innocence," *The New York Times Magazine* (January 26, 1969), p. 82.

[45] Fred Iklé, *How Nations Negotiate* (New York: Harper & Row, 1964), pp. 238–253.

In Iklé's analysis of Western and Soviet diplomacy Western states' national styles tend to be lumped together whereas the Soviet style is treated as distinctive. When dealing with regimes characterized by a Marxist-Leninist perspective, we no longer in fact speak of how the communists do this or that; rather we speak of Soviet communists, Chinese communists, Yugoslav communists, and Rumanian communists in order to stress the fact that the perceptions of any set of communist leaders are infused with national attitudes. Yet can we really deny that certain American or British ways of perceiving and handling foreign-policy problems are uniquely national or that certain forms of behavior are common to most, if not all, communist elites?

A second problem is more obvious: Are we not really talking of the style of the policy makers, rather than of the nation? Policy is decided by a relatively few people on behalf of the nation; the people themselves do not make policy. At best, they have the opportunity to change their leaders every few years if they do not like the government's policies. Public opinion may also affect policy between elections, but by and large the public—in a democracy at least—reacts to decisions after they have been made and sets the outer limits within which the responsible officials make their decisions. Would it not, therefore, be analytically more useful to focus on the styles of these officials, as we did when we defined the Soviet style, rather than on broad national styles? Do the few who make policy share national preferences, attitudes, and ways of behaving? The difficulty of distinguishing an elite style from a national style is particularly apparent in the Soviet example, where it ought to be easier to separate the communist and national elements because of the narrow base and indoctrination of the Soviet elite.

Is Russian expansion due to Soviet or Russian influences? Is communism merely a tool of a long-standing, pre-Bolshevik expansionist tradition? Edward Crankshaw, a British observer of Russian affairs, argues that "Russia has been an expanding power since the foundation of the Muscovite state in the fourteenth century"[46] because of strategic, economic, and missionary factors. Like Louis Halle, Crankshaw suggests that Russia has been expansionist for essentially defensive reasons, because it is not protected as are England and the United States by oceans or as are Italy and Spain by mountain barriers. "The Russians voyaged across the [Russian] plain, much as Tudor seamen explored the oceans. It is hard to know where to stop. If the Muscovites themselves had not expanded outwards from their centre and deep into the plain, their neighbors would have done so in their place."[47] Russian leaders have thus become obsessed with security and have expanded along lines of least resistance to keep "the enemy at the gates" as far away as possible.[48] Economic reasons, especially the search for maritime outlets, plus visions of Moscow as the third Rome (the true heir to Christian leadership and exponent of the Christian faith after the fall of Constantinople), reinforced this expansionist tradition and even gave it a strong missionary or messianic flavor. Experience in the state system, geographical position, and strategic and economic considerations are all concrete. In contrast, ideology tends to be abstract and subject to many different,

---

[46] Edward Crankshaw, *Cracks in the Kremlin Wall* (New York: Viking, 1951), p. 58.

[47] *Ibid.*, p. 59.

[48] *Ibid.*, p. 60.

346   usually conflicting interpretations; indeed, the practical relevance of ideology to foreign-policy decisions is questionable. Is ideology not invoked more often to rationalize decisions than to influence them? What then, is Soviet in Soviet Russian foreign policy? What is Russian? What in American policy is American and what is unique to the policy-making elite? Indeed—if we wish to be even more empirical and careful in our analysis—we can ask what is unique to liberal policy makers like Truman and Kennedy as distinct from more conservative ones like Eisenhower and Nixon?

Third, does not the concept of national style suggest that characteristics are carried from one generation to the next? Common sense tells us that even if there is such a thing as national style, some of its characteristics will change over time. The Vietnam war, it has been suggested, was the product of a crusading style, but other critics have suggested that this costly tragedy may at least have had the beneficial result of sobering this country up, of changing its style so that in the future American policy makers will take longer and harder looks at American vital interests, will not define an adversary by ideology alone, but by who that adversary is, and the extent to which it threatens American interests. The American missionary style will, it is hoped, be tempered, and the United States, having finally been socialized into the state system, will behave more as other nations do. This point, of course, raises the question: What will be American about the United States' international conduct? Did Nixon and Kissingers' emphasis on the balance of power mean that the old national style has already been largely abandoned?

Elite style is also subject to change as perceptions change. Soviet commentators and ideologues have shown increasing awareness that the American government, rather than acting simply as an instrument of Wall Street, has a high degree of autonomy on foreign-policy issues.[49] The bourgeoisie may share common interests and attitudes, but it is divided over which foreign policy to pursue. The idea of a united and cohesive group of monopoly capitalists with a single policy, enacted on their behalf by an "executive committee," has been replaced by a focus on Washington, D.C., as at least semi-independent of Wall Street. And in Washington itself the government is now divided between different sets of policy makers with varying interests and points of view on the conduct of foreign policy. Instead of an organized "power elite," there is a pluralistic decision-making system. The Soviets view American policy makers as divided into two groups, reflecting a division within the bourgeoisie itself: the "realists" and the "madmen" or "maniacs."[50] The former wish to avoid a war, are cautious while seeking reduction of international tensions, and recognize American power and influence as limited; the latter prefer military solutions to international problems, are militantly anticommunist, and seek a *pax americana*. They also recognize such nonbourgeois groups as trade unions and churches as seeking to influence policy.

---

[49] William Zimmerman, *Soviet Perspectives on International Relations, 1956–67* (Princeton: Princeton University Press, 1969), pp. 214–218. For Kennan's own reassessment of Soviet foreign policy, see Gati, "Mr. X Revisited: An Interview with George Kennan" and "Mr. X Reassessed: The Meaning of Containment," *Caging the Bear*, pp. 27, 40.

[50] Zimmerman, *op. cit.*, pp. 221–225.

(By and large, then, American foreign policy, as conducted by the realists, is aimed not at destroying the Soviet Union and risking nuclear warfare but at preserving the state system and peaceful coexistence with Russia.) In terms of our own previous analysis of the changed nature of American-Russian relations, the leaders in Moscow view the contemporary pattern as a relationship incorporating both conflict *and* cooperation. Although the Soviets are still committed to the vision of a communist world, they appear to perceive it as more distant. In the early 1960s Khrushchev still believed that there would be significant advances toward that goal during the next two decades; within a few years his successors were stressing the several centuries that it had taken capitalism to supplant feudalism. In short, the leaders of the Soviet Communist party—like the leaders of the British Labour party after World War II—have become increasingly "socialized" by the state system. Indeed, "it is to structural changes in the Soviet Union's position in the international system that one must look, first of all, for an explanation of the evolution of Soviet perspectives on the international system."[51] As one of the two superpowers, the Soviet Union has increasingly acted as other great powers have always done—that is, it has shown a keener concern for its place in the existing system than for the conversion of this system into a new order. As it has become a "have" power, an equal of the United States, the Soviet Union's interest in managing the state system, in the survival of which it has acquired a vested interest, has risen. And this reason has been reinforced by nuclear weapons, which have made it necessary to think of "peaceful coexistence" in more than tactical terms.[52] Revolutionary ambitions have had to be adjusted to the realities of the existing system.

Fourth, these results of the confrontation between style and reality raise the question of how the outside observer can distinguish between national style and responses to the distribution of power in the state system. We noted earlier that, when Britain, France, and Germany collapsed after World War II, the United States emerged as the only power capable of counterbalancing the Soviet Union in Eurasia. Emerging bipolarity generated the containment policy. To be sure, the ability of American policy makers to mobilize popular support for this policy in terms of the traditional dichotomy between Old World and New World, authoritarianism and democracy, was very helpful in these circumstances. But can it be claimed that the United States would not have reacted as it did in the context of external bipolar pressures except for its national style?

This question in turn raises the fifth and final question about national style as an analytical tool: Is style, to the extent that it exists, to be defined by what policy makers say, by what they do, or by particular patterns of behavior that they and their predecessors have exhibited before? Does the United States really act according to its style, or does it merely verbalize in a certain way in order to disguise a policy

---

[51.] *Ibid.*, p. 282.

[52.] Risk taking in Soviet foreign policy from 1955 to 1966 has been analyzed by Michael P. Gehlen, *The Politics of Soviet Coexistence: Soviet Methods and Motives* (Bloomington: Indiana University Press, 1967), pp. 116–127; and Hannes Adomeit, *Soviet Risk-Taking and Crisis Behavior: From Confrontation to Coexistence* (Adelphi Paper 101; London: International Institute for Strategic Studies, 1973).

348 dictated pretty much by "power politics" and first-level considerations? When Secretary of State John Foster Dulles spoke of a "moral crusade against communism," was he really sincere, or was he trying to mobilize congressional and public opinion according to a rather old but successful formula? When presidential candidate Carter spoke of replacing balance-of-power politics with "world-order politics," was he suggesting a different kind of foreign policy or merely setting himself and the Democrats off from the Republican administration and Secretary of State Kissinger's "realist" philosophy? Is Russia's "adversary partnership" with the United States consistent with its ideological outlook, or is ideology invoked merely to justify a policy dictated by the necessity of coexistence in a nuclear state system? The Peking leaders certainly left no doubt that they believe the Soviet Union has betrayed the faith in establishing its relationship with the United States. But, then, have not the Chinese done the same thing because of typical balance-of-power calculations?

THE CLASH OF SYSTEMIC SOCIALIZATION AND STYLE

Despite all the analytical problems inherent in the concept of style, its impact on foreign policy is difficult to deny altogether. Indeed, one way of interpreting a state's foreign policy is as the product of the interactions and tensions between systemically and stylistically influenced behavior. As suggested for both the Soviet Union and the United States, the system has been a moderating or restraining factor. It has tended to socialize both states, regardless of their internal structures. The Soviet Union therefore finds itself today in a paradoxical position. As a *communist* state, it has increasingly faced situations that, from the point of view of a *national* state, have been counterproductive.[53] It is clear that the expansion of communism to states that the Soviets did not control was not necessarily a blessing. To have an ally like China was to need no enemies. It was the government in Peking, not those in Washington, London, and Bonn, that actually claimed Russian territory. It was Mao who challenged Soviet leadership of the communist movement and called for the overthrow of Soviet rulers.

An outside observer must surely ask himself what the men in the Kremlin perhaps dare not ask themselves: Does the Soviet Union really want a communist world? Such a world would encompass not only such troublesome states as Yugoslavia and China but also other states not likely to do Soviet bidding. The Communist parties in Italy and France have declared publicly that, if they receive a sufficient popular vote and become members of coalition governments, their countries will remain members of the Common Market and the North Atlantic Treaty Organization (NATO)—as well as faithful to their democratic and pluralistic traditions with full respect for individual civil and political rights. These countries

---

[53.] This point is made by Ulam, "Communist Doctrine and Soviet Diplomacy: Some Observations," *International Negotiation* (testimony before the Jackson Subcommittee on National Security and International Operations of the Committee on Government Operations, United States Senate; Washington, D.C.: Government Printing Office, 1970), pp. 4–6.

could be troublesome to the Soviets if their communism, too, becomes nationally oriented. But, above all, does Soviet Russia want to see the establishment of a communist United States? If national style counts at all, this country would then seek to be the leading communist state in the world. After all, it has long considered itself "God's country" and it would certainly seek to be number one; regardless of ideology, it would have the economic clout to achieve this status. And, if elite style has meaning, American Communist party leadership, even if it were half as ruthless, tough, and assertive as that in Russia, would drive very hard bargains with "fraternal Russia," whether the issue was arms control, food, trade, or credits. Moscow's leaders might then have good grounds for screaming about "imperialist" Washington; they would soon adopt and apply to the United States China's favorite phrase for denouncing its northern neighbor—"social imperialism" (social because it is a socialist state and imperialism because it is behaving just as a capitalist one does).

Increasingly, Russia has become two-faced. On one hand, it has continued to consider itself an enemy of capitalism, seeking the transformation of what it sees as the American-dominated state system to a communist one. Moscow's leaders have not yet surrendered the idea that, until that point is reached, the irreconcilable struggle with capitalism will go on. They thus approve of "peaceful coexistence," which means that they wish to avoid a nuclear war, and reject "ideological coexistence," which means that they do not want reconciliation and an end to competition with the Western states, expecially the leading Western power. Adam Ulam has emphasized that the Soviet Union cannot completely abandon this rivalry.

> Political and psychological exigencies compel the Soviet regime to persist in [its] official and unrealistic view of the world: Communist China, while temporarily hostile, cannot in the long run have interests antagonistic to the USSR, whereas the United States, while not an immediate threat to Russia, must be considered a constant danger because of the nature of her system. [The reason is] the psychological inability of the Soviet leaders to admit to their people, perhaps even to themselves, the true dimensions and dangers of the Chinese problem. To do so would be to reveal how obsolete are the premises of Communism in today's world, to acknowledge unmistakably that the main danger to the security of the USSR comes not from the capitalists but from the growing power of a fellow Communist state. This acknowledgement, in turn, *would challenge the domestic rationale of the Communist regime, the whole structure of the Soviet power, the position of the ruling elite*—all this would be put in jeopardy.[54]

On the other hand, the Soviet Union, fearful of nuclear war and increasingly a "have" nation with a stake in the system and an interest in joining in comanagement of that system, behaved in the 1970s increasingly as any great power would have done. Of course, the American-Soviet rivalry was not about to end and be replaced by harmonious relations. For, as the state-system level of analysis has suggested, great powers, given their sense of insecurity and their desire to enhance their influence, remain the primary actors on the international stage. Russia, even if it were a nonrevolutionary state, would continue to be one of the

---

[54.] *Ibid.*, pp. 3–4 (emphasis added).

350   world's two greatest powers, with ambitions and interests of its own which are bound to clash in many areas and on many issues with those of the United States. Furthermore, over the last decade, Soviet strategic and conventional power has grown spectacularly. This is symbolized by a surface fleet that can be moved into the Mediterranean, the Red Sea, and the Indian Ocean—from which long-range naval patrols can be extended beyond Singapore—and it has shown "the flag" in the Caribbean and in the Gulf of Mexico.

Three questions are raised by this vast increase in Soviet power and the emergence of the Soviet Union as a global power able for the first time to project its military forces anywhere in the world. First, will the Soviet Union, with its immense new strategic strength, make greater demands and seek to use its power to realize more political dividends—as Khrushchev sought to do by exploiting a still nonexistent nuclear missile might in the late 1950s and early 1960s? Will Soviet leaders not become bolder in their policies and take greater risks, feeling more assured of the nation's capacity to face down the United States? Second, will such assertiveness and risk taking—as well as the ability to limit American options in local crises—be enhanced by the ability to extend conventional power across the oceans to almost any area of the world? Communist Russia, like czarist Russia, has until the 1970s basically been a Eurasian land power; the possibilities of its expansion have been limited largely to areas bordering on its frontiers. Even as one of the two superpowers to emerge from World War II, Russia failed to assert its claim to administer one of Italy's former colonies in North Africa; and, even as a nuclear superpower, it failed in the early 1960s to hold its advance position in Cuba or to consolidate its influence in the Congo or Ghana: Russia remained land-locked. But today with a sizable navy and air-lift capability, it has the means to expand Russian influence beyond Eurasia.

The third question is whether or not a siege mentality is useful to a regime seeking to preserve its domestic structure in the face of challenges from artists and intellectuals, the questioning attitude of many youths, and increasing nationalism among important Soviet minorities. By equating even the tolerance of dissent, as in Czechoslovakia, with a threat to the survival of the communist regime, foreign adversaries provide the regime with the justification that it needs for imposing strict censorship and persecuting nonconformists. External tension and enemies provide justification for the continued monopoly of power by the Communist party and insistence on ideological orthodoxy. Détente, because it may threaten to weaken the party's domestic position, has been accompanied by greater internal controls, watchfulness, and emphasis on ideological faithfulness and conservatism. Will the decreasing attraction of Communist ideology and the Soviet political system not, therefore, tempt Soviet leaders to follow the advice of Shakespeare's Henry V "to busy giddy minds with foreign quarrels" at a time of growing military strength?"

[55.] In the final analysis, here as in subsequent chapters, the questions we ask and the interpretations of the behavior of political systems we present depend on our individual view of these systems. For a representation and analysis of the ways in which leading American scholars of the Soviet Union have interpreted Russian behavior—as "the great beast," "the mellowing tiger," or "the neurotic bear"—see William Welch, *American Images of Soviet Foreign Policy* (New Haven; Yale University Press, 1970); and Jan F. Triska, "Soviet Foreign Policy Studies and Foreign Policy Models," *World Politics*, July 1971, pp. 704 ff.

At a time when Americans' attitude toward foreign involvements and commitments is weary as well as wary, such a course must be appealing. Before 1914 the declining legitimacy of the czarist regime led it to resort to nationalist appeals and a risky foreign policy to mobilize popular support; the disintegration of Austria-Hungary led its imperial government to do the same thing, including an attempt to crush Serbia, a Slavic state that Russia felt compelled to protect. Russia and Austria-Hungary precipitated World War I. Will the present Soviet leaders, needing foreign enemies, feel increasingly compelled to mobilize popular support by means of foreign successes and thus resort to ever riskier policies to gain such successes?[56]

The state system also raises a key question for American foreign policy, which has in the past been characterized by a crusading style. The United States, it has been argued, is essentially an inward-oriented society that has concentrated on domestic affairs and welfare issues and has considered foreign policy burdensome and distracting. Therefore, in order to mobilize public support and to unify the country for external ventures, the struggle for power and security endemic in the state system has had to be disguised as a struggle for realization of the highest values. Because, from the beginning of its existence, the United States has felt itself to be a post-European society—a shining example of democracy, freedom, and social justice for the Old World—anticommunism has been an obvious means of mobilizing congressional and public support for postwar policy. (*The United States could thus practice "power politics" while disguising it as "ideological politics."*[57]) Power politics requires ideological justification in a nation that has always viewed power as evil and corrupting. Domestically, power has been legitimated by the democratic purposes for which it has been used, and by the same token externally it has been justified as making the world safe for democracy. After 1945 anticommunism did not define American foreign-policy objectives; rather, American democracy needed anticommunism as a tool for conducting traditional foreign policy.

In the bipolar world, power politics was easy to moralize precisely because bipolarity involved both power and values. Globalism, which made sense as long as any communist expansion meant an addition to Soviet strength, could thus be explained in terms very understandable to Americans—democracy versus dictatorship. It is one thing, however, to "fight communism" as long as there is only one communism, and another to fight it once communism was a many-splintered thing. Which communism did the country "fight"? Are all communist states enemies *because* they are communist? Or does the United States now have to distinguish among them and determine which are hostile, friendly, or neutral and therefore which may or may not pose threats to American interests? What changes in the distribution of power can the United States safely allow in these new circumstances, and where and against whom must it still draw lines? Answers to these questions are more difficult than they were during the simple days of bipolarity because each situation confronts policymakers with different alternatives, thus arousing debate, perhaps intense controversy, and social division within the United States. In such

---

[56] J. Hackett *et al.*, *The Third World War: August 1985* (New York: Macmillan, 1978), pose a similar problem in relation to a possible World War III.

[57] Huizinga, *op. cit.*, offers a perceptive analysis of the problems confronting the United States once it could no longer disguise its "power politics."

352   debates, anticommunism is no longer particularly useful as a means of eliciting popular support and uniting the nation.

American policy makers thus confront a double dilemma. First, in the absence of anticommunism or some other missionary ideal, will the United States "dirty" its hands by playing power politics, straight and unadorned? Or will it, having become disillusioned by the Vietnam war and disenchanted with a world in which the forces of good and evil are no longer in simple confrontation, vacillate between moral crusading and moralistic isolation?[58] When power politics was synonymous with ideological politics, it was easy to be a leader and to organize various coalitions whose basic task was to push back when pushed. But can a nation that his historically condemned power politics adapt its outlook and style, once it is no longer possible to justify foreign policy in terms of an ideological crusade? Is it possible to "play the game by no other name"? The pressures for long-range continuing involvement show no sign of slackening. New issues, ranging from South African race problems to nuclear proliferation and threats to the oil supplies from the Persian Gulf to crowd the international agenda and pull the United States ever deeper into the international system. However powerful domestic tendencies to withdraw from the world and however great the desire to shift attention and resources to domestic problems, the world will not leave the United States alone. But if the American government continues to believe it important for this country to play a major role in the world, will it not have to portray the Soviet Union as evil, as a power whose promises and words cannot be trusted and with whom true détente is impossible?

The second part of the dilemma arises from the first part. Even if a missionary goal and all the proper slogans to arouse the nation could be found, would they in fact unify a people largely disillusioned by the Vietnam war and other revelations of American misdeeds, or would they divide the population even more deeply? Indeed, however desirable it may be to mobilize the country, crusading zeal has hardly been an undisguised blessing in the past. Its "highs" have time and time again led the nation into trouble by stimulating demands for unconditional surrender, which have made it more difficult to establish postwar balances of power or by overreacting to external threats, overextending commitments and power, and refusing to recognize or negotiate with adversaries that seem evil.

And the postwar (including Cold-War) "lows," following such excessive zeal, have repeatedly led to psychological demobilization, arising either from plain weariness or from cynicism about a world that clearly does not wish to be morally saved or improved by the United States. Massive military demobilization, as after World War II; disillusionment about the benefits of diplomacy as a means of solving the world's problems once the great expectations built up by summit conferences and periods of détente have not been quickly realized; reluctance to deal with a globe obviously not yet good enough for the United States since it resists America's

---

[58.] See Donald R. Lesh, A *Nation Observed* (New York: Potomac, 1974), for a series of Gallup polls on American attitudes toward foreign affairs, especially the increase of isolationalist attitudes in the early 1970s.

proclaimed noble intentions (or, as the post-Vietnam version would have it, an America so corrupted by "power politics" and so hypocritical about its purposes that it is no longer good enough to "save the world") have rendered the nation incapable of dealing in timely and effective fashion with the genuine security problems that confront it.

In addition, missionary zeal is unlikely to be helpful in the protracted multilateral negotiations required by the new socioeconomic agenda. Zeal is especially useful as a spur in arousing the country for a crusade against an obvious foe, in encouraging to military action against the enemy, as distinct from political negotiations. But in dealing with resources, food, population, and environmental issues involving many countries including allies and friends, zeal can be only divisive and politically counterproductive.

If a new missionary basis for American foreign policy is neither possible nor particularly desirable, on what basis then can the United States conduct its foreign policy? A balance of power? The Nixon administration apparently thought so. Even though, in his career as congressman, senator, and vice-president, the president had had a long record of staunch anticommunism, shared the belief in the "illusion of American omnipotence," and displayed an inflexible moralism which tended to reject having anything to do with communists lest one be tainted with an "un-American" virus, he and Kissinger, a German-born Jewish immigrant and exponent of "realism" in international politics, rejected the moralistic American justification for participation in foreign affairs.

International politics was not in their view a fight between the good and bad sides. All states, communist as well as noncommunist, have the right to exist and to pursue legitimate interests and aspirations. Crusading, which was based on the assumption that differences of interests represented a conflict of virtue and evil, was rejected. It therefore seemed better to learn to live with other states, to defend American interests if encroached upon, and to attempt to resolve differences and build on shared interests. Differences would not necessarily be easily or quickly resolved. Conflicting views based on different definitions of national interests are not normally easily reconciled. But, unlike conflicts of moral principles, differences of interest are reconcilable. Summit conferences are important as part of the effort to bridge such differences, but a single summit meeting is unlikely to solve all problems; to raise false hopes that it will do so produces cynicism and disillusionment that, in turn, endanger future negotiations. Furthermore, although good personal relations among national leaders may smooth the diplomatic process, they are no substitute for hard bargaining; accords basically reflect the ratio of power among nations.

Can the United States deal with a Soviet dictatorship whose values and practices are abhorrent? The answer is that the most the United States can expect is to influence Russia to behave responsibly and moderately in foreign policy. The United States is not omnipotent, and it cannot therefore demand the transformation of another nation's domestic structure; a nation's domestic affairs are its own business. To make agreements dependent upon internal reforms in the Soviet Union is counterproductive and raises tensions. American demands will be resisted, which

354   will jeopardize accords on international issues that might otherwise have been resolved. (The United States must abandon its habit of attempting to democratize its adversaries.) Negotiating with a communist regime like that of the Soviet Union is not a matter of morality, requiring internal purification before discussions and agreements. It is a matter of dealing with a powerful state with which the United States must discuss issues if peace is to be preserved. If one needs groceries one does not require the grocer first to reform his character; as long as he is honest in his business dealings, does it matter how he behaves in his personal life?

Internationally, especially in the nuclear age, is maintaining peace not itself a moral goal, even though it demands cooperation with a power like Russia? Peace can be kept only through a balance of power, which also, of course, protects the democratic nations. Within the parameters of such a balance, however, it is necessary to try to accommodate the legitimate needs of the adversary while opposing its expansionist aims and aggressive behavior. Power neutralizes power, but satisfying the interests of another great power is more likely to produce acceptance of the international system. No state can be completely satisfied, but each can be relatively satisfied.

Still, the very fact that, when the Carter administration took office, this logic was already widely under attack suggests that the American style, like the Soviet elite style, had not yet been thoroughly adapted to the state system. How can the United States pursue "just" a balance of power? Does it not stand for something more? Can it forsake its heritage and keep quiet about other countries' domestic affairs—specifically their violations of "human rights"—in order to get along with them internationally? Even if it were possible to conduct American foreign policy on the basis of a strict balance-of-power logic, the question would remain whether or not that would be desirable for American democracy. Alastair Buchan, a noted English observer, has argued that "it would be a sorry world and one that risked alienating not only the lesser powers but our own younger generation as well if they were asked to believe that a balance of power is the highest political achievement of which the new great powers are capable."[59] The tension between foreign policy as a means of influencing other states' behavior and as a register of virtuous attitudes thus remains.

---

[59] Alastair Buchan, *Power and Equilibrium in the 1970's* (New York: Holt, Rinehart and Winston, 1973), p. 111.

The Less-Developed Countries: The Primacy of Domestic Concerns

14

FOREIGN POLICY AS THE CONTINUATION OF DOMESTIC POLITICS

During the Cold-War years, the term "third world" was used to describe the former colonial, mostly non-Western, largely nonwhite, less-developed countries (LDCs). These nations did not, of course, constitute the unitary bloc implied by the label. There was considerable diversity among them: in history and experience, in religion and culture, in population and resources, and in ideology and political and economic systems. Some nations were more developed than others. Some had very large populations, whereas many had small populations. Some possessed sizable resources; others were not well endowed. Nevertheless, in their anticolonialism and determination to modernize and to fulfill the "revolution of rising expectations," they were distinct from the first, or Western industrial, world, and the second or Soviet-led communist, world. In their foreign policies, the third-world states have generally preferred nonalignment.

Since the opening of détente in the early 1970s, there has been increasing emphasis on the conflict between the first and third worlds, usually called the North-South conflict. This emphasis results from the greater frustration among the LDCs (except for the oil producers) over the continued division of the world between rich and poor nations. What unites the poor nations is a set of common attitudes: anger against the Western industrial nations and a sense that the LDCs do not control their own destinies. The embargo of the Oil Producing and Exporting Countries (OPEC) in 1973 against the United States and the quadrupling of oil

355

356 prices dramatically united the LDCs, even though the higher oil prices hurt most of them more than the Western industrial nations. But all have supported OPEC because, for the first time, they have sensed that the industrial West is vulnerable and can be pressured by means of producer cartels. It is their firm belief that they are the victims of the Western-dominated international economic system and that they must stand together to regain control over their fates that has led the third-world nations to move from nonalignment closer to confrontation with the West. The division between rich and poor nations may be somewhat oversimplified; in fact, a continuum between very rich and very poor is a more accurate image. But while the distance between the extremes is growing, that between the developed countries and the top level of the LDCs (those with more than $600 per capita annual income) is narrowing.(Nevertheless, nonalignment has shifted to alignment against the West.)

(The desire to modernize largely molds the LDCs' foreign policy and perceptions of the world. The foreign policies of the newer nations reflect their preoccupation with nation building. It has been said that, for a "new state, foreign policy is domestic policy pursued by other means; it is domestic policy carried on beyond the boundaries of the state."[1])

DEPRIVATION, DESPERATION, AND DEGRADATION

The right to national self-determination, conceived in the West but denied by Western industrial powers to their overseas territories, became a key issue after World War II. Throughout Asia and Africa former colonies have sought national independence and most have gained it.(The common denominator of this global nationalist revolution has been a fundamental urge to be "free from" the control of former colonial powers. From the beginning, colonialism contained the seeds of its own destruction. Humiliation and resentment of foreign domination stirred "reactive nationalism," which asserted itself in terms of the very values by which the Westerners justified their rule—national self-determination, dignity, and equality. A nation must be master of its own destiny; no one must ever dominate it again or treat it condescendingly.)

(Accompanying this drive for national independence has been the determination to achieve a higher standard of living and to abolish the abject poverty and misery of past centuries.)In the economically underdeveloped countries, people have continued to live on subsistence agriculture because they have not possessed modern tools—factories, machinery, dams, and so forth—with which to increase productivity. Even more important, they have lacked the cultural values, social structure, and political order necessary for industrialization. Less-developed nations

---

[1] Robert C. Good, "Changing Patterns of African International Relations," *American Political Science Review*, September 1964, p. 638.

do not necessarily lack natural resources, however. In that sense they can be divided between those that possess plentiful supplies of resources (like the oil states) and those fourth-world countries that either control less desirable raw materials or control very little of nature's wealth at all. Many of the latter are, like the industrialized countries, victims of higher oil prices. (But the hallmark of an LDC is its inability to attain *continued* economic growth.) The dividing line between developed and less-developed societies is usually pegged at an average annual income per person of $500. For the 70 percent of the world's population living in the new nations, the per capita income figure is far lower—less than $280 a year, or 77 cents a day.

In contrast, the annual average per capita incomes in western Europe, Japan, and the United States were astronomical by the end of 1978. The American figure stood at $7,572, or $20.74 a day (West Germany was even higher). Furthermore, these incomes have been constantly rising while those in the LDCs, with the exception of the OPEC countries, have been at a virtual standstill. The industrial West has had the capital for further growth; the new nations have suffered from lack of capital. (But the dividing line between developed and underdeveloped countries is not purely economic; it is also reflected in differences in infant mortality, life expectancy, general health, availability of housing and consumer goods (especially, bathing facilities and living space), calorie intake per person, and sources of energy.)

For the affluent middle-class American who has never known what it is to be poor—and who spends a minimum of $100 a year on recreation and about $500 on tobacco and food—it is impossible to conceive of the life led by a typical family in a developing nation. In the early 1960s Robert Heilbroner graphically conveyed what such an existence would mean to an American suburban family then living on a $9,000–$10,000 a year:

> We begin by invading the house of our imaginary American family to strip it of its furniture. Everything goes: beds, chairs, tables, television set, lamps. We leave the family with a few old blankets, a kitchen table, a wooden chair. Along with the bureaus go the clothes. Each member of the family may keep in his "wardrobe" his oldest suit or dress, a shirt or blouse. We will permit a pair of shoes to the head of the family, but none for the wife or the children.

> We move into the kitchen. The appliances have already been taken out, as we turn to the cupboards and larder. The box of matches may stay, a small bag of flour, some sugar and salt. A few moldy potatoes, already in the garbage can, must be hastily rescued, for they will provide much of tonight's meal. We will leave a handful of onions, and a dish of dried beans. All the rest we take away: the meat, the fresh vegetables, the canned goods, the crackers, the candy.

> Now we have stripped the house: the bathroom has been dismantled, the running water shut off, the electric wires taken out. Next we take away the house. The family can move to the toolshed. It is crowded, but much better than the situation in Hong Kong, where (a United Nations report tells us) "it is not

uncommon for a family of four or more to live in a bedspace, that is, on a bunk bed and the space it occupies—sometimes in two or three tiers—their only privacy provided by curtains."

But we have only begun. All the other houses in the neighborhood have also been removed; our suburb has become a shantytown. Still, our family is fortunate to have a shelter; 250,000 people in Calcutta have none at all and simply live in the streets. Our family is now about on a par with the city of Cali, Colombia, where, an official of the World Bank writes, "on one hillside alone, the slum population is estimated at 40,000 —without water, sanitation, or electric lights. And not all the poor of Cali are as fortunate as that. Others have built their shacks near the city on land which lies beneath the flood mark. To these people, the immediate environment is the open sewer of the city, a sewer which flows through their huts when the river rises."

And still we have not reduced our American family to the level at which life is lived in the greatest part of the globe. Communication must go next. No more newspapers, magazines, books—not that they are missed, since we must take away our family's literacy as well. Instead, in our shantytown we will allow one radio. In India the national average of radio ownership is one per 250 people, but since the majority of radios is owned by city dwellers, our allowance is fairly generous.

Now government services must go. No more postman, no more fireman. There is a school, but it is three miles away and consists of two classrooms. They are not too overcrowded since only half the children in the neighborhood go to school. There are, of course, no hospitals or doctors nearby. The nearest clinic is ten miles away and is tended by a midwife. It can be reached by bicycle, provided that the family has a bicycle, which is unlikely. Or one can go by bus—not always inside, but there is usually room on top.

Finally, money. We will allow our family a cash hoard of five dollars. This will prevent our breadwinner from experiencing the tragedy of an Iranian peasant who went blind because he could not raise the $3.94 which he mistakenly thought he needed to secure admission to a hospital where he could have been cured.

Meanwhile the head of our family must earn his keep. As a peasant cultivator with three acres to tend, he may raise the equivalent of $100 to $300 worth of crops a year. If he is a tenant farmer, which is more than likely, a third or so of his crop will go to his landlord, and probably another 10 percent to the local money lender. But there will be enough to eat. Or almost enough. The human body requires an input of at least 2,000 calories to replenish the energy consumed by its living cells. If our displaced American fares no better than an Indian peasant, he will average a replenishment of no more than 1,700–1,900 calories. His body, like any insufficiently fueled machine, will run down. That is one reason why life expectancy at birth in India today averages less than forty years.

But the children may help. If they are fortunate, they may find work and thus earn some cash to supplement the family's income. For example, they may be employed as are children in Hyderbad, Pakistan, sealing the ends of bangles over a small kerosene flame, a simple task which can be done at home. To be sure the pay is small: eight annas—about ten cents—for sealing bangles. That is, eight annas per gross of bangles. And if they cannot find work? Well, they can scavenge, as do the children of Iran who in times of hunger search for the undigested oats in the droppings of horses.[2]

It is not surprising that, as a former Pakistan finance minister once said, for the children who survive the age of five years in the underdeveloped countries, life is a matter of "deprivation, desperation, and degradation. It is an intense, but mercifully a short struggle, as their life expectancy is no more than thirty years."

THE WESTERNIZATION OF THE INTELLIGENTSIA

(Although the developing countries generally tend to blame Western capitalism for these conditions, the role played by the Western industrial nations in forging their nationhood cannot be ignored. Usually it has been "territorialization" by the colonial powers that has defined the present frontiers of these nations. The Western powers have drawn arbitrary lines on the map, often straight through tribal or ethnic boundaries, and then imposed single administrative and legal structures upon the resulting territories. All who lived within a particular structure were treated as if they belonged to a single nation.) A graphic example of the impact of such actions on the new nations is provided by Indonesia. When Indonesia received its freedom, it did not receive the territory of Dutch New Guinea, or West Irian. The Dutch claimed that the people of New Guinea were ethnically, racially, and culturally distinct from the Indonesians. Nevertheless, Indonesia persisted until, in 1963, it acquired West Irian. The territory had been part of the old Dutch East Indies empire, and Indonesia defined its territorial limits by the former imperial frontiers. Similarly, India, in its quarrel with China over precisely where the Sino-Indian boundary lies in the Himalayas, has defined its claim by the line drawn by British colonizers.

(Another by-product of colonialism has been the construction of harbors, roads, railroads, airports, telephone and telegraph lines, and factories, as well as the development of natural resources. These facilities have provided what economists call the infrastructure, or capital overhead—the prerequisite for any major industrialization.[3]) To be sure, Europeans did not undertake such projects for the

---

[2.] Robert L. Heilbroner, *The Great Ascent* (New York: Harper, 1963), pp. 23–26. Used by permission of the publisher and A.D. Peters & Co.

[3.] The disruption of traditional colonial society by Western industrial nations' economic behavior is analyzed in Max F. Millikan and Donald L. M. Blackmer, eds., *The Emerging Nations* (Boston: Little, Brown, 1961), pp. 3–17; and Immanuel Wallerstein, *Africa: The Politics of Independence* (New York: Vintage, 1961), pp. 29–43.

360   benefit of the natives. The roads and railroads were to carry resources or crops from the interior to the harbors; they were also used for troop movements to quell uprisings and riots. Nevertheless, their impact upon the traditional native economy and society was disruptive. The traditional patterns of life and expectations of the vast majority of peasants who had migrated from the land were altered in the cities. European-built centers of government, business, and communications offered the peasants who came there to work a new way of life and new values. Urban life provided the "demonstration effect."[4] The Europeans lived better and longer. Why, the natives wondered, could they not live as well and as long? They could hardly avoid awareness of the technical and scientific knowledge, tools, and skills that had given the Europeans their higher material standards, as well as their power. Why, the natives asked themselves, could they not learn these secrets? One point was especially noteworthy: Europeans believed that life could be improved here on earth and that poverty need not be accepted as one's fate.

(The urge to transform backward societies into modern societies thus began with the European introduction of urbanization, industry, wage-labor forces, and exchange economies. But the most significant contribution of Western colonialism was education of the social groups determined to lead their shackled nations into freedom and modernity.)A relatively small and youthful group, this nationalist intelligentsia produced the leadership of revolutionary movements in the under-developed countries. Its members were doctors, journalists, civil servants, lawyers, and so forth; what they had in common was their "Westernization." Educated in Europe or the United States—or in Western schools in their own countries—they had learned Western ways: language, dress, and conduct. Even more significant, in the course of their professional training they had learned to think in character-istically Western rational and secular terms. This "scientific" and "material" pattern of thought has revolutionary implications; for the LDCs' intelligentsias, it provided an escape from the traditions, customs, and privileges that had held their societies in the tight grip of economic, social, and political backwardness.(Materialism, with its simple but powerful message that human beings can be the masters of their own destinies, was exhilarating, a promise of intellectual liberation from religious su-perstition; it substituted rationalism for obsolete traditions and institutions. It had been the absence of just such a material attitude that had been responsible for these nations' economic underdevelopment.)

(Education, then, was the chief means by which Western political and social thought was diffused to non-Western peoples.) As one political analyst has observed, "The future will look back upon the overseas imperialism of recent centuries, less in terms of its sins of oppression, exploitation, and discrimination, than as the instrument by which the spiritual, scientific, and material revolution which began in Western Europe with the Renaissance was spread to the rest of the world."[5] It was this Westernization that had transformed members of the intelli-

---

[4] Barbara Ward, *The Rich Nations and the Poor Nations* (New York: Norton, 1962), p. 54.

[5] Rupert Emerson, *From Empire to Nation* (Cambridge, Mass.: Harvard University Press, 1960), p. 6.

gentsia into leaders of the nationalist and modernist movements of their countries.[6]

But, as intensely aware as the first generation of leaders and their successors were of the underdeveloped condition of their countries and as determined as they have been to initiate development, they have faced almost insuperable obstacles to the necessary economic "takeoff" and self-sustaining economic growth. Lack of national cohesion, far too rapidly growing populations, dearth of capital, inability to feed their people, and traditional social structures and values all have impeded the modernization of their societies, with grave foreign-policy implications.

THE ABSENCE OF NATIONAL UNITY

The Westernized intellectuals have become rulers of new nations, but few of their subjects share their nationalism. Concepts of nation, of national loyalty, of national governments making decisions for the benefit of the entire community, and of national laws and regulations taking precedence over local rules and tradition are new and strange to most of the peoples of the less developed areas. The first requirement of leaders of the new nations has been to construct the very nations in whose names they have revolted against colonial domination. They must be "nation builders." The masses' lives have been rooted in smaller communities, and their first loyalties are to tribes, regions, or religious, racial, or linguistic groups.[7] Loyalties are parochial, and attitudes are particularistic. They stand as formidable barriers to the formation of national consciousness and devotion to national symbols and may, in fact, reach such intensity as to cause civil war. Men from other regions are regarded not as fellow nationals but as "strangers," "foreigners," "outsiders." Disunity, rather than unity, is the spirit of most new nations. The communities created by the colonial powers may have become "national" in the sense that the people living in them have rid themselves of foreign rulers. But their common

---

[6.] "The term 'intelligentsia' [is thus] used to denote specifically those intellectuals who are experiencing internal conflict between allegiance to traditional cultures and the influence of the modern West. Within these terms of reference it is not the amount of knowledge or education that determines membership in the intelligentsia. . . . No man, no matter how learned, is classified as a member of the intelligentsia if he has retained his identify with his national background. As long as he remains integrated in his society and accepts the values of that society as his own, he is likely to remain essentially a conservative without that revolutionary spark which . . . would class him as a member of the intelligentsia. If, on the other hand, he is an intellectual who has felt the impact of Western civilization and has been drawn into the vortex of conflicting ideas, he enters the ranks of the intelligentsia. . . . Within the intelligentsia, however, rebelliousness is a common characteristic. Beset with doubts about traditional cultural values, its members have felt a driving need to search for something new." Klaus Mehnert, "The Social and Political Role of the Intelligentsia in the New Countries," in Kurt London, ed., *New Nations in a Divided World* (New York: Holt, Rinehart and Winston, 1964), pp. 121–122.

[7.] See particularly Emerson, *op. cit.*, pp. 89–187, 295–359; Clifford Geertz, "The Integrative Revolution," in Geertz, ed., *Old Societies and New States* (New York: Free Press, 1963), pp. 105–157; and Walter Connor, "Nation-Building or Nation-Destroying?" *World Politics*, April 1972, pp. 319 ff.

362 resentment and aspiration to be free has not developed into shared allegiance to nations with artificial frontiers previously drawn by Europeans.)

(Integrating diverse masses into a new nation, forming a national consensus, is therefore crucial. Race is one element impeding this "integrative revolution.") For example, many of the countries of southeast Asia, like Thailand, Malaya, and Singapore, contain numerous and sizable minority groups, chief among them the overseas Chinese. Almost everywhere in Southeast Asia the Chinese function as middlemen. They are distributors of consumer goods, bankers, investors, shopkeepers. And, while dominating southeast Asian economic life, they have retained their language and customs, tending to isolate themselves; they remain foreigners in the nations where they live. But centuries of Chinese invasion and conquest have left a residue of suspicion that is only intensified by this cultural separatism. The result is fear, jealousy, discrimination, accusations of "alien exploitation," and occasionally (as after the abortive Indonesian Communist party coup in 1965) the slaughter of the Chinese population. Another example is the cruel expulsion of the Chinese population from Vietnam in the late 1970s. The majority were forced out on unsafe boats after most of their money had been taken from them. Many drowned on the high seas; most of these "boat people" found refuge in other southeast Asian countries. Vietnam's anti-Chinese sentiment was one of the factors contributing to the short Vietnamese-Chinese war in 1979.

(There are also religious animosities.)When these spark religious wars and lead to massive dislocation of millions and slaughter of hundreds of thousands, they seem incomprehensible—at least to Westerners who have long since forgotten the Thirty Years' War. When India gained its independence, it was partitioned into Hindu India and Muslim Pakistan because the Muslim minority wanted its own nation. The division was accompanied by a great bloodbath. Over half a million people died.[8] Religious divisions do not, of course, have to be disastrous. But internal religious differences have hampered "nation building" in such nations as Lebanon and Burma. In Nigeria the religious differences between the Muslim Hausas and the Christian Ibos have fueled conflict that also reflects tribal, regional, and economic divisions.

(Regional differences also tend to be divisive, particularly when they are accompanied by uneven distribution of resources and wealth) An example is Indonesia, a nation of islands; the main islands are Java (on which the capital, Jakarta, is located), Sumatra, the Celebes, most of Borneo, and about half of New Guinea. Sumatra is the source of Indonesia's oil and rubber wealth, and the Sumatrans have little use for the Javanese, whom they believe they are subsidizing. The inhabitants of the Celebes, on the other hand, are suspicious of both the Javanese and the Sumatrans. Finally, the people of West Irian have little, if anything, in common with the people of the other islands. In Indonesia, as well as in new African countries like Zaïre and Nigeria,("Regionalism is understandable because ethnic loyalties can usually find expression in geographical terms. Inevitably, some regions

---

[8] Michael Brecher, *Nehru: A Political Biography* (New York: Oxford University Press, 1959), pp. 362–363.

will be richer than others, and if the ethnic claim to power combines with relative wealth, the case for secession is strong."[9])

As if these three factors contributing to disunity were not sufficient, there is yet(a fourth—tribalism.) Particularly in Africa,(the tribe is still the psychological, economic, and political touchstone for many, for it is the social organization closest and most familiar to them.) The colonial powers— particularly Britain, which ruled its colonies "indirectly" (through traditional chiefs)—helped to preserve this tribalism. The African tribes generally are not small groups of a few hundred or a few thousand members. The larger tribes would be considered ethnic or national minority groups in any Western state. The problem is not the large numbers of tribes but rather the large sizes of some tribes. The cohesion of new nations may be weakened by the desires of tribal chieftains to invoke the same claim of national self-determination that intelligentsias previously invoked on behalf of their nations. Additionally, because Europeans often split up tribal groups when they drew their artificial boundary lines in the conference rooms of Berlin, London, and Paris, the new nations' frontiers tend to be unstable. Tribes freely cross frontiers in search of water and grazing lands; one part of a tribe may try to break away from its "nation" in order to join the rest of the tribe in the neighboring nation. The result may be a frontier war like that between Ethiopia and Somalia in 1977; neither nation can allow secession, which would weaken it and perhaps cause it to disintegrate. Clashing national and territorial ambitions are thus potentially troublesome issues. The issue of national integrity touches almost all African nations. In the late 1960s, when those who had left Katanga after their unsuccessful attempt to secede from the Congo (now Zaïre) crossed from neighboring Angola back into Katanga (now Shaba), they raised again the issue of secession in many states with their own "Shabas." French, Belgian, and Moroccan troops intervened to repel them.

(The new nations' lack of political and cultural cohesiveness is clear in the language problem. Language is one of the most important factors in forming and preserving a sense of nationality, and uniformity of language not only helps people to communicate with one another but also promotes common attitudes and values. Group consciousness and common interests are stimulated in turn; people learn to think in terms of "we," as opposed to "they." Yet in many LDCs several languages are spoken, and any attempt to impose a single language is resisted. The prospects for national cohesion in these circumstances are not promising.)

(The question for new nations is less whether or not they will develop economically than whether or not they will survive as national entities. For, when people obey racial, religious, or tribal authority instead of legitimate national authority, secession and civil war can result. Ironically, the new nations face the task of "nation building" at a time when some Western states are once more confronting similar demands for independence and greater self-government.) In Canada the French-speaking population has been pressing for independence, and even in the United Kingdom, the Scots have been making similar demands; in other societies, like Belgium and Ireland, communal hatred remains deeply divisive.

---

[9] Wallerstein, *op. cit.*, p. 88.

OVERPOPULATION AND THE MALTHUSIAN PROBLEM

(The second problem for the modernizing intelligentsia is overpopulation. Not all underdeveloped nations, to be sure, have this problem, but many do; and overpopulation casts doubt on whether or not they can make any economic progress at all. Obviously, if there are always more mouths to feed, the increment in national income is likely to be eaten up. World population has already passed the 4 billion mark and is increasing at an annual rate of just over 2 percent.)On the average, 207,000 children are born each day, almost 1.5 million a week. But the European average increase is only 0.8 percent (excluding Russia, with 1 percent), and the American rate is 1.3 percent. It is in the underdeveloped areas that the rate is highest: 2.9 percent in Latin America (which means 7 million people per year), 2.3 percent in Asia, and 2.5 percent in Africa. Mexico's population in 1945 was 20 million; thirty years later it was more than 60 million. China's population grows each year by a sum greater than the total population of Canada; its population, estimated at 700 million, is expected to reach the billion mark by the year 2000, if not earlier. In 1900 there was one European for every two Asians; in 2000, the ratio will probably be one to four. It is also estimated that by 2000 there will be two Latin Americans for each North American—and this estimate is based on a 300 million population in the United States.

(There is, then, a "population explosion.")It was in 1830 that world population first reached 1 billion. By 1930 it had doubled; in 1970 the total was 3.5 billion people, and nearly half the world's population was under twenty years old. By the year 2000 the population is expected to be between 6.2 and 6.7 billion people. Although the people of the third world (including China) constitute 70 percent of the world's total population, by the turn of the twenty-first century they will constitute about 80 percent. After that it is expected that an additional billion will be added every five years or less if the rate of population growth does not decrease sufficiently.[10] Can our "crowded earth" continue to sustain such enormous increases of population?

(The underdeveloped countries have thus come face to face with the realities of the Malthusian problem: the constant hunger and grinding poverty that result when the population grows faster than do the means of subsistence.)More than 150 years ago the Reverend Thomas Malthus, who was also an economist, predicted this fate for the Western world—unless population growth was limited by "positive checks" (like wars and epidemics) or "preventive checks," (like sterilization and contraception). The great economic progress of the West—despite the huge population increase since 1800—had seemed to refute the Malthusian prediction. Agricultural production developed to provide a plentiful supply of food, and in-

[10] Michael S. Teitelbaum, "Population and Development," *Foreign Affairs*, July 1974, p. 746; Robert S. McNamara, "Population and International Security," *International Security*, Fall 1977, pp. 22–55.

dustrial production raised the standard of living to new heights. For years, therefore, Malthus's dire warning was ignored by all save diehard pessimists.

Unfortunately, the conditions that confront the underdeveloped nations are quite dissimilar to those experienced in the West. First, the Western industrial countries had far smaller populations when they began industrializing, and their subsequent population increases did not outdistance their economic gains. Ironically, the pattern in the LDCs has been to a significant degree brought about by the colonial powers. In the precolonial period the Malthusian "positive checks" had, in their own cruel way, contributed to some sort of balance between population and resources. The typical pattern was simple: Once a tribe had eaten most of the available food in the area it inhabited and had overfarmed the land so that soil erosion had begun, it would invade the preserve of neighboring tribes; in ensuing battles, members of both tribes would be killed, thus decreasing the numbers left to be fed. Periodic famine and pestilence also helped to maintain a balance between births and deaths. This seemingly eternal cycle of peace and population growth succeeded by violence and population decline was broken by the entry of the colonial powers. (The Western colonial states, by preserving peace in the areas they ruled and introducing modern medicine, upset the balance: More of the newborn survived, and people lived longer; populations began to increase at much greater rates.)

(The very poverty of the LDCs hinders birth-control programs. Children in many of these countries are a religious, social, and even economic necessity.) In India, for instance, Muslims believe that children are a "gift of Allah," and the childless couple is pitied or despised; a woman does not even establish herself with her husband or his family until she has borne a son. A Hindu man needs a son to perform certain rituals after his death, and during life he needs sons to fight in village feuds or in tribal warfare. Furthermore, there is a fear of having *too few* children, for they may be needed to work in the fields and support their parents as—and if—the latter grow older. Children are in this sense a substitute for the social-security payments or endowment policies common in the West. (People, in short, are not poor because they have large families; they have large families because they are poor.) Birth controls can be economically disastrous in these circumstances. The family is also the hub of life for Indian villagers. Weddings and births are festive social occasions, important village events. A woman's prestige may even be measured by the number of children, especially sons, that she bears. A voluntary reduction in the size of her family would in these circumstances strike at the very basis of her life.

At the 1974 international conference on world population problems, the LDCs were hardly willing to recognize that their growth, which is doubling their population every twenty years, is a problem. They shifted the focus of attention from birth control, which they saw as an infringement of their sovereignty, to economic and social development. Arguing that fuller exploitation of the world's resources could comfortably support ten times the present global population of 4 billion, they placed responsibility principally upon the industrialized nations to waste fewer resources in support of their already very high standards of living and

PROJECTED POPULATION GROWTH FOR SELECTED COUNTRIES

Third World Countries	Population Growth Figures (to nearest million)		
	1968[x]	1977[x]	Projected by 2000[xx]
Egypt	32	39	65
Nigeria	52	67	135
Mexico	46	65	132
Brazil	88	112	213
China	747	866	1,148
India	516	626	1,059
Pakistan	57	75	147
Indonesia	113	143	237

Note: [x] *United Nations Demographic Yearbook*, 1977, p. 137
[xx] *Statistical Abstract of the United States, ibid.*

to accelerate development in the LDCs. They emphasized that a declining birth rate would come as modernization occurred. Despite this public position, many LDCs have begun birth control programs. But the central question remains: Can these countries develop rapidly enough to keep ahead of their growing populations?

(For the LDCs, the following maxim may be painfully true: "Industrial revolutions may be defeated by Malthusian counter-revolutions."[11] In countries that have achieved economic growth, as many LDCs have done, population increases have canceled most, if not all, of the hoped-for increase in living standards or savings for capital investment.) How can the LDCs possibly provide housing, education, and jobs for all these people? The Aswan dam, planned in 1955 and completed in 1970, added 25 percent to Egypt's arable land, but in those fifteen years, Egypt's population increased by 50 percent to more than 30 million. By the year 2000 the Egyptian population will double to more than 65 million if the present rate of growth continues. During the nineteenth century Europe's population rose by approximately 0.5 percent per year; today, the poorer countries grow at 2.6 percent per year, or about 200,000 each day.(Fertility, once the key to survival, seems to have become the curse of humankind. Who said "love makes the world go around"?)

THE PROBLEM OF FOOD

(The paradox of the LDCs is that, although the overwhelming majority of their populations live on the land, the peasants have great difficulty producing enough food.)The emphasis on industrialization and visible projects like steel factories and

---

[11] Alexander Gerschenkron, *Economic Backwardness in Historical Perspective* (New York: Holt, Rinehart and Winston, 1965), p. 28.

automobile plants has too often led to a neglect of agriculture, which requires costly long-term investment in land reclamation, irrigation, and fertilizer plants. Furthermore, to the leaders of these countries, agriculture means poverty; it is a constant reminder of colonial subjugation and of their continued status as suppliers of raw materials. Given the continued swings in the prices of agricultural commodities, investing more in food is, not surprisingly, viewed with some reluctance. Yet food production must be raised dramatically not only to feed the rapidly growing populations, both rural and urban-industrial, but ideally also to earn foreign exchange with which to buy required goods and services. An industrial revolution requires a prior or simultaneous agrarian revolution. Instead of being separate and distinct processes, agricultural development and industrial development are intertwined. An industrial revolution cannot occur without the provision of extra food, and to raise food production above the subsistence level requires the application of machinery and science to farming. England, the first nation to industrialize, also had the highest agricultural productivity.

(Such productivity is difficult to achieve in traditional societies, where peasants have for centuries tilled the soil by the same methods.)Unlike the Western farmer—who produces cash crops for market and is therefore alert to technical innovations that may increase production, enabling him to buy other goods, including food items that he does not grow—the peasant is all too often a subsistence farmer, producing primarily for one family, exchanging with village neighbors any surplus for necessities. Usually, the peasant is the last person to be touched by the currents of modernization. Poorly educated and physically isolated from the growing urban centers, he has no contact with the latest trends in politics, with the new intellectual and technical currents that sweep the cities. The peasant is subject mainly to conservative influences: to religion, which tells him that he must bear his lot patiently, and to the landowner, who is the local political leader and the man to whom the peasant traditionally pays deference as well as portions of his crop.(Not surprisingly, it is usually the city dweller who is the activist and organizer of revolutionary movements; the peasant tends to be politically passive.)

(Not that the peasant has no grievances that can be manipulated by revolutionary leaders in attempts to break the power of the landowners and to undermine existing society. For the peasant has an intense "land hunger." He wants to own the land he tills.) In both Russia and China it was this land hunger that finally brought about the revolutions that destroyed the czarist and Nationalist Chinese governments, both dominated by landowners. Today there are still areas where most of the land that peasants hold by tenure is owned by a few wealthy landlords. In Latin America in the 1960s, 90 percent of all land was owned by 10 percent of the landowners,[12] years after Castro had taken power in Havana. Furthermore, land-tenure systems were frequently subject to such abuses as excessive payments in crops (generally from 10 to more than 50 percent, sometimes even 90 percent) or in work to be done on the landlord's estate. On the other hand, peasants who

---

[12.] Tad Szulc, *The Winds of Revolution* (New York: Holt, Rinehart and Winston, 1965), pp. 54–55.

368 own their own land are handicapped by the small size of their holdings, as well as by their crude methods of cultivation. Even if the backward and impoverished peasant owns his land, he is compelled to borrow money in order to survive. Usually he can do so only by paying a moneylender—usually a local landowner—extremely high interest rates (ranging from 20 to 40 percent or even more). The peasant is thus condemned to live in a state of continued indebtedness if he is to have fertilizer and other things he needs.

(The technical backwardness of the peasant, his small holdings of land, and the concentration of ownership all stand as formidable obstacles to agricultural development. Consequently, the dispossession of the old landowning class where it is still in control is not simply a matter of social justice. It is a political and economic prerequisite for modernization that a nation destroy the traditional social structure, founded upon a grossly uneven distribution of wealth, channel investments into industrialization, and encourage increases in agricultural production.)

(Such changes involve not simply reform but revolution.) Ownership of land in traditional society is bound up with social status, wealth, and political power; "land reform" therefore involves complete and profound alteration of the very basis by which society allocates status, wealth, and power. Those who receive these benefits do not surrender them voluntarily. Growing more food in societies in which the modernizers are not yet in power requires wholesale rearrangement of the social order, a more complex matter than simply sowing more seeds.

Fundamentally, the peasant must be granted his own land. But, even if in the future the governments of the LDCs shift their priorities to agricultural development and redeploy their resources accordingly, crop production may still be insufficient because of small farms and rapidly increasing populations. Small farms are simply too unproductive. Mechanical equipment is too costly and too inefficient for use on small farms. There are no easy solutions, then, even after political and social barriers have been overcome. Collectivization of the land has not been very successful where it has been tried, largely because of bitter peasant opposition; after almost half a century, agriculture remains the weakest area in the Soviet economy. More land must also be brought into cultivation. Of the potentially arable land, only 22 percent in Africa, 11 percent in South America, and approximately 45 percent worldwide is now being cultivated.[13]

(At any rate, whatever the size of the farm, if the peasant is to till his soil and produce a surplus that can be siphoned off to feed the city population, it is absolutely essential that a good part of the population be moved off the land. Population growth has crowded the land with small, inefficient subsistence farms. With fewer peasants on the land, it would be possible to form larger farming units and thus to raise overall output. At the same time, such a shift of population could provide the necessary labor force for a growing industrial sector. But this possibility raises another dilemma: Cheap food for urban workers means keeping prices down, but low prices provide little incentive for farmers to raise production. Higher prices for farmers may, however, bring trouble, even rioting, in town.)

[13.] *Gainesville Sun*, December 2, 1979. These estimates were reported from a study by Earl O. Heady, a well-known agricultural economist at Iowa State University.

For the present, the threat that population will outstrip food supplies remains. The Green Revolution, so-called because of its use of high-yield strains of grain and rice to increase production per acre, has been remarkably successful in several countries. Between 1954 and 1973 the food supply increased sufficiently to feed an extra 1.3 billion mouths. Starvation—as distinct from malnutrition—has not threatened Latin America, East Asia, and East Africa. It has struck mainly in the Sahel, or Central West Africa, and the Indian subcontinent. Still, if population continues to grow at present or near present rates in the LDCs, the Green Revolution may have only postponed the global food crisis. Africa, according to the U.N. World Food Council, may be facing a permanent food crisis. Some 440 million Africans, a tenth of the world's population, have less to eat in 1980 than in 1970.[14] Some writers have gone so far as to favor a policy of "triage."[15] This term was was adopted from the French army's World War I policy of sorting its wounded into three groupings: those who would probably recover even without medical assistance, those who would die regardless of medical treatment, and those who would recover if cared for right away. Because of the limited availability of medical personnel, medicine, and facilities, priority was given to the last group. The analogy suggests that in countries that outgrow their food supplies, starvation will be nature's way of correcting this imbalance and reducing the numbers of people. To intervene by sending relief supplies for humanitarian reasons would simply worsen the problem by creating even greater food crises and needs in the future until eventually even relief would not suffice. It is to be hoped that this awful choice—a moral choice—will be avoidable. At the beginning of the twentieth century the world population was 1.5 billion; three quarters of a century later it was 4 billion. A Malthusian pessimist would have predicted an inability to feed so many mouths. Will contemporary pessimists be equally wrong?

ACCUMULATING CAPITAL FOR MODERNIZATION

Beside problems caused by the gap between national leaders and tradition-bound masses and by overpopulation are the overwhelming problems of backward, even stagnant, economies. It is upon such bases that the new nations must build industrial economies to banish poverty, end economic dependence on the former colonial powers, and achieve international standing. Industrialization is a symbol of modernity. It is also a means of escaping a past as "raw-materials appendages" to the industrial powers. Eager for economic "takeoff" and transition to modern societies, the LDCs must somehow accumulate the requisite capital.

They are basically, as we already know, exporters of primary products, or raw materials. Many of them rely on single commodities for export; others have two or three resources each. Table 14.1 shows some examples of exports from LDCs.

---

[14] *Gainsville Sun*, July 10, 1980.

[15] William Paddock and Paul Paddock, *Famine—1975!* (Boston: Little, Brown, 1967).

TABLE 14.1
Developing-Country Dependence on Primary Products for Foreign-Exchange Earnings

Source: Department of State, *The Trade Debate*, inside front cover.

Theoretically, these countries should be able to earn sufficient capital from their exports to carry out large-scale industrialization, for, ideally, as Western industrial nations continue to consume more, their demand for raw materials should rise.

In practice, however, it has not usually worked out that way. (The LDCs' dependence on export of raw materials has limited their earning capacities, for their exports reflect every fluctuation of the Western business cycle.) As Western industrial ecnomies approach full employment, the demand for raw materials rises, and so do prices; when these economies turn downward, demand declines, and so do prices. A drop of just one cent in copper or coffee prices can result in the loss of millions of dollars, sometimes tens of millions of dollars. As the Mexicans used to say, "A sneeze in the American economy could lead to pneumonia in Mexico." (A second reason is that advanced Western industrial technology has, in many instances, made it both possible and profitable to develop synthetics and other substitutes. Industries are thus released from dependence on certain natural raw materials; demand then decreases, and prices drop. A final reason for the LDCs' difficulty in earning money through their exports is their efforts to compensate for low prices by means of greater production. The result is a glut on the international market and lower prices than before.)

The dilemma of the LDCs is agonizing. They desperately need capital. They rely on their raw-material exports to earn capital. But the harder they work to enlarge their volume of exports to enhance their earnings, the more prices may fall. At the same time, because of their difficulties in producing enough food for their rapidly growing populations, they must buy food. They must also import the machinery required to start their industrialization—Western machinery, the prices of which are always rising. The "terms of trade," the LDCs' earnings from their exports versus the cost of their imports, are thus against them. Exports of raw materials, then, do not seem a likely route of escape from poverty for the LDCs. American farmers faced a similar bind in the 1930s at a time when farm prices were low: They overproduced in order to enhance their earnings, thus glutting the market, forcing prices even lower, and reducing their own living standard far below that of city dwellers. The laws of the domestic laissez-faire market, having produced politically unacceptable results, were therefore amended in order to guarantee farmers higher prices and a decent standard of living through parity prices. Internationally, such steps have not yet been taken.

The international economy is, however, in the process of major change. Whereas in the past the developed states imported only raw materials and agricultural products from the LDCs, they are now increasingly importing manufactured goods from them. This change results partly from a vast increase in the activities of multinational corporations (MNCs); it also reflects the combination of rapid economic growth, near full employment, and very low population growth in the industrial West since World War II.[16] The resulting availability of high-wage jobs, often protected by union and other regulations, has attracted workers from the low-wage sectors of the industrial economies, creating shortages of unskilled workers. Western Europe, for example, has run short of policemen, bus conductors, hotel and hospital workers, and other unskilled personnel. There are, of course, several ways to meet such shortages: employing younger people, women, labor-

---

[16] Arthur Lewis, *The Evolution of the International Economic Order* (Princeton: Princeton University Press, 1977), pp. 31–37.

372   saving devices, and low-wage foreign labor (for example, Asians and southern Europeans). Of all the possible solutions the best long-term solution is to import cheaper manufactured products from the LDCs, thus freeing the national unskilled labor force for more productive sectors. During the 1960s, therefore, the international economy began to be turned on its head as rich nations invested in the poor nations in order to produce manufactures for export. By 1985, it is estimated, more than half the LDCs' exports will be manufactured goods. The rich (industrial) nations now export agricultural goods to the poor states, a startling change from the previous pattern. In discussing the United States, Richard Barnet and Ronald Müller have called this phenomenon the "Latinamericanization of the United States."

> . . . Production of the traditional industrial goods that have been the mainstay of the U.S. economy is being transferred from $4-an-hour factories in New England to 30 cents-an-hour factories in the "export platforms" of Hong Kong and Taiwan. Increasingly, as the cars, TVs, computers, cameras, clothes, and furniture are being produced abroad, the United States is becoming a service economy and a producer of plans, programs, and ideas for others to execute. . . .

> The United States trading pattern is beginning to resemble that of underdeveloped countries as the number one nation becomes increasingly dependent on the export of agricultural products and timber to maintain its balance of payments and increasingly dependent on imports of finished goods to maintain its standard of living. . . . (Unlike poor countries, however, the U.S. also exports "software"—i.e., technical knowledge.)[17]

(Of course, this situation involves only a few LDCs, the so-called "export platforms." Most LDCs unfortunately remain dependent on raw-materials exports. For 110 third-world nations seventy five percent of their total exports are still raw materials, which are processed and consumed elsewhere. Half the LDCs depend on single commodities for their earnings on the international market.)

THE CULTURAL AND SOCIAL TRANSFORMATION

It should be obvious by now that the term "economic development" suggests a one-dimensional picture of the actual process of transition from a traditional rural society to an advanced modern nation. "Economic development" implies that the only requirement is industry, that industrialization follows automatically from capital formation, and that mobilizing capital is therefore the crucial problem. Even when agricultural growth is included, as it must be, the term "economic development" implies an oversimplification—indeed, a distortion—of the complex realities of modernizing a traditional society. (Modernization) is more than simply

---

[17.] Richard J. Barnet and Ronald E. Müller, *Global Reach* (New York: Simon & Schuster, 1974), pp. 216–217.

building steel mills and constructing dams. It means, *above all else,* changes in values, aspirations, and expectations. The necessary changes are thus not simply economic; they are also political, social, and cultural. Economic development is multidimensional; modernization aims at the complete transformation of society, including revolutionary changes in class structures and the centralization of political authority.

Because the kind of modernization that LDCs are currently undergoing is in some respects comparable to earlier Western development, it will perhaps be instructive to review briefly some of the principal changes involved in the transition from medieval feudalism to the "modern," centralized, monarchical states. In this way, we can understand the scope and depth of the cultural and social changes involved.[18] It has been pointed out that traditional societies do not regard economic activity as a prime concern of life. Surprising as it may seem, even in Western history money making was not always the chief pursuit. In the Middle Ages religion was the principal concern. Earthly existence was considered merely a short prelude to eternal life, for which people prepared themselves through adherence to the moral code of the Roman Catholic Church. Every aspect of behavior was subject to the spiritual authority of the Church; in the economic sphere, the Church condemned the charging of interest—a basic necessity in a monetary economy— as usury. The desire for profit was equated with greed, and economic competition was simply not part of the accepted way of life.

This attitude toward interest and profits was, of course, inimical to business. Economic competition, profits, savings, investments, and the whole concept of economic growth were alien ideas in the Middle Ages. The merchant and craft guilds, which existed in the towns that had grown up by the eleventh century, functioned to prevent competition and to regulate the economic life of the towns. Membership in a guild was prerequisite to the establishment of oneself in "business" as a craftsman, and it was no easy task to become a member. The guilds regulated the age at which apprenticeship began, the cost and duration of training, and the number of apprentices that each guild master could have at any specific time. No master could have more helpers than his competitors and thus could not threaten their survival. Furthermore, the guilds regulated prices—which, according to the Church, had to be "just." A merchant was expected to be satisfied with a price that covered no more than the cost of materials plus labor. Economically, socially, and politically, the aim of medieval life—apart from its overriding religious purpose— was stability, security, and subsistence for everyone. Nowhere was this set of values more apparent than in the countryside, where the vast majority of people lived. The manor was the center of organized rural life and loyalties. Feudalism, which lasted approximately from 850 to 1200, arose after the decline of Charlemagne's empire. The dissolution of larger units of economic and social organization had resulted in widespread chaos, disorder, and violence. The resulting search for security led to establishment of the manorial system, within which people produced enough food, to provide them with government and protection. The lord of the manor, whose title and position derived from his ownership of the land, fulfilled

---

[18.] See R. H. Tawney, *Religion and the Rise of Capitalism* (Baltimore: Penguin, 1947).

374   many functions. He was governor, judge, and military defender; in the absence of a central government, no one else could undertake these tasks. But the lord of the manor was not an entrepreneur. The manor did not produce for a national market; agricultural methods and practices were dictated by custom, and only enough food for local subsistence was grown.

The serfs owned no land, nor could they buy it. Land was inherited, and inherited land was the basis of the entire social order. The lords, precisely because they owned the land, were the social, political, and military elite. There was no chance for the landless serf or his children to acquire land and rise socially. The relationship between lord and serf involved mutual responsibilities and obligations. In return for the stability and security provided by the lord, the serfs performed manorial labor. Bound to the land, they owed their master certain traditional services, like work in his fields and taxes (paid in kind from the crops grown by the serfs on the lord's land). There was no exchange economy; the medieval economy was essentially a "natural" one.

In order to modernize, Europe had to shift its emphasis from the spiritual afterlife to the temporal, replace the landowning nobility with a class eager for capital accumulation; achieve a more fluid social structure to permit upward mobility on the basis of achievement; and finally, create a larger political, social, and economic framework. None of these changes came quickly. The first thorough break with the medieval attitude came with Calvinism. The core of Calvinist doctrine, belief in predestination, meant that God had already selected those who would gain salvation. All others had been condemned to damnation and could do nothing to redeem themselves. The Calvinists naturally believed that they were among the few slated for salvation in the hereafter. In the meantime, they would dedicate their lives on earth to the glorification of God, demonstrating their spiritual devotion to Him—not simply by prayer but also by action. Calvinism, in contrast to Roman Catholicism, did not reject secular activities as unimportant; rather, it assigned priority to them. The vigor with which a person pursued his or her "calling" was a token of dedication to God and individual spiritual worth.

As wealthy as a person might become, though, he or she could never forget that he or she was "ever in the great Taskmaster's eyes." People were exhorted not to spend money frivolously but to save it and use it to produce more and even greater "good works." Industriousness, profits, savings, and investments were thus legitimized by religion. Thrift, character, and hard work represented the Calvinist's earthly trinity. A person's energy had to be focused on the work to which God had called him or her. Luxury, leisure, entertainment, and sexual enjoyment where to be shunned. In order not to succumb to temptation and become morally corrupted, each person had to exercise stringent discipline over his or her own weaknesses and emotions.

It is hardly surprising that this "Protestant ethic" and capitalism became so closely identified, for Calvinism dictated a "new scale of moral values and a new ideal of social conduct." It was but a short way from John Calvin to Adam Smith, whose theory of capitalism was based upon recognition of the acquisitive passion that the Church had earlier condemned. Smith accepted the desire for gain as a fact of life, calling it "enlightened self-interest." Laissez-faire capitalism was merely to harness this acquisitive instinct to the public welfare:

> Calvin did for the bourgeoisie of the sixteenth century what Marx did for the proletariat of the nineteenth. . . . He set their virtues at their best in sharp antithesis with the vices of the established order at its worst, taught them to feel that they were a chosen people, made them conscious of their great destiny in the Providential plan and resolute to realize it. The new law was graven on tablets of flesh; it not merely rehearsed a lesson, but fashioned a soul. Compared with the quarrelsome, self-indulgent nobility of most European countries, or with the extravagant and half-bankrupt monarchies, the middle classes, in which Calvinism took root most deeply, were a race of iron.[19]

The rise of capitalism and the bourgeoisie was, furthermore, accompanied by the centralization of political power in the state. The bourgeois settled in the new towns on or near rivers and roads and were thus well located for the conduct of trade. They considered themselves free men and women, not subject to the control of local lords. The conflict between feudal nobility and commercial middle class led to an alliance between the king and the bourgeoisie. Because of the decentralization of power in medieval Europe, the king was the supreme lord largely in name only. To consolidate power in his own hands, he had to break the power of the nobility, upon which he depended for his wealth and his army. The bourgeoisie proved an alternative source of wealth. It was willing to furnish money and to give the king its allegiance, for its aims coincided with his. First, it sought town charters specifying the citizens' freedom and their rights. Second, it wanted a larger area in which to trade. A powerful monarchy and establishment of a sovereign state were thus in its interests. By the early sixteenth century England, France, and Spain were already ruled by strong kings. Greater size, single codes of law, security of travel, common sets of weights and measures, and common currencies were all to the advantage of the bourgeoisie.

The bourgeoisie particularly benefited from the king's desire to enhance the power and prestige of the new state. As the index of power was wealth—with which the monarch could pay the bureaucracy administering the state, maintain a strong army, and build a sizable fleet—mercantilism was aimed at the development of a more self-sufficient economy. State policy was to maximize exports and minimize imports. Governments subsidized everything from porcelain manufacture to armaments production. This ever-growing economy in turn provided the foundation for the increasing political and social cohesion of the state. Governments also sponsored great voyages of exploration and granted charters to trading companies to exploit the wealth of the New World and the Orient. The result was a shift in trade from the Mediterranean to the Atlantic. Gold, silver, jewelry, spices, tobacco, ivory—and, of course, slaves—were transported to Europe from these lands, most of which had been colonized. This "commercial revolution" trans-

---

[19.] *Ibid.*, p. 39.

376   formed Europe into the economic center of the globe, the cockpit of world power. But this result would not have been achieved without previous changes in values and social structure and the establishment of a central government.

NATION BUILDING AND CIVILIAN AND MILITARY AUTHORITARIANISM

The task of nation building is thus enormously difficult and complex. (A new state must first create a nation within boundaries probably inherited from colonial days.) The secular intelligentsia may be intensely nationalistic, but the mass of the population may not share its dedication. There are, of course, exceptions. Algeria and Vietnam had to struggle for their independence in wars against colonial powers and their allies, but most LDCs have been "given" their independence; they have not had to win it in wars that might have aroused popular feelings of nationalism. For this latter and largest category of LDCs, the problem of achieving national cohesion after independence remains the primary problem. Citizens of the new nation have shared only the experience of colonial rule, and only the desire to gain national freedom has enabled various internal groups to cooperate. Once the colonial power has been ejected, however, these groups have little sense of belonging to a distinct cultural entity with certain shared expectations about the future. When the opponent against which they united is gone, there is little else to hold them together in a political, economic, and administrative entity; centrifugal forces then begin to exert themselves. Ironically, the resulting disintegration is given impetus by the very principle of national self-determination in the name of which the anticolonial revolution was carried out.

(The second task under these circumstances is not only to centralize power in order to counter the tendency toward political and social fragmentation but also to create a set of political institutions that can not only keep order but also represent the many factions and interests in society, mediate conflicting views and aspirations, and enable the government to act on behalf of society as a whole.) The task is thus to create legitimate governmental institutions through which conflict can be channeled peacefully and compromise achieved. Otherwise, *coups d'état*, rioting, revolutions, assassinations, and civil wars will remain the methods of resolving differences. As noted much earlier, without a government to exercise effective authority, as well as a common political culture or values widely shared by the people in the society, the domestic politics of a nation begins to resemble international politics, in which there is a high expectation of violence as a means of conflict resolution.

The term "less developed" refers not only to economies but also to political institutions. As Sam Huntington has put it, "The most important political distinction among countries concerns not their form of government but their degree of government."[20] The United States, Britain, and the Soviet Union have different forms of government, but they all do govern. Many, perhaps most, of the LDCs are characterized not only by poor health, education, food, productivity, and income but also by an even greater "shortage of political community and of effective, authoritative, legitimate government."[21]

(A third task is economic development.) For new nations, the response to the "revolution of rising expectations" is important not only for humanitarian reasons but also for political reasons and the cause of nation building. (The degree to which expectations are satisfied will be proof of the effectiveness of the new national government. Economic development produces a better life for the citizen; its significance is its *political* payoff.) To the people of a new nation not yet solidly knitted together, the nationalist intelligentsia must prove that what it is seeking to establish will be beneficial to them. Otherwise, why should they transfer their loyalty to it? Economic development can in this way help strengthen the fragile bonds of national unity and give the new nation legitimacy. It can also contribute to this goal in other ways. An industrial economy, because of specialization and division of labor, links different sectors of a country together; people of different ethnic backgrounds and religious beliefs work together because of the imperatives of economic interdependence. As these people interact economically, travel to other sections of the country, and communicate with people in different areas, they become more aware that they are all part of one nation and that unity is essential if their common hopes for the future are to be realized. An advancing economy also creates a new pattern of interests. The old farming interests are supplemented by a host of new economic and professional interests. In this context, individuals define their roles less in terms of ethnic or religious allegiances than in terms of "interests." The rise of new social classes (the urban, middle, and working classes) is of key significance, for such classes are national, rather than regional. Human beings thus become nationally self-conscious.

(A fourth task is dealing with the consequences of modernization, specifically the enormous social ferment that accompanies the collapse of tradition and customs, a ferment that can lead to political discontinuity and instability.) Because the old ways of doing things no longer suffice, new ways must be adopted. The result for most people is bewilderment and intense frustration. They find it difficult to adjust lifelong behavior and attitudes to the changing environment. The peasant's sense of security (which arises from knowing his place in society) and sense of belonging (which results from being part of an old way of life) collapse—particularly if he is forced off the land and herded into the city and a new factory, where he must learn the values and habits of industrial civilization. He resents the factory, with its discipline and monotony, long hours, and low pay, and he hates the vast slums where he lives in filth, poverty, and disease, with tens of thousands of other uprooted peasants. He feels degraded. As a peasant, poor as he is, he at least has

---

[20] Samuel P. Huntington, *Political Order in Changing Societies* (New Haven: Yale University Press, 1968), p. 1.

[21] *Ibid.*, p. 2.

status and a role in society; as a peasant worker, torn loose from his traditional and religious moorings and submerged in the anonymity of the labor force, he feels his individuality denied.[22] He has become an isolated atom in a secular mass society.

The peasant who stays on the land is also subject to frustration, hostility, and impatience. The transformation from subsistence peasant producing for his family to commercial farmer producing for a market is difficult. He must learn to operate new farm machinery and to try new methods. If herded into a collectivized farm, he will feel deprived of "his" piece of land and his personality. Furthermore, even if he is not herded into a collective farm, he will be resentful if the state takes away his surplus crops at low prices in order to feed the workers in the cities and to earn foreign exchange. His consumption, like that of the factory laborer, then, does not materially improve.

Before independence, the masses were constantly told by the leaders of the independence movement that, once the colonial rulers had been ousted, life would improve. But this better life cannot come for a long time, for capital formation requires postponement of consumption. The greater the gap between expectation and satisfaction, the greater each person's frustration. Only a gradual closing of this gap, providing each person with some improvement in life and some personal security, can relieve this dissatisfaction. (In Iran, for example, the reaction to modernization, including industrialization and the Western values that come with it, has led to a new emphasis on religion and the rejection of foreign "atheism" and materialism as alien to traditional culture; not surprisingly, this reaction was led by the clergy who combined their traditional views with a fervent nationalism to mobilize popular enthusiasm and support.) A society in transition is thus fraught with discontent, bewilderment, and insecurity.

(How does the nationalist intelligentsia cope with these problems? One way is to "nationalize" the people—to inculcate in them national consciousness and loyalty, recognition of the national government as *their* government, of its laws as reflecting *their* will and requiring *their* adherence. The majority must acknowledge that they are citizens of one nation and that the national government has the

---

[22.] Karl Marx, who confused capitalism as a mature economic system with the early phase of capital accumulation under any economic and political system, caught the essence of these peasant-laborers' protests. The bourgeoisie, he said, "has pitilessly torn asunder the motley feudal ties that bound man to his 'natural superiors,' and has left remaining no other nexus between man and man than naked self-interest, than callous 'cash payment.' . . . It has resolved personal worth into exchange value." Marx might more appropriately have used the words "Industrial Revolution" for "bourgeoisie." Indeed, he did say: "Owing to the extensive use of machinery and to division of labor, work of the proletarians has lost all individual character, and, consequently, all charm for the workman. He becomes an appendage of the machine. . . . Modern industry has converted the little workshop of the patriarchal master into the great factory of the industrial capitalist. Masses of laborers, crowded into the factory, are organized like soldiers. . . . Not only are they slaves of the bourgeois class, and of the bourgeois state; they are daily and hourly enslaved by the machine, by the supervisor, and, above all, by the individual bourgeois manufacturer himself. The more openly this despotism proclaims gain to be its end and aim, the more petty, the more hateful, and the more embittering it is." Quoted in Arthur P. Mendel, ed., *The Essential Works of Marxism* (New York: Bantam, 1961), pp. 15, 19–20; see also Adam B. Ulam, *The New Face of Soviet Totalitarianism* (Cambridge, Mass.: Harvard University Press, 1963), pp. 19–20.

legitimate authority to make decisions on behalf of the entire population. Such popular consciousness cannot be developed overnight. An entire people must, in a sense, go to school—to learn their nation's language and history (much of it mythical, devised for the purpose of fostering national identification) and to be brought into the mainstream of national life. Only then will the national symbols stimulate deep emotion; only then will a truly national community emerge.)

(In the meantime, if the nation is to be held together, the leader must be a "hero," the single person who more than anyone else symbolizes the new nation.[23] If he led the nationalist movement before independence, he may have agitated for freedom for years, propagated national mythology, and served time in jail as a result. He and the nation are thus in a very real sense identical. As "the founder of the nation," he provides a kind of symbolic presence without which the unity of the new nation would erode. Loyalty can usually be felt more keenly toward an individual who incorporates an idea—like the "nation"—than toward the idea itself. The hero in a new nation is a transitional figure in a transitional society. He serves the indispensable function of encouraging a shift from traditional, parochial loyalties to tribe or region to broader loyalties to the impersonal nation-state. The hero usually has charisma—"a quality of extraordinary spiritual power attributed to a person . . . capable of eliciting popular support in the direction of human affairs."[24] He is, in fact, a *substitute* for the nation and for the national institutions that have yet to be built; he also confers legitimacy upon the new nation and its government.)

Such a hero is usually supported by a single party as the principal instrument of national integration.[25] Unlike Western political parties, the primary function of which is to represent the various interests within the nation, the single party in a developing country has a double rationale.(First, the party is an effective means of socializing the traditionally "tribalized" people on a national basis.)Once the masses in the towns and countryside have been organized in provincial and local cells, the party, by drawing them into national life, tries to instill in them a sense of identification as citizens of a distinct national community. Just as the charismatic hero replaces the traditional chieftain, the nation is supposed to replace the tribe. The party claims to represent the nation. National elections, in this context, may not have much meaning as rituals of democratic choice among different parties and potential rulers. But the ritual of elections is nevertheless not, theoretically at least, without meaning. Elections are supposed to reflect involvement in the affairs of the nation and to establish meaningful links to national leaders. One effect, though, is that, to the degree that political participation does mobilize the masses, their desire for greater economic "payoffs" or welfare greatly increases the pressures on the rulers to succeed.

(The second rationale of one-party rule is its alleged efficiency in mobilizing

---

[23] Wallerstein, *op. cit.*, p. 98.

[24] *Ibid.*, p. 99.

[25] Three fourths of Africa's 345 million people, for example, lived under one-party rule in 1970—in twenty-nine of forty states. *The New York Times*, June 14, 1970.

380   the economic and human resources of a nation for the purpose of modernization.)
As one African leader said:

> Once the first free government is formed, its supreme task lies ahead—the building
> up of the country's economy, so as to raise the standards of the people, to eradicate
> disease, to banish ignorance and superstition. This, no less than the struggle against
> colonialism, calls for the maximum united effort by the whole country if it is to
> succeed. *There can be no room for difference or division.* In Western democracies,
> it is an accepted practice in times of emergency for opposition parties to sink their
> differences and join together in forming a national government. *This is our time
> of emergency,* and until our war against poverty, ignorance, and disease has been
> won, we should not let our unity be destroyed by a desire to follow somebody
> else's "book of rules."[26]

By American standards, such a one-party system is, of course, undemocratic. In
the United States the opposition is a loyal opposition whose allegiance is to the
same nation and values as the governing party. But in a new African nation the
opposition's allegiance is often regional and tribal, and it thus represents the centrifugal forces in society. In these circumstances, a change in the form of government favoring greater democracy could result in disintegration of the state. The
choice is *not* between democracy and dictatorship but between nationhood and
disintegration. The problem is not one of restraining power to ensure freedom but
one of accumulating sufficient power to ensure that the government will be obeyed
throughout the nation.[27]

Because of the tenuous nature of the bonds holding the nation together
and the immense difficulties inherent in modernization, civilian one-party governments often give way to military governments In LDCs the trend toward
military control of government is widely established. In Africa, over half the nations
were governed by the military in the middle 1970s. More than two thirds of the
countries of Asia, Africa, the Middle East, and Latin America have experienced
varying levels of military intervention since 1945.(Several conditions are frequently
cited favoring military intervention in politics.[28] First is the low level of political
culture and legitimacy in the new states.)Whereas in a modern society with developed and accepted political institutions, which contain and mediate conflict in
society, the military would find it difficult to justify seizing power and demanding
public obedience (or proving it possessed legitimate authority), in a new country
in which political obligation still follows largely along ethnic, religious, and racial

---

[26] Julius Nyerere, quoted in Paul E. Sigmund, Jr., *The Ideologies of the Developing Nations*
(New York: Holt, Rinehart and Winston, 1963), p. 199 (emphasis in original).

[27] Wallerstein, *op. cit.*, p. 96.

[28] General analyses of the role of the military in new nations are Morris Janowitz, *The
Military in the Political Development of New Nations* (Chicago: University of Chicago Press, 1964);
S.E. Finer, *The Man on Horseback* (rev. ed.; Baltimore: Penguin, 1976); John J. Johnson, ed., *The
Role of the Military in Underdeveloped Countries* (Princeton: Princeton University Press, 1962); Hun-
tington, *op. cit.*, pp. 192–263; Edward Feit, "Pen, Sword and People: Military Regimes in the Formation
of Political Institutions," *World Politics*, January 1973, *pp. 251 ff:* Feit, *The Armed Bureaucrat* (Boston:
Houghton Mifflin, 1973).

lines and there is little agreement about the rules of the game, the military can seize power. Instead of being regarded as a usurpation, such a seizure can be claimed as legitimate if embryonic political institutions and politicians appear to the public to have failed. Civilian leaders, overwhelmed by the massive problems confronting them, have often proved themselves inept and indecisive.

(In addition, the one-party system may not have provided the necessary organizational cohesiveness and discipline to mobilize the population for the difficult tasks of modernization. More frequently, in the absence of any opposition, single-party governments have grown lax, self-indulgent, and corrupt. Political instability, deteriorating or stagnant economic conditions, and national humiliation in international conflicts, tend to undermine popular faith in politicians, political institutions, and "politics." The people turn instead toward the army, another symbol of the nation it is sworn to defend. The army, opposed to lack of discipline and widespread dishonesty in government and usually somewhat contemptuous of politicians (particularly self-enriching, incompetent, and squabbling ones), often interprets public opinion in this way, for it tends to perceive itself as the true protector and guardian of the public, even though its interventions are motivated primarily by its own corporate interests. Having the coercive means to seize power, it has an advantage over other institutions.)

(A second condition favoring domestic military intervention is the low level of economic development.) In contrast, a Western army, regardless of its organization and technical sophistication, could not run a society as complex as Britain or the United States—probably not even New York City. When, after 1945, the army ran the occupation of Germany, for example, it did so only with the help of the top men in American business and professional life. Even then, its responsibility was limited to repair and reconstruction work. But, in a far less developed society, the military has an advantage over its civilian competitors. Armies are, by and large, microcosms of modern industrial societies. They are technically and rationally oriented to their occupational activities. They cannot function without engineers, mechanics, communications specialists, and so forth; even the operation of jeeps, tanks, guns, and other military equipment by the ordinary soldier demands elementary "industrial" skills. Military units have, in fact, on occasion been used for such tasks as the construction of roads, bridges, and harbors (recall the role of the U.S. Army Corps of Engineers in the development of the American West).

(Third, the army in a new nation is often said to be in a good position to organize the nation for its economic "takeoff" and to surmount the turbulent transition from the traditional agrarian to modern society.)An army is founded on centralized command, hierarchy, and discipline, the very characteristics that Communist parties claim will allow them, and only them, to modernize an underdeveloped nation successfully and rapidly. The army may, in fact, be the only organization that can compete with the communists in the capacity to break the power of the landowning classes, carry out land reforms, organize the nation's human and natural resources for development, and control the unhappy masses from whom capital savings must be collected.

Finally, it is claimed that the real power in many of the new armies lies

382

with the younger, highly nationalistic officers, who are dedicated personally and institutionally to the modernization of their nations. In the past, the senior officers usually came from the landed upper class, which had a vested interest in preserving traditional society. Today it is not the generals but the captains who play the key role in control of the army. As sons of small landowners and low-grade civil servants, they consider themselves the true "sons of the land" and despise the traditional ruling class where it still governs. They are aware of the comparative weakness of their armies, a weakness reflecting not only the absence of modern weapons but also the preindustrial nature of their societies. They also know from experience that, whereas in a traditional society a man's status is decided at birth, in the Westernized or modern army, personal advancement is possible. For this reason, these young and ambitious individuals, whose prospects of social advancement and economic reward are cut off as long as civilian society is highly stratified, have entered the armies, where their status in many instances is determined not by birth and family but by ability and hard work. The fact that there is a relationship between effort and reward in the military highlights the injustice of the surrounding civilian society and the need for reform. The younger military leaders thus tend to share the nationalistic and modernizing desires of the Westernized secular intelligentsia; indeed, they are usually called the "military intelligentsia" or the "intelligentsia in uniform."[29]

Yet, the performance of military governments falls far short of the expectations arising from conditions in the country and the organizational and social characteristics of the military.[30] Soldiers overthrow governments basically because they see the corporate interests of the armed forces threatened, whether from channeling of funds elsewhere or from attempts to deprive them of their autonomy and to politicize them. To be sure, the military, given its traditional perception of itself as the servant and protector of the state, finds it easy to justify political intervention in patriotic and selfless terms and, undoubtedly, believes what it is doing is in the national interest. Furthermore, the fortunes of many countries with low levels of development and single-resource economies are, of course, affected by external economic forces beyond their control. Military regimes have all too often demonstrated little success in promoting economic growth.

Not unnaturally, given the armed forces' organizational interests, the share of the national budget going to the military goes up quite dramatically in most instances of takeover (usually 50 to 75 percent of the previous budget), thus eating up whatever small increases in productivity may have been gained. Although economic growth is viewed as desirable, the military's interests come first—even at the cost of modernization. Furthermore, however apt soldiers are at managing barracks and infantry regiments and flying airplanes, they do not necessarily have the skills

[29] The degree to which the military leaders' perception of their role is influenced by the values they have learned in Western military academies is analyzed in Robert M. Price, "A Theoretical Approach to Military Rule in the New States," *World Politics*, April 1971, pp. 399–430.

[30] See Eric A. Nordlinger, "Soldiers in Mufti," *American Political Science Review*, December 1970, pp. 1131 ff.; and Nordlinger, *Soldiers in Politics* (Englewood Cliffs, N.J.: Prentice-Hall, 1977) for the best overall evaluation of the military in power. Our analysis has been heavily influenced by Nordlinger's judgments.

of economists and businessmen in assessing alternative economic-growth strategies, understanding fiscal policies, and directing large sectors of the economy. The economic record of military governments is hardly an enviable one, certainly no better than that of civilian governments.

Even the reputation of military regimes as reformers is, on the whole, undeserved. Although nationalistic military governments frequently claim to be progressive, determined to bring about redistribution of land and wealth and to enhance the people's welfare, their often militant rhetoric is in direct conflict with their corporate aggrandizement. In economies of scarcity, in which a gain for one group means a loss for other groups, increased military spending leaves less to redistribute. In addition, armies more often than not represent one or two tribal or ethnic groups, rather than a mixture of all the different groups in the nation. Attempts to favor the communities from which much of the military leadership comes serve only to deepen the already existing social divisions.

Yet the image of many military regimes as progressive persists, largely because in areas where the traditional landed elite still governs, as in much of Africa, Asia, and the Middle East, the military does, upon coming to power, redistribute land and wealth. The breakup of landed oligarchies, which does provide greater social mobility and economic opportunities, clearly favors the rural and urban middle classes with which the officers identify themselves. But where, as in Latin America, there already exists a relatively high level of modernization and where the lower class of peasants and especially workers is more politically self-conscious and mobilizable, military regimes will crack down if challenged. As a contender for sharing the power and wealth in society, a mobilized lower class is viewed as a threat to the military's corporate interests and middle-class interests in general. The result is that the military government is transformed into a defender of the social and economic status quo.

The military thus plays different roles in different societies. In traditional society, the middle-class military becomes radical, and its coups are "breakthrough" coups; in middle-class society, the military becomes a participant and arbiter; in mass society, the military becomes the conservative guardian of the prevailing order, and its coups are "veto" coups. The more underdeveloped the society, in other words, the more progressive the military's role; the more developed that society, the more conservative and reactionary that role.[31]

Still, however poorly or well what S. E. Finer has called the "armed modernizers" govern and advance their nations' economic growth and welfare, military regimes are likely to be common throughout the underdeveloped areas for some time to come. Civilian governments' inability to handle communal strife and advance economic development, plus their propensity for self-indulgence and corruption, will continue to weaken or destroy their legitimacy and incite the military to coups d'état while much of the population cheers and welcomes the new governors in uniform. It is the presence or absence of legitimacy that, in the final

---

[31.] Huntington, op. cit., pp. 192–263. The Huntington-Nordlinger view of the different roles the military plays in different societies is questioned by Robert W. Jackman, "Politicians in Uniform," *American Political Science Review*, December 1976, pp. 1078–1097.

384 analysis, permits translation of motives to intervene into action. "Where public attachment to civilian institutions is strong, military intervention in politics will be weak. . . . By the same token, where public attachment to civilian institutions is weak or nonexistent, military intervention will find wide scope . . . "[32] and not be regarded as a usurpation of power. Coups d'état are symptoms of the failing of civilian rulers, especially to modernize their nations. In these circumstances, the new nations' domestic problems will continue to affect profoundly the conduct of their foreign policies.

THE PURPOSES OF NONALIGNMENT AS A FOREIGN POLICY

The leaders of the new states clearly confront problems that are vast and seemingly insoluble—at least without arousing a great deal of popular anger—so that, rather than concentrating on their nations' domestic needs, they are tempted to play dramatic and popular roles on the international stage. (Indeed, foreign policy may help them accomplish their various internal aims. First, it may help them to "nationalize" their peoples.) As often the only force that united the people was hatred of the former colonial power—and this "reactive nationalism" tends to lose its force as a socially cohesive factor soon after independence—the only way to arouse them and keep them united is to continue the struggle against European colonialism or "imperialism" in general. The more tenuous the bonds uniting the members of a society, the more ardent will be the campaign against "vestiges of imperialism." By asserting that the nation is once more the victim of the Dutch, French, or British—or even all the industrialized West acting through NATO or Western-dominated international banking institutions—the leaders seek to arouse their peoples and unite them against a common external danger. Anticolonialism thus does not end with the achievement of national independence. The struggle against vestiges of colonialism or "neocolonialism" must be continued until a measure of national unity and economic progress has occurred. ". . . [A]nti-colonialism is a cement that holds together otherwise incompatible domestic factions. The cohesive function of the "common enemy' must be perpetuated even when the foreign 'enemy' is no longer a real threat. . . . This, perhaps, is the reason why opposition to colonialism frequently grows more intense *after* independence."[33] (Foreign policy thus serves as *a continuation of the revolution against colonial rule in order to preserve the unity of the new nation.*)

(Second, and closely related, the foreign policy of the LDCs involves a search for identity, status, and dignity.) Many of these countries are new nations, former colonies, with no national history, no commonly accepted political institutions, no domestic unity, and almost no strong national commitment among

---

[32] Finer, *op. cit.*, p. 21.

[33] Good, "State-Building as a Determinant of Foreign Policy in the New States," in Laurence W. Martin, ed., *Neutralism and Nonalignment* (New York: Holt, Rinehart and Winston, 1962), p. 5.

their populations. Even if they have had a glorious past and are at present independent, the feeling that they are still subject to Western influence may lead to an assertive foreign policy.

> (In short, the state's legitimacy is more easily asserted through its foreign policy than through its domestic policies and it is more apparent when performing on the international than on the national stage. Domestic issues divide the nation and disclose how little developed is its consciousness of itself; foreign issues unite the nation and mark it as a going concern.[34])

(Foreign policy is thus also an effort *to discover and establish the new state's personality and to reaffirm its identity as a nation separate from the former colonial power.)*/ Third, foreign policy is aimed at maximizing foreign aid that the LDCs receive for their development.)By the late 1970s, the third world accounted for 75 percent of the world's population but received only 10 percent of the world's revenues. Unable to earn sufficient funds to support their people, who frequently live in poverty and hunger, many LDCs have no choice but to seek external assistance. Indeed, it was widely believed in the industrial West during the 1950s and 1960s that the LDCs would need considerable foreign aid until they achieved self-sustaining economic growth. More specifically, on the assumption that communism thrives on misery, Western leaders believed that they ought to supply most of that aid, so that the LDCs could advance from traditional societies through the various stages to the "drive for maturity." (The critical stages were believed to be the pretakeoff and the takeoff stages; if the LDCs could not progress through them, then they might turn toward communism. In any event, for the LDCs, one aim of foreign policy has been to *attract the external funds necessary for their domestic transformation from rural, economically backward societies to urban-industrial societies with high standards of living.*)

(Fourth, nationalist leaders also aim to divert popular attention from domestic problems.)At home only painfully slow progress can be made, the task of development is bound to be long and arduous, and the masses will tend to become increasingly restless and dissatisfied. The gap between their rising material expectations and satisfaction seems unbridgeable as increasing numbers of people become politically conscious and demand satisfaction of their needs, even during the initial capital-accumulation phase. In addition, increased movement from the country to the impersonal and unfamiliar cities disrupts the traditional loyalties and ties of the people; unable to find substitutes, they live isolated in a mass society. And the tendency to political fragmentation remains ever present. The pressure on national leaders from the continuing need to improve living conditions and build the new nation is thus unrelenting, particularly because elections mobilize the masses and raise their hopes for a better life. If these demands remain unsatisfied, however, the revolution of rising expectations turns into a revolution of rising frustration, and the leaders and their government suffer declining prestige and support. In order

---

[34] *Ibid.*, pp. 8–9.

386 to preserve or recapture the people's support, stay in power, and stabilize the government, they are tempted irresistibly to assert themselves in foreign policy. In circumstances of economic stagnation, cultural alienation, and governmental insecurity, political leaders will be tempted to preserve their power by externalizing domestic dissatisfaction; foreign scapegoats will be required to relieve internal stresses and strains. It is easier for leaders to play prominent and highly visible international roles before their countrymen than to undertake the difficult work of modernizing their nation. Foreign policy, therefore, serves the *purpose of exporting domestic dissatisfaction and mobilizing popular support for the government.*

CHARACTERISTICS OF NONALIGNMENT

Nonalignment favors the implementation of all these aims. As noted much earlier, bipolarity made nonalignment feasible. By taking a neutral position, a new state could maximize its appeal to both the Soviet Union and the United States, as well as to their respective allies. The two superpowers acted as if they were two suitors seeking to win the hand of the beautiful, but still unattached, maiden. By occasionally seeming to promise itself without actually making a commitment, the new nation could gain leverage, despite its lack of power. For each suitor was compelled to show its ardor and "prove its love"—with its pocketbook. This approach tended to maximize the economic aid that the new nation received. The further it moved away from the West, the more eagerly the Communists would offer it assistance; the nearer it moved to the West, the greater the number of Western loans or grants that were offered.

Nonalignment also favored realization of the LDCs' other goals. It permitted them to carry on the anticolonial revolution, as well as to find their identities by continuing to reject their European "father" or "mother" countries. (The infant United States had done the same thing in formulating the Monroe Doctrine in which it publicly declared the separation of the New World from the Old World.) Obviously, in its search for nationhood an LDC cannot align itself, for it can assert itself and find its identity after many years as a colony only by emphasizing its independence from the West and, usually, the Soviet bloc as well.

> Insofar as foreign policy serves to further the establishment of national identity, nonalignment presents attractive possibilities. Before independence, a colony was related to the external world only through the foreign office of its metropole. It participated in the international community only by proxy. Once independent, it wants to pick up its own franchise, speak with its own voice, and demonstrate its own capacities. Alignment with a bloc means a renewed loss of voice and identity. Nonalignment means an uninhibited voice, an independent role, and a sense of uniqueness—particularly in relation to the former metropole (and, one might add, the United States as the West's premier power and ally of the former colonial ruler).[35]

---

[35] Good, "State-Building as a Determinant of Foreign Policy in the New States," p. 8.

(Although bipolarity favors nonalignment, not all nonaligned countries practice this approach in the same way.)The Yugoslavs consider themselves non-aligned; so do the Egyptians, Indians, Ethiopians, Malaysians, and Tunisians. Yet the dispositions of these countries range from sentiments that might be described as pro-Soviet to those that might be called pro-American. In a way, the problem of classifying the varieties of nonalignment is one of *time*. A regime may be looking eastward one moment yet normalize its relations with the West the next. Ethiopia is pro-American one year; then a new regime shifts toward the East. Egypt for many years seemed to be a Soviet pawn—indeed, in 1971 it formalized its association with a treaty of friendship and cooperation—but a year later it threw out its Soviet advisers and within two more years its president had reestablished diplomatic re-lations with the United States, called American Jewish Secretary of State Kissinger his "good friend and miracle worker," and denounced the treaty of friendship with Russia. Similarly, in the early 1970s India under Indira Gandhi signed a friendship treaty with Russia. But a few years later, after she had been defeated in a general election, her successor declared that his government would adopt a foreign policy of "proper nonalignment" and that the Indian-Soviet friendship treaty would not be allowed to interfere with India's relations with other countries—presumably the Western states. After her reelection, Mrs. Gandhi shifted again somewhat toward Russia.

(Nonalignment is even more a matter of *issue areas*.[36] One such area is military.)Egypt and India received vast amounts of military equipment from Russia; on the other hand, Singapore was willing to make its naval base available to the West in the event of hostilities, and Tanzania once relied upon the former mother country's (Britain's) military forces to restore domestic order. Yet all these countries consider themselves nonaligned. Some seek and gain military aid from both sides. The same is true for such other issue areas as economic assistance and trade, diplomacy, and ideology. Country A may be leaning westward because it places a high priority on democratic values, receives most of its military hardware from the West, receives about equal amounts of economic aid from both sides, and gravitates more toward Western than Soviet diplomatic positions (although India, for example, democratic tradition notwithstanding, has often gravitated the other way). Country B, in contrast, is politically sympathetic to the East, from which it receives military hardware, obtains much of its economic aid and trade from the West, and leans notably eastward on diplomatic issues (although again, a one-party state like Egypt, with its "Arab socialism," has switched from a pro-Soviet stance toward rapprochement with the United States, beside dismantling much of it brand of socialism in order to release private initiative and attract foreign investments while retaining some public ownership over certain sectors of the economy).

Even when a nonaligned country seems to lean more toward Russia or the United States, however, one must be careful: the term "pro-Soviet" may reflect a general attitude and preference on the part of national leaders, but it may also indicate positions that those leaders would have taken even in the absence of a cold

---

[36] Cecil V. Crabb, *The Elephants and the Grass* (New York: Holt, Rinehart and Winston, 1965), pp. 20–38.

388 war—anticolonialism or anti-apartheid, for example—and with which the Soviets seek to identify themselves. The same is true of a country that seems pro-American: Anwar Sadat is an Egyptian nationalist first, and when he leans toward the United States, it is because in his view Washington leaders can better help him achieve his goal of recovering Egyptian lands lost in 1967 because they have influence in Israel and the Soviets do not. On balance, however, nonalignment more often than not has seemed—and may continue to seem—to be pro-Soviet because of continuing anti-Western feelings.

Apart from still unfaded feelings about Western colonial governments, the new countries still attribute all sorts of ills, from white minority control and racism in South Africa to the continued role of the LDCs as raw-material suppliers for Western industries, to the West's indirect, or "neocolonial," control by economic means. The conviction that, despite their political independence, the distribution of power between the first and third worlds is still stacked against them and that the industrial West continues to determine the rules of the economic game in order to keep them poor and dependent has led the nonaligned countries to take increasingly anti-Western stands. In the sense that the many countries of Asia, Africa, and Latin America can be thought of as a cohesive bloc, despite regional and national differences, it is because they share this set of attitudes and feelings. As they are already anti-Western, all the Soviet Union has to do is to sympathize and identify itself with third-world causes.

FROM NONALIGNMENT TO THE NEW INTERNATIONAL ECONOMIC ORDER

The LDCs' anti-Western sentiments appear to be growing as the gap between the rich and poor nations widens. Aid has not helped to bring about self-sustaining growth. Trade has not earned sufficient funds to permit the LDCs to diversify their economies and make them less dependent upon single commodities for exports. The domestic problems that impede modernization remain enormous. Increasingly, therefore, the LDCs have argued that they cannot possibly overcome these obstacles and modernize themselves because they are victims of an international economy dominated by the industrial West. The causes and cures of underdevelopment, they claim, are not internal but external.

We have already noted the difficulties that most LDCs face in earning money on the international market. They are too dependent on single resources; the prices of these resources fluctuate with the Western industrial economies; competition among producers tends to lead to oversupplies, forcing prices downward; and, when Western industries substitute other resources or synthetics, prices are further depressed. In the meantime, the manufactured goods bought in the West tend to rise in price. The "terms of trade" do not therefore favor the LDCs.

It is in this context that the LDCs have increasingly claimed publicly that their relations with the industrial West have not changed much since colonial days. Formerly the colonies were governed directly from London, Paris, or other Western capitals. Since independence, the former colonies have achieved self-government but, they insist, their independence is only formal, rather than meaningful (Indeed, this formal independence masks the fact that *real* self-government does not exist, that the LDCs remain tied to their former masters by the same economic chains that characterized the colonial era. It is these chains that have kept and continue to keep them dependent on the industrial West.[37])

Their economies are as a result not oriented toward their national needs, toward improving the lives of their own peoples. Their resources were originally developed by the West and then used by Western industry for the production of goods that have raised the *Western* standard of living to the highest in the world. LDCs' economies are still tied to exports of cheap raw materials. North America, Europe, and Japan thus benefit enormously from resources from the southern half of the globe and dominate the international economy. The free market, which in theory benefits all nations, clearly favors the strong; the laws of supply and demand are not neutral. Rather, they work to keep the LDCs in a subordinate position. The LDCs are raw-material appendages and are likely to remain so, because keeping them underdeveloped benefits the advanced industrial countries of the West. The international economy thus limits the possibilities for their development.

(Dependency is a relationship characterized by asymmetry, in which the LDCs' economic growth is conditioned by events in the industrialized nations' economies. (Interdependence, on the other hand, is characterized by symmetry.)) (More specifically, the LDCs' dependence takes several forms. One is trade dependence.) They depend on the industrial states for markets in which to sell their commodities and are obviously both sensitive and vulnerable to levels of demand in the latter. Another form is investment dependence. Western investors control key sectors of the LDCs' economies: production of natural resources and any manufacturing that may have been developed. Foreign aid creates yet a third form of dependence. And, if these economic chains were not sufficient, they are usually supplemented by political alliances and military and police link to the LDCs' ruling elites, which often have vested intersts in preserving the dependent relationship. If the power of an elite is threatened, covert or overt foreign intervention cannot be ruled out. In these ways, the LDCs are managed by the Western industrialized countries, the real beneficiaries of the free market.

(The political objective of the LDCs is to change the international economy so that international wealth is more equitably distributed. The LDCs seek several concrete goals: higher and stable commodity prices (to provide steady income "decoupled" from Western economic fluctuations) so that they can plan for several years ahead, diversify their economies, and become less dependent on the sale of single resources; the protection of their purchasing power through "indexing," linking the sale of resources to Western inflation rates and rising prices for Western machinery, weapons, and food; doubling or tripling capital contributions from such

---

[37.] See Ward, Lenore D'Anjou, and J.D. Runnalls, eds., *The Widening Gap* (New York: Columbia University Press, 1971); Karl P. Sauvant and Hajo Hasenplug, eds., *The New Inter-National Economic Order* (Boulder, Colo.: Westview, 1977); and Jagdish Bhagwati, ed., *The New International Economic Order* (Cambridge, Mass.: M.I.T. Press, 1977).

390   international institutions as the International Monetary Fund, the International Bank for Reconstruction and Development, and the World Bank (in all of which they seek greater membership and voice); preferential Western tariffs for LDC exports, which would give them a competitive edge and enhance their earning capacity; a voice in controlling the levels of production and prices of alternative sources of minerals (like those found on the sea beds); deferment of debts—a debt which had increased from $142 billion in 1974 to $315 billion by 1978 for the non-OPEC LDCs[38]—which means postponing the costs of servicing these debts; and greater control over the multinational corporations (MNCs).) Although satisfaction of these demands would hardly constitute a revolutionary transformation of the international economy, it would constitute a New International Economic Order (N.I.E.O.), in which the industrial West's perceived control of the economic rules of the game would be reduced. The demands reflect the LDCs' struggle to end past humiliations, and their determination to stand on their own feet and control—or at least actively participate in—the determination of their own futures.

    Essentially a rational policy, from the perspective of the LDCs, the call for an N.I.E.O. is also a highly emotional issue, and it is therefore very difficult to deal with, especially for the United States, which finds itself the chief target of this anti-Western and anti-neocolonial movement. Pointing to its own history as the first "new nation," exhibiting the Declaration of Independence as an inspiration for foreign leaders, and stressing its understanding of the humiliation involved in being a colony and its record of support for self-determination do little good. Nor is it useful to point out that the poverty of the LDCs is not basically the result of Western exploitation but rather the result of their not yet having experienced the "stages of economic growth"—that is, the modernization process by which the large Western states were transformed into the urban-industrial, rich, and usually democratic states that they are today. It is even less useful to criticize the common disregard for individual dignity, human rights, and human life, and instances of discrimination and exploitation in the LDCs themselves.

    The third and fourth worlds are deeply resentful of their past treatment and present lot in the state system. It may be said that the poor and plentiful people of the southern half of this planet are no longer willing to be the "hewers of wood and drawers of water" for the rich states of the northern half. It is worth repeating that this attitude is the main reason why the poorer LDCs, though the hardest hit by OPEC policies, have continued to support OPEC enthusiastically. The louder the rich Western countries squeal, the greater is the delight of all the LDCs. As William Wordsworth wrote of the French Revolution, "Bliss was it in that dawn to be alive/But to be young was very heaven." A fourth world poet might have written those lines in the winter of 1973–1974. Throwing off the alleged chains of economic dependence may be the major task for the LDCs. But, though economics can be discussed rationally, the issues being negotiated are only partly economic. The discussion of terms of trade is deeply symptomatic of a general assertion of non-Western nationalism against the West. The economic bargaining

---

[38] *The New York Times*, April 14, 1980. Most of these debts were held by Western banks.

has been taking place, therefore, between parties who are all too frequently and too deeply separated by wide psychological and cultural barriers.

(The Western industrial countries maintain that the LDCs' problems are primarily internal: arising from population growth, low priority for agricultural development, unfavorable attitudes toward private enterprise and entrepreneurial initiative, and frequent condemnation of MNCs as tools of neocolonial exploitation, rather than acceptance of them as sources of technology, jobs, capital, and marketing skills. The first world notes that the poorest nations of the world are those not involved in international trade, whereas the most advanced LDCs are those nations that are deeply involved in international trade—nations like South Korea, Taiwan (Nationalist China), Hong Kong, Singapore, and Brazil. The developed countries do not deny that more could be done to help the LDCs, for example, helping to stabilize export earnings, lowering or elimination of tariff barriers, agricultural assistance, and channeling more economic aid through international agencies. But they do reject the charge that they are deliberately pursuing a policy of keeping the LDCs weak, poor, underdeveloped, and mere sources of raw materials.

The LDCs, on the other hand, are not simply arguing that in the international economy the rich and the strong have an advantage over the poor and weak; they are also insisting that they are poor because they have been robbed and exploited by the Western industrial powers. It is obviously more emotionally satisfying to blame one's unfortunate condition on external causes than to labor hard in the domestic arena and to achieve little in the face of so many obstacles. Equally, it is a shrewd bargaining tactic. The LDCs have, after all, little leverage: OPEC has leverage, and therefore most of the rest of the LDCs have attached themselves to OPEC. They hope that, in return for their support, the cartel will bargain on their behalf for better terms for their own commodities and manufactured goods. The LDCs also use the United Nations and other international bodies as forums in which to air their grievances and aspirations, to bring themselves more closely together, and to place the West on the defensive. Morality, no less than arms, can be an effective "weapon." Moral outrage is an especially attractive instrument of policy for the weak, which possess few sticks and carrots and hope that moral appeals will gain for them what strength cannot.

Insisting that their poverty is the result of Western exploitation, the LDCs claim that the West therefore owes them a moral debt for past colonial sins, which it must pay off in more earthly coin. Charging that the West plundered them in the past and continues to do so today, they repeat over and over again that such "imperialistic exploitation"—the slogan of the LDCs—is wrong. Presumably, in their view, Western political organization, economic ideas, scientific inventiveness, and technological skills have had little to do with creating Western prosperity. The attempt to induce a sense of Western guilt for past behavior is shrewd because many Westerners do feel ashamed and morally culpable for what their forefathers did, even though the political standards and moral codes were quite different in the colonial age. Reparations for past errors thus seems "the right thing to do"; helping the poor by narrowing the gap between them and the rich constitutes, for

392   these Westerners, a morally worthy cause, a way of gaining national redemption and of living up to the promise of a democratic way of life.

In a sense, OPEC, by redistributing income to the needy, is seen by the LDCs as doing what the rich countries have failed to do with foreign aid. How can the industrial West oppose the poorer nations' efforts to remedy the vast differences in standards of living and bring about more eqitable distribution of the world's goods? It has thus been placed in a morally ambiguous, if not indefensible, position by its own commitment to national self-determination and an egalitarianism in which inequality is equated with injustice and poverty is considered morally unacceptable. Are not all men—not just Americans—endowed with equal rights? The LDCs have exploited this sense of guilt and compassion: They have argued that the industrial West is consuming more than its fair portion of the world's resources, rather than unselfishly sharing its wealth with the poorer countries, and spending on armaments billions upon billions of dollars that could—and should—be spent on improving the lot of mankind. Here is Cuba's Castro speaking on behalf of the LDCs at the United Nations right after the ninety-two professed nonaligned nations met in Havana in 1979:

> The nonaligned countries stress the fact that it is imperative to do away with the enormous inequality that separates the developed from the developing counties. We are struggling for an eradication of poverty, of hunger, disease and illiteracy from which hundreds of millions of human beings still suffer. We aspire to a new world order—one based on justice, on equity and peace, one that will replace the unjust and unequal system which prevails today in which . . . "wealth is still concentrated in the hands of a few powers whose wasteful economies are maintained by the exploitation of labor as well as the transfer and the plunder of the national and other resources of the peoples of Africa, Latin America, Asia and other regions of the world. . . . "

> Arms expenditures are irrational. They must cease and the funds thus released be used to finance development. . . . The world is making an annual investment in military expenditures of more than $300 billion. With $300 billion you could in one year build 600,000 schools with a capacity for 400 million children, or you could build 60 million comfortable homes for 300 million people, or you could build 30,000 hospitals with 18 millions beds, or you could build irrigation systems to water 150 million hectares of land, which with the appropriate technology, could feed a billion people.[39]

Can any man of conscience really disagree? It is not wholly surprising, then, as the LDCs' frustration and at anger have risen since 1973, that nonalignment has increasingly appeared to be alignment with the Soviet Union and its ideological friends against the West. The Soviets had charged all along that the poverty and misery of the non-Western world have been the results of Western capitalism and imperialism. Still, it seems odd to find Vietnam, Afghanistan, North Korea, and Cuba accepted as nonaligned nations, odder still that the 1979 conference was held in Havana; and oddest that, when Vietnam was cruelly driving its Chinese pop-

---

[39.] *The New York Times*, October 13, 1979.

ulation out of the country, usually in boats that would not survive long ocean journeys, its behavior was not condemned as racist and that neither Vietnam's invasion of Cambodia nor the starvation of the Cambodian people in order to gain diplomatic recognition for the Vietnamese puppet regime in Cambodia was condemned as aggression or a crime against humanity.[40] The Soviets and the LDCs would not have hesitated to use such phrases had the United States acted in similar ways. Nevertheless, this coalition between the Soviet Union and the nonaligned nations is probably temporary and tactical. The latter are nationalistic, and they have not fought for national independence only to lose it to Soviet imperialism.

FROM N.I.E.O. TO INTERNATIONAL CLASS WAR?

In the original Western rationale for economic aid to countries of the third world, it is clear that, beside simple humanitarian sentiments, security considerations were uppermost. Perhaps the basic reason for such concern sprang from a logic frequently articulated by government spokesmen, academicians, and journalists and thus often implicit in policy: that a world divided between rich and poor nations is an explosive world in which the majority, which is poor, is set against the privileged minority. Such a gap is no more acceptable internationally than within each of the Western nations 100 years ago.

The two situations are believed to be so similar that the "lesson" of the previous experience can be applied to the international division of wealth. As the Industrial Revolution gathered momentum in the European countries and the United States, it created a privileged minority, which owned most of the wealth. The distribution of income was, to say the least, unequal. Laborers, including many children and women, worked fourteen to sixteen hours a day six or seven days a week, earned little beyond subsistence, and lived in overcrowded slums. The rich became richer, and the poor became poorer. This trend was so obvious that Benjamin Disraeli spoke of England as not one nation but two.

But, according to the prevailing free-market, or *laissez-faire*, philosophy, nothing could be done to alleviate this situation. Government intervention, whether to end the grosser forms of exploitation or to redistribute income to help the poor lead more decent and dignified lives, was rejected as contrary to the "laws of economics." Any outside interference with the workings of the market, it was said, would stifle the private incentive and initiative that stoked the competitive capitalist system. These "laws," which condemned a large section of the population to hopeless and miserable existence, received even further support from Charles Darwin's theory of evolution, with its emphasis on the "struggle for survival" and the "survival of the fittest." The philosophy of Social Darwinism was based on the very simple proposition that the rich are rich because they are the most fit; conversely, the poor are destitute because they are unfit. It never occurred to Social Darwinists to ask whether or not everyone had an equal start or opportunity in this struggle.

[40.] *The New York Times*, September 12, 1979.

394

These philosophical justifications for permitting abject poverty were ultimately rejected in all Western societies. The long working hours, unsanitary and unsafe working conditions, and teeming slums were blots on the national conscience. Permitting them to continue would also have been politically short-sighted and economically foolish. Politically, the permanent division of people into "haves" and "have nots" could end only in revolution, with the industrial middle class, or bourgeoisie, being overthrown by the working class, or proletariat. The bourgeoisie could, perhaps, retain its power by surrendering democratic beliefs and values and establishing authoritarian governments to crush proletarian protests and uprisings. Neither of these alternatives seemed attractive to the ruling middle classes. Nor did the policy of squeezing the workers for maximum profit make sense economically, for, the less money people have, the fewer things they can buy. Industry needs consumers. Social justice thus made sense—morally, politically, and economically.

In the late nineteenth century government in every Western society began to intervene increasingly in the economy. Growing public awareness of social problems and ills eventually led to the regulation of business: passage of minimum-wage and maximum-hours legislation; abolition of child labor and "sweatshop" working conditions; recognition of trade unions; measures to counteract the swings of the business cycle; implementation of a progressive income tax; and the initiation of unemployment insurance, public-works programs, and other "pump priming" projects to increase the purchasing power of the people during depressions and thus to stimulate renewed demand and production. These measures helped to create the twentieth-century mass market and gave the working class a vested interest in the existing social and economic order.

It is the same problem of inequitable distribution of income that is now plaguing the world. But this time the problem exists not within nations but among nations. The rich countries are becoming richer, the poor countries poorer. The unfettered operation of the "laws of economics" seems as dangerous now as it was in the nineteenth century. The Marxist prophecy that the exploited proletariat will overthrow the bourgeoisie may have been incorrect as far as Western industrial societies are concerned, but will it be fulfilled on the global plane? Will the poverty-stricken nations of the world, the international proletariat, rise up in revolution against the privileged and wealthy Western countries, the international bourgeoisie?

Indeed, this question loomed all the more ominously because of the growing Western dependence on OPEC oil and several non-OPEC oil producing countries. For most non-OPEC LDCs the expectations for modernization will be adversely affected; for some development will be slowed, but for many it is more likely to be set back,[41] polarizing the division between rich and poor nations, even though the rich may be becoming less rich as their economic growth rates slow down too, and the poor nations no longer include the OPEC and other oil-producing states, many of whom remain classified as "less developed countries." Such polarization will surely be accompanied by growing confrontation between the

---

[41] The retiring president of the World Bank predicted in 1980 that the average annual growth over the next four years would be 1.8 percent, compared to 2.7 percent during the 1970s and 3.1 percent in the 1960s. *The New York Times*, October 1, 1980.

haves and have-nots. (In short, the era of tighter oil supplies and ever higher oil prices, of slow economic growth or recession in the West—which means a lower demand for non-oil resources from the LDCs and lower prices for those sold by them, as well as less foreign aid from the Western states as their prosperity declines—may well be the era of international class war.) Some will gain at the cost of others in this age of increasing scarcity; the strong will survive and the weak must suffer in a world in which there is not enough to go around. But they may not suffer in silence and acquiesce in their lot. After all, were the meek—the vast majority, *les misérables*—not supposed to inherit the world?

15

Imperialism: The Marxist and Devil Versions

THE ECONOMIC INTERPRETATION OF POLITICS

Another analytical framework, in which the domestic system is the principal basis for explaining and predicting national foreign policy, is Marxism-Leninism. Specifically, Marxism-Leninism suggests only one responsible factor—the economy. The basic thesis is that a nation's foreign policy reflects the nature of its economic system and the corresponding class structure. This explanation, unlike those based on national and elite styles, is not intended to account for all nations' foreign policies. It claims a special insight into the foreign policies of a few states—in this instance, developed or industrial states with capitalist economies. Essentially it is argued that a capitalist state, because of its economy, is compelled to be expansionist, militaristic, interventionist, and reactionary; the capitalist search for profit leaves no choice but to extend control beyond national frontiers. (By definition, a socialist state, one that does not have an economy based on the search for profit, is not expansionist and is concerned only with guarding itself against the capitalist enemy.)

Such Marxist-Leninist explanations gained some popularity in the United States during the Vietnam war because the supposed "real reasons" for American intervention seemed more plausible and persuasive than those based on balances of power and systemic drives. North Vietnam was hardly in a position to threaten this country; its power was negligible compared to that of the United States. The need to stop communism was an unacceptable explanation to many critics in the middle and late 1960s. Therefore the only possible reason for the intervention, it was claimed by some of the more radical critics, was internal and economic: American leaders must have thought that intervention would be profitable. Indeed, these critics argued that the fundamental nature of the economy—including production, employment, and prosperity—not only could not be doubted but also provided the most revealing explanation for all American foreign policy, not just that in Vietnam. What Marxists call "the mode of production" was viewed as *the* determining cause of American policy. In the words of Gabriel Kolko, a historian:

> The way Americans define the causes of the Indochina debacle will determine whether they shall be intellectually prepared to anticipate future crises. Conventional wisdom still attributes America's role in Vietnam to accidents or bureaucratic myopia, thereby slighting the real meaning of the consistency of American interventions in the Third World in suppressing radical forces and preserving semi-colonial societies.
>
> Vietnam was an "accident" along a much older, intrinsically dangerous route only insofar as Washington's goals there far exceeded its power to attain them, and it eventually became profoundly dysfunctional to the U.S.'s global priorities and needs. But to divorce Vietnam and numerous interventions from the specific goals of American capitalism in the world, assuming that the needs and values of capitalism are irrelevant to the range of policy options decision-makers consider, is sanctioned ideology but poor history and debilitating to our capacity to anticipate our future.
>
> *War, from preparations through aftermath, is the central element in defining the essential quality of capitalist societies* as well as their relative power throughout this century, and it has also become the main catalyst to revolutionary movements and changes in vast areas.[1]

If it was the war which conferred upon this type of view a certain degree of popularity in this country, it ought to be noted that in the Soviet Union, in many less developed countries (LDCs) and some sectors of European academia, Marxism-Leninism is widely accepted as a way of viewing and understanding the world. Thus we need to know more about the background and intellectual content of this analytical framework.

THE MARXIST BACKGROUND: THE CLASS STRUGGLE AND THE GRAVEDIGGERS

Marxism arose as part of a general protest movement—which ranged from revolutionary anarchism to utopian socialism, from the Luddites to the Christian Socialists—against nineteenth-century industrial capitalism. Although industrialization

---

[1] Gabriel Kolko, "A War from Time to Time," *The New York Times*, March 6, 1973 (emphasis added).

eventually led to rapidly rising standards of living for the masses, the principal goal in its early stages was sustained economic growth. The reason was inherent in the process of industrialization itself, for accumulation of capital (what economists call capital goods)—that is, factories, machinery, and other durable equipment—is basic. This of course, is an oversimplification of the nature of industrialization. (Industrialization is basically a process of economic growth, but it is also vastly more than that; without an accompanying cultural, political, and social revolution in which the old rural and static society is uprooted, no industrial revolution can occur.) The industrialization of a society is thus more than a "technical" problem. Nevertheless, the essence of industrialization remains the increase of a society's industrial capital, for it is that capital, when combined with human labor, that will permit an increase in productivity. The machine allows the worker to raise his or her industrial output, producing in a day what he or she might otherwise have produced in a week. This higher productivity can more adequately meet consumer demands for whatever goods are required. The result is better living conditions.

Ironically, capital can be accumulated only if consumption is postponed. In order to build a factory, expand an already existing factory, or buy more machinery, a businessman must invest money. But where does the investor obtain this money? The answer is that the sum invested comes primarily out of profits. Although the business proprietor could simply save this money, the desire for more profit leads him or her to reinvest it. And to acquire maximum profits, he or she pays workers as little as possible and makes them work as long as possible. Otherwise, the profit margin will be lower, and money for investment will be less—which, in turn, will slow the rate of industrialization. The industrial working class thus pays a large part of the price of industrialization. The farmer, too, pays a price, for, if industrial wages are to be kept low, the cost of staples in the laborer's diet must also be kept low. The process of industrialization is essentially the same, regardless of the nature of the economic system. Even a communist society accumulates capital in this manner; there, however, it is the state, rather than the private entrepreneur, that accumulates the capital and squeezes it out of the general population.

The terrible effects of industrialization on workers in the nineteenth century have been vividly described in many works, including Karl Marx's *Das Kapital*. Edmund Wilson, in his recreation of the arrival of Friedrich Engels in Manchester, described it thus:

> He saw the working people living like rats in the wretched little dens of their dwellings, whole families sometimes more than one family, swarming in a single room, well and diseased, adults and children, close relations sleeping together, sometimes even without beds to sleep on when all the furniture had been sold for firewood, sometimes in damp, underground cellars which had to be bailed out when the weather was wet, sometimes living in the same room with pigs; ill nourished on flour mixed with gypsum and cocoa mixed with dirt, and their wailing children with laudanum; spending their lives, without a sewage system, among the piles of their excrement and garbage; spreading epidemics of typhus and cholera which even made inroads into the well-to-do sections.

The increasing demand for women and children at the factories was throwing the fathers of families permanently out of work, arresting the physical development of the girls, letting the women in for illegitimate motherhood and yet compelling them to come to work when they were pregnant or before they had recovered from having their babies, and ultimately turning a good many of them into prostitutes; while the children, fed into the factories at the age of five or six, receiving little care from mothers who were themselves at the factory all day and no education at all from a community which wanted them only to perform mechanical operations, would drop exhausted when they were let out of their prisons, too tired to wash or eat, let alone study or play, sometimes too tired to get home at all. In the iron and coal mines, also, women and children as well as men spent the better part of their lives crawling underground in narrow tunnels, and emerging, found themselves caught in the meshes of the company cottage and the company store and of the two-week postponement of wages. They were being killed off at the rate of fourteen hundred a year through the breaking of rotten ropes, the caving-in of workings due to overexcavated seams and the explosions due to bad ventilation and to the negligence of tired children; if they escaped catastrophic accidents, the lung diseases eventually got them. The agricultural population, for its part, deprived by the industrial development of their old status of handicraftsmen and yeomen who either owned their own land and homes or were taken care of with more or less certainty by a landlord on whose estate they were tenants, had been transformed into wandering day laborers, for whom nobody took responsibility and who were punished by jail or transportation if they ventured in times of need to steal and eat the landlord's game.

It seemed to Engels that the medieval serf, who had at least been attached to the land and had a definite position in society, had had an advantage over the factory worker. At that period when legislation for the protection of labor had hardly seriously gotten under way, the old peasantry and hand-workers of England, and even old petty middle class, were being shoveled into the mines and the mills like so much raw material for the prices their finished products would bring, with no attempt even to dispose of the waste. In years of depression the surplus people, so useful in years of good business, were turned out upon the town to become peddlers, crossing-sweepers, scavengers or simply beggars—sometimes whole families were seen begging in the streets—and, almost as frequently, whores and thieves.[2]

Marxism was a legacy of the Industrial Revolution. Specifically, it was one of many moral protests against the cruelties and miseries suffered by the worker. Such exploitation of human beings by human beings had to be ended, for it violated the whole Western humanitarian tradition from its Judaeo-Christian beginnings to the French Revolution. Professed equality of human beings had become meaningless in a society so deeply divided between the privileged few and the underprivileged many. The dignity and freedom of the individual had little reality, for

---

[2] Edmund Wilson, *To the Finland Station* (Garden City, N.Y.: Anchor, 1953), pp. 134–136. Used by permission of the author. For revealing documents of the period, see E. Royston Pike, *"Hard Times": Human Documents of the Industrial Revolution* (New York: (Holt, Rinehart and Winston, 1966); and Albert Fried and Richard M. Elman, eds., *Charles Booth's London* (New York: Pantheon, 1968).

400   the majority of men and women were paid only subsistence wages if they found any employment at all. Capitalism had enslaved people economically.

A system based on production for the "profit of the few" had to be changed to one based on production for the "use of the many." To be sure, capitalism had brought mankind great benefits. And no one praised its success more openly than its greatest critic: "The bourgeoisie, during its rule of scarce one hundred years," Marx wrote in *The Communist Manifesto*, "has created more massive and more colossal productive forces than have all preceding generations together. Subjection of nature's forces to man, machinery, application of chemistry to industry, and agriculture, steam-navigation, railways, electric telegraphs, clearing of whole continents for cultivation, canalisation of rivers, whole populations conjured out of the ground—what earlier century had even a presentiment that such productive forces slumbered in the lap of social labour?"[3] But, though the bourgeoisie had created the industrial machinery, it was itself the greatest obstacle to mass production for the benefit of society. Marx believed that capitalism could never abolish poverty by providing human beings only with basic necessities, for an economic system based upon the profit motive could result only in inequitable distribution of income. It was the desire for profit that itself caused workers' poverty and degradation, and profit was the outcome of private control over means of production. Capitalism therefore had to be replaced by a more just system—socialism—if the "acquisitive society" was to be transformed into a society concerned with social justice for the underprivileged. In a socialist society the working class would own the means of production and would therefore receive a fair share of the national income.

But Marxian socialism was more than a moral protest; it was also "scientific." Indeed, Marxism can be defined as that school of socialism that seeks to prove that the coming of socialism is inevitable.[4] In that respect, it is a natural outgrowth of the general Western belief in the inevitability of progress and the widespread equation of progress with improvement. This optimism was itself an offspring of the eighteenth century Age of Reason. A reaction to medieval society and philosophy, the Age of Reason—the Enlightenment—stood in direct contradiction to the religion-dominated and tradition-bound ethos of feudal Europe. The Enlightenment substituted reason for God, and the material world became the chief human concern; the creation of a better life was the chief goal. The perfect society was to be created here and now. The human condition, the result not of sin but of ignorance, was to be altered through reason, not grace. As controllers of their own fate, human beings could create the kind of world they wanted because God had given them reason with which to build paradise on earth; secular, rather than spiritual, activities were to be the chief focus of human strivings. The thinkers of the Enlightenment posited a rational universe, which could be mastered through knowledge. Knowledge would reveal comprehensible laws. Once those laws had been discovered, all problems of human existence could be solved. (The Age of Enlightenment thus stressed "materialism," defined simply as "realism," the ra-

---

[3] Arthur P. Mendel, *The Essential Works of Marxism* (New York: Bantam, 1961), pp. 17–18.

[4] Alfred G. Meyer, *Communism* (rev. ed.; New York: Random House, 1967), p. 12.

tional inquiry into the secular universe, composed of matter, in order to discover its laws.)

(Marx inherited this mental "set," and it was as a realist that he claimed that the capitalist system is historically doomed.) Capitalist thinkers asserted that the individual responds to economic self-interest in the same way that an individual atom responds to gravity. Given self-interest as the basic human motivation, the "economic laws" that supposedly will maximize society's economic benefits are the laws of supply and demand operating through the free market. The capitalist argument is simple. The individual wishes to augment his or her wealth; the desire for profit therefore leads him or her to produce whatever product consumers demand. Naturally, he or she will try to charge as much as possible. But, because others, in their search for profit, may produce the same item, the price must be competitive. If he or she charges more for the same item, no one will buy it. And what price can he or she charge? Each producer, hoping for increased sales, will try to undersell competitors. But no producer can sell at less than cost and stay in business. And, if costs are higher than those of the competitors, the producer must go out of business or find a more efficient method of production. Free competition thus has four results: supplies of products that consumers demand, sale of goods at minimal cost to consumers, profit for producers, and the continuation of only efficient operations in business. The "economic laws" supposedly channel each individual's self-interest in socially beneficial directions, and the competitive mechanism of the market is said to provide for the "greatest good of the greatest number." The free market as a way of organizing an economy for production and distribution thus theoretically guarantees harmony of interest between producers and consumers.

(Marx accepted this description of the capitalist market and the assumption that economics is the primary motivation for human behavior; he therefore focused his criticism on what he considered the central feature of the market: the transformation of all relations among individuals into exchange or monetary relations.) In a market society, it seemed to Marx, such relations were the only meaningful bonds among individuals. The consumer, in order to obtain the goods he or she wants, offers a cash incentive; the producer, to sell his or her goods, responds to the consumer's demands. Human beings are thus linked to one another as buyers and sellers through money, but they are also linked as employers and employees, and again the relation is a monetary one. For, in fact, the employer *buys* labor power, which the worker sells in order to obtain money with which to buy the goods necessary to sustain himself or herself. For Marx, the distinguishing feature of capitalism was the fact that not only goods but also *people* were sold on the market. Indeed, human labor was sold as was any other product. The bourgeoisie, as Marx bitterly remarked, "has left no other bond between man and man than naked self-interest, than callous 'cash payment.' . . . It has resolved personal worth into exchange value, and in place of the numberless indefeasible chartered freedoms, has set up that single, unconscionable freedom — Free Trade."[5]

In the end, the exploitation of the workers is the result of this treatment of human beings as commodities. Marx, like laissez-faire economists, maintained

---

[5] Quoted in *ibid.*, p. 15.

402   that the value of a product is equivalent to the amount of labor expended in its production. How then, he asked, is profit derived? If the exchange value, or cost, of a product equals its labor cost, then profit can be gained only by raising the price above market value or by paying the worker less. The latter option, he claimed, was the one chosen. The worker received only a subsistence wage—enough to keep him or her alive and able to work and reproduce; to the employer, a person's labor was worth no more than it took to keep him or her alive. The difference between what the worker should have been paid in terms of the cash *value* of his or her labor invested in the product and what he or she was actually paid represented the profit, or "surplus value."

(The significance of Marx's theory of value lies in its sociological implications. His analysis of the free market emphasizes not only the production and exchange of commodities, but also the *social organization* for production. Capitalists and proletariat need each other; both classes are compelled to cooperate. Each contributes a specific function: one the capital goods (what Marx called the "means of production"), the other the labor power. But, although the two classes are functionally interdependent, they are also mutually antagonistic. The capitalists exploit the proletariat because the market transforms human relations—whether between buyer and seller or between employer and employee—into exchange, or monetary, relations. The capitalists, to maximize their profits, will squeeze as much surplus value out of labor as possible; and, although they constitute only a minority of the population, they can continue their exploitation of the majority because they own and control the means of production and thus the power of the state.)

Political philosophers from Aristotle onward have analyzed the interaction between private power and control of the state. It has long been understood that groups organize to protect their interests and to extend their reach into the political arena. In some ways, Marx was furthering this interpretation when he noted that the bourgeoisie controls not only economic but also political power. But for Marx capitalism was more than an attempt to manipulate the apparatus of the state by private interests; the state is, in his words, nothing but the "executive committee of the bourgeoisie," a superstructure that reflects and reinforces the economic arrangements (capitalism) of the substructure. The state thus perpetuates capitalist exploitation of the proletariat. The result can be no less than a class struggle between the exploiters and the exploited.

Nor is this class struggle, according to Marx, unique to capitalism. (In every economic system, the "forces of production" produce corresponding "relations of production," or social structure.) In the Greek and Roman slave system, which succeeded the stage of "primitive communism" (in which all production and distribution had been communal), there were slaveowners and slaves. In medieval feudalism there were landowners and serfs. And in industrial capitalism there are capitalists and proletarians. In each system the "superstructure"—the state and the law, the moral and religious code, even art and family life—have reflected the economic substructure. (Every economic system has been divided between "haves" and "have nots," and consequently all have been racked by class struggle.[6]) Because

---

[6.] *Ibid.*, pp. 13–14.

the political system has been controlled, a political solution to the class struggle has been foreclosed; political reforms are meaningless, for in the end the haves will never willingly relinquish control. Will the worker ever achieve abundance and freedom from his or her "economic slavery"? Not by means of reforms, according to Marx. The "laws of economics," he argued, will however, assure his liberation.

(The bourgeoisie and the proletariat, then, are not fated to face each other eternally. "Judgment day" for the capitalist class will come, Marx predicted, for the proletarian revolution is *historically inevitable.* The economic forces that caused the death of the slave and feudal systems will do the same for capitalism. From the theory of surplus value, which for Marx was the axle around which the capitalist wheel revolved, Marx derived three economic laws, by which he explained the behavior of the system—and predicted its doom. The first was the law of "capitalist accumulation." Each capitalist, seeking to maximize profits, expands output in order to sell more than competitors sell. To do so, the capitalist must hire more workers, but, as the labor supply is bought up, labor costs will rise and, in turn, cut into profits. Each employer must therefore install labor-saving machinery to reduce costs and preserve profit margins. He or she thus accumulates capital. But he or she is simultaneously working against himself or herself. The source of surplus value is the very worker whom he or she must now replace. The increasing proportion of machinery to labor therefore produces the very thing that the introduction of machinery was supposed to prevent: a decline in profits. The second law—the "concentration of capital"—follows logically. The competitive process arising from the struggle for profits drives weaker capitalists into bankruptcy, thus concentrating capital in fewer and fewer hands. Eventually, this process ends in the establishment of monopolies. Together, these two laws produce the third, the law of "increasing misery." On one hand, as the capitalists are driven out of business and the workers are displaced by machinery, there will be large-scale unemployment and, simultaneously, an increase in the size of the proletariat, caused by entry into it of all capitalists who have lost out. On the other hand, the capitalist, compelled to compensate for falling profits, must intensify exploitation of the workers by further decreasing their subsistence wages. Because the unemployed—Marx called them the "industrial reserve army"—have no other means of existence, they have little choice but to accept work at any price. The wage level is then driven down for all workers. Surplus value increases but only for a time. The competitive process begins again, further decreasing profits, concentrating capital, and increasing the size and misery of the proletariat. And, through a series of recurring crises, each more severe than the preceding one, capitalism arrives at the final stage of its development— the proletarian revolution.)

(Capitalism, Marx held, would be its own gravedigger—for through industrialization it has fathered the very class that will overthrow it when it reaches economic maturity. The laws of the free market, ironically, will result in the overthrow of its main advocates. The forces of production will then no longer be privately owned. The exploitation of human beings by human beings will be ended forever, for society will no longer be divided between "haves" and "have nots." Industry, publicly owned by the "dictatorship of the proletariat," is to be used for the benefit of the proletariat. The dictatorship, however, is to be only temporary. Once its

404 principal purpose—the liquidation of the bourgeoisie—has been accomplished and private property, (the source of class formation and the class struggle) eliminated, the state is to "wither away," and a new period of history is to begin. Human beings will then be able to live in harmony, and the classless society will finally fulfill the ideals of fraternity, liberty, equality—and affluence—for the vast majority.)

LENIN, IMPERIALISM, AND GLOBAL REVOLUTION

The fundamental error committed by Marx was confusing capitalism with democracy. Because the state is the "executive committee" of the bourgeoisie, he said, capitalism cannot reform itself; the parliamentary institutions of capitalist states are merely façades for the "dictatorship of the bourgeoisie." According to Marx, the bourgeois minority will continue to use the power of the state to preserve its dominance over, and exploitation of, the proletariat and to quell any worker's disturbances or riots. This state of affairs will end only on the day that the proletariat rises up to overthrow its exploiters; because reform within the system is impossible, revolution is the only means of changing the system. This conclusion was perhaps natural at the time when Marx wrote, for the bourgeoisie was politically very powerful and the reform movement very weak. Certainly ruling groups or classes have not in the past willingly surrendered their power. The French Revolution, a bourgeois revolution against the traditional order, offers good evidence to support this conclusion.

Democracy, however, has helped to avoid the violent revolution that Marx forecasted. Capitalism might well have precipitated such a revolution had it been left unreformed. Workers did feel exploited. If a democratic reform movement had not responded to their grievances and needs, there would have been no alternative left to them but to seek satisfaction outside the system by nondemocratic and violent means. Capitalism, if it was to survive, had no choice but to accept democratic reforms. By accepting them, indeed, it consolidated its position, for its response to widespread needs won it popular allegiance. By meeting the aspirations of the workers through the creation of the welfare or social-service state, it "derevolutionized" them. As a result, the labor parties in central and western Europe abandoned the proletarian revolution. Revolution was replaced by democratic gradualism and peaceful change through the ballot box. And revolutionary Marxism became evolutionary socialism.

Marxists, therefore, had to ask themselves why the proletarian revolution had failed to occur. Democratic reform was the one answer they would not accept. Something that is evil cannot be made less evil by means of "reform." Perhaps its outward appearance can be altered, but it will remain basically unchanged. If capitalism is still evil and if it remains an exploitative order, why has it not collapsed, as Marx predicted? The usual explanation for the failure of the revolution is that the workers' rising living standards have given them a vested interest in the capitalist system and has been the principal reason why democratic socialists have given up their plans to overthrow capitalism. In Lenin's view, however, a movement to abandon the revolution and to acquire a larger share of the capitalist pie was no longer Marxist. Lenin recognized that higher wages for workers had undermined their proletarian consciousness and had made them reform-minded; in order to improve their material standards, they had developed what he called a "trade-union consciousness." The crucial question posed by this development was: What had made it possible for capitalists to raise paychecks, rather than, as had been predicted, being forced to decrease them further?

(As the ability of capitalism to reform itself had already been excluded, the answer had to be found in external circumstances. Colonialism, or imperialism, provided the key.[7] The "internal contradiction" of capitalism—the class struggle between the bourgeoisie and the proletariat—had been resolved by means of the capitalist indulgence in imperialism. It was imperialism that had changed the first and third laws of capitalism. The second law remained in force: Capital *was* concentrated in fewer and fewer hands. The era of imperialism was, indeed, the era of monopoly capitalism. But the law of capital accumulation, that had forecast declining profits, had been reversed. Imperialism was the source of huge profits— so huge, in fact, that Lenin called them "superprofits." Colonies provided inexpensive raw materials and cheap labor. They also provided markets in which goods produced in the metropolitan countries could be sold and investment opportunities for surplus capital.)

(It was now clear why the European workers' living standards had risen, despite the law of increasing misery. For the proletariat had shared in the society's enormous increase of wealth. In the age of imperialism, capitalists could afford to make economic concessions to their laboring classes in order to gain their support. They could even permit political concessions. Once the workers' allegiance to the capitalist system had been won, they could be allowed to vote, as voting had become meaningless once the choice had come to involve only two parties representing the capitalist class; the choice was which group of capitalists should exploit workers, not whether or not to abolish exploitation. The working class became increasingly "embourgeoisied," losing its revolutionary drive and spirit and acquiring a vested interest in the preservation of capitalism. This commitment to capitalism was reinforced by new and intense nationalistic feelings among the proletariat. Although it had been hostile to the capitalist class in the preimperialist phase, the proletariat acquired nationalistic feelings as it came to identify its interests with capitalist imperialism.)

Lenin's explanation for the failure of the proletarian revolution implied pessimism about the future. While imperialism continued the capitalists would reap sufficient superprofits with which to "buy" the support of the working classes. Only if those profits were eliminated would the capitalists have to resume their

---

[7] V. I. Lenin, *Imperialism, the Highest Stage of Capitalism* (rev. ed.; New York: International Publishers, 1939).

406   preimperialist domestic exploitation. (Then the class struggle would resume and would finally result in the proletarian revolution. This end was exactly what Lenin predicted, for, through imperialism, the "inner contradiction" of capitalism had been projected onto a global plane. Just as the capitalist class had exploited the proletarian class for profit, so the capitalist countries came to exploit the proletarian (colonial) countries for "surplus value." *Imperialism had, through its conquest of most non-Western areas, transformed the fight against capitalism into a global conflict.* The domestic class struggle had become an international class struggle. Indeed, because the uprising of workers in developed capitalist nations had come to depend upon elimination of colonial holdings, the prerequisite for the proletarian revolution had become the anti-imperialist revolution of the precapitalist colonial countries. "National liberation" thus became the most immediate task of communism.)

Lenin thus turned Marx upside down. The proletarian revolution was to begin in nonproletarian societies. The workers' revolution would arise in lands with economies that were basically agrarian, where peasants (not workers) constituted the vast majority of the poulations. Marx had said that the proletarian revolution would occur spontaneously when the capitalist economy has become mature. Lenin observed that, when the economy had become mature, the capitalists had nonetheless avoided revolution by means of imperialism. In those circumstances the consciousness of the proletariat was transformed from a revolutionary to a reformist cast. Conversely, the proletarian mood—the awareness of people that they are exploited—had become most intense in the colonial countries. Marx had declared that economic maturity and political consciousness are parallel developments that will precipitate the proltetarian revolution, but Lenin recognized that in the age of imperialism they are *inversely* related. The contrast was stark: Marx had stressed *economic* maturity as the prerequisite for the revolution; Lenin emphasized *political* consciousness. Josef Stalin later said, in his lectures on Leninism:

> Where will the revolution begin? Where, in what country, can the front of capital be pierced first?
>
> Where industry is more developed, where the proletariat constitutes the majority, where there is more culture, where there is more democracy—that was the reply usually given formerly.
>
> No, objects the Leninist theory of revolution; *not necessarily where industry is more developed*, and so forth. The front of capital will be pierced where the chain of imperialism is weakest, for the proletarian revolution is the result of the breaking of the chain of the world imperialist at its weakest link; and it may turn out that the country which has started the revolution, which has made a breach in the front of capital, is less developed in a capitalist sense than other, more developed, countries, which have, however, remained within the framework of capitalism.[8]

---

[8] Joseph Stalin, *The Foundations of Leninism*, quoted in Mendel, *op. cit.*, pp. 228–29 (emphasis in original).

AMERICAN CAPITALISM, IMPERIALISM AND THE COLD WAR

(Marxism-Leninism gives its believers another way of viewing and explaining American foreign policy and the nature of contemporary international conflicts. Fundamentally, the United States, as the world's most powerful capitalist state in the period since 1945, is seen as the leading Western imperialist power and guardian of the international capitalist order. The motives of American imperialism were the same as those of the European imperialists before World War II: opportunities for profitable investment, new markets, and cheap raw materials for home industries.)As Dutch, Belgian, and French imperialism collapsed before the onslaught of Hitler's armies and British imperialism weakened during the period of wartime cooperation with the United States and collapsed shortly after the common victory, the United States took over.[9] Having already worked assiduously to speed up Britain's imperial decline, the United States picked up almost all the pieces after the war.

(The United States has thus, in the Marxist-Leninist view, become the great exploiter of the underdeveloped areas of the world. American control of resources in those areas is, they assert, essential to the continued health of the American economy.[10])With only 6 percent of the world's population, the United States produces nearly 50 percent of the world's goods. To manufacture only the items for which it possesses the raw materials would reduce the capitalists' profits, cause large-scale unemployment, and reopen the class struggle, which would end in proletarian revolution in the United States. The "new" nations therefore function essentially as they did before they were granted formal political independence. They are still serving as suppliers of raw material for the most advanced industrialized capitalist nation. A capitalist state, like the United States, *must* expand abroad if its rulers wish to stave off domestic revolution. The only difference from the European imperialism of an earlier age is that the United States cannot, as its predecessors could, invade new areas and set up governmental or colonial rule. In the age of nationalism, in which the non-Western countries have achieved statehood, such direct control is no longer feasible, nor is it necessary for the United States. For, despite political independence, the new nations (as noted in Ch. 14) have become American dependencies. National self-determination has been a sham; the new states' fates have in fact been determined by external power.

(The principal means of alleged "neocolonial" control by the United States are essentially economic: American markets are essential to these new nations for the sale of their raw materials; American exports of food, machinery, and technology are important for their development; the size and distribution of American foreign aid, either direct or channeled through international financial institutions in which the United States has a major voice, are decided by governments in Washington;

[9.] Kolko, *The Politics of War* (New York: Random House, 1968).

[10.] Kolko, *Roots of American Foreign Policy*, pp. 48–87; and Carl Oglesby and Richard Shaull, *Containment and Change* (New York: Macmillan, 1967), pp. 72–111.

408   and the operations and investments of American-based multinational corporations (MNCs) are allegedly manipulated by the American government. These economic means are, furthermore, supplemented by various political ties: the support of the dominant political class in the new nation, which often has a vested interest in the socioeconomic status quo and in perpetuating its country's role as a commodity supplier for the industrial nations; American training, financing, and supplying of national military and police forces, whose task it is to suppress the "forces of disorder"—that is, of revolution; and the establishment of the Central Intelligence Agency (CIA), which can be used covertly to help shore up a weak regime or to reverse undesirable changes, if necessary by means of such "dirty tricks" as bribes, arms, private armies, assassinations, and coups d'état.[11] In a real emergency American forces are available for overt intervention to shore up America's "empire." Hence American policy in the LDCs as seen through Marxist-Leninist glasses is reactionary, usually supporting conservative political rulers who depend on Western capital for their fortunes and Western imperialism for their political power; serving foreign masters rather than their own people, they govern their countries on behalf of American capitalism.)

But if Lenin had been correct, the policy of imperialism only served as a temporary reprieve for capitalist states; in the long run there was no escape. By projecting the class struggle on a global scale through the policy of imperialism, the capitalist states only assured themselves that the exploited, poor "proletarian" nations would eventually become their executioners, even though they were agrarian-peasant states. History would not be denied.("National liberation" became the goal of the LDCs.)The imperialist chains were to be cut and these nations, finally independent of colonial control, could begin to develop themselves and use their resources to serve their own people. The days of their underdevelopment, during which they had served basically as cheap raw material providers for Western colonial and industrial countries, would be over.

(American imperialism also explained the outbreak of the Cold War. It was the determination of American imperialists to drive Russia out of eastern Europe and to restore that area as part of the larger European market that helped to precipitate the Cold War. Even more basically, the cause for this conflict was simply the existence of Soviet Russia as an anticapitalist state. The U.S.S.R. represented the wave of the future, an anticapitalist state which would be the nucleus of a postimperialist socialist world order in which all states would be liberated and their regimes be dedicated to the popular welfare. Thus it was necessary for the United States to try and destroy the Soviet Union while the former was still strong; failure to do so would doom it and the socioeconomic system it represented to defeat. Thus Stalin is absolved of all responsibility for the eruption of the Cold War. Rather, Russia is represented as the victim of American policy: Stalin was merely a nationalist with limited and historic security interest in the area to Russia's

---

[11.] For an "inside" account by a former agent, see Philip Agee, *Inside the Company* (New York: Bantam, 1976).

immediate west. It was the United States, pursuing an expansionist anti-Soviet policy and motivated by greed, rather than by a legitimate concern for its own safety, that was the aggressor. The United States, after all, had "the bomb"; the Soviet Union did not. How could one believe that Moscow threatened America?[12]

In the resulting Cold War with Russia anticommunism was invoked to justify American imperialism and to condemn striving for political and economic independence by the LDCs, upon the continued exploitation of which the prosperity of the United States depends. As a result, the United States has become the citadel of the *ancien régime*, the supporter of reactionary dictatorships and military cliques throughout the third world as part of its effort to prevent the rise of nationalist and revolutionary regimes that would claim control over their own resources and foreign investments on behalf of their peoples, who under imperialism continue to suffer poverty and misery. United States policy, not unnaturally under these circumstances, was virtually global in scope, militaristic and interventionist. Interpreted in this context, the war in Vietnam seemed unavoidable, despite its costs and despite the fact that South Vietnam was of so little economic value to the United States. The stake was nothing less than American control of the economies of the underdeveloped countries. Should Vietnam demonstrate that a genuinely nationalist, revolutionary movement could throw off imperialist shackles, it would set an example for all the other colonial countries. American leaders therefore had to intervene to crush the Vietcong. If South Vietnam had fallen, a *global* domino reaction would have followed.[13]

The logical conclusion of such an analysis is that a Vietcong victory and an American defeat were preconditions for the eventual emergence of a world in which despotism, hunger, and war would be abolished. The end of American imperial control will also permit the emergence of a truly just and peaceful United States, for, once the capitalists have lost their huge profits, resulting mass dissatisfaction will produce the revolutionary conditions that will finally liberate the American people. Imperialism, the last stage of capitalism, disintegrates as its chains are broken in the areas that are economically most underdeveloped but politically most conscious of their exploitation—and therefore most revolutionary.

[12.] *Ibid.*, p. 49. See, for example, David Horowitz, *The Free World Colossus* (New York: Hill & Wang, 1965); William Appleman Williams, *The Tragedy of American Diplomacy* (rev. ed.; New York: Delta, 1962); Lloyd C. Gardner, *Architects of Illusion* (Chicago: Quadrangle, 1970); Joyce and Gabriel Koko, *The Limits of Power* (Nw York: Vintage, 1968); Walter La Feber, *America, Russia and the Cold War* (New York: Wiley, 1967); Gar Alperovitz, *Atomic Diplomacy* (New York: Vintage, 1965); and Harry Magdoff, *The Age of Imperialism* (New York: Monthly Review Press, 1969).

For evaluations of this thesis, see Arthur Schlesinger, Jr., "Origins of the Cold War," *Foreign Affairs*, October 1967, pp. 22–52; and John Lewis Gaddis, *The United States and The Origins of the Cold War 1941–1947* (New York: Columbia University Press, 1972).

For criticism of some of the imperialist school's scholarship, see Robert James Maddox, *The New Left and the Origins of the Cold War* (Princeton: Princeton University Press, 1973); and Raymond Aron, *The Imperial Republic* (Cambridge, Mass.: Winthrop, 1974).

[13.] G. Kolko, *Roots of American Foreign Policy*, pp. 85–87.

A CRITIQUE OF THE IMPERIALIST
INTERPRETATION

How valid is this economic theory of imperialism as a general explanation of a nation's foreign policy, especially American foreign policy? One fundamental criticism is that conflict and war were occurring among independent political units— empires, city-states, dynasties—long before industrial capitalism developed. How then can we attribute wars in general to fundamental economic causes and especially to the profit motive? Once it is admitted that perhaps not all wars are caused by capitalism, the basic thesis is gravely weakened and can no longer stand as a broad explanation; even though specific wars may have been profitable, can we say that profits were the *motivation* for even those wars? And even if we could, would we be justified in raising these instances to the level of a universal historical law? Most Western colonial expansion, in fact, occurred in the period from the sixteenth to the eighteenth century, the period before the rise of industrial capitalism. Even most of the strife and hostilities in the nineteenth and early twentieth centuries— the three Prussian wars against Denmark, Austria, and France; the Russo-Turkish and Russo-Japanese wars; and World War I—can hardly be attributed to capitalist rivalries. In fact, Russia and Italy, active imperialist states in the sense that they were expansionist and used their superior power to exploit the weak, were not capitalistic at all. (Soviet behavior after World War II throws even more doubt on the presumed relation between industrial capitalism and war.)

Second, other students of Western imperialism have claimed that

> . . . international friction over private investments has been a good deal more frequent and dangerous where private investments have been pressed into service as instruments, tools, of a larger political purpose which the investments themselves did not originate. Investments used in the quest for national glory, and the like, have been more productive of international friction in the past than investments actuated solely by private profit motives.[14]

(Specifically, acquisition of colonies often served the state's political, rather than its economic, purposes.) In a system in which states felt insecure and were thus constantly concerned with relative power, colonies represented more than profits: They enhanced the master nation's prestige. For Germany, which was nationally unified only in 1870, far later than the other great powers, colonies represented a means of gaining a "place in the sun." Some German colonies in the South Pacific were not only not profitable—the Germans actually had to spend money to maintain them. But this money was considered well spent because colonies had the same importance that atomic bombs have had since 1945 as signs of rank and power. On the other hand, for France, defeated by Germany in 1870, colonial

---

[14.] Eugene Staley, *War and the Private Investor* (Garden City, N.Y.: Doubleday, 1935), pp. xv–xvi.

expansion in Africa was a way of regaining lost status and disguising national humiliation. Germany had a far larger population, but the manpower of the colonies meant that France had more soldiers to balance its neighbor's army. Tunisia may thus have "paid off" economically, but the colonies in equatorial Africa generally did not; the French government had other purposes in mind in acquiring them.

(Although economics should not therefore be discounted as a motive for nineteenth-century Western imperialism, it should also not be exaggerated as the driving force behind political expansion; very clearly, the state system and power considerations were then—as before—fundamental in explaining state expansion.) (Indeed, Benjamin Cohen, in a detailed analysis of imperialist theory and Western colonialism, finds the taproot of imperialism in the anarchical organization of the international system: "Nations yield to the temptations to domination because they are driven to maximize their individual power position" by their uncertainty and insecurity.[15] Imperialism, which Cohen defines as "any relationship of effective domination or control, political or economic, direct or indirect, of one nation over another," is the offspring of competing national sovereignties.[16] The "logic of dominion" is a rational operational strategy for a nation to adopt in these circumstances. It was also logical that governments would use corporations to advance their political purposes and bring pressures to bear on them if they were reluctant to comply.)

An interesting postwar instance was the 1953 CIA overthrow of the Mossadegh nationalist government in Iran and the restoration of the shah who had fled his country earlier. Rather than testifying to the dominance of big business—notably the large oil companies over foreign policy in America, this CIA operation was undertaken in support of broader national security goals, not to rescue private investments or enhance corporate profits. Mossadegh, who had received medical treatment at Walter Reed Hospital, had nationalized the Anglo-Iranian Oil Company in 1951. This in itself did not alienate the United States, which in both 1951 and 1952 gave sizable foreign aid funds to Iran. What led the United States to reconsider its support of Mossadegh was his quarrel with Britain and the virtual cutoff of Iranian oil shipments.

It should be noted that at the time the United States was an oil exporter and that American oil companies were not present in Iran. Oil for the United States or private investments were not, therefore, considerations affecting Washington's policy. And the loss of Iranian oil had been made up by production elsewhere. The American government did not even become involved until it became clear that Iran would not accept an exclusively British-owned operation. Hence the proposal for an international consortium including American, French, and British companies, to produce and ship Iranian oil; the American oil companies were unenthusiastic but finally acceded to governmental pressure after receiving relief from a criminal antitrust suit that had been brought against the oil companies

---

[15] Benjamin J. Cohen, *The Question of Imperialism* (New York: Basic Books, 1973), p. 67.

[16] *Ibid.*, p. 16.

412   by the Justice Department. The United States wanted to see Iran's oil flowing again so that Iran could maintain a stable, noncommunist regime. Short of cash, Iran appeared increasingly unstable and on a leftward path. (For the American oil companies, the resumption of Iranian production meant a cutback in their production—and profits—in order to prevent an oil glut.) Street riots had already burst out in 1951 and 1952, and in 1952 Mossadegh had concluded oil sale agreements with Eastern Europe. It was in this context that the CIA restored the shah and ended the life of the weak, increasingly radical nationalist Mossadegh regime. The impetus for action came from the government in Washington, not the oil companies who, in the absence of political pressure, would have stayed out of Iran. And (the CIA coup was the result of fears of growing communist influence in Iran.[17])

    Third, even though capitalism cannot generally be held responsible for interstate conflicts and wars, and even though power and prestige were important factors in the colonialism of the late nineteenth century, cannot *American capitalism after World War II* be held to blame for the outbreak of the Cold War and, even more important in the radical perception of American foreign policy, the alleged subjugation of the third world? On the origins of the Cold War, we can be brief for we have already examined the causes of American-Soviet rivalry and found them in the state system and emerging bipolarity after the defeat of Germany. Not only had the United States, still unsocialized by the state system, sought during the war to overcome the Soviet leaders' suspicions of the West in order to lay the foundations for postwar cooperation and peace, but also, as the war drew to a conclusion, its principal concern had been not to eliminate the self-proclaimed bastion of world revolution and enemy of Western capitalism or to push Russia out of eastern Europe and convert that area into a market for American corporations (poverty-stricken eastern Europe would not in fact have been a very profitable market for American goods) but to forestall a complete return to historic isolationism. The public mood was all too apparent in hasty military demobilization. For the United States to have pursued an assertive foreign policy complete with atomic threats, as the revisionists have claimed it did, would have required a dictatorial disregard for the widespread demands of the public, which very definitely set limits on what the administration could do.

    It was not until a year and a half after World War II had ended that the Truman Doctrine was enunciated. Only after further attempts to reconcile differences with Moscow leaders and after continued Soviet pressure, denunciations, and vilifications was the policy of containment launched. (Hostile Soviet behavior was the reason for the gradual shift of American policy and public opinion from amity to enmity; American policy was not the product of a virulent and preexisting anticommunist ideology.) Indeed, it was Soviet policy that had reflected an anticapitalist animus predating both the Bolshevik Revolution of 1917 and subsequent

---

[17.] Stephen D. Krasner, *Defending the National Interest* (Princeton: Princeton University Press, 1978), pp. 119–128.

Western anti-Soviet behavior. (Even before the Bolshevik leaders had seized power, they had judged capitalist states hostile simply because they *were* capitalist.[18])

But what about the charge of American domination of the third world as the cause of its continued poverty and misery, and the military interventions as in the Dominican Republic and Vietnam, or the more subtle economic and political interventions in countless other countries like Greece and Brazil, where United States imperialism supports what Gabriel Kolko has picturesquely called the "local *compradors* [sharks] and oligarchies."[19] Is the American economy so dependent on the underdeveloped countries' natural resources that it must control them lest they withhold those resources and thus lower the rates of American economic growth, employment, and prosperity? Is the likely result large-scale unemployment, an end to the economic "trickle-down" from the corporations' "superprofits," and massive social and political unrest as a prelude to the proletarian revolution?

Clearly, the United States, with more than half the world's productive capacity, does need extensive natural resources to stoke its industrial machinery. Kolko has argued that not even the total volume of resources that the United States imports is the cause of American imperialism in the third world. The American economy is "so intricate that the removal of even a small part, as in a watch, can stop the mechanism."[20] Each ton of steel, he claims, requires the addition of about thirteen pounds of manganese. "The same analogy is true of the entire relationship between the industrial and so-called developing nations: the nations of the Third World may be poor, but in the last analysis the industrial world needs their resources more than these nations need the West."[21]

In fact, there is simply no evidence that any communist country or nationalist regime of the third world will not sell its resources to the West—although, as the Organization of Petroleum Exporting Countries (OPEC) has shown, the LDCs do want higher prices and what they consider a fairer return for the resources that keep Western industry running. In addition, the sources of these raw materials are numerous and frequently in politically safe areas. In Kolko's example of manganese, he notes that it is available from Brazil, India, Gabon, and South Africa and that more than half the world's known reserves are in Russia and China. In any event, it is unlikely that all these sources will cut off their supplies to the West

---

[18.] An interesting characteristic of the imperialist interpretation of post-World War II American foreign policy is that it is based on examination in depth of the American economic system and social structure, in which every nook and cranny of the White House, the State Department, and the Pentagon have been searched for evidence of anti-Soviet motivation. Yet there has been hardly a look at the Soviet system and the dynamics of Soviet foreign policy since 1917; the latter is portrayed as primarily a reaction to American policy. Soviet policy apparently has no inherent purpose apart from the limited security interests in eastern Europe. Anything that does not fit the view of Soviet policy as legitimate and defensive is omitted by revisionist critics; first-level analysis in which the American-Soviet conflict is viewed as a product of bipolarity is conveniently rejected because it would preclude the possibility of blaming the Cold War solely or primarily on Washington leaders and absolving Moscow leaders of at least half the responsibility.

[19.] G. Kolko, *Roots of American Foreign Policy*, p. 86.

[20.] Kolko, *op. cit.*, p. 50.

[21.] *Ibid.*

414   or to the United States at the same time. As Robert Tucker has caustically noted, "Radical intellectuals may harbor such romantic notions but governments, revolutionary governments included, do not"—because they need the capital.[22] Finally, as we know, the United States—while increasingly importing such key resources as oil, bauxite, tin, and natural rubber from the LDCs—possesses many of the raw materials that it needs. We need only look at current attempts to find new sources of energy, to exploit more fully domestic oil deposits, and to clean an old source, coal, of which the United States has a vast supply. Indeed, most raw material production in the world occurs in the West, whereas the poorer and more populated of the LDCs remain net importers of natural resources. The need for the LDCs' resources was thus hardly a cause for American policies toward the third world during the Cold War days, an era in which the United States was an oil exporter, and more self-sufficient in resources than today.)

(There is thus a major theoretical weakness in the imperialist thesis: the claim that the capitalist state must exercise imperial domination over the third world. The theory is that either it controls these raw material sources, or it has no access to raw materials at all. Clearly, this either-or proposition is false.)As Jerome Slater has noted, an inverse relationship between "imperialism" and prosperity in the postwar period has indeed been demonstrated. It has been the least imperial countries, countries that have had to buy more of their raw materials than the United States on the international market, that have exhibited the highest rates of economic growth (West Germany, Japan, Canada, Norway, and Denmark), whereas those countries that have more slowly shed their former colonies (France and Britain until the 1950s and Portugal in the 1970s) have done far less well.[23]

    (What has been true of the United States' alleged dependence on third-world natural resources has been equally true of its alleged need of the LDCs' markets and investment opportunities. American exports in the past have found their principal markets in the rich Western states) Only in the 1970s, as Vietnam was winding down, did the United States sell more manufactured goods to the LDCs than to western Europe and Japan; similarly, the LDCs became an important market for American wheat, cotton, and rice exports. But in 1968, at the height of the Vietnam war,(American exports represented 4 percent of the gross national product (GNP); 67 percent went to western Europe, Canada, and Japan, whereas exports to the LDCs had decreased between 1955 and 1968.[24] American investments also went primarily to Western industrial countries, even though the American government attempted to control the outflow of dollars to minimize the negative impact on the balance of trade. By the beginning of the 1970s, 60–70 percent of American direct investments were in Europe and Canada; Latin America and the

---

[22] Robert W. Tucker, *The Radical Left and American Foreign Policy* (Baltimore: Johns Hopkins Press, 1971), p. 126.

[23] Jerome Slater, "Is United States Foreign Policy 'Imperialistic' or 'Imperial'?" *Political Science Quarterly*, Spring 1976, pp. 185–186.

[24] Tucker, *op. cit.*, pp. 134–136.

rest of the underdeveloped world were far behind. Direct investments abroad as a percentage of total investments were only 6 percent, although the return on foreign investment was 9.3 percent, a figure higher than domestic corporate profits (and explainable largely by the high concentration of investments in petroleum).[25] These export and investment figures, therefore, do not explain why the United States should seek control over the LDCs.)

(One additional point is certainly clear from this analysis, which suggests, contrary to the imperialist thesis, that the industrial countries are not structurally dependent on the third world: Although all the societies mentioned are capitalist—and they all do exhibit certain common economic structures like the free market and private property—it is clear that they handle their socioeconomic problems in quite different ways.) The United States may be the archetype of capitalism and imperialism, but Norway is hardly imperialist, Denmark's society is not divided between rich and poor, West Germany before 1973 had not suffered from the recurrent unemployment problems common in the United States, and Switzerland hardly has a foreign policy, let alone an expansionist one. (Noneconomic factors, therefore, seem critical to the manner in which capitalist states manage their domestic and foreign problems. But to stress social and political forces and to abandon the Marxist faith in the determining drive of economic forces is to surrender the belief that the future course of capitalist states can be predicted on the basis of their economic structures.)

(Fourth, perhaps the greatest irony of the imperialist theory is that, after the Nixon administration moved toward détente with Russia, the business community became one of its strongest supporters—just as it had looked forward to close American-Russian relations after 1945. There seemed to be money in this approach. It was not the capitalists who had precipitated the Cold War, nor did they oppose détente.) Businessmen are interested in making profits, and just as the church wants to save souls the world over, whether in democratic or nondemocratic societies, MNCs prefer cold cash to cold war. MNCs have no political preferences; they focus on what Marx once called, in another connection, the "cash nexus." Indeed, they seem anxious to prove correct Lenin's famous dictum that the capitalists would sell him the rope with which he would hang them. And so the corporations have sought contracts, and businessmen-farmers who grow the wheat that the Soviets want have usually opposed using economic boycotts to advance American political purposes. (After Afghanistan, farmers reluctantly went along, but their general unhappiness clearly indicated that this sanction could not be used frequently.) Indeed, as we saw in our discussion of MNCs, businessmen have as frequently been portrayed as pacifists as they have been seen as exploiters and warmongers. (The pacifist attitude results from the belief that "war does not pay" and that peace does pay because it permits international trade and therefore enables businessmen to earn profits. In any event, whether this interpretation is correct or incorrect, American industrial and agrarian capitalists are most likely to act as a

---

[25.] *Ibid.*, pp. 126–131.

416 constraining force on the American government if the latter should decide to take a harder line against Soviet leaders on some specific issue. If the capitalists sought to destroy the bastion of world revolution, they had chosen a strange way of "making the world safe for capitalism.")

(The real blow to the theory of imperialism surely comes from the Middle East. There the oil companies, which, according to the theory, should have determined American policy in the area, have very clearly had virtually no influence at all. American policy has been consistently favorable to Israel; the oil companies obviously have favored the Arabs.)Even after 1973, when American policy became more even-handed, the Nixon administration was heavily influenced by the desire to avoid yet another Arab-Israeli war that might lead to Soviet-American confrontation and possible nuclear war. In 1973 the two superpowers almost did clash, as the Soviets apparently threatened to send in their troops unilaterally when the Israelis were about to defeat the Egyptians. If Israeli-Arab differences had not been resolved, if their conflicts of interest had continued to smolder, and if the Arabs had gone to war again and had been humiliated again, the world might have witnessed a Soviet-American confrontation on the brink of nuclear war. Hence the sustained efforts to find a basis for peace in the area; Western oil needs, of course, reinforced the determination to seek accommodation between the Arabs and Israel. In any event, American policy has until recently reflected economic concerns less than cold-war concerns, and even the latter would have been avoidable had American aims not aligned the United States with Israel. Indeed, had anticommunism been the overwhelming American motivation, the national interest would have been identical with that of the oil companies. It was American support of Israel that alienated the Arabs and provided Soviet leaders with the opportunity to link themselves with the latter. Once Soviet influence had flowed into the area, the Cold War was extended to the Middle East.

IMPERIALISM WITHOUT EMPIRICISM

In the final analysis, as this example has shown, the best argument against the imperialist interpretation of American policy is the lack of empirical evidence for it.[26] If the United States is an imperialist power and if economic power confers political control, as the theory of imperialism maintains, then where is the American empire? We would certainly expect that, at the very least, the United States could protect MNCs abroad. Yet, since the 1960s, almost everywhere in the third world, American corporations have been nationalized while Washington's leaders have been helpless to prevent it; only going through the ritual of protest whenever sufficient compensation has not been offered. Especially in Latin America, where the United States has presumably most effectively extended its imperialist tentacles, nationalist regimes have expropriated billions of dollars worth of Amerian corporate property: in Argentina, Peru, Bolivia, Ecuador, even Chile. Seventy, or even fifty,

---

[26] See Aron, *op. cit.*, Part II, for a general evaluation of American postwar "imperialistic" policy.

years ago the marines would have been sent in. Today the label "dependency" can hardly be applied any more.

To be sure, the United States has intervened in Guatemala, Cuba, the Dominican Republic, and Chile, but these interventions have been intended not to rescue corporate or private investments but to destroy governments that American leaders have perceived—rightly or wrongly—as aligning themselves with the communist world. The motives have thus been political, related to security. Even in the Caribbean area and Central America, anti-Americanism and greater national assertion have characterized national behavior: in Jamaica, Trinidad, Nicaragua, Guatemala, El Salvador, and—symbolically most important for all the Latin American countries—in Panama, where control of the Canal is to be turned over to the Panamanians.

In addition, the terms of trade and investment have been changing in favor of the LDCs since 1973. The Western industrial powers, including the United States, have accepted this change and have not resorted to force—strange behavior indeed for so-called imperialists! Similarly, American, European, and Japanese MNCs have increasingly accommodated themselves to host countries' gradually tightening requirements, the purpose of which has been to compel foreign corporations to contribute more to the host countries' economic plans. Corresponding to this growing MNC–host-country alliance has been an increasing estrangement between MNCs and the home country, so that, when MNCs are subjected to more stringent host controls, they do not normally appeal for help to their home governments, as the oil companies demonstrated after 1973. Once the masters of the little oil kingdoms, the MNCs then became their servants when majority control was transferred to the Persian Gulf states; in the process, the companies learned that what benefited their hosts benefited them, even though it did not benefit their home countries. A significant shift of power between the MNCs and the host countries' governments which control the MNCs' access to and prices of the resources they extract has thus occurred. Higher oil prices have already been followed by higher prices for tin, copper, and bauxite, though they are not nearly as high as those for oil. (It must be emphasized at this point that it is the home country that is increasingly hurt by the relation between MNC and host nation, because investments abroad mean export of jobs and can affect the home country's balance of payments negatively. The situation is bound to result in efforts to establish controls over MNCs' foreign investments, for national and corporate interests are often at odds. For further analysis of this issue, see Chapter 19.)

If only the so-called imperialist powers did control the third world! If the proponents of the imperialist theory were logically consistent, they would have changed their tune after 1973, for Saudi Arabia should, according to that theory, today be the world's leading imperialist power and the Western countries, especially Japan, its dependencies, or "neocolonies."

> The growing acceptance of the "imperial" model or metaphor to the contrary notwithstanding, we may boldly but confidently conclude that the United States today does not "control" any country anywhere, and in only a slightly more

418

qualified manner we may also reject the notion of United States "domination." That the United States has varying degrees of influence in the Third World is of course undeniable, but it is a declining influence, and limited in scope and effectiveness to only certain matters. The United States has been all but powerless to stop rising nationalism and radicalism, as well as attacks on its interests and policies around the world. How does the United States today typically react to the nationalization of property, to dramatic increases in the prices of critical raw materials, to demands that it remove its military bases, to anti-American riots, to insults and contempt? On increasingly rare occasions with suspension of economic assistance to the offending state, more typically with mere diplomatic protest, and, increasingly, simply with silence—a sullen silence born of futility, perhaps, but significant precisely for that reason. "Imperialism" should be made of sterner stuff—and certainly it used to be.[27]

(As already noted, a more accurate description of American relations with the LDCs would be one of "*mutual* dependence, *mutual* power, and *mutual* vulnerability."[28])

An analyst who wishes to use the capitalist-imperialist model cannot therefore simply posit an economic motivation because it seems persuasive to him or her and because whatever situation he or she seeks to explain seems clear in the light of such analysis. Although it is true that economic factors may contribute to interstate conflict and war, so do other factors. The real question, then, is whether or not a specific conflict can be explained primarily or exclusively in economic terms. In order to do that, the analyst must show that economic motives have actually been converted into aggressive and expansionist policies, including the outbreak of hostilities. (As Vernon Van Dyke has argued:

> Those who approach the question of the causes of imperialism and war through a study of the formulation and execution of foreign policies in concrete situations rarely emerge with an answer that is exclusively economic. Almost always non-economic factors are found to be heavily involved, and very often they appear to play a decisive role.[29]

(The devotees of "American imperialism" will not admit this, although they may themselves focus on the policy-making process. But their logic has predetermined their perception: first, the identification of the political elite as members of the corporate elite; and second, the assumption that this elite, once in office, maintains its connections with industrial firms and allied law and banking firms. These policy makers supposedly form a small, cohesive group whose career experiences and expectations color their perceptions. Business, therefore, serves as the source of personnel and of assumptions shaping foreign, as well as domestic, policies. The third perception follows: As servants of corporate capitalism seeking profits both at home and abroad, the policy makers adhere to "free-world imperialism." To quote Kolko once more:

---

[27] Slater, *op. cit.*, p. 86.

[28] *Ibid.*

[29] Vernon Van Dyke, *International Politics* (2d ed.; New York: Appleton, 1966), p. 110.

. . . foreign policy decision-makers are in reality a highly mobile sector of the American corporate structure, a group of men who frequently assume and define high level policy tasks in government, rather than routinely administer it, and then return to business. Their firms and connections are large enough to afford them the time to straighten out or formulate government policy while maintaining their vital ties with giant corporate law, banking, or industry. The conclusion is that a small number of men fill the large majority of key foreign policy posts. Their many diverse posts make this group a kind of committee government entrusted to handle numerous and varied national security and international functions at the policy level. Even if not initially connected with the corporate sector, career government officials related in some tangible manner with the private worlds predominantly of big law, big finance, and big business.[30]

Yet, to reinforce a point made earlier, the deduction of an economically motivated expansionist foreign policy from policy makers' professional origins is not persuasive. A mid-1970s empirical study of businessmen concluded that their foreign-policy views were less influenced by economic considerations than by "shared images"—that is, by perceptions of the world and the role that the United States ought to play in it that are also shared by military officers, political leaders (in both the executive and legislative branches), and a variety of professional groups.[31] Businessmen tended to support the consensus favoring an anticommunist, internationalist, activist, and interventionist containment policy before the Vietnam war; since then they have favored a lower profile in foreign policy and spending less money for defense. Businessmen are thus not, as the imperialist thesis would have it, "hawkish"; those who may be hawks are likely to be so for *non*economic reasons. Economic interests most often led members of the business community to oppose war, which they view as unprofitable and damaging to the domestic system upon which a stable and expanding economy is based. Indeed, the authors of this study found that businessmen at the time shared the general lack of interest in foreign policy. A president cannot today, as during the cold-war days, look to them for sustained support of a vigorous foreign policy or high defense expenditures.

These findings tend to support the view that businessmen and their lawyers were not the *cause* of the United States' extensive postwar role in the world; rather, they were attracted to government service when the nation perceived itself to be in danger. They flocked to Washington in 1940, when the enemy was on the right, not on the left. Their motivation can hardly therefore be said to have derived from anticommunist ideology; rather, it arose from concern for national security, regardless of whether the threat came from the right or the left. This is also why business during the Cold War days accepted, although not necessarily gladly, governmental prohibition of trade with communist states, especially Russia and China. Such policy, intended to serve U.S. political interest, clearly did not serve

---

[30.] Kolko, *Roots of American Foreign Policy* pp. 3–26; Richard J. Barnet, *The Economy of Death* (New York: Atheneum, 1969), pp. 87–97; and G. W. Domhoff, *The Higher Circles: The Governing Class in America* (New York: Vintage, 1971), pp. 111–155.

[31.] Bruce M. Russett and Elizabeth C. Hanson, *Interest and Ideology* (San Francisco: Freeman, 1975).

420 business interests. (Business's acceptance of official policy hardly supports the contention that business dominates government; if anything, the reverse would appear more correct) The imperialist interpretation also overlooks the fact that when men go from big business, big law, or big finance to the State or Defense Department, their perceptions of their roles change and so do their outlooks and policy preferences. And, as a person's role (the behavior that is expected in a specific position, whether that of parent, professor, or secretary of state) changes, prediction of his or her behavior based on past roles and class identifications are likely to be off the mark. The expectations of society and of political superiors and peers, as well as the official's own perception of his or her role, will be among factors affecting his or her behavior. For a secretary of state coming from a corporation or law firm, the role will be defined by his or her conception both of it and of his or her "reference group." Secretary of State Dean Acheson's perceptions of the international system and the Soviet Union's aims after World War II were not influenced by his previous legal experience on behalf of big business. He certainly did not consider himself the spokesman for corporate capitalism and the architect of free-world imperialism. Not the demands of the economic system but his image of the state system governed his actions.[32]

Even more fundamentally, this radical interpretation of United States foreign policy since World War II makes another incorrect assumption: that of the unity of business. Asserting a single business interest does not make it so. Business is highly pluralistic—for example, big business and small business, export business and import business. Since different businesses and, even further, the separate sectors of each industry (for example, steel and auto industries), will be affected differently by such matters as tariffs, there is no unified business position. Steel may seek protection from foreign competition but the computer industry may want to export and may fear protectionist policies that encourage other nations—potential computer buyers—to protect themselves. Even then, however, note that the business concern is limited to such a topic as tariffs. It is not seeking to influence the overall "grand design" of United States foreign policy.

THE MILITARY-INDUSTRIAL COMPLEX

Whereas in Marxism-Leninism the conduct of a capitalist state's foreign policy is attributed to the nature of its economic system, a "devil" theory is focused upon a presumed conspiracy which is said to explain a capitalist state's external behavior. The Marxist-Leninist theory is based upon an elaborate intellectual structure; the "devil" theory is based on the assumption that certain men and groups—the so-called military-industrial complex (MIC)—profit from war and therefore are re-

---

[32.] Dean Acheson, *Present at the Creation* (New York: Norton, 1969); and Ronald J. Stupak, *The Shaping of Foreign Policy: The Role of Secretary of State as Seen by Dean Acheson* (New York: Odyssey, 1969).

sponsible for high international tensions and interventionist policies.[33] It is not the system that is viewed as the cause of capitalist expansionism but rather a group of "war profiteers." In contrast to the Marxist-Leninist interpretation, the "devil" theory recognizes capitalism as quite compatible with the status quo and peaceful policy—if only the MIC could be held politically responsible.)

(Who are the members of the MIC? They include, first of all, the professional military, whose roles, status, and shares of the budget all depend on "peace not breaking out," and, second, the managers of industrial corporations that serve the military and gain handsomely by it. The relationship is one of mutual need.) Some industries are extremely dependent on the armed services: Lockheed Aircraft, General Dynamics, McDonnell-Douglas, and Boeing would not survive without military orders. They employ large numbers of retired officers to help solicit contracts and to find out what kinds of weapons are wanted. Others, like General Motors, International Business Machines, and Standard Oil of New Jersey, also make great profits, though they are not strictly dependent for their economic well-being on the production of arms. The military, in turn, needs the corporations, especially those that are virtually public corporations, for they have the managerial talent, technological ability, and production lines to function as military arsenals.

(Other groups, however, also supposedly possess vested interests in the continuation of the Cold War.) They include those whom Richard Barnet has labeled "national security managers," including not only military leaders but also the more influential "militarized civilians" or "homicidal bureaucrats."[34] These men and women come from the world of corporations, high finance, and corporate law and they keep the United States at "permanent war," both because their economic goals are necessarily expansionist and because they perceive and operate in much the same ways as do professional military leaders. "The principal militarists in America wear three-button suits."[35] Examples cited include Secretary of State Acheson, who before the Korean war had counseled a buildup of military strength and later was the first to recommend fighting in that country; Secretary of State John Foster Dulles, who built extensive American alliances outside Europe. Having embraced military "realism," these officials and their subordinates supposedly gained a sense of accomplishment, public stature, and deference, as well as contacts for their later professional lives; they therefore did not favor relaxation of international tensions or resolution of conflicting interests, which were their *raison d'être*. There is a fourth segment as well: the labor unions, whose members find employment and paychecks in defense industries; the universities, where physical

---

[33] Sidney Lens, *The Military-Industrial Complex* (Philadelphia: Pilgrim, 1970); Barnet, *op. cit.*; Ralph Lapp, *The Weapons Culture* (Baltimore: Penguin, 1968); William Proxmire, *Report from Wasteland* (New York: Holt, Rinehart and Winston, 1970); Seymour Melman, *Pentagon Capitalism* (New York: McGraw-Hill, 1970); Melman, *The Permanent War Economy* (New York: Simon & Schuster, 1974); Adam Yarmolinsky, *The Military Establishment* (New York: Harper & Row, 1971); Steven Rosen, ed., *Testing the Theory of the Military-Industrial Complex* (Lexington, Mass.: Lexington, 1973); and Anthony Sampson, *The Arms Bazaar* (New York: Viking, 1977).

[34] Barnet, *The Roots of War* (Baltimore: Penguin, 1973), pp. 13–22.

[35] Barnet, *Economy of Death*, p. 79.

422   and biological scientists are engaged in government "research and development" and social scientists have contracts for policy-oriented studies; and the various states where economic growth is spurred by military installations and defense plants. Indeed, few segments of society seem to be exempt: Even local real-estate dealers, contractors, and retail merchants all profit from the population influx that defense installations bring to their communities.

(Defense is thus good business. Vested interests pervade American life, which is reflected in Congress, the fifth element of the MIC. Mobilizing support for arms production and a tough international stand is easy. Until recently, anti-communism was the means for arousing the evangelistic spirit and enthusiasm of the American people; their crusading behavior served the national-security managers well. Few congressmen asked questions about the defense budget or argued for lower force levels, different strategies, and fewer weapons. To do so was to risk being accused of neglecting the nation's defenses against communism; perhaps to risk one's constituents' welfare; certainly to risk the disapproval of colleagues, many of them with bases and defense industries in their constituencies, who controlled one's political future in Congress; and to risk the ultimate accusation, that of being "un-American."[36])Yet defense spending has benefited the entire economy. It has constituted a huge subsidy for stability and growth. Without it, the nation could have expected sizable unemployment and a decline in profits. According to the devil theory, the United States cannot afford peace, for too many powerful participants in the policy process have a stake in the system as it now operates. The world's first democracy, dedicated to human life, is thus now committed to an "economy of death." Private enterprise has been replaced by "Pentagon capitalism" and a "weapons culture," and the efficiency of the private sector has been replaced by highly inefficient "military socialism." Weapons are produced years after their target dates—if produced at all—and all too frequently they turn out to be unreliable and very expensive. The "overruns" on cost estimates often mount into the billions.

This interpretation of American foreign policy—like the earlier imperialist interpretation—provides a very satisfactory explanation for its advocates. It furnishes them with a key that appears to unlock the mysteries and problems of the world, for it constitutes a complete analysis of all domestic and foreign events. Economics seems such an obviously fundamental force. For an American especially, the striving for monetary success and material abundance (even for one who deliberately rejects such pursuit) is ever present. Explanations of American domestic politics have often been based upon assumptions about economic competition among business, labor, agriculture, and the military. Americans have been viewed as the "people of plenty," and American politics as largely a question of division of the bounty. (An analysis of American foreign policy in terms of the quest for profits by big corporations thus suggests a tangible and demonstrable underlying motivation for the continuing arms race and large-scale investment in the military.)

As with the imperialist theory, the MIC thesis omits all, or at least most,

---

[36.] The correctness of these assumptions by believers in the power of the "military-industrial complex," as well as congressional voting behavior in relation to defense issues, is analyzed in Bruce M. Russett, *What Price Vigilance?* (New Haven: Yale University Press, 1970).

analysis of the state system; the thesis rests on a vacuum. It thus takes on the conspiratorial tone of the virtually identical "merchants of death" interpretation of the United States' entry into the war in 1917.[37] The financiers, the munitions manufacturers, and the Eastern establishment, with its anti-German and pro-British sentiments, were said to be to blame for American entry into that war. Had it not been for those groups, the United States would supposedly have stayed neutral and spared "the people" from war. German hegemony in Europe and the threat to American security that it constituted were ignored. The contemporary version of this thesis also defines those forces with a vested interest in the Cold War, and it is again suggested that, if political control were exerted over them, the American people could once more live in peace, cut the defense budget, reduce military influence in government, and rearrange priorities between foreign and domestic policies. In both instances it is asserted that, if the United States but wills abstinence, it can abstain. And, arising from this peculiar version of "the illusion of omnipotence" is the claim that no threat, or certainly no great threat, to American vital interests exists. The perceived threat is largely imaginary, deliberately created and manipulated to arouse fear and hysteria. This tension meets the needs of the MIC, which has established itself as a very expensive and dangerous kind of Frankenstein, escaping from traditional democratic restraints.

It is hard to understand, however, how this conclusion can be arrived at if there are in fact so many millions of both influential and working Americans who benefit from the continuation of the arms race. Indeed, there is a contradiction at the heart of the theory of the MIC. On the one hand, it is suggested that American foreign policy is too interventionist, too involved, and too expensive and that it distorts national priorities. The emotional appeal of the MIC explanation lies in the belief that the United States' allegedly overextended and dangerous policy is contrary to the interests of the vast majority of Americans, who would benefit from a cutback in external commitments and concentration on domestic affairs. The MIC is, in fact, presented as a conspiracy blocking the "real interests" of the majority. On the other hand, almost every group in the United States seems to have a cash interest in international tension, including the growers who supply flowers for battle monuments; if so, the nation must have an interest in continued cold-war policies.

---

[37] A characteristic description of the role of the military was "the alliance of the military with powerful economic groups to secure appropriations on the one hand for a constantly increasing military and naval establishment, and on the other hand, the constant threat of the use of that swollen military establishment in behalf of the economic interests at home and abroad of the industrialists supporting it. It meant the subjugation of the people of the various countries to the uniform, the self-interested identification of patriotism with commercialism, and the removal of the military from the control of civil law."

This statement, which could have been spoken by a liberal senator or a representative of Students for a Democratic Society, is from conservative Senator Nye's investigations, held during the 1930s, attributing American involvement in World War I to the military-industrial complex of its time. "Munitions Industry," *Report on Existing Legislation*, Senate Report No. 944, Part 5, 74th Congress, 2d Session (Washington, D.C.: U.S. Government Printing Office, 1936), pp. 8–9; quoted in Hans Morgenthau and Kenneth Thompson, eds., *Principles and Problems of International Politics* (New York: Knopf, 1950), pp. 62–63.

It is therefore difficult to understand how such policies can be changed. Yet they have been changed: the percentage of GNP spent on defense at the end of the Carter administration is lower today than at any time since the Korean war in 1950, defense-related employment is half the 10 percent it reached during the 1950s, a number of large aerospace firms have been in serious financial trouble (Lockheed had to be rescued from bankruptcy by the government), and defense profits are down in relation to nondefense earnings.[38] How can we explain this? Or, how do we understand the elimination of 1,500 Strategic Air Command (SAC) bombers in the late 1950s and early 1960s with hardly a whimper, or the virtual elimination of the antiballistic missile (ABM) in the strategic-arms limitation treaty (SALT I)? It goes without saying that defense spending is profitable for some industries, labor unions, and even states (like California and Texas). But this admission is certainly not tantamount to a theory of arms races that explains the start or resumption, conduct, and termination of such races. For one thing, if the MIC thesis has any validity, how can we explain why arms races ever start, slacken, or stop? Arms races would be never ending. To attribute war to industries seeking profit is, in fact, a bit like saying that doctors and pharmaceutical companies deliberately encourage disease in order to earn higher salaries and profits.

Similarly, whether or not defense spending is a crutch for the economy is at least debatable; if the skilled personnel and technology devoted to weaponry had been devoted instead to the growth of the nonmilitary sector of the economy (assuming no external threat), would not the economy have grown more rapidly? Seymour Melman has argued that the "permanent war economy"—his term for an economy devoting over $100 billion to defense—has resulted in technical stagnation in many of the principal productive sectors of the economy, like manufacturing, transportation, and energy. He has estimated that the total investment in military hardware since World War II has exceeded industrial investment in plants and machinery in the same period! The American military establishment's demands for capital have left only 10 percent of the national income to be plowed back into productive investments, whereas Japan, for example, has plowed back 30 percent and West Germany almost 20 percent. Despite the widely accepted radical wisdom that war production is necessary for a capitalist economy to maintain high employment, a war economy in fact slows economic growth and reduces the capacity to generate prosperity and jobs. As various industries become noncompetitive with firms in other countries that invest proportionally less in defense and more in nondefense industries, American unemployment goes up.[39] Melman's own later estimates are shown in Table 15.1.

In addition, defense expenditures create fewer jobs than the same amounts of money spent in civilian fields. In January 1975, the U.S. Bureau of Labor Statistics estimated that $1 billion spent on defense had created 51,000 jobs. The same $1 billion would have created 61,000 jobs in public housing, 88,000 jobs in Veterans Administration health care, and 136,000 jobs if spent on manpower training.[40]

[38] Philip Odeen, "In Defense of the Defense Budget," *Foreign Policy*, Fall 1974, pp. 94–95.

[39] Melman, *Pentagon Capitalism* (New York: McGraw-Hill, 1970).

[40] Melman, "Go Civilian or Go Broke," *The New York Times*, December 14, 1976, p.

TABLE 15.1

EXAMPLES OF JOBS LOST IN AMERICAN INDUSTRIES BECAUSE OF NONCOMPETITIVENESS

Industry	Jobs Replaced by Imports 1964	1972
Men's and boys' suits and coats	800	7,100
Men's and boys' shirts and nightwear	4,000	18,200
Children's outerwear	15,300	31,700
Wood products	4,800	9,800
Furniture and fixtures	2,600	11,900
Rubber and plastic footwear	4,100	13,300
Men's and women's footwear	6,500	32,600
Fine earthenware food utensils	2,000	5,600
Pottery products	2,100	5,100
Fabricated metal products	2,900	7,200
Textile machinery	3,500	16,400
General industrial machinery	3,400	6,700
Typewriters and office machines	3,400	17,400
Calculating and accounting machines	1,300	5,300
Sewing machines	3,600	5,200
Current-carrying wiring devices	900	6,100
Radio and television receiving sets	7,600	37,700
Radio and television communication equipment	2,300	9,700
Semiconductors	700	11,800
Motor vehicles, bodies, parts	13,700	95,900
Motorcycles, bicycles, parts	4,500	28,300
Measuring and controlling devices	400	7,800
Watches, clocks, watch cases	4,100	7,100
Games, toys, children's vehicles	2,900	6,600
Sporting and athletic goods	2,500	8,100

And because military jobs pay money to workers without also expanding the supply of available goods—few individuals buy tanks or missiles—military spending results in inflation. More money chases fewer goods, driving prices up on the items people do buy. During the Vietnam War the sudden sizable increase in military spending following Johnson's intervention resulted in a sharp increase in inflation because the government did not raise taxes to soak up the additional purchasing power.

A better perspective on the military-industrial complex can be gained in the context of the state system. In a bipolar system in which both powers, regardless of their domestic structures or values, are highly sensitive to the slightest shift in the balance of power, lest it result in the opponent's hegemony, the emphasis is on demarcating spheres of influence and on defusing confrontations and managing crises. Not surprisingly, policy makers are concerned with their nations' military strength. Nor should it be surprising that civilians, especially secretaries of state, favor a military buildup and the fighting of a limited war, as in Korea. They are, after all, the chief foreign-policy advisers, and the nation's objectives and the means to achieve them are bound to be of concern to them. Ideally, policy makers balance

426   means and ends. "Militarized civilians" may thus favor development of a new weapon, a military doctrine, or higher force levels, just as they may favor the opposite if it seems necessary or desirable.) An understanding of the massive American bomber buildup in the 1950s or the large scale deployment of missiles during the early 1960s must be related to American concerns about Soviet behavior in the wake of the Korean war and resulting American fears of Soviet aggression in Europe—including continuing pressure on West Berlin from 1958 to 1961. To perceive the American-Soviet arms competition as essentially an "action-reaction" process in which each side's development of weapons leads to the adversary's counterdevelopment, weapon for weapon, is oversimplified, if not analytically distorted, for it tends to divorce acquisition of arms from foreign-policy developments.

Beside being affected by bipolarity in the period from 1945 through 1962, policy makers were also greatly affected by rapidly changing technology. The possibility of a technological breakthrough by the opponent was bound to worry those whose main concern was deterrence of an enemy believed to be expansionist. As ever newer delivery systems are invented, a series of arms races is at least understandable. For deterrence to remain effective, the offense must stay ahead of the defense; the deterrer can never leave its adversary in doubt that second-strike forces could eradicate it. Military influence on the policy process thus reflects the international situation; given the responsibility of policy makers in what still remains a bipolar nuclear system as well as the nature of modern technology, they have to play their cards conservatively. When the nation's security is at stake, great risks are unlikely. When a new missile or bomber replaces an older one, the decision is guided by that fact, rather than by corporate profits.

In addition to the state system and technology, the MIC thesis conveniently ignores both the actual policies pursued and the policy process. During the early years of the Cold War, the principal instrument of national policy was economic aid. Not until the Korean war erupted and the fear of other communist military attacks, particularly in Europe, heightened the Truman administration's estimate of the external threat to American security, did American and North Atlantic Treaty Organization (NATO) rearmament begin in earnest. After the Korean war, the fiscally and politically conservative Eisenhower administration, composed largely of businessmen, again cut back military spending drastically (as a percentage of annually growing GNP). The desire to balance budgets at lower spending levels and the conviction that the United States might well spend itself into bankruptcy led policy makers to concentrate on spending for the air force, with its capacity for "massive retaliation." On the whole, military appropriations and strategy during the Truman and Eisenhower years were decided by the "remainder method"—that is, they constituted the sum left after the national income had been calculated, the cost of domestic programs provided for, and nonmilitary foreign expenditures decided.[41] Only since the election of Kennedy have administrations drawn up defense budgets in an opposite fashion: deciding national strategy first and then determining the missions of the various services, the weapons they need, and the overall costs.

[41.] *The New York Times*, December 19, 1976.

Civilian policy makers have always remembered the maxim that, if you listen to a doctor, you are never healthy; to a minister, never without sin; and to a military man, never secure. Consequently, although the services have been consulted, they have rarely stopped grumbling about all the weapons that they have *not* received. Skepticism about military demands is surely warranted. But a questioning attitude does not mean that the military services should not be heard on policy and weapons, as some MIC critics seem almost to be suggesting in their denunciations of military influence. Even though it is, on the other hand, legitimate for the views of the four services to be expressed, the question of their influence on various policies and the acquisition of arms will surely vary from issue to issue and from time to time. For instance, the services normally have had to compete with one another for money and weapons because the military budget, though large in absolute figures, is nevertheless finite. One service's gain is frequently another's loss; the resulting interservice rivalry is usually fierce. The Defense Department's constituents—the industrial corporations and the political supporters of the services and corporations in Congress—have been involved in the policy process, though not necessarily in the way usually claimed. For example, although it is normally believed that congressmen whose constituencies include industries producing military hardware will vote for high military budgets, the voting records of such congressmen do not support this belief; many, indeed, vote for lower defense budgets. The principal correlation is between voting for arms and those representatives whose districts or states include military bases.[42] In any event, to the degree that corporations support weapons production and congressmen vote for military forces, their role is basically limited to supporting particular services in conflict with other services for contracts *after* the basic issue of funds and strategy has been decided by the president, whose control over the military is, in fact, strengthened by the normal and often intense interservice and intercorporate rivalry. He rules because they are so deeply divided. There is no military-industrial complex dictating higher budgets, more weapons, and more hawkish foreign policies; there are instead a *number of* military-industrial complexes that are usually in competition with one another.

For the president, then, the principal factor affecting decision remains his perception of the deterrent balance and technology. Even when Soviet military strength rises, it takes some *action* by Russia or its friends to bring about an American buildup. It took a Korean attack or a threat to Berlin to raise the executive and legislative branches' perceptions of external threat and to make it politically feasible to propose postponement of new domestic programs or new taxes for more weapons. Before the Korean war, Truman refused to enhance the nation's military capability; Eisenhower, even after the launching of the Soviet satellite Sputnik, did little, despite grave warnings about a potential missile gap and SAC's new vulnerability. It was the liberally oriented Kennedy administration that launched a large missile-production program and preparations for limited war in order to ensure itself policy

---

[41.] Samuel P. Huntington, *The Common Defense* (New York: Columbia University Press, 1961); and Walter Millis, *Arms and the State* (New York: Twentieth Century Fund, 1958), Part 2.

[42.] Russett, *op. cit.*

428   options after Khrushchev's tough behavior at the Vienna summit meeting in 1961 and the renewed Soviet challenge in Berlin. The Nixon administration was virtually unique among postwar American administrations in deciding upon major arms production and deployment in the absence of an obvious and visible security threat—and this decision aroused vigorous criticism. In response, the president could only assert the possibility of grave future danger, but in the absence of aggressive Soviet behavior there was no proof. He was therefore unable to rally widespread political support and to still the critics of his plans for deployment of ABMs and multiple independent reentry vehicles (MIRVs), both weapons the utility of which was difficult to demonstrate, as the test of their effectiveness lay in their nonuse.

One key point also follows from the bureaucratic decision-making model (which will be presented in Chapter 16): The military does not generally live up to its popular warlike image. Hitler once remarked of the German military that, before he became the Führer, he had thought he would have to put a leash on his soldiers to hold them back; instead he had constantly to push them forward. An army or navy is a bureaucracy. It is obviously interested in the expansion of its capabilities and influence in decision making, but, like any bureaucracy, it has a tendency to play safe. War, as the Prussian general Clausewitz said, is a gamble; it is risky and can spell defeat for a country and loss of influence, if not collapse, for the military bureaucracy. It is, in a real sense, easier to play soldier in peacetime. For example, the U.S. Army perceived its prime role in the post-1945 period to be the defense of Europe. Believing that it never received sufficient resources, the army was always aware that commitments could outrun strength; generally, therefore, it was not particularly enthusiastic about taking on new commitments. Army leaders preferred to concentrate on what they believed to be primary obligations.

For another example, the army (and the other services) did not favor intervention in Korea; it was the civilian leaders who thought it necessary to intervene. After China's entry into the war, when pressure to retaliate against it became intense—from General MacArthur in the field and from the Republican party—it was the military as a whole that took a leading role in opposing this move. Russia was the primary enemy; the United States should not therefore invest excessive resources against a secondary opponent and weaken itself in such a struggle. The air force, for instance, opposed using its big bombers to attack China, for, if too many were shot down, the air force's deterrent capacity against the Soviet Union would be weakened. The services have hardly been war dogs straining at the leash and seeking to promote further commitments and interventions.

The Korean War was not the only example of this attitude. The military was not the prime force in the Bay of Pigs operation; the American blockade of Cuba a year later; or intervention in the Dominican Republic; nor, despite the military headquarters established in Saigon and Kennedy's commitment of military advisers, was the military in Washington enthusiastic about intervention in Vietnam. After the disillusioning experience in Korea—a limited war in which the military leaders believed that they had been improperly restrained politically—a clique called the "Never-Again Club" was formed. On the other hand, once the civilians had decided to intervene *with* limits, the military went in and, hardly unexpectedly, sought to increase its strength and a relaxation of restraints to enhance the pressure on the enemy. One study of military advice on the use of force has in fact concluded that the Joint Chiefs have exercized the greatest influence on issues of intervention when they vetoed it.[43]

Theorizing and Faith

On the whole, it is probably correct to say that the MIC thesis is primarily a "devil theory," a polemical tool rather than an analytical one. The writings of the MIC theorists tend to run to a pattern: they decry both the nature and methods of American foreign policy, what the United States has done to the world, how it has done it, and the price it has paid in terms of delaying the fight against poverty and injustice at home. They hold the military and business interests and their "servants" in Congress responsible for starting the Cold War and/or continuing hard-line policies and escalating the arms race; in brief, the MIC is invoked to discredit the policies and institutions responsible for these policies. Someone must be to blame for the mess; clearly international tension and domestic injustice are not in the majority's interests. Logically, therefore, it follows that this minority of privileged men act as a conspiracy. Note also that the logic of this argument is backwards: the substance of the policies is condemned first; the MIC analyst then reasons from that back to those allegedly to blame. The whole argument rests on the rather questionable ground of guilt by association: if someone has an interest in arms, bureaucratically or economically, this must be the cause of arms races and increased international tensions.

Arms do, of course, acquire vested domestic interests, but does this mean that arms races are initiated by those interests, or that they will stoke such a race and prevent its slowing down or cessation? The 1972 ABM treaty, for example, was further reduced by the 1974 protocol agreed to at the Brezhnev-Nixon summit meeting that year; a lot of jobs and some vested interests, including some in the Soviet military, lost out in these agreements, which were made by two determined political leaders who could not be blocked. The same was true for the B-1 bomber which the U.S. Air Force wanted as a replacement for the aging B-52. Despite intensive lobbying by its contractor and by other groups such as labor with a vested interest in building the B-1 and despite support for the bomber in Congress, including a specific House appropriation for it, President Carter decided not to go ahead with the construction and deployment of a B-1 bomber fleet of 224 planes. In the final analysis, the military's influence on American foreign policy and defense spending was more a symptom of the bipolar situation in which the United States found itself for most of the post-1945 period than of any illegitimate pressures brought to bear on the government. In fact, this emphasis on illegitimate policy

---

[43.] Richard K. Betts, *Soldiers, Statesmen and Cold War Crises* (Cambridge, Mass.; Harvard University Press, 1977).

430   processes is precisely the common thread that runs through both the Marxist-Leninist and MIC views of American policy.) As John Sloan has suggested about dependency theory, the advocates of these approaches or theories have "dealt with their conclusions more as true believers than as social scientists." Accepting these models with something akin to "religious fervor," such scholars "have resembled self flagellating monks atoning for the sins of their nation in Vietnam, Cuba, Guatemala, and the Dominican Republic." Unlike most scholars, they appear to "enjoy the luxury of having their social theory perfectly congruent with their normative beliefs" and continue to believe with great conviction and no uncertainty that one key explains virtually any nation's foreign and domestic policies.[43] As E. H. Carr said several decades ago about the realist approach to international politics: it lacked an ultimate goal and vision which gave it both a strong emotional appeal and grounds for moral judgment, especially for condeming current policies.[44] (The imperialist and "merchants of death" theories lack none of these characteristics. Hence their appeal, in the U.S. and even more so elsewhere, regardless of the evidence which may or may not support them; truth with a capital T is a matter of faith, even if it is poor social science. Empirical study of the policy process suggests a quite different model, one that is pluralistic, competitive, and open, exactly what the Marxist-Leninist and MIC explanations deny.)

---

[43] John W. Sloan, "Dependency Theory and Latin American Development: Another Key Fails To Open The Door," *Inter-American Economic Affairs*, Winter 1977, p. 30.

[44] Carr, *The Twenty Year Crisis*, pp. 89–94.

Decision Making and the "Games Bureaucrats Play" 16

THE ROLE OF PERCEPTION AND BUREAUCRATIC POSITION

T he decision-making approach to understanding the foreign policy of a country is based on the assumption that we should look at the *specific personnel and departments officially responsible for making external policy*.[1] When we speak of a state's doing this or that, we are really speaking of those officials, the policy decisions they make, and how they implement them. The state, in short, equals the official policy makers whose decisions and actions constitute the policies of the state. Decisions are the "outputs" of the domestic political system. By focusing on the decision makers, this approach emphasizes, first, how they *see* the world. What is important is not what the international system is really or objectively like but rather how the policy makers perceive it. For it is on their perceptions that these officials act or, for that matter, do not act; reality thus does not exist independent of the policy makers' definitions of it.

As we noted much earlier, a balance-of-power analysis allows prescriptions of what Chamberlain should have done to counter Hitler in the 1930s but not what he did. Without studying the prime minister and his advisers within the cabinet

---

[1] See Roger Hilsman, *To Move a Nation* (Garden City, N.Y.: Doubleday, 1967); Graham Allison, *The Essence of Decision* (Boston: Little, Brown, 1971); Morton H. Halperin, *Bureaucratic Politics and Foreign Policy* (Washington, D.C.: Brookings, 1974); and Halperin and Arnold Kanter, eds., *Readings in American Foreign Policy* (Boston: Little, Brown, 1973).

432 and outside it, and without analyzing their perceptions of Hitler, the goals of Nazi Germany, and the Versailles peace treaty, first-level analysts could not tell why the British did what they did and did not do other things or why they bungled and brought on the very war they had hoped to avoid. Such an analysis was thus not very helpful. A useful analysis would have included Chamberlain's misperception of Hitler as a simple German nationalist who, while seeking some territorial adjustments, had otherwise only limited ambitions; once satisfied, Chamberlain believed, he would accept the European system, instead of seeking to overthrow it. Such an analysis would also have been focused on the pacifist nature of British public opinion, still guided by memories of horrible manpower losses during World War I; this opinion acted as a constraint upon British political leaders, even had they wished to contain Germany.

Similarly, even if another concept can properly explain some particular event, as the concept of national style can account for the American intervention in the Vietnam war, such an explanation may be rejected as too broad and vague. How can we attribute the war to national style without scrutinizing the officials who have made the decision to fight it, the departments in which they have served, organizational pressures to intervene or not to intervene, and legislative and public pressures. As national style presumably affects all policy makers, was the Vietnam intervention inevitable? If not, then, despite the alleged impact of the American style, we must examine the personnel, sometimes described as "the best and the brightest" that the United States had to offer, who made the decision to intervene. Had the United States not intervened in Vietnam, would that abstention also have been attributed to national style? If whatever a nation does arises from its style, then style is too encompassing a concept; by explaining everything, it explains nothing. The same can be said of economic explanations, especially Marxist-Leninist determinism. An event is ordained by history, or it is not ordained. A skeptic rightfully chooses to study the specific officials who make the specific decisions.

One model of decision making—the rational-actor model—has been central to first-level analysis, in which each state is viewed as a unified actor, making foreign-policy choices in four clearly separate steps: selecting objectives and values, considering alternative means of achieving them, calculating the likely consequences of each alternative, and selecting the one that is most promising. As Henry Kissinger wrote in 1957, if American policy is to seek security and peace, it cannot rationally be based on a strategy of massive retaliation against the U.S.S.R. when confronted with limited challenges. To respond in this manner would only ensure American suicide; not to respond at all would be tantamount to surrender. Both courses are therefore irrational. The only rational option in these circumstances is "limited war."[2] This rational model, as ought to be clear, underlies not only analyses of international politics and specific foreign policies but also other spheres of decision making. In the competitive "games nations play," with their informal rules, but also in other games, like courtship and politics, each player must make a set of decisions if he or she is to "win." There are usually several options; he or

---

[2] Henry A. Kissinger, *Nuclear Weapons and Foreign Policy* (New York: Harper & Row, 1957).

she must at each point in the game decide which play is the best in terms of ultimate goals.)

(The other model is that of governmental politics. It is focused on the executive branch of government and especially on the bureaucracies whose official responsibility is to formulate and execute foreign policy. It is also focused on the legislature, at least in free countries, and on many interest groups, the mass media, and the various publics that together constitute public opinion. The bureaucracy is thus viewed in its broader governmental and societal setting. The emphasis is on the *pluralistic nature of decision making* in which, in general, the actors' views reflect their positions and interests. As one motto has it, *"Where you stand depends on where you sit."* Policy in these circumstances is formulated, on one hand, through conflicts among many actors with different perceptions, perspectives, and interests and, on the other, through reconciling these differences. These two elements of the policy struggle will determine who receives what and when. Such a political way of making policy generally applies to noncrisis security policies, which express continuing goals and involve continuing sets of actors, including the Congress (because security policies often need funding).)

(Graham Allison has aptly illustrated the difference between rational and bureaucratic policy making.[3])When in the late 1950s, the Soviet Union tested its first intercontinental ballistic missile (ICBM), American leaders became very concerned about a possible "missile gap" favoring the Soviets. Following the rational model, they concluded that Russia would exploit this technological breakthrough, mass-produce ICBMs, and use them to pressure the United States to concede territorial changes in central Europe, specifically in the symbolically significant western half of Berlin. In terms of the balance of power, the Soviets had achieved a major technological breakthrough, which, if fully exploited before the United States could test and deploy an ICBM, could give them superior power. Rationally, in terms of the rules of the game of the international system, that is what the Kremlin leaders should have done—at least, that is what American policy makers expected them to do. Had the United States been the nation to test the first ICBM, it would have gone into large-scale production which would have strengthened the American hand in relation to the Soviet Union. It would have seemed the logical thing to do. If the same American policy makers had used the pluralistic policy-making model, however, they would have been more cautious in drawing this conclusion. The Red Army controlled the missiles, and it was unlikely to abandon suddenly its traditional definition of its role on the ground in favor of intercontinental strategic deterrence with ICBMs. The very thought would be alien to an organization preoccupied with land defense and a role limited to Eurasia. A dramatic shift to deterrence within the army would certainly have been accompanied by an observable policy struggle, as more traditional officers, whose role had been ground combat, would have been down-graded and would presumably have fiercely resisted. Similarly, the development of a large ICBM force would have required a vast transfer of funds from other services and their requirements, thus creating

---

[3.] Allison "Conceptual Models and the Cuban Missile Crisis," *American Political Science Review*, September 1969, p. 716.

434   interservice rivalries and quarrels. The different models, then, offered grounds for quite different assessments of what the Soviets would do and implied quite different American defense and foreign policies. The incoming Kennedy administration, acting upon the rational model, initiated a more numerous missile deployment than it might otherwise have done; the Russians' reaction, after the Cuban missile crisis in 1962, was an extensive buildup that has resulted in the achievement of strategic parity.

We shall now examine these two models in more detail. But it must first be noted that, although the decision-making models can be used in explaining other countries' foreign policies, we shall use American examples and focus on the American policy process because of more readily available materials, the many decisions that have been made in Washington since World War II, and the greater familiarity of American readers with recent history in which the United States has been actively involved. Later we shall return to the comparative usefulness of the models in decision making and, indeed, to their analytical limitations as well.

CRISIS DECISION MAKING

The rational-actor model is probably the most relevant to explaining and understanding crisis decisions. A crisis, as already suggested, is characterized by a number of features, one of which is a perceived threat to vital interests, usually surprise, and urgency to make decisions.[4] Most important and always present in the situation, in which one state has confronted another with a demand for a change in the status quo, is the possible use of violence, possibly of nuclear war. One characteristic of the decision-making process is therefore that decision making rises to the top of the governmental hierarchy, specifically, to the president and his closest advisers. Some will be statutory advisers, like the secretaries of his chief foreign-policy agencies; others will be people both in and out of government whose judgment he particularly trusts. During the potentially very explosive Cuban missile crisis of 1962, the Executive Committee, which managed the crisis, included as members the president and vice president; the secretaries of State and Defense; their seconds in command; the director of the Central Intelligence Agency (CIA); the chairman of the Joint Chiefs of Staff; the president's special assistant for national security affairs; and certain other individuals like the secretary of the Treasury, the Attorney General (the president's brother), the president's special counsel (perhaps his closest friend after his brother), an ambassador just returned from Moscow, and President Truman's former Secretary of State.[5] During the 1972 spring offensive of North Vietnamese troops, when the defeat of the South Vietnamese army seemed imminent,

---

[4] Oran Young, *The Politics of Force* (Princeton: Princeton University Press, 1968), pp. 6–15; and Charles F. Hermann, ed., *International Crises* (New York: Free Press, 1972).

[5] For the Cuban missile crisis, see Elie Abel, *The Missile Crisis* (New York: Bantam, 1966), Alexander L. George *et al.*, eds., *The Limits of Coercive Diplomacy* (Boston: Little, Brown, 1971); and Robert F. Kennedy, *Thirteen Days* (New York: Norton, 1967).

the decision-making process was more narrowly confined. Partly as a result of the concentraton of foreign-policy decision making in the White House under Kissinger, partly as a result of President Nixon's style as a "loner," and partly as a result of the President's tactic of confronting a Senate increasingly critical of the continuation of the Vietnam war with *faits accomplis* (which could not be done if leaks occurred before action), decision making seems to have been confined largely to these two men, although the members of the National Security Council were consulted formally.[6]

(A second characteristic of crisis decisions is the central role of the president; it is primarily he who interprets events and evaluates the stakes in the crisis.) Kennedy's and Nixon's "readings" of the situations that they confronted, the consequences that these situations might have for American security, and their own political futures and abilities to lead the nation were responsible for their actions. ((The latter two can hardly be separated, for the external challenges, as the president sees them, do not really leave a choice of accepting a loss of personal prestige without a loss of national prestige. For the president of the United States, personal and national cost calculations tend to be identical.))Kennedy saw the installation of Soviet missiles in Cuba as a personal challenge, with potentially damaging national effects. In response to earlier congressional and public clamor about possible Soviet offensive missiles in Cuba—as distinct from ground-to-air or ground-to-ship defensive missiles—Kennedy had publicly declared that the United States would not tolerate offensive missiles on the island 90 miles off the Florida coast. Intended primarily as a declaration to cool American domestic criticism that had come largely from Republicans, Kennedy's statement had also led Moscow leaders to respond that they had no intention of placing missiles in Cuba; Russia had, they said, more than enough missiles at home. The president had thus initially deemphasized the possibility that the Russians would install such weapons in Cuba, and the Russians had then signaled their understanding of his declaration. Privately they had further reassured him that they had no intention of installing missiles anywhere outside the U.S.S.R. Kennedy was thus publicly pledged to act if the Russians lied—as it turned out they had—unless he wished to be publicly humiliated. If he did not act, the Soviet leaders would not believe other pledges and commitments that the president had made or taken over from his predecessors. At least, that is how the president perceived the situation.

The consequences were judged very dangerous by Kennedy, who already feared that Khrushchev had interpreted previous acts— the abortive Bay of Pigs invasion of Cuba and the inaction of American troops when the Berlin Wall went up—as signaling lack of will, an absence of sufficient resolution and determination to defend American vital interests.(Khrushchev spoke openly of an American failure of nerve. The United States, in his view, spoke loudly but carried a small stick) (It was not so much the effect of the Soviet missiles upon the military equation between the two powers that mattered, though that was important; it was the political consequences of the *appearance of* a change in the balance of power that

---

[6] Tad Szulc, "Behind the Vietnam Cease-Fire Agreements," *Foreign Policy*, Summer 1974, pp. 39–40.

436   were deemed critical by Kennedy. The Soviet Union was supposed to be on the short end of the missile gap, but American inaction would, Kennedy feared, be widely recognized as a persuasive answer to Soviet claims of missile superiority and would lead allied governments to fear that, in the new situation in which the United States would be highly vulnerable to nuclear devastation, they could no longer count on this country to defend them. Above all, it might tempt the Soviets to exploit the situation and to seek to disrupt American alliances—especially NATO, since Khrushchev had already restated his determination to eject the western allies from West Berlin. If Khrushchev succeeded in Cuba, why should he take seriously Kennedy's pledge to defend West Berlin? And, if he did not, would not Soviet and American troops soon be clashing in an area where they would be hard to separate?

       The real irony of the Cuban missile crisis is that Kennedy was also determined that, during his years in office, he would try to seek a more stable and restrained basis of coexistence with the Soviet Union. This long-range goal, which hardly had the massive support it has today, could not be realized if Khrushchev would not take Kennedy seriously and tried to push him around. Then serious negotiations, in which each party recognized the other's legitimate interests, would be impossible. A major change in the cold-war atmosphere was thus at stake, in addition to the United States' reputation for power and willingness to keep commitments already given: domestically, of course, another "defeat" in Cuba discrediting Kennedy's foreign policy was bound to affect his personal standing with his party, the Congress, and the public and to lead to strong right-wing Republican pressures to be more forcible in the future and to the endangerment of New Frontier liberal domestic reforms.

       Nixon also saw the central issue in Vietnam as the United States' reputation for power, its prestige.[7] When he came into office, there was little question that Americans were weary of the high costs, especially in casualties, of the Vietnam war. These costs seemed totally disproportionate to the continuation of a war that promised no successful end in the near future. For Nixon, the crux of the problem was not whether or not the United States should leave Vietnam but, as he repeatedly stressed, *how* it should leave. If its chief adversaries, Russia and China, were to be deterred and contained, if fruitful negotiations with Russia over arms control were to occur, if relations were to be established with the Peking government, and if a more stable and peaceful "structure of peace" were to be worked out with those nations, then the United States' reputation in the two major communist countries was the crucial factor. If it were humiliated in Vietnam, it would be viewed as a "pitiful, helpless giant" that could be pressured, with which it was not necessary to negotiate seriously, and that offered few attractions as a potential partner for either Russia or China against the other.

       Nixon's strategy was therefore to "Vietnamize" the war. The South Vietnamese army was increasingly taking over the fighting, but it would receive large-

---

[7.] The process of Nixon's decision making has been reconstructed from *ibid.*, from *The New York Times* of the period, and from Henry Branden, *The Retreat of American Power* (Garden City, N.Y.: Doubleday, 1973). Also Henry Kissinger, *White House Years* (Boston: Little Brown, 1979), pp. 1097–1123, 1165–1200.

scale American air support to help preserve a noncommunist government in South Vietnam. If American public opinion would support a strategy that would lead to few casualties for the United States and if the pressure to leave Vietnam completely could thus be greatly reduced at home, then the Hanoi regime would presumably have an incentive to negotiate a compromise settlement. Confronted by continued use of American air power and—it was hoped—an increasingly better-trained South Vietnamese army equipped by the United States, Hanoi's leaders would find their hopes for all-out victory in the South dimming and would prefer to end hostilities and settle for political competition in order to gain a share of the power in Saigon.)

This strategy, however, brought the United States to the brink of disaster in spring 1972, just after Nixon's dramatic visit to Peking and just before his extremely important visit to Moscow to negotiate limitations on defensive and offensive missiles and other key topics. Nixon, like Kennedy, rejected the possibility of inaction, even though the Moscow summit meeting with its potential for a dramatic change in the nature of the American-Soviet adversary partnership might be jeopardized if he took strong action against the Soviet Union's fraternal socialist state. But the president believed that the Soviet government, having supplied the government of Hanoi with much of its modern military paraphernalia, including ground-to-air missiles and tanks for conventional offensives, should have restrained the North Vietnamese leaders just before the summit meeting. As Nixon perceived the situation, whether or not Moscow had been aware of the timing of the North Vietnamese offensive, the fact of the offensive seriously endangered his Vietnam- ization policy and humiliated him on the eve of vital negotiations; the president did not intend to enter these negotiations under the cloud of defeat and failure. The failure of Vietnamization also would, of course, undermine his prestige and lead- ership at home. He had already ordered the bombing of North Vietnam; he now ordered that its harbors be mined in order to stop incoming Russian and Chinese supplies. President Johnson had always refused to take this step, for the risk of a confrontation with the Soviets was high. Did the latter not have the right to supply their friends? Would the United States have permitted Russia to blockade American supplies to South Vietnam? In any event, Nixon took the risk of a confrontation. Negotiations with Hanoi's leaders had not gone anywhere; Vietnamization did not seem much more successful. The president therefore re-Americanized the war and, by risking a direct confrontation with the USSR, hoped to compel it to pressure Hanoi leaders to settle the war—if the USSR wanted better relations with the United States. The Russians did not call off the Moscow summit meeting.

Nixon apparently did not consider other courses of action; he rejected inaction as the price for the Moscow summit. Kennedy had considered alternative responses to the Soviet missiles in Cuba, everything from diplomatic pressures and a secret approach to Castro to surgical air strikes at the missiles, invasion, and blockade. Feeling strongly that he had to act in order to impress Khrushchev, however, Kennedy had chosen the blockade as the option most likely to attain the removal of the Soviet missiles. Although the blockade could not by itelf achieve this objective, it was a sign of American determination, permitting the United States the option of increasing the pressure on the Soviet regime later if the missiles were

438   not removed; providing a relatively safe middle course between inaction and invasion (or an air strike), which might provoke the Russians; and placing on Khrushchev the responsibility for deciding whether to escalate or deescalate. It is significant that, thanks to a U-2 "spy plane," the administration had a whole week to debate the meaning and significance of the Russian move, what its military and political effects on American security interests were likely to be, what the different courses of action open to the United States were, and which was most likely to achieve removal of the Soviet missiles without precipitating nuclear war. Many crises simply do not afford such time for preparation and the careful consideration of alternatives. Even during the missile crisis, the initial reaction of most of the president's advisers had been to bomb the missile sites. Slowing down the momentum of events is crucial if impulsive actions are to be avoided.

Nixon apparently made his decision to bomb and mine in Vietnam during the week before he announced it—that is, after Kissinger had flown to Moscow to talk to Russian leaders and after he had, upon the latter's urgings, met privately with the top North Vietnamese negotiator in Paris—to no avail. At a subsequent Nixon meeting with his principal cabinet officers, only the vice-president and Secretary of the Treasury John Connally were strongly in favor of attacking North Vietnam; the secretaries of State and Defense and the director of the CIA were opposed or unenthusiastic. Kissinger was apparently of two minds on the issue. Nixon thus had less time than Kennedy had had in Cuba; rather, his position was more like that of Truman after the North Korean invasion of South Korea, that of Kennedy when the Berlin wall went up, or that of Johnson when the internal Dominican situation erupted and the embassy began reporting the likelihood that "Castro communists" would gain control.

As we might imagine, a third characteristic of crises is the subordination of bureaucratic interests to the need to make a decision to safeguard the "national interest." The crisis is accompanied by a sense of urgency, as well as by the policy makers' perception that the nation's security is at stake and that war looms. Furthermore, decision making has risen to the top levels of the government, and the men and women in those positions, though reflecting their departmental points of view, do not necessarily feel themselves limited to representing those points of view. Organizational affiliation is not *per se* a good predictor of those points of view. Senior participants in crises behave more as "players" than as "organizational participants." Robert McNamara did not reflect the Joint Chiefs' readiness to bomb and invade during the Cuban missile crisis (just as later in Vietnam he was increasingly to disagree with their views and recommendations); he became the leading proponent of the blockade. Other players in that crisis did not even represent foreign-policy bureaucracies—the two men closest to the president, the Attorney General, and the president's special counsel, along with the secretary of the treasury and a former secretary of state, for example, represented only themselves. The bureaucratic axiom that "you stand where you sit" is thus not necessarily correct, at least during a crisis.

Finally, crisis decision making is characterized by congressional noninvolvement. Congressional leaders are usually called in and informed of the president's decision just before he announces it publicly. This form is followed as a matter of courtesy. But their advice is not requested. Presidents consider themselves more representative than any senator or House member and as representative as Congress as a whole.) Interestingly enough, Kennedy, after informing a congressional delegation of his decision to blockade Cuba, did ask for its opinions. When the response was to question the utility of the blockade and to propose an air strike instead, Kennedy reacted angrily. After the congressmen left, he consoled himself by saying that, had they had more time to think it over, they, like he, would also have decided on the blockade.(If presidents assure themselves like this, why indeed consult members of the legislative branch? In any event, in crises what choice do they have but to support the only president the country has at the moment?)

DECISION MAKING AS A PLURALISTIC POWER STRUGGLE

(The governmental model of decision making is characterized first by multiple institutional actors: the three branches of the federal government. In foreign-policy matters, the principal participants are the executive and legislative branches. Within these institutions there are a multitude of departments, organizations, staffs, committees, and individuals concerned with foreign policy. Within the executive branch, there are the president, his assistant for national-security affairs, and his staff; the senior foreign-policy departments (the State and Defense Departments and the CIA); the junior departments (Agency for International Development or AID, U. S. Communications Agency, and Arms Control and Disarmament Agency or ACDA); and departments with domestic jurisdictions that occasionally deal with foreign-policy issues falling within their areas of expertise (Departments of the Treasury, Commerce, and Agriculture). Similarly, Congress consists of the Senate and the House, and each is further divided into different party groupings and committees—the latter being subdivided even further into subcommittees. In 1978, there were 385 subcommittees in Congress.[8] Often several committees and subcommittees hold hearings and issue reports on the same policy.)

(This institutional pluralism is supplemented by organized groups representing many economic, ethnic, racial, and religious interests. As for foreign policy, however, "it is questionable, in fact, whether we are really entitled to talk about group influence on 'foreign policy'; with very rare exceptions, the influence of nongovernmental groups is on particular, discrete, rather highly specialized matters, which, even if they may be deemed to be within the foreign-policy field, are very far from constituting or defining that field."[9])Business groups and labor may be

[8.] For elaboration, see John Spanier and Eric M. Uslaner, *How American Foreign Policy Is Made* (third ed.; New York: Holt, Rinehart and Winston, 1981).

[9.] Bernard C. Cohen, "The Influence of Non-Governmental Groups in Foreign Policy-Making," in Andrew Scott and Raymond Dawson, eds., *Readings in the Making of American Foreign Policy* (New York: Macmillan, 1965), pp. 96–116.

440   interested in particular tariff issues when certain industries and their employees are exposed to foreign competition; an ethnic group may be stimulated by disputes involving a specific country, like Israel or Greece. Yet continuing concern with foreign policy as a whole is lacking; it is intermittent and tied to special issues.

The reason for this more limited interest in security policy than in domestic affairs is easy to understand. Interest groups have abundant knowledge and experience of internal affairs, but on foreign-policy issues they rarely show comparable information and skill; they must therefore rely on foreign-policy experts, who provide a powerful counter to lay involvement. In addition, whereas interest groups are regularly consulted by the respective executive departments while domestic legislation is being drawn up (they, after all, constitute the department's clientele), in foreign policy the departments tend to be their own constituencies and spokesmen. Institutional interests (within the government) therefore predominate over associational interests (outside it). The responsible agencies have their own experts and are in contact with other experts, be they at the RAND Corporation or at Harvard University. Although there is a fairly stable structure of societal interest groups concerned with domestic policies, the comparable structure in the traditional area of foreign policy concerned with security issues is weak and at times even ephemeral.

(A second characteristic of decision making is conflict among actors. Because the president is both the nation's chief diplomat and the commander in chief of its armed forces, this conflict occurs primarily within the executive branch, between executive departments responsible for foreign policy formulation and those responsible for implementation.[10])We can speak, for example, of the State Department versus the Defense Department, though conflict between the executive and legislative branches of government also occurs. Actually, as must be clear, the executive departments and the two houses of Congress rarely speak with a single voice. At the State Department, the head of the European desk may express a view quite different from those of the heads of the Asian and African desks. In the Defense Department, the position of the air force may differ from those of the army and navy. Indeed, within each service there are differences, as between the Strategic Air Command and Tactical Air Command, the surface navy and strategic submarine navy and aircraft-carrier navy. In the Senate, the Foreign Relations Committee may be in conflict on a specific issue with the Armed Services Committee, and subcommittees of each committee may disagree with one another. This situation must be multiplied by the other committees and subcommittees in both houses.(Each of these institutions, bureaucracies, committees, and interest groups develops intense organization identifications, and all are determined not only to survive but also to expand their influence in the policy process. Furthermore, each, viewing a problem from a special perspective, is likely to develop strong convictions about the content of policy, especially when "national interests" are involved and the organization or department thinks that it has a vital contribution to make. Institutional struggles between the executive and legislative branches, as well as

---

[10.] See Samuel P. Huntington, *The Common Defense* (New York: Columbia University Press, 1961), pp. 123 ff., for formulation of defense policy.

within each branch and within executive departments, are consequently the norm.)

(This kind of policy process is often condemned as "parochial," on the assumption that more comprehensive solutions—that is, more "correct"solutions—to all policy problems could be found were it not for the selfish and narrow points of view of the various participants in the foreign-policy process. Adherents of this view ignore the fact that, in any pluralistic institution, different convictions compete; competing policy recommendations are offered as solutions to the problems being considered, and these recommendations represent a fairly broad spectrum of choice. Just as in a democracy different groups and individuals have the right to articulate their values and interests, so the various parts of the executive and legislative branches articulate their own policy views and seek to protect their own interests. The issue is not which policy position and recommendations are correct; *clearly there is not a single correct policy. The issue is how to reconcile conflicting interpretations of what the correct policy ought to be.* Reconciliation of the policy preferences of the various "players" is complicated by the many players outside the executive branch.)

(The third characteristic of decision making, resulting from the first two, is a reconciliation of these different points of view in order to build a "consensus" or majority "coalition" from these so that decisions can be made.) Negotiating thus occurs throughout the executive branch as officials and agencies in one department seek support in another or attempt to enlist the aid of the president or his advisers in order to achieve their goals. The process is one of widening the base of support within the executive branch and then seeking further support in the two houses of Congress, gaining allies through continual modification of the proposed policy. (The official policy "output" that emerges represents the victory of one coalition formed across institutional lines over an opposing coalition of the same kind.)

More specifically, a coalition across institutional lines can be, for example, an alliance among the personnel of a particular desk in the State Department, of a specific service in the Defense Department, and of various bureaus in the Departments of the Treasury and Commerce, as well as of several committees in Congress; it may be opposed by personnel of other desks, services, bureaus, and committees in the same or other departments and the legislative branch. Such a coalition, furthermore, usually holds together only for the specific issue being considered. (A different kind of issue requires mobilization of a different coalition. The reason is that in the United States political parties are undisciplined and party loyalty cannot automatically be counted upon for any given presidential policy. Great energy must thus be expended on this task.)

(Roger Hilsman has compared this process of making policy through conflict, on one hand, and cooperation, on the other, with the behavior of states in the international system.[11]) Politics, as we noted earlier, is distinguished by three features: the existence of multiple groups or organizations; an accompanying set of different and conflicting perspectives, values, and interests; and different amounts of power. (Policy is thus not only a matter of which point of view seems to have the most merit and pertinence, it is also a matter of who has power and exercises it most*

[11.] Hilsman, *op. cit.*, pp. 552–555.

442   *effectively*. The resulting policy struggle—as in international politics—can be summed up as a conflict among different actors over their conflicting power and purposes; the intragovernmental negotiations involved in this struggle are every bit as difficult and tedious as intergovernmental negotiations.

A fourth characteristic of decision making is the effect of conflict and coalition building on policy output. One of the most important results of continuous bargaining within the "policy machine" is that policy in any area moves forward one step at a time and tends to focus on fleeting concerns and short-range aims. [12] This is usually called "incrementalism." Another word is "satisficing." Policy makers, this word suggests, do not sit down each time that they have to make a decision and go through rational procedure of decision making. They do not try to isolate which values and interests they wish to enhance, examine all the means that might achieve these goals, calculate the consequences of each, and then select the one most likely to be successful. Policy makers have neither the time nor the resources to go through this process. Instead, they pick the policy that is likely to be most satisfactory, and they judge this point by whether or not the policy has been successful in the past. If so, why not take another step forward on the same path?

The presumption is that what has worked in the past will work now, as well as in the future. In addition, once a majority has been forged, after hard struggle and probably much "bloodletting," the "winning" coalition will normally prefer modification of existing policy to another major fight. The assumption is, of course, that there will be policy outputs, which is not necessarily true. Negotiations among different groups with conflicting perspectives and vested interests can produce a stalemate and a paralysis of policy.

As a result, policy tends to vacillate between incrementalism and crisis, either because incrementalism is not adequate to a developing situation or because stalemate produces no policy at all. It may be said with reasonable correctness that, during "normal" periods, low external pressure on the policy machine favors continuation of existing policies; during crises, high pressure tends to produce innovative reaction, perhaps because a stalemated policy machine must have an *external* "*trigger*" in order to undermine the coalition supporting the status quo. A crisis may break up coalitions, may awaken a sufficiently great sense of danger to dampen the pluralistic struggle, even if only for a short time, and may create a feeling of urgency—and therefore a common purpose—among the various participants in policy making. Additionally, as already suggested, crisis policy is decided in an inner circle, composed of the president and a few top officials and trusted advisers; at a time of perceived danger these officials function relatively free of departmental points of view and interests, which are likely to be subordinated to the perceived need for rapid decision making. The usual process of consensus or coalition building is thus short-circuited. [13] There are, then, two policy processes: the pluralistic advocacy system and the crisis-management system, the latter involving top officials (assistant secretaries and up), the former a broader mix of interests.

[12] Charles E. Lindblom, "The Science of Muddling Through," *Public Administration Review*, Winter 1959, pp. 79–88.

[13] Theodore J. Lowi, *The End of Liberalism* (New York: Norton, 1969), pp. 160–161.

It took the bombing of Pearl Harbor in 1941 to harness the strength of the United States and direct it toward warding off German and Japanese threats to the nation's security. Symbolically, after December 7, 1941, Franklin Roosevelt, who had called himself "Dr. New Deal"—the physician called in to cure a sick economy—became "Dr. Win the War." Similarly, after World War II, it was the overwhelming Russian threat that allowed Truman to mobilize the country for containment; before the threat became so obvious that it could no longer be ignored, Truman had been unable to take the necessary countermeasures. Again, it took Castro and his attempts to stir anti-American revolutions in Latin American countries to produce the Alliance for Progress in order to help relieve some of the problems in the Southern Hemisphere.

(A fifth characteristic of the policy process, implicit in our analysis so far, is its time-consuming nature. Incrementalism suggests a policy machine in low gear, moving along a well-defined road rather slowly in response to specific short-run stimuli.) A proposed policy is normally discussed first within the executive. It then passes through official channels, where it receives "clearances" and modifications as it gathers a broader base of support on its way "up" the executive hierarchy to the president. (Constant conferences and negotiations among departments clearly slow the pace.) (The process takes even longer when the policy requires congressional and public approval.) On domestic policy particularly, potential opponents can occupy many "veto points" to block legislation within Congress; such veto points are the numerous House and Senate committees and subcommittees that hold hearings on legislation, and the floor debate and votes in both chambers. Should both houses of Congress pass the legislation, the differences between the two versions must be compromised and resubmitted to both for final approval. Only then does the legislation go to the president for his signature. Should he veto it, it will go back to Congress, which can override his veto, but only by a two-thirds vote. The advantage of this slow process lies with those who oppose specific pieces of legislation, for it is difficult to jump all the hurdles along the route to final approval and enactment. It is because there are so many points along the way at which a policy proposal can be stopped, watered down, or compromised beyond recognition that they are called "veto points." This process, admittedly, is more common in domestic than in foreign policy because of the president's greater responsibility and freedom to make policy in the latter area.

Given this slow negotiating process, the formidable obstacles, and great effort needed to pass a new major policy, old policies and the assumptions upon which they are based tend to survive longer than they should. For example, policy based on the assumption that the communist world is cohesive continued even after the Russian-Chinese conflict had surfaced in the late 1950s, and preoccupation with strategic deterrence persisted long after the need for a limited war capacity had been painfully demonstrated in the Korean war. It can be argued that urban decay, racial discrimination, and environmental pollution are all problems that have been neglected for such long periods that crises have been bound to occur. Indeed, it may well be that many of the nation's external and internal problems cannot be solved by a time-consuming process that does not produce policy until

444 conflicts among clashing interests have been resolved and compromises struck. In the end, time—an ingredient that large-scale governmental policy processes consume in abundance—may run out, and the government, confronted by growing problems and incapable of meeting them with sufficient effectiveness and timeliness, may find itself "overloaded," perhaps breaking down under the strain.

(Sixth, the competition among various groups involved in the policy process is also likely to place a premium on attractive and appealing packaging and advertising, which means that, rather than presenting complex and sophisticated reasons for a particular policy position, proponents will try to make it more acceptable by oversimplifying the issues, tying their "product" up with a pretty moral ribbon, and overselling it by insisting that it will definitely solve the buyer's problems. The sellers may indeed exaggerate these problems in order to enhance the buyer's feeling that he or she absolutely needs the policy "product" being offered.[14] In foreign policy, the presentation of issues in terms of communism versus anticommunism, good against evil, hardly helped the understanding of the real issues involved and made it difficult to adjust policies to a changing international environment and a changing communist world.)The threat of Russia, simply as a great power, was real enough; that it was a communist Russia, furthermore, was an even greater threat.(Nevertheless, the menace of "international communism" was exaggerated, partly because it was an effective device for persuading various governmental agencies to accept certain policies, as well as for mobilizing majority support in Congress and the country for those policies.)

(More specifically, as Morton Halperin and Arnold Kanter have suggested, the commonly shared assumptions upon which the decision makers operate— their biases, or images—help to determine which decisions are made.)If anticommunism is the bias—the belief that communism is expansionistic and aggressive, that it must be contained rather than appeased, that military force is to be used to effect containment wherever and whenever necessary—those who try to "sell" their preferences in terms of these "shared images" have a good chance of putting together a majority coalition. On the other hand, those whose preferences are not in line with these assumptions lose out. Other writers have said the same thing more crudely: They have suggested that the toughest anticommunists, posing as the most vigorous "operators," have won the bureaucratic and wider governmental struggle. (Bureaucratic *machismo* is the easiest policy to sell. Those who question the "shared images" lose influence.)

All proponents of specific policy preferences especially seek to sell their "products" to their potentially best customer—the president. His approval and support are obviously decisive. The competition is therefore intense. All important policies are likely to come to the president's attention and to require decisions. The president, as the sole nationally elected official, holds the only position in which all the many considerations bearing on policy can be balanced against one another. There is no other point at which conflicting views and interests so converge; in his office, nonmilitary and military programs, foreign policy and domestic claims conflict, are weighed, and are compromised. Yet the very fact that the president

---

[14.] *Ibid.*

is central to the policy process and that demands upon his time are therefore overwhelming means that he cannot give many issues the time they deserve. He may have little time for them until a crisis erupts. A remote problem will usually be ignored or receive scant attention until it reaches a crisis level; then it will be managed.

(Seventh, one further characteristic of American foreign-policy decision making is that it is usually public. In a democracy publicity is inevitable. Although policy may be made primarily by the executive, its confines are established by public opinion.)No British government before 1939 could have pursued a deterrent policy toward Hitler, and no American government before the fall of France could have intervened in Europe to preserve the balance of power.(In general, however, public opinion tends to be permissive and supportive as far as presidential conduct of foreign policy is concerned.[15])The public is aware that it lacks information and competence in this area, which is remote from its everyday involvement, and it therefore looks to the president for leadership. (In the area of domestic policy, the public is much better informed and public opinion more structured.) Only when setbacks arise or painful experiences pinch the voters will public opinion on foreign policy be expressed, the limits of public tolerance be broadly clarified, and perhaps the party in power be punished. Even though most of the time public opinion does not function as a restraining factor, policy makers are always aware of its existence, however amorphous it may be. Because mass opinion does not tend to take shape until *after* some foreign event has occurred, it can hardly serve as a guide for those who must make policy; nonetheless, the latter will take into account what they think "the traffic will bear," because they know that, if a decision is significant enough, there is likely to be some crystallization of opinion and possibly retribution at the polls.

Reflecting public opinion, Congress was, until the Vietnam war, usually *supportive* of the president's foreign policy. Throughout most of the postwar period, Congress had followed the president's lead, and its role had been essentially reactive and peripheral.(The executive initiated and devised foreign policies, which Congress rarely rejected; primarily, its role was to legitimate those policies in either the original or amended form.[16])The record of American foreign policy since 1945 shows clearly that all major presidential initiatives, from the Truman Doctrine and the Marshall Plan to the Alliance for Progress and the Nuclear Anti-Proliferation Treaty, have been accepted and supported by Congress.[17] This has changed since

---

[15] Francis E. Rourke, "The Domestic Scene," in Robert E. Osgood, ed., *America and the World: From the Truman Doctrine to Vietnam* (Baltimore: Johns Hopkins Press, 1970), pp. 147–188; William R. Caspary, "The 'Mood Theory': A Study of Public Opinion and Foreign Policy," *American Political Science Review*, June 1970, pp. 536–547; and James N. Rosenau, "Foreign Policy as an Issue Area," in Conference on Public Opinion and Foreign Policy, *Domestic Sources of Foreign Policy* (New York: Free Press, 1965).

[16] Former Secretary of State Dean Acheson offers some amusing and somewhat sarcastic comments on the way that Senator Arthur Vandenberg helped to legitimate presidential policy during the crucial days after 1945. *Present at the Creation* (New York: Norton, 1969), p. 223.

[17] James A. Robinson, *Congress and Foreign Policy-Making* (rev. ed.; Homewood, Ill.: Dorsey, 1967). For the early postwar period, see Daniel S. Cheever and H. Field Haviland, Jr., *American Foreign Policy and the Separation of Powers* (Cambridge, Mass.: Harvard University Press, 1952), pp. 106 ff.

446 the Vietnam war, however, as the Congress became more skeptical of presidential wisdom in foreign policy and became more assertive on the many issues facing the United States with Russia, its allies, and third-world countries. The result was considerable public debate and executive-legislative conflict.

THE ABM AND VIETNAM

The seven points discussed in the preceding section by no means exhaust the characteristics of the foreign-policy process in the federal government, but they are the most obvious. If we consider the Johnson administration's decisions on the antiballistic missile (ABM) and Vietnam, they are clearly visible.[18] Opposed to the ABM were Secretary of Defense McNamara and Secretary of State Rusk, plus the A.C.D.A.; all believed that the decision to deploy an ABM would mean a spiraling and costly arms race and would destroy all chances for a stabilization of the American-Soviet deterrent balance. McNamara believed that an American decision to deploy the ABM would virtually preclude any possibility of initiating arms-limitations talks with the Soviets. He was also skeptical of the technical feasibility of the proposed ABM. The secretary, however, was in a minority position within his own department on the question of feasibility. The Pentagon's Office of Defense Research and Engineering, concerned with development of modern weapons, and its Office of Systems Analysis both supported deployment. Within the Defense Department only the Office of International Security Affairs joined McNamara in opposition to the ABM.

The principal bureaucratic supporters of the ABM were those in the armed services. In contrast to the situation on most defense issues, the ABM debate found the three services united in support of a weapons system. Although the army, navy and air force each "saw a different face of ABM and reached different conclusions,"[19] the very fact of this interservice agreement is worth noting. Previously, McNamara had taken advantage of divisions among the services in order to prevail on issues of defense spending. Their united front however, compelled him to go above the services and to appeal directly to the President. Different departments and, indeed, different bureaus within the various departments thus all saw different "faces" of the same ABM problem and had different stakes in the issue.

Others, too, had interests and stakes in the ABM debate. Supporting the services were several senior members of the Senate Armed Services Committee, including Chairman Richard Russell and such other influential members as John Stennis and Henry Jackson. These senators were supporters of Johnson's Vietnam policy and had been friends of the president while he had been Democratic Majority

---

[18] In this section we rely heavily on the account by Halperin, "The Decision to Deploy the ABM: Bureaucratic and Domestic Politics in the Johnson Administration," *World Politics*, October 1972, pp. 62 ff. For the development of the ICBM, see Edmund Beard, *Developing the ICBM* (New York : Columbia University Press, 1976).

[19] *Ibid.*, pp. 67–69.

Leader in the Senate during the Eisenhower administration. Indeed, Johnson had served with them on the Armed Services Committee and trusted their judgment. He was particularly close to Russell.

In arguing their case, proponents and adversaries often stressed different factors. Supporters stressed the fact that the Soviets had already developed such a system, that it threatened the American deterrent capacity, and that the ABM would save American lives. They argued that an ABM would provide Americans with an extra bargaining chip in any negotiations on a mutual defensive-weapons limitation. Opponents, on the other hand, were less concerned about the Soviet deployment of ABMs than about the potential for a new arms race. Another factor that concerned them was the price tag. Estimates of the cost of an ABM system ranged from $30 to $40 billion.

In the presence of these opposing pressures, no decision was possible at a level below that of the president; only he could decide. But a president's stake in any given issue is always greater than that of anyone else, and his perspective is different from that of any other player. For one thing, he wants to maintain unity in his administration and thus Johnson sought to avoid, if at all possible, a direct break with McNamara. The two men were already at odds over the war in Vietnam, but the president still valued his Secretary of Defense too highly to reject his advice out of hand. McNamara viewed the ABM choice as a direct confrontation between himself and the Joint Chiefs of Staff, and he therefore would have seen a decision to deploy the system as a direct rejection. In addition, a president also needs congressional support for his foreign and domestic policies. A negative decision on the ABM would have alienated key senators who were also long-time friends and colleagues whose opinions and convictions Johnson respected. But a president is also more than the chief officer of his administration and chief architect of legislation to be submitted to Congress. He is also head of his party and therefore concerned with his own reelection and his party's fortunes at the polls. The Republicans were already talking of an ABM gap, threatening to do to the Demo rats what Kennedy and Johnson had done to Nixon in 1960—to use the potentially powerful charge of neglecting the nation's defenses. Johnson, who had not yet decided not to run again for the presidency, nevertheless had to be worried about the possible impact of such an accusation.

But there are still other considerations and pressures that a president must take into account. He knows that in the final analysis he is responsible for the country's security and protection; others can advise him, but only he can make the required decisions, and it will be he who will be judged not only by the people he governs but also by history.[20] And that judgment is his ultimate stake. He will go down in history with George Washington, Thomas Jefferson, Abraham Lincoln, the two Roosevelts, Truman, and others; no one who occupies the White House (or its equivalent in other countries) can possibly ignore his future historical reputation. Johnson, whose involvement in Vietnam was already arousing popular and congressional criticism and casting doubt on his place in history, was thus keenly interested in a major arms-limitation agreement with the Soviet Union to

---

[20] Halperin, *Bureaucratic Politics and Foreign Policy*, pp. 81–82.

448 help his standing at that time and in the future; he needed a major breakthrough in the area of international reconciliation.

In this situation, given the "pitfalls" he saw in the ABM issue and the stakes he had in it, yet buffeted by conflicting pressures, the president would have preferred to make no decision at all and to allow the proponents and opponents of ABM to reach some kind of compromise among themselves. The problem of gaining the president's support for one of the contending coalitions is thus not limited to reaching him but also includes persuading him to make a decision at all. His tendency is to procrastinate or to make only a "minimal decision." Warner Schilling's apt phrase, in connection with another important presidential decision, is "how to decide without actually choosing":

> The President did make choices, but a comparison of the choices that he made with those that he did not make reveals clearly the minimal character of his decision. It bears all the aspects of a conscious search for the course of action which would close off the least number of future alternatives, one which would avoid the most choice.[21]

> . . . One of the major necessities of the American political process [is] the need to avert conflict by avoiding choice. The distribution of power and responsibility among government elites is normally so dispersed that a rather widespread agreement among them is necessary if any given policy is to be adopted and later implemented. Among the quasi-sovereign bodies that make up the Executive the opportunities to compel this agreement are limited.[22]

Truman put this need for gaining support to decide policy in fewer and more picturesque words: "They talk about the power of the president, how I can push a button and get things done. Why, I spent most of my time kissing somebody's ass."[23]

The critical question thus became What would be the nature of this compromise? At least part of the answer became clear in a meeting between Johnson and McNamara, on one hand, and Soviet Premier Kosygin, on the other, at Glassboro, New Jersey, in June 1967. Johnson pressed the Soviets for a date for the opening of arms-limitations talks. This declaration would allow him to postpone the decision on the ABM. But Johnson did not receive an answer. Kosygin, described the Soviet ABM as a defensive weapon and therefore unobjectionable. As a weapon that would save lives, it was in the Russian premier's judgment a good weapon that would not destabilize the arms balance and was thus not a proper subject for a strategic-arms limitation treaty (SALT). McNamara's principal objection to the ABM had been refuted by the Soviets. Consequently, Johnson no longer saw the ABM as a possible stumbling block to beginning arms-limitations talks.

---

[21] Warner R. Schilling, "The H-Bomb: How to Decide Without Actually Choosing," in Halperin and Kanter, *op. cit.*, p. 253.

[22] *Ibid.*, p. 255.

[23] Quoted in *Time*, January 25, 1968.

Johnson then made his minimal decision: to adopt a small anti-Chinese ABM system. McNamara announced the decision in a contradictory speech: On one hand, he announced that the most effective way to overcome a Soviet ABM was to saturate the defense with offensive missiles, suggesting that the Soviets could do that to the United States as well. On the other hand, should the Chinese be as irrational as their militant revolutionary rhetoric suggested, a small ABM system might help to deter a strike. In one sense, McNamara had won a major victory against the Joint Chiefs of Staff and ABM supporters in Congress, who favored a nationwide anti-Soviet (and more expensive) ABM system. The very fact that he made the speech showed that he had by no means suffered a major defeat on this issue. He could view the President's decision as leaving open the possibility that the system would never be deployed at all if the Russians would later agree to limitation of mutual defensive weapons. The administration had come out *not* in support of deployment but only in support of increased funding for the procurement of certain ABM parts that would require a long lead time. On the other hand, the very fact that the administration had publicly changed its position represented a victory for ABM supporters in Congress and the Joint Chiefs. Proponents of the more extensive system viewed the change in the administration's position as a hopeful sign and expected that they could accomplish their goal later. There were as yet no "winners" or "losers." Compromises had prevented that. The fight was to continue into the Nixon administration, when it was decided that, in the absence of any agreement on the Soviet SS-9 missile, minimal protection for American Minutemen missiles and a bargaining chip for the forthcoming SALT talks was necessary.

This series of events furnish a good illustration of how a decision emerges from the interactions of multiple actors with conflicting perspectives and different stakes; the Vietnam war is an equally good example of the incremental nature of policy making. A commitment of sorts to Vietnam had begun during the period when the French were still engaged in reestablishing their colonial control after World War II. After an initial period of nonsupport for this colonial effort, the United States began to supply economic and military assistance to the French, in return for French support of American policy in Europe, an area of vital interest to the United States. This aid was stepped up after the outbreak of the Korean war and the later Chinese military intervention in Korea. It was during this period, just after the birth of Communist China, its alliance with Russia, and the outbreak of war in Asia, that the bipolar image of the world held by American policy makers seemed most valid (it was certainly shared by leaders in Moscow and Peking). As the expansion of any communist country's power was thus viewed in Washington as an expansion of Russian power and as a gain of power and security for Russia was equated with a loss of power and security for the United States, it is not surprising that the possible loss of Vietnam was viewed in terms of a domino image. If Vietnam fell, the rest of the dominoes in Southeast Asia were expected to fall. The other countries of the area either would turn toward procommunist neutralism or would themselves be taken over because of communist revolutions or communist pressures from outside.

The second Indochinese war, which began in the late 1950s, was thus to be a problem for the Kennedy administration. But Kennedy, during his years in office, never really had time for Vietnam. He was swamped by other foreign-policy crises, as well as by an increasingly tense domestic racial situation. Cuba, Berlin, Laos, Vienna (where he had a tense confrontation with Khrushchev), and the Alliance for Progress preoccupied him. Vietnam was not then in crisis, though the situation was deteriorating. Because of Kennnedy's essentially bipolar view of the international conflict, his perception of "wars of national liberation" as instigated by Mosċow's leaders, and his desire to avoid further foreign-policy setbacks and accusations of being soft on communism, he committed military advisers to help shore up the Saigon government and avoided making a clear-cut decision about what to do in Vietnam. After Kennedy's assassination in 1963, Johnson also sought to procrastinate, hoping for the best even while planning escalation. His time was primarily devoted to restoring domestic calm and unity in the wake of national tragedy, to persuading Congress to pass the largest volume of progressive domestic legislation in a single term in the century, and to the forthcoming election campaign.[24] The president's experience, expertise, and interests were domestic. His attempt to win time and to convince Hanoi leaders of the futility of persisting in the struggle may have been understandable, but in the meantime South Vietnam was nearing total collapse. By early 1965 procrastination was no longer feasible. The choice had become one of either withdrawing from the war or expanding and escalating it. Johnson at that point decided to follow what he and his advisers saw as a continuing American commitment to the Saigon government begun by Truman, continued by Eisenhower, escalated by Kennedy (who sent 16,500 American military personnel), and expanded further by himself when he ordered air strikes against the North after an alleged attack on two American destroyers in the Gulf of Tonkin in August 1964.[25]

Johnson had inherited a situation in which only ad hoc decisions had been made in response to immediate problems. Only piecemeal economic and military commitments had been made; each constituted the minimally necessary step to prevent a communist victory.[26] At no point were the fundamental questions and long-range implications of increasing involvement in Vietnam analyzed: Was South Vietnam vital to American security? Would its fall simply lead to consolidation of one country under a nationalist leader, or would it be the first step in the communization of all of Southeast Asia? Did the political situation in South Vietnam warrant or preclude American intervention? Were political conditions both in the

[24] Tom Wicker, *JFK and LBJ: The Influence of Personality upon Politics* (Baltimore: Penguin, 1969), pp. 151–182.

[25] See *The New York Times*, June 13 and 14, 1971; and Joseph C. Goulden, *Truth Is the First Casualty: The Gulf of Tonkin Affair—Illusion and Reality* (Chicago: Rand McNally, 1969).

[26] Chester L. Cooper, *The Lost Crusade* (New York: Dodd, Mead, 1970); Hilsman, *op. cit.*, pp. 413 ff.; and, especially, David Halberstam, *The Best and the Brightest* (New York: Random House, 1972), a good though not unbiased account of the incremental nature of the American commitment. See also Daniel Ellsberg, *Papers on the War* (New York: Simon & Schuster, 1972), and Paul M. Kattenburg, *The Vietnam Trauma in American Foreign Policy, 1945–75* (Brunswick, N.J.: a Transaction Book 1980).

United States and in South Vietnam conducive to effective military action? How large a commitment would the United States be required to make, and what costs should be expected? What role should the Saigon government and its forces play? If these questions were even asked by President Kennedy and other responsible foreign-policy officials as they sent military advisers into South Vietnam—thus creating a powerful military bureaucracy in Saigon that had a vested interest in succeeding and that fed deliberately overoptimistic reports to the Washington government in order to acquire more arms, men, and money—the answers did not provide guidelines for the policies that were ultimately followed. The assumption was that South Vietnam was vital, a test of the credibility of American commitments and power. Policy was built upon that assumption. (The approach was incremental, and, as the overall situation deteriorated badly, Johnson, like Kennedy before him, continued to react to the symptoms of the problem and to apply short-range solutions: covert operations, followed by increasingly frequent "retaliatory" air strikes against North Vietnam, followed again by round-the-clock bombing, and, when none of these measures had compelled Hanoi's leaders to "cease and desist" in the South, ultimately the use of American ground forces in South Vietnam.)

(Yet counterrevolutionary warfare is political first and military second; its success depends upon the development of relations of trust and support between the government and its citizens) The failure of Diem, followed by the American agreement to depose him and tacit acceptance of his murder, convincingly demonstrated that the political situation in South Vietnam was not conducive to success. Indeed, intervention was frequently advocated to boost the South Vietnamese government's morale! But how American intervention could infuse that government with the will and determination to fight was never discussed; should morale in Saigon not have been a prerequisite for American help? In any event, a sizable contingent of American advisers was already involved, and American prestige had been committed. The war had already become "Americanized."

(Up to that point incrementalism had occurred within the broader context of cold-war perceptions of American policy makers, from Truman to Johnson; then the pressure from the military intensified the general pressures and escalated the conflict.) Indeed, it may well be that the tendency to oversell—along with Johnson's obvious political interest in ending the war as quickly as possible, certainly by 1968—placed military considerations uppermost. Despite much evidence to the contrary, the military considered the war a modified, limited form of conventional warfare. For example, in 1962, General Wheeler, then Army Chief of Staff and later chairman of the Joint Chiefs of Staff, said:

> Despite the fact that the conflict is conducted as a guerrilla warfare, it is nonetheless a military action. . . . It is fashionable in some quarters to say that the problems of Southeast Asia are primarily political and economic rather than military. I do not agree. The essence of the problem in Vietnam is military.[27]

American commanders in Vietnam agreed. Vietnam would not be much different from Korea, they claimed. It was just a matter of Americanizing the war a little

---

[27] Hilsman, *op. cit.*, p. 426.

452 more than it already had been. The Joint Chiefs of Staff assured Johnson that a couple of years and 200,000 troops should do it. (This sloppy evaluation by the JCS and its advice to Johnson contrasted strongly with the approach of former Army Chief of Staff Matthew B. Ridgway, who in 1954 had sent teams to Vietnam to calculate what would be required if the United States should intervene. His report to President Eisenhower, a former general himself, was a principal reason why the United States had stayed out of the war at that time.)[28]

There were few opposing arguments from other senior officials or organizations. Secretary of State Rusk largely concurred in the conclusion that the Vietnam war would be essentially conventional and that since it would therefore be a military affair he should stay out of it. Walt W. Rostow, the presidential assistant for national security affairs, was particularly concerned with the problem of supplies infiltrated from external areas or "sanctuaries" and therefore suggested that only attacks on the "ultimate source of aggression" would bring such a war to an end. What opposition there was came from the CIA (whose predictions were remarkably accurate), the State Department Bureau of Intelligence and Research, Assistant Secretary for Far Eastern Affairs Averell Harriman, and some of the bright young Turks he had brought with him, as well as certain Pentagon military officers working on counterrevolutionary strategy and tactics. But their efforts were in vain, and gradually most of them, especially in the State Department, lost their jobs, were replaced, or simply lost much of their influence, as did the CIA.[29]

In these circumstances, it is not surprising that the air force managed to oversell the benefits of bombing North Vietnam. The U.S. Air Force was essentially fighting for its identity. In World War II strategic bombing had had limited effects until the late stages; during the Korean war, the tactical bombing of the communist supply lines had also had only limited impact. Vietnam was thus viewed by the air force as a test. In the words of a former Assistant Secretary of Defense for Public Affairs, "the bombing of North Vietnam became the symbol of the importance of air power."[30] Even though, as noted earlier, Vietnam, an unindustrialized country with external sources of military supplies and supply routes often hidden by jungles, was a poor place for such a test, the air force was determined to prove itself at least capable of tactical interdiction. Rivalry with the navy, which was trying to demonstrate the capability of its carrier-based air power, only intensified the resolution of the air force to prove itself and to demonstrate its superiority over the navy. Both services thought future missions, morale, and budgets to be at stake. Indeed, the navy had supported the air force bombing campaign in its initial stages in order to participate in it and demonstrate *its* competence in its rivalry with the air force. But why did the army support the air force? The answer appears to be "so that the air force could fail"! General Wheeler and General William Westmoreland probably knew that air power could hardly accomplish the goal of compelling North Vietnam's leaders to desist in the South or cutting off the supplies flowing to the

---

[28] Melvin Gurtov, *The First Vietnam Crisis* (New York: Columbia University Press, 1967).

[29] Halberstam, *op. cit.*, pp. 361–378.

[30] Quoted by Robert L. Galucci, *Neither Peace Nor Honor* (Baltimore: Johns Hopkins University Press, 1975), p. 72.

South.[31] But the very failure of the air force would mean greater subsequent military commitment so that the United States would be successful, and this commitment was bound to mean the involvement of the army. The president, on the other hand, hoped that bombing would frighten the North Vietnamese into desisting and that the conflict could be won "on the cheap", without the heavy losses that would be involved if ground forces were committed. Diverse actors with different interests thus formed a coalition in support of the bombing. If air power then failed, as the navy and army expected, they would be sent in; if it succeeded, as the president hoped, the ground war with its heavy casualties would be unnecessary. For all, however, the

> bombs were dropped as a necessary political prerequisite to the engagement of American troops. . . .[F]or those who had to concern themselves with the bounds of public opinion, the function of air power was to fail openly so that large scale losses of American lives on the ground in Asia could be justified.[32]

The public nature of decision making was also apparent in the Vietnam war, certainly more so than in connection with the ABM. But, apart from Johnson's general knowledge from the Korean war that a long war would not be popular, public opinion was not much of a guide at the beginning of the escalation in Vietnam. What was important throughout 1964 and the first months of 1965 was how the president perceived public, as well as congressional, opinion: his conclusion was that neither the general public nor its representatives in Washington wanted the United States "to lose South Vietnam to communism." This view placed an especially powerful pressure on Democratic presidents, as they saw it; the party that was sensitive to charges of having "lost" China was anxious to avoid the accusation of also having "lost" Indochina. The president did not want to be placed on the defensive by these vicious charges and to jeopardize the rest of his foreign policy and perhaps his Great Society domestic program as well. Johnson certainly received widespread popular approval for his action during the Gulf of Tonkin episode, and, by and large, he continued to receive majority approval during the initial period of open intervention.

Nonetheless, Johnson never went to the public or to Congress to explain either the seriousness of the situation in South Vietnam as he perceived it or the necessity, as he saw it, of large-scale American intervention—and very probably a long war. Increasing intervention was thus not accompanied by much public debate; neither was there much public criticism. But, the longer the war lasted, the greater the dissatisfaction with American policy became, and the more extensive and intensive were the criticism and dissent expressed both in Washington and in the country as a whole. Administration officials frequently explained their policy; officials who disagreed sometimes resigned but more often leaked their points of view or expressed them to newspaper correspondents. Members of Congress artic-

---

[31] *Ibid.*, p. 49.

[32] *Ibid.*, p. 53.

454 ulated their views more and more. Well-known Democratic and Republican liberals voiced their increasing opposition. Senator J. William Fulbright held Senate Foreign Relations Committee hearings to give critics, frequently former government officials and concerned and informed scholars, a forum.[33] The Senator also offered his own wide-ranging critique of American foreign policy in two books.[34] Two other senators went directly to the public: Senator Eugene McCarthy, who decided to oppose President Johnson in the primaries; and, after McCarthy's surprisingly strong showing in New Hampshire, Robert Kennedy, President Johnson's principal rival in the party and by then already a powerful critic of the war, who also entered the primaries to contest Johnson's renomination. The Republican leadership, on the other hand, increasingly attacked the administration for its military restraint and favored the full unleashing of American air power; in these attacks, they were joined by a number of powerful conservative Democrats, especially in the Senate.

Criticism and dissent were, of course, not limited to Washington. Support and, more often, opposition spread to many college campuses and cities. Demonstrations, teach-ins, marches, vigils, and, on occasion, riots accompanied this widening opposition. The administration, of course, counterattacked.[35] General Westmoreland and Ambassador Henry Cabot Lodge, for example, were called home and appeared before Congress and the public—on such shows as *Meet the Press* —where they presented optimistic forecasts and belittled Vietcong achievements. The president gave speeches defending his policies and denouncing his critics as "nervous Nellies." After the Vietcong's Tet offensive had revealed the fallaciousness of official optimism about victory, the criticisms grew even more widespread and pointed. The press was by then very hostile, and congressional opposition to mobilizing larger reserves and an even more costly war was clear. The immediate issue around which much of the debate revolved was the bombing of North Vietnam. It had been initiated to bring Hanoi leaders to the negotiating table, but its cessation became the precondition for holding talks about ending hostilities. On March 31, 1968, the president announced a bombing halt, which, most significantly, signaled an end to the previously open-ended commitment to South Vietnam, implicitly acknowledged repudiation of military victory as the objective, and began the shifting of ultimate responsibility for the conduct of the war to the Saigon government. He also announced that he would not run for a second term. This example leaves little doubt that, the longer an issue persists, the more congressional and public opinion will become involved. In contrast, a crisis can be handled mainly by the President and a few of his most trusted advisers and is over quickly.

---

[33] *The Vietnam Hearings* (New York: Vintage, 1966).

[34] J. William Fulbright, *Old Myths and New Realities* (New York: Vintage, 1964); and Fulbright, *The Arrogance of Power* (New York: Vintage, 1967).

[35] The battle within the executive over Vietnam, and especially over halting the bombing of North Vietnam, is told in some detail in Townsend Hoopes, *The Limits of Intervention* (New York: McKay, 1969).

A CRITIQUE OF THE DECISION-MAKING APPROACH

In contrast to the first-level model in which each state is considered as an individual actor, in the decision-making literature each government is viewed as composed of multiple actors; instead of regarding foreign policy as a product of a rational choice among several options that maximize a chosen value like security, analysts focus on the many conflicting values, perspectives, and interests that result in a specific policy. Two scholars have gone so far as to suggest that

> a focus on the international objectives of a state is essentially misleading, in that the participants' attention primarily is focused on domestic objectives. . . [T]he scholar requires an understanding of a nation's domestic political structure and of its national security bureaucracy in order to explain or predict the foreign policy actions it will take.[36]

"The games nations play" are the result of "the games bureaucrats play" to enhance their personal influence, as well as that of their own agencies; the same can be said of nonbureaucratic players.

Clearly, a noncrisis decision like that President Johnson made to go ahead on the anti-Chinese ABM system is not easily explainable in terms of the rational-actor model. The decision might not have been made had it not been for congressional and bureaucratic pressures, for the president really was primarily interested in starting the SALT talks and avoiding another expensive and possibly destabilizing arms race. But, even for the president, there are constraints. Specifically, Johnson wanted to avoid a break with influential senators, as well as with his own Secretary of Defense, over the ABM. The political costs of breaks with either were greater than he was willing to pay at the time. He also had to consider the probable electoral costs if he decided to avoid any ABM decision. So he compromised; he made a minimum decision, satisfactory to all the chief actors, who all thought that they had "won" the President over to their position. In fact he had kept his options open for more definite decisions in the future.

The "foreign policy" decision that emerges from this bureaucratic system, set in its turn in the broader governmental system,

> . . . is not necessarily "policy" in the rational sense of embodying the decisions made and actions ordered by a controlling intelligence focusing primarily on our foreign policy problems. Instead it is the "outcome" of the political process, the government actions resulting from all the arguments, the building of coalitions and countercoalitions, and the decisions by high officials and compromises among them. Often it may be a "policy" that no participant fully favors [for the system is] more responsive to the internal dynamics of our decision-making process than to the external problems.[37]

[36.] Halperin and Kanter, *op. cit.*, p. 3.

[37]. I. M. Destler, *Presidents, Bureaucrats, and Foreign Policy* (Princeton: Princeton University Press, 1972), pp. 64, 74.

(This point certainly raises a key issue: How can one judge the substance of policy—its wisdom and its potential contribution to the security of the country—by the fact that a consensus has been reached among multiple actors? As Galucci has aptly observed, "A wretched policy for the United States may be perfectly understandable as a superb compromise among competing interests, but it must ultimately be evaluated as undesirable by some criteria of what is in fact good for the nation."[38] But what is the point of making such a judgment if policy is not made rationally? At best, the result would be to underline the gap between policy as it is "really made" and how it perhaps ought to be made.)

(One reason for this gap is the lack of presidential leadership; the president is merely one of many players. To be sure, he may be "first among equals," but his ability to impose his decisions is limited by the other players. Johnson did not want an ABM but was pushed into taking the first minimal step toward acceptance of it. The Joint Chiefs' coalition with powerful leaders in the Senate was not one that the president could ignore. A president, according to the organizational charts of the executive branch, may be "the boss" and presumably can order the Joint Chiefs, for example, to do or not to do what he chooses. In reality, the relationship is more equal, and the participants bargain with one another; the close relation between military leaders and a powerful congressional committee and ranking legislative leaders or the threat of resignation by military leaders (which reportedly occurred during the Vietnam war) makes it necessary for the president and the Secretary of Defense to persuade their subordinates. One writer has argued that the maxim "where you stand is where you sit" applies even to crisis decisions. There is no evidence, he claims, that, as the stakes become bigger, the various decision makers remove the "tinted glasses" through which they habitually examine issues.[39]

It must often seem to presidents that statements about their enormous power are exaggerated; they are very sensitive to the limits on it. President Carter, it has been reported, could not even get rid of the mice in the Oval Office! When a couple of mice ran across the carpet one evening, a call went out to the General Services Administration (GSA), the official housekeeper for federal buildings. A few weeks later, however, another mouse apparently died in the wall of the Oval Office. The resulting odor became quite noticeable just as the President was preparing to receive a foreign dignitary. An emergency call was made to the GSA, but it refused to come back. It insisted that it had already exterminated all the "inside" mice in the White House! The mouse that had died therefore must have come from the outside and was therefore a matter for the Department of the Interior. The Department, however, refused jurisdiction because the mouse had died *in* the White House. President Carter exploded: "I can't even get a damn mouse out of my office."[40] He can, however, declare an American commitment to keeping the Persian Gulf open and undertake actions that can affect war and peace.

(Three criticisms may however be made of the government-politics model. The first is that it overemphasizes the constraints, especially within the executive

---

[38.] Galucci, *op. cit.*, p. 142.

[39.] *Ibid.*, p. 153.

[40.] *The New York Times*, January 15, 1978.

branch, on presidential leadership and initiative in foreign policy.[41] Rational policy making, as we have noted, is the key to crisis decision making, but it can also occur in other areas of policy, especially when policy makers strike out in new directions. The reasons why the presidential perspective is preeminent in what Robert Art calls "innovative policy" were exemplified in the first Nixon administration. First, the president can seize for himself certain specific policy areas (like SALT or negotiating the end of the Vietnam war and rapprochement with China). "The ability of bureaucracies to independently establish policies is a function of Presidential attention. Presidential attention is a function of Presidential values. The Chief Executive involves himself in those areas which he determines to be important."[42] In contrast to the emphasis in the bureaucratic model, it is more correct to say that, to a large degree, bureaucratic influence is a function of presidential—and, it ought to be added, congressional and public—inattention. The bureaucracy thus plays its largest role in routine daily affairs, its smallest during crises.

A president can also structure the organization for making foreign policy decisions. Nixon did so by making Kissinger his special assistant on national security affairs, a kind of supersecretary of foreign affairs; giving him a fairly sizable staff; and clearly ignoring the established bureaucracy or subordinating it to the White House. Kissinger's staff presented the established bureaucracy with questions on areas or policies on which it wanted policy papers, gathered them together, evaluated the alternatives, and once the president had selected the best policy, sent the decision back to the bureaucracy for implementation.[43] The Nixon experiment was an attempt to institutionalize rational policy making. As he said, "I refuse to be confronted with a bureaucratic consensus that leaves me no options but acceptance or rejection and that gives me no way of knowing what alternatives exist."[44] Foreign-policy decisions that are primarily the outcomes of bureaucratic infighting and compromise, rather than of rational responses to perceived external challenges and problems, were to be avoided. Bureaucratic interests, though not totally eliminated, were thus greatly limited and subjected to presidental perspectives and interests—at least, until the Watergate scandal in 1973.

A president also chooses his cabinet officials. And, though they do come to represent the various bureaucracies and agencies in government, they also normally reflect the president's general views and values, for they owe their places in the history books to the man who appointed them and are likely to feel some gratitude. They know too that the president, if displeased, can fire them and that most of them are expendable. Short of exercising the ultimate sanction, of dismissing high officials, the president decides whom to listen to and whom to exile

---

[41] For the critique that follows we are indebted to Robert J. Art, "Bureaucratic Politics and American Foreign Policy: A Critique," *Policy Sciences* 4 (1973), 467–490; and Stephen D. Krasner, "Are Bureaucracies Important?" *Foreign Policy*, Summer 1972, pp. 159–179.

[42] Krasner, op. cit. p. 168; Krasner's emphasis on the state as a unified actor pursuing its "national interest" is elaborated in Krasner, *Defending the National Interest* (Princeton: Princeton University Press, 1978).

[43] Destler, *op. cit.*, pp. 118–53.

[44] *Ibid.*, p. 199. Also see George, "The Case for Multiple Advocacy in Making Foreign Policy," *American Political Science Review*, September 1972, pp. 751 ff.

458   from the policy-making circle) Kennedy picked Secretary of Defense McNamara, rather than Secretary of State Rusk; Nixon, during his first term, selected his national-security assistant and paid little attention to his Secretary of State. During the Vietnam war, Johnson eliminated powerful and respected men like McNamara from his administration when they increasingly opposed his bombing policy, and he simply did not listen to others. He appointed as his national-security assistant W. W. Rostow, a man who reportedly filtered out dissenting views before they could reach him. An observer who has stressed the constraints on Johnson admits: "Lyndon Johnson was surrounded, or more accurately, *surrounded himself with loyal advisors who supported him in what he thought he had to do. . . . The President himself was clearly setting the tone and choosing isolation."*[45] That is, the president was structuring his decision-making environment. The limits on presidential initiatives and preferences in crises and other key policy areas have thus probably been overstated in much of the literature on decision making.

(A second criticism of the government-politics model is that it also exaggerates the degree of conflict among the multiple actors.)Throughout the Cold War the policy makers, both senior political appointees and bureaucrats, tended to be united, despite their varying institutional responsibilities, by a set of commonly shared assumptions or "shared images" of the external world. These shared images minimized conflict and indeed usually made the executive branch and government appear similar to the unitary actor that the government-politics model had rejected. Among these images were the central conflict in the international system between the United States and Soviet Russia (or the "free world and the "communist world"); the expansionism of communist Russia; the increment to Russian power and the loss to American power whenever a country "fell"; and the unique economic and military strength of the United States and the resulting responsibility for defending the free world ("free" meaning noncommunist, not necessarily democratic) and preserving the balance of power against mighty Russia (and after 1949 for over two decades a potentially strong China as well). These images were held throughout the long cold-war period and were reassessed only after the disaster in Vietnam had left the country no choice but to reexamine the assumptions that had led it into war. These assumptions, amounting to a virtual consensus among policy makers, help to account for the tenacious continuity of American foreign policy over two decades, and they set outer boundaries to the conflicts within the government. Those who did not fully share this set of images and thus did not take a tough anti-Soviet stand were generally unable to influence policy. A psychologist has argued that uniformity was especially common within the relatively small circle of leading officials because there is a great deal of pressure to conform to "groupthink";[46] "dovish" views were suppressed among a group whose members were trying to impress one another with their "toughness." Whether this interpretation is correct or incorrect, it is true that, during the period from the declartion of the Truman Doctrine to the Vietnam war, top government officials reflected these views in

---

[45]. Galucci, *op. cit.*, pp. 99, 105 (emphasis added).

[46]. Irving Janis, *Victims of Groupthink* (Boston: Houghton Mifflin, 1972).

arguing for an expanded American role far more frequently than their organizational or bureaucratic interests dictated.

Indeed, it is questionable that, for "senior players," the axiom "where you stand is where you sit" does indicate what positions they will take in a policy debate. Rather, as Art has stressed, institutionally motivated policies are primarily reflected in decisions

> that have direct, immediate, clearly predictable results for the structural set-up of institutions and for their long-term prosperity—those decisions which we may call the "bread and butter choices" that determine the long-term competitive position of an institution, decisions regarding career advancement in the foreign service or in the uniformed military, budgetary allocation decisions, or those regulating the instruments by which institutions will carry out the tasks assigned to them (like weapon systems for the services).[47]

(Third, and perhaps most important, the government-politics model may also have downplayed domestic politics. Although it has been generally true that in foreign policy Congress has supported presidential policy, largely because of a shared set of images, electoral politics particularly has been bound to intrude.) In 1960 Kennedy had run on the issue of the "missile gap"; in 1968 Johnson (though he did not run) did not wish to hand the Republicans the "ABM gap" issue. Summit meetings and major diplomatic achievements (for example, a SALT agreement) may be necessary in themselves, but they are hardly unrelated to important— especially presidential—elections, as the timing of such announcements or events frequently demonstrate.

The critical foreign-policy conflicts induced by domestic political consid- erations have, as noted, come in the area where general executive-legislative col- laboration has broken down: Far Eastern policy in the wake of Nationalist China's collapse and the birth of Communist China. Subsequent Republican efforts to exploit this issue electorally led to vicious attacks upon the administration for supposedly deliberately selling out China, continued indictments of the Democrats for the "fall of China," and widespread hunts for alleged traitors in government (and universities and the media) who had "sold China down the river." Two-party competition and the natural temptation to exploit the in-party's setbacks paralyzed American policy in Asia for two and a half decades. Later presidents—even Ei- senhower, the moderate Republican, but particularly Democratic presidents—re- mained fearful of improving relations with Communist China and, more broadly, of any "appeasement of communism." Knowing the great difficulties that they would have with Congress if they defied it, they were afraid to take any but strong positions against Communist China and for Nationalist China. Johnson, informed within hours of becoming president that South Vietnam was collapsing, responded that he was not going to be the president who saw Southeast Asia go the way of China. Congressional and public pressures—or the anticipation of such pressures— have repeatedly affected the content of American foreign policy.

[47.] Art, *op. cit.*, p. 484.

460   The price in this instance has obviously been very high. Had China been recognized in early 1950, before the Korean war, and had an exchange of diplomatic personnel between the two countries taken place, might the Truman administration not have heeded the Peking leaders' threats to intervene in Korea if American forces continued to advance toward China's frontiers, rather than dismissing those threats as bluffs? Had American observers been stationed in Peking, would the Kennedy and Johnson administrations not have known that the war in South Vietnam was not part of "Asian communism's expansionism" and did not therefore constitute any threat to American vital interests? Would the Vietnam war not then have been avoided? More broadly, could better relations with China not have been established earlier in order to exploit the increasing Sino-Soviet conflict and to help bring about a parallel reduction in American-Soviet tensions?

Instead, it took a long and costly war and a new president, a Republican, to open the door to The People's Republic of China. The years of fighting in Vietnam, with no victory in sight, had made the country weary of inflexible anticommunism. President Nixon himself believed that the problems of Asia could not be solved without Communist China; certainly the Vietnam war could not be ended unless Peking leaders would help. As an old-time "hardliner," Nixon could hardly be accused of coddling or appeasing communists. But, just in case of strong opposition from within his own party (vice-president Spiro Agnew, for example, was opposed) and from the powerful China lobby, which had long been arousing millions in the country and in Congress against Communist China and mobilizing support for the Nationalist Chinese, he made the decision alone and confronted the bureaucracy, Congress, and public opinion with a *fait accompli*, announcing that he would visit The People's Republic. The subsequent trip symbolized a basic and irreversible change of direction in American foreign policy. In terms of enhancing American security, this rapprochement was highly rational and a long-overdue adjustment to the changing international distribution of power. For far too long, American China policy had been hostage to domestic and congressional politics.

Even with the weakening of anticommunism, domestic politics has continued heavily to affect American foreign policy. Indeed, congressional questioning and criticism of—and willingness to undermine—presidential policy has grown during the 1970s.[48] The Vietnam war discredited the leadership of the executive branch and its expertise in foreign policy; the Watergate scandal and other revelations of CIA and Federal Bureau of Investigation (FBI) activities added to congressional determination to be more assertive in foreign policy in a period in which there was no new consensus on which to base policy. In the early days of détente, when Kissinger wanted to supplement the military stick with economic carrots in order to induce more restrained Soviet behavior, the Senate added the Jackson-Vanik amendment on Jewish emigration from Russia to a commercial treaty; because of this attempt at interference with its domestic jurisdiction, Moscow rejected the treaty, thus reducing the economic leverage that the United States might have

---

[48.] Spanier and J. Nogee, eds., *Congress, the Presidency and Foreign Policy* (Elmsford, N.Y.: Pergamon, 1981).

gained. The Senate also almost undermined the Panama Canal treaties and failed to vote on SALT II, which effectively killed it. Congress as a whole imposed an arms embargo against Turkey to punish it for its invasion of Cyprus, which had been intended to protect the Turkish minority there from a Greek attempt to unite Cyprus with Greece. The Congress itself is now more splintered than ever before: Party loyalty has further declined; the authority of committee chairmen has been reduced; and subcommittees have become more numerous and influential. Given this high degree of decentralization, pressure groups have gained increased access to congressional policy makers. Especially active are ethnic groups, like the Greek-Americans, who favor the Turkish embargo, and American Jews, who have dissuaded American governments from pressing Israel to be more conciliatory in the Middle East peace negotiations. It has thus become much more difficult for a president to mobilize Congress on foreign-policy issues; obstructing, delaying, changing, and even emasculating policy have become considerably easier.

(It therefore appears that the decision-making approach requires two modifications. First, analysts must distinguish between different kinds of policies. Second, it should be more focused on presidential preferences, the shared images among the principal executive and legislative officials, and domestic politics, including party competition and executive-legislative relations. This assessment does not deny the relevance of bureaucratic politics. It suggests, however, that it must be viewed within the broader context of the state system, because the making of foreign-policy decisions occurs within this international context, which places limits upon what countries can do, regardless of their power, their leaders' ideological commitments, public opinion, and the conflict among the many actors involved in the decision-making process. Emphasis on presidential preferences and shared images among governmental leaders, leading to essentially rational decisions on key issues, also permits the outside observer to make independent judgments on what is in the "national interest."[49])

"INTERMESTIC" DECISION MAKING

One major exception must be emphasized, however. To the degree that international politics will in the future shift its focus from security-territorial to socioeconomic issues, the governmental-bargaining model will become more relevant for analytical purposes. The issues themselves are those that have normally fallen within the arena of domestic politics, as distinct from international politics. But clearly food production, birth rates, access to raw materials, price levels, and fishing and drilling rights under the oceans can no longer be neatly categorized as domestic issues. They are also on the international political agenda. Yet, unlike the more traditional type of foreign-policy issue, on which the executive is the leading actor, the congress and public opinion have in the past generally been supportive or at

[49.] Galucci, *op. cit.*, pp. 153–154; Art, *op. cit.*, pp. 486–487.

462   least permissive, and the structure of the interest groups generally weak, these newer "intermestic" issues—the term telescopes the words "international" and "domestic"—involve far larger numbers of actors. In order to come up with satisfactory solutions, departments and agencies of government with domestic expertise and jurisdiction must be consulted; similarly, many congressional domestic committees and interest groups will be activated. On these issues the foreign-policy process will be the same as on domestic policies. The larger number of actors, the important stakes that key legislators, committees, and lobbyists will now perceive in foreign policy—ranging from billions of dollars in profits in resources and food through such noneconomic stakes as concern for the environment, human dignity, and social justice to the influence and status of the various actors—will make it far more difficult to arrive at policy decisions.

Negotiations will be long and very difficult, and compromises acceptable to so many involved parties will not be arranged without immense effort, if they can be arranged at all. Vested interests are easier to defend than to challenge successfully in a system of dispersed institutional power. The State Department proclaiming the "national interest" will hardly be heard above the din of voices emanating from the Departments of Commerce, the Treasury, Agriculture, and Labor, the respective committees in the Congress, and the range of clienteles, or interest groups involved. All these actors, too, will articulate their respective points of view and will have far more "clout" in the political arena. Many will be well-organized and well-financed groups representing millions of constituents or voters. In these circumstances, in which formerly uninvolved executive agencies are actively involved and Congress, interest groups, and public opinion exert powerful influences, the president's ability to initiate, lead, and maneuver will be seriously circumscribed. In contrast to many security issues in which no immediate tangible interests are perceived to be at stake and in which the president is generally acknowledged to have greater expertise, the new issues involve many concerns, especially material ones, that arouse many actors who believe they are just as expert and experienced as the executive.

Presidential involvement does not guarantee successful domestic negotiations. On some key issues, he may, lacking votes, be reluctant to enter that specific policy arena at all, lest he fail and his reputation for "getting things done" be impaired. In the past, on most foreign-policy issues, he could normally count on achieving his aims, thus building a successful record, benefiting his party, and presumably helping the nation. But, if we multiply the immense difficulties involved in arriving at acceptable compromises or tradeoffs on serious domestic issues by the number of other countries participating in such negotiations, at least one point becomes clear: the American national style—which intersects with the decision-making process—will be severely tested.

Americans like to win and win big; but more often these gains, though genuine, will not be huge; in some instances the problem will be not how much we gain but rather how to minimize our losses. We look for quick results, no matter how difficult the issues and how stubborn the interests involved, even when mutual good will is present; lengthy negotiations with no spectacular results tend

TABLE 16.1

POLICY CHARACTERISTICS

Type of Policy	Chief Characteristics	Primary Actors	Principal Decision Maker	Role of Congress	Role of Interest Groups	Relations Among Actors
Crisis	short run; bureaucracy and Congress short-circuited; common stake in all winning or losing together	President, responsible officials, and individuals from in and out of government	executive (presidential preeminence)	postcrisis legitimation	none	cooperation
Noncrisis (security)	long run; bureaucratic-legislative participation; winners and losers	President; executive agencies; Congress; interest groups; public opinion	executive bureaucracy	congressional participation	low to moderate	competition and bargaining
Intermestic (welfare)	long run; bureaucratic-legislative participation; winners and losers	President; executive agencies; Congress; interest groups; public opinion	executive-congressional sharing	high	high	competition and bargaining

This table is modeled on one in Randall B. Ripley and Grace A. Franklin, *Congress, the Bureaucracy, and Public Policy* (Homewood, Ill.: Dorsey, 1976), p. 17.

464   to end either in lack of interest or in frustration. And there will always be the spokesmen, interests, congressmen, and rival politicians complaining of "sellouts" and "giveaways." On the so-called "new agenda," then, the government-politics model is likely to prove a handy guide to analysis and understanding, though it will not provide solutions to stalemates that will occur on many issues. For a country that has long believed in its omnipotence and self-sufficiency, in its moral right and ability to have its way, and in its choice whether to involve itself or abstain from involvement in world affairs, a system of more than 150- odd states divided by politics, ideology, and legal and moral differences, yet presumably interdependent, will be profoundly taxing.

COMPARATIVE IMPLICATIONS

Two more points should be mentioned. First, although we have chosen the American government as an example of pluralistic decision making, the same type of tool can be applied to analyzing the purposes of the Soviet or British governments. In Russia, too, there are multiple bureaucratic interests behind the totalitarian facade: party, army, police, and industrial and agricultural interests, all of which have spokesmen to represent their needs and grievances. Conflict among these actors thus occurs in the Soviet government as well, but, in contrast to the American government, these bureaucracies are unable to mobilize interest groups or legislative and popular support for their policy preferences. Outside the government, such groups as the trade unions do not have autonomous existence; the communist party controls all appointments, promotions, and demotions. Obviously, the party also commands the legislature; the Supreme Soviet has no independent role. And there is no freely expressed public opinion in Russia. Within overall party control and the context of "shared images," however, bargaining and coalition building presumably occur in the making of foreign policy.[50]

In the British government, despite the prime minister's control over his or her parliamentary followers, owing to the disciplined nature of British parties in the House of Commons, he or she must first resolve differences among members who represent different institutional and associational interests in the cabinet. Then he or she must woo the backbenchers, for the party cannot be led where it does not want to go. Ken Waltz has argued that a prime minister tends to avoid innovations in policy unless he or she has gained support from cabinet colleagues and the rank and file.

> Seldom will a prime minister try to force a decision widely and genuinely unpopular in his party. The prime minister must preserve the unity of the party, for it is not possible for him to perpetuate his rule by constructing a series of majorities whose

---

[50.] Zbigniew K. Brzezinski and Huntington, *Political Power: USA/USSR* (New York: Viking, 1964), pp. 196–197. Also see Arnold L. Horelick, A. Ross Johnson, and John D. Steinbruner, *The Study of Soviet Foreign Policy: Decision-Theory-Related Approaches* (Beverly Hills: Sage, 1975), for an evaluation of decision-making models as they have been used in studying Soviet politics.

composition varies from issue to issue [as in the United States]. He is, therefore, constrained to crawl along cautiously, to let situations develop until the necessity of decision blunts inclinations to quarrel about just what the decision should be.[51]

(Incrementalism thus seems to be as much a feature of British as of American government. Continuity of policy, slow adjustment to changing circumstances, policy deadlocks, and evasion of issues until they become crises are features in common. Innovations in policies are few and far between.)

Second, it must be added that this model holds several implications for international negotiations. For one thing, it suggests how difficult they are likely to be, quite apart from the substantive complexity of the problems being negotiated. For misunderstandings, failures of communication, disappointed expectations, and even failure of the negotiations between two countries may easily result when each set of national foreign-policy makers is so deeply engaged in its own bureaucratic and governmental "games" that it does not pay sufficiently close attention to the other side. Even between countries as close as Britain and the United States, negotiations can break down because the Londoners are negotiating with other Londoners and Washingtonians with other Washingtonians in trying to formulate policy. "Their self-absorption is a day-and-night affair; it never flags. They calculate accordingly and act to suit. So do their counterparts inside the other government. . . . Comprehension of the other's actual behavior is a function of their own concerns."[52]

Just one example: The NATO countries want to standardize their weapons, which would allow elimination of duplicates, while also allowing the forces of one country to exchange arms and spare parts with those of another and reducing the cost of individual weapons through mass production for the entire alliance. Such a move would make the alliance more efficient on the battlefield. A common battle tank for the United States and West Germany is one of the weapons that was suggested. But neither army was very happy with the idea. The U.S. Army has been particularly opposed, for the tank brings great prestige like the aircraft carrier for the navy. In a comparative test of the American and West German tanks conducted by the army it was found that, even though the German tank reportedly had greater range, consumed less fuel, was more reliable, and had a 30 percent greater target-hitting capability than the American version, the German tank failed "to satisfy several requirements" while the American tank "meets essential program objectives and the majority of specific program requirements."[53] Each service has continued to play its own game, even though it has been official policy to standardize the main battle tank. And this game has ended in a watered-down compromise: The American and West German tanks will share a common engine produced in the United States and a German gun.

---

[51] Kenneth N. Waltz, *Foreign Policy and Democratic Politics* (Boston: Little, Brown, 1967), pp. 59–62.

[52] Richard E. Neustadt, *Alliance Politics* (New York: Columbia University Press, 1970), p. 66.

[53] *The New York Times*, March 8, 1977.

466

Whether or not such comparative analyses allow us to make conclusive judgments about the relative merits of different political systems is a matter of debate. They are, of course, a popular pastime: Totalitarian governments are said to be more effective in making foreign policy than democratic ones because they are allegedly more able to respond rapidly to new situations and thus to exploit sudden opportunities or minimize the damaging effects of other states' policies. Britain's cabinet system, with its unity between executive and legislative and party discipline, is often claimed to be superior to the American presidential system, with its separation of executive and legislature and lack of party cohesion. Waltz has suggested that these propositions ought to be reversed. Yet we need to be careful in making such judgments. A prime minister may have to preserve party consensus and to make some compromises. Yet every member of Parliament is selected to run in his or her constituency by party leaders on the basis of his or her party loyalty; those who eventually work up to cabinet status are those members who have worked diligently and loyally for the party. The prime minister, in short, controls careers, and no British government in this century has been voted out of office by a combined vote of the opposition party plus defecting members of the ruling party. Party discipline is not lightly flouted if one cares for a political career.

In any event, between adversaries, the problems of negotiation are likely to be even greater, especially as one side likely knows less about the other's government than about its own ally's government. Nondemocratic governments tend to hide their internal differences better than democratic ones do. Yet our model suggests that such differences must exist even in dictatorships. The Nixon administration agreed to a whole series of projects with the Soviet Union in order to create in parts of the Soviet bureaucracy vested interests in cooperation with the United States. Should the Soviet political leaders decide once more to confront the United States, several segments of the bureaucracy, it was hoped, could be counted on to restrain them. The key question, of course, in such an interdependent relationship is, Who will influence whom more? In any event, in negotiations between two highly bureaucratized governments, the international negotiations are only one of *three* simultaneous sets of negotiations—including those between the governments and those among the various participants within each government. Kissinger used to utter the complaint that it was easier to negotiate with the Soviet leaders than to negotiate an agreed-upon policy in Washington; this complaint may be common in many capital cities.

V

FROM STATE SYSTEM TO INTERDEPENDENCE AND THE "NEW INTERNATIONAL POLITICS"

17

Preserving Peace in the
State System: The United
Nations, Disarmament, and
International Norms

THE RESTRAINT OF STATE BEHAVIOR?

The outlook for peace in a system of more than 150 states certainly does not appear bright. The hierarchy of great powers that historically maintained the international version of "law and order" has been eroded through the birth of so many states; the assertiveness of many of them, especially those with ambitions for regional leadership; the diffusion of modern conventional arms and possibly also nuclear weapons; the instability of many third-world regimes; the likelihood of conflict—even violent conflict—among them because of ethnic, racial, and religious differences; the probability that the superpowers will be drawn into these quarrels; the increasing reluctance of Western industrial states to use force in their disputes with smaller, non-Western nations; and the spread of terrorism. This weakening of the hierarchy that has served as a stabilizing influence is bound to be disruptive. But, whatever the future may hold, the past has taught us that no previous balance in history has in the long run prevented war permanently; no deterrent strategy has been proof against failure. Two world wars and a cold war in something over thirty years are evidence enough; and, although the possibility of Armageddon is ever-present, will it be sufficient to guarantee perpetual peace in a world characterized by more states, more civil strife, more international conflicts, more conventional arms, more nuclear weapons, and more terrorism?

Furthermore, can human welfare any longer be advanced by states within their national frontiers? Inflations and recessions cut across frontiers; no nation can

470   any longer promote economic growth and prosperity on its own, for all have become dependent upon uncontrollable forces from which they cannot insulate themselves. The less-developed countries (LDCs) have problems with too many people, too much poverty, and too little food, but similar problems affect all states. The inequitable distribution of wealth in the world is a source of potential revolution, especially as more and more LDCs come to view the international economic order as controlled by the West and stacked against them. One analyst has drawn an interesting comparison on this point:

> In a sense, the United States is a tenant occupying the largest, most elegant, most luxuriously furnished penthouse suite in a global cooperative apartment house. The hundred or so other tenants occupy premises of varying sizes and degrees of attractiveness. As one tenant among many, the United States does not have any direct concern with how other tenants decorate their apartments. . . . The United States does, however, have a basic interest in the structural soundness of the building as a whole. It is precisely that soundness which is in question. The condition of the building is beginning to deteriorate rapidly, and drastic action is needed to correct crumbling foundations, defective wiring, corroded plumbing, leaking roofs, not to mention overcrowding in some apartments and muggings in some stairwells. Unless these basic repairs and maintenance are undertaken, the building is liable to collapse or to go up in smoke. As the wealthiest tenant in the building, the United States has more to lose than anyone else from the deterioration of the living conditions in the building. The United States has a clear interest in insuring that the structure as a whole is sound and that minimum conditions for decent human existence prevail in the building.[1]

Until recently most solutions have been focused on peace and security. Given the nature of the state system and the increasing destructiveness of modern technology, avoidance of war has been given precedence over welfare issues, which are of more recent origin. Only in this century, especially since the 1930s, have Western states established social services at home and demonstrated to the rest of the world the high standards of living that can be achieved. The nuclear revolution and the emergence of the third world have, however, drawn attention to the urgency of *both* abolishing warfare and relieving human misery generally. These tasks are novel, for the balance of power cannot ensure eternal peace; in the age of scarcity before the development of mass-production techniques human beings did not think of global abundance and individual affluence as feasible aspirations.

How can these basic problems of peace and welfare be approached *within* the existing state system? How can state behavior be restrained and made more responsible? We shall examine two approaches, one internal (see Chapter 18), the other external. The former represents an effort to modify the game of nations through domestic reform; the latter represents an attempt to achieve the same goals—especially peace—through cooperation among states in the United Nations, through disarmament agreements, and through international legal and moral

---

[1.] Samuel P. Huntington, "Foreign Aid: For What and For Whom." *Foreign Policy*, Spring 1971, pp. 130–131.

norms. For many advocates of international organization, the United Nations symbolizes the expectation that war will be abolished, for, ideally at least, it represents the embodiment of a new spirit of internationalism that will supposedly replace national egotism. In former Senator J. William Fulbright's words, the United Nations is an institution intended to protect "humanity from the destructiveness of unrestrained nationalism" and therefore to be strengthened by subordination of shortrun national needs to long-run human needs.[2]

In contrast, disarmament agreements are not addressed to the problem of conflict resolution; their purpose is the extermination of the weapons with which conflicts may be waged. Whereas the United Nations approach stresses a spirit of accommodation and the peaceful settlement of disputes, the disarmament approach is based on the assumption that differences in interests will continue but that, if nations no longer possess arms, wars will not occur. The third approach stresses self-restraint by states in obeying international law or behaving more morally. How realistic are these three approaches to making the state system safe for humanity? If they offer practical solutions, the abolition of the state system may not be necessary; if they do not, the case for the creation of a new world order may be stronger.

THE THREE PHASES OF THE UNITED NATIONS

To understand the United Nations, it is necessary to understand what it is *not*. It is not the "great peacemaker" and solver of all problems. It is not a superstate, usurping members' sovereignty and imposing its will on them. Nor is its behavior independent of states' national interests and political considerations. United Nations decisions are not made according to some impartial, nonpolitical, and therefore purportedly superior standard of justice. The organization is not above politics because it cannot exist or act independently of its members' politics. Rather, it reflects the political interests, attitudes, and problems of its member states. It is only the channel through which the power and purposes of its members are expressed. The United Nations is not a substitute for power politics; it only registers the power politics of the state system. It is a mirror, not a panacea; there is no magic wand by which it can resolve all international problems. It cannot transcend the cold war or anticolonial struggles. It must function in the world as it exists, and it cannot solve any problems that its members, because of conflicting interests, are not prepared to solve. Its failures demonstrate only its members' inability to reach agreement.

Because the United Nations is not a superstate but a body registering its members' political interests, attitudes, and problems, its functions can best be understood in terms of the changing conditions of the state system. In its first phase

---

2. J. William Fulbright, "In Thrall to Fear," *The New Yorker*, January 8, 1972, p. 59.

472   the United Nations reflected wartime hopes that, once victory over Germany had been won, cooperation among great powers would continue and peace would be maintained. Primary authority for the preservation of peace and security in the United Nations was vested in the Security Council (originally composed of eleven members, six of them on two-year rotation; the total membership has since been raised to fifteen). Real authority, however, was to be exercised by the five permanent members, the United States, Russia, Britain, France, and China (at first Nationalist China and subsequently Communist China). With the votes of seven members of the Security Council, including all the permanent members, the Council could take enforcement action against aggression, and its decision was then supposed to be obeyed by all members of the United Nations; each permanent member of the Council could veto such action. Through an oligarchical structure that reflects the global distribution of power, the great powers were able to become the masters of the United Nations. Indeed, the United States and the Soviet Union, actually the only two great powers remaining in 1945, were the real masters. Britain was exhausted, France was still recovering from defeat and the German occupation, and China was a weak country embroiled in civil war. As long as the two superpowers could maintain harmony, peace would be preserved.

The security system was thus directed only against the smaller nations; if they disturbed the peace and if the great powers could agree to take punitive action, they could be squashed. The United Nations was, in the words of one delegate to its first conference, "engaged in establishing a world in which the mice could be stamped out but in which the lions would not be restrained."[3] The purpose of the veto was to prevent one of the great powers from mobilizing the United Nations against another great power. Because a decision to punish a great power for aggression would precipitate global war, the

> insertion of the veto provision in the decision-making circuit of the Security Council reflected the clear conviction that in cases of sharp conflict among the great powers the Council ought, for safety's sake, to be incapacitated—to be rendered incapable of being used to precipitate a showdown, or to mobilize collective action against the recalcitrant power. The philosophy of the veto is that it is better to have the Security Council stalemated than to have that body used by a majority to take action so strongly opposed by a dissident great power that a world war is likely to ensue.[4]

Conflicts among great powers were to be handled *outside* the United Nations under collective self-defense arrangements, which did not require prior Security Council authorization for individual or joint military action in response to an attack.

As the two superpowers took opposite sides at the beginning of the Cold War, the United States sought to mobilize the support of the United Nations for the containment of Russia and thus to associate its own policies with the human-

---

[3] Quoted in Inis L. Claude, Jr., *Power and International Relations* (New York: Random House, 1964), p. 59.

[4] *Ibid.*, p. 160; and Claude, *Swords into Plowshares* (rev. ed; New York: Random House, 1964), pp. 80–86.

itarian, peaceful, and democratic values underlying the organization. The transition from the first to the second phase was most dramatically illustrated in Korea. The United States had no choice but to oppose the Soviet Union, but it acted under United Nations auspices. Soviet absence from the Security Council on the day of the vote to intervene enabled it to do so. But such an absence was not likely to occur a second time. The United States therefore introduced the "Uniting for Peace" resolution in November 1950, the purpose of which was to transfer primary responsibility for the preservation of peace and security to the General Assembly should the Security Council be paralyzed by the veto. Constitutionally, this transfer of authority should not have been possible. The General Assembly had authority only to debate, investigate, and make recommendations on issues of international peace and security. Even then, it could offer no recommendations affecting matters on the Security Council's agenda; by placing an issue on the agenda, then, the Council could supposedly reduce the Assembly to a debating society.

The Americans argued, however, that the United Nation's responsibility for the preservation of international peace and security could not be abandoned just because the Security Council was paralyzed. If the Council could not fulfill its "primary responsibility" for this function, the Assembly would have to assume the task. It need hardly be added that in the Assembly, as it was then constituted, the United States could easily muster the two-thirds majorities needed for important resolutions from among members of the North Atlantic Treaty Organization (NATO) countries, the older British dominions, the Latin American republics, and one or two Asian states. The Soviet Union, with no veto in the Assembly, was of course consistently outvoted, though it was still able to use the body as a forum for its own point of view.

American use of the Assembly to support anticommunist policies did not last long. Just as the configuration of power underlying the original Security Council—the wartime alliance—had changed shortly after the establishment of the United Nations, so the political alignment at the outbreak of the Korean war was not destined to survive even that war, despite the "Uniting for Peace" resolution. The United States had received United Nations support at first for two reasons. First, an overwhelming number of member nations, including the nonaligned states,[5] saw in the North Korean aggression a test of the United Nations itself. If the organization had failed to respond, it would follow the League of Nations into the dustbin of history. Second, the smaller powers saw in the transfer of authority on security matters to the Assembly an opportunity to play a larger role in United Nations affairs than assigned to them in the original charter, much to their resentment. But Communist Chinese intervention in late 1950 made American-sponsored use of the United Nations as an instrument of collective enforcement against the communist bloc more difficult. The involvement of a major communist power and the possibility that the American government might accede to strong domestic pressures to extend the war to China by air bombardment, naval blockade, and the landing of Nationalist Chinese forces on the mainland, dramatized the

---

[5.] Egypt, because of its complaint that the United Nations had not supported it in the war against Israel in 1947–1948, was an exception.

474   wisdom of the United Nations architects' original effort to prevent the organization's involvement in military conflicts among great powers. The danger of a larger war, which might even bring in Russia, was simply too great.

In addition, twelve Arab-Asian members of the General Assembly were determined to remain nonaligned in the Cold War. Their earlier support for American intervention in Korea had been motivated by their concern for the United Nations as an institution. It was essential that North Korean aggression be met, and, because the United States had the strength to take appropriate measures, the Arab-Asian members had approved of the original American reaction. But they had no desire to participate in collective measures against one side or the other, which would in effect have forced them to become allied to one of the cold-war blocs through the mechanism of the United Nations voting procedure. The problem was to prevent a military clash between the great powres and, simultaneously, to avoid becoming aligned in the Cold War themselves. The answer was to shift the function of the United Nations from enforcement to conciliation.[6] The United Nations was to serve as an instrument of mediation in conflict situations between the great powers. The original assumption that peace could be preserved by having five lions, headed by the two biggest lions, act as world guardians was replaced with recognition of the imperative need to keep the lions from mauling one another to death—and trampling the mice while they were at it.

A third phase of the United Nations was thus initiated. In the first, the members had been dedicated to preserving the wartime Grand Alliance; in the second, it had become an American instrument for prosecuting the Cold War. This phase had begun to fade during the Korean war. By exerting great pressure, the United States could still, in the spring of 1951, obtain the two-thirds majority needed in the General Assembly for a condemnation of Communist China. Already, though, it had to make concessions in order to muster these votes—the price being that it not follow the condemnation with additional military or economic measures. Instead, the United States was to give primary emphasis to conciliatory efforts of the Arab-Asian bloc—supported by most of the NATO allies, which were also concerned about possible escalation of the conflict—to end the war. By 1955 the United Nations had reached adolescence; and, as the number of newly independent members, especially African ones, grew rapidly after 1955, it matured quickly. In 1955 six new Asian and North African states were admitted to membership; the next year four more were added. In 1960 the number of new states admitted was seventeen, mainly from sub-Saharan Africa. By 1974 Asian, African, and Latin American states made up three quarters of the 138 members. Both the American and the Soviet blocs had previously used the United Nations for their own cold-war purposes, but the neutral bloc was now using the organization to erase the vestiges of Western colonialism as quickly as possible. The General Assembly was a particularly good forum in which to voice anticolonial sentiments and to keep pressure on the West by passing, or trying to pass—with the help of the Soviet bloc—resolutions favoring national self-determination.

---

[6] Ernst Haas, "Types of Collective Security: An Examination of Operational Concepts," *American Political Science Review*, March 1955, pp. 40–62, examines this transition from "permissive enforcement" to "balancing."

In this third phase, the United Nations could not, however, help becoming involved in the Cold War. The United States and the Soviet Union, to be sure, did not allow the organization to interfere in *their* clashes. The Soviets had no intention of permitting the United Nations to intervene in Hungary or Czechoslovakia. Nor would the United States permit it to become involved in negotiations over the post-1958 Berlin crises, Cuban problems,[7] and the war in Vietnam. East-West issues were debated only; no action was taken. The superpowers handled their own direct confrontations. But, on the periphery of the Cold War, the United States and the Soviet Union were constantly tempted to interfere in the conflicts arising from the end of colonialism. Such interference, by threatening the peace and involving neutrals in the Cold War, was bound to lead the nonaligned nations to take protective action. The United Nations was for them more than a political platform. It was also a shelter in which they sought refuge from great-power pressure. In this third phase, they thought of the United Nations as *theirs*, and they were determined to use it to remain nonaligned. The chief function of the United Nations thus became "preventive diplomacy"[8]—that is, the stabilization of local conflicts *before* either of the superpowers could become involved and thus provoke its antagonist's intervention as well. To state this point negatively, preventive diplomacy was intended to keep American-Soviet clashes from extending beyond the cold-war zone. At the same time, by containing the Cold War, the small nations could safeguard their independence and control their own future to some extent. The mice were thus to keep the lions apart so that they could not grapple with each other and trample the mice. The chief means of stabilization was establishment of a "United Nations presence" in these peripheral quarrels; the organization thus functioned as a fire brigade, devoted to minimizing potential fire hazards. It could not douse the fire, but its presence could signal that fire was imminent or had already broken out and should be controlled quickly.

PREVENTIVE DIPLOMACY

In a real sense, the United Nations has thus performed a crucial function in a highly combustible world. But in order to perform this role, it has needed not only support, or at least acquiescence, from the superpowers but also active support and participation of the third-world countries. The contribution of the latter to systemic stability was in response to two conditions. The first is the tendency of their problems to spill over into the international arena. One example is the disintegration of a

---

[7.] In Cuba, only after the Cuban missile crisis of 1962 had already been resolved was the organization to be used—and then it was to check that all Soviet missiles had been removed from Cuba. But, because Fidel Castro refused to submit to international inspection and the United States had no doubts that all the missiles had been shipped back to Russia, the United Nations remained uninvolved.

[8.] Andrew Boyd, *United Nations: Piety, Myth and Truth* (Baltimore: Penguin, 1962), pp. 85 ff; Claude, *The Changing United Nations* (New York: Random House, 1967), pp. 23 ff; Arthur L. Burns and Nina Heathcote, *Peace-Keeping by U.N. Forces: From Suez to Congo* (New York: Holt, Rinehart and Winston, 1963); and Linda B. Miller, *World Order and Local Disorder* (Princeton, N.J.: Princeton University Press, 1967).

476   state, as happened in the Congo after it attained independence in 1960; in the resulting attempts to reunify it, competing factions sought outside help. Another is a clash among states in a region when each party has friends in the superpower camps. This kind of clash occurred during the Israeli-Egyptian war in 1956, when France and Britain intervened militarily on Israel's side and the Soviet Union supported Egypt diplomatically—and even talked of firing missiles at Paris and London. The second condition is that these types of problem tend to attract the attention of the Soviet Union and the United States, thus possibly leading to confrontation, with all the attendant dangers of military conflict. The two superpowers are attracted, of course, because these problems may bring to power groups favorable to one side and thus inimical to the other, or they may lead to a regional expansion that would benefit one side and hurt the other. If one of the two superpowers is unwilling to tolerate what it may consider a local or regional setback, it will intervene; if it fears that its opponent may intervene, it may move first in a preventive intervention. In either instance, it risks counterintervention. The conflicts that have arisen on the periphery of the American-Soviet rivalry have thus tended to feed into the major confrontation between the two superpowers.

    Further analysis of the Suez crisis of 1956 can be instructive in this connection. Egypt had been a British protectorate from 1881 to 1936, when it was granted independence. Britain retained control of the Suez Canal, though, and in effect maintained a dominant position. But mounting Egyptian nationalism and a corresponding rise in anti-British feeling eventually led Britain to relinquish its Suez military base, though not its control of the canal, in 1954. The moment that British troops had withdrawn, President Nasser launched an energetic anti-Western campaign to eliminate all "colonial" governments from the Middle East and North Africa. Success would, of course, have made him the leader of all Arabs and would have given him control of most Arabian oil. Once Egypt had become the strongest Arab state, it would have had tremendous bargaining power, for Europe, especially Britain, was dependent on Middle Eastern oil. The United States and Britain were alarmed by these attempts to eliminate Western influence in the economically and strategically vital Middle East, particularly as Nasser was leaning more and more toward the Soviet Union, for which the Middle East offered a means of outflanking NATO without a shot being fired. Shortly after Nasser extended diplomatic recognition to Communist China, therefore, the United States withdrew its offer to finance the Aswan dam, which was to provide irrigation for much of Egypt's weather-beaten soil and thus to promote its economic development. Nasser's response was to nationalize the Suez Canal, claiming that he would use income from it to build the dam.

    Britain then felt compelled to act. If Nasser were allowed to seize the Suez Canal with impunity, the British believed, then other Arab governments would also expropriate Western property—particularly oil property. Furthermore, no pro-Western Arab government would be safe from overthrow by pro-Nasser elements within its own country. Britain was joined by France, which sought to stop Egyptian shipments of arms to Algerian nationalists to be used against France. They found their opportunity when Israel attacked Egypt. This moment occurred after Nasser's famous arms deal with Russia, the stated purpose of which was to drive Israel into the sea. The consequent hostilities threatened to develop into major war, as the Soviet Union, which shared Egypt's interest in expelling the West from the Middle East, threatened to send volunteers to Egypt and even to rain atomic rockets on London and Paris.

The possibility of Soviet intervention naturally elicited an American response. The United States disapproved of its allies' attack on Egypt, which smacked of nineteenth-century colonialism and might alienate the new nations. American support for the British and French action would have allowed the Soviet Union to pose as the friend and defender of those new nations. The United States therefore voted with the Soviet Union in the Security Council to condemn Britain and France's aggression and to call upon them to desist. At the same time, it could not stand by and let the Soviet Union send military "volunteers" into the Middle East, let alone attack Britain and France; a warning note was therefore sent to Moscow. Yet the Soviet Union, posing as Egypt's protector, could hardly have remained inactive in the event of American intervention without endangering its good relations with the other nonaligned states. At the very least, then, the situation was dangerous.

In 1973 there was almost a replay of this crisis. In October Egypt and Syria attacked Israel during the highest Jewish holiday, Yom Kippur, the Day of Atonement. Egypt was then governed by Anwar Sadat, an Egyptian nationalist but a more moderate figure than Nasser, who had been an Arab nationalist, or pan-Arabist, before his death. The country had become increasingly frustrated by Israel's continued occupation of Egyptian territory on the east bank of the Suez Canal. This territory, captured in the Six-Day War in 1967 after Nasser had precipitated a showdown through a series of political and military moves, seemed likely to remain in Israeli hands for a long time. Israel had no incentive to surrender it. After the war in which it had gained its independence, Israel had had to fight for survival in 1956 and 1967. The Arab states continued to be hostile to it, and Nasser, the only Arab leader of stature who could have mobilized popular support throughout the Arab world for a compromise settlement that included recognition of Israel's existence, had refused to play the role of peacemaker. Instead, allying himself with the rulers of Jordan and Syria, he had proclaimed in 1967 that Egypt was ready for the "final struggle." Even after losing yet another war, he refused to sit down with Israeli leaders and negotiate a settlement; Egyptian defeat therefore had brought not peace but only another cease-fire.

For Israel, however, that was a peace of sorts. It thought itself militarily superior and therefore not likely to be attacked. The American-Soviet *détente* also benefited Israel, for the United States did not press it to give up the captured Egyptian and Syrian territories. The Soviet Union, needing American technology, investments, and trade goods to bolster its own sagging economy and also wanting a strategic arms-limitation treaty (SALT), was in no position to press Israel or to give active political and military support to the Arab states. Moscow's leaders, by limiting their support for North Vietnam, despite the American blockade and bombing in the spring of 1972, had achieved better relations with Washington's

478   leaders and were not about to permit the Cairo government to jeopardize them. Indeed, having supplied North Vietnam with the arms that had helped it to launch the spring offensive and thus jeopardized better Soviet-American relations, the Russian leaders made sure that the offensive arms needed for an attack on Israel were not delivered; only Egypt's defenses were bolstered. The territorial status quo thus became frozen.

But Sadat was unwilling to live with that status quo. For one thing, he was subject to increasing domestic pressures, especially from the army and university students, to seek revenge on Israel; external pressures from the more militant Arab states, like Libya, and from nonstate actors, including the various Palestinian guerrilla movements, were also severe. Sadat, an unglamorous figure after the charismatic Nasser, was thus in danger of being overthrown; pro-Soviet Egyptian leaders were particularly anxious to replace him as he began to reduce and then to eliminate their influence and undertook measures to attract foreign, including American, private capital to rescue the stagnant Egyptian economy from the "Arab socialism" introduced by Nasser. Above all, Sadat recognized that, if Israel was to be compelled to abandon Arab territory captured in 1967, he had to look elsewhere than to Moscow for support. Only the United States, Israel's friend, could help him to achieve this goal, and this emphasis on the return of the lost territory suggested a reciprocal willingness to recognize Israel's existence. But Israel, skeptical after its previous bitter experiences, the victim of constant guerrilla attacks and continual denunciations by Arab militants, did not respond. Israel believed that Sadat was merely talking and that the return of captured Egyptian territory would only strengthen him for yet another war. The United States, too, did nothing after Sadat threw out his Soviet military advisers in 1972, in an effort to take the initiative toward a peace agreement and to attract support from the United States.

Frustrated, Sadat, whose power was in danger, therefore launched the Yom Kippur war, taking Israel by surprise and achieving initial success in crossing the Suez Canal and driving into the Sinai Desert. But, once Israel had recovered from the shock and had driven Egypt's Syrian allies back from the Golan Heights, its forces concentrated on Egypt; they crossed the Suez Canal to the west bank, cutting off supplies to the Egyptian forces on the east bank and encircling them. At that point, the United States and Russia agreed upon a cease-fire resolution in the U.N. Security Council. The United States agreed because it thought that no peace could be arranged if Egypt were again humiliated in war—indeed the psychological boost derived from its initial successes had to be preserved if it were to be expected to make any concessions in a peace settlement—and Russia agreed in order to avoid an Egyptian defeat that might compel the Soviets to enter the war to rescue what it still regarded as a client state.

Indeed, the Soviets almost did enter as the shooting continued and the Israelis tried to encircle and destroy the Egyptian army on the eastern side of the Suez Canal. Sadat then requested the United States and the Soviet Union to use their own forces to impose a cease-fire. When the United States declined to intervene with its forces and Russia threatened to do so unilaterally, the two superpowers found themselves in confrontation. American military forces were placed on a worldwide alert, and another highly inflammable situation had suddenly arisen.

As for the Republic of Congo (now Zaïre), it became an independent state in 1960. But the Belgians, unlike the British and the French in most of their colonies, had not trained native leaders to take over from them. Complete disorder soon broke out and the native army rioted. The Belgian settlers fled, and to protect them Belgium flew in troops. Congolese Prime Minister Patrice Lumumba interpreted the Belgian action as an attempt to restore colonial rule. He appealed to the United Nations to compel the Belgians to withdraw. The Soviets immediately supported his appeal and condemned Belgium, accusing it of acting as a front for "NATO imperialism." An even more serious situation developed when the province of Katanga (now Shaba) seceded. Katanga's rich copper mines were the Congo's main source of revenue, and secession thus threatened the survival of the entire nation. The Katanga mines were, however, owned by the powerful Union Minière du Haute-Katanga, which supported secession. This company, representing Belgian and British capital, helped provincial President Moïse Tshombe build up a large army, led by Belgian and other European officers. Lumumba demanded that the United Nations crush Tshombe's mercenary army and help to restore Congolese unity.

When his demand went unheeded, Lumumba appealed to the Soviet Union for help against the "colonialists." He received both Russian diplomatic support and Russian military supplies, and it looked as if the Soviet government was about to establish a base from which it could further expand its influence in Africa. Lumumba was dismissed from office by Congolese President Joseph Mobutu, whom the United States supported in order to prevent establishment of a Soviet foothold in central Africa. The Soviets, however, refused to recognize Lumumba's successor, insisting that only Parliament had the right to dismiss Lumumba and that, as it had not done so, he was still the legitimate Congolese Prime Minister and must be restored to his office. The subsequent murder of Lumumba exacerbated the situation.

The national coalition government of the Congo, formed in early 1961, thus faced a major crisis from the beginning, a crisis that could only benefit the Soviet Union unless a solution was found. The government, committed to a policy of nonalignment, had as its first objective national reunification. Failure to achieve this goal would undermine its authority and lead to collapse from political and financial weakness. The transfer of power to a more radical procommunist government would then be a real possibility. The central government, to head off its own collapse, might turn toward Russia, just as Lumumba had done. In either instance there would be a Soviet-American confrontation in the Congo.

It is in such situations in which the two superpowers are drawn into confrontations that threaten the peace of the world, and that the United Nations in its third phase can play its most important role. Just as the Security Council had been intended as the focus of authority in the first phase and the General Assembly had become the focus in the second phase, the secretary-general was to be the principal actor in the third phase. No longer merely the prime administrative officer

480   of the organization, the secretary-general, largely through his partnership with the nonaligned nations, had become its leading political officer. It was Dag Hammarskjöld who, by establishing the precedent of the United Nations presence in troubled areas, first assumed the role of "custodian of brushfire peace." The most dramatic expression of this custodianship has been the "nonfighting international force," the purpose of which is basically not military but political. The size of the force, drawn primarily from states not involved in the particular dispute, and its firepower are not as significant as its political presence, which forestalls the use of Soviet or American forces. During the Suez crisis in 1956 a U.N. Emergency Force (UNEF) thus supervised the withdrawal of British, French, and Israeli troops from Egypt. It did not seek to *compel* withdrawal through combat. The cease-fire agreement was the prerequisite for its use, yet the mere fact that it was available made it easier to obtain British, French, and Israeli agreement to withdraw. Once withdrawal had been completed, fewer than 5,000 United Nations soldiers were left to guard the Israeli-Egyptian frontier and to maintain peace in that area. Symbolically, it was Nasser's demand that these forces be withdrawn in 1967, leaving Egypt and Israel to confront each other directly, that led to the Six Day War. Similarly, the interposition of United Nations forces between Israeli and Egyptian troops ended the crisis emanating from the American-Soviet confrontation during the 1973 war; it was these forces that stood between the hostile troops on both the Egyptian and Syrian fronts as American Secretary of State Kissinger patiently negotiated disengagements of the combatants as a prelude to more comprehensive peace negotiations.

       At least three conditions are imposed on such an international force. First, as already mentioned, it must be neutral and must therefore exclude permanent members of the Security Council. Second, the nation upon whose territory the force is to show its "presence" must grant permission for such entry. The host nation, as a sovereign state, thus exercises some control over the composition of the international force and can exclude troops from nations that it considers unfriendly or undesirable. It can also demand the withdrawal of these troops, as Egypt did in 1967. Indeed, Nasser's army simply shunted them aside. Even had the secretary-general not agreed to their withdrawal, he would have had no option; UNEF was a small force and not fit for fighting. Israel had refused to accept United Nations forces on its side of the frontier with Egypt; had it done so, it would have been protected against an Egyptian strike by their very presence. The third condition is that the United Nations force may not intervene in any purely internal conflict and become party to the dispute. In Egypt in 1956 and 1973, the force was thus not used to impose a specific settlement on Nasser or Sadat in order to calm the international situation. It merely disentangled the combatants. The United Nations presence was not intended to deal with the causes of the two wars; it was to deal only with their effects. The same was true in the Congo, though with a special twist. It was precisely the United Nation's refusal to interfere in the domestic politics of the Congo that created most of the difficulties. After the Congo had disintegrated, the head of the "national" government insisted that the U.N. Operations in the Congo (UNOC) crush the secession of Katanga. In the end, the international organization could not isolate itself from the Congolese civil war. The effect of United Nations *non*intervention was to freeze the Congolese schism and, because Katanga's rich copper mines were the major source of national revenue, ensure the collapse of the Congo government. United Nations forces therefore eventually did fight to crush the secession of Katanga. The third condition of domestic nonintervention is thus a qualified one.

The nations of the third world, it must be noted, can use this preventive diplomacy function *only* if the superpowers permit them to do so. The assumption underlying the pacifying role of the nonaligned states is that both the United States and the Soviet Union wish to avoid new areas of conflict in the Cold War because of the high risk. Their desire to avoid nuclear war gives them a vested interest in keeping peripheral conflicts under control. They will thus at least acquiesce in the establishment of a United Nations presence: "It cannot be done *against* the major parties; it cannot be done *by* them; it can only be done *for* them and by their leave."[9]

Four alternative courses of action are possible in conflicts not involving direct American Soviet confrontations, especially in order to achieve preventive diplomacy. The United Nations may take a pro-Western action, an impartial action, no action at all, or a pro-Soviet action. Obviously, the American preference is in that order; the Soviets prefer the exact reverse. Neither extreme is really feasible, but the difficulty is that between the remaining alternatives the United States prefers impartial, neutralizing action, whereas the Soviet Union prefers inactivity. The reasons are obvious. The United States fears that inactivity will lead either to a Soviet advantage or a collapse requiring American intervention—and Soviet counterintervention. It also hopes that impartial action will accomplish pro-American results. Conversely, the Soviets hope that inaction will produce pro-Soviet results and prevent American intervention. The Soviets fear that the course preferred by the United States may indeed yield results detrimental to Soviet interests.

Preventive diplomacy, by limiting the scope of marginal conflicts and seeking to stabilize conflict situations, has on the whole served American purposes better than Soviet ones. In Egypt in 1956 and 1973 United Nations forces helped to preempt possible Soviet intervention. In the Congo in 1961 United Nations intervention eliminated the bridgehead that the Soviets had established. The Soviet Union was therefore frustrated. From its perspective, the moving force in both crises, especially the Congo, had been the secretary-general of the United Nations, and the results only served to demonstrate the need for a Soviet veto over his actions. In the aftermath of the Congo the Soviets proposed a "troika" plan, which would provide for the appointment of three secretaries-general, each of whom would represent one of the major blocs in the world. The Soviets thus sought to supplement their actual veto in the Security Council and their virtual veto in the General Assembly (where the Soviets can now usually find enough votes among the nonaligned states to prevent a two-thirds majority vote against them) with a

---

[9] Claude, "Containment and Resolution of Disputes," in Francis O. Wilcox and H. Field Haviland, Jr., eds., *The U.S. and the U.N.* (Baltimore: Johns Hopkins Press, 1961), pp. 101–128 (emphasis in original).

482   hidden veto at the top of the Secretariat. This veto would ensure that the United Nations could not do anything that is in any way detrimental to Soviet interests.

The Russian leaders' reaction to the United Nations intervention in the Congo was growing disenchantment with the international organization, as far as its peace-keeping operations were concerned; in fact, Russia refused to contribute any funds for those operations. The nonaligned states, to be sure, have shown no such disenchantment. They unanimously opposed the "troika" plan to hamstring the secretary-general, for they value the organization as the bastion of their independence and "neutralist" positions in the Cold War. Because of Russia's refusal to pay for United Nations peace-keeping operations and American insistence that Russia must pay if it was not to lose its voting rights in the General Assembly, the international body became deadlocked and remained so until American leaders saw that they would receive little support for stripping Russia of its voting rights in the Assembly. They were then willing to recognize instead the principle that no great power must pay for operations that it regards as detrimental to its interests.

It is inconceivable that the United States would be more likely than the Soviet Union to support financially operations that were injurious to its national interests. Indeed, at the time that the United States abandoned its position, it declared that it too reserved the right not to pay for future peace-keeping operations of which it disapproved. Although this move may at the time have been a face-saving way out of an awkward situation, the United States went further than the Russians and reduced its contribution to the United Nations as a whole, not only for peace-keeping forces, but also in 1971, when Peking was seated in the international organization. At a time when President Nixon was seeking rapprochement with the leaders of Peking, the U.S. House of Representatives reacted by deciding unilaterally, and in clear violation of the U.N. Charter, to cut the American share of the United Nations budget from 31 to 25 percent. The Senate eventually restored the cut, but the American government did notify the General Assembly, which assesses the member states, that the United States wished to negotiate a reduction in its contribution to no more than 25 percent.

Another interesting result of the clash of the superpowers over the Congo was the revival of the Security Council as the main United Nations organ concerned with security issues. If Russia cannot be assured of majority support in the General Assembly—and the 1971 vote on seating the Peking government demonstrated that the United States can also no longer count on majority support—and if Russia cannot control the secretary-general, then it seemed better to keep peace-keeping operations in the Security Council, where, with judicious use of the veto, the Russian government can keep some degree of control and influence over whatever is decided. But, if Russia does not act with restraint in the Council, as the history of the United Nations has shown, the Council's function will merely be shifted to another U.N. organ in which Russia has less influence and no veto. Like Russia, the United States cannot be certain of controlling the Security Council, as it was able to do in the first phase, because in 1966 its nonpermanent membership was expanded. Events in 1974 suggested a similar loss of American influence in the

General Assembly and the adoption by that body of purposes detrimental to American interests. It is thus not surprising that during the Yom Kippur war of 1973 the two superpowers cooperated in the Council to pass a cease-fire resolution, to sponsor jointly under United Nations auspices the Geneva peace conference between Arabs and Israelis, and to follow a similar procedure when Greece and Turkey almost came to war over Cyprus in 1974.

Although the United Nations has managed to prevent the continuation and escalation of hostilities in which one or both of the superpowers have not been directly involved, it should be emphasized that this is not to be confused with the prevention of war. That is the clear lesson of the war in 1967, when Egypt exercised its sovereign right to expel United Nations forces from its territory. Sometimes wars are not even under the jurisdiction of the United Nations. In 1971 Pakistan brutally crushed an attempt by East Pakistan to secede and become independent. Claiming that the proposed secession was a domestic matter, the Pakistani government rejected United Nations intervention and killed 3 million people. India, burdened by 10 million refugees from East Pakistan and eager to eliminate its only rival on the subcontinent, helped to establish the state of Bangladesh and sent the refugees back; it, too, rejected United Nations intervention. When the Vietnamese invaded Cambodia in order to overthrow the pro-Chinese Pol Pot regime and imposed a pro-Vietnamese government, and when subsequently Chinese forces crossed its frontier with Vietnam in order to teach the Vietnamese a lesson, none of these communist states wanted a debate on aggression in Indochina. It would have been too embarrassing. Nor have all conflicts in Africa received attention in the halls of the United Nations. When in 1977 Somalia was actively supporting, perhaps even sponsoring, an uprising in the Ogaden area of Ethiopia and when later the Ethiopians, with Soviet-Cuban support, were driving to Somalia's border, no debate occurred. Nor was there debate when Idi Amin of Uganda provoked Tanzania and, in the subsequent war, Tanzanian troops deposed Amin. The United Nations' role in issues of security and peace, though useful, thus remains very limited.

Civil wars, with their potential for spilling over into interstate conflict, or the barbarous treatment of people by their own governments may also not be placed on the international agenda. While the Nigerian government was engaged in civil war against the Ibos in the seccessionist state of Biafra from 1967 to 1970, approximately half a million people died; the issue was not debated in the United Nations because many LDCs did not wish to legitimate Biafra and encourage secession in their own countries. After their victory in Cambodia, the communist government of Pol Pot adopted a barbarous policy of genocide against its own people, yet this problem never appeared on the United Nations agenda; 3 to 4 million of Cambodia's 8 million people reportedly died as a result of these policies before the regime was forcibly replaced in 1979 by a Vietnamese puppet regime. The United Nations consists of sovereign states, which means that each has the right to exclude any intervention aimed at protecting the rights of individuals among its citizens.

A FOURTH PHASE OF THE UNITED NATIONS?

Several points about the United Nations are worth restating. First, the organization is *not* a substitute for power politics. To idealize the United Nations, to expect it to rise "above that sort of thing" and to be superior in morals and general demeanor to the nation-states that are its members is not only unwarranted but also likely to breed disillusionment and cynicism. Unrealistically high expectations, when disappointed, result in declining support for its highly important "preventive diplomacy." The United Nations is not simply a debating society. Speeches there serve the purpose of articulating conflicting views and making the world more aware of key issues that are likely to be troublesome. United Nations representatives from various nations are also able to gather informally, to try to reconcile differing interests, and to arrange compromises out of the limelight.

Second, although the United Nations is neither a world government nor totally impotent, it is not very powerful in dealing with the superpowers. In 1979 the General Assembly demanded that Vietnam withdraw its troops from Cambodia after two attempts to censure Vietnam in the Security Council had been vetoed by Russia. The Assembly resolution, sponsored by Vietnam's noncommunist neighbors and supported by many LDCs, was ignored by Vietnam. In 1979–1980, the Security Council agreed that Iran ought to release the American hostages held in the embassy in Teheran. Because seizure of diplomatic personnel threatened to make diplomacy itself impossible, such unanimity was to be expected. If the United Nations could not speak for the safety of diplomats, what could it speak for? But, when Iran continued to hold the hostages, economic sanctions were vetoed by the Soviets in the Security Council. The United States did not then take the issue to the General Assembly, allegedly because a supportive vote there would have no legal force but actually because a majority could not be obtained. Support for American military action against Iran was also lacking. Conversely, after a Security Council resolution calling for Soviet military withdrawal from Afghanistan was vetoed by the Russians, the Assembly did vote 104–18 (with thirty states not voting) to condemn the Soviet move, a rare occurrence in the United Nations, but one that reflected the LDCs' anger at the nation that had so persistently claimed to be their "natural ally" and supported their nonalignment. As important as this resolution was symbolically, however, it had little practical effect on Russia's continued military involvement in Afghanistan.

Third, because the United Nations reflects the real world and not the ideal world that many observers and proponents seek, it should not be surprising that all its member nations continue to follow their national interests, regardless of how moralistic and altruistic their rhetoric. When Russia was in a minority in the first phase, it could counter majority resolutions in the Security Council only through its veto power as one of the five permanent members. It did indeed cast many vetoes, partly because the United States, using diplomacy as a tool of propaganda, repeatedly introduced resolutions to which it knew Russia would object. Precisely because the United Nations is associated in the popular mind with idealism, the

United States was able to place the Soviet Union in a position of seeming to obstruct the peaceful work of the organization, and to align itself with the majority in the pursuit of all that is good and true.Conversely, the United States did not have to cast a single veto; it had majority support in the Security Council. In using majority votes to reject Soviet proposals, the United States was exercising what has been called a "hidden veto"—a negative vote hidden beneath a democratic cloak.

Not until 1966, when enough nonpermanent members had been added to the Security Council to jeopardize American control of that body, did the United States begin to cast vetoes itself. Both superpowers now negotiate with other Council members to obtain majority support, though it is still easier for the United States to do so. The national interests of a member dictate its voting behavior, as we have already suggested. American voting behavior in the Council, despite its few vetoes until now, is thus not fundamentally different from Russian behavior. And, faced with the possibility that the majority of LDCs may form an anti-Western coalition, the United States in late 1974 warned the General Assembly of the erosion of popular and congressional support for the United Nations in the United States.

Fourth, as the United Nations does represent its constituents and as these nations pursue their national interests through the organization, it follows that the United Nations will occasionally reflect a double standard of judgment. When Israel retaliates upon one of its Arab neighbors for brutal guerrilla attacks and outright murder, it is likely to find itself condemned by a majority of members, for the Arab states, both as LDCs and as Muslim nations, have lots of friends. The guerrillas and the Arab states harboring them will not be similarly condemned. The United States cast its second veto when Israel, having exacted reprisals for the murder by Palestinian terrorists of several members of the Israeli Olympic team in Munich in 1972, was about to be condemned in the Security Council. And, although South Africa is frequently condemned, the LDCs never condemned Idi Amin for as many as 300,000 murders or the persecution and expulsion of 60,000 Asians from Uganda, or Burundu for over 100,000 Hutus reported killed within its borders.

"The countries of the Third World are not subject to criticism or attack, even by each other, while any part of the rest of the world which can be labelled racist or imperialist must be held accountable."[10] An early, and blatant, example was India's invasion of the Portuguese colony Goa in 1961. India argued that the colony represented "imperialism," which automatically constituted "aggression." The Indian invasion was thus an act of liberation and completely legitimate. A majority of the United Nations' members supported India's claim. When Vietnam invaded Cambodia in the late 1970s and replaced the Pol Pot regime with a communist government acceptable to Hanoi leaders, the new government refused to allow the United States and other countries to feed the Cambodian people, or only pretended to do so, even though it was estimated that as many as 2 million people might starve without massive outside assistance. Yet no resolutions de-

---

    10. Rupert Emerson, "The Fate of Human Rights in the Third World," *World Politics,* January 1975, p. 224.

TABLE 17.1

UNITED NATIONS MEMBERSHIP AT FIVE-YEAR INTERVALS

Year	Members
1946	55
1950	60
1955	76
1960	99
1965	107
1970	127
1975	144

These figures are taken from successive issues of the *United Nations Yearbook*.

nouncing this behavior as barbaric were passed in the General Assembly. Had the United States, however, sent troops into Iran in 1979–1980 to liberate fifty hostages—held in total violation of international law, under which embassies and diplomatic personnel are immune, a tradition long honored by all nations—it would undoubtedly have been condemned in the United Nations, and anti-American riots would have occurred in many of the LDCs. But in the Iran-Iraqi war of 1980, the latter was not condemned for the attack on its neighbor.

Fifth, the United Nations does not represent "world public opinion," which allegedly restrains state behavior. Most states can hardly be considered democratic, although many of them claim to be. Most states are authoritarian, whether civilians or military officers are in charge; public opinion has no means of expression on national issues in such countries. Nor do they allow competing parties or a free press and other mass media; the masses hear only what their governments wish them to hear. In addition, a government's public statements may not reflect its private views. For example, during the Vietnam war, Indian leaders were officially condemning the United States, but they told Vice-President Hubert Humphrey privately during a 1966 visit that it was essential that the United States was there. Otherwise, China would become a menace. The Chinese threat was all they could see. (That was the view of Presidents Kennedy and Johnson as well, and, if India perceived civil war in Vietnam in the context of Communist China's expansion, it is perhaps less surprising that the American government did so as well after 1961.)

In any event, the absence of a world public opinion reflects the existence of many nations with varied historical traditions, philosophies, ideologies, and political and moral standards. There is little consensus among countries on what is moral and what are acceptable standards of behavior. Certainly there is nothing equivalent to those that exist in modern Western political systems. What does exist is a set of *governmental* views and opinions, which are often mistaken for "world public opinion." When a government solemnly declares in the United Nations that "our people wish to express their outrage" or whatever else, it is presenting its own opinion as the *vox populi*.

A state is admittedly sensitive to what other states think of its actions, and it may take prospective reactions into account in deciding on its aims, how they are to be achieved, and how publicly to explain them. Concern for other states' opinions is an everyday affair of which extensive public-relations and propaganda efforts are the symptom. And no state relishes a United Nations vote against it, for the popular image of the United Nations as a "good" organizaton, symbolic of man's desire for peace, is deeply rooted. Nevertheless, when governments feel genuinely strongly about an issue, they will go ahead, regardless of the *national* opinions expressed in the General Assembly and Security Council. The Soviet invasions of Hungary, Czechoslovakia, and Afghanistan are examples. Iran continued to hold American hostages, despite a disapproving vote in the Security Council. A United Nations resolution approved by a majority of states is the result of a tradeoff, in which some states support other states on issues that are of no concern to them in return for votes on issues that do interest them.

Sixth, and perhaps most significant, the United Nations has been very adaptable in the world in flux. Like the American Constitution, it has proved flexible and pragmatic. It was originally established on the assumption that the great powers would cooperate, with the added safeguard that, if they could not cooperate, it was better to cast a veto than to attempt to ride roughshod over a great power. It seemed preferable to paralyze the Security Council and to prevent action, for that would reflect the genuine stalemate outside the United Nations; to have abolished the veto might have cured the Security Council's impotence, but it would also probably have meant war. When one great power opposes another, it is the better part of wisdom to attempt to negotiate differences, rather than to outvote one of the parties and then to try to enforce the majority decision. In any event, the United Nations was not permanently paralyzed in its area of primary responsibility, peace keeping. This function was first shifted to the General Assembly, then to the secretary-general, and then back—or so it seems—to the Security Council. Thanks to this flexibility, the United Nations has demonstrated a vitality that its predecessor, the League of Nations, never exhibited during the period between the two world wars. It has survived and performed some vital functions during three decades of changing American-Soviet relations, the appearance of many new states, and the subsequent division between rich and poor countries. Presumably it will continue to survive in the rapidly changing world of the future.

One of its current problems arises from the fact that it is the forum in which the LDCs publicize their causes. It is there that they voice their demands for the new international economic order (global redistribution of wealth and power between rich and poor countries) and raise various specific issues related to this demand: management of food reserves, setting of commodity prices, ownership of ocean mineral resources, curbing population growth, and meeting minimum human needs. The years after the 1973 war in the Middle East were years of confrontation between Western industrial countries and the third world, in which rhetoric often became strident and the double standard plain. The Western countries were continually criticized for past and present exploitation even while they were being called upon for assistance; the communist countries, which offered virtually no material help, suffered no rebuke and even enjoyed acclaim for their view that poor countries are poor because they have been exploited by the rich. The temper of the LDCs, most of which had in the past prided themselves on nonalignment,

488   was symbolized by their 1979 meeting in Cuba. Vietnam and North Korea, which, like Cuba, were not nonaligned at all, attended this meeting and tried to influence the assembly to support Soviet policy. The subsequent unexpected Soviet invasion of Afghanistan aroused overwhelming disapproval, however.

The main danger to the vitality and viability of the United Nations arises from its failure to observe its own charter and decisions. The dangerous Middle Eastern situation first suggested the possibility that the United Nations is entering a fourth, anti-Western phase. The Assembly invited the head of the Palestine Liberation Organization (PLO), a nonstate actor whose acts of terrorism and hijacking it had debated only a few years earlier, to address it. It treated Arafat as a head of government and greeted him with sustained applause while limiting the time for an Israeli reply, which was delivered to a virtually empty auditorium. Simultaneously, the Arab-African-Asian majority, supported by the communist states, barred Israeli participation in the previously nonpolitical United Nations Educational, Scientific, and Cultural Organization (UNESCO). In addition, the Assembly ousted South Africa from its sessions because of that nation's racial practices after the Security Council, which exercises ultimate suspension power, had refused to do so. It was the General Assembly's Algerian president who had decided to treat the PLO chief as a head of government and to curb Israel's right to speak on the Palestinian issue, a ruling that was upheld by a large Assembly majority. Previous Assembly presidents had acted with greater restraint and balance, regardless of their personal preferences or their nations' official positions.

It was in 1975, however, that the most dramatic confrontation in the General Assembly occurred. That was the year Amin, then president of Uganda and chairman of the Organization for African Unity (OAU), a man who had voiced approval of the slaughter of Israeli atheletes at the Munich Olympics and had said that Adolf Hitler's only error had been not killing more Jews, claimed to speak on behalf of forty-six African members when he charged that the United States had been colonized by Zionists and that Israel had no right to exist. The coalition of African, Asian, Arab, and communist nations also was able to pass a General Assembly resolution equating Zionism with "racism." A similar resolution was passed almost unnoticed in the closing weeks of the 1979 session. The earlier resolution, sponsored by the Arab states, also proclaimed the Palestinians' right to independence and sovereignty but failed to recognize the same right for Israel. The resolution thus represented acceptance by the majority in the General Assembly of the rights of Palestinians, as defined by leaders who refused to accept the rights of the nation of Israel, over the birth of which the United Nations had presided. A 1980 special session of the General Assembly similarly called for the formation of a Palestinian state without any reference to Israel's right to exist. Concern for human rights had become very selective, shaped by national and racial criteria.

In 1976, on the initiative of Cuba, the U.N. Decolonization Committee once more affirmed Puerto Ricans' "inalienable rights" to self-determination and independence, a move clearly intended as a sharp slap at the United States. The relationship between the United States and Puerto Rico was characterized as "colonial" and "imperialistic." This attack was almost an annual ritual; in 1973, for example, the resolution had been approved in the General Assembly by a vote of 104–5, with 19 abstentions, despite the fact that the official Independence party in Puerto Rico had polled less than 5 percent of the vote in several elections. The rest of the population, exercising the right to self-determination that most members of the General Assembly do not allow their own people, had consistently voted for commonwealth status. In 1975 Ambassador Daniel P. Moynihan (now a senator from New York) had headed off a similar resolution in the General Assembly.

The danger of such votes, *if* they represent a trend, are several. The United Nations was founded as an organization of states. Guerrilla leaders, including those of Algeria, had not in the past been invited to the organization or given observer status, even when it seemed likely that they might someday establish governments. More important, members of the United Nations govern certain territories and populations; they were not admitted because they enjoyed certain kinds of government or practiced certain enlightened or virtuous policies. The Fair Deal United States, Democratic Socialist England, Stalinist Russia, and Nationalist China had been among the founding members; membership had clearly not then been a question of the purity or nobility of governments. To begin to exclude governments—of Israel, of South Africa, perhaps in the future even of Egypt—or to limit their right to speak because a majority of members of the General Assembly objected would signify a radical transformation in the aim of the United Nations, which was originally to provide a forum for the views of all nations and an arena where informal exchanges of opinion might occur. The issue had been universal membership, not the domestic or foreign policies of specific states.

In addition, the relevance of future General Assembly resolutions, which are of an advisory nature only, may be placed in doubt. The authority of a majority composed of many small nondemocratic states, whose financial contribution in the United Nations' upkeep is minimal, will be widely questioned—at least in the West. A possible fourth phase of the United Nations, in which the majority of its members are anti-Western and especially anti-American, will almost certainly alienate American opinion and financial support, which has already been reduced. As Ambassador John Scali, Moynihan's predecessor, explained in 1974:

> These resolutions are sometimes adopted by Assembly majorities which represent only a small fraction of the people of the world, its wealth, or its territory. Sometimes they brutally disregard the sensitivity of the minority. . . . Each time that this Assembly makes a decision which a significant minority of members regard as unfair or one-sided, it further erodes vital support for the United Nations among that minority. But the minority which is so often offended may in fact be a practical majority, in terms of its capacity to support this organization and implement its decisions.[11]

Ironically, a weakening of American support for the United Nations may occur just when the organization's services may be most needed to separate combatants and mediate conflicts. Indeed, the world may become more explosive as

---

[11] *The New York Times*, December 7, 1974.

military power is diffused and economic rivalries are multiplied. The United Nations at present provides a meeting ground where the first and third worlds can hold meaningful discussions. Heated confrontations and exchanges of recriminations are unlikely to produce fruitful negotiations.

In an increasingly polycentric world, in which an ever-larger number of problems confront all states, there remains a need for the United Nations as a forum. This forum is particularly needed for the new agenda of socioeconomic issues. United Nations and United Nations-sponsored conferences like the World Food Conference and the special session on proposals for the new international economic order, are natural places for states to meet, form coalitions on different issues, and bargain. It is especially the third-world countries that gain influence in the General Assembly, where each country, regardless of size or wealth, has one vote; the poor countries who constitute a majority, can thereby place the first world, which believes in majority rule, on the defensive.

In contrast to the very limited, though not insignificant, role that the United Nations can play in the area of security issues, its almost universal membership may mean a larger and more visible role on the new agenda of issues. The organization can influence the priorities of its members by calling special conferences or scheduling certain issues for debate; it can be instrumental in the formation of coalitions that can negotiate with one another, especially as LDCs cannot afford to maintain embassies in all countries but can send delegates to the United Nations. It can also publicize specific issues to help educate the governing elites and attentive citizens in the many member countries. The U.N. role in the state system may therefore be greater in the future, but the sovereignty of the member states will continue to limit its contribution to resolving nations' security and welfare problems.

DISARMAMENT AMONG STATES

From the moment that the first atomic bomb was exploded, the central question has been whether or not "absolute" weapons can be compatible with the continued existence of humanity organized in nation-states. If nations are unwilling to relinquish their sovereign rights or at least to adopt a new spirit of accommodation within the United Nations, might not some future quarrel spark a global conflagration that will leave the world in ruins, its smoldering ashes a monument to human scientific genius and human malevolence? The Spanish philosopher José Ortega y Gasset once wrote that man is "lord of all things, but he is not lord of himself." The devil in George Bernard Shaw's *Man and Superman* put the point even more poignantly, long before the bombing of Hiroshima:

> And is man any less destroying himself for all this boasted brain of his? Have you walked up and down upon the earth lately? I have; and I have examined Man's wonderful inventions. And I tell you that in the arts of life man invents nothing but in the arts of death he outdoes Nature herself, and produces by chemistry and

machinery all the slaughtered, of plague, pestilence, and famine . . . when he goes out to slay, he carries a marvel of mechanism that lets loose at the touch of his finger all the hidden molecular energies, and leaves the javelin, the arrow, the blowpipe of his fathers far behind. In the arts of peace Man is a bungler. . . . I know his clumsy typewriters and bungling locomotives and tedious bicycles: they are toys compared to the Maxim gun, the submarine, torpedo boat. There is nothing in Man's industrial machinery but his greed and sloth: his heart is in his weapons. This marvelous force of life of which you boast is a force of Death: Man measures his strength by his destructiveness.[12]

If Shaw is correct, our first level of analysis may lead us only to a rather gloomy prediction for the future. For, given the conflict inherent in the state system, nuclear war is only a matter of time. But we can logically draw several other conclusions from our model that may help us to deal with the power and security dilemma inherent in the state system and to avoid ultimate catastrophe. One recommended solution is general and complete disarmament. Even before the bombing of Hiroshima, it was apparent that, in a competitive system, political conflict is accompanied by arms buildups; these "arms races" tend to erupt in warfare. The question has been whether or not it would be safer for all nations to disarm. If nations continue to accumulate arms, is war not inevitable sooner or later? Have not all previous arms races ended in wars? The answer seems obvious, and disarmament seems an obvious solution, particularly in the nuclear age. Armaments are no longer a means of protecting nations, and only disarmament could guarantee national security. Failure to disarm means that sooner or later the nuclear powers will clash. Arms control cannot prevent that; cannot save the world from destruction. The goal therefore, according to some analysts, must be total or quantitative disarmament; even partial or qualitative disarmament, aimed at specific types of weapon, like nuclear arms, will not suffice.

Yet however *theoretically* feasible disarmament may seem, it is nevertheless unlikely to provide the answer to the problem of nuclear weapons in political conflict. In the first place, there can be no such thing as *total* disarmament. The problem is not just a semantic one. In assessing a nation's strength and capacity to wage war, as we know, we must take into account—along with number of men under arms and the weapons they possess—geographical position, population, natural resources, productive capacity, and scientific ability, all equally important. Military power is only one aspect of a nation's overall strength, and that strength cannot be artificially eliminated. Even total disarmament would leave a "war potential" that could be mobilized after a declaration of war. International quarrels would not cease with the abolition of armaments. Second, no disarmament treaty can eradicate knowledge of nuclear physics and the ability to construct atomic or hydrogen bombs. In any event, even elimination of nuclear weapons would leave countries possessing such vast resources and skills as the United States and the Soviet Union possess with more than enough potential power to conduct a long and very destructive war.

---

12. George Bernard Shaw, *Man and Superman* (Baltimore: Penguin, 1952), p. 145.

492   The belief that disarmament is the solution to war in the state system is based on the assumption that arms races cause wars. In order to protect itself, a nation increases its military strength; another nation then builds up its military power to guard against possible attack from the first nation. The ensuing arms race develops its own momentum and creates a war psychology; at a favorable moment, when one country believes that it is stronger than the other—or that the other side is beginning to pull ahead—it will attack. Interaction between the contestants is thus considered to produce an arms spiral that, when it reaches a critical point, automatically precipitates hostilities through a sort of "spontaneous combustion." But, because in the state system arms accompany competition, the critical question is why wars sometimes occur and sometimes do not. The answer requires an examination of political causes.

To attribute wars to the simple existence of arms is to confuse cause and effect. An arms race does not follow a logic of its own. It is not an autonomous process divorced from the political context in which it occurs. Capabilities cannot be artificially separated from intentions. Military power serves the political ends of the state.[13] An arms race reflects political tensions between nations; it does not cause those tensions. States need armaments to protect what they consider to be their interests; they do not fight simply because they possess arms. Rather, they possess arms because they believe it may someday be necessary to fight. Indeed, it can be shown that, when nations involved in political quarrels fail to arm, they invite aggression. Although it is true that, when power confronts power, there may be danger, it is certain that, when power meets weakness, there will be far greater danger. It is all too easy to attribute conflicts to arms races. It is much more difficult to mention wars that have been prevented because nations have armed themselves.

As arms are a *symptom* of interstate political conflict, it is illusory to expect nations to disarm while conflict persists. *The prerequisite for disarmament is political agreement on issues separating the nations involved in the arms race.*[14] How can nations be expected to agree to total elimination or major reduction of the instruments with which they seek to protect themselves and gain their ends? If nations cannot settle their political differences, they cannot end the arms race. If the differences could be resolved peacefully, the arms race would not have begun. In the absence of reliable substitutes with which states can defend and seek their objectives, states need arms. This need is bound to influence their disarmament proposals. If a nation is already stronger than its opponent, it will want to preserve and even enhance this superiority, and its disarmament proposals will contain that

[13.] On the nature of the arms race, see Huntington, "Arms Races: Prerequisites and Results," in Carl J. Friedrich and Seymour E. Harris, eds., *Public Policy: A Yearbook of the Graduate School of Public Administration, Harvard University* 7 (Cambridge, Mass.: Harvard University Press, 1956), pp. 41–86; George H. Quester, *Nuclear Diplomacy* (New York: Dunellen, 1971); Colin S. Gray, "The Arms Race Phenomenon," *World Politics*, October 1971, pp. 39 ff.; Gray *The Urge to Compete: Rationales for Arms Racing,*" *World Politics*, January 1974, pp. 207 ff; Gray, *The Soviet-American Arms Race* (New York: Heath, 1976); Albert Wohlstetter, "Is There a Strategic Arms Race?" *Foreign Policy*, Summer 1974, pp. 3–20; and Wohlstetter, "Rivals, But No Race," *Foreign Policy*, Fall 1974, pp. 48–81.

[14.] Merze Tate, *The United States and Armaments* (Cambridge, Mass.: Harvard University Press, 1948), makes this point very well in analyzing the only reasonably successful disarmament agreement in history, the Washington Naval Conference of 1921–1922.

built-in bias. If it is weaker, it will want to catch up with and, if possible, surpass its opponent, and its proposals will reflect those objectives. An attempt to freeze the status quo will arouse anger and frustration in a revisionist state; on the other hand, efforts to erode the status quo will be a source of annoyance and worry to a state that benefits from the status quo. Disarmament negotiations in these circumstances are merely another form of the arms race itself, in which each nation aims to increase its relative power position.

The lack of mutual trust in these circumstances becomes an impediment to agreement on disarmament. The United States has since 1945 been proposing inspection as a substitute for trust. States are not going to rely on good faith for the implementation of whatever accords may be reached, especially in the nuclear era. Any form of disarmament, whether involving strategic nuclear arms or conventional weapons, is in itself an incentive to cheat, for gaining an advantage over the adversary may result in a significant political "payoff." But all states, including the Soviet Union until 1974, have rejected calls for inspection and have denounced them as attempts at espionage. (It is doubtful, for instance, that Washington leaders would have been more willing to tolerate Soviet personnel's inspecting American industrial plants and military installations than Soviet leaders have been willing to tolerate American inspectors in Russia.) Although the consequence was that both superpowers were compelled to rely primarily on remote means of inspection, which became increasingly feasible with newer technology, the conflict over inspection demonstrated the underlying distrust between them. Mutual confidence is thus the necessary prerequisite for inspection to work; it is precisely the absence of this confidence that—given the conflicts of interest among states—makes statesmen believe it imperative to possess arms. And that is exactly where the problem lies: Arms in an essentially anarchical state system serve useful functions; without reliable alternative means of achieving the same purposes, potential adversaries are unlikely to surrender or accept significant restrictions on their arms. It is perhaps symbolic that the very first disarmament conference, in 1899, was called by the Russian czar to discuss "the most effective means of assuring to all peoples the blessing of real and lasting peace, and above all of limiting the progressive development of existing armaments."[15] It was born out of fear that Russia was falling behind Germany in the European arms competition because it was unable to afford to keep up. Underneath the noble words about a "real and lasting peace," the first disarmament conference was actually called to keep Russia *in* the arms race.

Why, then, do states pursue disarmament at all? The fundamental reason is that disarmament *negotiations* are, as already suggested, a form of arms competition. It could not be otherwise. In the state system, each nation must defend itself against attack. As the possibility of war is inherent in the conflict of national wills, each state must pay attention to its armed strength. As Salvador de Madariaga has remarked:

> All disarmament conferences are bound to degenerate into armament conferences. In all of them discussion is based on the assumption of war, and they all reveal

---

[15.] *Ibid.*, pp. 35–36.

494

the inevitable conflict between the ardent endeavors of the delegations present, each of which has for its main aim to secure the highest possible increase of its relative armaments in a general reduction of absolute forces, if such a reduction there must be.[16]

A parable about a disarmament conference held by animals illustrates this point. The animals, having decided to disarm, convene in order to discuss the matter. The eagle, looking at the bull, suggests that all horns be cut off. The bull, looking at the tiger, says that all claws should be clipped. The tiger, looking at the elephant, is of the opinion that tusks should be either pulled out or shortened. The elephant, looking at the eagle, thinks that all wings should be clipped. Then the bear, glancing around at all his brethren, says in tones of sweet reason: "Comrades, why all these halfway measures? Let us abolish everything—everything but a fraternal, all-embracing hug." All countries need arms, but, because of the importance of arms, they usually cannot agree on the ratio of power that ought to exist among them.

A second reason for pursuing disarmament is propaganda. Disarmament is like motherhood, the flag, and apple pie: Who can be against it? Does not everyone desire it? Disarmament conjures up an image of peace and harmony among states, a willingness to coexist amicably and to resolve disputes with reason, to act with restraint, to radiate good will, and to show concern for all people, not just those of one's own nation. Disarmament is good, moral, clean, and virtuous; to be against it is to be in favor of war, conflict, and national egotism and against humanity. What nation wants to be labeled a warmonger? Disarmament is thus an issue on which diplomacy is concerned to a very large extent with propaganda. Because disarmament is a popular goal, no nation is willing to reject a disarmament conference. Disarmament plans, however, frequently contain a "joker" that the opponent cannot possibly accept.[17] The "joker" serves a dual function: compelling rejection of the entire plan (while placing the onus for the resulting diplomatic deadlock on the other side) and protecting the vital interests of the proposing side.

A third reason for disarmament negotiations is economic. Earlier we spoke of the choices that governments, especially governments of great powers, must make between guns and butter. The arms bill for the superpowers is enormous and continuous. Furthermore, it rises with increasing technical complexity—at least in industrialized Western economies. Since World War II the United States and the Soviet Union have produced nearly $20 trillion in gross national product (GNP), approximately $15 trillion in the United States alone. Of this amount more than $2 trillion had been spent on arms by the end of the Vietnam era, about $1.3 trillion by the United States and an estimated $1 trillion by Russia."[18] Costs remain high. Soviet spending has totaled 12–14 percent of its GNP for the past several years. It is estimated that Soviet leaders outspent the United States by $100 billion

---

[16] Salvador de Madariaga, *Disarmament* (New York: Coward-McCann, 1929), pp. 62–63. For an account of the disarmament negotiations as part of the postwar arms race, see John W. Spanier and Joseph L. Nogee, *The Politics of Disarmament* (New York: Holt, Rinehart and Winston, 1962).

[17] Spanier and Nogee, *ibid.*

[18] U.S. Department of State News Release, August 1972.

during the 1970s. And, after declining to just below 6 percent of GNP for several years (the lowest since before the Korean war), American defense spending is slated to go up again.

The costs of weapons are enormous.[19] A single nuclear aircraft carrier costs between $2 and $3 billion. One C-5A transport plane costs $60 million. The track for the proposed MX missile costs more than $4 billion, and the total system, including 200 missiles, will ultimately cost $25 billion (each MX costs about $100 million). Here are some costs for less exotic hardware (note how much inflation has driven them up during the 1970s):

M-16 rifle bullet: 6 cents to 19 cents (up 217 percent)

M-16 rifle: $82 to $260 (up 217 percent)

Hand grenade: $2.06 to $6.49 (up 215 percent)

Army jeep: $2,835 to $9,067 (up 220 percent)

8-inch howitzer: $173,246 to $463,000 (up 167 percent)

Airplane jet engine: $262,000 to $677,000 (up 158 percent)

CH-53A helicopter: $1.9 million to $10.4 million (up 447 percent)

Defense is therefore not surprisingly a source of controversy in the United States. As Senator McGovern, the Democratic candidate for president in 1972, said during debate over the defense budget in that year:

> Our people are alert to threats abroad. But they are equally concerned with the deterioration of our society from within.
>
> They see decaying cities, wasted air and water, rampant crime, crumbling housing and failing transportation. . . . And they are tired of seeing their needs starved to underwrite corrupt governments overseas, to pay more than our share of alliances with the rich nations of Europe and to buy shiny new airplanes that don't fly, guns that don't fire and missiles that only increase the terror.
>
> I suggest that the most serious national security questions today involve such questions as the health of our people, the quality of our schools, the safety of our streets, the condition of our environment, the vitality of our economic system and most of all the confidence of our society that this nation cares about its own.[20]

But it is not only the superpowers and their allies that spend large sums on arms. The developing countries, too, are buying arms, including the most advanced conventional arms, on a large scale, for both protection and prestige.[21]

---

[19] *Time*, October 29, 1979.

[20] *The New York Times*, August 2, 1972.

[21] See, for example, "Poor Nations Spend Fortune on Arms Purchases," *The New York Times*, August 2, 1974, pp. 1, 14, for the situation as these nations entered the 1970s.

496   Ironically the poor countries are growing poorer—in part, at least—because they are buying more weapons. In 1974, for example, India exploded a nuclear device and, despite its claim that it had no intention of building a nuclear force, starkly raised the issue of national priorities in an LDC. In 1964 India had had a population of 580 million, growing at a rate of 13 million a year. Approximately 30 percent was illiterate. The nation's industrial production was stagnant. Three fourths of its university graduates could not find employment, and unemployed intellectuals are a sure source of trouble. After its nuclear explosion ten years later *The New York Times*, in an editorial, was very blunt: It remarked that India had placed "considerations of national power and presitige above the needs of its people," that the Indian explosion was "another monument to human folly" in general, and that the appropriate reaction was "one of despair that such great talent and resources have been squandered on the vanity of power, while 600 million Indians slip deeper into poverty. The sixth member of the nuclear club may be passing the begging bowl before the year is out because Indian science and technology so far have failed to solve the country's fundamental problems of food and population."[22]

Perhaps these words smack a little too much of the moral outrage of a nation that already had the bomb, yet they do address a basic dilemma: The cause of disarmament is very often advanced not only in order to increase the amount of domestic "butter" but also with the idea that the rich countries can give money that would normally be spent on weapons to the poorer nations for economic development. A prominent economist has indeed claimed precisely that: "The only tangible "reserves" that could be used to break decisively the grip of poverty throughout the world are the huge amounts of labor, capital and natural resources that are being devoted year in and year out to the maintenance and gradual expansion of military establishments."[23]

In the final analysis, however persuasive the economic reason for disarmament is, considerations of security are greater. Symptomatic of the failure to solve the problems of interstate conflict is the fact that disarmament negotiations do not even occur until nations are locked in political struggle, and by then they are too late. Settlement of differences, political agreement, and the existence of some degree of mutual confidence are the ingredients necessary to achieve a successful disarmament agreement among states that believe that otherwise they may have to go to war with one another. In the absence of these ingredients, disarmament negotiations are bound to fail, for the conflicting nations will insist that, in the absence of reliable substitutes, they need arms for defense and realization of their goals.

    States will not disarm so long as they insist upon maintaining their national sovereignty intact. . . . A sovereign state invariably asserts the power to be the

---

[22] *The New York Times* , May 20, 1974.

[23] Wassily Leontief, "Cutting U.S. and Soviet Military Outlays", *The New York Times*, March 24, 1977.

ultimate judge in its own controversies, to enforce its own conception of rights. . . . Moreover, sovereignty necessarily implies the right to make war in the national interest."[24]

INTERNATIONAL LAW AND MORALITY

In our earlier presentation of the model of the state system, international politics was called "politics without government" because in the system there are none of the institutions of government—legislative, executive, or judicial—that in domestic systems perform the functions of regulating society and distributing goods. Even more fundamentally, there is no shared set of values and no common political culture in the international community. In this decentralized, or anarchical, state system, the principal restraint on states is the balance of power. Power unmet is power abused; power must therefore restrain power. If this model of the state system is essentially correct—as our analysis has shown in detail—then it becomes easy to understand why state behavior is so little tempered by international law and morality when vital interests are at stake. These elements may on occasion reinforce restraints imposed by calculations of power and prudence, but usually they are secondary and supplementary. The limited impact of international legal and moral considerations is symptomatic not of inherent lack of merit but of the primitive nature of the state system.

This conclusion may appear surprising in connection with international law, for states are themselves the principal source of that law. Most international law is customary. Certain norms of conduct that have evolved over a long period of time at some point become accepted as binding by the states that have followed them; new states then tend automatically to accept them. One other principal kind of international law is treaty law. Unlike customary law, which is applicable to all states, treaty law binds only the parties that sign and ratify the treaties. As two states alone can hardly establish a rule of conduct, treaty law can be created only by a larger number of states.

States usually obey international law, despite widespread opinion to the contrary, because they need it. The rise of states as independent political units made the development of law necessary. Each sovereign state enjoyed complete jurisdiction and authority over its own territory and people, but it enjoyed neither beyond its boundaries. As states are compelled to coexist, however, they have to regulate their relations. If they are to stay in official contact, they must exchange representatives, which means that the rights and immunities of diplomats have had to be defined so that they can be protected on foreign soil. Other matters that have had to be covered include how title to territory is acquired (which, retains some

---

[24.] Tate, *op. cit.*, p. 3.

498 importance because of continuing frontier disputes), ceded, and recognized; a state's jurisdiction over territorial waters, air spaces, and aliens on its soil; conditions under which treaties come into effect and are terminated; legal methods for resolving disputes; and conduct of warfare and determination of the rights of neutrals. It should be obvious now why states do not normally violate international law— indeed, why it is virtually self-enforcing, except, increasingly, in the area of warfare. The legal norms provide a degree of order and predictability in an all too uncertain and chaotic environment. States expect to benefit from the reciprocal observance of obligations; if a particular state gains a reputation for not keeping its agreements, other states will be reluctant to sign further agreements with it, and reprisals may also occur.

This rule is as true for Western states, among which customary international law originated, as for non-Western states. It has sometimes been held that Western-derived international law is unacceptable to the third world and that, therefore, the law must be developed further to reflect the values and interests of the latter. But this view has led to confusion: On the one hand, the non-Western states are attempting to articulate their economic and political interests, shaped mainly by their desire for modernization, so that they can play a more influential role in the state system; on the other, they seek to express their resentment of a legal order that mirrors primarily the interests of the rich and powerful Western states. The new countries have thus accepted the prevailing law, invoking it when it favors them in disputes with other states, while seeking certain changes, for example, in the areas of foreign investments and property and the settlement of claims after expropriation and nationalization of such holdings. Yet, even on the latter issue, we suspect that, if some of the newer states gain greater stakes in the international system and become exporters of capital, their views will move closer to those held by the more industrialized Western states.

Because of the anarchical nature of the state system, however, international law has shortcomings. The international legal system, unlike a national or municipal one, exists in the absence of a supranational legislature. Customary and treaty law is a substitute for legislated rules. The difficulties inherent in a decentralized system are clear: States may disagree about when a custom becomes a legal norm; they may differ in defining their obligations; and there is no accepted authority to impose a uniform interpretation. Law that evolves over time is also, of course, slow to adapt to rapidly changing conditions; as a result, it may become obsolete. Treaty law may not be subject to such obsolescence, but it does not apply to nonsignatories. Treaty law may also suffer from a lack of specificity. Nor is there a supranational executive to impose sanctions when international law is violated, as in domestic systems, though, as one noted English international legal expert noted:

> . . . the weakness of international law lies deeper than any mere question of sanctions. It is not the existence of a police force that makes a system of law strong and respected, but the strength of the law that makes it possible for a police force to be effectively organized. The imperative character of law is felt so strongly within a highly civilized state that national law has developed a machinery of

enforcement which generally works smoothly, though never so smoothly as to make breaches impossible. If the imperative character of international law were equally strongly felt, the institution of definite international sanctions would easily follow.[25]

In a sense, the word "law" is a misnomer in this context. A proper designation would be "norm," a prescribed rule of conduct that one *ought* to follow; not to follow it may bring a bad conscience, disgrace, or even social ostracism. A law is similar, except that violation also leads to legal sanctions (fines, jail sentences, or executions). But there is no international government with superior force to apply to those states that break the law. The principal shortcoming of international law, in these circumstances, is that its subjects decide when it applies! No state is indicted, tried, and punished. States normally obey international "law" and accept their obligations under it because the law applies to everyday relations; on the whole, the routine business of coexistence makes light demands on states. When the law is violated, it is because of issues that involve high political stakes, and the offended party usually applies its own sanctions.

Such violations are relatively few in number but tend to be dramatic and sensational when they occur, thus giving rise to the impression that international law is "weak." For example, during the 1950s the United States sent U-2 intelligence planes over Russia in the name of national security, even though Russia has legal jurisdiction over its own air space and had given no permission for such flights. Cuba, as a sovereign state, has a perfect right to welcome the strategic missiles of the Soviet Union on its soil, and the United States has no legal right to demand their withdrawal. Yet American security interests and the balance of power with the Soviet Union were perceived to require such a withdrawal in 1962. The United States therefore blockaded Cuba, but, as a blockade is legally a *casus belli*, this action was called a quarantine. In these and similar instances, it would be more correct to say that international law is *restricted* in the range of its application, rather than that it is weak; this limited range of application is the reverse of the broad freedom of independent action that states claim for themselves.[26]

The great powers, the principal actors involved in maintaining the balance of power, thus ignore international law when it would restrain them from doing what they believe they must do to preserve the balance. When Italy invaded Ethiopia in the 1930s, international lawyers thought that Italy had violated the League of Nations covenant and that sanctions ought to be invoked. Yet Britain and especially France wished Italy to remain a friend and potential ally against the new Germany of Hitler. To apply sanctions would be to alienate Italy and would thus make it more difficult to keep the balance. International law is also a problem for smaller states concerned with regional balances, rather than the systemic balance. Israel, for example, was surrounded in the 1950s and 1960s by states that were clearly hostile and refused to recognize its right to exist; it therefore struck preemptively

---

[25] L. Brierly, *The Law of Nations* (New York: Oxford University Press, 1949), p. 73. Also see Werner Levi, *Law and Politics in the International Society* (Beverly Hills: Sage, 1976).

[26] Brierly, *op. cit.*, p. 74.

in 1956 and 1967, when it believed that its enemies were about to attack. Yet such a war is generally considered illegal.[27]

In an instance having little to do with the balance of power, Iran seized the American embassy in Teheran in 1979, even though, according to international law, embassies are to be regarded as parts of the nation they represent and diplomats are legally immune to seizure and captivity. The militant Islamic regime, insisting that it was the United States that had violated international law since World War II by interfering in Iran's domestic affairs by supporting the Shah, demanded his return for trial and presumably execution for what it condemned as his cruel tyranny and alleged subservience to the United States. In order to obtain "justice," Iran claimed both that the United States had violated international law and that seizure of the American embassy and its personnel—labeled spies, rather than diplomats—was therefore legitimate.

All disputes, then, are not "justiciable." Disputes can be categorized in two types: disputes that are justiciable or amenable to settlement on a legal basis and those that are nonjusticiable or political.[28] Political disputes are usually nonjusticiable not because there is no law that can be invoked but because they involve vital interests. If a state is dissatisfied with the status quo—for example, the settlement imposed upon it by victor states at the end of a war—it does not appeal to the law for a remedy because the law upholds the status quo. On the basis of existing law, an appeal for legal revision would have to be disallowed. But the question of change is not a judicial one; consequently, adopting judicial methods would be of no avail. The question of revision is political. The dispute may be resolvable peacefully, by negotiations and compromise. The distinction between a legal and a political problem is therefore somewhat arbitrary, reflecting the state's attitude toward the status quo. Nevertheless, it is a critical distinction.

The anarchical nature of the state system also limits the impact of moral norms on the competition and rivalry of states. Indeed, probably in no sphere of human endeavor is there a greater gap between professions of moral principles and declarations of noble intentions on the one hand and actual behavior on the other, than in international politics. A frequent definition of a diplomat is "an honest man sent abroad to lie for his country." A man or woman who slays another human being is normally called a killer; if apprehended, tried, and, convicted, the killer is isolated from society in prison or, in many countries, put to death. But a person who kills a lot of other people called enemies on behalf of his or her country is hailed as a hero, presented with medals, and sometimes even immortalized in a statue or on a postage stamp. Ordinary soldiers receive veterans benefits from a grateful country.

The usual explanation for the alleged immorality of states is that their concern for their security requires them to do "whatever must be done." In a domestic system of law and order, the resulting sense of security allows individuals and groups to act with at least some degree of morality; but, in the international system, the absence of law and order means that all states, like the cowboys in a

---

[27] Hedley Bull, *The Anarchical Society*, pp. 143–144, 108–109.

[28] P. E. Corbett, *Law & Society in the Relations of States* (New York: Harcourt, Brace, 1951), pp. 77–79.

lawless western town, must figuratively go armed and must be prepared to shoot when their lives are endangered. In Thomas Hobbes' philosophy, the war of every man against every other man in a state of nature arose not from fear of death but from fear of *violent* death at the hands of his fellow man; in the resulting state of perpetual war nothing was unjust. The idea of right and wrong, justice and injustice, simply had no place. The state system is essentially a Hobbesian jungle; in a jungle one must behave appropriately. The "nice guy" is devoured.

In such a system it is perhaps the better part of wisdom to adapt and to play the game of nations, however rough that game is at times. For a statesman, being a good man and possessing moral intentions are not enough. Prime Minister Chamberlain of Great Britain was such a man. Above all, he wanted to avoid another war with Germany and to spare his people another such awful bloodletting as World War I had been. Surely preserving the peace was a moral goal. Peace is precious, not to be lightly sacrificed, to be forfeited only if absolutely unavoidable. Had Chamberlain been a less noble individual, more willing to take up arms and risk surrendering peace, he might have saved the peace he so treasured.

This line of thinking suggests that power and morality are antithetical. If a state is concerned with security and power, it must throw off morality as so much excess baggage; if, on the other hand, it seeks to act morally, it will suffer badly in the international struggle. This position is, however, false. Acts by individuals and groups, subnational or national, all involve moral considerations; decisions involve choices, and in choosing one course over another moral predispositions that are inherent in larger social values do have effects. In an international context, it is more accurate to say that, *the closer relations among states move to the pole of enmity, the more likely the states are to adopt policies normally considered immoral; on the other hand, the closer those relations move to the pole of friendship and the more secure the states feel, the more moral will be the conduct of their foreign policies.*[29]

Whatever the degree of morality that influences states in different situations, the source of this morality lies within the states themselves. A number of points are worth mentioning in this connection. First, states, singly or collectively when they share certain common interests, identify those interests with morality. Clearly, no state is going to admit publicly that its actions are unethical. President Julius Nyerere of Tanzania once said on behalf of his country and the "poor nations" of the world:

> I am saying it is not right that the vast majority of the world's people should be forced into the position of beggars, without dignity. In one world, as in one state, when I am rich because you are poor, and I am poor because you are rich, the transfer of wealth from the rich to the poor is a matter of right; it is not an appropriate matter for charity. . . . If the rich nations go on getting richer and richer at the expense of the poor, the poor of the world must demand a change, in the same way as the proletariat in the rich countries demanded change in the past.[30]

[29.] Wolfers, *Discord and Collaboration*, p. 54.

[30.] Quoted in P. T. Bauer and B. S. Yamey, "Against the New Economic Order," *Commentary*, April 1977, p. 27.

502   The LDCs are thus believed to be poor because the Western industrial states are rich; the former thus have a legitimate grievance based on the latter's plunder of their resources and continued "capitalist" exploitation. The Western countries owe them reparations and help as a moral obligation and historic duty. This formulation is the essence of the claim for a new international economic order. The definition of what is moral and what is immoral is egocentric—and obviously very practical if it induces guilt feelings among the former colonial powers so that they seek to relieve those feelings by means of "alms for the poor."

Second, states define morality differently, as President Nyerere's words illustrate, according to whether or not they are satisfied with their positions in the state system. A "status-quo state," which benefits from the current power distribution, will espouse a morality identified with the interests of the larger state system and will emphasize peace. If its interests coinside with those of most other members of the system, there is no occasion for challenges from the latter: upholding peace will give the state a political and psychological advantage against challengers, which must threaten war or actually go to war to effect change and can therefore be denounced as aggressors and warmongers. The status-quo state stresses the need for diplomacy, claiming that no problem is insuperable, that all can be settled by patient and sincere negotiations, rather than by unjustified intimidation or force. The peace of a region—of the world—should be everyone's prime consideration; no injustice or wrong, however strongly felt, is worth the even greater injustice of war and the sacrifice of peace.

In contrast, a revisionist state that seeks to transform the status quo to its own advantage will attempt to avoid being morally discredited by claiming that it is underprivileged, a "have not" state, and that it seeks only equality or national self-determination. A good example occurred at the November 1976 U.N. General Assembly meeting, when a resolution linking South African *apartheid* with Western governments and especially with the government of Israel was passed. This resolution called the South African government "illegitimate," having "no right to represent the people of South Africa." It declared support for "the legitimacy of the struggle of the oppressed people of South Africa and their liberation movement, by all possible means, for the seizure of power by the people."[31] This resolution was thus an open call for the use of violence, justified in this instance by the morality of the goal—the end of discrimination and the equality of all people, black and white. The challenger must thus convince other states that the status quo demands alteration because it is no longer morally justifiable.

Note again how very practical an instrument morality can be. The weak usually have few other weapons, and appeals to morality in states where public opinion is accessible to foreign persuasion can be effective. If the international system could be made to function according to moral principles, the inequality of power among states would not matter. It would even work to the advantage of the weak. Note also that the moral issues raised publicly in international forums and those not raised reflect political circumstances and, in international organizations, votes. The issue of the human rights of blacks in South Africa has been made an

---

[31] *The New York Times*, November 10, 1976.

international issue by black African states in the United Nations; the issue of the
human rights of black Africans in some black African states, the rulers of which
have hardly been among the world's leading respecters of the political and civil
rights of their subjects, has not been raised in the same forum. Black leaders do
not want to raise the issue of human rights in their own states, and they have
enough votes to prevent it.

Third, although we should not be surprised that states try to justify themselves, it would be a mistake to assume that "anything goes" just because officials
who decide specific policies stamp them "morally approved." The domestic principles of a state can and do act as restraints on its behavior. For example, many
Englishmen, as well as many people throughout the English-speaking world, disapproved of the British intervention at the Suez Canal in 1956 because they believed
colonialism no longer legitimate and the invasion of Egypt unjustifiable in an age
of nationalism. Similarly, many people in the United States—and in much of the
rest of the world—found American support of the Saigon regime in Vietnam
illegitimate; in that "civil war" the Hanoi leaders were widely identified with the
principle of national self-determination.

How could the democratic United States support an autocratic regime that
denied every democratic principle to which the United States professed commitment, in a war against those who were fighting for national unity and independence?
In addition, the often massive use of force against a small unindustrialized country—
on which the United States dropped more bombs than it had dropped on Germany
and Japan combined during World War II—seemed outrageous. The means used
to wage the war and the destruction wrought seemed to many excessive in the light
of the proclaimed moral purposes of the intervention. Both the ends and the means
of American policy in Vietnam were thus widely questioned.

These two examples demonstrate a growing normative restraint anchored
in the values of Western democratic societies, especially the principle of national
self-determination, in military confrontations between the first and third worlds.
The use of force in such conflicts, short of a clear threat to national security or
prestige, is now widely regarded as illegitimate in the West. Force, or the threat
of it, is justifiable only to ward off or respond to "aggression," that is, in clashes
between the first and second worlds. This more restricted definition of justifiable
force has not yet become rooted in either the communist states or the LDCs.

Note the different uses made of the principle of national self-determination.
The West has conceded to the Organization of Petroleum Exporting Countries
(OPEC) their *right*, individually and collectively, to deny the Western states access
to oil, an indispensable source of energy for many. OPEC can deny this access by
means of an embargo and, perhaps less provocatively, by means of restricted production. What would happen if Saudi Arabia did cut production? Even without
a sizable cut, the price increase in 1979 alone was almost 100 percent over an
already extremely high price. This rise ensured several years of little or no economic
growth in the industrial nations. But a Western use of force was ruled out. The
OPEC states knew that they could do anything short of final "strangulation" of the
West and "pushing the industrial West into sheer economic chaos."

In contrast, the Soviet Union is not restrained by the principle of self-determination. It does not regard this principle as virtually absolute. In the West, when this principle is violated, it is usually violated so clumsily (as in the American interventions in Cuba in 1961 and in Chile a decade later) and the violations receive so much bad publicity, that it is rarely attempted. It is not that Soviet leaders do not subscribe to national self-determination; rather, they simply do not recognize anti-Soviet self-determination. When Hungary in 1956 or Czechoslovakia in 1968 sought greater independence from Soviet control, the Red Army intervened. Self-determination was not viewed as the issue in the Kremlin; military intervention was justified by condemning these efforts at self-determination as "reactionary." The Soviet intervention in Afghanistan in late 1979 was justified as protecting that country's Marxist regime from alleged "counterrevolutionary forces." In fact, the regime was losing a civil war in which the United States was not involved at all. But many Muslim Afghans did not like the Marxist government. In fact, this intervention outside Russia's postwar sphere of influence in eastern Europe was a flagrant use of force for territorial expansion. The Soviet Union has justified recent interventions in Angola and Ethiopia, as well as in South Yemen across the Red Sea, by claiming that it has been supporting "national liberation" movements—even though, in Angola, for example, the nation had already received its independence from Portugal. When national self-determination can be invoked in the context of the anti-Western struggle—what Russian leaders call the "anti-imperialist" struggle—force is practicable.

Arthur Schlesinger, Jr. rather picturesquely remarked once that a nation's foreign policy is the face that it wears to the world, and, if this policy embodies values that appear incompatible with the nation's ideals, either the policy will lose public support and have to be abandoned, or the nation will have to toss its ideals overboard. A nation, like an individual, must in the final analysis be true to itself, or the "consequent moral schizophrenia is bound to convulse the homeland."[32] During the Cuban missile crisis in 1962, to cite only one example, when the President and his advisers were debating whether to attack or blockade the island, Robert Kennedy argued strongly against the former course on the grounds of American tradition. A surprise attack, which would kill thousands of Cuban civilians, seemed inconsistent with that tradition. The United States was not like Japan, and his brother, the president, was not a Tojo, who had launched the surprise attack on Pearl Harbor that had brought the United States into World War II. There were, of course, other reasons—"practical" ones—that helped the government to decide in favor of the blockade option, but the moral one was brought into the discussion and unquestioningly contributed to the decision. Note that the moral factor was also perceived by Robert Kennedy as politically beneficial. A surprise attack, he declared, "could not be undertaken by the U.S. if we were to maintain our moral position at home and around the globe. Our struggle against Communism throughout the world was far more than physical survival—it had as its essence our heritage and our ideals and these we must not destroy."[33]

---

[32] Arthur Schlesinger, Jr., "National Interests and Moral Absolutes" in Ernest W. Lefever, *Ethics and World Politics* (Baltimore: Johns Hopkins Press, 1972), p. 35.

[33] Robert E. Kennedy, *Thirteen Days* (New York: New American Library, 1968).

A nation, particularly a democratic nation, can on occasion thus find itself in a dilemma, caught between its values and its security interests, at least in terms of its immediate foreign policy. It is, after all, always easier to justify short-term deviations from the nation's values if it can be maintained that in the long run these deviations enhance those values. We noted earlier the tensions inherent in any American policy that, in the name of democracy, calls for alliance with undemocratic states in order to enhance American security. Similarly, but more shocking to many Americans, is the tension between the democratic ethos and security that has been revealed in a number of other ways: assassination plots by the Central Intelligence Agency (CIA) against foreign leaders, especially Castro, the overthrow of a legitimately elected government in Chile, and the "secret bombing" of Cambodia. The dilemma of making foreign policy in the face of conflicting pressures and values is finding a way to *enhance some of the principal objectives with minimum sacrifice of other equally important objectives.* As we asked earlier, in our analysis of competition among objectives, how does a state mix, and in what proportions, security and welfare; security, democracy, and individual liberty; and security and peace? The choice is *not* a simple choice between one or the other, between what is good and what is bad.

No more dramatic or tragic illustration of this dilemma could have occurred than the Iranian seizure of the American embassy in 1979. The shah, who had been both dictatorial and ruthless, had also been strongly pro-American. He had supported Egyptian President Sadat in his search for peace after 1973, and he had long supplied oil to Israel, even during the 1973 war. There is no question about the firm support that the United States had given to the shah over the years; in the early 1950s, the CIA had restored him to power after he had been forced to flee his country. Nor is there much doubt that the shah's secret police used torture or that his relatives and aides made millions of dollars. It was always clear that the shah was quite unpopular. American interests, however, were equally clear: control of the strategic Persian Gulf and plentiful supplies of oil. In 1979 Iranian oil constituted only 4 percent of American consumption, but the allies in Europe and Japan were principal consumers of Iranian oil.

Could there have been a bigger disaster for the United States and its allies than the shah's collapse? Oil prices shot up virtually 100 percent in one year because of reductions in Iranian oil supplies and the resulting tight world market. Egypt lost a staunch friend and now must buy its oil elsewhere; so must Israel, which feels even more insecure now that Iran is also militantly anti-Israel. Furthermore, the security of the Persian Gulf, which the United States had counted on the shah to guard, is now endangered by a zealous religious regime bent on fomenting an Islamic rebellion against the United States, including the overthrow of pro-Western Arab Muslim leaders in the oil kingdoms along the Persian Gulf. It is also questionable that the Iranians themselves are better off under this regime, which is bent upon restoring traditional customs. It has banned Western music, dance, and drink; has sought to crush all opposition; and has killed its enemies in ways all too reminiscent of the shah's own dictatorial rule. Modernization is falling by the wayside, the economy is in decline, and large-scale unemployment and inflation are growing worse. Furthermore, the government must devote a large part of its

506   energies to resisting forces of disintegration, as represented by the Kurds and other ethnic groups that are seeking autonomy. In view of these complexities, was American support for the shah "criminal"?[34]

If morality generally serves as a constraint on state behavior, despite the frequent dilemmas involved in moral choice, it can also result in "unrestraining" or unleashing foreign policy. One point in Kissinger's rebuttal to critics of his détente policy focused on attempts to transform Russia's domestic structure; Kissinger argued that the critics' attitude was counterproductive because it could result only in a stiffening of Soviet foreign policy, making it less flexible and less amenable to compromise and raising international tensions. Kissinger might have elaborated this argument by suggesting that it was precisely this type of attitude that had led in the past to a crusading style.[35] For an attempt to impose moral values on another state means that conflicts among states become transformed from conflicts of interest, which may be resolvable through hard bargaining, to conflicts of moral philosophies, between good and evil, which tend not to be resolvable peacefully. Viewing the international arena as one in which St. George must always be slaying dragons leads to a complete misunderstanding of the nature of international politics. Instead of a method by which to analyze the behavior of states in terms of their sense of insecurity, their legitimate interests and aspirations, the great difficulties involved in coexisting, and their common and conflicting interests, politics among nations becomes a matter of virtue and vice, in which purity is to vanquish villainy. And, if the struggle among states is viewed as a struggle between right and wrong, those who *know* that they are right all too often become zealots and crusaders. Like a religious fanatic, a state convinced that it represents morality easily and rapidly strikes poses of absolutism and self-righteousness.

Translated into foreign policy—as postwar American foreign policy has amply demonstrated—such moralism has several undesirable results, two of which are failure to recognize other governments because of moral disapproval and unwillingness to meet with adversaries to reconcile conflicting interests. ("One does not compromise with the devil"—to do so would be to become tainted oneself.) In addition, states that view themselves as moral arbiters also exhibit a crusading spirit in peace and war, which makes it difficult for their governments to distinguish between vital and secondary interests and may even entice them into disputes that involve only peripheral interests (as in the American intervention in Vietnam). Finally, a nation imbued with the crusading spirit is likely to transform war into total war, to seek the unconditional surrender of the infidel. Crusaders remain oblivious to the fact that total military victory may make a postwar balance of power much more difficult to attain. Moralism thus not only results in misunderstanding of international politics but, when applied to policy, also guides it on a course that in most instances will be detrimental to the state's own interests. Countries in which fanaticism has led to rigidity and self-righteousness are intolerant of other

---

[34.] If so, most of the world's leaders can be called "criminal," for few have not supported regimes that have jailed domestic opponents and violated human rights. Indeed, many rule their own countries in this manner.

[35.] See Chapter 13 for a discussion of national styles.

countries; coexistence with them—the minimal basis for peace—then becomes very difficult, if not impossible. Zeal and peace are virtually mutually exclusive, for zeal gives rise to intervention in order to reshape and reform other states. Do democratic states have a moral mandate to remake other states in their own images? Indeed, can any state really expect—should it have the right to expect—to do more than influence the external behavior of another state when the latter impinges on its interests? Is foreign policy to be a barometer for virtuous attitudes? In international politics it may be less important to create moral norms for governing the relations among states than to temper moral self-righteousness and moralizing!

In a world composed of many nations, then, there are many different historical traditions, philosophies, ideologies, and political and moral standards. There is little consensus among countries on what is moral and immoral, good and bad. Let us refer again to the LDCs' claim that the industrialized West has a moral duty to help them eliminate the inequalities and injustices of international life that keep them poor. To limit ourselves to only one aspect of this issue, we can ask, are the non-Western states poor *because* of past colonial rule and the extraction of their natural resources at low cost? If they are, perhaps the former colonial countries do owe reparations to their former colonies. But the fact is that many states like Tanzania were not only not states but were also poor before Western colonialism. Whatever economic progress they have made—indeed, their very search for modernization—is because of the impact of Western ideas, capital, technology, and enterprise. The colonial states extracted copper or tea, but they also founded the mines and plantations, and it was Western industrialization and demand that gave economic value to their products. The non-Western states now stress nationalism and the right to self-determination, economic development and the welfare society, all values reflecting those of the Western colonial states that brought these values with them. There is no reason to believe the LDCs' claim that they would have improved their standard of living on their own but for the exploitation of colonialism; the very idea of progress has been inherited from colonial days.

The most backward third-world countries are those that have not had any or much contact with the industrial West. The most advanced—whether the standard of measurement be literacy, life expectancy, economic wealth, or the presence of modern industry—are former colonies with extensive economic links to the West. Not that poverty does not continue to exist throughout the less-developed areas. What is questionable is that poverty exists solely or mainly *because* of past colonialism.[36] Many Western industrial states therefore reject the idea that the underdeveloped nations have a moral claim on their treasuries. Richard Cooper, Undersecretary of State for Economic Affairs in the Carter administration, has complicated this question of exploitation even further. In those instances in which living standards have declined, rather than risen, as a result of Western contacts, he has argued, the decline has resulted principally from rapid population growth. This growth directly reflects the introduction of Western medicine and standards

---

[36.] Richard N. Cooper, "A New International Economic Order for Mutual Gain," *Foreign Policy,* Spring 1977, pp. 81–86.

508   of sanitation (Cooper cites the population of the Indonesian island of Java, which increased from 4.5 million to 63 million between 1815 and 1960, an increase of fourteen times, while the population of England increased only five or six times.[37]) Is the West therefore responsible for poverty resulting from larger populations? Should it not have introduced modern medicine? And, we may ask, next time there is a food shortage in the underdeveloped world, should the industrial West allow starvation in order to bring population, food, and other resources back into balance? Or would that course be immoral, even though the additional population will hamper efforts at modernization even further?

      Indeed, the question is even more complex because the governments of underdeveloped countries often pursue policies *after* independence that are highly inefficient. President Nyerere of Tanzania, who has claimed that his country—like other third-world countries—is poor because the West is rich, has forgotten that Tanzania was always poor and probably would be poorer still today had it not been for British colonial rule; furthermore, his government, unlike that of his relatively well-to-do neighbor Kenya, has chosen to pursue a policy hostile to private enterprise. Although drought and higher oil prices are partially responsible, governmental policy has also played a role in reducing the per capita agricultural yield. In Uganda, former president Amin's policy of driving out the Asians, who had lived in the country for generations and constituted its business community, helped shatter that nation's economy. Algeria, one of the third world's more radical states and one of the OPEC members annually seeking high price increases for oil, was once an exporter of wheat. Seventeen years after independence, it imports more than two thirds of its domestically consumed cereals, paying for them with two thirds of its earnings from oil and natural gas.[38] Governments are not always blameless for their countries' poverty; although many LDCs do face problems in earning their keep and being able to modernize, the domestic policies they pursue frequently contribute to their continued lack of economic progress.

      Moral questions and claims, then, may be simple to put forth, but they are not simple to answer. Moral judgments that seem at first glance easy often turn out not to be clear-cut. Furthermore, what one party calls moral is not necessarily moral to another. There are no universal standards of morality or of justice. This lack of agreement in turn reflects the decentralized nature of the state system. There do not, then, appear to be systemic or external solutions to security problems in the state system. But what about internal solutions? Can state behavior not become more restrained and responsible as a result of changes *within* states?

[37.] *Ibid.*, pp. 86–87.

[38.] John P. Entelis, "Algeria, Myth and Reality," *The New York Times*, December 1, 1979, p. 21.

18

Modernization, Misperceptions, and the Prospects for Peace

HOMOGENEITY AND MODERNIZATION

When there are so many states with different political, economic, and ideological arrangements, it is perhaps not too surprising that another frequently suggested solution to international conflict and the security dilemma is conversion of all states to a single set of arrangements. A state system whose members are all homogeneous—sharing the same types of political, social, and economic arrangements—is said to be a peaceful one. After the French Revolution in 1789, for example, democrats, assuming that power politics is the offspring of selfish princes and that "the people" who have to fight and die are essentially peaceful, insisted that harmony among states and peace would follow once the small group of European rulers who had profited from a system composed of aristocratic states had been overthrown. After the Bolshevik Revolution, the communist leaders believed that, once the minority of capitalists in the Western states had been overthrown, and private property and the profit motive eliminated, the people would no longer be exploited and made to fight for their rulers' benefit. There would then no longer be any reason for hostilities among states. Leon Trotsky, the new Foreign Commissar, claimed that he had taken the job so that he would have more time for his Party activities; all he had to do was to publish the secret treaties signed by the czarist regime and call for the poor and the downtrodden everywhere to rise up in revolt.[1] Then he could close the Foreign

---

[1] Edward Hallett Carr, *The Bolshevik Revolution, 1917–1923* (London:Macmillan, 1953), p. 16.

510 Office—permanently! "Rulers bad, people good," seems a common diagnosis of the ills of the world; "all power to the people," or at least to their representatives— usually self-proclaimed, rather than elected—appears to be the prescribed remedy. A world of democracies (or of communist states) is thus expected to be a peaceful world.

Modernization has sometimes been advanced, at least implicitly, as the contemporary Western remedy for the diversity of social structures and political and economic systems. Former presidential adviser W. W. Rostow has suggested that states, like individuals, pass through certain "stages of growth" as they mature. These stages include the traditional society, whose economy is agrarian and static; the pretakeoff phase, in which economic growth begins; the takeoff phase, in which economic development becomes a continuing matter; maturity, in which the economy is diversified; high mass consumption; and, finally a post-mass-consumption phase, in which economic and quantitative concerns give way to a greater focus on the quality of individual and social life.

Rostow has argued that, in the first two stages, states are not yet strong enough to resort to war. But, during the transition from traditional, socially fragmented society to a modern urban-industrial society, political leaders tend to invoke nationalism. And nationalism tends to give rise to regional aggression.

> Historically, it has proved extremely tempting for a part of the new nationalism to be diverted on to external objectives, notably if these objectives looked to be accessible at little real cost or risk. These early aggressive exercises were generally limited in objective, aimed at territories close to the new nation's own borders— within its region—rather than directly at the balance of Eurasian power: thus, the American effort to steal Canada during the French wars; Bismarck's neat military operations against Denmark, Austria, and France from 1864 to 1871; the Japanese acquisition of primacy in Korea in 1895; and the Russian drive through Manchuria to Vladivostok, leading to the test of strength with resurgent Japan in 1904–5.[2]

The modern version of such "bloody shirt" politics is viewed as a product of the need to enhance national cohesion for the purpose of modernization and is found among the charismatic first-generation leaders of independence movements. Rostow advises us to be reasonably cheerful about this stage of development, for in the past external adventures have given way as the task of modernizing the economy and society absorbed more time and energy. He thus provides us with a certain historical perspective on our age. The behavior of some of the new nations is to be viewed as merely part of a transitional phase.

Of course, even when this phase has passed, peace will not be guaranteed. During the takeoff phase, the state's resources will still be relatively limited, and expansion will therefore tend to be only regional. But, once a state has become industrially developed and powerful, it can, if it chooses, pursue far greater expansion. Germany, Japan, and Russia chose such a course, even though the high

---

[2] For the effects of economic growth on society, see W. W. Rostow, *The Stages of Economic Growth* (Cambridge, Eng.: Cambridge University Press, 1960), p. 113; and Rostow, *Politics and the Stages of Growth* (Cambridge, Eng.: Cambridge University Press, 1971).

mass-consumption phase is supposed to impose a certain uniformity on the principal states and make the world less prone to war. Domestic preoccupations and affluence are supposed to be the society's chief concerns, in that stage, not foreign policy and war. Values, too, are supposed to change. During this stage, human beings are no longer regarded as objects of exploitation or aggression; the emphasis is on dignity and welfare.

In this context, according to Rostow in 1960 when he wrote his book on the stages of economic growth, Russia was a nation about to make a choice between world primacy and high mass consumption. In essence, he declared, "Communism is likely to wither in the age of high mass consumption."[3] Soviet foreign policy would once more become *Russian* foreign policy as the Russian people become preoccupied with their material comforts and the missionary ideology eroded. Revolutionary proclamations would become merely routine declarations of an increasingly irrelevant liturgy; rhetoric aside, however, the Soviet Union would actually be undergoing transformation into a typical nation-state, concerned more with the protection of Russian *national* interests than with the advancement of communist interests. With the "end of ideology," the revolutionary refusal to recognize the right of states to enjoy different social and political persuasions would end as well. Russia would take its rightful place in the state system, a system that it would now regard as legitimate. But, according to this logic, not only Russia and other militant communist states but also the new, economically less developed states would join the ranks of well-behaved states bent on maintaining the international system, as the emerging nationalism of earlier days was transformed into mature, cooperative nationalism coupled with successful modernization.

It has seemed, then, that the relationship between economic and political development would be most significant in shaping the world of the future. The problem, however, is that no one really knows much about this relationship. The few attempts at propounding theories of modernization have been based largely upon Western experience, and, because the United States and England have been posited as models of modern systems, there has been a certain circularity in these arguments. These two nations have been *the* most highly developed societies—politically, economically, and socially. They have served as examples that other nations could—and supposedly would—imitate if they wanted to become modern, affluent societies. It is questionable, however, that these two Western societies can usefully serve as models for the rest of the world.

Some of the models of modernization rather ironically reflect non-Marxist versions of economic determinism. Whereas Marxism predicts that capitalism will be replaced by socialism and the dictatorship of the proletariat, a more contemporary thesis is that totalitarian rule by the self-proclaimed vanguard of the working class will be replaced by more liberal institutions. Proponents of each claim that peace will follow the replacement or erosion of the old regime. They share not only a common conclusion but also common assumptions: that economic and technological factors make their own demands and that the industrial way of life molds society accordingly. Presumably the processes of industrialization blur differences

---

[3.] Rostow, *Stages of Economic Growth*, p. 133.

512   in political structures, historical experiences, and cultural values and produce similar political systems.

But that all industrialized and urbanized societies are indeed so similar that they can be embraced by the concept of "modern society" is unclear. The United States and Russia, for example, are unlikely to "converge" and become virtually identical societies.[4] The historical development of nations remains a key factor, and economic growth will not automatically create a homogeneous world. The state system will continue to be characterized by diversity, though, even if it were not, current relations among communist states—like past relations among Greek city-states or the dynastic states of Europe before the French Revolution—would cast doubt on the assumption that peace is likely among similar states.

Perhaps most misleading is the notion, often unspoken, that at the end of the process of development stands a democratic society. In a way, this expectation may not seem unreasonable. Western states have not always been democratic, and we know from history that only among "people of plenty"—when "plenty" is distributed reasonably equitably among most classes or sections of society—can democracy flourish. In comparison, the absence of a middle class and the existence of social imbalance between the privileged few and the deprived majority provide ideal breeding grounds for political instability and revolution. Nevertheless, inherent in this line of thinking are the characteristic modern Western association of economic development with the growth of the middle class and democratic institutions and the connection of democracy with peaceful behavior. Yet we also know from the examples of Germany and Japan that modernization does not by itself produce political democracy; rather, it can strengthen semifeudal authoritarian systems. In the United States the term "grass-roots democracy" is still current—referring to the agrarian origins of American democracy. Modernization may have strengthened this democratic system, but it did not produce it. Democratic institutions and political culture have not evolved *since* industrialization *because of* industrialization. In countries that had not already developed traditions of limited government, industrialization has not created such traditions and the associated liberal values. If a nation already had a constitutional tradition when the modernization process started, that tradition has been strengthened. The key, then, is not economic growth but the political traditions and norms already existing. Neither economic growth nor homogenization is therefore likely to help resolve international political conflicts.

MISPERCEPTION AND CONFLICT RESOLUTION

Responsible political and bureaucratic leaders, as we saw in our analyses of style and decision making, play the principal roles in policy formulation and implementation. Of particular importance are the images of the external world and of

---

[4.] For a comparative study of these two countries and an evaluation of the possibilities of "convergence," see Zbigniew K. Brzezinski and Samuel P. Huntington, *Political Power: USA/USSR* (New York: Viking, 1964).

national aims and roles in the international system held by the nation's chief decision makers and key advisers. No issue has done more than the Vietnam war to spotlight this issue of how principal decision makers view the world beyond their own national boundaries. President Johnson was called a "cold warrior." Because of his anticommunism, he perceived the world—especially the communist world— through distorted lenses and therefore pursued policies unsuited to the contemporary world. One observer noted at the end of the Johnson administration that "The deficiencies of American foreign policy, epitomized by Vietnam but evident in events in many other parts of the world, result from faulty modes of thought rather than from defects of personality or errors of execution." Washington's leaders were still living on the "intellectual capital" accumulated in 1947, even though "these policies have become obsolete, and the United States has been unable to devise new policies capable of dealing successfully with the issues of a different age."[5] Correct perception of the fragmentation of the communist nations and of the nature of the war in South Vietnam would presumably have resulted in more accurate assessments of American interests in Vietnam, which in turn would have precluded massive intervention in 1965.

Obviously misperceptions do play a role in a nation's foreign policies. Khrushchev badly miscalculated President Kennedy's determination when he placed missiles in Cuba; President Truman and Secretary of State Acheson were unable to understand the position of Communist China's new leadership in 1950 and to see that the latter might view the advance of American troops in North Korea toward China's border as threatening to its security. Kennedy sent the first advisers to South Vietnam and escalated American involvement and prestige. We can multiply such examples. Perhaps the most famous and interesting was that of the bombing of Pearl Harbor in 1941. The American government, and especially the army and navy commands in Pearl Harbor, which had received war warnings from Washington and should have been on the alert and taken other appropriate steps, could not believe that the Japanese would be so foolish as to attack the United States. America was the stronger nation, and war would certainly result in Japan's defeat. Why should Japan not therefore concentrate on expanding into Southeast Asia, picking up the pieces of empires belonging to the European powers that had just been defeated by Germany or were still preoccupied with fighting Germany? Such expansion would be a high-gain, minimal-risk strategy. In fact, the Japanese did expand into Southeast Asia. But they also attacked Pearl Harbor, because they assumed, first, that the United States would oppose their expansion and, second, that, if they sank the American battle fleet they could conquer all East Asia (including China) before the navy could be rebuilt. The United States, faced with a *fait accompli* and an offer of peace, would then have to accept. This miscalculation was eventually disastrous for Japan.

It is one thing, however, to argue that misperceptions lead to errors of policy, even grave errors on occasion; it is quite another to claim that misperceptions are *the* cause of international conflicts and tensions. The latter approach strongly

---

[5.] Hans J. Morgenthau, *A New Foreign Policy for the United States* (New York: Holt, Rinehart and Winston, 1969), pp. vii, 3.

514   suggests that *conflicts among states have no "real" causes and would be resolvable if policy makers would only correct their misperceptions. Much of this thinking betrays a strong normative bias. If only policy makers perceived each other correctly, there would be peace and relative harmony in the world.*

Ralph K. White is typical of this school of thought. "Misperceptions might explain how normally sane human beings can unwittingly, without intending the consequences, involve themselves step by step in actions that lead to war."[6] War is thus considered to erupt only as the result of mistakes. Misperceptions or distorted "cognitive maps" seem to provide the only sensible explanation of why states continue to resort to warfare when the world "desperately wants to avoid it" and "only a madman could start a war." White, indeed, has entitled the opening chapter of his book "Misperceptions as a Cause of Two World Wars," suggesting that the two most significant twentieth-century wars resulted from mistakes and that the world would have been better off had they not occurred. (In 1939 E. H. Carr wrote that this view, though characteristically Anglo-Saxon, would come as news to Czechs and Poles, who owed their national existence to World War I; to the French, who had regained Alsace-Lorraine in 1918; and to the Germans, who had regretted only that they had lost World War I, not that they had entered it.)[7] Misperceptions of reality, White stresses, can result from any of six kinds of distorted thinking:

1. The image of a diabolical enemy

2. A virile self-image

3. A moral self-image

4. Selective inattention

5. Absence of empathy

6. Military overconfidence[8]

These six distortions involve black-and-white thinking in which consciously or unconsciously, evidence is distorted, facts selected to fit preconceived images, and the interpretation of events slanted. Such "irrational" thinking is supposedly what creates "unnecessary wars." White admits that not all wars do result from irrationality and that not all devils are imaginary; some "semimad semidevils" are dangerous and must therefore be restrained. And analysts may sometimes, by means of "realistic, evidence-oriented thinking," rather than "biased thinking," arrive at a genuine black-and-white picture. As all perception is selective, however, how can we tell when our perceptions are correct and when they are distorted? Winston Churchill was right in his view of Nazi Germany in the 1930s, but few in England shared that view; the logical conclusion to his thinking, after all, meant risking war with Germany. Neville Chamberlain's view seemed far more reasonable; satisfying

---

[6] Ralph K. White, *Nobody Wanted War* (Garden City, N.Y.: Doubleday 1968), p. 3.

[7] Carr, *The Twenty Years' Crisis 1919–1939* (New York: Macmillan, 1961), pp. 51–52.

[8] White, *op. cit.*, p. 6.

Hitler's legitimate nationalistic aims would make it possible to avoid war. Had White written in 1935–1938, one suspects that he would have found Churchill's thinking "irrational" and that of Chamberlain realistic and reasonable. In any event, hindsight has made it clear that Chamberlain was grievously wrong; if only the prime minister had possessed the correct perception of the Nazi regime and risked war! But the major emphasis of the literature on misperception is the opposite: *misperception has led to conflict and war, whereas correct perception has prevented strife.*

For more recent examples we need only study two prominent postwar American statesmen. In a biography of Dean Acheson, one of two distinguished secretaries of state who served President Truman, Gaddis Smith has argued that the assumptions underlying Acheson's thought and policy advice were "an extraordinarily articulate expression of thoughts which guided American foreign policy for a third of a century after outbreak of the Second World War. An appraisal of Acheson must therefore be an appraisal of the nation's behavior in world affairs for an entire generation."[9] In Smith's interpretation, Acheson's general image of the world and what ought to be the American role in it was shared by other secretaries of state, including his successor, John Foster Dulles, and such later presidents as Eisenhower, Kennedy, Johnson, and Nixon. All were heavily influenced by their generation's experiences and perceptions. Postwar American leaders had been tempered in the crucible of the 1930s; the career of Hitler and the appeasement at Munich, as well as the Nazi-Soviet pact, had made deep impressions on them. More specifically, one lesson that the generation thought it had learned from the interwar period was that the American isolationist stance had helped to bring on World War II and that American participation in western European defense after World War I would have helped to deter Hitler. Isolationism therefore no longer seemed a feasible policy; expansionistic totalitarian movements, whether Nazi or Soviet, had to be contained. A second lesson was that appeasement only whets a dictator's appetite; it seemed better to stand firm against his demands and to "present arms." Soviet policy was expansionist and aggressive and had to be resisted, by force if necessary. "Driven by the ghost of Hitler,"[10] by memories of failure to understand the enemy's point of view, of concessions made from a position of weakness, and of failure to match the adversary's military strength, this generation had learned that "peace cannot be preserved by good intentions and a small army." Acheson therefore approached American-Soviet relations as a deadly contest in which a gain in power for the United States was good, a gain for the Soviet Union bad. Negotiations with the devil were to be avoided. Soviet totalitarianism had to be contained and its expansionist attempts dammed, until some day it would inevitably mellow. Inflexible American policies, distrust of all Russian and other communist states' aims and interests, and inability to recognize the diversity within the communist world were purportedly the results, as was the unnecessary continuation of the Cold War.[11]

---

[9] Gaddis Smith, *Dean Acheson* (New York: Cooper Square, 1972), p. 414.

[10] *Ibid.*, p. 423.

[11] Smith, "The Shadow of John Foster Dulles," *Foreign Affairs*, January 1974, pp. 403–408.

516   Whereas analysts like Smith have attributed misperceptions to drawing the wrong lessons from history, others like Townsend Hoopes and Ole Holsti have attributed them to other factors. In focusing on Acheson's successor, Secretary of State Dulles, they have emphasized his rigid personality and his equally inflexible anticommunist view. That point of view has been well summed up by a British ambassador to Washington during the Dulles period:

> Three or four centuries ago . . . it was not rare to encounter men of the type of Dulles. Like them, in vigorous and systematic reflection, he had come to un-shakeable convictions of a religious and theological order. Like them, he saw the world as an arena in which the forces of good and evil were continuously at war. Like them, he believed that this was the contest which supremely mattered.[12]

Hoopes entitled his biography of the secretary *The Devil and John Foster Dulles*.[13] Communism, of course, was the devil. Since he was not to be given his due, Dulles pursued a rigid anticommunist policy, resisting negotiations and a search for accommodation. Hoopes' biography criticizes the "tenacious continuity" of American foreign policy at a time of changing external and internal conditions, which "cried out" for a "searching reappraisal" of the assumptions underlying that policy. If only Eisenhower, Hoopes has regretfully complained, had not been so seriously ill during much of his second term and had taken charge of the nation's foreign policy, détente might have been achieved earlier, for the president's instincts were more conciliatory, and he had a broader perspective and a better sense of proportion about American interests and broader global needs. (Hoopes assumes, without offering any proof, that Dulles did not faithfully represent the president's policy preferences.)

          In a behavioral analysis, with conclusions not very different from those of Hoopes, political scientist Holsti has argued that Dulles drew a distinction between the Russian state and the governing Communist party, between Russian national interests and Marxist-Leninist ideology with its universal revolutionary goals, and between the Russian people and Soviet leaders. The consequence of these distinctions, Holsti claims, was that in Dulles' mind the American quarrel was with the Soviet leaders, whose aims reached beyond legitimate and limited Russian interests; the United States had no conflict with the Russian people, who, had they been represented by a democratic, rather than a totalitarian, government, would have followed only limited national interests, rather than global expansionism. This expansionism was, in Dulles' view, the cause of the Cold War. The United States had to prevent the expansion of "atheistic communism" and be constantly on guard against communist attempts to lull the West.

          Given Dulles' black and white image of the world—and this is of central importance to the misperception approach—all incoming information had to be

---

[12] Quoted by Ole R. Holsti, "Cognitive Dynamics and Images of the Enemy: Dulles and Russia," in Holsti *et. al.*, *Enemies in Politics* (Chicago: Rand McNally, 1967), p. 37.

[13] Townsend Hoopes, *The Devil and John Foster Dulles* (Boston: Atlantic/Little, Brown, 1973).

filtered through his particular perceptions; what fitted his preconceived image was accepted, and what did not fit was filtered out. The image thus remained intact. "Psychologic" is the term sometimes used to describe this tendency to see what we want to see and to reject contrary evidence; psychologists call it a "reduction of cognitive dissonance." The consequence, Holsti argues from Dulles' public statements, is that various Soviet pronouncements and moves, including a major reduction in the size of the Red Army during Dulles' tenure as secretary of state, were not recognized as possible concessions and attempts to relax tensions. They served only to reinforce Dulles' preexisting picture of Soviet Russia and were interpreted as signs of Soviet weakness, attempts to win a respite in order to recoup strength for a more effective and successful future struggle with capitalism. A more flexible, less suspicious personality, Holsti has suggested, might have been more receptive to new and conflicting information and presumably would have made more serious and sustained efforts to test Soviet intentions and perhaps to bring about what is now popularly known as détente.

John Stoessinger has made the same point in different terms. Statesmen like Dulles are crusaders. Policy is the product of missionary zeal to eliminate evil from the world and to transform the world itself into a better and more peaceful place. The crusader bases his or her decisions not on experience but on ideological views dogmatically interpreted and tenaciously held. In contrast, the pragmatist is guided by his or her experience and is flexible in policy making. Unlike the crusader, the latter encourages advisers to state opposing views to test his or her own and is quite willing to change a point of view and policy if criticisms seem warranted and his or her own convictions not as sound as they had seemed initially. (Of course, Stoessinger has assumed that policy makers can be neatly categorized as essentially one or the other of these two types.)[14]

Sometimes, instead of attributing misperceptions to individual leaders' images or personalities, analysts attribute them to nations as a whole. Nations, claims John Stoessinger in another book, "live in darkness." Great gaps appear between image and reality as they respond not to realities but to fictions—what Fulbright called "myths"—that they themselves have created. "[G]reat nations struggle not only with each other, but also with their perceptions of each other."[15] These misperceptions are not easily changed. As in pluralistic decision making, with its incremental development of policy, change comes mainly after disasters like the Vietnam war; only at such moments are old perceptions and policies reexamined. In the absence of disaster, however, Chinese, American, and Russian self-images and images of one another and other states remain intact. Clearly, nations are in need of "light."

One popular version of this theme is that of the "mirror image:"[16] two

---

[14] John Stoessinger, *Crusaders and Pragmatists* (New York: Norton, 1979), especially pp. xiii–xvii.

[15] Stoessinger, *Nations in Darkness* (New York: Random House, 1971), p. 5, and Stoessinger, *Why Nations Go to War* (New York: St. Martin's Press, 1974).

[16] White, "Images in the Context of International Conflict," in Herbert C. Kelman *et al.*, eds., *International Behavior: A Social-Psychological Analysis* (New York: Holt, Rinehart and Winston, 1965), pp. 238–275.

518   adversaries find it impossible to resolve an arms race, for example, because they bring to the negotiating table the distrust and fear that they have acquired as opponents. Each has come to believe that it represents wisdom, virtue, and morality and that the other is the embodiment of evil seeking its destruction. The United States views the Soviet Union as a communist dictatorship that exploits the masses at home and is bent on a global crusade for communism. The Soviet Union is equally convinced that the United States is a dictatorship of the bourgeoisie that has enslaved the proletarian majority and seeks to export capitalism by force. Americans, of course, know how false this image of the United States is. At the same time, the Soviets claim that they do not exploit their masses, that the austerity of the period of intensive industrialization is being replaced by increased attention to the welfare of Soviet citizens, and that in international politics they seek only to be left alone to complete their industrialization. Their large armies and powerful rockets are needed only because of the threat of American attack (paralleling the American claim that military forces are needed only to deter Soviet attack). On the basis of these distorted images, then, both act belligerently, thus bringing the world to the precipice of utter destruction—and for no "sane" reason.

As Erich Fromm has said, each side views the other "pathologically"—in terms of paranoia, projection, fanaticism, and Orwellian "doublethink."[17] Fromm and others think of war and peace in terms of individual psychology and see war as a deviation comparable to personal psychotic behavior. In such a framework, there is no objective reason for conflict, which exists only because of distorted perceptions, unhealthy attitudes, and outmoded ways of thinking.[18] If only political leaders would abandon such "dysfunctional" thinking, nations would no longer misperceive one another; they would then see one another as defensively oriented, harboring no expansionist aims, possessing only peaceful intentions.

Sometimes it seems that peace is not simply a matter of correct vision but also a matter of mental health. Some political analysts, in fact, have tried to psychoanalyze leading personalities like President Woodrow Wilson; the first secretary of defense after World War II, James Forrestal, who committed suicide; and President Nixon. In the process they have found personality traits that may have adversely affected these figures' conduct in office. We are all aware that among policy makers, as among the rest of us, there are normal amounts of hostilities, repressed urges, and anxieties that could be expressed in policy. It is not surprising, therefore, that one psychologist, after noting that many Nazi leaders could be professionally diagnosed as mentally ill, suggested that a person entrusted with domestic or international leadership should first undergo psychological tests; such tests, designed to separate the normal from the maladjusted, would be devised and administered by a group of psychiatrists and clinical psychologists in order to minimize the possibility of error.[19] If the president and other leaders have personal

---

[17] Erich Fromm, *May Man Prevail?* (New York: Doubleday, 1961).

[18] For an analysis of alleged distorted American perceptions of the Soviet Union and an attack upon the foundations of "realist" thinking, see Anatol Rapoport, *The Big Two: Soviet-American Perceptions of Foreign Policy* (New York: Pegasus, 1971).

[19] Otto Klineberg, *The Human Dimension in International Relations* (New York: Holt, Rinehart and Winston, 1964), pp. 65–66.

physicians on their staffs to take care of their physical health, why not psychiatrists to watch over their mental health as well? Rulers ought to be "psychologically disarmed" if we are all to remain safe and sane. It has been seriously suggested in this connection that new drugs capable of controlling emotions and aggressive behavior might, indeed, prove helpful as a supplementary device for curbing leaders' hostile impulses.

The problem with this solution is threefold. First, in many instances psychiatrists differ among themselves; who, then would psychoanalyze the psychiatrists, not only to ensure that *they* were of "sound" mind and "reasonable" judgment but also to determine *which* opinions were "correct"? How can the citizens of a nation be assured that the psychiatrists' judgments about their leaders' psychological fitness and characters are valid and reliable, not simply expressions of personal political preferences disguised as expert opinions; nuclear scientists have often expressed individual political views when requested to give objective, technical advice on arms control issues. Even if the psychiatrists could keep their political biases out of their professional opinions, however, it would have to be asked not only whether or not a leader suffered from a current mental or character deficiency but also whether or not he or she was likely to develop one in the future. What risk of a future mental breakdown or character flaw could be regarded as acceptable before a leader could be certified as fit for office?[20]

Second, it is one thing to psychoanalyze a historical figure at a distance—a hazardous undertaking in itself—and quite another to conclude that his or her mental state negatively affected the formulation of objectives and the choice of means for achieving them. Stalin may have been paranoid, as Khrushchev claimed, but in his behavior he was hardly rash or prone to disastrous miscalculation; when he did miscalculate, his errors were those that *any* policy maker might have made. Indeed, even though, as outside observers we may be tempted to label Stalin's fantastic suspicion of other states as paranoid, ordinary intelligence cautions us: Did his policies reflect a personality problem, the ideological perspective through which he perceived the United States as an enemy, the totalitarian system in which he held absolute power yet continuously feared being overthrown, or the natural suspicion of any ruler aware of the nature of the state system and of Russian history? Stalin may have had a distorted image of the United States, but his misperception was not necessarily the offspring of a sick personality.

Third, the idea of mentally sanitizing leaders, perhaps by coming up with a character profile—as James Barber's fourfold typology of presidential character—in order to eliminate those who do not fit it from even being nominated for office, smacks of Plato's exclusion from government of all those who are incorrectly trained. But do psychiatry and behavioral engineering really have better answers to the problem of power than, for example, those given by political theorists throughout the ages or by the American Founding Fathers, who relied upon balancing competing interests, parties, and institutions? Participation of contending groups in the

---

[20] Alexander L. George, "Assessing Presidential Character," *World Politics*, January 1974, p. 237, a review essay on James D. Barber, *The Presidential Character: Predicting Performance in the White House* (Englewood Cliffs, N.J.: Prentice-Hall, 1972).

520   policy process tends to reduce, if not to eliminate, views that reflect compelling personal needs. Even if an important policy maker holds opinions based upon extremely distorted perceptions, it is unlikely that these views will prevail in continued confrontation with more "realistic" policy prescriptions. "Insofar as a decision is made within a group context in which the individual's decision or attitude is visible to others, the opportunity for a decision or attitude to perform personality-oriented functions will be limited."[21] Although there is no guarantee that what Irving Janis has called "groupthink"[22]—a unified policy position that emerges after insufficient consideration of alternative policy options—will not occur, it need not occur and can be guarded against, as presidents like Franklin Roosevelt, Kennedy (especially during the Cuban missile crisis), and Nixon have repeatedly demonstrated.

Some of these comments are especially applicable to decision making in crises, in which, as we have seen, the president becomes the preeminent decision maker. Personal disorders or misperceptions should, if present, make themselves felt then, if ever. In the Cuban missile crisis case, the Kennedy administration had a number of options: to do nothing, to protest at the United Nations, to arrange a blockade, or to undertake an air strike or an invasion. Although the blockade was finally chosen, the air strike had been recommended by a number of the president's advisers, who, upon further consideration, then changed their minds. All the alternative courses of action were carefully sifted. Indeed, to promote the frankest possible discussion, the president absented himself from many of the discussions, for his presence and opinions tended to stifle opposing or critical views. Such collective decision making tends to filter out distortions of perception and irrational judgments. The very urgency of the decision and the catastrophic consequences of a wrong decision, are incentives to the policy makers to do so. Clearly, in the Cuban crisis time was the important variable. Had the decision been made in a great hurry, it might well have been the wrong one. For example, an air strike might have killed Russians, humiliating Khrushchev and compelling him to avenge Russian honor. But, even had the decision been made more quickly than it was and even had it been a disastrously wrong decision, we still could not say that the hostility and grossly distorted perceptions of some policy makers had been *the* cause. Among the multiple factors that account for a given decision, how does the outside observer assess the weight to be given to any single factor? Why, for example, should personality needs be considered decisive?

Even as powerful and dominant a policy maker as Henry Kissinger—of whom a wit has said that he was served by two presidents—could hardly express his personal needs through policy decisions, although much has been made of his youth in Nazi Germany. But the policy of détente was not new; it was a continuation

---

[21] Sidney Verba, "Assumptions of Rationality and Non-Rationality in Models of the International System," *World Politics*, October 1961, p. 103.

[22] Irving L. Janis, *Victims of Groupthink* (Boston: Houghton Mifflin, 1972). See George, "The Case of Multiple Advocacy in Making Foreign Policy," and *Presidential Decisionmaking in Foreign Policy* (Boulder: Westview, 1979); and I. M. Destler, *Presidents, Bureaucrats and Foreign Policy* (Princeton: Princeton University Press, 1972), for analyses of how "groupthink" can be avoided.

of policy initiated after the Cuban missile crisis as the United States and the Soviet Union turned increasingly from confrontation and competition to cooperation on certain issues—for example, arms control. Nixon and Kissinger accentuated and broadened the scope of this policy. However, their policies were bounded to a large degree by what Congress and the public were willing to tolerate. A policy of détente with Russia and rapprochement with China was made almost necessary by the many years of fighting and frustration in Vietnam. Even in Vietnam the only option was to leave; although the administration won time by reducing American participation in the ground war and lowering the attendant casualty rate, it never had the choice of continuing to wage a vigorous war with primarily American ground forces.

In an institutional and political environment that encourages competition of views, the effects of the "sick" personality or extreme views tend to be filtered out. In any event, how do we know whether or not a particular policy maker is being misled by his perceptions? One difficulty in analyses like those applied to Acheson and Dulles is that they involve reconstructions only from public statements of how individual policy makers saw reality in general and certain situations in particular. Another, more severe problem is that of knowing whether a policy maker's image of an adversary can be attributed to a rigid personality, religious attitudes, false historical analogy, or thinking based on experience in the state system. Was Acheson's historical analogy between Stalin and Hitler really that far-fetched in 1945–1950? Was it based on false perceptions or correct perceptions of Stalin's behavior? Did not Stalin's brutal takeover of eastern Europe; the show trials, executions, and disappearances of noncommunist leaders; and his unending vilification of the West *generate* the widely held perception of him as cruel and inhuman, seeking to expand Soviet power westward? If, in fact, he had only limited security aims, then was he himself not responsible for Western misperceptions?

Were Dulles' moralizing and anticommunism really determined mainly by his personality and religious views or were they simply means of mobilizing congressional and public support for an essentially pragmatic foreign policy in a bipolar system? Even if he was unduly rigid in his foreign policy, was he not simply responding to constant attacks upon the "softness" of American foreign policy by the dominant right wing of the Republican party in Congress and to the Republican administration's desire to unify the party and avoid the kinds of attacks that had paralyzed the Truman administration's ability to conduct foreign policy after 1950? [23]

Furthermore, to what degree can the strongly anti-Soviet and anticommunist views of Acheson and Dulles be attributed to external conditions? In a system characterized by a high level of mistrust, even a defensive act may be interpreted by the opponent as hostile. In a bipolar system, such perceptions are especially frequent. The result, of course, is the growth of mutually hostile images that tend, on the whole, to resist contradictory evidence; indeed, friendly gestures may be

---

[23.] Michael A. Guhin, *John Foster Dulles* (New York: Columbia University Press, 1972), pp. 3–10.

522   dismissed as attempts to hoodwink the opponent into relaxing its guard or as signs of weakness.

The greatest difficulty, however, arises from the possibility that the analyst is *merely substituting his or her own judgment for that of the policy maker. As a critic of official policy, he or she tends to attribute that policy to the distorted views of the decision makers and therefore concludes that the remedy is to correct the distortions.* To paraphrase Professor Higgins of *My Fair Lady,* "Why can't the policy makers be as smart as I?" If those who formulate policy were more "flexible," continuously "testing reality" and adjusting their perceptions to that reality (as defined by the critics), there would presumably be less and possibly no reason at all for conflict.[24] It cannot be denied, of course, that decision makers, like most individuals, tend to see the world through colored glasses and by and large to select the facts that confirm their preconceptions. But it is also true that, "if we consider only the evidence available to a decision-maker at the time of decision, the view later proved incorrect may be supported by as much evidence as the correct one— or even by more."[25] The evidence is often ambiguous and subject to more than one interpretation. As Alexander George has noted:

> . . . for example, when the investigator disagrees with the policy a leader continues to pursue despite evidence of its mounting costs, he is more likely to judge that leader as rigid and stubborn than when he supports that policy. Similarly, a leader who takes a firm stand and draws the line in disputes with political opponents may be judged to be engaged in highly adaptive behavior by an investigator who believes that such behavior is required by the situation; but the same behavior may be judged to be irrationally aggressive by a different investigator whose system of values leads to a different perception of the requirements and dangers implicit in the same situation.[26]

Nevertheless, it remains popular to explain conflict as if it were the offspring of false images held by one of the parties and perhaps by both. Not that such images are not present; in our earlier analyses of the American national style and of Soviet perceptions and elite style have shown that they frequently are. But, instead of claiming that such images cause or greatly magnify conflict, it may be more correct to conclude that the opposite hypothesis is true: *Conflict among states demonstrates not that the adversaries misunderstand one another but that they understand one another only too well.* While Chamberlain misperceived the nature of Hitler's aims, Britain tried to appease Hitler; once the prime minister's misperception had been

---

[24] For example, see Ross Stagner, *Psychological Aspects of International Conflict* (Belmont, Calif: Brooks/Cole, 1967), pp. 1–16; and Klineberg, *op. cit.*

[25] Robert Jervis, "Hypotheses on Misperception," *World Politics,* April 1968, p. 460. For a more detailed analysis of the effects of perception, one in which, however, institutional and political constraints are underestimated, see Jervis, *Perception and Misperception in International Politics* (Princeton: Princeton University Press, 1976).

[26] George, "Assessing Presidential Character," pp. 235–236.

corrected by events, however, Britain declared war on Germany. It was Roosevelt's incorrect image of Stalinist Russia that resulted in a policy focused on Germany's defeat without anticipation of possible conflict with the Soviet Union. As Soviet Russia expanded into the center of Europe after Germany's defeat and then pressured Iran and Turkey after 1945, it was Truman's correct perception of what had to be done in a two-power world that produced the Truman Doctrine and the containment policy.

As conditions change, so do perceptions. Within a year of announcement of the Truman Doctrine, the United States was proffering aid to Yugoslavia after its break with Russia; this offer was the first of several attempts to "build bridges" to eastern Europe, which began in earnest in 1956 with the Polish and Hungarian upheavals. Similarly, after Nationalist China's collapse in 1949, the allegedly indiscriminately anticommunist Acheson recognized the potential for differences between the two communist giants and planned, once Chiang Kai-shek on Formosa had been eliminated by Mao Tse-tung, to recognize the new Chinese regime. Even during the Korea war, Acheson believed that crossing the thirty-eighth parallel would be safe *because* the Peking government was already too absorbed with the Russian threat in the north to pay much attention to events in Korea.

As the situation changed again, the United States and the Soviet Union began to cooperate with each other on arms control; they shifted from a total adversary relationship to a limited adversary relationship. Perhaps one of the best proofs that perceptions change with external circumstances is President Nixon's pursuit of détente with Russia and rapprochement with China. During the 1950s Nixon had been a militant anticommunist; no so-called psychohistorical analysis has yet satisfactorily explained how a man allegedly so loaded with misperceptions, character defects, and inner anguish could have conducted such a flexible, non-ideological, pragmatic balance-of-power foreign policy.[27] In addition, China's revolutionary and anticapitalist posture and rhetoric did not stand in the way of improvement in relations with the United States when Russia had come to seem a potential threat, nor did they inhibit China from supporting capitalist European integration and a strong capitalist North Atlantic Treaty Organization (NATO) to balance Russian power in the West. The philosophies of Karl Marx and of Mao had become subordinate to the balance of power. As Hans Morgenthau has commented more generally, "the assumption that the issues of international conflict, born as they are of misunderstandings, are but imaginary and that actually no issue worth fighting about stands between nation and nation" is wrong.

> Nothing could be farther from the truth. All the great wars which decided the course of history and changed the political face of the earth were fought for real stakes, not for imaginary ones. The issue in these great convulsions was invariably: who shall rule and who shall be ruled? Who shall be free, and who, slave?[28]

[27.] Bruce Mazlish, *In Search of Nixon* (New York: Basic Books, 1972).

[28.] Morgenthau, *Politics Among Nations*, p. 504.

ON TO MACROPOLITICS

We thus turn back from the state system in which there seems to be no solution to conflict and war, to world order. In the final analysis it is the necessity for solutions—for instance, to the "arms race"—that compels us to shift away from the state system. The logic is straight-forward. The overriding issue, it is argued, is preventing the death of the earth. When the problem of the arms race is stated in these apocalyptic terms, there can be no choice: Because the problem *must* be resolved, it must be *resolvable*. To admit that it may not be possible to disarm is to discourage further efforts to seek agreement and to encourage complacency that can end only in disaster. In this view, obstacles blocking the way to disarmament should not be considered insurmountable; they are seen merely as difficulties to be overcome. If the problem of nuclear fission could be solved why cannot human ingenuity—applied to the abolition of weapons rather than to the production of ever-more destructive ones—solve the problem of disarmament? Why should human beings not for once apply their reason to constructive, rather than destructive, purposes?

Because disarmament is so desirable, its advocates conclude that it is technically and politically possible.[29] Disarmament may not be the usual way to resolve conflicts, and politicians may reject it outright as "impractical and impossible," but our unique times demand bold solutions. However impossible disarmament may have been in the past, these observers argue, there is no alternative to it today. The search for disarmament is therefore not idealistic; it is highly realistic. The admonition to "love thy neighbor" becomes "Love thy neighbor *if* you love thyself."[30] No great power can afford *not* to love its neighbor if it values its own life. The world must not destroy itself simply because the leaders of the great powers still think in outdated terms of "national interests," rather than in realistic terms of the "common interest of mankind" in preserving peace. What the world needs is not more old-fashioned "power politics," which in the past has always led to war; rather it needs imaginative and radical solutions. Nuclear bombs make it mandatory for statemen to change habits and ways of thinking inherited from the prenuclear age. If the world is not to be engulfed in nuclear flames, political leaders must be objectively concerned about the needs of humanity, regardless of their own subjective prejudices and national ideologies; which pale into insignificance beside the overwhelming central issue of survival.

The alternative to such a "common sense" solution is thus disaster. The abolition of all weapons and the weakening of sovereignty may involve risks, but disaster from nuclear warfare is unthinkable. And—as this logic may also be aplied to overpopulation, environmental hazards, or diminishing resources—no "sane" man would hesitate between such risks and the certainty of catastrophe. For these observers, it is a simple "either-or" problem, and the solution is just as simple. All

---

[29] Robert Gilpin, *American Scientists and Nuclear Weapons Policy* (Princeton: Princeton University Press, 1962).

[30] Herz, *International Politics*, p. 333.

people have to do is to recognize the peril to their existence, the stark alternatives, and the urgency of the remedy.

Implicit in this line of thinking is a clear-cut division between those who have vested interests in the preservation of the nation-state—after all, what jobs would there be for soldiers, diplomats, and "merchants of death," for example, if the nation-state and arms were abolished?—and the vast mass of "humanity." The former obviously oppose disarmament and cannot successfully participate in negotiations, for their patterns of thought are rooted in the state system. But the future of the world demands that statesmen or at least scholars think as if the state system had *already* been transcended.

It can be argued therefore that *our concepts of state behavior are outdated. Reflecting the experiences of the historical state system, our thinking has not yet caught up with the "necessities" of a rapidly changing world.* The central point is that we cannot afford any longer to focus on the states in the system, their objectives, and their interactions. The focus of international politics must be enlarged from the individual nation-state—the "micropolitics" that we have been studying up to this point— to global society, or "macropolitics," in which the fate of each nation is tied to the fates of all other nations. According to Richard Sterling, macropolitics

> is the understanding that the world is becoming too small and vulnerable to survive unless global needs are recognized and acted upon with the same commitment and energy that have traditionally characterized responses to national needs . . . [for] the survival and prosperity of the globe is the necessary condition for the survival and prosperity of its parts. The negative corollary is easily deduced: unconcern for the whole will jeopardize its continuing existence, with the parts suffering the necessary consequences.
>
> Macropolitical analysis must therefore begin with the questions central to its global concerns: What is the *international* interest? What policies and institutions appear to benefit all men, and what appear to benefit some but not others? What is likely to disadvantage them all? It must ask what any given nation-state contributes to the international interest and judge the value of any particular national interest in terms of the answer to that question.[31]

[31.] Richard W. Sterling, *Macropolitics* (New York: Knopf, 1974), pp. 5–6.

Peace Through the Transformation of the State System 19

WORLD GOVERNMENT AND ORDER AND THE ABOLITION OF CONFLICT

I f conflict cannot be abolished in the state system, the *abolition* of that system may be the only hope for the future existence of mankind. Many observers believe that the anarchy of the state system must be replaced by *world government*. Governments preserve peace and maintain law and order on the domestic scene. If a government could be created that would supersede the governments of sovereign nations, could it not, like national governments in their own spheres, ensure global peace once and for all? It is often argued, by analogy, that under the American Articles of Confederation, the states retained their sovereignty and continued their quarrels. But, under the Constitution, the states were reduced in status to nonsovereign members of a new federal system in which the national government could apply national law directly to individuals and had the responsibility and the authority to ensure domestic tranquility. Can we not argue, then, as advocates of world government do, that the American Constitutional Convention was the great rehearsal[1] for a global convention that will transfer the sovereignty of all nations to a world government, the purpose of which will be to ensure global peace through establishment of the "rule of law"? Such partisans seem to believe that, wherever a "legal order"

---

[1] Emery Reves, *The Anatomy of Peace* (New York: Harper & Row, 1945), pp. 253–270. See also Carl Van Doren, *The Great Rehearsal* (Nw York: Viking, 1948), for a discussion of American constitutional nation building as an example for the world.

is established—that is, wherever government applies law directly to its citizens—government functions as a peace-keeping institution. What leads them to this conclusion?

Inis Claude has suggested that one factor is the attractiveness of certain terms and the images that they produce in people's minds—terms like "government" and "law and order":

> A clue may perhaps be found in the intimate association between the idea of world government and the fashionable theme of world rule of law. *Law* is a key word in the vocabulary of world government. One reacts against anarchy—disorder, insecurity, violence, injustice visited by the strong upon the weak. In contrast, one postulates law—the symbol of the happy opposites to those distasteful and dangerous evils. Law suggests properly constituted authority and effectively implemented control; it symbolizes the supreme will of the community, the will to maintain justice and public order. This abstract concept is all too readily transformed, by worshipful contemplation, from one of the devices by which societies seek to order internal relationships, into a symbolic key to the good society. As this transformation takes place, law becomes a magic word for those who advocate world government and those who share with them the ideological bond of dedication to the rule of law—not necessarily in the sense that they expect it to produce magical effects upon the world, but at least in the sense that it works its magic upon them. Most significantly, it leads them to forget about politics, to play down the role of the political process in the management of human affairs, and to imagine that somehow law, in all its purity, can displace the soiled devices of politics. Inexorably, the emphasis upon law which is characteristic of advocates of world government carries with it a tendency to focus upon the relationship of individuals to government; thinking in legal terms, one visualizes the individual apprehended by the police and brought before the judge.[2]

Apart from the seductive quality of certain terms and the favorable images they create, the key argument of proponents of world government is that peace depends primarily upon the creation of a government that, because of its superior power, will be able to enforce the law upon individuals. This argument, however, shows that these proponents misunderstand the function of government and exaggerate the coercion necessary to maintain law and order. Admittedly, government power does play a role in preserving peace. To repeat an earlier phrase, a peaceful society is—at least to a degree—a policeful state. At the same time, however, as we have seen in our own analysis,[3] this power is not the principal factor in achieving peace; particularly in democratic societies. There have simply been too many civil wars; coups d'état, revolutions, and secessions to justify as much trust as world federalists place in the establishment of government as a solution for the disorder inherent in the international system. If government fails to produce "law and order" and is unable to keep the nation united, as we have seen often in the last few

---

[2] Inis L. Claude, Jr., *Power and International Relations* (New York: Random House, 1964), pp. 260–261.

[3] See Chapter 5.

528   decades, then what confidence can we have that world government is the answer to anarchy and war?

The fact is that domestic peace results from political negotiations and compromises required by the constantly changing distribution of power among conflicting, usually organized, interests within a common political culture. It is not the application of law to individual violators and their imprisonment for disobeying the law that are primarily responsible for domestic peace. Neither is it the policeman swinging his or her club or the judge to whom citizens basically owe "law and order." Most citizens obey most laws not out of fear but out of habit, respect, and recognition of their legitimacy. Peace is essentially the result of constant political adjustment and accommodation, accomplished through the efforts of the much-maligned politicians. When groups and classes have what they consider genuine grievances and unfulfilled aspirations for which they seek—but are unable to find—redress, then disorder, rioting, and civil war are likely. Applying a law that sanctifies the status quo becomes an incitement to conflict, not a solution. The issue then is not what the law is but what it should be. The analogy of catching the individual lawbreaker and applying sanctions is hardly appropriate; indeed, it is irrelevant.

The example of American nation building—from confederation to federation—in fact offers evidence that the belief that the mere creation of government as a solvent of conflict is mistaken. Even more necessary than political adjustment among contending interests is a common political culture or sense of community. Such a sense of community is apparent in the Preamble to the U.S. Constitution, in which it is declared that the purpose was to establish a "more perfect union." There was already a union, formed during the long colonial period and tested in the War of Independence; it had only to be made "more perfect." By 1787 Americans already shared a language, a common cultural tradition, and a democratic heritage.

> The thirteen colonies formed a moral and political community under the British Crown, they tested it and became fully aware of it in their common struggle against Britain and they retained that community after they had won their independence . . . . The community of the American people antedated the American state, as a world community must antedate a world state.[4]

The final test of this union came during the Civil War, which had to be fought before the United States could become a durable political community. It is, then, precisely the absence of an equivalent sense of global community or political culture that makes it impossible to establish a world government—along with, it ought to be added, a historical amnesia in which the civil wars and political disorders of the West have been forgotten and the past, especially that of the United States and England, romanticized.

Ironically, in an essentially anarchical or Hobbesian state system that exists in a state of potential war, a world government, if it could be established at all,

---

[4] Hans J. Morgenthau, *Politics among Nations* (4th ed; New York: Knopf, 1967), pp. 498, 499. See also Crane Brinton, *From Many One* (Cambridge, Mass.: Harvard University Press, 1948).

would have to be a dictatorship. When a sense of community is absent, the only government capable of restraining the various nations would have to wield immense power, thus creating what Hobbes called a Leviathan. This kind of government is not what world federalists want, however; they want a democratic world state. But a constitutional or limited government based upon the consent of the governed is dependent— as shown by the American experience—on a preexisting community. Proponents of world government are thus caught in an insoluble dilemma: To emphasize the urgency of transforming the existing state system, they describe the latter in Hobbesian terms, but then they seek a democratic result, rejecting the logical consequences of their own analysis. World government may be not only impossible to create but may also be undesirable—at least for democrats.

This contradiction has not discouraged some analysts of world affairs, however. Indeed, their goals have become more ambitious. Given the "endangered planet" on which we are said to live, they claim that even if a world government is impossible a new *world order* is more than ever necessary.[5] Specifically, four values are emphasized in this new thinking about world order. The first is peace. The superpowers, to be sure, are already concerned about peace and systemic stability, as is shown by their avoidance of nuclear war and attempts to reduce the tensions among themselves. But the present definition of peace as the absence of a destructive total war, although it allows for high levels of interstate conflict (as during the Cold War) or lower levels of tension (as in détente), is no longer sufficient for many proponents of a world order, because it is quite compatible with continued tolerance of poverty and social injustice in the world.

The other values to be embodied in a "world order," as Richard Falk has presented them, are economic well-being, the antithesis of the large-scale poverty in the underdeveloped nations and the lower social reaches of the rich nations; social and political justice, the recognition of "inalienable rights" to freedom, self-expression, and human dignity, as well as the collective claim to self-determination and self-government; and ecological balance to prevent the pollution of "spaceship earth" and the depletion and waste of the globe's finite resources.

Given the critical importance of preventing war and building a more decent and humane world without poverty and social injustice, many people believe that it is more important today than ever before to think of world order as the best alternative to the present state system. Even if it remains practically a utopian solution—attainable only in the distant future, if at all—it still can serve as a goal toward which we can build. Given the strength of nationalism in the real world the prospects for laying the foundation for a future world order are admittedly not bright—at least, they have not been bright so far. But the new interdependence presumably increases the prospects for it. Creating a new world order is, then, no longer entirely a matter of wishful thinking and naïveté. Human beings cannot

---

[5.] Saul H. Mendlovitz, *On the Creation of a Just World Order* (New York: Free Press, 1976); Louis René Beres and Harry R. Targ, eds., *Planning Alternative World Futures* (New York: Holt, Rinehart and Winston, 1975); Richard A. Falk, *A Global Approach to National Policy* (Cambridge, Mass.: Harvard University Press, 1975); and Falk, "Future Worlds," *Headline Series* no. 229 (New York: Foreign Policy Association), February 1976.

530 afford to indulge any longer in old patterns of thinking and behaving. Balance-of-power statecraft is outmoded, and to cling to it is only "romantic adherence." Says Falk boldly, "the new utopians are the old realists and vice versa."[6] Even a former U.N. secretary-general has commented in 1970:

> I do not wish to seem overdramatic but I can only conclude from the information that is available to me as Secretary General that the members of the United Nations have perhaps ten years left in which to subordinate their ancient quarrels and launch a global partnership to curb the arms race, to improve the human environment, to defuse the population explosion and to supply the required momentum to development efforts.
>
> If such a global partnership is not forged within the next decade, then I very much fear that the problems I have mentioned will have reached such staggering proportions that they will be beyond our capacity to control.[7]

Unfortunately, the mere fact that a goal is necessary and desirable does not render it attainable, no matter how "fragile" the world's security, how its population burgeons, however rapidly its resources diminish, how vast the "widening gap" between rich and poor countries grows, and how "calamitious" the future may appear. There is no evidence that states are yet placing international interests ahead of national interests.

In the final analysis, a deep pessimism is common among proponents of world order. There is a veneer of optimism, and Falk, for example, views the 1970s, 1980s, and 1990s as the decades of consciousness raising, mobilization, and transformation respectively, so that at midnight on January 1, 2000, the new order is to be born. But, apart from such marvelous timing, we sense a deep gloom. If "spaceship earth" does in fact confront military, economical, and environmental self-destruction, talk of raising consciousness of future dangers and of "world order modeling" and exhorting nations to think of "international interests" seem rather futile and desperate, given the scope and nature of the transformation in attitudes and structures required.[8]

SUPRANATIONAL COMMUNITY BUILDING THROUGH FUNCTIONALISM

If the establishment of a world government by means of federation, on the model of American nation building, or the creation of a global order to deal with the common and pressing problems of humanity, is hardly likely to occur in the near future, is there any other way to overcome nationalism and to build such a government and a supportive global community that presumably would be democratic,

---

[6] Falk, "Future Worlds," p. 47.

[7] These words of U Thant were reported by James Reston, *The New York Times*, October 22, 1970.

[8] See, for instance, Harold D. Lasswell, "The Promise of World Order Modelling Movement," *World Politics*, April 1977, pp. 425–437.

rather than dictatorial? Several political scientists have decided to study this issue empirically. How have political units in the past been integrated into larger political organizations, the authority of which then superseded their own? How relevant are these historical instances to the contemporary problem of integrating nation-states into a supranational political community?

Note three terms that we have just used: "integrating," "supranational," and "political community." Karl Deutsch and several associates who analyzed various instances of integration of political units in the *preindustrial* era defined integration as "the attainment, within a territory, of a 'sense of community' and of institutions and practices strong enough and widespread enough to assure, for a 'long' time, dependable expectations of 'peaceful change among its population.'"[9] Closely related is the term "supranational," which refers to the formation of a community and institutions above those of the integrating states; this community would have the authority to make political decisions on behalf of the states that would require their obedience (as the American federal government has authority superior to that of the individual states). "Supranational," then, is not to be confused with the word "international." An international or intergovernmental organization is an organization composed of states. Its decisions are reached through negotiation and compromise among the states, not imposed from above. Finally, according to Amitai Etzioni, a "political community" is

> . . . a community that possesses three kinds of integration: (a) it has an effective control over the use of the means of violence (though it may "delegate" some of this control to member-units); (b) it has a center of decision-making that is able to affect significantly the allocation of resources and rewards throughout the community; and (c) it is the dominant focus of political identification for the large majority of politically aware citizens [10]

Among states the threat of violence remains a key element in the resolution of differences, but the chief characteristic of a supranational organization is the absence of intimidation and war from bargaining over important issues. *The anarchical model of the state system*, which is focused on negotiations through threat and counterthreat—or force and counterforce—*is no longer applicable.* Deutsch and his colleagues have therefore called such an enlarged supranational organization a "security community."[11] Historically they distinguish between two kinds: the *pluralistic* security community, composed of states that retain their national autonomy while forming certain specific and subordinate agencies of cooperation on particular matters (as do the United States and Canada or Norway, Denmark, and Sweden), and the *amalgamated* security community, in which states surrender autonomy to new set of political institutions, as did the provinces of Italy and Germany at the time of unification. Deutsch found that pluralistic security communities are easier to achieve and more durable; amalgamated security communities are more difficult to establish and more likely to fail.

[9.] Karl Deutsch *et al.*, *Political Community and the North Atlantic Area* (Princeton: Princeton University Press, 1957), p. 5.

[10.] Amitai Etzioni, *Political Unification* (New York: Holt, Rinehart and Winston, 1965), p. 4.

[11.] Deutsch *et al.*, *op. cit.*

The movement toward a united Europe since World War II, the principal historical experiment by industrialized states in supranation building, falls into the latter classification, though in reality it remains closer to the former. What Deutsch and his colleagues were interested in first were the *conditions* essential to produce a successful amalgamated security community. Not surprisingly, some of the conditions that had been present in preindustrial amalgamations were also present in the experiment that began in 1950 with the formation of the European Coal and Steel Community (ECSC) and produced eight years later the European Economic Community (EEC), or Common Market. And it is on this important—perhaps revolutionary—experiment that we shall concentrate here.

One condition was a compatibility of values and expectations among the amalgamating states. The original Inner Six certainly had such a compatibility; all were pluralistic societies (though Germany and Italy had recently been fascist states), and each had representative political institutions. In the larger countries, West Germany, France, and Italy, as well as in smaller Belgium, the governing Christian Democrats shared a European outlook and held similar views on social welfare, the free market, and other issues. A second condition was that the political elites of the integrating countries believed their way of life to be distinctive. The Iron Curtain was to them more than an ordinary political division; it separated the "West" from the "East," thus forming two distinct geographical and cultural entities. Christian Democrats were particularly disposed to think of the East-West conflict in terms of the historic struggle between Christendom and the "barbarian" invaders from the East (like the Mongols and the Turks). Russia, usually regarded in the past as non-European, now fitted the latter role, and, for the Christian Democrats, the defense of "civilization" once again required Western countries to subordinate their own differences, in order to unite in the struggle against communist Russia.

A third condition of particular significance in amalgamation was the expectation of mutual economic benefit. For the Inner Six this benefit was to be realized in two ways: through formation of a common market through the mutual elimination of trade barriers, import quotas, and other restrictions, and through establishment of a common tariff to protect this market. European industry would then enjoy an enormous potential market, and efficient enterprises would presumably expand and modernize their plants to take advantage of this enlarged market. By the same token, inefficient plants unable to compete—and unwilling to make the effort—would be closed. Business in general would profit; European integration would thus be in the interest of business. Labor would acquire a similar stake in the new Europe as production rose and the level of employment and real wages followed. To be sure, workers in less efficient industries would lose their jobs, and they might have to move to other areas in search of new employment. But in general the Common Market would produce more jobs. The consumer would also benefit from the expanding economy. As he or she saw national economic barriers tumbling and industry converting to techniques of mass production—large-scale production at reasonable cost and with wages sufficient to enable consumers to buy in quantity—he or she, too, would recognize the advantages of the Common Market.

These conditions, then, are some of the principal conditions for the existence of a supranational community. Others include superior economic growth, high political and administrative capabilities in the participating units, unbroken links of social communication, broadening of the political elite, mobility of individuals, and multiple ranges of communication and transaction.[12]

But how about the *process* of integration? How does it occur? Functionalists think they know. David Mitrany, the father of this school of thinking, assumed that the *vertical* divisions between states, which produce conflict and war, can be overcome by tying the various functional areas of the economies of different countries together *horizontally*, in order to resolve their common social, economic, and humanitarian needs.[13] These needs, he believed, can be regarded as essentially nonpolitical and noncontroversial, for they involve welfare and social justice, rather than national security and prestige. As each area of need is tackled, a transfer of state authority to supranational institutions will occur; as the satisfaction of more needs is undertaken, more and more authority will be transferred to international institutions. Sovereignty is thus to be whittled away until at some point, nations will find themselves brought very close in this ever-expanding web of activity. They will then have a greater stake in maintaining peace and transfering national authority to new supranational organs. In Frederick Schuman's apt phrase, integration of the various functional areas could bring "peace by pieces."[14] Mitrany called it a "working peace system," distinct from peace safeguarded by the balance of power; clearly, the emphasis is on social and economic tasks that cut across national boundaries and the establishment of supranational institutions to which governments relinquish their authority to deal with those tasks. In Mitrany's words, "the problem of our time is not how to keep nations peacefully apart but how to bring them actively together."[15]

Ernst Haas was the first to study this process of integration in great detail after the start of the movement toward a greater Europe. Like Mitrany and Jean Monnet, the French master planner of the New Europe, Haas found the driving force behind integration to be economic self-interest. There had to be "something in it for everyone." Haas also emphasized, as did the French government when it launched ECSC, the importance of approaching economic integration step by step. Rather than attempting immediate integration of the entire economies of all member nations—which would have been politically impossible to accomplish— they suggested beginning with the coal and steel sector. In 1950 French Foreign Minister Robert Schuman proposed that the Six pool their coal and steel industries in the ECSC. The choice of coal and steel, the backbone of industry, was deliberate, for it would tie together German and French heavy industry to such an extent that it would become impossible to separate them. Germany would thus never again be able to use its coal and steel industries for nationalistic and militaristic purposes.

---

[12] *Ibid.*, pp. 46–58.

[13] David Mitrany, A *Working Peace System* (London: National Peace Council, 1946).

[14] Quoted by Claude, *Swords into Plowshares* (New York: Random House, 1964), p. 376.

[15] Mitrany, *op. cit.*, p. 7.

534   The political and military power of the Ruhr valley would no longer be accessible for purely German purposes. War between Germany and France would become not only unthinkable but also impossible under these circumstances.

Because the coal and steel sector forms the basis of the entire industrial structure, its isolation after the establishment of ECSC was only apparent. This sector was chosen for the very reason, Haas suggested, that it would have an economic "spillover." ECSC would exert pressure on the unintegrated sectors of the economy, and, as the benefits of the pooling of heavy industry became clearly observable, these other sectors would follow suit. ECSC was thus the first stage in an attempt to create a wider market. It was expected that this approach would be gradually extended to other functional areas of the economy, like agriculture, transportation, and electricity, with the eventual creation of a federal European state enjoying a huge market and a highly developed mass-production system. Once integration had been set in motion, it would pick up momentum on its own.

Such economic spillover first occurred in 1958, when the Six established the Common Market. Their aim was the formation of an economic union. All tariffs, quotas, and other restrictions hampering trade among themselves would be completely eliminated; in turn, they would establish a common tariff to reduce imports and to keep as much of the market for themselves as possible. Furthermore, they would gradually abolish restrictions on the movement of labor, capital, and services within the community and would set up a number of funds to help realize the Common Market. Finally, the Six established a third community, Euratom, for the generation of industrial energy. Together, ECSC, EEC, and Euratom would constitute a European political community.

Functional integration thus rested on the theory of free trade. Each nation would specialize in those commodities that it could produce best, and the resulting trade would maximize consumer choice and national prosperity for all the member nations. The results of this free trade, however, were also to include the significant ingredients of integration. Apart from economic spillover, the most important effect, which Haas stressed, was the *political* spillover. If there was to be a Common Market and if it was to be more than just a customs union, there had to be a uniform set of rules to govern the economic and social policies of the member countries.[16] For example, if one nation should adopt a deflationary policy, its industries would be able to undersell those of its partners and capture their markets. Clearly, this kind of development had to be guarded against. Or, if a nation, after abolishing its tariffs for a specific industry, then subsidized that industry's production or imposed an internal tax on competitive foreign goods, it would gain an obvious advantage for its own industry. Such discrimination by a single government had therefore to be forbidden. Uniform rules could not be established, however, simply for preventing deviant behavior; affirmative action was also required. Because prices

---

[16.] Two of the better early discussions of the expected harmonization of national policies were Michael Shanks and John Lambert, *The Common Market Today—and Tomorrow* (New York: Holt, Rinehart and Winston, 1962), pp. 56–105; and U. W. Kitzinger, *The Politics and Economics of European Integration* (New York: Holt, Rinehart and Winston, 1963), pp. 21–59. See also Emile Benoît, *Europe at Sixes and Sevens: The Common Market, the Free Trade Association, and the United States* (New York: Columbia University Press, 1961).

reflect production costs, which in turn partly reflect national regulation of wages, hours, working conditions, and social-welfare programs, the industries of a nation with lower standards possess a great advantage over competitors in neighboring states. A single set of standards in such areas as minimum wages, maximum hours, and welfare programs was thus considered necessary. In addition, as workers would be able to move from one country to another in search of employment and better jobs, there had to be a single social-security program for all six nations. If labor was to be mobile, its welfare programs had to be Community-wide. This increasing need to harmonize the social and economic policies of the Six would demand a single governmental center for policy formulation in continental Europe. Common policies would require common institutions with supranational authority.

In real terms, such supranational authority, one observer has noted, "starts to come into play when a state agrees . . . to carry out decisions to which it is itself opposed. Most obviously, such a situation arises when it has agreed to be outvoted if necessary by other states—either by a simple or by some weighted or qualified majority."[17] Common institutions with supranational authority extending beyond trade and tariff matters play a central role in furthering the larger political community. Because of this stress on institutions, Haas' theory of functionalism, as distinct from Mitrany's theory, has been named "neofunctionalism":

> If economic integration merely implied the removal of barriers to trade and fails to be accompanied by new centrally made fiscal, labor, welfare, and investment measures, the relation to political integration is not established. If, however, the integration of a specific section (e.g., coal and steel), or of economics generally (e.g., the "General Common Market") goes hand in hand with the gradual extension of the scope of central decision-making to take in economic pursuits not initially "federated," the relation to the growth of political community is clear.[18]

The development of a political community is most readily demonstrated by interest-group activity. In a developed supranational economy those whose interests are affected by the decision-making institutions, adversely or otherwise, will organize to lobby at the supranational level in order to influence particular decisions. An economic institution thus affects political life, expanding the scope of the full community. One is reminded of the United States, where various interest groups lobby at the state and the federal levels. In an open, pluralistic society interest groups and political parties (as aggregates of interest groups) normally act at whatever level of government important political policies are decided; this pattern has indeed been the aim of the EEC's founders. Interaction between decision-making institutions and the multitude of interest groups was considered of vital importance to the political integration of the Six.[19]

In the long run, however, the self-interest of various groups will not suffice. A truly federal Europe must have popular support as well, and in step three the

---

[17] Kitzinger, *op. cit.*, pp. 60–61.

[18] Ernst B. Haas, *The Uniting of Europe* (Stanford: Stanford University Press, 1958), pp. 12–13.

[19] *Ibid.*, p. xiii.

536   political spillover leads to social integration: transfer of national loyalty to the supranational community.

> As the process of integration proceeds, it is assumed that values will undergo changes, that interests will be redefined in terms of a regional rather than a purely national orientation and that the erstwhile set of separate national group values will gradually be superseded by a new and geographically larger set of beliefs. . . .
>
> As the beliefs and aspirations of groups undergo change due to the necessity of working in a transnational institutional framework, mergers in values and doctrines are expected to come about, uniting groups across former frontiers. The overlapping of these group aspirations is finally thought to result in an accepted body of "national" doctrine, in effect heralding the advent of a new nationalism. Implied in this development, of course, is a proportional diminution of loyalty to and expectations from the former separate national governments. Shifts in the focus of loyalty need not necessarily imply the immediate repudiation of the national state or government. Multiple loyalties have been empirically demonstrated to exist.[20]

Based upon "the logic of integration," the EEC was thus designed to develop into a United States of Europe through three stages: *a customs union*, an *economic union*, and a *political and social union*.

The fundamental assumptions underlying this logic were three: first, that economic and social, or low-politics, problems could be separated from political and security, or high-politics, issues; second, that the ever-widening vested interests and habits of cooperation formed in the low-politics area would spill over into high politics; and, third, that there would be a massive shift of loyalty from the nation to the new supranational community, as citizens—producers, laborers, farmers, and consumers—came to recognize the economic benefits from the new and larger community.

The ups and downs of the European movement reflect on the validity of these assumptions. Economic integration did pick up momentum in Europe, but the very success of the Six may ironically be one of the greatest obstacles to the political spillover. As the national wealth of EEC members rose, the urgency of further integration declined. Contrary to the expectations of the functional analysts—who emphasized that fulfillment of some needs would result in growing support for the integration of other sectors of the economy and further development of new supranational attitudes—economic gains through the customs union seem to have led to protection of the status quo and reduction in support for further integration.[21] Indeed, the final irony may well be that the citizens and interest groups who gain economically from the European movement attribute those benefits largely to their own governments, thus once more enhancing the confidence in nation-states supposedly lost as a result of defeat in World War II and the postwar economic collapse.

---

[20] *Ibid.*, pp. 13–14.

[21] This result is explained by the concept of "equilibrium"; see Leon N. Lindberg and Stuart A. Scheingold, *Europe's Would-Be Polity* (Englewood Cliffs, N.J.: Prentice-Hall, 1970). See also Joseph S. Nye, Jr., *Peace in Parts* (Boston: Little, Brown, 1972).

National loyalties thus remain; only in the long run may generational changes result in greater attraction to a new Europe for those born after World War II, whose values are said to be largely "postbourgeois."[22] (Bourgeois values are largely based on individual material and physical security, whereas postbourgeois values are based more on community values and intellectual and esthetic satisfaction. Adherents of the latter tend to be more cosmopolitan than parochial—that is, nationalist—in their identifications.)

Even more important, high politics and low politics are more difficult to separate in reality than in theory. This discovery should not occasion surprise. As Claude has asked:

> Is it in fact possible to segregate a group of problems and subject them to treatment in an international workshop where the nations shed their conflicts at the door and busy themselves only with the cooperative tools of mutual interests? Does not this assumption fly in the face of the evidence that a trend toward the politicization of all issues is operative in the twentieth century?[23]

States have remained jealous guardians of their sovereignty, national identities, and military strength; the more an economic policy has seemed to infringe on security issues, the greater the difficulties in achieving a united policy and the less likely that the cooperative habits learned in low politics will be transferred to high politics. France and the other five countries may pool their coal- and steel-producing facilities (even here France also had the high-politics goal of trying to insure itself against German rearmament and aggressive policies), but it is quite another story when it comes to pooling their foreign and defense policies.

The functionalists, believing in "the victory of economics over politics," have incorrectly minimized the significance of political decisions and the will of individual leaders, like the Christian Democratic premiers and chancellors of Italy, France, and West Germany, who initiated the European integration movement, and Charles de Gaulle, who slowed it down. Indeed, a study of Britain's decision to enter into the Common Market persuasively demonstrates that this decision was not—and could not be—the result of interplay among the various subnational interest groups; the decision was clearly a high-politics decision, based upon broader criteria than merely economic interests, however important the latter.[24] These political-security issues grew out of concern for Britain's status and influence in the world. Would continuing to "go it alone" mean a reduction in Britain's influence in this age of superpowers? Conversely, would its influence be enhanced if it were a member of a larger political unit?

Indeed, Britain's entry into the Common Market, as well as the impetus toward European integration among the Inner Six illustrates the functionalist ne-

---

[22] Ron Inglehart, "An End to European Integration?" *American Political Science Review*, March 1967, pp. 91–105; and Inglehart, "The Silent Revolution in Europe: Intergenerational Change in Post-Industrial Societies," *American Political Science Review*, December 1971, pp. 991–1017.

[23] Claude, *Swords into Plowshares*, p. 385.

[24] Robert J. Lieber, "Interest Groups and Political Integration," *American Political Science Review*, March 1972, pp. 53–67; and for more detail, Lieber, *British Politics and European Unity* (Berkeley: University of California Press, 1970).

538 glect of external conditions. After World War II, in an international environment dominated by two superpowers, the European nations saw that they would be helpless unless they formed a United States of Europe and became the world's third superpower. This entity would be able to define and achieve its own ends, instead of remaining a disunited object of American-Soviet competition. For France, the original sponsor of the ECSC, it would also serve several foreign-policy aims: to gain equality of status and influence with the "Anglo-Saxons" and not to fall behind England and West Germany in influence within the Western community. The American interest in the European movement was to add Europe's power to the Western scales in the balance with the Soviet Union. Just as the external threat had spurred the European movement, the momentum has slowed as the threat from the East has diminished. As the defeated and discouraged continental states recovered and the unique circumstances in which integration was launched passed, the larger vision seems to have dimmed somewhat. Will withdrawal of large numbers of American troops some day or a renewed sense of insecurity as a result of growing Russian military help to revitalize this vision?

The need for a common policy was dramatically illustrated during the early 1970s. On one hand, there were indications of new life in the European-union movement. First, the Six became the Nine, as Britain, Ireland, and Denmark joined in 1973 (Norway refused). Portugal, Spain, and Greece are also slated to join. Second, the enlarged European community may not develop as expected. It will in all probability be focused on the cooperation of governments, leading to negotiated collective policies. The building blocks of Europe will remain the states, but the Community will speak increasingly with one voice, though in different tongues.[25] The Community has shown some evidence of ability to move toward united foreign-policy positions, on both Atlantic European and Middle Eastern issues.

On the other hand, events since the 1973 oil crisis have called into question the cohesion of the EEC, even its viability. In a surprisingly frank declaration on the state of the Common Market in February 1974, EEC officials declared:

> Europe is being put to the test. It is faced with a new situation which is pitilessly highlighting its weakness and its dependence, but which is also revealing how badly it is in need of unity.
>
> It is facing this situation in a state of crisis: A crisis of confidence, a crisis of will and a crisis of lucidity. . . .
>
> Now that it is put to the test, Europe must show the world its common resolve. Over the last few weeks, setbacks and failures have, on the contrary, disturbed us and have raised doubts as to the will of the governments to make progress and as to the ability of our institutions to fulfill their tasks. . . .
>
> At a time when international relations are undergoing a far-reaching transformation, with vital consequences for us all, is there a single European

---

[25.] Theo Sommer, "The Community Is Working," *Foreign Affairs*, July 1973, pp. 748–749.

country which can exercise real influence and carry weight comparable to that of
a united Europe?[26]

This question and questions about the additional cost of oil, resulting balance-of-payment deficits for all member states, and measures to erase these deficits without harming economic growth, employment, and social justice, the Commission suggested, require a single economic strategy. Will Europe show a will to unite, or will it flounder? That is the critical question. The original threat from the East has waned, and the specific cold-war conditions in which the Europe of Six was launched have passed. The European states are looking increasingly inward. The vision of a united Europe seems to have faded. The growing economic and financial strength of the Common Market, like that of Japan, has not yet been translated into political and military terms. Admittedly, "Europe" is not yet dead. In 1979 the member states held elections for the European Parliament, a move that was at least symbolic and may someday enhance the Parliament's rather limited authority. The acceptance of Greece, Spain, and Portugal as eventual members to help their fragile democracies survive was also significant, as was the common position they took on a comprehensive peace for the Middle East.

But there is another way of looking at this question. Europe is engaged in an experiment in building a "supranation" the complexity of which is even greater than that of the United States. Considering the far shorter period that the Europeans have had, it is perhaps extraordinary that the disappearance of national interests should have been expected to occur so quickly. The danger will come if the member governments no longer believe that community action can fulfill their purposes better than individual national action. At present, the Commission, the executive of the EEC, does not possess the authority to deal with the important issues confronting the European states, and the various governments have hardly demonstrated the will to grant this authority. Economics has not yet triumphed over politics, and a United States of Europe remains a distant objective. The 1973 oil crisis has led to renewed emphasis on national sovereignty and an attitude of "every state for itself" as each scrambles to make oil deals with OPEC members.

If integration in Europe, where political, economic, and social conditions favored formation of a supranational community after World War II, has fallen far short of expectations, how can the experiment succeed in less developed areas, so that regional integration can serve as a basis for world government? According to Haas, the factors favoring integration are an urban-industrial level of development, a pluralistic society in which the masses express their aspirations and grievances through interest groups and political parties, political elites competing with

---

[26] "State of the Community," *European Community*, April 1974, pp. 12–14. On elite and mass attitudes toward European unification, generally showing the softness of support for a united Europe, see Werner J. Feld and John K. Wildgen, eds., *Domestic Political Realities of European Unification* (Boulder: Westview, 1977). On the future of the European community and its impact on economic and political relations in the world, see Feld, *The European Community in World Affairs* (Port Washington, N.Y.: Alfred, 1977).

one another for control of the government, and relations between elites and masses that are governed by constitutional and democratic rules. Clearly, the European experience with functional integration is not applicable to the LDCs, with their low industrialization, tenuous national integration, and absence of pluralism and democracy. The prospects for an East African Community or a Central American Common Market have never been very bright.

As a process of achieving a world state and community, then, functional integration remains of doubtful utility. Even if it is eventually successful in Europe and in some non-Western areas, the result will be simply to increase the number of superpowers. Surely, the likelihood of their competing with one another is just as great as the possibility that they will serve as stepping stones on the path toward a global state. If the need for a world state is really so urgent as its advocates suggest, if the contemporary globe is indeed in such awful straits and the time in which to save ourselves so short, then, even if regional integration can create such building blocks, disaster will still lie ahead—for the process of integration is clearly very time-consuming, and time apparently is one commodity that is running out.

Even though the functional model, based on European experience, seems limited in its applicability, as well as in its explanatory relevance to non-Western areas, it remains true, as Robert Lieber has observed, that

> Even with such extensive criticism of the functionalist theory of integration, we are still left with what one of its sharpest critics has termed an empirical theory of considerable analytic power and predictive ambition. . . . It effectively calls our attention to the way in which integration can grow as an unintended product of incremental decisions; it identifies the spillover process that does operate within the realm of welfare politics; it indicates how integration can thrive despite divergent interests and orientations; and it correctly predicts group behavior across national boundaries. Functionalism offers a useful means for making sense of the complex and sprawling integrative enterprise. It provides organizing concepts and helps us to formulate questions, explanations and even predictions. We are thus considerably better off than if we approached this enterprise with only a critical stance and no theory at all.[27]

TRANSNATIONAL ACTORS AND THE NEW GLOBALISM

In contrast to international and supranational organizations, transnational actors can be defined as organizations that carry on "significant centrally directed operations in the territory of two or more nation-states." One of the most potent of these actors is the gigantic business enterprise or multinational corporation (MNC) like General Motors, an American-controlled and -directed MNC that carries on

---

[27.] Lieber, *Theory and World Politics* (Cambridge, Mass.: Winthrop, 1972), pp. 49–50.

activities in many different countries. Such a corporation pursues its purposes *across* international boundaries in many different markets. Although, to be sure, business organizations, banks, churches (notably the Roman Catholic Church), and revolutionary groups are not new to the international scene, in the years since World War II there has been a vast proliferation and growth in size of transnational actors, and expansion of their operations to a virtually global scale. Lester Brown, in comparing the sizes of multinational corporations with the sizes of nation-states at the beginning of the 1970s, ranked them according to gross annual sales and gross national product (GNP) respectively. He found that the first twenty-two entries were the twenty-two largest nations, ranging from the United States to Argentina. Number 23 was General Motors, followed by Switzerland and Pakistan; Exxon and Ford Motors ranked twenty-seven and twenty-nine. Of the top fifty, forty-one were nations and nine were MNCs; of the second fifty, eighteen were nations and thirty-two were MNCs. In the top 100, countries barely outnumbered corporations, fifty-nine to forty-one.[28] Another indicator of size revealed that Standard Oil of New Jersey at that time (now Exxon) had three times more employees overseas than the United States State Department and a tanker fleet larger than that of Russia. Clearly, many MNCs' resources are much greater than those of most members of the United Nations, and many operate on a geographical scale exceeding that of the great empires of the past. Oil has enhanced these trends. Since 1973 Exxon has overtaken General Motors as the world's largest corporation. The oil companies have all profited enormously; so, of course, have the oil-producing states, raising them in the rankings. Banks, too, have done well, as a result of "petrodollars," the internationalization of business, the flow of money across frontiers, and consumer financial services. The Bank America Corporation (which issues VISA cards) and Citicorp (which issues Master Cards) have each achieved resources of $100 billion, equivalent to the total 1978 output of Belgium, a prosperous country. No more than two dozen states in the world have such output.

What has made it possible to speak of a "transnational organizational revolution in world politics"?[29] Modern means of fast transportation and communication are one factor, and another is the technical and organizational capabilities to operate across long distances. Particularly in business, because of the emergence of strong consumer-oriented economies in the industrialized first world and because of high-technology industries like electronics, this revolution has become very visible. Exporting may also have become increasingly disadvantageous for many industrial concerns because of lower local labor costs and transportation costs to that country; a corporation may therefore decide that it can remain competitive only if it establishes production facilities in that country. Pepsi-Cola, for example, has 512 plants in 114 countries, and in 1973 it was the 119th largest MNC. The extension of production facilities has been especially important in

---

[28] L. Brown, *World Without Borders*, pp. 213–215, 216.

[29] Samuel P. Huntington, "Transnational Organization in World Politics," *World Politics*, April 1973, pp. 333 ff. See also Luiz Simmons and Abdul Said, eds., *The New Sovereigns* (Englewood Cliffs, N.J.: Spectrum, 1974); and Charles P. Kindleberger, ed., *The International Corporation* (Cambridge, Mass.: M.I.T. Press, 1970).

542   western Europe, where the Common Market has provided a dynamic market but where non-Market goods are subject to import duties. The purpose of the tariffs was to restrict the market to industries of the member countries, among which tariffs had been eliminated as an incentive to growth. Yet it is behind this common tariff wall that extensive American capital investment and business growth have taken place in Europe, a growth so large that we can speak of *two* American economies, one in the United States and the other in Europe; in the noncommunist world the latter is second only to the former.

American corporations, accustomed to operating in many American states with their different regulations, have adapted better than many of their European competitors to operating within the Common Market; European firms, which have historically confined themselves to protected national markets, have consequently lagged behind American corporations.[30] The transnational business organization operating in multiple markets shifts its resources from one country to another as needed; its aim is to maximize profits, and the various national markets thus appear as parts of a single larger one, in which capital, technology, and other resources can be shifted at will. American firms, thinking in continental terms, have thus become more "European" than European firms; the largest corporations in Europe are American.[31] This overseas investment pattern suggests that the growth of the MNC is a rational response to new business opportunities, as well as a defensive move to protect overseas markets to which these firms had previously exported. Given the kind of managerial talent, financial resources, and technical skills that American MNCs possess, telexes, telephones, and jet liners have enabled them to coordinate operations and pursue a virtually global business strategy. (Some European and Japanese MNCs have responded in the same manner in other markets; some European cars, for example, are manufactured in the United States).

The vast reach of the MNC has aroused a great deal of speculation about the impact of such transnational actors on the state system. There is a *Marxist-Leninist*, or anti-imperialist, interpretation, of course, in which it is claimed that the capitalist class, having long exploited the domestic proletariat and squeezed all possible profits out of the third world, has now found a larger, better-organized, and more effective organization to continue its exploitation. The MNCs thus represent a further stage of corporate capitalism, serving as an instrument of an expansionist foreign policy based on resources and cheap labor from the third world and dependent upon investment opportunities for "surplus capital." The state, controlled by the capitalist class, is the chief actor, the MNC its tool, the best means in an age of rapid transportation and instant communication for rich "monopolists" to exploit the vast majority of the world's population and to keep it in poverty.

A second interpretation is the *liberal* one, in which it is suggested that the MNCs will create a new world of plenty for all and conflict for none, a view popular with the MNCs' own managements and supporters. Each MNC is viewed as an

---

[30] Robert L. Pfaltzgraff, *The Atlantic Community* (New York: Van Nostrand Reinhold, 1969), pp. 108–110.

[31] *Ibid.*, p. 80.

independent actor, not as a tool of the state, and with its managerial skills and technology it can stoke the fires of economic development, eventually abolishing poverty throughout the less developed areas. In its search for profits, it neither blocks economic development nor perpetuates destitution. Indeed, its corporate selfishness leads to maximum global welfare as long as there is no political interference. Furthermore, it is argued that, in a world divided by nationalism, the MNCs can provide the impetus for creation of a world community. Former Undersecretary of State George Ball has argued that the MNC, which he calls "Cosmocorp," has outgrown the state; national boundaries are anachronistic, for they confine its activities.[32] Unlike traditional imperialism, which presumably encouraged the state to open up new lands for business to exploit, the new business corporation seeks not territorial and political control but access to different markets. In this multinational context, the Cosmocorps' managers are the new "globalists," the "advance men" of "economic one-worldism" who view the globe as a single market—or, in Peter Drucker's phrase, a "global shopping center."

Dependent upon foreign states for permission to produce and sell within their frontiers, these managers regard states, national egotism, and assertively militarist foreign policies as contrary to their own interests. Their primary loyalty is to the corporation, rather than to the nation, and global corporate interests take precedence over national interests. MNCs need peace; national rivalries are economically too costly from their perspective. MNCs, the devils of anti-imperialist theory, are the angels of the liberal theory, for they provide a major restraint on foreign adventures as peace and profits become interdependent.[33] The MNCs thus seem likely to replace nation-states as the most visible and potent actors on the world scene, and welfare will then replace power politics. The MNCs have burst through the confining jurisdictions of national sovereignty and will bring a better life to all peoples. Unable to fulfull their citizens' expectations, nation-states have become anachronisms. The managers of IBM, General Motors, Exxon, GE, Coco-Cola, Lever Brothers, and other large MNCs make decisions daily that appear to have a more immediate and visible impact on consumers' lives than governments do.

It is easy to understand why states are anxious and concerned about the MNCs on their territories. Even advanced industrial states are wary. MNCs represent high technology. Will other industrial economies become their "technological colonies," that is, dependencies of the country whose MNCs possess the most advanced technology and skills? As one French observer has written:

> . . . electronics is not an ordinary industry, it is the base upon which the next stage of industrial—and cultural—development depends. In the nineteenth century the first industrial revolution replaced manual labor by machines. We are now living in the second industrial revolution, and every year we are replacing the labor of human brains by a new kind of machine—computers.

---

[32] George W. Ball, "Cosmocorp: The Importance of Being Stateless," *Atlantic Community Quarterly*, Summer 1968, p. 168.

[33] Richard J. Barnet, *The Roots of War* (Baltimore: Penguin, 1973), pp. 229–238.

544

> A country which has to buy most of its electronic equipment abroad will be in a condition of inferiority similar to that of nations in the last century which were incapable of industrializing. Despite their brilliant past, these nations remained outside the mainstream of civilization. If Europe continues to lag behind in electronics, she could cease to be included among the advanced areas of civilization within a single generation.[34]

By the early 1970s, American MNCs controlled 80 percent of Europe's computer business, 90 percent of its microcircuit industry, 50 percent of its transistor industry, and 65 percent of its telecommunications. In addition, they controlled sizable portions of more traditional industries, like automobiles (40 percent), synthetic rubber (45 percent), and petrochemicals. Concern that the MNCs will come to control the technologically most advanced, most rapidly growing, and most profitable sectors of industrial economies is understandable, even though American firms own only 5 percent of overall European corporate assets.

There is also great concern because of the huge size and assets of MNCs compared with the GNP of the host states. This issue is particularly sensitive in the LDCs, which fear that MNCs will dominate their economies, "repatriating" their excessive profits and thus draining capital from already capital-hungry states. Additional complaints are that they fail to produce the goods needed for modernization; for example, Coca-Cola attracts money that could be spent on necessities like milk, meat, vegetables, educational materials—even cars in countries with hardly a road system. MNCs are also said to impose Western cultural and consumer-oriented values (the term "cultural imperialism" is often used).[35]

But whether the MNC operates a manufacturing plant in Europe or an extractive industry in the third world—and it is the former that has attracted most American investment capital[36]—the common fear in the host country is that it will exploit its power in a way that will hurt national interests. For example, if an MNC no longer finds the investment climate suitable in one country, as a result, perhaps, of governmental policy or labor troubles, it can pick up its chips and move to another country, leaving behind unemployment and a lot of ill feeling. Because other states seek to attract the MNC, it can play off one state against the other. During the Cold War, American laws forbade shipment of certain products to designated countries. If a country hosting an American MNC wished to pursue a more friendly policy toward the United States' adversaries or simply to improve its balance of payments through trade, it might not be able to do so if such a move involved restricted products manufactured by a subsidiary of an American MNC. The apprehensions of nations about their control over their own economies have been strengthened by MNCs' political interference, like ITT's efforts at subversion in Chile and bribes offered and subsidies paid by Lockheed and other firms to

---

[34.] J. J. Servan-Schreiber, *The American Challenge* (New York: Avon, 1969), p. 42.

[35.] A strong indictment of the M.N.C.s may be found in Barnet and Ronald E. Müller, *Global Reach* (New York: Simon and Schuster, 1974).

[36.] Blake and Walters, *The Politics of Global Economic Relations*, pp. 78–80; and Nye, "Multinational Corporations in World Politics," *Foreign Affairs*, October 1974, p. 162.

TABLE 19.1

A COMPARISON OF MARXIST, LIBERAL AND MERCANTILIST IDEAS ABOUT THE MULTINATIONAL CORPORATION AND THE INTERNATIONAL ECONOMY

	Marxist	*Liberal*	*Mercantilist*
Actor	capitalist class	multinational corporation	state
Nature of economic relations	clashing interests and conflict	common interests and harmony	clashing interests and conflict
Goal of economic activity	maximization of class interest	maximization of global welfare	maximization of national welfare
Economic-political assumption	that economics does determine politics	that economics should determine politics	that politics determines economics

Adapted from Gilpin, U.S. *Power and the Multinational Corporation* (New York: Basic Books, 1975), p. 27 (by permission of the publisher).

governmental and political leaders in many countries for orders or the right to sell their products. Host governments are very sensitive to infringements of their right to maintain control over their economies for their own purposes.

Still, it is doubtful that the MNCs are a threat to the survival of the state system. The rumors of the imminent death of the state are premature for two reasons. The first is that politics still precedes economics: The growth of transnational corporations to a large extent reflects American political power and influence in most regions of the world. During the Cold War the United States used alliances in every region to contain Russia and China. American military and political organizations, as well as private economic ones, followed in the wake of political commitments in western Europe, the Middle East, South Asia, East Asia, and Latin America. Trade, so to speak, followed the flag. Historically, this process has been called *mercantilism*. The state encourages the activities of its businessmen—whether in trade with foreign countries or in overseas investment—in order to create greater wealth at home. Robert Gilpin has argued strongly that "political values and security interests are the crucial determinants of international economic relations. . . . Throughout history each successive hegemonic power has organized economic space in terms of its own interests and purposes."[37] Although it is true that transnational actors are the products of modern technology, it is American power that has created the conditions for their expansion. Most MNCs are controlled by Americans. The implication is that a reduction in the American political role in the world will bring a decline in MNCs' activities, though the increasing numbers of European and Japanese MNCs will be even more active.

[37.] Robert L. Gilpin, "The Politics of Transnational Economic Relations," in Robert O. Keohane and Nye, eds., *Transnational Relations and World Politics* (Cambridge, Mass.: Harvard University Press, 1972).

The second reason why the state may well survive the challenge of the new transnational business actor is that, although some conflict between the two is unavoidable, they need each other. Their conflict is complementary.

> It is conflict not between likes but between unlikes, each of which has its own primary set of functions to perform. It is, consequently, conflict which, like labor-management conflict, involves the structuring of relations and the distribution of benefits to entities which need each other even as they conflict with each other. The balance of influence may shift back and forth from one to the other, but neither can displace the other.[38]

Indeed, the transnational actor appears to strengthen, rather than to weaken, the state, for it needs the latter's permission for access to its territory. The multinational corporation may well be one of the leading reasons for the increasing role of the state in economic affairs and the extension of state power into the economic realm. In Europe, for example, governments intervene in the economic sphere in order to create domestic competitors to counterbalance the size and influence of American corporations; governments remain sensitive to retaining national control over their economies and are concerned that their goals not be upset by corporate decisions made on a multinational basis. As John Fayerweather has noted, "at critical points every nation-state finds that its objectives of national military security, domestic economic stability, protection of particular national groups, and even national pride become more important than potential economic increments from full participation in global economic optimization."[39]

Host countries have therefore increasingly set the terms of access and thus established relations in which they benefit from the presence of MNCs in terms of employment, taxes, balance of payments, transfer of technology, and managerial skills, while simultaneously permitting the latter to earn enough to provide an incentive to stay. Some hosts establish employment quotas for nationals, require MNCs to establish themselves in so-called depressed areas (for which they may, however, receive tax incentives), forbid layoffs, and demand the training of whatever local workers are required (which may, however, be subsidized). Almost all host countries set dates for achieving complete or majority ownership; they may also set export figures for the MNCs (which some may be reluctant to comply with in order to avoid competing with their own brands in other countries). In return for access to markets, MNCs have in recent years increasingly complied with these types of demands by the host countries. The result has been greater cooperation between host states and MNCs. Indeed, the host country's strength in setting the terms of MNCs' access has been increased by the fact that American management, finance, and technology now face increasing competition from the Europeans and Japanese.

> In short, sovereignty is no longer at bay in most countries. To be sure, the degree of this shift in power differs from country to country, and from industry to industry.

[38.] Huntington, *op. cit.*, p. 366.

[39.] John Fayerweather, "The Internationalization of Business," *Annals of the American Academy of Political and Social Science*, September 1972, pp. 6–7.

It is virtually complete in most industrial host countries and some developing countries as well, and is well underway in many other developing countries.[40]

Symbolic of this trend is the terms that the oil producing states have set for the once-powerful oil companies.

The "state centric" model of international politics is thus likely to remain our principal explanation of what occurs in the international environment. The MNC continues to operate in a system in which the peace so necessary to business operations is preserved by states. It is the states that control the terms of access–if there is access—and remain the focus of citizens' loyalties; it is they who will determine the future of the MNC and not the reverse.

A dramatic instance of control by a host government came to light during the 1973 war between Israel, on one hand, and Egypt and Syria, on the other, when the Arabian American Oil Company (Aramco), the world's largest petroleum producer, refused to supply oil to American military forces in the Mediterranean and other areas of the world on instructions from Saudi Arabia, its only source of crude oil. Aramco, composed of four of the largest American oil companies, claimed that it really had no choice but to follow Saudi instructions. As a result, the U.S. Defense Department had difficulty in obtaining oil for its military forces at a time when Israeli-Arab hostilities posed a danger of confrontation with the Soviet Union (which did in fact occur). Was Aramco's compliance with the Saudi embargo against the United States a flagrant instance of lack of corporate patriotism or merely evidence of the sound business practice of loyalty to the company first? On the other hand, Japan and all communist states until recently refused to admit American investment capital at all. In addition, American-owned corporations abroad are subject to the laws and commands of the host countries.[41] When in 1974 Argentina wanted to sell thousands of vehicles made by Ford, General Motors, and Chrysler subsidiaries in that country to Cuba, it was not the companies that blocked the deal; they wished to comply with Argentina's wishes. It was the American government that opposed the deal until Argentina threatened to nationalize the companies.

The fact that Aramco has responded obediently to the wishes of Saudi Arabia, even though that has helped the Arabs in their economic warfare against the United States, is a clear demonstration that MNCs tend to obey host governments. Clearly, the MNC is hardly a docile instrument of "U.S. imperialism," serving national policy by preying upon other nations' resources and undermining the capacity of their governments to further the welfare of their peoples.[42] In fact, although the MNC may have its headquarters in the United States and may control a sizable part of the American market, it has in a genuine sense become "dena-

---

[40] C. Fred Bergsten, "The Coming Investment Wars?" *Foreign Affairs*, October 1974, pp. 135 ff.; and Bergsten, Thomas Horst, and Theodore Moran, *American Multinationals and American Interests* (Washington, D.C.: Brookings, 1978).

[41] Raymond Vernon, *Sovereignty at Bay* (New York: Basic Books, 1971), pp. 241–247.

[42] For an argument for the imperialist and exploitative character of MNCs, see Müller, "Poverty Is the Product," *Foreign Policy*, winter 1973–1974, pp. 71 ff.; and Barnet and Müller, *op. cit.* For an evaluation, see Chapter 12.

548   tionalized," belonging not to any one nation but to the many nations in which it operates. The preferences of the American government do not necessarily carry much weight with the MNC. For example, during the Johnson presidency American companies invested millions of dollars in Europe, establishing and expanding their activities there while simultaneously the American government sought to reduce dollar outflow in order to cut the balance-of-payments deficit and the export of American jobs. If a branch of an American automobile company abroad is required to export a certain percentage of its production, automobile exports from the United States and the American balance of payments may be adversely affected. "What is good for General Motors" is not necessarily good for the country any longer.

    Corporations essentially want to be left alone to do their business; they are not interested in politics, which means that an MNC will work with a democratic government in a democratic society and—despite the howls of its critics—with despotic and even racist governments in other countries (just as the Roman Catholic Church historically has come to terms with virtually every conceivable type of government in order to have access to their territories and to save the souls of their citizens).[43] In the short run, the MNCs may well reinforce the status quo in the societies in which they operate. In the long run, however, they may help to undermine the status quo—in noncommunist societies, at least—by making visible new technology, ideas, social and cultural values, and ways of life that challenge especially the LDCs' more traditional cultures, as Western colonialism once did.

> There is little evidence to substantiate the argument that the multinational corporation as an independent actor has had a significant impact on international politics.
>
>   While the evidence is indisputable that the multinational corporation is profoundly important in the realm of international economic relations, its political significance is largely confined to its impact on domestic politics where it is an irritant to nationalistic sentiments. . . .
>
>   Where these business enterprises have influenced international political relations, they have done so, like any other interest group, by influencing the policies of their home governments. . . .
>
>   Contrary to the argument that the multinational corporation will somehow supplant the nation-state . . . it is closer to the truth to argue that the role of the nation-state in economic as well as in political life is increasing and that the multinational corporation is actually a stimulant to the further extension of state power in the economic realm.[44]

    This point is well illustrated by the relationship between the MNC and its home country. As relations with host nations become closer, relationship with the home nation grows more and more distant. Labor particularly has become protectionist, opposing what the unions call the "export of jobs" to LDCs, especially Taiwan, Hong Kong, South Korea, and Singapore. The home government may

---

[43] Ivan Vallier, "The Roman Catholic Church: A Transnational Actor," in Keohane and Nye, *op. cit.*, pp. 135–140.

    [44] Gilpin, *op. cit.*, pp. 68–69.

increasingly seek to restrict the outflow of investment capital when it is suffering high unemployment and balance-of-trade deficits (more money going out to pay for imports than coming in from exports). Ironically, the relations may well worsen, for the "stake is nothing less than the international division of production and the fruits thereof." As the American government more and more experiences the shift of benefits to other countries—and the same is true for other home countries of MNCs—domestic political pressures to restrict the MNCs will increase. The American government is bound to intervene at some point to protect the nation's prosperity. According to Fred Bergsten, intervention may be the only way to avoid "the threat of investment wars."[45] Note that states will be interfering and negotiating with one another, in order to resolve this and other issues; that is, it will be the states that will seek to avoid conflicts resulting from the very economic forces that some proponents of MNCs believe will bring the world together in prosperity and render national divisions essentially meaningless.

---

[45] Bergsten, *op. cit.*, p. 148.

Interdependence as a Substitute for Power Politics

20

THE HALFWAY HOUSE

State behavior may be restrained primarily by the balance of power, and international organization and legal and moral norms may supplement this balance to some degree, but the essentially anarchical nature of the system appears likely to continue; so do emphasis on national self-help and national egotism. On the other hand, perhaps, these consequences of the system may be eliminated if the anarchical structure can be transformed and replaced by a world government and order that will allow for peaceful change, provide for the security of member states, and engender a more prosperous world with a decent standard of living and justice for all people. But this possibility does not seem feasible. The outlook for the world may therefore be bleak. "Interdependence"[1] is a sort of halfway house between the anarchy of the contemporary system and the promise of a world state in the future. Believers in the promise expect the state system to continue but with the fangs of national interest drawn; even before world government comes into existence, they expect some of its benefits—greater cooperation, rather than conflict; less emphasis on violent resolution of conflict; more emphasis on joint solutions peacefully arrived

[1] Some of the basic books and articles on the nature of interdependence and the role of power are Seyom Brown, *New Forces in World Politics* (Washington, D.C.: Brookings, 1974); Robert O. Keohane and Joseph S. Nye, *Power and Interdependence* (Boston: Little, Brown, 1977); and Stanley Hoffmann, "Choices," *Foreign Policy*, Fall 1973, pp. 3–42. More popular treatments can be found in Lester R. Brown, *World Without Borders* (New York: Vintage, 1972); and Dennis Pirages, *Global Ecopolitics* (North Scituate, Mass.: Duxbury, 1978).

550

at—to become common. States may even remain the principal actors and a world state only the ultimate objective, but interdependence will increasingly bind all states together, catch them in its web and make their individual security and especially their economic fortunes dependent on one another. Whatever the problems confronting a single state, solutions will no longer be national solutions achieved at the cost of other states. Instead, they will be reached collectively and will benefit all states. The maxim of the historic state system "His gain is my loss" is to be replaced by the maxim "We shall all lose or gain together" in the new interdependent state system.

There is, in this view, nothing idealistic about relying on interdependence. It already exists to a degree, and every day human beings become increasingly aware of it, regardless of the states they live in. Simultaneously, historic concern with security issues and old ways of conducting international politics ("power politics") are becoming outmoded. Except for nuclear proliferation, the new international agenda is focused on such issues as resources (especially energy resources), population and poverty in the LDCs, the growing gap between rich and poor nations, the environment, and human rights. Such issues are economic, technological, and social—even moral, to the extent that the morality of the gap between rich and poor is being questioned.

This kind of interdependence will be discussed and analyzed here in three parts: first, a set of examples to illustrate what is meant by interdependence; second, a more detailed analysis of the character of interdependence and exactly how behavior in the old state system is said to differ from that under interdependence, and, third, an evaluation of the validity of the interdependence thesis.

THE IMPACT OF OIL

Oil, perhaps even more dramatically than nuclear weapons, offers an illustration of interdependence. The impact of the policies of the Organization of Petroleum Exporting Countries (OPEC) on the first world include the following:

> *Double-digit inflation.* OPEC's continual price rises are not the only cause of inflation, but they are a major stimulus. Pumping the oil out of the ground cost $0.25 a barrel, but as the 1980s began, the cost OPEC charged was over $30 a barrel.

> *Recession and substantial unemployment.* Economic growth rates are at their lowest since the Great Depression of 1929–1930. Millions have lost jobs.

> *Stagflation.* Inflation and recession are occurring simultaneously. Policies to reduce inflation raise unemployment, and policies aimed at reducing unemployment heighten inflation. There seems no way out, and economists are baffled. They know how to "cure" inflation or recession but not both at the same time, and their inability to solve this problem is

intensified by the political pressures to lower the rate of inflation and to raise employment.

Reduction in the standard of living. The cost of living exceeds wage settlements; less can be bought with wages; and powerful union attempts to keep up with or stay ahead of inflation simply stimulate inflation. For nonunionized workers, the white-collar middle class, the elderly, and the poor, cuts in current living standards and future expectations are largely unavoidable.

Inability to plan national economic growth, employment levels, and inflation rates. A government can do all the planning that it wishes, but foreign states still have a major, perhaps a decisive, influence on the way of life of its people.

Threats to the "welfare state" and political democracy. Rapid economic growth after World War II provided the wealth and the taxes to fund the many social services of modern democratic countries, as more and more groups in society gained bigger slices of the ever-expanding "economic pie," social conflicts were eliminated or kept to acceptable levels. In a shrinking, stagnant, or only slowly growing economy, one sector can gain only at the expense of another, intensifying social conflicts, setting class against class, region against region, union workers against nonunion workers, and so on. Can the democratic rules operate in an environment of stagflation, with every group struggling to maintain or improve its position?

Changing life styles. Perhaps the most immediate impact is visible in smaller cars, lower speed limits, adjustments in heating and air conditioning, and the curtailing of trips and vacations. Especially in the United States in which the population is sprawled all over suburbia, without good mass transportation systems, the worst effects of future oil shortages and much more expensive gasoline may be still to come.

Vulnerability to events. The fall of the shah of Iran led to a disruption of oil supplies. Even when Iranian production was resumed (at a lower level), oil supplies were stretched tightly. Prices shot up almost to 100 percent in 1979. Gas lines appeared in several places in the United States (California and Washington, D.C., among others) and prices for heating oil rose sharply. That the collapse of a monarchy halfway around the world should have such a dramatic impact conveys inescapably the meaning and profound impact on each one of us of "interdependence."

Threats to Western unity. Paying for oil year in and year out may be beyond the financial ability of some nations and may incite "trade wars" among Western states, as each seeks to maximize exports and reduce imports to earn sufficient money to pay oil bills that may bring some of them to the brink of bankruptcy. They may also seek to gain advantages over their allies in the scramble for oil. The strains on the North Atlantic

Treaty Organization (NATO) could become intolerable and its ability to deter the Soviet Union in Europe seriously impaired.

Reduction of Western defense capabilities. The Western democracies, even the United States, West Germany, and Japan, cannot afford to maintain sizable military forces and equip them with modern arms. The days of many guns and much butter simultaneously appear to be over. A strong defense may have to be paid for by money taken from domestic welfare programs, conversely, any increase in social services is likely to mean less money for defense.

Effects on international currency stability. As more dollars flow to OPEC to pay for oil, the flood of oil dollars—"petrodollars"—reduces its value. There are simply too many dollars in the world market. The American responsibility for this glut is great, for it has been primarily the continued expansion of American demand and the failure of conservation measures that have produced this outflow of dollars.

Rising costs of imports. As dollars flow outward and decline in value, the cost of imported goods rises. American manufacturers, instead of undercutting the competition, have also raised prices, partly to compensate for their higher costs, and partly to raise their own profits. The spiral of inflation has thus been pushed even higher, while the dollar continues to decline.

Absence of solutions. There are no "escape routes" or "miracle cures." Discovery of more oil will require long periods of exploration and the investment of enormous amounts of capital. Even if plentiful supplies can be found, they will not be available in the short run. In the meantime, drilling and transportation of oil in ships continue to pose major environmental hazards. Nor are other alternatives likely to be available soon: coal, shale oil, and nuclear energy. Furthermore, all pose environmental problems: The use of coal means stripmining and air pollution; shale rocks must be dumped after the oil has been squeezed out; and nuclear energy threatens safety both immediately and through waste disposal. Solar energy is still in a technologically primitive stage, not yet ready to be harnessed in major ways. Nor has any Western society, especially the United States, yet decided the key tradeoffs between these various types of energy and economic and environmental costs.[2]

The impact of continuing and occasionally sharp increases in oil prices on less-developed countries (LDCs) that do not themselves produce oil is also severe:

Menace to their economic development. As more money has to be spent on oil just to keep up with price hikes, the LDCs have borrowed $119 billion from commercial banks in the West; extra costs in 1979 alone were over $10 billion.[3]

[2.] Robert Stobaugh and Daniel Yergin, eds., *Energy Future* (New York: Random House, 1979). The authors recommend increasing reliance on the sun, but the National Academy of Science has questioned this recommendation and favors coal and nuclear energy.

[3.] *The New York Times,* July 4, 1979.

Threat to the food supply. Especially those states where modern oil-dependent technology is used in agriculture may find it difficult to grow sufficient food for their rapidly increasing populations.

Reduction in ability to "earn their way." As demand in the industrial West for the commodities of the LDCs decreases, the prices of those commodities also decline. Yet the countries need foreign exchange and earnings to buy machinery and food that they cannot grow themselves.

Less foreign aid. The Western economies can afford less assistance for the poorer nations.

Threat of Western tariffs. It is likely that Western nations will even raise tariffs to keep out the few products young industries can export. Western labor, already suffering from unemployment, is not committed to the free flow of trade when domestic jobs are at stake.

Increased costs of Western exports. Western machinery, food, and consumer items will become less available to the LDCs as their foreign earnings shrink in amount and value.

Social and political turmoil. Especially for the LDCs already living close to the subsistence level, worsening conditions may bring to power radical and authoritarian regimes, which will probably also be highly nationalistic and anti-Western.

Clearly, then, not only do OPEC's activities affect Western economies and the LDCs' prospects directly but also the Western response to them has a further impact on the LDCs and the reverse. Even the OPEC countries themselves are not unaffected.

They must export their oil.

They need Western technology and trade to modernize their societies.

Some of them may need Western—especially American—political support to protect their political regimes from external attack, subversion, and *coups d'état.*

They may seek to buy modern arms for their defense, thus becoming dependent on Western technicians to maintain the equipment and train their men in its use.

They presumably have an interest in Western economic stability and prosperity because of the heavy investment of OPEC earnings in the West.

To sum up, then, every state's actions have an impact on all other states.

One final comment on oil: Should the lot of the LDCs actually improve and the gap between rich and poor nations narrow, the strain on the world's nonagricultural resources will certainly be intensified. If, for example, the Western industrial nations were once again to experience high rates of economic growth, along with declining unemployment and inflation, the demand for oil would rise steeply; one factor holding down world demand for oil after 1973 was that the West, which uses the bulk of the world's oil, was in an economic slump. Until the fall of the shah in 1979, oil prices had been rather steady, increasing only rather slowly after the initial quadrupling in 1973–1974. (Indeed, real prices had gone down because the value of the dollar was declining.) We need only imagine the pressures on world oil supplies if many LDCs were to become highly industrialized and thus great energy consumers; even the possible entry of the Soviet Union, at present still self-sufficient in oil, into the world market in the mid-1980s is likely to lead to yet another round of price increases. In a highly industrialized world, how long—regardless of price—will the world's oil (and other resources) last?

More than a decade ago, two writers said about the newborn American child:

> Every 7½ seconds a new American is born. He is a disarming little thing, but he begins to scream loudly in a voice that can be heard for seventy years. He is screaming for 26,000,000 tons of water, 21,000 gallons of gasoline, 10,150 pounds of meat, 28,000 pounds of milk and cream, 9,000 pounds of wheat, and great storehouses of all other foods, drinks, and tobacco. These are his lifetime demands of his country and its economy. . . .
>
> He is requisitioning a private endowment of $5,000 to $8,000 for school building materials, $6,300 worth of clothing, $7,000 worth of furniture. . . . He is yelping for a Paul Bunyan chunk, in his own right, of the nation's pulpwood, paper, steel, zinc, magnesium, aluminum and tin.[4]

But that calculation was based on prices in the middle 1960s. This child, now grown up, is now surrounded by petroleum by-products; disposable plastic knives, forks, plates, and packaging; styrofoam cups and containers; and the like, most of which have been substituted for china, glass, metal, and wood objects. In 1978 alone, discarded plastics totaled more than 1.5 billion pounds, which is equivalent to the weight of 10 million human beings! All these products are made from oil.

The point is that each new person makes a claim on the earth's food, energy, and other resources. Yet can we assume that resources are infinite or that technology will always find substitutes or new resources as the old ones run out?

POPULATION AND FOOD

The term "population explosion" refers to the doubling of the world's population approximately every thirty-five years. In 1930 there were 2 billion people; in the 1960s that figure had reached 4 billion, and by the year 2010, the projected figure is 8 billion. Recently, however, there has been a decline in population growth from

---

4. Robert and Leona Rienow, *Moment in the Sun* (New York: Dial, 1967), p. 3.

556   1.98 percent for the period 1965–1970 to 1.88 for 1975–77.[5] Estimates for the year 2000 now vary from 6 to 7 billion people, though most are nearer to the 6-billion mark.

The problem, however, is not the simple increase of population but the fact that most of the new people are being born in the third world. The fertility rate of Western industrial societies is already low and may be declining further. In the United States the rate in 1977 had dropped from 1.1 percent to 0.8 percent; in Britain, there was zero population growth, and in both parts of Germany deaths exceeded births. The current overall growth in the first world is estimated at 0.7 percent. This figure contrasts sharply with 2.3 percent in the LDCs, which means that the mid-1967 world population of 3.5 billion had risen to 4.3 billion by 1977. Even a decline in the non-Western birth rate will, if it continues, leave an enormous population. Nine tenths of the approximately 2 billion people who will be born between now and the year 2000 will live in the third world; about 80 percent of the world's population will then be living in the LDCs.

The world division between rich and poor will then be even more striking than it is now. The rich will be richer and fewer, and the poor will be poorer and more numerous. Such a division, which would certainly lead to revolution within a single society, is hardly likely to be a stabilizing force in international politics. For example, according to a report prepared by the U.N. Fund for Population Activities,[6] the population in the LDCs by the year 2000 will further burden countries where malnutrition already affects 20 percent of the population, where 30 percent do not have proper health care or access to clean water, where 40 percent do not have jobs or are underemployed, and where more than 50 percent of the population over fifteen years old is illiterate. There has also been a major shift of population from country to city. The urban population of the world doubled between 1950 and 1978 and will have doubled again by 2000. In addition, the decline in fertility, combined with lengthening life expectancies, has pushed up the average age of the world's population; by the turn of the century there will be twice as many people in their seventies and eighties as there are now. Between young people seeking education, jobs, housing, and food and demands of an aging population, the strain on the resources of the LDCs will be immense.

The United Nations reports that these trends "are bound to have radical-to-revolutionary implications for national economic and social structures"—and, we may add, for the entire international system, as the LDCs' domestic problems are sure to spill over into the international arena. Even today, when the industrial nations have only 30 percent of world population and the LDCs have 70 percent, the former are affected; as the ratio changes, perhaps to 20 to 80 percent by 2000 or 2010, the demands of the poor will become more insistent and more radical.

One of the more serious consequences of such an increase in population will be shortages of food. Interdependence in this connection has been dramatically demonstrated already. In the early 1970s there was a food shortage, which may be repeated and become worse.

---

[5] *The New York Times*, June 18, 1979.

[6] *The New York Times*, June 18, 1979. See also Georges Tapinos and Phyllis T. Piotrow, *Six Billion People* (New York: McGraw-Hill, 1978).

If the projected end-of-century world population of 6.5 were to materialize, food production would have to double present levels merely to maintain current inadequate consumption levels. The increase in the earth's food-producing capacity over the next three decades would have to equal that achieved from the time agriculture originated to the present.[7]

Oil-price increases, however, are making energy-intensive farming, usually called the Green Revolution, more difficult to sustain because oil is needed for fertilizer, irrigation pumps, pesticides, mechanical farm tools, and transportation and distribution of food.

The race between food and people has, moreover, been intensified by the way that people eat, especially in the industrialized world. In LDCs the staple is grain or rice, but with economic advancement comes a shift to meat. It takes about eight pounds of grain to produce one pound of beef. The demand for meat—which has spread to Russia as well—strains the supply of animal feeds, forage, and fertilizer. The point is that food that goes to feed the cattle, pigs, and chickens which more than 200 million Americans eat could probably feed seven times that many Chinese. In the 1950s and 1960s the United States kept large food surpluses because American farmers were enormously productive. In the early 1970s these surpluses were sold off, with a large share going to the Russians who had a bad harvest in 1972. Some other countries, like India, also needed large occasional American food shipments to feed its vast population. So demand was great and the supply so tight that two poor harvests between 1972 and 1974 cut heavily into all grain stocks, spreading hunger across the globe.[8] The American stocks have now been rebuilt; Russia has had some good (as well as some poor) harvests; and India, Pakistan, and Bangladesh have all improved their food production. But the aim of the 1974 World Food Conference in Rome—to establish an international grain reserve—remains a dead letter.

The LDCs, in their efforts to modernize—that is, to industrialize and to urbanize—have, with some exceptions, placed agricultural development lower on their scale of priorities. This approach has been understandable because of the association between colonial status, on one hand, and agriculture and development of natural resources, on the other. Steel factories, automobile plants, and other glamorous industries remain desired symbols of modernity and of a promised better life, but in the meantime they drain funds away from agricultural investment.

Providing cheap food has been one way that the governments of many LDCs have attempted to curb social unrest among the teeming millions in their cities. High food prices would—and at times have—caused rioting and generally explosive situations. But cheap food is hardly an incentive for native farmers to produce more. When farmers can earn only a little, they will produce only a little. For the LDCs this situation poses a real dilemma. It is intensified by increasing evidence that improved nutrition results in a lowering of the birth rate. If children have a better chance of surviving birth and reaching their productive years—when

---

[7] L. Brown, *op. cit.*, p. 95. Also see Georg Bergstrom, *The Hungry Planet* (New York: Collier, 1972).

[8] *The New York Times*, November 11, 1978.

558 they can help to provide for their parents in old age (in a kind of family social-security system)—then fewer children will be conceived.

In the meantime, occasional starvation and, more seriously, widespread malnutrition remain. It has been estimated that each day almost 900 million people fall at least 250 calories short of a proper diet, and 1.3 billion are chronically undernourished.[9] Among the effects of malnutrition are the stunting of physical growth and of mental development.

THE MODEL OF INTERDEPENDENCE

What is the main point of all the foregoing examples? First, we have tried to illustrate over and over again that the meaning of interdependence is *mutual vulnerability*. The United States and the Soviet Union, the two most powerful states in the world, are also militarily the two most vulnerable. Each can destroy the other; each holds the other's population hostage. What one or the other of the superpowers does—from deploying weapons to conducting research on and development of future arms—is thus of utmost concern to its adversary. Political conduct, too, is a matter for worry because, should one superpower infringe upon the other's vital interests, confrontation could result. The two nations have thus become interdependent; the behavior of each profoundly affects the other and determines whether or not it will survive. They will either die together or exist together.

Similarly, OPEC's actions have affected the economies of all noncommunist states. Developed or underdeveloped, they have all been seriously dislocated, as plans for economic growth have been transformed into efforts to prevent further stagnation and to regain economic momentum. Both industrial and agricultural sectors have been affected; inflation and recession have left no nation untouched. Yet the OPEC nations, which need to sell their oil and which invest their capital in the West, cannot afford to hurt the industrial states too much without hurting themselves—through lost sales and interest payments and curtailment of assistance in their development. Should they go too far, of course, they might even drive the Western industrial states to resort to force in sheer desperation. Economic growth, then, apparently can no longer be carried out on a national basis but requires coordination with other economies. No state remains immune to events elsewhere; national economic autonomy is a thing of the past. The nations of the first and third worlds—and in the latter both the resource-rich countries and the resource-poor nations often called the fourth world—are tied together. Each is sensitive to the other's needs and actions and can hurt the other. What A does will quickly affect B; for example, an oil price increase by A results in further inflation and unemployment in B. How seriously A's decisions will affect B depends upon alternative available oil supplies, other energy sources, and whether or not the increases in inflation and unemployment occur in small steps or in a single big

---

[9] Pirages, *op. cit.*, p. 77.

jump. If alternative oil is available, A's action may not hurt much. B may be sensitive to A but not too vulnerable. If B, on the other hand, has no other sources of energy and must pay large price increases it will be hurt. It will be very vulnerable. Interdependence includes both these elements—sensitivity and vulnerability.[10]

A second point is the interrelations among issues. In an earlier chapter we noted how the dangers of nuclear proliferation have been accentuated by the world oil situation and the temptation of countries to look to nuclear energy to help them cut back on oil imports. Yet the nuclear-fuel cycle, especially the enrichment and reprocessing procedures, can produce the materials for building nuclear bombs and thus endanger the state system itself. Similarly, we have noted that oil prices are interrelated with economic growth, food production, population growth, monetary stability, environmental integrity, and other issues. No one issue can anymore be viewed as seperate, for each affects and is affected by a series of other issues.

Third, with the exception of the diffusion of nuclear weapons, all the issues named here are essentially economic and social (including moral). For example, in the industrial nations, high oil and natural-gas prices are obviously a major problem for low-income people, who may have to give up food in order to heat their homes in the winter or freeze if there is not enough money left after the rent has been paid. Whether such people should be allowed to go hungry or cold or both for reasons beyond their control or whether they should be assisted with government subsidies is a social and moral issue. Indeed, on a much broader scale, do human beings *as* human beings have a fundamental right to sufficient food? Is it acceptable that in the West, especially the United States, people tend to overeat and that therefore dieting and exercising in order to fight obesity are major concerns, while in the LDCs millions suffer from hunger and malnutrition? Is the sizable gap in wealth between the first and third worlds not, in the final analysis, a moral issue?

Of the importance of these socioeconomic, or "low politics," issues, also often called prosperity, welfare, or bread-and-butter issues, there can now be no doubt. Since 1973 OPEC has erased any doubt that existed. But the proponents of interdependence are arguing something far more important: that most analysts of international politics have neglected economic issues, relegated trade and financial matters to a subordinate place in the scheme of things, and that economic problems are basically technical and should be resolved by experts who understand such matters. These proponents argue that interdependence among states is the principal characteristic of the contemporary international system (indeed, as other actors, like multinational corporations [MNCs] are prominently featured, the words "global system," rather than "state system," are usually used). This interdependence will supposedly lead to more peaceful and collaborative behavior among states; proneness to conflict and resorts to violence or threats of violence will at the very least be curbed somewhat. Above all, the new interdependent system will be characterized by cooperation. States that are mutually vulnerable *have* to work together; they cannot, as in "power politics," seek advantage at the cost of potential adversaries.

---

[10] Keohane and Nye, *op. cit.*, pp. 11–13.

Let us look in more detail at the building blocks of this interdependence model, in order to understand more fully why "the logic of interdependence" supposedly will lead to a more peaceful and harmonious world. The first block consists of nuclear arms, which, precisely because of their suicidical nature, have engendered a greater sense of security, which, though not absolute, has diminished the importance of the security issue. Deterrence works, and threats of violence have taken the place of unrestrained violence; when force is used, it is circumscribed so that escalation between the superpowers will not occur. The awesome nature of nuclear weapons has thus led to an increasing reluctance to use force. Furthermore, in both limited conventional and unconventional warfare, a superpower has no advantage just *because* is is a superpower; indeed, the increasingly high costs of using force against third-world states inhibit the superpower even more. Never before in history, then, have the old symbols of great-power status been so useless, aside from defending the status quo.

The second building block is the change in the principal aim of national foreign policies. The single best word to describe this change is "modernization." The harnessing of labor to machinery in order to enhance productivity and to increase standards of living began in western Europe in the nineteenth century, spread to North America, and has now been extended to the third world. Low-politics issues are, for citizens of most lands, more important than high-politics issues. These citizens want to improve their material way of life. In democratic countries, where the "revolution of rising expectations" began, governmental concern about improving their peoples' lives has reflected electoral pressures. But their very example has led even nondemocratic nations to seek the same goals. Initially the presence of the colonial power, with its superior standard of living, longer average life expectancy, lower infant mortality, greater literacy, and technological and scientific prowess, offered vivid demonstrations of alternatives to the colony's way of life; the conquering foreigners' guns were symbols of a superior way of life and technology. The West was therefore to be emulated.

Governments thus have had to be increasingly responsive to low-politics issues. Their choices have had to satisfy people's material needs and desires; their success has been judged by their provision of social services and the growth of the gross national product (GNP). The management of the economy— even a free-enterprise economy—by government is thus politically necessary in order to ensure high employment, rapid economic growth, economic stability, and equitable distribution of income, as well as minimum wages, maximum hours, and other social measures. Governmental incompetence in economic management is not easily forgotten or forgiven at election time.

Because low politics, or domestic welfare, has assumed priority over traditional security concerns, the third building block is the recognition that states are no longer self-sufficient. The days of autonomy, when at least the great powers had most of the resources they needed and controlled their own economic destinies, are gone. If governments are to satisfy their people's demands for greater prosperity, they will have increasingly to enter into the international economy. To fail to do so will be too costly politically; because economic growth will be slow. Governments thus are drawn farther and farther into interdependence. Note that implicit in this line of reasoning is the virtual elimination of the line between "foreign policy" and "domestic policy." The two are virtually indistinguishable in the real world. To satisfy its citizens, the government pursues domestic economic policies that depend for their success on events in the world beyond its own borders. Foreign policy is thus bound to be thoroughly enmeshed with issues of trade, aid, development, monetary stability, and exchange rates; more and more, ecological issues have been included too, for pollution knows no political boundaries.

The socioeconomic "game" thus reflects a new awareness that states have become economically interdependent and that each society's economic viability and prosperity depend on those of all other societies. Highly industrialized states and developing nations all must cope with limited supplies of raw materials, resource depletion, overpopulation, food shortages, and environmental spoilation. No nation is any longer, to paraphrase John Donne, "an island unto itself." The economic futures of all are inextricably intertwined, and the many economic links among nations constitute a web of interdependence.

The fourth block follows logically: Low politics involves coordinations, whereas high politics involves conflict. Nations have become so interdependent on bread-and-butter issues that a given nation has no choice but to cooperate if it wishes to promote its own prosperity. On security issues, states still operate as separate political units. A single nation's increase in power and security is still usually seen by a potential adversary as a loss of power and security for itself and thus something to be opposed. But an increase in welfare for the same nation depends on increases in welfare for other nations as well. In the new "socioeconomic game," states gain or lose together.

Building-block five is the fundamental irrelevance of force to low-politics issues. Interdependent states must cooperate over a long period; the use or threat of force, effective as it may once have been in managing conflict, is inefficient and counterproductive in a game of coordination. Coercion or violence may perhaps pay off on a single issue, but, given the need for long-term collaboration, anger and resentment following such tactics may lead to some sort of economic revenge. If another nation possesses a much-needed commodity, it is hardly helpless, even if it is militarily inferior. The gains from force would therefore be few, if any, and the costs probably quite high. Force, in short, is a clumsy weapon, not very cost-effective on socioeconomic issues, on which even the militarily weak have bargaining power that traditional means of calculating power hardly reveal. "Imagine, for example, one state threatening a resort to force if another did not comply with its demand for a currency devaluation. Or consider the likelihood of two neighboring states going to war over a question of pollutants that flow downstream or downwind across their common borders."[11] These issues call for a kind of bargaining in which force can play no role.

Sixth, the very meaning of power has changed, given the uselessness of force; the need for cooperative behavior if common problems are to be solved; and

---

[11] James N. Rosenau, "Capabilities and Control in an Interdependent World," *International Security*, Fall 1976, p. 39.

562   the complexity of such issues as population control, increased food production, development of alternate energy sources, monetary stability, and economic growth, all of which demand great technical expertise.

> Bargaining over differences, trading issues off against each other, promises of future support, threats of future opposition, persuasion through appeals to common values, persuasion through the presentation of scientific proof—these are the prime control techniques through which the problems of interdependence must be addressed. They are, of course, as old as diplomacy itself, but they have taken on new meaning in the light of the decline of force as a viable technique and in view of the complex nature of the interdependence issues. . . . The inclination to rely on appeals to common values, with a corresponding diminution in the tendency to threaten reprisals, appears especially likely to emerge as central to the conduct of foreign affairs.[12]

The seventh building block is this bargaining relationship, which, in contrast to the cold-war and détente relationships, is not bipolar but multipolar. Whether the issue is oil or some other resource, the environment, population, food, foreign investments, or the MNCs, many nations are involved, usually different nations on different issues. In Stanley Hoffmann's phrase, there are many "chessboards"; different players with different power resources negotiate on each issue.

This point in itself may not seem particularly novel. Yet, when many nations participate on many issues, and force is not a viable bargaining instrument, it seems that the historical power hierarchy based on security issues has been eroded and that all states are essentially equal on welfare issues. Surely this claim is audacious, if not revolutionary. The dominance of the superpowers and traditional power politics are said to have disappeared; security is now basically a "given," and the primary objective of states is welfare.

The envisioned interdependent world, then, is one in which states will still exist but not the kinds of states that we have been studying so far. Interdependence will have "tamed" them, drawing the "sharp teeth of sovereignty"; it will also have dissolved selfish "national interests" and bonds of national loyalty.[13] Genuinely equal states will live together in greater harmony and mutual understanding; at the very least, they will be disposed to resolve conflicts peacefully. Economic and technological forces will bind them together, and national frontiers will become increasingly irrelevant, for economic cooperation will cross borders. Geopolitics and security conflicts will thus become anachronistic. Interdependence may not engender world government, but it can make the nation-state and power politics irrelevant in a "world without frontiers." Nations can no longer adequately solve their own problems and serve their peoples' desires for better lives. Such

---

[12] *Ibid.*, p. 44.

[13] For a critique of the theory of interdependence as applied to relations between the first and third worlds, see Tucker, *The Inequality of Nations*. For a suggestion that the United States make a world order, rather than the balance of power, the focus of its policy, see Stanley Hoffmann, *Primacy or World Order* (New York: McGraw-Hill, 1978).

TABLE 20.1

CLAIMED DISTINCTIONS BETWEEN POWER POLITICS AND INTERDEPENDENCE

	Power Politics	Interdependence
Issues	high politics: security, balance of power, spheres of influence	low politics: natural resources, energy, food and population, environment
Actors	states (primarily in the first and second worlds)	states (primarily in the first and third worlds), multinational corporations
State relationships	conflicting "national interests"	interdependence, common interests, and transnational cooperation
Rule	conflict: "What you gain I lose" (balance of power)	cooperation: "We gain or lose together" (community building)
Management	bilateral	multilateral
Role of power	coercion	rewards
Role of force	high	low, if not obsolete
Organization	hierarchical (bipolar or multipolar)	more nearly egalitarian
Future	basic continuity	radical change

global problems as insufficient natural resources and energy, overpopulation, poverty, and shortages of food, as well as the potential revolutionary situation created by the division between rich and poor nations, can be solved only at the global level. National solutions are no longer possible.

This model certainly embodies a radically different international system from the one we described earlier. The *structure* has been transformed and the power hierarchy replaced by a new egalitarianism; force is no longer "thinkable," and the key values of national security, prestige, and power have been replaced by economic welfare, consumerism, social justice, and environmental concerns. Table 20.1 sums up the basic distinction between the old "security game" and the new "socioeconomic game."

"NEW" COOPERATION OR "OLD" STRIFE?

Before we begin our critique of the interdependence model, a preliminary note is in order. The assumption is that humanity is facing critical problems, which will overwhelm it unless nations learn to cooperate to find solutions. We ought to remember, however, that forecasts about the future of humanity are basically

564　guesses, even when based on fairly reliable data about the current world. Who would have believed in 1900 that the 1.5 billion people living then would be increased by 4 billion in less than a century? Thomas Malthus warned 200 years ago that there were too many people then living and that they could not all be fed; already in 1750 Tertullian had advised that "the remedy for nations is to let famine take its course."[14] Who can now say that feeding even 6–7 billion people is out of the question?

In any event, it is ironic that only a few years after the United States was widely criticized—often by current proponents of interdependence—for pursuing a global foreign policy and extending American commitments beyond the nation's alleged capacities, including the costly "adventure" in Vietnam, globalism has reappeared in a new form. Only the agenda has changed, and, as the new welfare issues cannot be managed by single nations, "foreign policy leaders schooled in the old arithmetic of national security will have to learn the formula of economic interdependence, the advanced calculus of planetary bargains and global welfare."[15]

In evaluating interdependence, Robert Paarlberg has raised a fundamental issue when he questioned this emphasis on managing national welfare at the global level, stressing instead that the prerequisite for prosperity is improvement in domestic policy leadership. It may sound convincing to say that global problems require global solutions, but fertility, for example, is hardly amenable to agreement among states. The problem of rapidly growing populations is still primarily a national responsibility. What can foreign governments do in the absence of domestic will to manage this issue? Similarly, emergency food shipments or worldwide food reserves are no substitute for national policies emphasizing agricultural development. Food production and distribution, nutrition, and population control require greater national commitments and shifts of internal priorities and resources than most LDCs have been willing to make in the past; for many, painful and difficult structural reforms in landowning patterns will also be necessary. Discipline, organization, efficiency in government and administration, and considerable financial investment are all necessary, yet such qualities are in short supply—and not just among the LDCs.

The energy problem may require cooperation with other nations, it is true, but even then the solution will have to begin at home. The United States could go far toward solving its energy problems if its government and people would conserve more oil and act with greater dispatch to find alternative sources of energy. The basic energy problem partly reflects failure to reduce demand, to produce more domestic oil, and to develop other energy sources. Only if these and other measures are undertaken can international cooperation be of some help. "So it is that global welfare cannot be properly managed abroad until it has been tolerably managed at home. Without a prior exercise of domestic political authority, the global welfare crisis will not admit to efficient interstate control."[16]

[14] Quoted by Alan Berg, "The Trouble with Triage," *The New York Times Magazine*, June 15, 1975, p. 30.

[15] Robert L. Paarlberg, "Domesticating Global Management," *Foreign Affairs*, April 1976, p. 563.

[16] *Ibid.*, p. 571.

Indeed, we may add to Paarlberg's comment our own observation that, when the distinction between foreign and domestic policies has been blurred, weak domestic efforts to encourage economic growth and promote prosperity will lead to corresponding tendencies to pin the blame for domestic problems on other nations. The appeal to nationalism and the search for foreign devil figures will increase tensions among the states whose alleged interdependence is supposed to create more harmonious relations. The incentive to externalize domestic failure will surely be very strong if the LDCs do not modernize fairly rapidly. For such failure is very likely to produce more activist, radical, authoritarian regimes that will be more disposed to confrontation than to conciliation. Beleaguered governments, struggling with massive domestic dissatisfaction, may well adopt intensely nationalistic and aggressive policies out of desperation.

A 1976 United Nations report entitled *The Future of the World Economy* declared that, to halve the income gap between rich and poor nations by the year 2000 would require first, "far-reaching internal changes of a social, political and institutional character in the developing countries, and second, significant changes in the world economic order."[17] Each alone would be insufficient; the two types of change must be combined. But it is highly doubtful that the LDCs possess the will or governmental authority and capacity to take the "drastic measures" called for in the agricultural or capital-reinvestment sectors (30–35 percent, even 40 percent, of gross national product is called for). Even more doubtful is their ability to carry out the accompanying "significant social and institutional changes." To read the report is to recognize that its goal is unattainable.

Second, although there can be little doubt that welfare issues have become prominent on the international agenda, the assumption that they have achieved priority because security can be taken virtually for granted is overstated: The threat of global war has not at all vanished because the nuclear balance has so far guaranteed the peace. Both superpowers still use the threat of force and from time to time have precipitated crises that could have gone further. Miscalculation in future crises remains a distinct possibility. In addition, technological innovations in offensive or defensive weapons or the emergence of asymmetrics in force structures may undermine the strategic balance. Or the use of conventional forces may increase in an era of nuclear stalemate. Projecting mutual deterrence into the distant future and assuming that the issue of security is no longer relevant or at least no longer of primary importance may be premature. Most LDCs still believe that they have security problems, and there are few constraints on their use of violence.

Even more fundamental though, is the fact that the "security game" is not some antique remnant from the dark age, which is now best forgotten; the "socio-economic game," may be more worthwhile, but it is not the only game in the system. The superpowers still give priority to their relations with each other. China pays a great deal of attention to Russia and to Asian security in general. Western Europe must focus on its relations with Russia and the question of Atlantic security. Even in the third and fourth world preoccupation with regional security, compe-

---

[17.] *The New York Times*, October 14, 1976,

566   tition for leadership, maintenance of military strength, and alignments with extra-
regional powers typify international politics. The "socioeconomic game" is, in fact,
played within the larger framework of the "security game." Instead of economic
interdependence generating a new kind of international order that will weaken
traditional reliance on forcible means of conflict resolution, it is likely that historical
security problems will condition the character of interdependence.

Indeed, as Robert Gilpin has argued, it was American power that created
the conditions for the expansion of American MNCs. Similarly, it can be argued
that American postwar security policy, which was focused on alliances with Europe
and Japan, established the conditions for the high degree of interdependence that
exists today within the European Economic Community (EEC) and between its
members and the United States and Japan. Multiple public and private links in
trade, investment, and currency bind these highly industrialized states together.
But for the American-Soviet security conflict, American protection of Europe, and
the European integration movement, the present measure of interdependence might
not have come to exist. Symbolically, the chiefs of governments of the major
nations of the Atlantic community (which includes Japan) have met regularly at
economic summit conferences for years. The degree of interdependence once led
West German Chancellor Helmut Schmidt to tell President Gerald Ford bluntly,
when the president was thinking of letting New York City go bankrupt, that such
an occurrence would have profound international repercussions and could not
therefore be allowed.

It may well be, therefore, as John Weltman has said, that

> If major conflagration between the superpowers is avoided, if lesser conflicts are
> kept from spreading, if indeed governments are able to devote their energies to
> solving those planet-wide economic, social, and ecological problems which un-
> deniably call for universal cooperation, it will be *because* of successful management
> of the strategic relationships between the superpowers.[18]

Third, the degree of interdependence among states also varies. The United
States is in some ways the least vulnerable of the Western states. Militarily, it
provides security for its allies around the world: they are thus dependent upon the
United States, which, in turn, is interdependent with the Soviet Union. On economic issues, the United States is comparatively invulnerable, except for oil. It
produces abundant food and feeds much of the world. The shortage of global food
supplies thus benefits the United States which reaps considerable earnings from
exports; a crisis for some countries is thus hardly even a threat to the United States.
This country is also a major producer of raw materials and, thanks to superior
technology, has a significant capacity for making substitution for those raw materials
that it lacks. Even in energy, it possesses enormous coal reserves and the technology
to develop other sources. Issues like world population growth and the global division
between rich and poor have so far had little impact on the United States. They do

---

[18] John J. Weltman, "On the Obsolescence of War," *International Studies Quarterly*,
December 1974, pp. 413–414.

not at present threaten its national security or well-being; except for OPEC, the American need for the LDCs is not particularly strong. Europe and Japan, for example, are far more vulnerable on the resource issue. Or, to put it in different words: some states are more vulnerable than other states. There is nothing new about that; some states have always been able to use another state's vulnerabilities to influence their behavior. Even if it were granted that military power is less useful today in compelling the latter to do what they might otherwise not do; the fact that economic means are available to achieve the same purpose is surely not an argument that the fundamental nature of international politics has been transformed.

Fourth, the fact that states, while interdependent, may not be equally vulnerable, means that states have some choice of policies to pursue. The United States has pursued a deliberate strategy of *increasing* interdependence with Russia on arms control since 1960; this interdependence has accelerated since 1972 and has been fortified to some degree with agreements on technology and trade. The United States is also seeking to strengthen its ties with Saudi Arabia by helping it to modernize and by supplying it with extensive arms. Conversely, states can also pursue a policy of *decreasing* interdependence, like the various programs proposed by the Nixon, Ford, Carter, and Reagan administrations to make the United States more self-reliant in energy. During the 1970s many LDCs became increasingly concerned about their dependence on the United States for food and began to emphasize their agricultural-development programs, which had previously been secondary to industrialization.

The prospects of too much interdependence may thus provide the incentive for a state to make itself *less* dependent! Few states, if any, seem ready to accept any radical infringement of their freedom of choice and action. Russia still practices selective détente, and there is no available evidence that Soviet leaders have yet given much thought to the problem of interdependence and the supposedly obvious conclusion that their stake in a peaceful and orderly international system is growing for reasons having little to do with nuclear weapons. Indeed, the Russian economy, rich in resources, is less dependent on the rest of the world than are most Western economies. Given the nature of the Soviet regime, it will undoubtedly try to limit the political consequences of importing Western technology. Nor do countries like Libya, Algeria, or Iraq appear very concerned about the effects of their constant push for higher oil prices.

Fifth, as this example shows, political considerations remain primary in international politics. International economic relations have not yet pulled nations so close together that they have displaced politics; rather, economics remains the handmaiden of politics. Events in Iran since the shah's overthrow suggest that "interdependence" among nations is more than simply a matter of mutually beneficial exchanges of specific resources or products. It is also a matter of compatible regimes. The militantly religious Ayatollah Khomeini clearly considers his regime less "interdependent" with the West, especially the United States, than that of the pro-Western shah had been. Indeed, in Iran today there appears to be no awareness of interdependence at all. Khomeini is very much convinced that the United States, and even more Western Europe and Japan, are *dependent* on Iranian oil, and

568   American actions have confirmed this conviction: for example, the refusal to let the shah settle in the United States after he left Iran, as well as continuing shipments of spare parts for American military equipment to help Khomeini's forces crush the Kurds, who were seeking greater autonomy. Before the seizure of the American hostages in late 1979, everything was done to avoid arousing the Ayatollah's wrath and a break in oil shipments. Khomeini could therefore encourage the fanatical Muslim "students" in their invasion of the American embassy and their holding of its personnel as hostages. The fervently anti-American Khomeini regime has wanted little, if anything, from the United States other than the former shah and his money.

Indeed, events in the Middle East illustrate not interdependence but *Western dependence* and vulnerability. The following frightening words are from an editorial in *The New York Times*:

> Iran's revolution has stirred up Shiite Moslems around the Gulf. . . . Saudi Arabia feels a major threat from a Soviet-supported South Yemen. But it also fears revolutionary sentiment that might build up against the ruling dynasty. . . .
>
> In Iraq, meanwhile, a Shiite majority inspired by Ayatollah Khomeini has been seething. The unrest probably accounts for last summer's bloody purge by the new strongman, Saddam Hussein. He has retaliated by encouraging Iran's Arabs in their sabotage and abrogating a border agreement with Iran. Hostile Kurds and other domestic enemies pepper his pot.
>
> A sizable Shiite minority also troubles the sheikdom of Kuwait. Ethnic Iranians have been arrested or deported. Here as elsewhere in the region, anti-American voices call for big cutbacks in oil production to make the national treasure last. . . .
>
> The confederated united Arab Emirates, like Kuwait and Saudi Arabia, rely heavily on foreign workers, including Palestinians. They also confront Iran's claim to three strategic islands near the narrow Strait of Hormuz, a vital oil route. . . .
>
> Finally, in Oman, the ruling Sultan has lost the comforting shield of the Shah's troops against domestic opponents presumably armed by South Yemen. . . .
>
> In sum, a few well-aimed bullets around the Persian Gulf could cause a massive leak of Western-bound oil. There is no real prospect, let alone guarantee, of stability. The region's tensions are rooted in political, religious, national, dynastic and military rivalries only marginally related to the Arab-Israeli conflict and largely beyond American influence. No prudent nation would count on containing them. It would race to escape its dependence.[19]

Interdependence thus appears to be a matter not only of "objective necessity" but of compatible regimes as well. If the governments that sell oil to the West were replaced by anti-Western religious fanatics or radical secular leaders, oil shipments would be endangered. One shudders to think what would happen in the aftermath of a revolution in Saudi Arabia. If there were genuine interdepen-

---

[19.] *The New York Times*, November 8, 1979.

dence, the United States would not have to worry about an overthrow of the Saudi royal house.

Is it accidental that the highest degree of interdependence is among the Common Market countries and between them, on one hand, and the United States and Canada, on the other—that is, among primarily industrialized and democratic countries with closely linked political and security interests? Is it surprising that interdependence between the United States and the Soviet Union is much less likely to be successful? And is it really amazing that regimes in conflict with the United States and the West should reject claims of interdependence as attempts to prevent them from advancing their national purposes? Is interdependence not actually the goal of the vulnerable?

Sixth, much of the discussion in favor of interdependence is in fact *prescriptive*. The emphasis is on a strategy of increasing the degree of interdependence among nation-states; the more links there are, the more cooperation will be required, and the greater the restraints on states' freedom of action will be. And this point is really the crux of the interdependence thesis: *placing constraints on the national egotism and assertiveness of states by catching them in a "web of interdependence" in which they will become so deeply enmeshed that, on one hand, they will be unable to extricate themselves without suffering great harm and, on the other, they will be compelled to cooperate for the "good of humanity."* An argument supposedly based on description of the facts of interdependence, whether in security or in economics, thus shifts almost imperceptibly to advocacy of a course of policy intended to suppress conflict in the state system in favor of a focus on the welfare of all human beings. Says Lester Brown, "At issue is whether we can grasp the nature and dimensions of the emerging threats to our well-being, whether we can create an integrated world economy and a workable world order, and whether we can render global priorities so that the quality of life will improve rather than deteriorate.[20]

For those who are not optimistic about the feasibility of supranational integration and a possible new world order, but who despair of the ability of states to solve the security problems of nations in the nuclear age and achieve the welfare of the people living in these nations in an age of apparently declining resources, too many people and too little food, and the pollution of the world's land, sea, and air, interdependence becomes an argument for a "world without borders," a "unified global society," a halfway house. In short, *the advocacy of interdependence tends frequently to become a plea for a world "beyond the nation-state," for transcending the state system and building a better, more cooperative, and more harmonious world order, for subordinating "power politics" to "welfare politics" and national interests to planetary interests, for recognizing before it is too late that humanity shares a common destiny. It is essentially a normative, rather than a functional, argument for a revolutionary shift to a new world order from the current state system in which asymmetrical interdependence equals the capacity to coerce.*

It may be that appeals to global solidarity, moral imperatives, and hu-

---

[20.] L. Brown, *op. cit.*, p. 12.

570   manitarian motives are more favorably received today than in the past and that images of a "global village" and "planetary humanism" have been increasingly reflected in world conferences on the environment, population, food, and the new international economic order. But this receptivity does not constitute an

> effective consensus on global redistribution of income or wealth, or global guarantees of minimum human needs, or on global equality of opportunity. Those precepts have scarcely achieved a solid footing domestically, even in the most advanced societies, where democratic voting pushes governmental policies toward egalitarianism. At the international level, no corresponding political structure is either in hand or in prospect.[21]

The international cooperation needed to resolve the many issues of low politics depends upon the existence of a sense of community between rich and poor nations at least as strong as that *within* a highly industrialized nation with a tradition of political unity.[22]

Seventh, although these "relevant utopias," the purpose of which is to rescue humanity from becoming an endangered species, are Western and especially American intellectual constructs, with little appeal in the Socialist world or the third world, the latter would presumably be the principal beneficiaries of global reform as a result of a redistribution of wealth. Furthermore, the LDCs are very suspicious of some Western ideas about interdependence. When it is suggested that a major problem is overpopulation in the LDCs, the latter reply that birth control is tantamount to genocide. Supposedly the West is seeking to maintain a favorable ratio of white to colored peoples and to preserve its own high standard of living, which is allegedly based on the LDCs' resources. More people in the third world would mean the LDCs would keep these resources for themselves, thus interfering with Western patterns of consumption. When it is proposed that all nations show more concern for the environment, the LDCs reply that such concern would prevent them from industrializing. After decades of polluting the land, sea, and air freely, the hypocritical West now seeks to persuade the LDCs to remain simply raw-material suppliers. Suggestions that nuclear diffusion is dangerous to all states, are countered with arguments that efforts to limit proliferation of nuclear arms hinder the LDCs' development of nuclear energy for peaceful purposes—even while the nuclear powers continue to build up their arsenals.[23] Nationalism and national interests still appear to be the primary focus of most, if not all, states.

Let us be clear, then, what these examples show—namely, that Western suggestions as to how the LDCs might develop more quickly are not viewed by the LDCs as well-intended, helpful proposals but as a means of holding them down. The energy crisis is bound to accentuate this sense of bitterness, if not paranoia, about the contemporary distribution of wealth in the world. For many LDCs will be hard hit by the ever-increasing price of oil and will go either into further debt if Western banks continue to make them loans, or, more likely, lower their ex-

---

[21] Lincoln Jordon, *International Stability and North-South Relations* (Stanley Foundation Occasional Paper 17; Muscatine, Iowa: 1978), p. 7.

[22] Blake and Walters, *op. cit.*, p. 35.

[23] *The New York Times*, December 5, 1979.

pectations about modernization. This will hardly come easy to regimes whose claim to power is that they will develop their nations. A frustrated "revolution of rising expectations" will intensify the North–South conflict in two respects: first, between the rich and poor in general, and second, between the rich and OPECs *nouveau riches*, whose wealth and power will continue to grow as oil prices go up and they gradually take over from the oil companies the transportation, refining, and marketing of oil as well.

Eighth, it is not only that the issue of security is neither old-fashioned and out-dated nor guaranteed, but also that economic issues will underline and reemphasize the essentially Hobbesian character of international politics. The reaction to the oil crisis of the 1970s vividly demonstrated the continued stress on national interest, even if close allies and friends were hurt. Thus the United States sought, at least in words, greater energy independence; Canada decided to keep more of its oil and not send it to the United States; the various European states scrambled to make their own oil deals with OPEC countries, including offers of training manpower in nuclear engineering for oil (such as Italy's reported deal with Iraq). Cooperation fell victim to a "me-first" or "beggar thy neighbor" policy among the Western industrial countries. Other nations were hardly wiser or more virtuous, not least the OPEC countries, who regularly raised oil prices. Indeed, OPEC's more radical anti-Western states—whose declarations of policy were generally filled with denunciations of "imperialism" and sympathy for the lot of the poor deprived masses in the underdeveloped world—were frequently in the vanguard of the price hawks" seeking to maximize their earnings. They "beggared" all their neighbors, Western and non-Western; when oil supplies exceeded demand (which should have lowered oil prices) they simply cut supplies and raised prices further. In both security and economic terms, nations, by and large, continued to fear that another state's advantage was their disadvantage; one state's increase in security and/or wealth was perceived as a loss of security and/or wealth for themselves. To repeat: the energy crisis thus tended to reinforce the essentially Hobbesian nature of international politics, however noble the arguments for a new world order that would improve the lot of all mankind.

INTERDEPENDENCE, AMERICAN NORMS, AND ESCAPING FROM "POWER POLITICS"

The fundamental assumption underlying arguments for interdependence is that technological, economic and social forces operating transnationally are "inevitably" driving all nations toward greater cooperation. With a faith in the determinism of economic forces reminiscent of Marxism, proponents of this view are ready to abandon the troublesome world of politics. Perhaps their emphasis on economic necessities should not be surprising. Americans are especially prone to see economics as the universal palliative for the human condition. The basic assumption of laissez-faire capitalism is that human beings are economically motivated; the

572 laws of supply and demand will thus transform individual economic selfishness into social benefits, "the greatest good for the greatest number." The role of the government, according to laissez faire, is to stay out of the market; the best government is the one that governs least, for political interference with economic laws will upset the results those laws are said to produce. Economics is good, identified with human welfare; politics is bad, blocking the road to human progress.

Not surprisingly, when the logic of the free market is projected internationally, it is possible to conclude that a peaceful international society will be created by free trade and that an international laissez-faire policy will benefit all states just as national laissez-faire policies are believed to benefit all individuals within states. People all over the world have a vested interest in peace if they are to carry on their economic relations. Trade and war are supposedly incompatible. Trade, furthermore, depends upon mutual prosperity—the poor do not buy much from one another. War impoverishes and destroys, creating ill will among nations, whereas commerce benefits all participating states; the more trade, the greater the number of individual interests involved. Commerce is thus nationally and individually profitable and creates a vested interest in international peace. War, by contrast, is economically unprofitable and therefore obsolete. Free trade and peace are actually one and the same cause. This version of the argument for interdependence was already quite common at the time of the United States' birth.

> This feeling that one civilization now encompassed the whole world was reinforced by the astounding growth of economic interdependence. The [national political] barriers that existed seemed artificial and ephemeral in comparison with the fine net by which the merchants tied the individuals of the different nations together like "threads of silk." . . . [T]he merchants—whether they are English, Dutch, Russian, or Chinese—do not serve a single nation; they serve everyone and are citizens of the whole world. Commerce was believed to bind the nations together and to create not only a community of interests but also a distribution of labor among them—a new comprehensive principle placing the isolated sovereign nations in a higher political unit. In the eighteenth century, writers were likely to say that the various nations belonged to "one society"; it was stated that all states together formed "a family of nations," and the whole globe a "general and unbreakable confederation."[24]

During the later years of the Cold War, another variant surfaced. The thesis was that the economic development would create affluence, political democracy, and stability, as well as peaceful societies. Helping the LDCs to modernize with foreign aid thus seemed essential. Economic development was even expected to transform communist Russia; as that country became more industrialized and modern, Soviet ideology was expected to erode, its foreign policy to be "derevolutionized," and the country to become a "status quo" state willing to "live and let live." The United States had only to continue its containment policy while

---

[24] Felix Gilbert, *To the Farewell Address* (Princeton: Princeton University Press, 1961), p. 57.

waiting for the results of Russia's own energetic efforts to grow economically. A peaceful world was thus inevitable as the result of beneficial economic forces.

Just as the failure of free trade to bring about lasting peace had led people to pin their hopes on economic development, so the failure of economic development to narrow the gap between rich and poor nations and to generate a more stable and peaceful world has given rise to the thesis of integration, the "businessman's peace," and interdependence. The goal of a peaceful system of more harmonious states has remained constant; so has the focus on the economic forces that will purportedly bring it about. "Economics good, politics bad" appears to be the motto. Economics caters to people's needs and brings benefits; politics brings destruction and misery. Economics binds people together; politics drives them apart. Yet trade and economic development have each in turn failed to achieve this goal; and the current degree of interdependence has not yet replaced the "security game" inherent in the structure of the state system or passed beyond the stage of an asymmetrical interdependence which makes some states vulnerable and confers upon others the capacity to coerce.

The argument for interdependence thus reflects an attempt to escape from "power politics" into a calmer, more decent, and humane world. The Vietnam war intensified this urge to escape from the wicked world of "power politics" among many disillusioned supporters of American cold-war policies. Having in the past supported a policy which they believed was a crusade in defense of democracy against the anti-democratic forces of totalitarianism, they now looked for both forgiveness for past error and a new way to achieve the same goal of a better, more just and peaceful world. However, it would not be power—which was bad and divisive—but economics—which was good and healing—which would achieve this objective. Characteristically American, they argue that it is the United States' responsibility to lead the world into the new era. They remain crusaders for the moral cause, even though

> [T]he largest part of today's global welfare crisis originates within states, remains within states, and the most powerful tools for corrective action are internal instruments of nation-state policy. Until those instruments have been properly used, an attractive welfare bargain among states is beyond reach. Global welfare management turns out to be just like every other act of charity. It must begin at home.[25]

A FINAL WORD ON CONCEPTS

We began this book by setting up an analytical framework. It is perhaps appropriate, then, to end by commenting on that framework. First, it should be apparent that all three levels of analysis are ncessary if international politics is not to be oversim-

---

[25] Paarlberg, *op. cit.*, p. 576.

574   plified. The state-system model may help us greatly to understand the outbreak of the Cold War, but by itself it cannot lead us to the reasons for the scope and intensity of this conflict. On the other hand, to attribute the eruption of the American-Soviet conflict solely to the Soviet anticapitalism or to American anti-communism is to ignore the dilemmas of power and security confronting all members of the state system, and the environment in which states exist. The result is not only a restricted understanding of state behavior but also a misreading of history that could, if extended, result in a misreading of the future as well. To suggest, as American revisionist writers do, that, without an alleged American anticommunist animus predating Soviet postwar behavior, there would have been no Cold War is therefore to ignore the underlying realities of the state system. In the absence of a first-level perspective, the Cold War is bound to be misunderstood, for it will then be viewed solely as the result of American anticommunism or Soviet anticapitalism, or Truman's toughness or Stalin's paranoia, rather than as the result of the age-old game of "power politics," which members of the state system are compelled to play. And, of course, if the reasons for this conflict are perceived incorrectly, the lessons drawn—lessons that will influence future policy—will also be incorrect.

Second, although usually we need all three levels of analyses, they are not necessarily equally important. Which level may be most significant in any given analysis is partly a matter of the investigator's judgment. Whereas one analyst may tend to give greatest weight to the structure of the state system and the least to personality, such weighting cannot be applied regardless of circumstances. For example, an analysis of post-World War II American foreign policy based solely on changing distributions of international power is incomplete. For American decision makers, having successfully used anticommunism to mobilize public and congressional support once Soviet postwar aims had become clear, found themselves trapped in competitive two-party domestic politics: the mere possibility that the party out of office might accuse the other of being "soft on communism" drove the latter (especially the Democrats) to pursue more militant policies and allowed less flexibility in policy decisions. The impact of domestic politics thus contributed greatly to such preemptive actions as the 1965 Dominican intervention or the intervention in Vietnam the same year. These interventions were undertaken in large part to forestall opposition assaults on the administration's conduct of foreign policy.

Third, different levels of analysis may yield conflicting interpretations. In first-level analysis, based upon the structure or hierarchy of power in the system, those who are most powerful are equated with those who are most active. A small country under normal conditions is not going to be a principal troublemaker, no matter what its ideology or aims; it is the big and powerful countries whose conflicts will disturb the system. Strength derives from industry and modern technology. But our second-level developmental scheme holds out the expectation that modernized nations will be more peaceful. A world of urbanized industrial states would provide for consumer satisfaction and citizens' domestic orientation; war would no longer "pay." Will a multipolar world—a nuclear multipolar world—be more dangerous or more peaceful? The answer may be different in first-level and second-level analyses.

In another instance, according to the second-level interpretation, the American intervention in Vietnam was the logical result of the American economic system, based on profits. In third-level analysis, the war is viewed as the result of policy makers' distorted perceptions of the state system. In the former interpretation, the outbreak or avoidance of war is a question of the system; the changing of leaders makes no difference, for they are simply products and instruments of that system. Whether Johnson or McGovern was president is not important in explaining American military involvement in Vietnam; the system itself determined that intervention. It is an illusion that "one simply replaces individuals in office with other men . . . rather than solving problems with an altogether new system"[26] that will behave in a quite different manner. In our example, a socialist system would supposedly not be prone to military intervention and an expansive, aggressive foreign policy because it would not be committed to the search for economic profits abroad. According to the third-level analysis, however, who was President is important, indeed the key factor. The "system," whatever it may be, is not viewed as an automaton moving along a predetermined path; countries with the same types of system do not all act alike. Johnson intervened in Vietnam, McGovern probably would not have done so. Systems are not, these analysts insist, beyond human control and will; leaders' choices of policy drive the system.[27]

Fourth, although the various levels of analysis and the concepts used at each level are intended to help the analyst to understand state behavior better—regardless of whether or not he or she approves of that behavior—particular levels and certain concepts can also be used to cast blame. We observed earlier the fascination with economic explanations of conflict and war, particularly the capitalist-imperialist interpretation. More often than not, such explanations are invoked polemically, in order to cut through the complexities of reality and to reveal the "true" motivations behind policy. Usually based on contrasts between privileged and poor, "haves" and "have nots," "exploiters" and "exploited," evil oppressors and decent oppressed victims, these explanations lead to castigations, denunciations, and accusations—and usually simple solutions as well. It is important to be aware that the analytical levels can be used in this polemical manner and to guard against such use.

Fifth, concepts change. Bipolarity in the prenuclear period was traditionally unstable, and multipolarity was stable. Nuclear weapons, however, have led to a reversal of these correlations. However valid and persuasive a concept may seem at a given moment, it ought to be reexamined regularly, because in a world of rapidly changing conditions a concept that is valid today may be invalid tomorrow. Some concepts of development or modernization involving stages of economic growth and accompanying political stages, which are based upon Western

---

[26] Gabriel Kolko, *The Roots of American Foreign Policy* (Boston: Beacon, 1969), p. 134.

[27] Doris Kearns, in her biography *Lyndon Johnson and the American Dream* (New York: Harper & Row, 1970), places heavy emphasis on personality and psychological interpretation.

historical experience, are already being reassessed, as scholars learn more about the variety of Western experiences, as well as those of non-Western states.

Finally, an analysis of international politics, regardless of level, can be no better than the concepts on which it is based. But many of the concepts necessary for a study of contemporary international politics are still new—especially those related to modernization, regional integration, and deterrence. To understand the rapidly changing world in which we live, the social scientist has been compelled to grope for such new concepts. Even the language is sometimes new, reflecting the inadequacy of older terms for dealing with some of the unique problems of our time. To take only one example, our military vocabulary now includes the following terms, which were virtually unknown before World War II:[28]

nuclear exchange	limited war
nuclear stalemate	catalytic war
mutual deterrence	nth-country problem
balance of terror	nuclear proliferation
credibility	arms control
"soft" and "hard" weapons	tacit agreement
"passive" and "active" defenses	nuclear blackmail
preemptive, first, and second strikes	crisis management
assured destruction	nuclear threshold
countervalue	overkill
counterforce	death of earth (DOE)
damage limitation	

Other changes in the international environment are just beginning to be analyzed: for example, MNCs and the new economic agenda in international politics. Are the MNCs more powerful than many of the smaller or less developed states? Where and how, for instance, do they fit into the broader framework of systemic behavior? There is no comprehensive theory of transnationalism, at least not yet, and perhaps there will not be one as long as states remain the principal actors; the international system is defined in terms of interactions among states, and states basically set the rules by which other actors operate. On the other hand, as Kenneth Waltz has suggested, if the latter should at some future time begin to rival or surpass the major state actors, a new theory of international politics will be necessary.[29]

Of course, analysts like Hoffmann, Nye, and Keohane suggest a need for a "modern" theory of international politics based on socioeconomic or welfare issues.[30] Yet, although these issues may seem novel after several decades of focusing on security issues, states have long pursued economic aims by both economic and military means, just as they have sought political objectives. Is the distinction

---

[28] For a comprehensive dictionary of such terms, see Wolfram F. Hanreider, ed., *Words and Arms* (Boulder: Westview, 1979).

[29] Kenneth N. Waltz, "Theory of International Relations," in Fred I. Greenstein and Nelson W. Polsby, *International Politics* (Reading, Mass.: Addison-Wesley, 1975), p. 73.

[30] Hoffmann, "Choices," and Keohane and Nye, *op. cit.*

between welfare, or low-politics, issues and security, or high-politics, issues useful analytically, aside from simplifying reality? The proponents of interdependence emphasize change and dispensing with outmoded ways of thinking about international politics. There can surely be no question that many changes have occurred, but has this stress on the new not exaggerated their effects at the expense of the tenacious continuity of old ways and the state system's resistance to change? How much do arguments that traditional analysis of the state system is no longer relevant reflect the hopes and biases of observers, rather than clearly perceptible international trends? Is Klaus Knorr correct when he says that "we get understandably tired of old paradigms and wish to try out new ones" and "normative leanings run strong in academia, and wishfulness—the desire to escape from the prepotence of traditional international behavior—can induce a suitable perceptual selectivity"?[31]

All analysts have biases; none is "value free" or objective. Every analysis thus begins with certain assumptions or judgments; for example, in this book the persistence of basic behavior patterns among states has been stressed. Clearly there has to be more investigation of the degree to which a new international politics is likely to affect studies of international politics. The scholars mentioned and others have made stimulating contributions to this investigation and have suggested new directions. Although they have not yet come up with a new, broad theory, theoretical concern is high and theory in a state of flux.

In the meantime, this generation, like earlier generations, will be called upon—or condemned—to live with an ambiguous reality, it will have to forswear both cynicism and illusion in trying to deal with it. It must simultaneously avoid a seductive but futile escape into nostalgia for the past and imperious rage at a world that will not conform to its vision. Instead, like its predecessors, this generation must learn to live in a world where neither war nor peace is a constant, where the millennium remains a distant dream and the threat of nuclear Armageddon an ever-present fear. The beginning of wisdom is understanding the most difficult of all worlds—the *real* one. It is to that end that this book is dedicated.

---

[31] Klaus Knorr, "Is International Coercion Waning or Rising?" *International Security*, Spring 1977, p. 110.

A Selective Bibliography of Books†

INTERNATIONAL POLITICS AND THE STATE SYSTEM

ARON, RAYMOND, *Peace and War.** Garden City, N.Y.: Doubleday, 1966; London: Weidenfeld and Nicolson, 1966. Paperback ed., Holt, Rinehart and Winston.

BULL, HEDLEY. *The Anarchical Society.** New York: Columbia University Press, 1977.

CARR, EDWARD H. *The Twenty Years' Crisis 1919–1939.** New York and Basingstoke: Macmillan, 1961. Paperback ed., Harper Torchbooks.

DOUGHERTY, JAMES E., and ROBERT L. PFALTZGRAFF, JR. *Contending Theories of International Relations.** Philadelphia: Lippincott, 1971.

HERZ, JOHN H. *International Politics in the Atomic Age.** New York: Columbia University Press, 1962.

KAPLAN, MORTON A. *System and Process in International Politics.** New York: Wiley, 1964.

———, ed. *New Approaches to International Relations.* New York: St. Martin's Press, 1968.

KNORR, KLAUS, and JAMES N. ROSENAU, eds. *Contending Approaches to International Politics.* Princeton, N.J.: Princeton University Press, 1969.

MCCLELLAND, CHARLES A. *Theory and the International System.** New York: Macmillan, 1966.

MORGENTHAU, HANS J. *Politics Among Nations.* 5th ed. New York: Knopf, 1972.

ROSECRANCE, RICHARD. *Action and Reaction in World Politics.* Boston: Little, Brown, 1963.

---

*Indicates paperback.

†For articles, see chapter footnotes.

ROSENAU, JAMES N., ed. *Domestic Sources of Foreign Policy*. New York: The Free Press, 1967.

———, ed. *International Politics and Foreign Policy*. 2d ed. New York: The Free Press, 1969

———, ed. *Linkage Politics*. New York: The Free Press, 1969.

SINGER, J. DAVID, ed. *Quantitative International Politics*. New York: The Free Press, 1968.

SPIEGEL, STEVEN L. *Dominance and Diversity*. Boston: Little, Brown, 1972.

WALTZ, KENNETH N. *Man, the State, and War.* * New York: Columbia University Press, 1959.

———. *Theory of International Politics.* * Reading, Mass.: Addison-Wesley Publishing Co., 1979.

WIGHT, MARTIN. *Power Politics*. Edited by Hedley Bull and Carsten Holbraad. New York: Holmes & Meier, 1978.

WOLFERS, ARNOLD. *Discord and Collaboration: Essays on International Politics.* * Baltimore: The Johns Hopkins Press, 1965.

DETERRENCE AND ARMS CONTROL

Atomic Energy Commission. *The Effects of Nuclear Weapons*. Rev. ed. Washington, D.C.: Government Printing Office, 1962.

BRODIE, BERNARD. *Strategy in the Missile Age.* * Princeton, N.J.: Princeton University Press, 1959.

———. *War and Politics.* * New York: The Macmillan Co., 1973.

COLLINS, JOHN M. *American and Soviet Military Trends Since the Cuban Missile Crisis.* * Washington: Center for Strategic and International Studies, Georgetown University, 1978.

GEORGE, ALEXANDER L., et al. *The Limits of Coercive Diplomacy.* * Boston: Little, Brown, 1971.

——— and SMOKE, RICHARD, *Deterrence in American Foreign Policy.* * New York: Columbia University Press, 1974.

HOLST, JOHAN J., and UWE NERLICH. *Beyond Nuclear Deterrence*. New York: Crane, Russak, 1977.

KAHAN, JEROME H. *Security in the Nuclear Age.* * Washington: Brookings Institution, 1975.

KAHN, HERMAN. *On Thermonuclear War*. Princeton, N.J.: Princeton University Press, 1960.

———. *Thinking About the Unthinkable.* * New York: Horizon Press, 1962. Paperback ed., Avon.

KAUFMAN, WILLIAM W. *The McNamara Strategy*. New York: Harper & Row, 1964.

KISSINGER, HENRY A. *The Necessity for Choice.* * New York: Harper & Row, 1961.

———, ed. *Problems of National Strategy.* * New York: Holt, Rinehart and Winston, 1965.

KNORR, KLAUS. *On the Uses of Military Power in the Nuclear Age*. Princeton, N.J.: Princeton University Press, 1966.

LEVINE, ROBERT A. *The Arms Debate*. Cambridge, Mass.: Harvard University Press, 1962.

MARTIN, LAURENCE, ed. *Strategic Thought in the Nuclear Age*. Baltimore: Johns Hopkins University Press, 1980.

MORGAN, PATRICK M. *Deterrence.* * Beverly Hills, Calif.: Sage Publications, 1977.

NEWHOUSE, JOHN. *Cold Dawn*. New York: Holt, Rinehart and Winston, 1973.

580   Osgood, Robert E., and Robert W. Tucker. *Force, Order, and Justice.* Baltimore: The Johns Hopkins Press, 1967.

Schelling, Thomas C. *Strategy of Conflict.* Cambridge, Mass.: Harvard University Press, 1960. Paperback ed., Oxford (London).

Schelling, Thomas C., and Morton H. Halperin, *Strategy and Arms Control.* New York: Twentieth Century Fund, 1961.

Snyder, Glenn H. *Deterrence and Defense.* Princeton, N.J.: Princeton University Press, 1961.

Talbott, Strobe. *Endgame.* New York: Harper & Row, 1979.

Wolfe, Thomas W. *The SALT Experience.* Cambridge, Mass.: Ballinger, 1979.

CRISES AND LIMITED WAR (CONVENTIONAL AND REVOLUTIONARY)

Abel, Elie. *The Missile Crisis.* Philadelphia: Lippincott, 1966. Paperback ed., Bantam.

Blaufarb, Douglas S. *The Counterinsurgency Era.* New York: The Free Press, 1977.

Blechman, Barry M., and Stephen S. Kaplan. *Force without War.* Washington: Brookings Institution, 1978.

Galula, David. *Counterinsurgency Warfare.* New York: Holt, Rinehart and Winston, 1964.

Giap, Vo Nguyen. *Banner of People's War: The Party's Military Line.* New York: Holt, Rinehart and Winston, 1970.

———. *People's War, People's Army.* New York: Holt, Rinehart and Winston, 1962. Paperback ed., Bantam.

Greene, T. N., ed. *The Guerrilla—and How to Fight Him.* New York: Holt, Rinehart and Winston, 1962.

Heilbrunn, Otto. *Partisan Warfare.* New York: Holt, Rinehart, and Winston, 1962.

Kennedy, Robert F. *Thirteen Days.* New York: W. W. Norton, 1969. Paperback ed., Signet.

Kissinger, Henry A. *Nuclear Weapons and Foreign Policy.* New York. Harper & Row, 1957. Abridged paperback ed., Norton.

Mander, John. *Berlin.* Baltimore: Penguin Books, 1962.

Mao Tse-tung on Guerilla Warfare. Translated and with an Introduction by Samuel B. Griffith. New York: Holt, Rinehart and Winston, 1961.

Meyer, Karl E., and Tad Szulc. *The Cuban Invasion.* New York: Holt, Rinehart and Winston, 1962.

Osgood, Robert E. *Limited War.* Chicago: University of Chicago Press, 1957.

Paret, Peter, and John W. Shy. *Guerrillas in the 1960's.* Rev. ed. New York: Holt, Rinehart and Winston, 1962.

Smoke, Richard. *War: Controlling Escalation.* Cambridge, Mass.: Harvard University Press, 1978.

Snyder, Glenn H., and Paul Diesing. *Conflict Among Nations.* Princeton: Princeton University Press, 1978.

Spanier, John W. *The Truman-MacArthur Controversy and the Korean War.* Cambridge, Mass.: Harvard University Press, 1959. Rev. paperback ed., Norton.

Speier, Hans. *Divided Berlin.* New York: Holt, Rinehart and Winston, 1961.

Stern, Ellen P., ed. *The Limits of Intervention.* Beverly Hills, Calif.: Sage Publications, 1977.

TAYLOR, MAXWELL D. *The Uncertain Trumpet.* New York: Harper & Row, 1960.   581
THAYER, CHARLES W. *Guerrilla.** New York: Harper & Row, 1963.
WHITING, ALLEN S. *China Crosses the Yalu.* New York: Macmillan, 1960.
WILLIAMS, PHIL. *Crisis Management.* New York: Wiley, 1976.
WOLF, ERIC. *Peasant Wars of the Twentieth Century.** New York: Harper & Row, 1969.
YOUNG, ORAN. *The Politics of Force.* Princeton, N.J.: Princeton University Press, 1968.

THE VIETNAM WAR

COOPER, CHESTER L. *The Lost Crusade.* New York: Dodd, Mead, 1970.
DRAPER, THEODORE. *Abuse of Power.** New York: Viking Press, 1967.
FALL, BERNARD B. *Street Without Joy.* 3d rev. ed. Harrisburg, Pa.: The Stackpole Co., 1963.
_____. *The Two Viet-Nams.* 2d rev. ed. New York: Holt, Rinehart and Winston, 1967.
_____. *Viet-Nam Witness, 1953–66.* New York: Holt, Rinehart and Winston, 1966.
GURTOV, MELVIN. *The First Vietnam Crisis.** New York: Columbia University Press, 1967.
HOOPES, TOWNSEND. *The Limits of Intervention.** New York: McKay, 1969.
KATTENBURG, PAUL M. *The Vietnam Trauma in American Foreign Policy, 1945–75.* New Brunswick, N.J.: A Transaction Book, 1980.
LEWY, GUENTER. *America in Vietnam.* New York: Oxford University Press, 1978.
OBERDORFER, DON. *Tet.* Garden City, N.Y.: Doubleday, 1971.
*The Pentagon Papers.** Chicago: Quadrangle, 1971. Paperback ed., Bantam.
PFEFFER, RICHARD M., ed. *No More Vietnams?** New York: Harper & Row, 1968.
PIKE, DOUGLAS. *Viet Cong.** Cambridge, Mass.: The MIT Press, 1966.
SCHLESINGER, ARTHUR M., JR. *Bitter Heritage.** Boston: Houghton Mifflin, 1967. Paperback ed., Fawcett Crest.
SCHURMANN, FRANZ, et al. *The Politics of Escalation in Vietnam.** Boston: Beacon Press, 1966. Paperback ed., Fawcett Premier.
SHAPLEN, ROBERT. *The Lost Revolution.** New York: Harper & Row, 1966.
TANHAM, GEORGE K. *Communist Revolutionary Warfare.* Rev. ed. New York: Holt, Rinehart and Winston, 1967.
THOMPSON, SIR ROBERT. *No Exit from Vietnam.* New York: McKay, 1969.

NUCLEAR PROLIFERATION

BUCHAN, ALASTAIR, ed. *A World of Nuclear Powers?** Englewood Cliffs, N.J.: Prentice-Hall, 1966.
GOMPERT, DAVID C., MICHAEL MANDELBAUM, RICHARD L. GARWIN, and JOHN H. BARTON. *Nuclear Weapons and World Politics.** New York: McGraw-Hill (for the Council on Foreign Relations/1980s Project), 1977.
GREENWOOD, TED, HAROLD A. FEIVESON, and THEODORE B. TAYLOR. *Nuclear Proliferation.** New York: McGraw-Hill (for the Council on Foreign Relations/1980s Project), 1977.
LEFEVER, ERNEST W. *Nuclear Arms in the Third World.** Washington: Brookings Institution, 1979.

582 COMPARATIVE FOREIGN POLICY

BRZEZINSKI, ZBIGNIEW K., and SAMUEL P. HUNTINGTON. *Political Power: USA/USSR.** New York: Viking Press, 1964.

CLINE, RAY S. *World Power Assessment 1977.* Boulder, Colo.: Westview Press, 1977.

MACRIDIS, ROY C., ed. *Foreign Policy in World Politics.** 3d ed. Englewood Cliffs, N.J.: Prentice-Hall, 1967.

————. *Modern European Governments.** Englewood Cliffs, N.J.: Prentice-Hall, 1968.

NORTHEDGE, F. S., ed. *The Foreign Policies of the Powers.** New York: Holt, Rinehart and Winston, 1969.

WALTZ, KENNETH N. *Foreign Policy and Democratic Politics.** Boston: Little, Brown, 1967.

WILKINSON, DAVID O. *Comparative Foreign Relations.** Belmont, Calif.: Dickenson Publishing Co., 1969.

AMERICAN FOREIGN POLICY

ADLER, SELIG. *The Isolationist Impulse.** New York: Abrams, 1957. Paperback ed., Collier Books.

ALMOND, GABRIEL. *The American People and Foreign Policy.** New York: Holt, Rinehart and Winston, 1960.

BELL, CORAL. *The Diplomacy of Détente.* New York: St. Martin's Press, 1977.

BROWN, SEYOM. *The Faces of Power.** New York: Columbia University Press, 1968.

GADDIS, JOHN LEWIS. *Russia, the Soviet Union, and the United States.* New York: Wiley, 1978.

GATI, CHARLES, ed. *Caging the Bear.** New York: Bobbs-Merrill, 1973.

GILBERT, FELIX. *To the Farewell Address.** Princeton, N.J.: Princeton University Press, 1961.

HALLE, LOUIS J. *The Cold War as History.** New York: Harper & Row, 1967.

HILSMAN, ROGER. *To Move a Nation.** Garden City, N.Y.: Doubleday, 1967. Paperback ed., Dell.

HOFFMANN, STANLEY. *Primacy or World Order.** New York: McGraw-Hill, 1978.

HOWE, IRVING, ed. *A Dissenter's Guide to Foreign Policy.** New York: Holt, Rinehart and Winston, 1968. Paperback ed., Doubleday Anchor.

JONES, JOSEPH M. *The Fifteen Weeks.** New York: Viking Press, 1955. Paperback ed., Harcourt.

KENNAN, GEORGE F. *American Diplomacy 1900-1950.** Chicago: University of Chicago Press, 1951. Paperback ed., Mentor.

————. *Memoirs.** Boston: Little, Brown. 1967.

————. *The Cloud of Danger.* Boston: Atlantic-Little, Brown, 1977.

KOLKO, GABRIEL. *The Roots of American Foreign Policy.** Boston: Beacon Press, 1967.

LIPPMANN, WALTER. *U.S. Foreign Policy.* Boston: Little, Brown, 1943.

MORGENTHAU, HANS J. *In Defense of the National Interest.* New York: Knopf, 1951.

————. *A New Foreign Policy for the United States.** New York: Holt, Rinehart and Winston, 1969.

MUELLER, JOHN E. *War, Presidents, and Public Opinion.** New York: Wiley, 1973.

Osgood, Robert E. *Ideals and Self-Interest in America's Foreign Relations.** Chicago: 583
University of Chicago Press, 1953.

Seabury, Paul. *The Rise and Decline of the Cold War.* New York: Basic Books, 1967.

Smith, Gaddis. *American Diplomacy During the Second World War.** New York: Wiley,
1966.

Spanier, John. *American Foreign Policy Since World War II.** 8th ed. New York: Holt,
Rinehart and Winston, 1980.

Steel, Ronald. *Pax Americana.** New York: Viking Press, 1967.

Tsou, Tang. *America's Failure in China.** Chicago: University of Chicago Press, 1963.

Tucker, Robert W. *Nation or Empire?** Baltimore: The Johns Hopkins Press, 1968.

_____. *The Radical Left and American Foreign Policy.** Baltimore: The Johns Hopkins
Press, 1971.

MEMOIRS AND BIOGRAPHIES OF AMERICAN STATESMEN AND ADMINISTRATIONS

Acheson, Dean. *Present at the Creation.** New York: W. W. Norton, 1969. Paperback
ed., Signet.

Brown, Seyom. *The Crises of Power: Foreign Policy in the Kissinger Years.* New York:
Columbia University Press, 1979.

Byrnes, James F. *Speaking Frankly.* New York: Harper & Brothers, 1947.

Eisenhower, Dwight D. *White House Years: Mandate for Change.** Garden City, N.Y.:
Doubleday, 1963. Paperback ed., NAL.

_____. *White House Years: Waging Peace.* Garden City, N.Y.: Doubleday, 1965.

Ferrell, Robert H. *George C. Marshall.* New York: Cooper Square Publishers, 1966.

Gerson, Louis L. *John Foster Dulles.* New York: Cooper Square Publishers, 1967.

Hoopes, Townsend. *The Devil and John Foster Dulles.* Boston: Little, Brown, 1973.

Kissinger, Henry. *White House Years.* Boston: Little, Brown, 1979.

Nixon, Richard. *RN.** New York: Grosset & Dunlap, 1978.

Schlesinger, Arthur M., Jr. *A Thousand Days.** Boston: Houghton Mifflin, 1965.
Paperback ed., Fawcett Crest.

Sorensen, Theodore C. *Kennedy.** New York: Harper & Row, 1965. Paperback ed.,
Bantam.

Truman Harry S. *Memoirs.** 2 vols. Garden City, N.Y.: Doubleday, 1958. Paperback ed.,
Signet.

COMMUNIST THEORY

Bober, M. M. *Karl Marx's Interpretation of History.** New York: W. W. Norton, 1965.

Daniels, Robert V. *The Nature of Communism.** New York: Random House, 1962.

Hunt, R. N. Carew. *The Theory and Practice of Communism.** Rev. ed. Baltimore:
Penguin Books, 1963.

Lichtheim, George. *Marxism: An Historical and Critical Study.** 2d ed. New York: Holt,
Rinehart and Winston, 1965.

584   MARCUSE, HERBERT. *Soviet Marxism.* * New York: Columbia University Press, 1958. Paperback ed., Random House Vintage.

MENDEL, ARTHUR P., ed. *The Essential Works of Marxism.* * New York: Bantam Books, 1961.

MEYER, ALFRED G. *Leninism.* * Cambridge, Mass.: Harvard University Press, 1957. Paperback ed., Holt, Rinehart and Winston.

————. *Marxism.* Cambridge, Mass.: Harvard University Press, 1954. Paperback ed., University of Michigan Press.

POPPER, KARL R. *The Open Society and Its Enemies.* * Vol. II: *High Tide of Prophecy.* Princeton, N.J.: Princeton University Press, 1950. Paperback ed., Harper Torchbooks.

WILSON, EDMUND. *To the Finland Station.* * New York: Harcourt, Brace & Co., 1940. Paperback ed., Garden City, N.Y.: Doubleday Anchor Books, 1953.

SOVIET FOREIGN AND MILITARY POLICY

ASPATURIAN, VERNON V., ed. *Process and Power in Soviet Foreign Policy.* Boston: Little, Brown, 1971.

BRZEZINSKI, ZBIGNIEW K. *Ideology and Power in Soviet Politics.* * Rev. ed. New York: Holt Rinehart and Winston, 1967.

DALLIN, DAVID J. *Soviet Foreign Policy After Stalin.* Philadelphia: Lippincott, 1961.

DINERSTEIN, HERBERT S. *War and Soviet Union.* * Rev. ed. New York: Holt, Rinehart and Winston, 1962.

DOUGLAS, JOSEPH D. JR., and AMORETTA M. HOEBER. *Soviet Strategy for Nuclear War.* * Stanford Calif.: Hoover Institution Press, 1979.

GARTHOFF, RAYMOND L. *Soviet Military Policy.* New York: Holt, Rinehart and Winston, 1966.

————. *Soviet Strategy in the Nuclear Age.* * Rev. ed. New York: Holt Rinehart and Winston, 1962.

GEHLEN, MICHAEL P. *The Politics of Coexistence.* Bloomington: Indiana University Press, 1967.

HORELICK, ARNOLD L., and MYRON RUSH. *Strategic Power and Soviet Foreign Policy.* Chicago: University of Chicago Press, 1966.

KENNAN, GEORGE F. *Russia and the West under Lenin and Stalin.* * Boston: Little, Brown, 1961. Paperback ed., NAL.

KOLKOWICZ, ROMAN, et al. *The Soviet Union and Arms Control.* * Baltimore: The Johns Hopkins Press, 1970.

LEITES, NATHAN. *The Operational Code of the Politburo.* New York: McGraw-Hill, 1951.

————. *A Study of Bolshevism.* New York: The Free Press, 1953.

MACKINTOSH, J. M. *Strategy and Tactics of Soviet Foreign Policy.* London and New York: Oxford University Press, 1962.

MOSELY, PHILIP E. *The Kremlin and World Politics.* * New York: Random House, 1960.

SCOTT, HARRIET F., and WILLIAM F. SCOTT. *The Armed Forces of the USSR.* Boulder, Colo.: Westview Press, 1978.

SHULMAN, MARSHALL D. *Beyond the Cold War.* * New Haven, Conn.: Yale University Press, 1965.

————. *Stalin's Foreign Policy Reappraised.* * Cambridge, Mass.: Harvard University Press, 1963. Paperback ed., Atheneum.

SOKOLOVSKY, V. D., ed. *Military Strategy: Soviet Doctrine and Concept.** New York: Holt, Rinehart and Winston, 1963.

STRAUSZ-HUPE, ROBERT, et al. *Protracted Conflict.** New York: Harper & Row, 1959.

TRISKA, JAN F., and DAVID D. FINLEY. *Soviet Foreign Policy.* New York: Macmillan, 1968.

ULAM, ADAM B. *Expansion and Coexistence.** 2d ed. New York: Holt Rinehart and Winston, 1974.

VON LAUE, THEODORE. *Why Lenin, Why Stalin?** Philadelphia: Lippincott, 1964.

WHETTEN, LAWRENCE L., ed. *The Future of Soviet Military Power.* New York: Crane, Russak, 1976.

WOLFE, THOMAS W. *Soviet Power and Europe, 1945-1970.** Baltimore: The Johns Hopkins Press, 1970.

————. *Soviet Strategy at the Crossroads.* Cambridge, Mass.: Harvard University Press, 1964.

ZIMMERMAN, WILLIAM. *Soviet Perspectives on International Relations, 1956–1967.* Princeton, N.J.: Princeton University Press, 1969.

COMMUNIST CHINA

BARNETT, A. DOAK. *China and the Major Powers in East Asia.** Washington: Brookings Institution, 1977.

CRANKSHAW, EDWARD. *The New Cold War.** Baltimore: Penguin Books, 1963.

FLOYD, DAVID. *Mao against Khrushchev.** New York: Holt, Rinehart and Winston, 1964.

HALPERIN, MORTON. *China and the Bomb.** New York: Holt, Rinehart and Winston, 1965.

HINTON, HAROLD C. *Communist China in World Politics.* Boston: Houghton Mifflin, 1966.

HSIEH, ALICE LANGLEY. *Communist China's Strategy in the Nuclear Era.** Englewood Cliffs, N.J.: Prentice-Hall, 1962.

LOW, ALFRED D. *The Sino-Soviet Dispute.* Madison, N.J.: Fairleigh Dickinson University Press, 1978.

MEHNERT, KLAUS. *Peking and Moscow.** New York: G. P. Putnam's Sons, 1963.

OKSENBERG, MICHEL, and ROBERT D. OXNAM. *Dragon and Eagle.* New York: Basic Books, 1978.

SALISBURY, HARRISON E. *War between Russia and China.** New York: W. W. Norton, 1969. Paperback ed., Bantam.

WINT, GUY. *Communist China's Crusade.** New York: Holt, Rinehart and Winston, 1970.

ZAGORIA, DONALD S. *The Sino-Soviet Conflict, 1956–1961.* Princeton, N.J.: Princeton University Press, 1962.

LESS DEVELOPED COUNTRIES AND MODERNI-ZATION

ALMOND, GABRIEL A., and JAMES S. COLEMAN. *The Politics of the Developing Areas.* Princeton, N.J.: Princeton University Press, 1960.

BERLINER, JOSEPH S. *Soviet Economic Aid.* New York: Holt, Rinehart and Winston, 1958.

586

BLACK, C. E. *The Dynamics of Modernization.** New York: Harper & Row, 1966.

BLACK, EUGENE R. *The Diplomacy of Economic Development.** New York: Atheneum, 1963.

CRABB, CECIL V. JR. *The Elephants and the Grass.* New York: Holt, Rinehart and Winston, 1965.

DEUTSCH, KARL W., and WILLIAM J. FOLTZ, eds. *Nation-Building.* New York: Atherton Press, 1963.

EHRLICH, PAUL. *The Population Bomb.** New York: Ballantine, 1968.

EMERSON, RUPERT. *From Empire to Nation.** Cambridge, Mass.: Harvard University Press, 1960. Paperback ed., Beacon.

FICKETT, LEWIS P., ed. *Problems of the Developing Nations.** New York: Thomas Y. Crowell, 1966.

FINER, S. E. *The Man on Horseback.* New York: Holt, Rinehart and Winston, 1962.

GEERTZ, CLIFFORD, ed. *Old Societies and New States.* New York: The Free Press, 1963.

GERSCHENKRON, ALEXANDER. *Economic Backwardness in Historical Perspective.* Cambridge, Mass.: Harvard University Press, 1962. Paperback ed., Holt, Rinehart and Winston.

HANSEN, ROGER D. *Beyond the North-South Stalemate.* New York: McGraw-Hill (for the Council on Foreign Relations/1980s Project), 1979.

HEILBRONER, ROBERT L. *The Great Ascent.** New York: Harper & Row, 1963.

———. *The Making of Economic Society.** Englewood Cliffs, N.J.: Prentice-Hall, 1962.

HUNTER, ROBERT E., and JOHN E. RIELLY, eds. *Development Today.* New York: Holt, Rinehart and Winston, 1972.

HUNTINGTON, SAMUEL P. *Political Order in Changing Societies.** New Haven, Conn.: Yale University Press, 1968.

JANOWITZ, MORRIS. *The Military in the Political Development of New Nations.** Chicago: University of Chicago Press, 1964.

JOHNSON, JOHN J., ed. *The Role of the Military in Underdeveloped Countries.* Princeton, N.J.: Princeton University Press, 1962.

LEWIS, W. ARTHUR. *The Evolution of the International Economic Order.** Princeton: Princeton University Press.

LIPSET, SEYMOUR M. *The First New Nation.* New York: Basic Books, 1963.

LISKA, GEORGE. *The New Statecraft: Foreign Aid in American Foreign Policy.* Chicago: University of Chicago Press, 1960.

MARTIN, LAURENCE W., ed. *Neutralism and Nonalignment.** New York: Holt, Rinehart and Winston, 1962.

MILLIKAN, MAX F., and DONALD L. M. BLACKMER, eds. *The Emerging Nations.** Boston: Little, Brown, 1961.

MORAN, THEODORE H. *Multinational Corporations and the Politics of Dependence.** Princeton: Princeton University Press, 1974.

MYRDAL, GUNNAR. *Rich Lands and Poor.* New Yorker: Harper & Row, 1957.

———. *The Challenge of World Poverty.* New York: Pantheon, 1970.

NORDLINGER, ERIC A. *Soldiers in Politics.** Englewood Cliffs, N.J.: Prentice-Hall, 1977.

ORGANSKI, A. F. K. *The Stages of Political Development.* New York: Knopf, 1965.

PYE, LUCIAN W. *Politics, Personality, and Nation-Building.** New Haven, Conn.: Yale University Press, 1966.

ROSTOW, W. W. *Stages of Economic Growth.** London and New York: Cambridge University Press, 1960.

ROTHSTEIN, ROBERT L. *The Weak in the World of the Strong.* New York: Columbia University Press, 1977.

RUSTOW, DANKWART A. *A World of Nations.** Washington, D.C.: The Brookings Institution, 1967.

SHILS, EDWARD A. *Political Development in the New States.** 's-Gravenhage, The Netherlands: Marten & Co., 1962.

SIGMUND, PAUL E., ed. *The Ideologies of the Developing Nations.** 2d rev. ed. New York: Holt, Rinehart and Winston, 1972.

SIMON, SHELDON W., ed. *The Military and Security in the Third World.* Boulder, Colo.: Westview Press, 1979.

STALEY, EUGENE. *The Future of Underdeveloped Countries.** Rev. ed. New York: Holt Rinehart and Winston, 1961.

SZULC, TAD. *The Winds of Revolution.** Rev. ed. New York: Holt Rinehart and Winston, 1965.

TAPINES, GEORGES, and PHYLLIS T. PIOTROW. *Six Billion People.* New York: McGraw-Hill (for the Council on Foreign Relations/1980s Project), 1978.

TUCKER, ROBERT W. *The Inequality of Nations.* New York: Basic Books, 1977.

VON DER MEHDEN, FRED R. *Politics of the Developing Nations.** Englewood Cliffs, N.J.: Prentice-Hall, 1964.

WARD, BARBARA. *Five Ideas That Change the World.** New York: W. W. Norton, 1959.

––––––. *The Rich Nations and the Poor Nations.** New York: W. W. Norton, 1962.

WRIGGINS, HOWARD W., and GUNNAR ADLER-KARLSSON. *Reducing Global Inequities.* New York: McGraw-Hill (for the Council on Foreign Relations/1980s Project), 1978.

FOREIGN POLICY DECISION-MAKING (INCLUDING MILITARY-INDUSTRIAL COMPLEX)

ALLISON, GRAHAM T. *Essence of Decision.** Boston: Little, Brown, 1971.

BARNET, RICHARD J. *The Economy of Death.** New York: Atheneum, 1969.

––––––. *The Roots of War.** Baltimore: Penguin Books, 1973.

BERKOWITZ, MORTON, P. G. BOCK, and VINCENT J. FUCCILLO. *The Politics of American Foreign Policy.** Englewood Cliffs, N.J.: Prentice-Hall, 1977.

BETTS, RICHARD K. *Soldiers, Statesmen, and Cold War Crises.* Cambridge, Mass.: Harvard University Press, 1977.

DESTLER, I. M. *Making Foreign Economic Policy.* Washington: Brookings Institution, 1980.

GELB, LESLIE H., and RICHARD K. BETTS. *The Irony of Vietnam.** Washington: Brookings Institution, 1979.

GRABER, DORIS. *Public Opinion, the President, and Foreign Policy.** New York: Holt, Rinehart & Winston, 1968.

HALPERIN, MORTON. *Bureaucratic Politics and Foreign Policy.** Washington, D.C.: Brookings Institution, 1974.

HALPERIN, MORTON, and ARNOLD KANTER, eds. *Readings in American Foreign Policy.** Boston: Little, Brown, 1973.

HEAD, RICHARD G., FRISCO W. SHORT, and ROBERT C. MCFARLANE. *Crisis Resolution.* Boulder, Colo.: Westview Press, 1978.

HILSMAN, ROGER. *The Politics of Policy Making in Defense and Foreign Affairs.** New York: Harper & Row, 1971.

HUNTINGTON, SAMUEL P. *The Common Defense.** New York: Columbia University Press, 1961.

588   JANIS, IRVING L. *Victims of Groupthink.* * Boston: Houghton Mifflin, 1972.

KANTER, ARNOLD. *Defense Politics.* Chicago: University of Chicago Press, 1979.

KRASNER, STEPHEN D. *Defending the National Interest.* * Princeton: Princeton University Press, 1978.

LENTNER, HOWARD H. *Foreign Policy Analysis.* Columbus, Ohio: Charles E. Merrill, 1974.

LEVERING, RALPH B. *The Public and American Foreign Policy, 1918–1978.* New York: William Morrow, 1978.

MUELLER, JOHN E. *War, Presidents and Public Opinion.* New York: Wiley, 1973.

ROSEN, STEVEN, ed. *Testing the Theory of the Military-Industrial Complex.* Lexington, Mass.: Lexington Books, 1973.

RUSSETT, BRUCE M. *What Price Vigilance?* * New Haven, Conn.: Yale University Press, 1970.

SPANIER, JOHN and JOSEPH NOGEE, eds. *Congress, the Presidency and Foreign Policy.* * New York: Pergamon, 1981.

THOMPSON, JAMES CLAY. *Rolling Thunder.* * Chapel Hill: University of North Carolina Press, 1980.

YARMOLINSKY, ADAM. *The Military Establishment.* * New York: Harper & Row, 1971.

UNITED NATIONS

BAILEY, SIDNEY D. *The United Nations.* * New York: Holt, Rinehart and Winston, 1963.

BLOOMFIELD, LINCOLN P. *The United Nations and U.S. Foreign Policy.* * Boston: Little, Brown, 1960.

BLOOMFIELD, LINCOLN P., et al. *International Military Forces.* Boston: Little, Brown, 1964. 1964.

BOYD, ANDREW. *United Nations.* * Baltimore: Penguin Books, 1963.

BURNS, ARTHUR LEE, and NINA HEATHCOTE. *Peace-keeping by U.N. Forces.* New York: Holt, Rinehart and Winston, 1963.

CALVOCORESSI, PETER. *World Order and New States.* New York: Holt, Rinehart and Winston, 1962.

CLAUDE, INIS L., JR. *The Changing United Nations.* * New York: Random House, 1967.

_____. *Power and International Relations.* New York: Random House, 1964.

_____. *Swords into Plowshares.* 4th ed. New York: Random House, 1971.

DALLIN, ALEXANDER. *The Soviet Union at the United Nations.* * New York: Holt, Rinehart and Winston, 1962.

FRYE, WILLIAM R. *A United Nations Peace Force.* * Dobbs Ferry, N.Y.: Oceana Publications, 1957.

GOODRICH, LELAND M. *The United Nations in a Changing World.* New York: Columbia University Press, 1974.

HAAS, ERNST B. *Beyond the Nation-State.* * Stanford, Calif.: Stanford University Press, 1964.

MILLER, LINDA B. *World Order and Local Disorder.* Princeton, N.J.: Princeton University Press, 1967.

MILLER, RICHARD. *Dag Hammarskjold and Crisis Diplomacy.* * Dobbs Ferry, N.Y.: Oceana Publications, 1961.

NICHOLAS, HERBERT G. *The United Nations as a Political Institution.** 2d ed. London
and New York: Oxford University Press, 1962.

NYE, JOSEPH S., JR. *Peace in Parts.** Boston: Little, Brown, 1971.

STOESSINGER, JOHN G. *The United Nations and the Superpowers.** New York: Random House, 1966.

DISARMAMENT

BARNET, RICHARD. *Who Wants Disarmament?** Boston: Beacon, 1960.

BULL, HEDLEY. *The Control of the Arms Race.** 2nd ed. New York: Holt, Rinehart and Winston, 1965.

DOUGHERTY, JAMES E. *How to Think about Arms Control and Disarmament.* *New York: Crane, Russak, 1973.

NOEL-BAKER, PHILLIP. *The Arms Race.** New York: Oceana Publications, 1958.

SPANIER, JOHN, and JOSEPH L. NOGEE. *The Politics of Disarmament.** New York: Holt, Rinehart and Winston, 1962.

TATE, MERZE. *The Disarmament Illusion.* New York: Macmillan, 1942.

———. *The United States and Armaments.* Cambridge, Mass.: Harvard University Press, 1948.

INTERNATIONAL LAW

BOZEMAN, ADDA. *The Future of Law in a Multicultural World.* Princeton: Princeton University Press, 1971.

BRIERLY, J. L. *The Law of Nations.* 6th ed. New York: Oxford University Press, 1963.

CORBETT, PERCY E. *Law and Society in the Relation of States.* New York: Harcourt Brace Jovanovich, 1951.

DEUTSH, KARL W., and STANLEY HOFFMAN, eds. *The Relevance of International Law.* Garden City N.Y.: Doubleday, 1971.

HENKIN, LOUIS. *How Nations Behave.** New York: Holt, Rinehart and Winston, 1968.

KAPLAN, MORTON A., and NICHOLAS DeB. KATZENBACH. *The Political Foundations of International Law.* New York: Wiley, 1961.

INTERNATIONAL MORALITY

BUTTERFIELD, HERBERT. *International Conflict in the Twentieth Century: A Christian View.* New York: Harper & Row, 1960.

LEFEVER, ERNEST W., ed. *Ethics and World Politics.* *Baltimore: Johns Hopkins University Press, 1972.

HERZ, JOHN H. *Political Realism and Political Idealism.* Chicago: University of Chicago Press, 1951.

NIEBUHR, REINHOLD. *Moral Man and Immoral Society.** New York: Charles Schribner's Sons, 1932.

———. *The Children of Light and the Children of Darkness.* New York: Charles Scribner's Sons, 1944.

———. *The Irony of American History.** New York: Charles Scribner's Sons, 1952.

THOMPSON, KENNETH W. *Political Realism and the Crisis of World Politics.* Princeton: Princeton University Press, 1960.

WOLFERS, ARNOLD. *The Anglo-American Tradition in Foreign Affairs.* New Haven: Yale University Press, 1956.

590 PERCEPTION AND PSYCHOLOGY

FRANK, JEROME D. *Sanity and Survival.** New York: Random House, 1968.
HOLSTI, OLE R., et al. *Enemies in Politics.** Chicago: Rand McNally, 1967.
KELMAN, HERBERT C., ed. *International Behavior.* New York: Holt, Rinehart and Winston, 1965.
KLINEBERG, OTTO. *The Human Dimension in International Relations.** New York: Holt, Rinehart and Winston, 1964.
RIVERA, JOSEPH H. DE. *The Psychological Dimension of Foreign Policy.* Columbus, Ohio: Charles E. Merrill, 1968.
STAGNER, ROSS. *Psychological Aspects of International Conflict.** Belmont, Calif.: Brooks/Cole Publishing Co., 1967.
STOESSINGER, JOHN G. *Nations in Darkness.** New York: Random House, 1971.
———. *Why Nations Go to War.* New York: St. Martin's Press, 1974.
WHITE, RALPH K. *Nobody Wanted War.** Garden City, N.Y.: Doubleday, 1968.

FUNCTIONALISM AND COMMUNITY-BUILDING

DEUTSCH, KARL, et al. *Political Community and the North Atlantic Area.* Princeton, N.J.: Princeton University Press, 1957.
ETZIONI, AMITAI. *Political Unification.** New York: Holt, Rinehart and Winston, 1965.
HAAS, ERNST B. *The Uniting of Europe.* Stanford, Calif.: Stanford University Press, 1958.
LICHTHEIM, GEORGE. *The New Europe.** 2d ed. New York: Holt, Rinehart and Winston, 1964.
LIEBER, ROBERT J. *British Politics and European Unity.* Berkeley: University of California Press, 1970.
LINDBERG, LEON N., and STUART A. SCHEINGOLD. *Europe's Would-Be Polity.** Englewood Cliffs, N.J.: Prentice-Hall, 1970.

TRANSNATIONALISM, WORLD ORDER, AND ECONOMICS

BARNET, RICHARD J., and RONALD MULLER. *Global Reach: The Power of the Multinational Corporation.** New York: Simon & Schuster, 1975.
BERES, LOUIS R., and HARRY R. TARG. *Planning Alternative World Futures.** New York: Holt, Rinehart and Winston, 1975.
BERGSTEN, FRED, THOMAS HOLST, and THEODORE H. MORAN. *American Multinationals and American Interests.** Washington: Brookings Institution, 1978.
BLAKE, DAVID H., and ROBERT S. WALTERS. *The Politics of Global Economic Relations.** Englewood Cliffs, N.J.: Prentice-Hall, 1976.
BROWN, LESTER R. *World without Borders.** New York: Vintage Books, 1973.
———. *In the Human Interest.** New York: W. W. Norton, 1974.

BROWN, SEYOM. *New Forces in World Politics.* * Washington, D.C.: The Brookings Institution, 1974.

FALK, A. RICHARD. *A Global Approach to National Policy.* Cambridge, Mass.: Harvard University Press, 1975.

GILPIN, ROBERT. *U.S. Power and the Multinational Corporation.* New York: Basic Books, 1975.

JOHANSEN, ROBERT. *The National Interest and the Human Interest.* * Princeton: Princeton University Press, 1980.

KEOHANE, ROBERT O., and JOSEPH S. NYE. *Power and Interdependence.* * Boston: Little, Brown, 1977.

KEOHANE, ROBERT O., and JOSEPH S. NYE, JR., eds. *Transnational Relations and World Politics.* Cambridge, Mass.: Harvard University Press, 1972.

KINDLEBERGER, CHARLES P., ed. *The International Corporation.* Cambridge, Mass.: MIT Press, 1970.

LAQUEUR, WALTER. *Terrorism.* Boston: Little, Brown, 1977.

MANSBACH, RICHARD W., YALE H. FERGUSON, and DONALD E. LAMPERT. *The Web of World Politics.* * Englewood Cliffs, N.J.: Prentice-Hall, 1976.

MENDLOVITZ, SAUL H. *On the Creation of a Just World Order.* * New York: The Free Press, 1975.

PIRAGES, DENNIS. *Global Ecopolitics.* * North Scituate, Mass.: Duxbury Press, 1978.

SAID, ABDUL, and LUIZ R. SIMONS, eds. *The New Sovereigns.* * Englewood Cliffs, N.J.: Prentice-Hall, 1975.

SAMPSON, ANTHONY. *The Sovereign State of ITT.* New York: Stein and Day, 1973.

SPERO, JOAN E. *The Politics of International Economic Relations.* * New York: St. Martins's Press, 1977.

C. MAXWELL STANLEY. *Managing Global Problems.* * Iowa City: University of Iowa (for the Stanley Foundation), 1979.

VERNON, RAYMOND. *Sovereignty at Bay.* New York: Basic Books, 1971.

———. ed. *The Oil Crisis.* * New York: W. W. Norton, 1976.

WU, YUAN-LI. *Raw Material Supply in a Multipolar World.* * 2nd ed. New York: Crane, Russak (for the National Strategy Information Center), 1979.

A Selective Glossary

ABM An antiballistic missile that is designed to "knock-down" incoming missiles and/or their warheads (nuclear bombs) before designated targets can actually be struck.

Alliances Agreements among states to support each other militarily in case of attack and/or to enhance their mutual interests. Alliances supplement national power and clarify spheres of interest. NATO and the Warsaw Pact are examples.

Anti-Colonialism The rejection of the former "father" or "mother" country by a Third World (or Fourth World) state.

Appeasement In contemporary usage, a term of shame meaning one-sided concessions to an adversary. Prior to the Munich Conference of 1938, the term was "respectable" because it denoted a settlement of just grievances and consequent avoidance of war.

Arms Control In general, the process of securing international agreements which place restrictions upon numbers, types, and performance characteristics of weapons. In the nuclear context, the process is aimed at stabilizing mutual deterrence and avoiding mass destruction through the elimination of U.S. or USSR first-strike incentives.

Arms Race The attempt by a nation or alliance to attain military superiority over its adversaries through marked increases in the production of weapons and/or technological breakthroughs. Arms races are characterized by an action–reaction pattern among nations, resulting in costly expenditures for all the concerned parties.

Balance of Capability and Balance of Resolve The two mutually supportive components of the balance of power. While quantifiable military strength is important, the perception of a nation's willingness to use tangible power when threatened has assumed even greater significance in the crisis-prone nuclear era.

Balance of Power A relationship whereby nations strive to maximize their security through the establishment of an approximate systemic power equilibrium, thus reducing the probability of warfare or domination. In short, power checks power.

Bipolar System An international system dominated by *two* superpowers and/or coalitions. This system is characterized by a high degree of insecurity, clear distinctions between friend and foe, hypersensitivity to power shifts, the drawing of lines or "frontiers," arms races, and cohesiveness of each alliance camp.

Bipolycentrism A state system characterized by the "loosening" of rival blocs into less cohesive alliances and the simultaneous rise of nonaligned influential actors. While the dominant military powers remain the United States and the Soviet Union ("bi"), the growing influence from other ("poly") centers of influence heralds the possible transition to true multipolarity.

Bribery Aid Refers to American assistance which was intended to buy the support of the ruling classes and military, such as Latin America.

"Burning One's Bridges" Strengthening the credibility of a commitment by making it impossible to physically retreat or ensuring that your troops would be killed ("tripwire effect") if attacked by an adversary.

Bureaucratic Policy-Making Model A pluralistic decision-making approach that stresses the roles of the executive/legislative branches, nongovernmental groups, and foreign-policy agencies.

Capitalism An economic system that calls for private ownership of property, a free market based on the laws of supply and demand, a general absence of governmental interference, and the pursuit of individual profit.

Charismatic Hero In a developing country, the revolutionary leader who symbolizes national unity and confers legitimacy upon the new nation and its government.

Cold War The international climate of extreme tension and hostility that evolved between the United States (the West) and the Soviet Union (communist bloc) after World War II.

Comecon The Council for Mutual Economic Aid, founded in 1949 by the Soviet Union as a means of integrating the economies of the Eastern European states.

Common Market The European Economic Community (EEC), founded in 1958, the purpose of which was to create unified national economic policies (uniform external tariff wall, mobile labor and capital, and so forth) among its original members (Belgium, France, West Germany, Italy, Netherlands, and Luxembourg). Eventually, economic unity may "spill over" into a political federation of Europe. Now has four more members (Britain, Denmark, Ireland and Greece).

Communism A revolutionary ideology that seeks the destruction of capitalism and its replacement by a collectivist society in which private ownership of property is no longer necessary. Consequently, both social/economic classes and the state will cease to exist.

Compensation This is the division of a strategically located country in order to preserve the balance of power among the major states (example, the Russian-German division of Poland in 1939).

Containment This fundamental policy, coined by George Kennan in 1947, formed the core of post-World War II American foreign policy. A long-term, patient policy, containment was dedicated to blocking Soviet expansion through countervailing American economic/military power. Eventually, it was expected that the Soviet leadership would "mellow," abandon its expansionist drive, and accept the international status quo.

Counterforce Strategy Strategic weapons targeted at the adversary's military capabilities such as bomber bases, ICBM silos, air defense installations, and so on.

Countervalue (Countercity) Strategy Strategic weapons targeted at the adversary's population centers, industries, and social/political institutions.

"Credible Commitment" A nation's avowed obligation to an ally or friendly state that is *believed* (and perceived) to be significant and vital by adversaries. Such techniques as "staking one's reputation" or "relinquishing the initiative" are intended to enhance credibility.

594   **Crises**   Intense, relatively brief great-power confrontations that have become substitutes for war in the nuclear era. Crises involve vital national interests, a significant disturbance in the balance of power, and each party's reputation for power. From a decision-making perspective, a crisis is characterized by little planning time, elite executive-level deliberations, the central role of the president, paucity of reliable information, and the perceived need to react quickly and decisively.

Cruise Missile   A nuclear missile, resembling a pilotless aircraft, that operates entirely within the earth's atmosphere and is launched from the air or sea.

"Crusader" Statesman   A key policy maker whose views are characterized by an unshakeable missionary zeal to eliminate world evil or those adversaries who exemplify such values.

Cuban Missile Crisis   The 13 tense days in October of 1962 when the U.S. and the Soviet Union clashed over the issue of Soviet missiles emplaced in Cuba. The crisis ended with Khrushchev's promise to remove the missiles in exchange for President Kennedy's pledge not to invade Cuba.

Decision-Making Approach   The level of analysis that concentrates on the specific policy makers and governmental departments officially responsible for the conduct and implementation of foreign policy.

Détente   In general, a relaxation of previously strained relations or tensions between two or more countries. Specifically, in the United States détente meant that U.S.–USSR global competition could be "restrained" while maximizing cooperation in the areas of arms control, trade, technology, and so forth.

Deterrence (Nuclear)   In a bipolar nuclear context, the assumption that total war is synonymous with mutual destruction, since effective second-strike capabilities exist in both superpowers' arsenals. This nuclear standoff, if perceived as credible by rational policy makers on both sides, prevents the outbreak of war. Thus, the utility of nuclear forces rests in their *threatened* rather than actual use. The purpose of deterrence is to influence the adversary's intention not to attack.

Diplomacy   International negotiations and/or bargaining in order to decide upon the distribution of the things about which nations differ.

Disarmament   Agreement to reduce (or abolish) existing military forces and/or weapons. Disarmament is based upon the faulty assumption that arms races cause wars. Wars occur because of underlying political tensions, not the existence of weaponry.

Divide-and-Rule   A traditional technique where Nation A attempts to exploit existing differences among Nation B and its allies so as to gain a distinct balance of power advantage.

Domino Theory   A theory that originated in the post-World War II period, stressing the interdependence of a superpower's global commitments. Thus, "the failure to honor a commitment in one area may be seen by both the adversary and allies as an indication that other commitments also may not be honored." From this perspective, allowing a strategically located state to fall under communist control would eventually result in neighboring states succumbing as well.

Economic "Fat"   In cases where a nation's economy is blessed with great productivity and wealth, a significant amount of "butter" can be converted into "guns" and still leave the population with enough butter.

Economic Flexibility A nation's ability to convert its economy quickly from the production of peacetime goods to military hardware.

Economic "Slack" The amount of unused productivity in a nation's economy.

Embargo An economic weapon of a nation whose purpose is to prevent exported products and/or strategic technology from being sent to the embargoed party.

First World The world of the advanced urban-industrial societies and "mixed economies" of Western Europe, North America (Canada and the U.S.), and Japan.

Fourth World The world of the underdeveloped countries with few exploitable raw resources, who therefore require considerable amounts of foreign aid in order to survive (examples: Haiti, Egypt, Thailand).

Functionalism The theory that envisions economic and social cooperation among nations in various fields, which will eventually construct a new international political community.

Graduated Escalation A wartime strategy of incrementally increasing the scope and intensity of force levels in the hope that the enemy will at some point agree to negotiate an end to the war.

"Groupthink" A termed coined by Janis to indicate the tendency of decision-making groups to formulate policy on the basis of insufficient information and ineffective, unequal consideration of all available options.

Guerrilla Warfare, See **Revolutionary War**

"Guns vs. Butter" A competition of objectives which many states confront, involving spending on security (military-defense needs) concerns vs. welfare pursuits (schools, hospitals, education, housing, and so forth).

Human Rights The early theme of the Carter Administration's foreign policy, which stressed a moral dedication to individual freedoms and opposition to those governments that flagrantly violate these principles.

ICBM An intercontinental ballistic missile that can be launched over a range of 3000–4000 (or more) nautical miles (example: U.S. Minuteman III).

Ideology A set of beliefs that attempts to describe and explain contemporary reality while prescribing a desired future.

IGOs Intergovernmental organizations that may be classified as global (United Nations) or regional (OAS, Arab League). Military, social, and economic functions can also distinguish IGOs (North Atlantic Treaty Organization, World Health Organization).

Imperialism (general) "Any relationship of effective domination or control, political or economic, direct or indirect, of one nation over another."

Imperialism (Lenin) Lenin's theory argues that the proletariat (workers) revolution did not occur as expected in western capitalistic societies because of those societies' exploitation of poorer, underdeveloped countries. "Superprofits" obtained from these foreign markets were used to "buy-off" the political consciousness of western workers.

Incrementalism The tendency of policy makers to move forward very slowly while

596 concentrating upon momentary, short-run aims rather than comprehensive long-range planning.

Intangible Components of Power Components that do not lend themselves to accurate calculations or quantification, such as a nation's national morale, quality of leadership, or the efficiency of its political system.

Integration According to Karl Deutsch, "the attainment, within a territory, of a 'sense of community' and of institutions and practices strong enough and widespread enough to assure, for a 'long time,' dependable expectations of 'peaceful change' among its population."

Intentions vs. Capabilities A fundamental dilemma confronting decision makers when calculating the linkage between goals (intentions) and power (capability) of an adversary. For example, the reasons for the ultimate policy objectives behind the massive military build-up by the Soviet Union in the 1970s can be interpreted as either offensive or defensive in nature.

Interdependence The argument that because nations of the "global system" have become *mutually vulnerable* through an interrelationship of socioeconomic and technological issues ("low politics")—energy, overpopulation, poverty, ecology, food supplies, human rights, monetary exchanges—their future behavior will be oriented toward long-term collaboration rather than the old "balance-of-power security through the use of force" mentality ("high politics issues"). In short, the maxim of "we will all lose or gain together" will be stressed rather than "his gain is my loss."

Intermestic Policy Relating to issues that embrace *both* international and domestic politics, including food production, access to raw materials, and drilling rights under the ocean.

International or State System The "regular and observable" interactions of sovereign political units (primarily nations) within a basic global context of cultural and institutional anarchy.

Intervention Either overt or covert involvement in the affairs of a state by another state or alliance in order to influence policy and events.

Irredentism The desire of State A to annex territory in State B that contains peoples who possess linguistic, racial, or ethnic background similar to State A's citizenry.

Isolationism A foreign policy pursued by the United States especially during the nineteenth century and immediately prior to World Wars I and II. Isolationism generally refers to noninvolvement in the affairs of the international community, although the *degree* of disinterest varies considerably.

Kiloton Weapon A nuclear weapon, the yield of which is measured in thousands of tons of TNT. A ten kiloton weapon is equal to the explosive power of 10,000 tons of TNT.

"Kto-kovo" In Soviet ideological parlance, "Who will destroy whom?" The phrase signifies the belief in the irreconcilable struggle between capitalism and communism.

"Latinamericanization of the United States" A term that refers to a major shift or reverse in the international economy: the developed, industrialized countries (particularly the United States) are now exporting agricultural products while importing Third World manufactured products rather than the other way around.

LDCs The "less-developed" countries of the international system, usually categorized as belonging to the Third or Fourth Worlds. Economic backwardness and/or ineffective, weak political institutions are typical of these states.

Levels of Analysis Three explanatory levels—the state system (balance of power), the nation-state (its internal nature), and decision making (leadership elites)—collectively explain and describe how and why nations "play" the games they do. Each level of analysis derives its analytical power from selective variables and data, thus stressing *different* cause-and-effect relationships behind *similar* international events and behavior.

Limited War An armed conflict fought for limited political objectives and with definite restrictions upon military power. Additionally, limited warfare is characterized by noninvolvement of the superpowers, geographical and targeting constraints (sanctuaries), nonuse of tactical nuclear weapons, and forgoing total victory over the enemy.

Macropolitics The view that the *international interest* of mankind should replace the traditional national interest since global society has become increasingly interdependent.

MAD An acronym for mutual assured destruction, a doctrine that is at the heart of strategic deterrence, deterring all-out war. It is exemplified by the statement that "you may kill me if you strike me, but I will kill you before I die." Since theoretically neither side can win, nuclear war is prevented.

Marshall Plan A massive program of American economic aid (15 billion dollars) aimed at rebuilding war-torn Western Europe during the 1948–1952 period. An economically healthy Europe was perceived by American policy makers as being more resistant to communist inroads.

Marxism The "scientific" doctrine developed by Karl Marx and Friedrich Engels during the nineteenth century, which viewed historical development as a series of economic class struggles (society's "haves" vs. "have-nots"). Consequently, capitalism would inevitably be overthrown by a worker's revolution (proletariat) against the bourgeoisie (propertied, exploiting class), *eventually* ushering in a classless, nonpropertied, nonexploitive utopia.

Megaton Weapon A nuclear weapon whose yield is explosively equivalent to one million tons of TNT. For example, a five megaton missile warhead would equal the explosive power of five million tons of TNT.

Milieu Objectives State goals "concerned with shaping the environment of the state system in which all states live."

Military-Industrial Complex The alleged conspiratorial alliance of the professional military, defense corporation executives, national security managers, labor union members, university researchers, and pro-defense congressmen, which benefits economically and politically from sustained international tension and the resulting high levels of defense spending on strategic and conventional arms.

Mirror-Image An explanation for international violence resulting from misperception. Each nation sees itself as "good" while opponents are viewed as the embodiment of "evil."

MIRV A multiple independently targeted reentry vehicle: a single ballistic missile

598   that carries a cluster of warheads with each warhead capable of hitting a separate target.

Misperception   The theory that wars occur because decision makers have good and evil or black and white images of the world, thus filtering out any incoming information which conflicts with their preconceived "cognitive maps."

Models (Analytical Frameworks)   Simplified and selective representations of (international) reality that perform the functions of political classification, explanation, and prediction.

Modernization   The long, complex, and often painful transformation of a state from an agrarian, socially fragmented entity to a politically unified, urban-industrialized society. Economically, development is marked by a change from traditional society to one with high mass consumption. Above all, modernization involves fundamental changes in the population's values, expectations, and psychocultural orientation. In the view of some, modernization will convert politically unstable, totalitarian, or revolutionary states into mature, cooperative, and affluent (peace-loving) members of the international system.

Motivational Power   Signifies a nation's "political will" in actively employing its power and/or persuasive capabilities in the international system.

Multinational Corporations (MNCs)   Business enterprises that conduct their operations across international boundaries and in multiple markets, in effect creating a "global shopping center." American MNCs include Exxon, Pepsi-Cola, and General Motors.

Multipolar System   A system that has at least four approximately equal powers. In contrast to rigid and simple bipolarity, multipolarity is considered complex and flexible. Frequent alliance realignment and lowered sensitivities to changes in the balance of power are therefore characteristic of this international structure.

MX Missile   A "mobile" missile that may be deployed by the United States during the late 1980s in order to make the nation's land-based missiles less vulnerable to a potential Soviet first-strike.

National Interest   An ordering of priorities in accordance with national goals.

National Morale   An intangible component of power that refers to a population's patriotism, national loyalty, and willingness to sacrifice during times of war and/or international tension.

National Style   Each state's particular approach to foreign policy based on its historical experience, political and social values, economic status, and self-image. Invariably, national policy-making elites will selectively perceive world events, problems, and "solutions" through culturally colored "lenses."

Negative Power   The capacity to prevent unfavorable changes in the international status quo and/or a nation's perceived security interests.

Neutralization   A balance-of-power technique, opposite from compensation (see Glossary), that signifies a "hands-off" policy toward a strategically important country.

NIEO (New International Economic Order)   A demand made by the LDCs for a more equitable distribution of the world's wealth as just compensation for alleged past and present exploitation by the West.

Nonalignment A policy of noncommitment (particularly evident in the Third World) to either the communist or free world alliances.

Nuclear Diffusion The acquisition of national nuclear capabilities by a significant number of middle- and smaller-rank states in the international system.

OPEC The Organization of Petroleum Exporting Countries (Saudi Arabia, Algeria, Quatar, Kuwait, Libya, Iraq, Iran, United Arab Emirates, Nigeria, Indonesia, Venezuela, and Ecuador), a cartel whose purpose is collectively to fix the levels of production and the price of crude oil on the world market.

Peace A complex, multifaceted concept which, in its most general sense, denotes the absence of major warfare in the international system.

Peaceful Coexistence A Soviet doctrine acknowledging the dangers of nuclear war and therefore asserting that the communist-capitalist struggle could be channeled into nonmilitary areas of competition.

Per Capita GNP Signifies the Gross National Product, the sum market value of all consumer and capital goods and services produced in a year, divided by the population. It is one indicator or index used in calculating power rankings among nations.

Perceived (Subjective) vs. Actual (Objective) Power The distinction (or gap) between what others believe a nation's power to be and how much power that nation could really employ in a war situation. A nation's actual power will be "downgraded" or disregarded if adversaries believe it will not be used in the defense of national interests.

Petrodollars The vast amount of "oil" dollars paid to OPEC by the industrialized states (particularly the United States), resulting in devaluation of the dollar, increases in import prices, and renewed spirals in the rate of domestic inflation.

Pole In the international system, a major center of military/economic power incorporating an individual state or coalition, and thus capable of affecting the balance of power in an extensive area of the world. Each pole possesses vital interests distinct from other comparable poles.

Political Community A community that has effective control over the means of violence, a decision-making center that allocates resources, and a focus of political identification for the population under its jurisdiction.

Population Explosion Refers to the doubling of the world's population approximately every 35 years. Thus, the projected figure for the year 2010 will be eight billion people!

Positive Power The capacity to compel favorable alterations in the international status-quo, particularly (although far from exclusively) by a superpower.

Possession Objectives Objectives "which states cherish for themselves and which they pursue in a competitive situation." Security, the perpetuation of the territorial integrity and political independence of the state, is a prime example.

Power (among States) The ability to influence other nations in the state system to behave in a certain manner or to prevent them from taking a particular action.

Pragmatist Statesman A policy maker who is flexible and willing to modify his views after listening to opposing viewpoints.

600   **Prestige**   A nation's reputation for power among its fellow states and the degree of respect that is subsequently accorded.

Security Policy Decisions   Basic policy decisions of a noncrisis nature incorporating inputs and bargaining patterns among foreign policy bureaucracies, the White House Staff, Congress, interest groups, and the public.

Preemptive Strike   An attack launched by an aggressor in the belief that the other side is ready to launch its own first strike.

Preventive Strike   An aggressor's unprovoked, carefully calculated attack upon an opponent with the expectation that total victory can be achieved.

Psycho-milieu vs. Operational-milieu   Referring to the decision-making level of analysis, the gap that may or may not exist between the perceived world involving decision-maker's values and beliefs and the real world and its objective constraints.

Rational-Actor Model   A decision-making approach that stresses a clear definition of policy goals and an examination of the possible options that can attain those goals.

"Realists" vs. "Madman"   The Soviet perception of the division within American foreign policy elites, with the former preferring international caution and peaceful coexistence and the latter being militantly anticommunist and war-oriented.

Relinquishing the Initiative   The deterrer makes it known that he will stand firm and that the responsibility for starting any conflict rests on the other side.

Revolutionary or Revisionist State   A state in the international system (examples are late eighteenth-century France and twentieth-century Soviet Russia) whose leadership opposes the existing exploitive world order and seeks to liberate mankind, bringing it freedom, justice, and peace.

Revolutionary Warfare (Guerrilla Warfare)   Lengthy conflicts fought by a band of insurgents (or proclaimed liberators) whose primary goal is to capture state power as a means of transforming the nation's sociopolitical structure and economy. The key to the guerrilla's eventual success or failure is their ability to win the support of the native population.

SALT   The Strategic Arms Limitation Talks, negotiations begun in 1969 between the United States and Soviet Union.

"Search and Destroy"   The primary United States ground strategy in the Vietnam War in which American forces in helicopters searched for communist guerrillas in the countryside to destroy them.

Second-Strike Capability   The ability after absorbing a nuclear first-strike from the enemy to have sufficient remaining retaliatory forces (missiles, bombers, and so on) to deliver a counterattack resulting in the enemy's total destruction.

Second World   The communist states of Eastern Europe and the Soviet Union.

Security Council   The primary organ in the United Nations responsible for the preservation of peace and security. The fifteen-member council can take enforcement action against international aggression provided one of the five great powers (permanent members) does not exercise a veto.

"Security Dilemma"   In an anarchical state system, the "security dilemma" follows from a state guarding itself by increasing its power to enhance its security;

as its potential adversary does the same, the first state's sense of insecurity recurs, leading it to increase its power once more, and so forth.

Sino–Soviet Split The serious conflict between Communist China (People's Republic of China) and the Soviet Union over ideological interpretations, leadership of the international communist movement, disputed territories, and major strategic issues.

SLBM A submarine-launched ballistic missile, such as the United States' Poseidon or Trident.

Sovereign State The primary political actor in the international system. Each of the approximately 155 states is characterized by a territorial base, jurisdiction over its internal and external affairs, and, to varying degrees, a conception of self-identity (nationalism) and unity.

Spheres of Influence Areas under the influence of domination of a great power. (Example: Eastern Europe for the Soviet Union.)

Stable Deterrence The strategic nuclear American-Soviet balance in which the deterrent forces of both sides are invulnerable.

Stable State System A system characterized by minimal violence and generally by the peaceful settlement of national differences.

Stagflation The simultaneous occurrence of recession and inflation, caused, in part, by OPEC's increases in oil prices.

Staking One's Reputation A technique intended to enhance a commitment's credibility through the involvement of a nation's honor and prestige.

Stalemate A form of conflict resolution in which victory for either side is rejected due to *mutual* battlefield exhaustion, reluctance to invest further resources, or unwillingness to escalate due to the risks involved.

State System See **International System**.

Substructure In Marxist-Leninist theory, the fundamental economic forces of a society (the ownership of property and wealth).

Superpowers Nations that possess an extraordinary degree of power (military, economic, diplomatic) allowing them to pursue an independent role in global affairs and/or whose actions have a substantial effect upon the policies of other political actors throughout the entire state system.

Superstructure In Marxist-Leninist ideology, the political, social, and cultural institutions/beliefs that are creations or reflections of the underlying economic forces or substructure.

Supranational Actor Best exemplified by the European Economic Community (EEC), or Common Market, in which nine sovereign states—Belgium, France, West Germany, Italy, Luxembourg, Netherlands, Great Britain, Denmark, and Ireland—have transferred a degree of their sovereign authority on economic issues to a superior decision-making body. The EEC's ultimate goal, though far from being realized, is to transform the economic union into a United States of Europe.

Surplus Value In Marxist theory, the "difference between what the worker should have been paid in terms of the *cash value* of his labor in the product and what he was actually paid (profit)."

602

Tacit Negotiations   Informal, indirect bargaining activity among states as opposed to traditional face-to-face diplomacy.

Tangible Components of Power   Usually refers to components that can be "measured" or "quantified," such as a nation's population, size, military strength, and economic productivity.

Tet Offensive   The North Vietnamese-Viet Cong attack against the major cities of South Vietnam in early 1968. While the communist forces were eventually repulsed with heavy casualties, Tet symbolized a psychological turning point for the United States in the war. The offensive belied the Johnson Administration's assertion that the war would soon be won.

Third World   The world of the nonwestern, largely economically underdeveloped countries.

Total War   A war where the political objectives of complete victory over the enemy are matched by the full mobilization of nation's military, economic, and social resources (example: World War II).

Totalitarianism   A political system that attempts to control every aspect of a citizen's life.

Transnational Actor (NGO)   A nongovernmental organization that is characterized by headquarters in one country but that also conducts its centrally directed operations in two or more countries. The most prominent example is the multinational corporation.

Tripolarity   An international system in which three major power centers exist. Tripolarity may be considered more (or less) stable than a bipolar system (see Chapter 6 for elaboration).

Truman Doctrine   The 1947 pronouncement that "it must be the policy of the United States to support free peoples who are resisting subjugation by armed minorities or outside pressures." While originally directed at Greece and Turkey, the doctrine actually marked the beginning of the containment era and the acknowledgement of the United States role in preserving the balance of power in a bipolar world.

UNCTAD   The United Nations Conference on Trade and Development, sometimes equated with Third World coalition strategy.

Uniting for Peace Resolution   A United States-sponsored resolution in November 1950, which transferred peace-making power from the Security Council to the General Assembly; on which support for American anticommunist policies in Korea would not be blocked by a Soviet veto.

Unstable Deterrence   The American-Soviet nuclear balance, in which one or both of the deterrent forces has become vulnerable, thereby tempting the other side to preempt.

Unstable State System   A system very prone to the outbreak of war.

War   Hostilities between states that are conducted by armed force. War is the "instrument of last resort" and usually establishes the "actual ratio of power among existing states."

World Government   The (idealistic) concept of a supreme global authority who would make wars among states impossible.

INDEX